AMERICA'S OPIOID ECOSYSTEM

How Leveraging System Interactions Can Help Curb Addiction, Overdose, and Other Harms

EDITORS

BRADLEY D. STEIN | BEAU KILMER | JIRKA TAYLOR | MARY E. VAIANA

Dionne Barnes-Proby | Jonathan P. Caulkins | Lois M. Davis | Michael Dworsky
Susan M. Gates | Martin Y. Iguchi | Karen Chan Osilla
Rosalie Liccardo Pacula | Bryce Pardo | Tisamarie B. Sherry | Sierra Smucker

RAND
CORPORATION

For more information on this publication, visit **www.rand.org/t/RRA604-1**.

About RAND

The RAND Corporation is a research organization that develops solutions to public policy challenges to help make communities throughout the world safer and more secure, healthier and more prosperous. RAND is nonprofit, nonpartisan, and committed to the public interest. To learn more about RAND, visit www.rand.org.

Research Integrity

Our mission to help improve policy and decisionmaking through research and analysis is enabled through our core values of quality and objectivity and our unwavering commitment to the highest level of integrity and ethical behavior. To help ensure our research and analysis are rigorous, objective, and nonpartisan, we subject our research publications to a robust and exacting quality-assurance process; avoid both the appearance and reality of financial and other conflicts of interest through staff training, project screening, and a policy of mandatory disclosure; and pursue transparency in our research engagements through our commitment to the open publication of our research findings and recommendations, disclosure of the source of funding of published research, and policies to ensure intellectual independence. For more information, visit www.rand.org/about/research-integrity.

RAND's publications do not necessarily reflect the opinions of its research clients and sponsors.

Library of Congress Cataloging-in-Publication Data is available for this publication.

ISBN: 978-1-9774-1066-5

Limited Print and Electronic Distribution Rights

This book is dedicated to our dear friend and colleague, Martin Iguchi. From his early work implementing the first methadone program in Camden County, New Jersey, to his pioneering work on contingency management and his contributions to this volume, Martin was steadfast in his commitment to helping those most in need. He served as a mentor to several authors of this book, providing the insight, humor, and compassion that we all needed. Martin will be long remembered in the field and by the people he helped. He is missed by us all.

Martin Y. Iguchi
1955–2021

About This Report

In 2018, the RAND Corporation initiated a comprehensive effort—*Opioids Uncharted*—to better understand the problems and responses to help stem the tide of opioid overdose and addiction. The first product from this initiative, a book titled *The Future of Fentanyl and Other Synthetic Opioids*, remains the most comprehensive document written about the origins of this problem, the current situation, and possibilities for the future. The key message from this book was that decisionmakers in the United States must start thinking "outside the box" when considering solutions.

Since that book was released in late 2019, limited progress has been made. The coronavirus disease 2019 (COVID-19) pandemic pushed our problems with opioids and overdose deaths to the back burner, but they continue to boil over. Unfortunately, that book is just as relevant today as when it was published, and the recommendations and ideas discussed could still make a difference.

The second product from the *Opioids Uncharted* initiative is a more holistic and far-reaching effort, focused on what we refer to as "America's opioid ecosystem." Viewing the opioid crisis as an ecosystem requires adopting a comprehensive perspective. The book draws on the expertise of more than 15 RAND researchers in multiple areas, including drug policy, substance use treatment, health care, public health, criminal legal system, harm reduction, child welfare and other social services, education, and employment. Understanding the nature of the opioid ecosystem is a necessary step for decisionmakers seeking to continue to address the crisis. To craft sound policies, they need to pay attention to multiple parts of the ecosystem at the same time. They also need reliable information to understand how policies interact and what effects of the interaction are likely to be. Moving away from siloed thinking and adopting an ecosystem approach will not only help curb the opioid crisis. It should also help mitigate the harmful consequences of other drug problems.

We dedicated project resources and communications expertise to ensure that our products and dissemination activities are optimized for reaching our primary intended audiences: policymakers and other critical decisionmakers and influencers, including those in the public, private, and nonprofit sectors. This ambitious project will not be the last word on America's drug crisis, but it offers a unique perspective on how the country understands and responds to this grave public health challenge.

Funding

Funding for this venture was provided by gifts from RAND supporters and income from operations. We are especially grateful to the contribution made by Jack McCauley, whose support was critical in the late stages of the project.

Acknowledgments

This book would not have been possible without the vision of our former RAND President, Michael Rich. Michael encouraged us to think big about addressing America's issues with opioids and provided the guidance and support to make it happen. His leadership and investment in RAND's *Opioids Uncharted* initiative led to this volume and to our book on *The Future of Fentanyl and Other Synthetic Opioids*. We are deeply indebted to Michael for everything he has done for this initiative, for us personally, and for the larger RAND community.

There would also be no book if it were not for our brilliant chapter authors. Many of these chapters could have been developed into separate books, and we were amazed by the authors' abilities to crystallize the ecosystem interactions and key policy considerations for their respective chapters. We learned a tremendous amount from our colleagues during this process and are forever thankful for their wisdom (and patience!).

We are especially grateful for the extremely detailed and useful comments we received on the full volume from Ricky Bluthenthal, Jonathan Caulkins, Beth McGinty, and Susan Sohler Everingham. We are also indebted to those who reviewed stand-alone chapters, including Mahshid Abir, Dionne Barnes-Proby, Ray Barishansky, Shawn Bushway, Magdalena Cerda, Rajeev Darolia, Carrie Fry, Rebecca Kilburn, Jane Liebschutz, Nipher Malika, Aili Malm, Harold Pollack, Lucy Schulson, and Melanie Zaber. We also thank Rosalie Liccardo Pacula and Priscillia Hunt for their early contributions to this volume and Julia Dilley for her insights on drug possession decriminalization in Oregon. All these reviewers made this a much stronger book, but the views presented here reflect only those of the chapter authors.

Because parts of this book are rooted in two previous RAND publications, *Considering Heroin-Assisted Treatment and Supervised Drug Consumption Sites in the United States* and *The Future of Fentanyl and Other Synthetic Opioids*, we remain indebted to the more than 200 people who shared their experiences and opinions with us during interviews and focus groups for those projects.

Last, but certainly not least, we have many other colleagues at RAND who offered guidance and support throughout this process. We owe a tremendous amount to Anita Chandra, Rick Eden, Susan Gates, Jennifer Gould, Kimbria McCarty, Chris Nelson, Darleen Opfer, Jeanne Ringel, Dana Torres, Jason Ward, Chara Williams, and to Brian Dau, Blair Smith, Maria Vega, Emily Ward, and Pete Soriano, who provided editorial and design assistance.

Summary

Motivation

The United States has long grappled with multiple problems stemming from the use of alcohol and other drugs, but the number of individuals overdosing and dying from drugs has grown exponentially since 1979; provisional estimates from the Centers for Disease Control and Prevention (CDC) suggest that more than 100,000 individuals died from drug-involved overdoses between September 2021 and August 2022. Approximately 75 percent of the deaths involve opioids (mostly opioids that are illegally produced), and most death certificates for overdoses list multiple drugs.

But the problems are broader and deeper than drug fatalities. Reliable data are lacking on the number of individuals actively using drugs and those with substance use disorders (SUDs). Although most people who use drugs do not run into problems with them or suffer from SUDs, depending on the substances involved, there can be myriad physical and mental health consequences associated with being addicted to drugs.

And it is not just those with SUDs who suffer. Their substance use and related behaviors can significantly affect their families, friends, employers, and wider communities. Having a loved one suffer from addiction can bring with it substantial psychological, physical, and financial costs.

Opioids play an outsized role in America's drug problems, but they also play a critically important role in medicine. Thus, they deserve special attention. The dynamics of America's drug problem are also shifting, not only in the types of opioids being consumed but also in the populations most affected—especially in terms of race and ethnicity.

Of course, our primary focus on opioids does not mean we can ignore the country's issues with other drugs. To the contrary, the United States confronts multiple challenges, including long-standing problems related to alcohol and a dramatic rise in harms related to methamphetamine use. Correspondingly, some of the observations and suggestions made in this volume will be applicable to contexts other than opioids.

Focusing on America's Opioid Ecosystem

Many policies have been implemented to reduce opioid use, enhance effective treatment, and mitigate opioid-related harms. But confronting the crisis is not just about better pain management or treatment for opioid use disorder. Many widely adopted policies target individuals at highest risk for opioid misuse or opioid use disorder and focus on the role of the health care system in providing treatment for addiction and comorbid disorders. However, a broader swath of the population and many more governmental and nongovernmental systems are affected by problems related to substance use. These systems interconnect, often in unexpected ways. As a result, policies targeting one part of the system can have unintended consequences on other parts, affecting systems that they were not intended to target. A lack of a systems perspective also contributes to missed opportunities that could promote positive change.

This volume, which is arguably the most comprehensive analysis of opioids in 21st century America, offers a broader view by considering the opioid crisis in the context of an ecosystem.[1] Its component parts, linked by individuals and organizations, interact both directly and indirectly. Recognizing the ecosystem's major components and exploring how they do—and do not—interact allows us to

- understand how one component of the ecosystem can have a major impact on opioid-related outcomes in other components
- identify new policy opportunities that require interacting with or reducing barriers among multiple components of the ecosystem.

Multiple commissions, task forces, and research teams are working to reduce the harms associated with opioids. We applaud these efforts, acknowledging their important contributions. By necessity, our report covers much of the same ground. However, we extend the prior work on several important dimensions. We consider, more explicitly and in greater detail, the specific ways in which the opioid crisis affects systems that are less commonly considered, such as the child welfare and education systems; we also consider how policies in those systems may affect systems more commonly considered, such as the health care, harm reduction, criminal legal, and SUD treatment systems. We examine policies that would be implemented within systems that could have potential benefits in other systems; we also appraise policies that must be implemented across systems and offer ways to do so.

Major Takeaways

A major contribution of this study is to identify opportunities at the intersections of the ecosystem's components and to highlight other cross-sector initiatives that could mitigate the harmful effects of opioids. We offer nine portfolios of action addressing issues that arose

---

[1] Some have referred to this problem as the "opioid epidemic," "opioid crisis," or "overdose crisis," noting that the rise in overdoses is not limited to opioids. Those preferring the latter term are correct to note increases in deaths involving drugs other than opioids, but the problems extend beyond fatalities. This volume uses *opioid crisis* because it covers more than overdoses, is not limited to problems faced by people who use opioids, and signifies the unique role opioids play in American society. This is in no way meant to suggest that other drug problems should not be addressed or to downplay the medical benefits opioids provide millions of people in the United States. Indeed, an important aspect of the crisis is the barriers people confront when trying to obtain prescribed opioids to treat opioid use disorder and, increasingly, for chronic pain. (For sources on terminology, see Chapter One.)

across many ecosystem components. These portfolios could help decisionmakers prioritize and organize their efforts to address the opioid crisis.

Just because an idea appears in the volume does not mean that it is a priority option, or even a good option, for every community. We recognize the complexities, challenges, and potential downsides of implementing these ideas. For some ideas, there is a strong evidence base; others have potential and deserve consideration. That said, some of the ideas, if implemented, might not be as effective as envisioned or could have unintended consequences.

We offer four major takeaways:

1. **America's issues surrounding opioids are most appropriately viewed in the context of an ecosystem.** Like a biological ecosystem, it is dynamic, and its components (such as medical care, criminal legal system, harm reduction, and others, as depicted in Figure S.1) interact both directly and indirectly.

   Understanding these interactions is challenging but essential for effective policymaking. For example:

   a. *Ecosystem components often focus on individuals, but their families also lie at the heart of the ecosystem.* The family members, friends, and wider communities of those with SUDs can also suffer its harms. Family members who live with those with SUDs are often directly affected, and these relatives interact with the ecosystem components in a variety of ways, depending on the status and needs of the individual using drugs. Understanding these interactions can help us identify ways in which families can be better supported. Acknowledging the harms families experience could further justify devoting time and resources to helping them, potentially reducing the overall burdens imposed by opioid use disorder.

   b. *Each ecosystem component has its own mission, priorities, and funding, but policies furthering those priorities may hamper the efforts of other system components.* Furthermore, most of these components are designed to serve the broader population, not just people who use opioids, and that can leave the special needs of this group unmet. Lack of coordination and communication across ecosystem components poses a formidable challenge for many opioid-affected individuals and their families. In addition, decisions made in one component can ripple through the ecosystem; effects can be helpful, harmful, or unanticipated. To illustrate this point, we present the following three examples:

      i. Public housing policies that can exclude individuals misusing substances are intended to protect other residents, but housing instability is a significant barrier to successful treatment and recovery.

      ii. Making drugs illegal increases their price and reduces their availability. But a criminal record makes it harder for an individual to get a job and access social services, and fear may discourage individuals with opioid use disorder from identifying themselves and seeking help.

FIGURE S.1
The Opioid Ecosystem

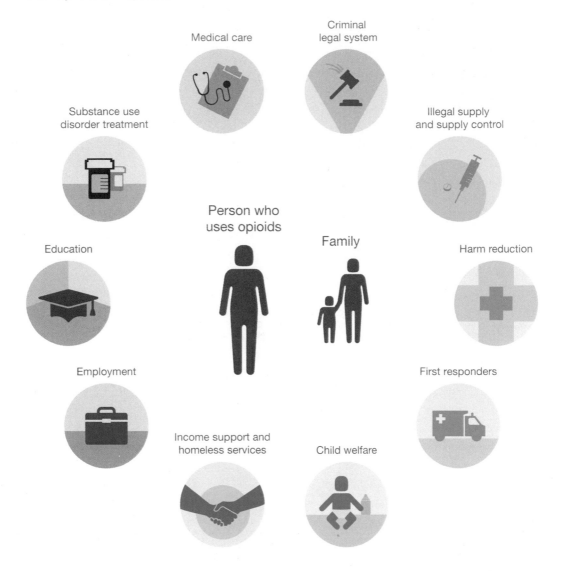

iii. Child welfare policies regarding parental drug use are intended to keep children safe, but fear of losing a child may prevent a parent who uses drugs
from seeking treatment.

2. **Current responses to opioid problems are insufficient—the United States need to
innovate.** The increased prevalence of such illegally produced synthetic opioids as
fentanyl has exacerbated the harms of drug use—and particularly of overdose—and
complicated the struggle with opioids.

a. *Increasing access to and use of high-quality treatment for SUDs remains the top
priority*, but it will not be enough to stem the tide of overdose deaths and addic-

tion. Even clients receiving high-quality treatment for opioid use disorder often cycle in and out of treatment, and those who return to using illegally produced opioids (and sometimes other drugs and counterfeit pills) carry a heightened risk of overdose in an era of synthetic opioids.

b. *Because criminalization of drug possession and/or use creates barriers in many components of the ecosystem, jurisdictions could consider alternatives ranging from changing enforcement practices to changing laws.* Each alternative has pros and cons, and the consequences will likely differ depending on local conditions (e.g., types of drug problems, service infrastructure, existing enforcement practices).

c. *The federal government should make it easier—not harder—for states or localities to pilot, implement, and evaluate interventions that are intended to help reduce overdose deaths.* Because the nature and character of current issues with opioids differ substantially across communities, giving state and local decisionmakers the latitude to design and implement local services is essential to ensuring that they address local needs and priorities.

d. *New approaches need not be permanent and should include objective evaluation.* There is considerable uncertainty and hesitancy regarding the introduction of new interventions. To assuage possible concerns, decisionmakers could implement sunset clauses to limit the duration of new policies and make their extension contingent on satisfactory evaluation results.

e. *Policy gaming exercises could stimulate leaders to consider new approaches* and the complexities of how they would affect other ecosystem components. The games could be coordinated by government officials, nonprofit organizations, and/or philanthropic foundations.

3. **Someone needs to take ownership of assisting people in their journey through the systems.**

a. *Individuals with opioid use disorders often touch multiple components of the ecosystem, but it is not always clear who is responsible for coordination among components or transition from one component to another.* Is it the system component from which an individual is coming that is responsible for managing the transition, or is it the system component to which the individual is going? Who takes ownership of assisting people in their journey or transition through the systems? (Examples include individuals with opioid use disorder being released from incarceration and needing to obtain employment or engage in treatment in the community; individuals receiving services from first responders or in emergency rooms who do not transition to treatment; and children who are informally moved to a relative's home because of parental substance use not being referred to services they may need.) By making clear who is responsible at these junctures and providing the resources necessary to meet the commitment of the additional responsibility, policymakers and stakeholders can diminish some of the disconnects that hamper the provision of treatment and support.

b. *A broader perspective allows us to identify policy opportunities generated by the interactions of components across the ecosystem.* For example, comprehensive case managers could help people with opioid use disorder navigate the landscape of existing service providers; develop a plan for appropriate services; and establish linkages and relationships with corresponding agencies, among other actions. These case managers also could remain involved with individuals throughout periods when more-traditional case managers are not involved, such as during an individual's incarceration, enabling managers to address needs proactively during high-risk periods, such as release from incarceration. Such a model would likely require new sources of funding, probably from state and local governments or foundations; therefore, case managers would be involved with individuals when they are uninsured and not involved with social services.

4. **The United States is often flying blind, which makes it difficult to evaluate existing interventions, invent new ones, or improve our understanding of ecosystem interactions.**

a. *The United States urgently needs to improve the data infrastructure for understanding people who use drugs, drug consumption, and drug markets.* There is a lack of credible information about the number of people with opioid use disorder and/or those using illegally produced opioids, let alone those who supply illegal opioids. This hampers policymakers' ability to allocate resources efficiently, monitor changes in drug markets, and conduct rigorous policy evaluations. The United States needs to step up efforts to learn more about the size and characteristics of this population and how they are changing.

b. *There is little information about what happens to individuals when they transition from one component of the ecosystem to another.* This, coupled with the data gaps mentioned earlier, hampers our ability to know how different components of the ecosystem interact and how that interaction affects individuals moving through the system.

c. *Unlike many prior public health challenges, the onset of the overdose crisis has not motivated substantial new surveillance efforts.* The HIV/AIDS crisis prompted large-scale investments in new data and monitoring systems. The overdose crisis, which now kills more than HIV/AIDS did at its peak, has not elicited a comparable investment in data infrastructure.

d. *Concrete opportunities for data improvements exist and could offer great value to policymakers and researchers alike.* For instance, administrative data already being collected by law enforcement agencies could be made more available to researchers so that they can learn about drug markets, especially for fentanyl. Valuable discontinued programs, such as the Arrestee Drug Abuse Monitoring (ADAM) program, could be resurrected. New data-collection efforts, such as wastewater monitoring, could be introduced to provide essential real-time data on trends and changes in drug consumption and to detect the emergence of new psychoactive substances.

Understanding the nature of the opioid ecosystem is a necessary step for decisionmakers seeking to move forward. They need to pay attention to multiple parts of the ecosystem at the same time. And they need reliable information to understand how policies interact and what effects of the interaction are likely to be.

Moving away from siloed thinking and adopting an ecosystem approach will help stem the current tide of addiction and overdose deaths. It also should help mitigate the harmful consequences of future drug problems.

Contents

Figures and Tables

Figures

Tables

CHAPTER ONE

Introduction

Opioids play an outsized role in America's drug problems, but they also play an essential role in medicine. The purpose of this volume is to inform ongoing policy efforts to reduce opioid-related harms, with a special focus on how individuals, organizations, and systems interact with respect to opioids.

We argue that the issues surrounding opioids are appropriately viewed as an ecosystem and, as in a biological ecosystem, parts of the ecosystem interact both directly and indirectly. This comprehensive view recognizes how decisions made in one part of the ecosystem can have a major effect—sometimes helpful, sometimes harmful, and sometimes unanticipated— in other parts of the system. A broader perspective also allows us to identify policy opportunities generated by the interactions of components across the ecosystem.

In the chapters that follow, we characterize the ecosystem, drawing on the knowledge of subject-matter experts, existing research, and some of our own analyses. In our concluding chapter, we identify barriers and opportunities that are common to many parts of the ecosystem and offer suggestions for prioritizing policy considerations.

We begin by sketching the broad contours of the country's struggle with drugs, giving special attention to opioids.

The National Context for U.S. Issues with Opioids

The United States has long grappled with multiple problems stemming from the use of alcohol and other drugs, but the number of people overdosing and dying from drugs has grown exponentially since 1979 (Jalal et al., 2018). Recent estimates suggest that more than 100,000 individuals died from drug-involved overdoses between September 2021 and August 2022 (Provisional data from the Centers for Disease Control and Prevention [CDC], 2023).[1]

But the harms run broader and deeper than drug fatalities. We lack reliable data on the number of individuals actively using drugs and the subset of them who meet the clinical

---

[1] The estimated total excludes those who may have died from drug-involved violence or accidents or medical conditions attributable to or exacerbated by substance use. This total also excludes deaths exclusively attributable to alcohol poisoning. CDC reports that there are about 2,300 alcohol poisoning deaths each year and roughly 100,000 deaths that are attributable to alcohol-related causes overall (CDC, 2019).

criteria for a substance use disorder (SUD).[2] However, one recent estimate suggests that, in 2019, at least 20 million Americans had an SUD in the past year (Substance Abuse and Mental Health Services Administration [SAMHSA], 2020b).[3] There are also myriad physical and mental health consequences associated with SUDs; their nature and severity vary with the drugs involved (Degenhardt et al., 2013; Mark et al., 2001; Nicosia et al., 2009).

It is not just those with SUDs who suffer. Their substance use—and behaviors related to that use—can impose mental, physical, and financial costs on their families, friends, employers, and wider communities. For example, although not everyone with an SUD engages in criminal behavior to support their habits, some do, and those who are victimized can also suffer greatly. Borrowing money from friends and family—sometimes with little prospect of repayment—is another burden.

There are many types of opioids, and they play multiple roles in the lives of millions of Americans.[4] Most prescription opioids are used to help control chronic or acute pain (Dahlhamer et al., 2018). Methadone and buprenorphine are opioids that are used primarily to treat opioid use disorder (OUD).[5]

Per capita prescription opioid rates increased dramatically in the 1990s as pharmaceutical companies promoted opioids aggressively, and pain was even promoted as the "fifth vital sign." Some pharmaceutical companies—including the Sackler-owned Purdue Pharmaceuticals, among others—also pursued deceptive and illegal activities to increase sales across the country (see, e.g., Keefe, 2021). For example, executives of InSys Therapeutics were convicted of criminal racketeering charges for essentially bribing doctors to prescribe fentanyl (Lopez, 2019). There have been efforts to reduce the number of opioid prescriptions, given the devastating consequences of oversupply. However, these efforts have inadvertently created barriers for some individuals who need the drugs for pain relief, even though most studies find that

---

[2] SUD and alcohol use disorder are two distinct diagnoses, according to the *Diagnostic and Statistical Manual of Mental Disorders* (DSM). Unless noted otherwise, when we use the term *SUD*, we refer to drugs other than alcohol and tobacco.

[3] For insights about the limitations of using National Survey of Drug Use and Health data to measure the number of people with SUD, and especially for the use of heroin, see Caulkins et al., 2015; Reuter, Caulkins, and Midgette, 2021; and Chapter 2 of this volume.

[4] Some have referred to this problem as the "opioid epidemic," "opioid crisis," or "overdose crisis," noting that the rise in overdoses is not limited to opioids. Those preferring the latter term are correct to note increases in deaths involving drugs other than opioids, but the problems extend beyond fatalities. This volume uses *opioid crisis* because it covers more than overdoses, is not limited to problems faced by people who use opioids (PWUO), and signifies the unique role opioids play in American society. This is in no way meant to suggest that other drug problems should not be addressed or to downplay the medical benefits opioids provide millions of people in the United States. Indeed, an important aspect of the crisis is the barriers people confront when trying to obtain prescribed opioids to treat opioid use disorder and, increasingly, for chronic pain (Zhang, Kilaru, et al., 2021; Zhang, Paice, et al., 2021; Lagisetty, Healy, et al., 2019).

[5] The 2023 Consolidated Appropriations Act (H.R. 2617), which was signed by President Biden on January 4, 2023, changed requirements related to prescribing buprenorphine.

the United States continues to lead the world in terms of total and per capita rates of opioid prescribing (further discussed in Chapter Two).

Most people who use prescription opioids—for prescribed purposes or not—do not experience problems because of their use (Higgins, Smith, and Matthews, 2018; Volkow et al., 2019). This is partly because most people use them for short periods and infrequently. Individuals who use the drugs for longer periods sometimes become physically dependent, meaning that "the body adapts to the drug, requiring more of it to achieve a certain effect (tolerance) and eliciting drug-specific physical or mental symptoms if drug use is abruptly ceased (withdrawal)" (National Institute on Drug Abuse [NIDA], 2018b).

Such dependence is not the same as addiction. *Addiction* is best characterized as compulsive use despite harmful consequences (NIDA, 2020, p. 4). People with opioid addiction are usually dependent on them (i.e., they need larger doses to achieve the same effect and can suffer short-term health consequences from stopping use), but not everyone who is dependent is addicted.[6] The risk of addiction from a short (e.g., seven-day) prescription is minimal, and short-term prescriptions account for a substantial share of all opioid prescriptions. However, a large portion of pharmaceutical company sales and profits come from supplying people who use prescription opioids on an extended basis, and prolonged use greatly increases risks, not only of becoming physically dependent but also of sustained use, leading to addiction and/or the use of other opioids, such as heroin or illegally produced fentanyl.

Similarly, most people who try heroin do not go on to experience a heroin use disorder (Anthony et al., 1994), in part because most people never use it regularly. There are also some people who regularly use heroin for pleasure without negative consequences (see, e.g., Kaplan, 1983; and Hart, 2021), but it is difficult to estimate the precise number (see Chapter Two). Nonetheless, for many, prolonged and regular heroin use results in addiction, which often creates great harms for themselves and others.

The spread of illegally produced synthetic opioids, such as fentanyl, since 2014 has massively exacerbated the harms from using illegal drugs, particularly overdose, and complicated the struggle with opioids. Although parts of the United States had temporary minor outbreaks of illegally produced fentanyl in the past, those outbreaks utterly pale in comparison with the contemporary mass production and importation of these substances from China and Mexico (Pardo et al., 2019). Synthetic opioids are both more potent and less expensive than heroin, giving wholesalers a strong financial incentive to mix them with heroin or put them in counterfeit pills or other drugs to cut costs and increase profits (Mars, Rosenblum, and Ciccarone, 2019; Pardo et al., 2019). As a consequence, many individuals who believe that they are purchasing heroin or other opioids are unknowingly using synthetic opioids and overdosing.

Fentanyl is also carving out its own place in the market. In some locations, such as Massachusetts and New Hampshire in the United States and British Columbia in Canada, fentanyl

---

[6] There is confusion about these terms. Formerly, those who were addicted to opioids were diagnosed with what was called "opioid dependence."

has largely replaced heroin (Scholl et al., 2019; Pardo et al., 2021; Shover et al., 2020), and there are growing reports of people specifically looking for fentanyl (Buresh et al., 2019; Gryczynski et al., 2019; Meier et al., 2020). There is a large market for illegally produced fentanyl powder—that is purchased separately from heroin—in San Francisco (San Francisco Office of Economic and Workforce Development, 2021), and there have been some reports that it is becoming harder for people who use drugs to find heroin in some cities in the western part of the country (see, e.g., Boiko-Weyrauch, 2021; and McCormick, 2022).[7]

As noted, of the 100,000 drug-involved deaths in the United States between September 2021 and August 2022, roughly 75 percent involved opioids (CDC, 2023). However, many of the deaths involve polysubstance use (Cicero, Ellis, and Kasper, 2020; also see Chapter Two). In addition, focusing on drugs detected by the coroner or medical examiner tells only part of the story. The thoroughness and accuracy of these assessments may be questionable (Ruhm, 2018; Slavova et al., 2019). More fundamentally, the substance whose use escalated into SUD and triggered a cascade of events may or may not be the individual's drug of choice at the time of death. For example, many individuals who are using illegally produced opioids such as heroin or fentanyl today began their opioid use with nonmedical use of prescribed opioids (Jones, 2013; Mars et al., 2014). Thus, many—and perhaps most—deaths attributed to heroin or synthetic opioids may have their roots in prior prescription opioid use.

Current Responses to U.S. Opioid Problems Are Insufficient

Noteworthy efforts have been made to address the country's drug problems. Access to quality treatment, especially medications for OUD (MOUD), has been expanding (Mojtabai et al., 2019; Wen, Borders, and Cummings, 2019), and more individuals with OUD have entered—and remained engaged in—treatment (Saloner, McGinty, et al., 2018; Sharp et al., 2018). The majority of those with OUD did not receive treatment in the previous year, and studies suggest that the share of those receiving MOUD could have ranged from roughly 14 percent to 28 percent in 2019 (Krawczyk et al., 2022; Mauro et al., 2022).[8] That gap does not stem solely from limited treatment access. Many people with OUD do not want or seek out treatment.

Naloxone, the overdose reversal drug, is also now more readily available (Lambdin et al., 2020), and an increasing number of police departments and other first responder agencies are training and equipping officers with it (North Carolina Harm Reduction Coalition, undated). Many states have facilitated access through third-party prescribing laws, in which naloxone prescriptions can be written for individuals who have not been examined by the prescriber,

---

[7] The McCormick article quotes Dr. Ricky Bluthenthal as follows: "What's happening is fentanyl is replacing heroin in most of the nation's largest drug markets. . . . As fentanyl has begun to replace heroin and become the only thing available, you have this increased mortality among African Americans."

[8] We put more stock in the lower number because it is not purely based on the National Survey on Drug Use and Health. For more on this, see Chapter Two.

and standing-order laws, in which naloxone can be distributed or dispensed from pharmacies without patient-specific prescriptions (Smart et al., 2020). However, the vast majority of individuals filling opioid prescriptions that put them at higher risk of overdose do not fill naloxone prescriptions (Guy et al., 2021; Stein et al., 2021).

Initiatives to reduce the supply of prescription opioids have been successful in reducing the amounts prescribed. Unfortunately, in some cases, restrictions have made it harder for patients to address their chronic pain (North Carolina Medical Board, 2018; Lagisetty, Healy, et al., 2019) and created new harms (see the box on opioid tapering and discontinuation). And despite reductions in the number of opioid prescriptions, the per capita prescription rate in the United States remains far higher than in any other high-income country (Organisation for Economic Co-operation and Development, 2019; see Chapter Two).

Despite these efforts, we continue to see increases in opioid-involved overdose deaths (CDC, 2021a), opioid-involved hospitalizations (Singh and Cleveland, 2020), and medical problems typically associated with injection drug use (Ronan and Herzig, 2016; Collier, Doshani, and Asher, 2018). The absolute number of people receiving treatment for OUD is increasing, but as noted, most individuals with OUD are not accessing that treatment (SAMHSA, 2018) and even fewer receive MOUD, the most effective treatment for many people (SAMHSA, undated). What is especially problematic from a resource allocation and policy evaluation perspective is that we do not know how the share of those with OUD receiving treatment is changing.

A major barrier to assessing progress is lack of information. We lack reliable national estimates of the total number of people who use prescription opioids (for nonprescribed purposes), heroin, and/or synthetic opioids (Kilmer and Caulkins, 2014; Caulkins et al., 2015; Reuter, Caulkins, and Midgette, 2021), let alone how many of them have OUD. There is also an urgent need for early-warning systems to detect synthetic opioid supply. The United States made major investments in surveillance and data collection in response to HIV/AIDS; a comparable effort has not been made for opioids (Pardo et al., 2019; Frank, Humphreys, and Pollack, 2021).

In short, although expanding MOUD and naloxone is critical, MOUD and naloxone are not adequate or complete responses in the sense that even after having pushed those priorities, the rates of OUD and death are still very high and will remain so for years to come unless other approaches are developed and implemented (Humphreys et al., 2022).

Efforts to Address Opioids Confront Both Old and New Challenges

Challenges surrounding substance use are not new, and neither are the larger issues related to health outcomes and social determinants of health, such as health care access and quality, education, and economic and community-level factors (including incarceration; CDC, 2021b). In this section, we highlight a few old and new challenges to addressing problems

Issues Surrounding Prescription Opioid Tapering and Discontinuation

Because of efforts to decrease clinically unnecessary and potentially harmful opioid pre-scribing, a key consideration is the manner in which such reductions in opioid prescrib-ing are achieved and how to avoid negative unintended consequences for individuals with chronic pain. Health care providers, patients, and advocacy groups have voiced concerns that growing "opioid hesitancy" might result in inadequate access to pain treatment for individuals with severe, disabling pain for whom other therapies have not been effective (Hoffman, 2018; Kertesz, 2017). There are also concerns that more-restrictive opioid pre-scribing policies might disproportionately harm patients from minority racial and ethnic groups, who are already less likely to receive opioids for pain and more likely to experience discontinuation of long-term opioid treatment (Burgess et al., 2014; Gaither et al., 2018; Phan et al., 2021; Singhal, Tien, and Hsia, 2016).

Furthermore, there is limited but accumulating evidence on the ways in which indi-viduals with pain might experience harm as a result of more-restrictive opioid prescrib-ing practices, especially patients with chronic pain on long-term opioid therapy, who are at increased risk of adverse health outcomes if opioid therapy is abruptly discontinued or tapered too quickly (Agnoli et al., 2021; Demidenko et al., 2017; DiPrete et al., 2022; Mark and Parish, 2019; Oliva et al., 2020).

A large study of individuals with commercial insurance or Medicare Advantage who were prescribed opioids between 2008 and 2017 found that dose tapering has become more common since 2016, including tapering at rates that exceed those recommended by CDC guidelines (Fenton et al., 2019). Similarly, a study of Medicaid beneficiaries in Vermont who received chronic high-dose opioid analgesic therapy between 2013 and 2017 found that more than 50 percent of patients who discontinued opioid treatment did so suddenly. This study also highlighted the potential risks of rapid discontinuation: 49 percent of patients who discontinued opioid treatment had an opioid-related emergency department or hospital visit, but the probability of these adverse events decreased by 7 percent with each additional week that dose tapering was extended (Mark and Parish, 2019). A national study of patients receiving care from the Veterans Health Administration found that all patients who were exposed to opioids had an increased risk of death because of overdose or suicide after stopping opioids and that the risk increased with the length of time an indi-vidual had been treated with opioids (Oliva et al., 2020).

Concerns about such unintended consequences and harms have led to efforts to clarify and revise chronic pain management treatment guidelines (Dowell et al., 2022) and are important considerations in any efforts to reduce risks associated with opioid pain man-agement. This issue is discussed throughout this volume, particularly in Chapters Five, Seven, Twelve, and Fourteen.

related to opioids that appear in multiple parts of this volume: systemic racism, stigma and discrimination, and the coronavirus disease 2019 (COVID-19) pandemic.

Racism

Systemic racism has plagued the United States for centuries, and deeply rooted racial and ethnic disparities affect many social determinants of health (Williams, Lawrence, and Davis, 2019; Bluthenthal, 2021, Volkow, 2021). With respect to opioids, people of color and those living in communities with a larger percentage of people of color are less likely to receive the most-effective treatments for OUD (Stahler and Mennis, 2018; Stein et al., 2021; Lagisetty, Ross, et al., 2019; Volkow, 2019). Black and/or Hispanic individuals who enter treatment for OUD are less likely than non-Hispanic White individuals to complete it (Saloner and Lê Cook, 2013).

In 2020, the U.S. federal government published a report entitled *The Opioid Crisis and the Black/African American Population: An Urgent Issue* (SAMHSA, 2020a). Noting the changing dynamics of the crisis, SAMHSA argued that "[a]ttention to this epidemic has focused primarily on White suburban and rural communities. Less attention has focused on Black/African American communities which are similarly experiencing dramatic increases in opioid misuse and overdose deaths" (SAMHSA, 2020a, p. 3).[9] Disparities in polysubstance deaths also deserve more attention, especially because the increase in deaths involving both synthetic opioids and cocaine disproportionately affect people of color (we further discuss this in Chapter Two; see also the box comparing the response to crack and opioids). Similarly, American Indians and Alaska Natives have seen disproportionately large increases in drug-related mortality, and there has been a comparative lack of attention paid to the situation in tribal communities (Joshi, Weiser, and Warren-Mears, 2018; Tipps et al., 2018).

---

[9] Changes in opioid-involved overdose deaths by race/ethnicity from 2000 to 2020 are documented in Chapter Two. A useful summary covering 1979–2015 is provided by Alexander, Kiang, and Barbieri, 2018, p. 712:

> The opioid epidemic can be divided into three waves between 1979 and 2015. During the first wave, from 1979 to the mid-1990s, opioid mortality was higher for the black population, but rates of increase were similar for both populations and largely driven by heroin. During the second wave, from the mid-1990s to 2010, the opioid epidemic expanded quickly within the white population while opioid mortality remained stable in the black population. As a consequence, the racial gradient of risk reversed in 2000, and by 2010, the opioid mortality rate were [sic] over 2 times higher for whites than for blacks. During this period, the opioid epidemic was driven largely by non-heroin and non-methadone opioids (i.e., prescription painkillers). Lastly, from about 2010 to 2015, the opioid mortality rate grew rapidly for both the black and white populations.

Comparing the Responses to Crack and Opioids

The racial dynamics in how the country has addressed opioids versus crack cocaine have been widely discussed (see, e.g., Gounder, 2016; Szalavitz, 2016; and Shachar et al., 2020). It has been argued that the country's response to the crack cocaine tribulations of the 1980s and 1990s—which disproportionately affected major cities and communities of color—was highly aggressive and implemented primarily by ramping up criminal justice efforts. In contrast, the response to opioids—which initially disproportionately affected White rural communities—has been more focused on treatment and public health approaches (Shachar et al., 2020).

There is truth in this narrative, but it is incomplete. There is no denying that policing intensified in response to the surge in violence that accompanied the spread of crack cocaine (this violence was often associated with crack markets and sellers, not so much with those using crack), and the application of mandatory minimum sentences and other forms of determinant sentencing increased in the 1980s, infamously so for crack offenses.[a] These policies contributed to a large increase in incarceration, disproportionately of young Black men. Public health was not completely absent from the scene: Insurance benefits for SUDs and specialty SUD treatment did expand (SAMHSA, 2016).

Public health interventions have played a much larger role in discussions of the 21st century opioid crisis, partially because escalation of prescription opioid use and its diversion were not in any meaningful way linked to violent crime, and perhaps more importantly, there were essentially no organized or high-level traffickers or distribution. Most of the diversion and sale of prescription opioids was by individuals with multiple prescriptions (i.e., it was PWUO who were often supplying, not multitiered international drug distribution networks). Furthermore, we have much better treatments for OUD than for cocaine use disorder. That has always been true, but the gap between OUD treatment in 2010 and cocaine treatment in 1985 is even wider than the gap between treatment capabilities for the two drugs at any specific point in time.

However, law enforcement is still playing a major role in the response: There are on the order of 200,000 to 300,000 arrests for opioid-specific offenses each year (i.e., arrests for production, sales, and distribution and for simple possession) and multiple times that for arrests for crimes related to opioid use (e.g., property crimes, which we discuss more in Chapter Two). There has also been an increase in charges related to drug-induced homicide laws, which apply additional sanctions on those who supply drugs to someone who overdoses and dies (Beletsky, 2019; Health in Justice Action Lab, undated).

---

[a] It is widely reported that sentences for crack were more severe than those for powder cocaine, but the more accurate description is that a sentence of a given length could be triggered by smaller quantities of crack than powder cocaine.

Stigma and Discrimination

Long-standing concerns regarding stigma and discrimination against PWUO and people who use other drugs also shape responses to the current crisis (Volkow, 2020b).[10] For example, a growing body of research suggests that stigmatizing labels, such as *addict* or *substance abuser,* can influence how individuals, including medical professionals, perceive people with SUDs (Kelly and Westerhoff, 2010; Ashford et al., 2019). Also, some clinicians simply do not want to provide MOUD (Kennedy-Hendricks et al., 2020), and, of clinicians who begin prescribing medication to treat opioid use disorder, most cease within a year (Cabreros et al., 2021). Research has also found that higher levels of stigmatized attitudes about people with OUD are strongly associated with lower rates of providing MOUD (Stone et al., 2021).

Drug laws and some criminal legal interventions seek to reify social disapproval of drug use. The stigmatization of people who use and/or sell drugs is a feature, not a bug, of the current system, as it is for other forms of criminal activity. However, this is only one component. There is also considerable stigma associated with alcohol use disorder (Kilian et al., 2021).

Although criminal justice agencies play an important role in preventing drug-related crimes, laws intended to reduce drug use and drug-related crime can create barriers to recovery, even though other criminal justice programs can increase uptake of treatment. Drug offense convictions entail much more than a criminal record; they can occasion additional sanctions, such as reduced access to or additional restrictions on public housing and nutritional support. Restrictions vary by state and locality (Polkey, 2019).

Some of these polices are well intentioned (e.g., protecting public housing or shelter residents from drug-related victimization), but there are trade-offs. Making it harder for those with SUDs to obtain shelter and other services makes it harder for them to stabilize their lives and engage in treatment.

COVID-19 Pandemic

The COVID-19 pandemic brought new challenges (Wang et al., 2021). It will take time before we really know how the pandemic has affected opioid-related harms, but early reports show an increase in fatal overdoses (American Medical Association, 2021; CDC, 2021a), possibly from more people using alone, although also possibly from expanded fentanyl supply. Experts worry that individuals will face barriers in accessing treatment because of concerns about contracting COVID-19 (Volkow, 2020a; Khatri and Perrone, 2020). That said, to maintain access to treatment for OUD at a time when the pandemic reduced face-to-face treatment,

---

[10] We are not aware of any longitudinal data on the extent of stigma in the United States. The General Social Survey has asked questions on the topic in the past, but regrettably not in a way that would enable comparisons over time. In a recent new effort, Shatterproof fielded a 2020 survey on addiction stigma to a nationally representative sample of nearly 8,000 individuals. In headline findings offered by the authors, three-quarters of respondents did not believe that individuals with SUDs were experiencing a chronic illness and nearly two-thirds of participants responded that they would not want a person with an SUD to marry into their family (Shatterproof and The Hartford, 2021).

the federal government and many state governments temporarily relaxed some of the restrictions requiring in-person visits (Andraka-Christou et al., 2021; Pessar et al., 2021), potentially enabling many individuals to maintain access to MOUD (e.g., via telehealth) (Cantor et al., 2021; Nguyen et al., 2021; SAMHSA, 2021). The extent to which these changes will ultimately become permanent remains to be seen.

Taking an Ecosystem Approach to Addressing Opioids

Multiple policies have been implemented to reduce opioid misuse, enhance effective treatment, and mitigate opioid-related harms (see, e.g., review by Schuler et al., 2020). But confronting the crisis is not just about better pain management or treatment for OUD. Many widely adopted policies target individuals at highest risk for opioid misuse or OUD and focus on the role of the health care system in providing treatment for addiction and comorbid disorders. However, a broader swath of the population and many more governmental and nongovernmental systems are affected. These systems interconnect, sometimes in unexpected ways. As a result, policies targeting one part of the system can have unintended consequences, affecting systems that they were not intended to target. Lack of a systems perspective also contributes to missed opportunities that could promote positive change.

In this report, we offer a broader perspective by considering the opioid crisis in the context of an ecosystem. Its component parts, linked by individuals and organizations, interact both directly and indirectly. Taking this comprehensive approach helps us identify

- **new perspectives:** The scope and persistence of the problem demands innovative new approaches, which require looking at the problem in a novel (or at least unconventional) way.
- **contradictions:** Policies designed to help in one arena can cause harm in others, counteracting each other and often wasting resources.
- **synergies:** Policies interact with each other in ways that can multiply their impacts.
- **unintended consequences:** Components of the opioid ecosystem interconnect, often in unexpected ways. As a result, policies targeting one part of the system can have unintended consequences, affecting systems that they were not intended to target.
- **transitions:** Policies need to be designed so that the targets of interventions do not get lost between components as their situations evolve.
- **the importance of families:** Families sometimes suffer because of a relative's substance use but also are key players in many components of the ecosystem.

Building on Previous Efforts

Multiple commissions, task forces, research teams, and other organizations and partnerships are working to reduce the harms associated with opioids (e.g., Barry, 2018; Kertesz, 2017; Kertesz and Gordon, 2019; Commission on Combating Synthetic Opioid Trafficking, 2022;

Humphreys et al., 2022). Our work builds on and extends this work. For example, Barry, 2018, recognized that changes in the illegal market related to the introduction of fentanyl would create challenges in multiple components of the opioid ecosystem, including criminal legal system, harm reduction, first responders, and SUD treatment. Furthermore, Kertesz and others have written about the potential dangers of focusing primarily on opioid prescribing within the medical care system, underscoring the need for policymakers to consider how efforts to address such prescribing can both affect and be affected by other systems (Kertesz, 2017; Kertesz and Gordon, 2019).

Several efforts have taken a broader view, exploring how social determinants of health create an environment that is likely to exacerbate opioid misuse and overdose while raising barriers to effective treatment. Researchers have also explored ways in which policies addressing some of these social determinants could improve the response to the opioid crisis in many dimensions of the system, including the specialty SUD treatment system, the criminal legal system, and community efforts at harm reduction (Park et al., 2020; Dasgupta, Beletsky, and Ciccarone, 2018). Saloner and colleagues, among others, have examined the variety of opioid-related harms across multiple systems. In their work, they argued that considering the crisis as a public health problem presents valuable opportunities across multiple elements of the overall system to implement policies addressing various aspects of the crisis (Saloner, McGinty, et al., 2018; Bingham, Cooper, and Hough, 2016).[11]

We laud these previous and ongoing efforts and acknowledge their important contributions. However, we extend the prior work on several important dimensions. We consider, more explicitly and in greater detail, the specific ways in which the opioid crisis affects system components that are less commonly considered, such as the education system, employers, and the child welfare system. We also consider how policies in those parts of the system may affect components that are more commonly considered, such as the health care system, criminal legal system, and SUD treatment system. We examine policies that would be implemented within systems that could have potential benefits in other systems; we also appraise policies that must be implemented across systems and suggest ways to do so.

The challenges associated with interactions across system components are not unique to opioids. Such concepts as coordination, redundancy, and unintended consequences are fundamental issues in the fields of public administration and business management.[12] In the case

---

[11] There is sometimes a tendency for discussions about drug policy to devolve into "criminal justice versus public health" debates. We find this framing too simplistic and not very helpful for promoting productive policy conversations. There are obvious tensions among various components of the ecosystem, but there are also some synergies, collaborations, and innovations that should be recognized. These debates can be more productive if the focus is on specific levers, agencies, and actions, and one goal of this report is to foster and inform these more specific discussions.

[12] Indeed, there have been numerous attempts to coordinate health services, and some look beyond traditional medical care settings. One example is the Robert Wood Johnson Foundation's Culture of Health Action Framework, which conceives of "a strengthened health care system in which medical care, public health, and social services interact to produce a more effective, equitable, higher-value whole that maxi-

of opioids, some of the system-related questions are "bread and butter" health systems issues. For example, are those receiving treatment for an OUD receiving nonmedical services (e.g., housing) that will improve the probability of sustained recovery?

But the systems questions around opioids become increasingly complex when one factors in profit-maximizing entities—be they pharmaceutical firms or illegal drug suppliers—that have an incentive to persuade people to use or misuse opioids. As noted earlier, there are some policies intended to protect potential victims of drug-related harms (e.g., children, public housing residents, employers) that can also create challenges for PWUO or people who are in recovery. Policymakers often have to balance these competing interests.

Major Components of the Ecosystem

At the core of the opioid ecosystem are the individuals who use opioids and their families; these are the topics of the next two chapters. We also explore the following ten major components of the opioid ecosystem, which are affected by and affect such individuals (see Figure 1.1):

1. **Substance use disorder treatment** covers services by providers who specialize in treating substance use disorders. These services include engaging individuals in treatment, providing effective treatment, retaining individuals in treatment for long enough for the treatment to be beneficial, supporting individuals in recovery, and facilitating reengagement with treatment among individuals in recovery who start using again.

2. **Medical care** covers physical and mental health care beyond specialty substance use disorder treatment. It encompasses health care providers, health care delivery organizations, insurers, pharmaceutical companies, medical training organizations, and various regulatory bodies.

3. **Criminal legal system** includes local, state, and federal laws; law enforcement agencies; lawyers and courts; corrections agencies (including community supervision); and the private and nonprofit organizations that support these institutions (e.g., drug-testing companies).

4. **Illegal supply and supply control** is a broad component, encompassing drug trafficking organizations, "pill mills," and people who use opioids but give or sell (some of) their prescription opioids to others. Supply control includes criminal justice agencies and regulatory agencies, such as the U.S. Food and Drug Administration.

5. **Harm reduction and community-initiated interventions** include interventions to reduce risks and stigma associated with drug use, such as naloxone distribution pro-

---

mizes health and well-being for all" (Martin et al., 2016, p. 1976). Our challenges with opioids, however, extend far beyond the health care system.

FIGURE 1.1
The Opioid Ecosystem

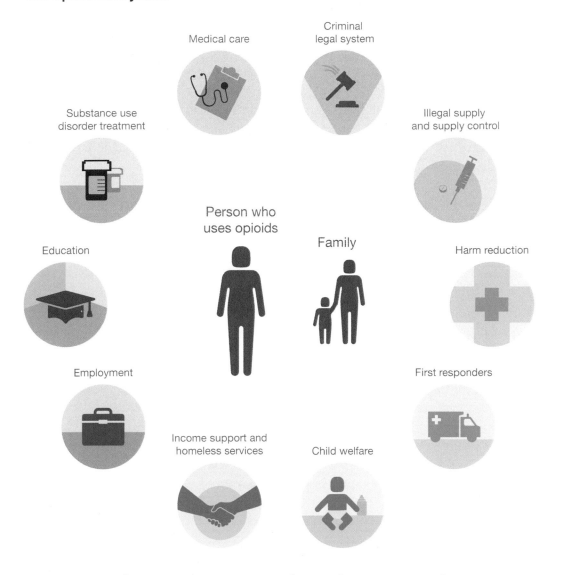

grams and syringe service programs, along with community coalitions to prevent and reduce the harms of drug use.

6. **First responders** covers professionals who provide medical assistance in emergency situations, including drug overdoses. Our discussion addresses three main types of first responders—law enforcement, fire and rescue, and emergency medical services.

7. **Child welfare** covers public and private services designed to ensure that children are safe and protected from abuse and neglect, ensure that they live in stable and permanent environments, and support child well-being.

8. **Income support and homeless services** covers public support programs, largely focusing on Social Security Disability Insurance, Supplemental Security Income, welfare (Temporary Assistance for Needy Families), and agencies that provide services to people experiencing homelessness.
9. **Employment** addresses the myriad ways in which labor markets affect and are, in turn, affected by opioids, including through the behaviors of both employees and employers.
10. **Education** is affected by the opioid ecosystem in many ways. Although it is not an explicit goal of the education system to address the opioid crisis or opioid use, the opioid crisis touches the education system in a variety of direct and indirect ways through its effect on individuals and communities.

The components we have identified are neither mutually exclusive nor exhaustive. For example, substance use disorder treatment is just one part of the medical care system; however, the issues surrounding the former are so central to the crisis that considering it a separate component of the ecosystem is justified. Similarly, the concept of illegal supply and how it is addressed are shaped by the criminal legal system.

We do not identify separate components for social services or public health because they are covered by other parts of the ecosystem. Social services are addressed in the chapters on child welfare (Chapter Ten), income support and homeless services (Chapter Eleven), employment (Chapter Twelve), and education (Chapter Thirteen). The traditional roles of public health agencies are addressed in the chapters on the specialty treatment system for opioid use disorders (Chapter Four), medical care (Chapter Five), and harm reduction and community-initiated interventions (Chapter Eight). Furthermore, surveillance is discussed in these chapters and in the chapters on the criminal legal system (Chapter Six) and illegal supply (Chapter Seven).

The components in Figure 1.1 are not inherently of equal importance; importance depends on the outcomes being considered. For example, if one were focused on issues related to the supply of opioids, the medical care, substance use disorder treatment, criminal legal system, and illegal supply components would be more prominently featured. If one were more focused on reducing harms related to drug use, the harm reduction and community-initiated interventions and first responders components deserve more attention.

The box on the next page offers three specific examples of how thinking about opioids as an ecosystem can enhance policy analyses and improve lives.

Humanizing the Ecosystem

The opioid ecosystem is more than macro-level interactions at the policy level; millions of people affected by opioids interact with many of the system components. Understanding these touchpoints can help identify barriers to effective interventions and policy opportunities.

To help bring the ecosystem concept to life, we offer several vignettes that begin with a focus on individuals and then highlight the system components with which they interact. The

Three Examples of How Thinking About Opioids as an Ecosystem Could Make a Difference

Acknowledging that family matters. OUD creates harms for those with that medical condition and can negatively affect family members and others close to the individual with OUD; however, most policies and programs neglect these other stakeholders. Indeed, most past economic studies of opioids have failed to account for this, largely because it is hard to quantify and collect data on the emotional, physical, financial, and mental health harms often associated with having a loved one who has an SUD and the effects that this situation can have on performance in school or productivity at work. Acknowledging these consequences would justify devoting time and resources to helping these families reduce the overall burdens imposed by OUD.

Making it easier for those with OUD to move across system components to obtain services. Several steps can be taken to address the challenges that occur as individuals with OUD move across system components (e.g., medical care, criminal justice, income support). At the juncture between components, it is unclear who is responsible for a successful transition. In many cases, this means that no one is responsible. Although many system components use case managers, some of whom work across components (e.g., treatment providers helping patients gain access to social services), too often individuals with OUD fall through the cracks between components. By clarifying who is responsible at these junctures and providing resources necessary to meet the commitment of the additional responsibility, we can diminish some of the disconnects that hamper provision of treatment and support.

Better understanding the far-reaching effects of changing drug laws and enforcement strategies. There is a growing discussion about decriminalizing the possession and use of all drugs in the United States. In November 2020, Oregon voters passed an initiative to not only decriminalize all drugs—including heroin and illegally produced fentanyl—but also redirect funds from cannabis tax revenues to provide health assessments and other services to those cited for drug possession. Other jurisdictions (e.g., Washington, Massachusetts) are discussing related measures. Now is the time to rigorously analyze the potential effects of these efforts. Better understanding how criminal laws and law enforcement actions affect the other components (e.g., eligibility for some health services, treatment referrals) can lead to more-rigorous and -informative analyses, and hopefully better policies.

vignettes are fictitious and do not represent specific individuals or families; however, they are consistent with the experiences of many individuals in communities throughout the country. Chapter Two, which describes individuals who use opioids, sheds further light on how individuals may find themselves in situations similar to those described in these vignettes.

Each vignette is accompanied by a version of Figure 1.1 that highlights the dimensions of the ecosystem that play the most active roles in the vignette.

Vignette 1: Becky and Mike

Becky (age 30) and her son Mike (age 9) lived in one of the seven states that drop individuals from Medicaid if they are imprisoned (Kaiser Family Foundation, 2019). Becky became dependent on the opioid pain medication Vicodin after extensive dental surgery that was covered by Medicaid. Her dentist stopped writing prescriptions six weeks after the surgery, but Becky started doctor shopping to obtain more opioid pain medications, and because prescribers were not required to check the Prescription Drug Monitoring Program in Becky's state, none of them realized that Becky was getting pain medications from multiple places. Becky's opioid misuse made her less productive at work, and she began stealing from her

FIGURE 1.2

The Opioid Ecosystem: Vignette 1

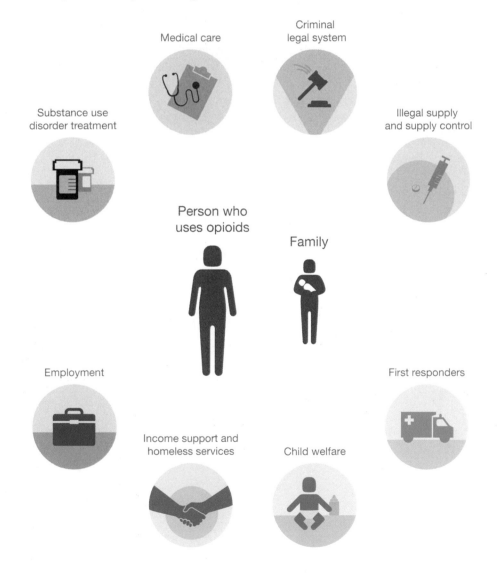

coworkers to feed her increasingly expensive habit. Ultimately, she lost her job and began to sell pills to pay the rent, buy groceries, and cover the costs of her own opioid consumption.

After running a red light while she was high, Becky was arrested for impaired driving. Because this was her first offense, she was sentenced to probation and mandatory attendance at a 12-step program. However, compliance was not consistently enforced, and Becky stopped attending. Within a month, she was convicted a second time for possession with intent to distribute (she had prescription bottles obtained from other people, whose names were on the label). She was remanded to a drug court, which ordered her to counseling, but it did not provide an option for medication treatment for her opioid use disorder.[13]

While in the drug court program, Becky was arrested, convicted for selling drugs, and sentenced to prison, where treatment for her opioid use disorder was not available. Becky's son Mike moved in with Becky's parents. Once she was released, Becky had nowhere to go and no source of income. She moved in with her parents but began to use drugs again. To finance her renewed use, Becky borrowed money from her parents under false pretenses but failed to pay them back. Shortly thereafter, she overdosed on opioids. Her parents called 911, the paramedic was able to revive her with naloxone, and Becky survived.

She was determined to get into treatment, but had no insurance coverage because she had been disenrolled from Medicaid when she was incarcerated. She had reapplied for Medicaid when she was released, but the process of being reinstated took time, and during that period without insurance, Becky was unable to get treatment. Furthermore, the drug convictions made it harder for her to obtain public income support or to find a job. After more than three months of struggling, Becky's mom found her after an overdose. This time, the paramedic could not revive her.

Vignette 2: James

James (age 55) worked in a refrigerator assembly plant in Ohio. He had a history of depression, which was exacerbated by his heavy drinking. Toward the end of a shift, he caught his sleeve in a conveyor belt and severely injured his arm and shoulder. The physician to whom he was referred through workers compensation prescribed OxyContin to help him with pain while he was in physical therapy. After six weeks, James was sufficiently recovered that he resumed work, although he still had chronic pain. He did not stop taking OxyContin because he enjoyed how it made him feel. As his body's tolerance to the medication increased, he needed a stronger dose. After several months, he started to crush the prescribed pills and snort them.

James then "traded down" to heroin; first smoking, then injecting. He was aware that injecting drugs was risky in terms of infection, disease transmission, and overdose, so he regularly visited syringe service programs to pick up sterile supplies.

---

[13] Efforts have been made to close this gap in many jurisdictions (see, e.g., California Health Policy Strategies, 2018).

FIGURE 1.3
The Opioid Ecosystem: Vignette 2

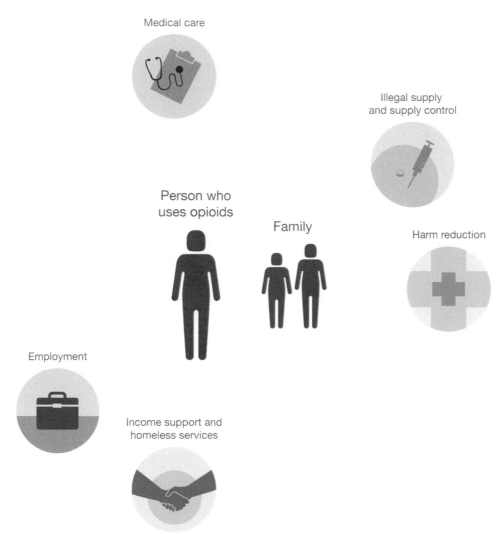

James continued to work in the factory, although he knew he was less productive (a phenomenon referred to as *presenteeism*). But he did not ask for help; he was not sure he had a "real" problem because he was working, and he knew that asking for treatment would brand him as a "junkie" among his managers and coworkers.

Eventually, his poor performance cost him his job. He continued to inject heroin. Physical labor was now prohibitively painful, but there were no vocational programs to help him make a transition to less physically demanding employment. Without a job, he could no longer afford his apartment. He lived in his car for a while, but it was stolen, so he lived on the street.

Dealers in the area started to adulterate heroin with fentanyl. James unknowingly injected a mixed bag and ended up overdosing. He survived, but examination in the emergency department revealed that he had contracted infective endocarditis, a dangerous infection of one of the heart valves, from injecting these substances. Treatment involved intravenous antibiotics for six weeks, which was covered by Medicaid.

With his endocarditis treated, James is back on the street. He continues to struggle with his opioid use disorder, drinks heavily, and has no available help for his mental health issues.

Vignette 3: Louie

Louie (age 17) was a high-school student in California who worked as a waiter at a local restaurant. He was a B-average student who was well liked by his classmates and teachers and very involved in school activities. He did not get in trouble other than one suspension when he and some friends were caught drinking at a high school football game. After taking Percocet at a few parties over the course of his junior year, he discovered that his mom had a bottle of prescription opioids left over from a medical procedure performed the previous year. The dozen or so pills remaining in that bottle lasted him a few weeks, and he really enjoyed the high. It was not interfering with his school or job, and no one suspected that he was using.

Most youth who experiment with opioid analgesics do not proceed to misusing them, but this was not the case for Louie. He started buying pills regularly from one of his coworkers and, after a few months, realized that he was feeling anxious and sometimes nauseous when he was not taking them. He started spending even more of his tips to buy pills. He knew that some of those pills were likely counterfeit, but they tended to be cheaper. As he ramped up his use over the next few months, his boss and parents noticed that he was acting differently and was generally less reliable.

After a friend overdosed from a counterfeit pill that contained fentanyl, Louie admitted to his parents that he thought he had a problem and was scared of overdosing like his friend. His parents acquired some naloxone to keep in the house and convinced him to see a doctor for treatment. As is all too common, his parents had a difficult time finding a doctor to prescribe buprenorphine to Louie because he was only 17, but after three months of searching, they finally found a physician willing to treat him.

Louis has been stable on buprenorphine for 18 months, graduated from high school, and started college. However, his college girlfriend keeps telling him that taking buprenorphine is "just trading one drug for another," so his parents are afraid he might stop taking it and go back to using counterfeit pills.

FIGURE 1.4
The Opioid Ecosystem: Vignette 3

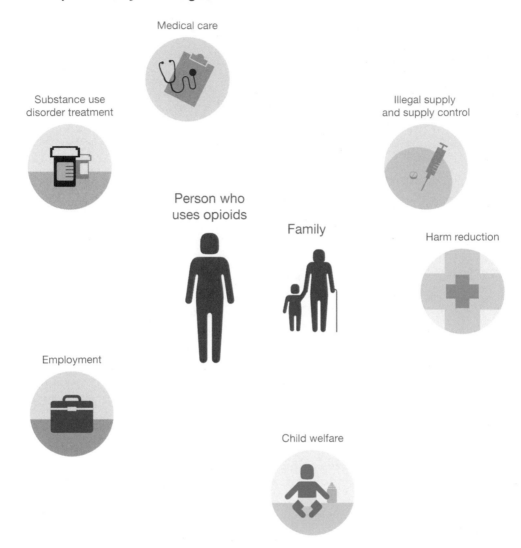

Vignette 4: Eleanor and Clare

Eleanor, a 38-year-old single mom, lives with her 15-year-old daughter Clare. Eleanor had a good job as a manager in a busy accountant's office. She occasionally snorted heroin. Eleanor's new live-in boyfriend was more than an occasional heroin user, and Eleanor started to use it more frequently. Heroin was only a phone call away in the city where they lived. When her boyfriend left her, Eleanor's drug consumption increased sharply.

Like the millions of children living in the households in the United States where a parent is using opioids for nonprescribed purposes (Bullinger and Wing, 2019), Clare was neglected because of her mom's substance use. She had been a good student, but now her schoolwork suffered. Her teachers saw the change and noticed that Eleanor no longer showed up for parent-teacher conferences. Clare had several close friends she hung out with, but now she was embarrassed to ask them to come over because she never knew what state her mom would be in. She felt increasingly isolated.

Eleanor's drug use spiraled out of control, and she began injecting even more than usual because the illegally produced fentanyl she started purchasing gave her a shorter high than heroin. Her elderly parents took Clare for a few months so Eleanor could enter an abstinence-based residential treatment facility. Clare was confused, and her grandparents really struggled to take care of her.

Eleanor emerged from treatment, remained drug-free for a time, and Clare moved back in with her. But the stability did not last. As is common with those completing treatment for opioid use disorder (NIDA, 2018a), Eleanor started using drugs again and became prone to angry outbursts as she despaired about her addiction. Child Protective Services and Child Welfare became involved. The agency recommended temporary foster care.

FIGURE 1.5
The Opioid Ecosystem: Vignette 4

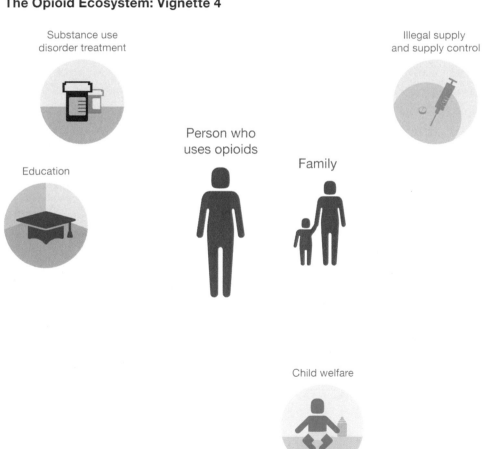

Eleanor eventually got medication treatment for her opioid use disorder. She had occasional relapses, but she made Clare's needs a priority and continued with treatment. However, she was unable to stay off drugs for long enough to meet the Child Welfare threshold. Ultimately, the agency recommended terminating Eleanor's parental rights. Because Clare could not stay with her grandparents, she will remain in foster care until she is 18, unless she is adopted.

Vignette 5: Doug

Doug (age 44) is an independent trucker. His wife Marie, a 42-year-old stay-at-home mother of two young children, has had opioid use disorder since shortly after a car accident, when she was prescribed opioids for chronic pain. Marie suffered four nonfatal overdoses over the prior two years, leading to multiple trips to the emergency department. During this time, Doug was anxious about Marie's well-being and changed jobs to local driving instead of cross-country trips to avoid prolonged separation from his wife. After Marie's second and third overdoses, the emergency department referred her to outpatient treatment. However, Marie stopped treatment in both instances after just a few weeks and unsuccessfully tried to hide this from Doug.

Despite his understanding of substance use disorder, Doug could not help but feel frustrated with the situation. Finally, after the fourth overdose, Marie was referred to a residential treatment program. Doug supports Marie's participation in residential treatment and tells Marie to put her health first.

To care for the children while Marie is in treatment, Doug will have to survive without a paycheck. He tells Marie not to worry about the cost, although their insurance does not cover residential treatment and child care will be an issue; he assures her that they will figure it out, likely through a bank loan or by borrowing money from friends and family.

Doug's parents, who live nearby, have offered to take care of the children so that Doug can resume work and cover the mounting costs. However, Doug knows that this would require his elderly parents, who live on a fixed income, to undertake a major lifestyle change. Thus, he would prefer to avoid this scenario. The stress eats at Doug, and he takes it out on the kids by yelling at—and sometimes hitting—them. The stress at home has also affected the children at school: Both have struggled with schoolwork over the past two years, and the youngest has been having more behavior problems at both home and school.

FIGURE 1.6
The Opioid Ecosystem: Vignette 5

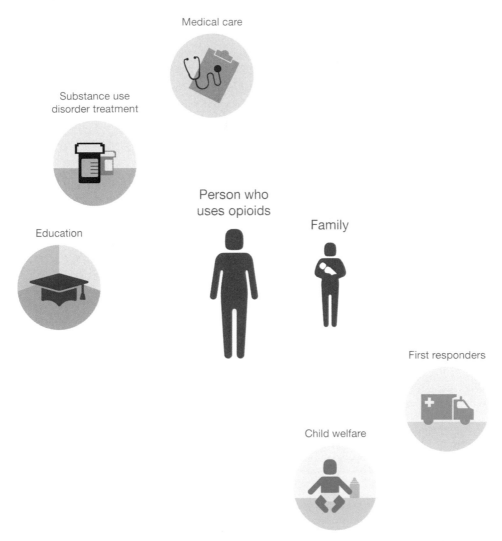

Approach and Structure of This Report

Our work and that of other researchers suggests that policy discussions most commonly focus on individual system components, giving short shrift to interactions between the components and the policy options available (Saloner, McGinty, et al., 2018; Stein, 2019; Park et al., 2020; Schuler et al., 2020). Much of this previous work has also largely focused on individuals with OUD and not on their families. This report is intended to help fill this gap, and more importantly, to help improve outcomes related to opioid problems.

The primary audience for this report is decisionmakers at the federal, state, and local levels. It should also be useful for foundations and philanthropic donors looking for opportunities to create change that have often been overlooked. Finally, we believe that this effort can help (1) researchers better understand the full consequences of policy changes with respect to opioids and other drugs and (2) members of the media identify the dynamics of interactions (or lack thereof) among parts of the system that deserve more attention and discussion.

We dedicate a chapter to each of the components of the ecosystem presented in Figure 1.1. Chapter Two provides background information about PWUO, who constitute the demand side of the market. There is an extensive and growing body of literature on the epidemiology of opioid use and polysubstance use in the United States. We do not attempt to present a systematic review of this work. Instead, we draw on some of these studies and on secondary data analyses to address nine questions that provide context for understanding our current problems with opioids and how those problems have evolved.

Chapter Three focuses on the family members and loved ones of those who use opioids. This is an underexamined topic that is critical not only for understanding the full consequences of opioid consumption (both the harms and benefits) but also for identifying opportunities for improving the lives of PWUO and those around them.

Chapters Four through Thirteen, which focus on the components of our ecosystem model, are written by RAND researchers with extensive experience in that particular domain. The chapters have a similar structure. The authors begin each chapter by describing the component and how it affects and is affected by opioids. They then highlight the other ecosystem components with which it interacts and present policy considerations. In some cases, the policy change would influence processes or outcomes within the system components highlighted in that chapter; in other cases, the changes could have their greatest impact in other parts of the ecosystem.

Some of the policy considerations we offer are motivated by existing peer-reviewed research, but for many, there is little or no empirical evidence evaluating anticipated policy effects; they are ideas we believe could make a positive difference in some—but not necessarily all—communities. That is why we describe them as considerations as opposed to full-throated endorsements.[14]

The final chapter, Chapter Fourteen, synthesizes the chapter-specific findings (with a special focus on barriers to progress), identifies common issues that affect multiple components of the ecosystem, and offers ideas for prioritizing policy considerations. These priorities likely will differ depending on whether one's perspective is federal, state, or local, and we highlight this issue in that chapter.

We do not limit our discussion of policy considerations to those mentioned in the previous chapters. Indeed, one of the advantages of producing this report is that it prompts one to assess the opioid policy landscape comprehensively and to think creatively about new ideas and missed opportunities involving multiple components.

---

[14] Appendix B lists all ideas discussed in these chapters and where the change would likely occur (e.g., at the federal, state, local, and/or nongovernmental level).

Throughout the report, we highlight extensive interactions between the various components. We note that "extensive" is a qualitative judgment rather than one based on a single formula. Because the components interact in different ways on multiple dimensions (e.g., flows of people, levels of government, timing and context of the interaction), it is difficult to apply a universal rule. The existence of more-extensive interactions is highlighted in a modified ecosystem graphic at the beginning of each chapter.

Our approach has limitations. First, the components displayed in Figure 1.1 are not the only ones affecting and affected by opioid use. (For example, we do not discuss the role of public transportation, which can play an important role in accessing treatment and other health services [Marsh, D'Aunno, and Smith, 2000; Syed, Gerber, and Sharp, 2013].) However, to make the ecosystem concept tractable and most useful to decisionmakers, we selected those components that we believe offer the most potential for creating positive change.

Second, our approach does not generate an exhaustive list of *all* options available to decisionmakers within each of the components. We focus primarily on policy considerations that could have the biggest impact on other components with respect to opioids and on those that require coordination and interaction across multiple components.

Finally, it is beyond the scope of this report to conduct a cost-benefit analysis for policy opportunities. In fact, one of the advantages of our approach is that it will generate new ideas for which there as of yet may be little or no empirical evidence. We highlight this issue in the synthesis chapter, making it clear which options have greater empirical support and which are new and may be worth piloting or deserving of additional analysis.

We anticipate that most individuals will focus on the chapter(s) that are most germane to their own interests and experience; however, we recommend that readers review the next two chapters on PWUO and their families before reading the others. We have structured our discussion to make it easy for readers to learn about the roles of other components. Thus, to the extent possible, each chapter is a stand-alone discussion of the opioid-related issues in that part of the ecosystem and of the component's interactions with other parts of the system. In the service of that goal, we have allowed some duplication of material across chapters.

This report is certainly not the final word on the opioid crisis. At its current pace, this evolving tragedy is expected to kill hundreds of thousands of people over the next five years and lead to addiction and burdens for millions more. However, we believe that focusing on the opioid ecosystem and the interactions of its components will enrich how policymakers, practitioners, and researchers understand this dynamic problem and enhance their choices about how to move forward. This will hopefully save lives and improve quality of life for both people with substance use disorders and their loved ones.

Abbreviations

CDC	Centers for Disease Control and Prevention
COVID-19	coronavirus disease 2019
NIDA	National Institute on Drug Abuse
MOUD	medications for opioid use disorder
OUD	opioid use disorder
PWUO	people who use opioids
SAMHSA	Substance Abuse and Mental Health Services Administration
SUD	substance use disorder

References

Agnoli, Alicia, Guibo Xing, Daniel J. Tancredi, Elizabeth Magnan, Anthony Jerant, and Joshua J. Fenton, "Association of Dose Tapering with Overdose or Mental Health Crisis Among Patients Prescribed Long-Term Opioids," *JAMA*, Vol. 326, No. 5, 2021, pp. 411–419.

Alexander, Monica J., Mathew V. Kiang, and Magali Barbieri, "Trends in Black and White Opioid Mortality in the United States, 1979–2015," *Epidemiology*, Vol. 29, No. 5, 2018, pp. 707–715.

American Medical Association, *Physicians' Actions to Help End the Nation's Drug-Related Overdose and Death Epidemic—and What Still Needs to Be Done,* Chicago, Ill., 2021.

Andraka-Christou, Barbara, Kathryn Bouskill, Rebecca L. Haffajee, Olivia Randall-Kosich, Matthew Golan, Rachel Totaram, Adam J. Gordon, and Bradley D. Stein, "Common Themes in Early State Policy Responses to Substance Use Disorder Treatment During COVID-19," *American Journal of Drug and Alcohol Abuse*, Vol. 47, No. 4, 2021, pp. 486–496.

Anthony, James C., Lynn A. Warner, and Ronald C. Kessler, "Comparative Epidemiology of Dependence on Tobacco, Alcohol, Controlled Substances, and Inhalants: Basic Findings from the National Comorbidity Survey," *Experimental and Clinical Psychopharmacology*, Vol. 2, No. 3, 1994, pp. 244–268.

Ashford, Robert D., Austin M. Brown, Jessica McDaniel, and Brenda Curtis, "Biased Labels: An Experimental Study of Language and Stigma Among Individuals in Recovery and Health Professionals," *Substance Use & Misuse*, Vol. 54, No. 8, 2019, pp. 1376–1384.

Barry, Colleen L., "Fentanyl and the Evolving Opioid Epidemic: What Strategies Should Policy Makers Consider?" *Psychiatric Services*, Vol. 69, No. 1, 2018, pp. 100–103.

Beletsky, Leo, "America's Favorite Antidote: Drug-Induced Homicide in the Age of the Overdose Crisis," *Utah Law Review*, Vol. 2019, No. 4, 2019, pp. 833–890.

Bingham, Kevin, Terri Cooper, and Lindsay Hough, "Fighting the Opioid Crisis: An Ecosystem Approach to a Wicked Problem," Deloitte Insights, 2016. As of April 1, 2021: https://www2.deloitte.com/us/en/insights/industry/public-sector/fighting-opioid-crisis-heroin-abuse-ecosystem-approach.html

Bluthenthal, Ricky N., "Structural Racism and Violence as Social Determinants of Health: Conceptual, Methodological and Intervention Challenges," *Drug and Alcohol Dependence*, Vol. 222, 2021.

Boiko-Weyrauch, Anna, "Fentanyl Is a Great Drug for Cartels. But Those Blue Pills Are Killing King County," NPR, December 3, 2021.

Bullinger, Lindsey Rose, and Coady Wing, "How Many Children Live with Adults with Opioid Use Disorder?" *Children and Youth Services Review*, Vol. 104, 2019.

Buresh, Megan, Becky L. Genberg, Jacquie Astemborski, Gregory D. Kirk, and Shruti H. Mehta, "Recent Fentanyl Use Among People Who Inject Drugs: Results from a Rapid Assessment in Baltimore, Maryland," *International Journal of Drug Policy*, Vol. 74, December 2019, pp. 41–46.

Burgess, Diana J., David B. Nelson, Amy A. Gravely, Matthew J. Bair, Robert D. Kerns, Diana M. Higgins, Michelle van Ryn, Melissa Farmer, and Melissa R. Partin, "Racial Differences in Prescription of Opioid Analgesics for Chronic Noncancer Pain in a National Sample of Veterans," *Journal of Pain*, Vol. 15, No. 4, 2014, pp. 447–455.

Cabreros, Irineo, Beth Ann Griffin, Brendan Saloner, Adam J. Gordon, Rose Kerber, and Bradley D. Stein, "Buprenorphine Prescriber Monthly Patient Caseloads: An Examination of 6-Year Trajectories," *Drug and Alcohol Dependence*, Vol. 228, 2021.

California Health Policy Strategies, *Collaborative Courts and Medication-Assisted Treatment in California*, Sacramento, Calif., October 2018.

Cantor, Jonathan, Andrew W. Dick, Rebecca Haffajee, Megan F. Pera, Dena M. Bravata, Bradley D. Stein, and Christopher M. Whaley, "Use of Buprenorphine for Those with Employer-Sponsored Insurance During the Initial Phase of the COVID-19 Pandemic," *Journal of Substance Abuse Treatment*, Vol. 129, 2021.

Caulkins, Jonathan P., Beau Kilmer, Peter H. Reuter, and Greg Midgette, "Cocaine's Fall and Marijuana's Rise: Questions and Insights Based on New Estimates of Consumption and Expenditures in U.S. Drug Markets," *Addiction*, Vol. 110, No. 5, 2015, pp. 728–736.

CDC—*See* Centers for Disease Control and Prevention.

Centers for Disease Control and Prevention, "Alcohol Related Disease Impact (ARDI) Application," webpage, 2019. As of April 1, 2021:
www.cdc.gov/ARDI

Centers for Disease Control and Prevention, "Provisional Drug Overdose Death Counts," webpage, 2021a. As of April 1, 2021:
https://www.cdc.gov/nchs/nvss/vsrr/drug-overdose-data.htm

Centers for Disease Control and Prevention, "About Social Determinants of Health (SDOH)," webpage, March 10, 2021b. As of April 1, 2021:
https://www.cdc.gov/socialdeterminants/about.html

Centers for Disease Control and Prevention, "Provisional Drug Overdose Death Counts," webpage, updated February 15, 2023. As of February 17, 2023:
https://www.cdc.gov/nchs/nvss/vsrr/drug-overdose-data.htm

Cicero, Theodore J., Matthew S. Ellis, and Zachary A. Kasper, "Polysubstance Use: A Broader Understanding of Substance Use During the Opioid Crisis," *American Journal of Public Health*, Vol. 110, No. 2, 2020, pp. 244–250.

Collier, Melissa G., Mona Doshani, and Alice Asher, "Using Population Based Hospitalization Data to Monitor Increases in Conditions Causing Morbidity Among Persons Who Inject Drugs," *Journal of Community Health*, Vol. 43, No. 3, 2018, pp. 598–603.

Commission on Combating Synthetic Opioid Trafficking, *Commission on Combating Synthetic Opioid Trafficking: Final Report*, Washington, D.C., February 2022.

Dahlhamer, James, Jacqueline Lucas, Carla Zelaya, Richard Nahin, Sean Mackey, Lynn DeBar, Robert Kerns, Michael Von Korff, Linda Porter, and Charles Helmick, "Prevalence of Chronic Pain and High-Impact Chronic Pain Among Adults—United States, 2016," *Morbidity and Mortality Weekly Report*, Vol. 67, No. 36, 2018, pp. 1001–1006.

Dasgupta, Nabarun, Leo Beletsky, and Daniel Ciccarone, "Opioid Crisis: No Easy Fix to Its Social and Economic Determinants," *American Journal of Public Health*, Vol. 108, 2018, pp. 182–186.

Degenhardt, Louisa, Harvey A. Whiteford, Alize J. Ferrari, Amanda J. Baxter, Fiona J. Charlson, Wayne D. Hall, Greg Freedman, Roy Burstein, Nicole John, Rebecca E. Engell, et al., "Global Burden of Disease Attributable to Illicit Drug Use and Dependence: Findings from the Global Burden of Disease Study 2010," *The Lancet*, Vol. 382, No. 9904, 2013, pp. 1564–1574.

Demidenko, Michael I., Steven K. Dobscha, Benjamin J. Morasco, Thomas H. A. Meath, Mark A. Ilgen, and Travis I. Lovejoy, "Suicidal Ideation and Suicidal Self-Directed Violence Following Clinician-Initiated Prescription Opioid Discontinuation Among Long-Term Opioid Users," *General Hospital Psychiatry*, Vol. 47, July 2017, pp. 29–35.

DiPrete, Bethany L., Shabbar I. Ranapurwala, Courtney N. Maierhofer, Naoko Fulcher, Paul R. Chelminski, Christopher L. Ringwalt, Timothy J. Ives, Nabarun Dasgupta, Vivian F. Go., and Brian W. Pence, "Association of Opioid Dose Reduction with Opioid Overdose and Opioid Use Disorder Among Patients Receiving High-Dose, Long-Term Opioid Therapy in North Carolina," *JAMA Network Open*, Vol. 5, No. 4, 2022.

Dowell, Deborah, Kathleen R. Ragan, Christopher M. Jones, Grant T. Baldwin, and Roger Chou, "CDC Clinical Practice Guidelines for Prescribing Opioids for Pain—United States, 2022," *Morbidity and Mortality Weekly Report*, Vol. 71, No. RR-3, 2022.

Fenton, Joshua J., Alicia L. Agnoli, Guibo Xing, Lillian Hang, Aylin E. Altan, Daniel J. Tancredi, Anthony Jerant, and Elizabeth Magnan, "Trends and Rapidity of Dose Tapering Among Patients Prescribed Long-Term Opioid Therapy, 2008–2017," *JAMA*, Vol. 2, No. 11, 2019.

Frank, Richard G., Keith Humphreys, and Harold Pollack, "Our Other Epidemic: Addiction," *JAMA Health Forum*, Vol. 2, No. 3, March 2021.

Gaither, Julie R., Kirsha Gordon, Stephen Crystal, E. Jennifer Edelman, Robert D. Kerns, Amy C. Justice, David A. Fiellin, and William C. Becker, "Racial Disparities in Discontinuation of Long-Term Opioid Therapy Following Illicit Drug Use Among Black and White Patients," *Drug and Alcohol Dependence*, Vol. 192, 2018, pp. 371–376.

Gounder, Celine, "Opioids Are a Bipartisan Issue Because They've Become a Mainstream, White One," *The Guardian*, June 9, 2016.

Gryczynski, Jan, Helen Nichols, Robert P. Schwartz, Shannon Gwin Mitchell, Paulette Hill, and Kim Wireman, "Fentanyl Exposure and Preferences Among Individuals Starting Treatment for Opioid Use Disorder," *Drug and Alcohol Dependence*, Vol. 204, November 2019.

Guy, Gery P., Andrea E. Strahan, Tamara Haegerich, Jan L. Losby, Kathleen Ragan, Mary E. Evans, and Christopher M. Jones, "Concurrent Naloxone Dispensing Among Individuals with High-Risk Opioid Prescriptions, USA, 2015–2019," *Journal of General Internal Medicine*, Vol. 36, No. 10, 2021, pp. 3254–3256.

Hart, Carl L., *Drug Use for Grown-Ups: Chasing Liberty in the Land of Fear*, New York: Penguin Press, 2021.

Health in Justice Action Lab, "Drug-Induced Homicide," webpage, undated. As of April 1, 2021: https://www.healthinjustice.org/drug-induced-homicide

Higgins, C., B. H. Smith, and K. Matthews, "Incidence of Iatrogenic Opioid Dependence or Abuse in Patients with Pain Who Were Exposed to Opioid Analgesic Therapy: A Systematic Review and Meta-Analysis," *British Journal of Anaesthesia*, Vol. 120, No. 6, 2018, pp. 1335–1344.

Hoffman, Jan, "Medicare Is Cracking Down on Opioids. Doctors Fear Pain Patients Will Suffer," *New York Times*, March 27, 2018.

Humphreys, Keith, Chelsea L. Shover, Christina M. Andrews, Amy S. Bohnert, Margaret L. Brandeau, Jonathan P. Caulkins, Jonathan H. Chen, Mariano-Florentino Cuéllar, Yasmin L. Hurd, David N. Juurlink, et al., "Responding to the Opioid Crisis in North America and Beyond: Recommendations of the Stanford–*Lancet* Commission," *The Lancet*, Vol. *399, No.* 10324, 2022, pp. 555–604.

Jalal, Hawre, Jeanine M. Buchanich, Mark S. Roberts, Lauren C. Balmert, Kun Zhang, and Donald S. Burke, "Changing Dynamics of the Drug Overdose Epidemic in the United States from 1979 through 2016," *Science*, Vol. 361, No. 6408, 2018.

Jones, Christopher M., "Heroin Use and Heroin Use Risk Behaviors Among Nonmedical Users of Prescription Opioid Pain Relievers–United States, 2002–2004 and 2008–2010," *Drug and Alcohol Dependence*, Vol. 132, No. 1-2, 2013, pp. 95–100.

Joshi, Sujati, Thomas Weiser, and Victoria Warren-Mears, "Drug, Opioid-Involved, and Heroin-Involved Overdose Deaths Among American Indians and Alaska Natives—Washington, 1999–2015," *Morbidity and Mortality Weekly Report*, Vol. 67, No. 50, 2018, 1384.

Kaiser Family Foundation, "States Reporting Corrections-Related Medicaid Enrollment Policies in Place for Prisons or Jails," webpage, 2019. As of November 5, 2020: https://www.kff.org/medicaid/state-indicator/ states-reporting-corrections-related-medicaid-enrollment-policies-in-place-for-prisons-or-jails

Kaplan, J., *The Hardest Drug: Heroin and Public Policy*, Chicago, Ill.: University of Chicago Press, 1983.

Keefe, Patrick Radden, *Empire of Pain: The Secret History of the Sackler Dynasty*, New York: Bond Street Books, 2021.

Kelly, John F., and Cassandra M. Westerhoff, "Does It Matter How We Refer to Individuals with Substance-Related Conditions? A Randomized Study of Two Commonly Used Terms," *International Journal of Drug Policy*, Vol. 21, No. 3, 2010, pp. 202–207.

Kennedy-Hendricks, Alene, Colleen L. Barry, Elizabeth Stone, Marcus A. Bachhuber, and Emma E. McGinty, "Comparing Perspectives on Medication Treatment for Opioid Use Disorder Between National Samples of Primary Care Trainee Physicians and Attending Physicians," *Drug and Alcohol Dependence*, Vol. 216, 2020.

Kertesz, Stefan G., "Turning the Tide or Riptide? The Changing Opioid Epidemic," *Substance Abuse*, Vol. 38, No. 1, January–March 2017, pp. 3–8.

Kertesz, Stefan G., and Adam J. Gordon, "A Crisis of Opioids and the Limits of Prescription Control: United States," *Addiction*, Vol. 114, No. 1, 2019, pp. 169–180.

Khatri, Utsha G., and Jeanmarie Perrone, "Opioid Use Disorder and COVID-19: Crashing of the Crises," *Journal of Addiction Medicine*, Vol. 14, No. 4, 2020, pp. e6–e7.

Kilian, Carolin, Jakob Manthey, Sinclair Carr, Franz Hanschmidt, Jürgen Rehm, Sven Speerforck, and Georg Schomerus, "Stigmatization of People with Alcohol Use Disorders: An Updated Systematic Review of Population Studies," *Alcoholism: Clinical and Experimental Research*, Vol. 45, No. 5, May 2021, pp. 899–911.

Kilmer, Beau, and Jonathan Caulkins, "Hard Drugs Demand Solid Understanding," *USA Today*, March 8, 2014. As of March 29, 2022:
https://www.usatoday.com/story/opinion/2014/03/08/
heroin-abuse-hoffman-research-column/6134337/

Krawczyk, Noa, Bianca D. Rivera, Victoria Jent, Katherine M. Keyes, Christopher M. Jones, and Magdalena Cerdá, "Has the Treatment Gap for Opioid Use Disorder Narrowed in the U.S.? A Yearly Assessment from 2010 to 2019," *International Journal of Drug Policy*, August 4, 2022.

Lagisetty, Pooja A., Nathaniel Healy, Claire Garpestad, Mary Jannausch, Renuka Tipirneni, and Amy S. B. Bohnert, "Access to Primary Care Clinics for Patients with Chronic Pain Receiving Opioids," *JAMA*, Vol. 2, No. 7, 2019.

Lagisetty, Pooja A., Ryan Ross, Amy Bohnert, Michael Clay, and Donovan T. Maust, "Buprenorphine Treatment Divide by Race/Ethnicity and Payment," *JAMA Psychiatry*, Vol. 76, No. 9, 2019, pp. 979–981.

Lambdin, Barrot H., Ricky N. Bluthenthal, Lynn D. Wenger, Eliza Wheeler, Bryan Garner, Paul Lakosky, and Alex H. Kral, "Overdose Education and Naloxone Distribution Within Syringe Service Programs—United States, 2019," *Morbidity and Mortality Weekly Report*, Vol. 69, No. 33, August 21, 2020, pp. 1117–1121.

Lopez, German, "Top Executives at Major Opioid Company Found Guilty of Criminal Racketeering," *Vox*, May 3, 2019. As of July 10, 2022:
https://www.vox.com/policy-and-politics/2019/5/3/18528123/
insys-fentanyl-trial-verdict-john-kapoor-opioid-epidemic

Mark, Tami L., and William Parish, "Opioid Medication Discontinuation and Risk of Adverse Opioid-Related Health Care Events," *Journal of Substance Abuse Treatment*, Vol. 103, 2019, pp. 58–63.

Mark, Tami L., George E. Woody, Tim Juday, and Herbert D. Kleber, "The Economic Costs of Heroin Addiction in the United States," *Drug and Alcohol Dependence*, Vol. 61, No. 2, 2001, pp. 195–206.

Mars, Sarah G., Philippe Bourgois, George Karandinos, Fernando Montero, and Daniel Ciccarone, "'Every "Never" I Ever Said Came True': Transitions from Opioid Pills to Heroin Injecting," *International Journal of Drug Policy*, Vol. 25, No. 2, 2014, pp. 257–266.

Mars, Sarah G., Daniel Rosenblum, and Daniel Ciccarone, "Illicit Fentanyls in the Opioid Street Market: Desired or Imposed?" *Addiction*, Vol. 114, No. 5, 2019, pp. 774–780.

Marsh, Jeanne C., Thomas A. D'Aunno, and Brenda D. Smith, "Increasing Access and Providing Social Services to Improve Drug Abuse Treatment for Women with Children," *Addiction*, Vol. 95, No. 8, 2000, pp. 1237–1247.

Martin, Laurie T., Alonzo Plough, Katherine G. Carman, Laura Leviton, Olena Bogdan, and Carolyn E. Miller, "Strengthening Integration of Health Services and Systems," *Health Affairs*, Vol. 35, No. 11, November 2016, pp. 1976–1981.

Mauro, Pia M., Sarah Gutkind, Erin M. Annunziato, and Hillary Samples, "Use of Medication for Opioid Use Disorder Among US Adolescents and Adults with Need for Opioid Treatment, 2019," *JAMA Network Open*, Vol. 5, No. 3, 2022.

McCormick, Erin, "'Historically Tragic': Why Are Drug Overdoses Rising Among Black and Indigenous Americans?" *The Guardian*, February 17, 2022.

Meier, Andrea, Sarah K. Moore, Elizabeth C. Saunders, Bethany McLeman, Stephen A. Metcalf, Samantha Auty, Olivia Walsh, and Lisa A. Marsch, "Understanding the Increase in Opioid Overdoses in New Hampshire: A Rapid Epidemiologic Assessment," *Drug and Alcohol Dependence*, Vol. 209, 2020.

Mojtabai, Ramin, Christine Mauro, Melanie M. Wall, Colleen L. Barry, and Mark Olfson, "Medication Treatment for Opioid Use Disorders in Substance Use Treatment Facilities," *Health Affairs*, Vol. 38, No. 1, 2019, pp. 14–23.

National Institute on Drug Abuse, *Principles of Drug Addiction Treatment: How Effective Is Drug Addiction Treatment?* Washington, D.C.: U.S. Department of Health and Human Services, January 2018a.

National Institute on Drug Abuse, *Principles of Drug Addiction Treatment: Is There a Difference Between Physical Dependence and Addiction?* Washington, D.C.: U.S. Department of Health and Human Services, January 2018b.

National Institute on Drug Abuse, "Drug Misuse and Addiction: What Is Drug Addiction," *Drugs, Brain, and Behavior: The Science of Addiction*, Washington, D.C.: U.S. Department of Health and Human Services, June 2020.

Nguyen, Thuy D., Sumedha Gupta, Engy Ziedan, Kosali I. Simon, G. Caleb Alexander, Brendan Saloner, and Bradley D. Stein, "Assessment of Filled Buprenorphine Prescriptions for Opioid Use Disorder During the Coronavirus Disease 2019 Pandemic," *JAMA Internal Medicine*, Vol. 181, No. 4, 2021, pp. 562–565.

Nicosia, Nancy, Rosalie Liccardo Pacula, Beau Kilmer, Russell Lundberg, and James Chiesa, *The Economic Cost of Methamphetamine Use in the United States, 2005*, Santa Monica, Calif.: RAND Corporation, MG-829-MPF/NIDA, 2009. As of May 25, 2022: https://www.rand.org/pubs/monographs/MG829.html

NIDA—*See* National Institute on Drug Abuse.

North Carolina Harm Reduction Coalition, "U.S. Law Enforcement Who Carry Naloxone," webpage, undated. As of May 25, 2022: http://www.nchrc.org/law-enforcement/us-law-enforcement-who-carry-naloxone/

North Carolina Medical Board, *North Carolina Medical Board Licensee Survey Results*, Raleigh, N.C., July 2018.

Oliva, Elizabeth M., Thomas Bowe, Ajay Manhapra, Stefan Kertesz, Jennifer M. Hah, Patricia Henderson, Amy Robinson, Meenah Paik, Friedhelm Sandbrink, Adam J. Gordon, and Jodie A. Trafton, "Associations Between Stopping Prescriptions for Opioids, Length of Opioid Treatment, and Overdose or Suicide Deaths in US Veterans: Observational Evaluation," *BMJ*, Vol. 368, 2020.

Organisation for Economic Co-operation and Development, *Addressing Problematic Opioid Use in OECD Countries*, Paris: OECD Health Policy Studies, 2019.

Pardo, Bryce, Jirka Taylor, Jonathan P. Caulkins, Beau Kilmer, Peter Reuter, and Bradley D. Stein, *The Future of Fentanyl and Other Synthetic Opioids*, Santa Monica, Calif.: RAND Corporation, RR-3117-RC, 2019. As of May 25, 2022: https://www.rand.org/pubs/research_reports/RR3117.html

Pardo, Bryce, Jirka Taylor, Jonathan Caulkins, Peter Reuter, and Beau Kilmer, "The Dawn of a New Synthetic Opioid Era: The Need for Innovative Interventions," *Addiction*, Vol. 116, No. 6, 2021, pp. 1304–1312.

Park, Ju Nyeong, Saba Rouhani, Leo Beletsky, Louise Vincent, Brendan Saloner, and Susan G. Sherman, "Situating the Continuum of Overdose Risk in the Social Determinants of Health: A New Conceptual Framework," *Milbank Quarterly*, Vol. 98, No. 3, September 2020, pp. 700–746.

Pessar, Seema Choksy, Anne Boustead, Yimin Ge, Rosanna Smart, and Rosalie Liccardo Pacula, "Assessment of State and Federal Health Policies for Opioid Use Disorder Treatment During the COVID-19 Pandemic and Beyond," *JAMA Health Forum*, Vol. 2, No. 11, 2021.

Phan, Michael T., Daniel M. Tomaszewski, Cody Arbuckle, Sun Yang, Candice Donaldson, Michelle Fortier, Brooke Jenkins, Erik Linstead, and Zeev Kain, "Racial and Ethnic Disparities in Opioid Use for Adolescents at US Emergency Departments," *BMC Pediatrics*, Vol. 21, No. 252, 2021.

Polkey, Chesterfield, "Most States Have Ended SNAP Ban for Convicted Drug Felons," National Conference of State Legislatures blog, 2019. As of September 9, 2021: https://www.ncsl.org/blog/2019/07/30/most-states-have-ended-snap-ban-for-convicted-drug-felons.aspx

Reuter, Peter, Jonathan P. Caulkins, and Greg Midgette, "Heroin Use Cannot Be Measured Adequately with a General Population Survey," *Addiction*, Vol. 116, No. 10, 2021, pp. 2600–2609.

Ronan, Matthew V., and Shoshana J. Herzig, "Hospitalizations Related to Opioid Abuse/Dependence and Associated Serious Infections Increased Sharply, 2002–12," *Health Affairs*, Vol. 35, No. 5, 2016, pp. 832–837.

Ruhm, Christopher J., "Corrected US Opioid-Involved Drug Poisoning Deaths and Mortality Rates, 1999–2015," *Addiction*, Vol. 113, No. 7, 2018, pp. 1339–1344.

Saloner, Brendan, and Benjamin Lê Cook, "Blacks and Hispanics Are Less Likely Than Whites to Complete Addiction Treatment, Largely Due to Socioeconomic Factors," *Health Affairs*, Vol. 32, No. 1, 2013, pp. 135–145.

Saloner, Brendan, Emma E. McGinty, Leo Beletsky, Ricky Bluthenthal, Chris Beyrer, Michael Botticelli, and Susan G. Sherman, "A Public Health Strategy for the Opioid Crisis," *Public Health Reports*, Vol. 133, Suppl. 1, 2018, pp. 24S–34S.

SAMHSA—*See* Substance Abuse and Mental Health Services Administration.

San Francisco Office of Economic and Workforce Development, *A Report from the San Francisco Street-Level Drug Dealing Task Force*, San Francisco, Calif., June 30, 2021.

Scholl, Lawrence, Puja Seth, Mbabazi Kariisa, Nana Wilson, Grant Baldwin, "Drug and Opioid-Involved Overdose Deaths—United States, 2013–2017," *Morbidity and Mortality Weekly Report*, Vol. 67, No. 5152, 2019, pp. 1419–1427.

Schuler, Megan S., Sara E. Heins, Rosanna Smart, Beth Ann Griffin, David Powell, Elizabeth A. Stuart, Bryce Pardo, Sierra Smucker, Stephen W. Patrick, Rosalie Liccardo Pacula, and Bradley D. Stein, "The State of the Science in Opioid Policy Research," *Drug and Alcohol Dependence*, Vol. 214, 2020.

Shachar, Carmel, Tess Wise, Gali Katznelson, and Andrea Louise Campbell, "Criminal Justice or Public Health: A Comparison of the Representation of the Crack Cocaine and Opioid Epidemics in the Media," *Journal of Health Politics, Policy and Law*, Vol. 45, No. 2, 2020, pp. 211–239.

Sharp, Alana, Austin Jones, Jennifer Sherwood, Oksana Kutsa, Brian Honermann, and Gregorio Millett, "Impact of Medicaid Expansion on Access to Opioid Analgesic Medications and Medication-Assisted Treatment," *American Journal of Public Health*, Vol. 108, No. 5, 2018, pp. 642–648.

Shatterproof and The Hartford, *Shatterproof Addiction Stigma Index*, Hartford, Conn., October 2021.

Shover, Chelsea L., Titilola O. Falasinnu, Candice L. Dwyer, Nayelie Benitez Santos, Nicole J. Cunningham, Rohan B. Freedman, Noel A. Vest, and Keith Humphreys, "Steep Increases in Fentanyl-Related Mortality West of the Mississippi River: Recent Evidence from County and State Surveillance," *Drug and Alcohol Dependence*, Vol. 216, 2020.

Singh, Jasvinder A., and John D. Cleveland, "National U.S. Time-Trends in Opioid Use Disorder Hospitalizations and Associated Healthcare Utilization and Mortality," *PloS One*, Vol. 15, No. 2, 2020.

Singhal, Astha, Yu-Yu Tien, and Renee Y. Hsia, "Racial-Ethnic Disparities in Opioid Prescriptions at Emergency Department Visits for Conditions Commonly Associated with Prescription Drug Abuse," *PLoS ONE*, Vol. 11, No. 8, 2016.

Slavova, Svetla, Chris Delcher, Jeannine M. Buchanich, Terry L. Bunn, Bruce A. Goldberger, and Julia F. Costich, "Methodological Complexities in Quantifying Rates of Fatal Opioid-Related Overdose," *Current Epidemiology Reports*, Vol. 6, 2019, pp. 263–274,

Smart, Rosanna, Bryce Pardo, and Corey S. Davis, "Systematic Review of the Emerging Literature on the Effectiveness of Naloxone Access Laws in the United States," *Addiction*, Vol. 116, No. 1, 2020, pp. 6–17.

Stahler, Gerald J., and Jeremy Mennis, "Treatment Outcome Disparities for Opioid Users: Are There Racial and Ethnic Differences in Treatment Completion Across Large Us Metropolitan Areas?" *Drug and Alcohol Dependence*, Vol. 190, 2018, pp. 170–178.

Stein, Bradley D., *Addressing the U.S. Opioid Crisis: Using an Integrated Systems-Based Approach*, Santa Monica, Calif.: RAND Corporation, CT-520, 2019. As of July 12, 2022: https://www.rand.org/pubs/testimonies/CT520.html

Stein, Bradley D., Rosanna Smart, Christopher M. Jones, Flora Sheng, David Powell, and Mark Sorbero, "Individual and Community Factors Associated with Naloxone Co-Prescribing Among Long-Term Opioid Patients: A Retrospective Analysis," *Journal of General Internal Medicine*, Vol. 36, No. 10, 2021, pp. 2952–2957.

Stone, Elizabeth M., Alene Kennedy-Hendricks, Colleen L. Barry, Marcus A. Bachhuber, and Emma E. McGinty, "The Role of Stigma in U.S. Primary Care Physicians' Treatment of Opioid Use Disorder," *Drug and Alcohol Dependence*, Vol. 221, 2021.

Substance Abuse and Mental Health Services Administration, "Table 5.40A—Received Medication-Assisted Treatment for Alcohol, Opioids, and Alcohol or Opioids in Past Year Among Persons Aged 12 or Older, by Demographic, Geographic, and Socioeconomic Characteristics: Numbers in Thousands, 2018 and 2019," undated. As of April 1, 2021: https://www.samhsa.gov/data/sites/default/files/reports/rpt29394/NSDUHDetailedTabs2019/NSDUHDetTabsSect5pe2019.htm#tab5-40a

Substance Abuse and Mental Health Services Administration, "Chapter 6: Health Care Systems and Substance Use Disorders," in *Facing Addiction in America: The Surgeon General's Report on Alcohol, Drugs, and Health*, Washington, D.C.: U.S. Department of Health and Human Services, November 2016, pp. 6-1–6-45.

Substance Abuse and Mental Health Services Administration, *Key Substance Use and Mental Health Indicators in the United States: Results from the 2017 National Survey on Drug Use and Health*, Rockville, Md.: Center for Behavioral Health Statistics and Quality, 2018.

Substance Abuse and Mental Health Services Administration, *The Opioid Crisis and the Black/ African American Population: An Urgent Issue*, Rockville, Md.: Office of Behavioral Health Equity, April 2020a.

Substance Abuse and Mental Health Services Administration, "2019 NSDUH Detailed Tables," webpage, September 11, 2020b. As of April 1, 2021: https://www.samhsa.gov/data/report/2019-nsduh-detailed-tables

Substance Abuse and Mental Health Services Administration, "SAMHSA Extends the Methadone Take-Home Flexibility for One Year While Working Toward a Permanent Solution," press release, November 18, 2021. As of July 12, 2022: https://www.samhsa.gov/newsroom/press-announcements/202111181000

Syed, Samina T., Ben S. Gerber, and Lisa K. Sharp, "Traveling Towards Disease: Transportation Barriers to Health Care Access," *Journal of Community Health*, Vol. 38, No. 5, 2013, pp. 976–993.

Szalavitz, Maia, "Addictions Are Harder to Kick When You're Poor. Here's Why," *The Guardian*, June 1, 2016.

Tipps, Robin T., Gregory T. Buzzard, and John A. McDougall, "The Opioid Epidemic in Indian Country," *Journal of Law, Medicine & Ethics*, Vol. 46, No. 2, 2018, pp. 422–436.

Volkow, Nora D., "Access to Addiction Services Differs by Race and Gender," National Institute on Drug Abuse blog, 2019. As of September 9, 2020: https://www.drugabuse.gov/about-nida/noras-blog/2019/07/ access-to-addiction-services-differs-by-race-gender

Volkow, Nora D., "Collision of the COVID-19 and Addiction Epidemics," *Annals of Internal Medicine*, Vol. 173, No. 1, 2020a, pp. 61–62.

Volkow, Nora D., "Stigma and the Toll of Addiction," *New England Journal of Medicine*, Vol. 382, No. 14, 2020b, pp. 1289–1290.

Volkow, Nora D., "To End the Opioid Crisis, We Must Address Painful Social Disparities," *Drug and Alcohol Dependence*, Vol. 222, 2021.

Volkow, Nora D., Emily B. Jones, Emily B. Einstein, and Eric M. Wargo, "Prevention and Treatment of Opioid Misuse and Addiction: A Review," *JAMA Psychiatry*, Vol. 76, No. 2, 2019, pp. 208–216.

Wang, Quan Qiu, David C. Kaelber, Rong Xu, and Nora D. Volkow, "COVID-19 Risk and Outcomes in Patients with Substance Use Disorders: Analyses from Electronic Health Records in the United States," *Molecular Psychiatry*, Vol. 26, No. 1, 2021, pp. 30–39.

Wen, Hefei, Tyrone F. Borders, and Janet R. Cummings, "Trends in Buprenorphine Prescribing by Physician Specialty," *Health Affairs*, Vol. 38, No. 1, 2019, pp. 24–28.

Williams, David R., Jourdyn A. Lawrence, and Brigette A. Davis, "Racism and Health: Evidence and Needed Research," *Annual Review of Public Health*, Vol. 40, 2019, pp. 105–125.

Zhang, Hao, Austin S. Kilaru, Zachary F. Meisel, and Yuhua Bao, "Prescription Drug Monitoring Program Mandates and Opioids Dispensed Following Emergency Department Encounters for Patients with Sickle Cell Disease or Cancer with Bone Metastasis," *JAMA*, Vol. 326, No. 3, 2021, pp. 274–276.

Zhang, Hao, Judith Paice, Russell Portenoy, Eduardo Bruera, M. Carrington Reid, and Yuhua Bao, "Prescription Opioids Dispensed to Patients with Cancer with Bone Metastasis: 2011–2017," *The Oncologist*, Vol. 26, No. 10, October 2021.

CHAPTER TWO

People Who Use Opioids

Beau Kilmer, Jirka Taylor, and Bryce Pardo

Introduction

This report offers a comprehensive assessment of how people who use opioids (PWUO) inter-act with various components of the opioid ecosystem and how these components interact with one another. This chapter provides some baseline information about PWUO and the major consequences of their opioid use, ranging from pain relief to overdose to adverse effects on others.

There is an extensive and growing body of literature on the epidemiology and conse-quences of opioid use and polysubstance use. Our discussion draws on this research and on our own secondary data analyses to address ten questions that provide context for under-standing the evolution and status of the opioid situation in the United States:

1. How many people use opioids in the United States, and which opioids are they using?
2. How does the rate of opioid prescribing in the United States compare with that of other countries?
3. What share of PWUO transition to opioid use disorder (OUD)?
4. How many people currently suffer from OUD?
5. What are the characteristics of those with OUD and the subset of them who receive treatment?
6. Who is dying from opioid-involved overdoses and how has this changed over time?
7. What is the scope of other health harms related to opioid use, including nonfatal overdoses?
8. What do we know about the families of those with OUD?
9. How many arrests can be linked to opioids each year?
10. For those with OUD who are justice involved, what share of their arrests are for drug law violations versus other crimes?

Our goal is not to present the results of a systematic review for each question; rather, it is to highlight some relevant studies and data sets. That said, the data needed to address many of these questions have substantial limitations (see the box that follows, "Popular Publicly Available Data Sources Used to Learn About People Who Use Opioids"), and the recency of data varies by source (e.g., the best data available on the number of people who use heroin are for 2016). However, enormous value comes from conducting rough calculations to help the reader understand the orders of magnitude involved. That is, we aim to provide rough estimates of very important quantities, even if available data do not address them directly. In the final section of the chapter, we offer some ideas for improving the data infrastructure needed to learn about PWUO and other drug market activities.

Popular Publicly Available Data Sources Used to Learn About People Who Use Opioids

National Survey on Drug Use and Health (NSDUH). The NSDUH is a nationally representative survey of those 12 and older in the United States (n = ~70,000). The sampling frame excludes those with no fixed household address (e.g., homeless or transient persons not in shelters) and residents of institutional group quarters, such as jails and hospitals (Substance Abuse and Mental Health Services Administration [SAMHSA], undated-b). Although the survey is useful for understanding the characteristics and consumption patterns for those who use alcohol, cannabis, and tobacco, it systematically underestimates the number of individuals who use heroin and other highly stigmatized drugs, particularly those who use heavily (Kilmer et al., 2014; Reuter, Caulkins, and Midgette, 2021). It is unclear how well the survey captures those with OUD who use prescription opioids, and as of 2020, it did not include questions about the use of illegally produced synthetic opioids like fentanyl (SAMHSA, 2021). Furthermore, people who use drugs do not even always know that they have used fentanyl when suppliers mix it into other powders or pills. This does not mean that NSDUH provides no useful information about those who use opioids; it is best to think that NSDUH describes a subset of those who led stable enough lives to participate in an audio computer-assisted self-interview and who were forthcoming about their opioid use. In terms of measuring OUD, the survey used questions based on the *Diagnostic and Statistical Manual of Mental Disorders*, fourth edition (DSM-IV), which measures substance "abuse" and "dependence" for specific drugs through 2019. Those meeting criteria for either "abuse" or "dependence" in NSDUH are often classified as having a substance use disorder (SUD) (e.g., Votaw et al., 2019; Wu, Zhu, and Swartz, 2016).

There were multiple changes made to 2020 NSDUH which make it difficult to compare OUD statistics before and after 2019 (SAMHSA, undated-a). Most importantly, the 2020 NSDUH uses a different measure of OUD (based on *Diagnostic and Statistical Manual of Mental Disorders*, fifth edition [DSM-V] criteria). Second, SAMHSA reports that virtually no data were collected from mid-March through September 2020 because of the coronavirus disease 2019 (COVID-19) pandemic. Third, the survey methodology changed when SAMHSA started using web surveys instead of in-home computer aided surveys in Quarter 4 (October through December 2020). SAMHSA concludes, "Because these changes in data collection coincided with the spread of the COVID-19 pandemic and any related behavioral or mental health changes, we cannot fully separate the effects of methodological changes from true changes in the outcomes" (SAMHSA, undated-c). Thus, we primarily focus on the 2019 data throughout this report.

Treatment Episode Data Set (TEDS). The TEDS data cover all admissions to substance use treatment facilities receiving public funding in the United States; there is also some information about discharges from treatment. Data may include some individuals who are privately funded if they are receiving treatment at a facility receiving public funds. In the past, TEDS covered approximately two-thirds of all treatment episodes in the country (Saloner and Lê Cook, 2013). However, this is probably no longer true, especially for those with OUD who are being prescribed buprenorphine by clinicians outside the specialty sector (further addressed in Chapter Four). Another limitation is that TEDS data are available only at the episode level, not the individual level. Thus, one person can account for multiple admissions in these data.

Multiple cause of death (MCOD) data. The MCOD data cover the universe of deaths in the United States, specifying the characteristics of the individual (including county of residence) and the cause of death. For deaths involving substance use, data include the International Classification of Diseases, tenth revision (ICD-10) codes for all substances detected, allowing analysts to understand the extent to which polysubstance use may have played a role in the death. However, when polysubstance use is detected, the data do not provide information about whether the substances were used at the same time or on the same day. Researchers have also raised questions about the accuracy of these data. For example, Ruhm, 2018, argues that the "rates of any opioid and heroin/synthetic opioid-involved drug deaths are 20–35% higher in every year than reported figures." This is in part a function of the quality of testing for specific drugs in overdose deaths, which vary across places and over time.

How Many People Use Opioids in the United States, and Which Opioids Are They Using?

As noted in Chapter One, the medical community most commonly prescribes opioids to address acute and chronic pain and to a lesser extent uses multiple opioids in the treatment of OUD. Opioids have multiple effects. Notably, they can (1) relieve pain, (2) produce euphoria, and (3) increase the risk of respiratory failure and overdose (especially when consumed with other drugs), all in a dose-dependent way. Although it is not surprising that we have better information on those who receive opioids from authorized sources compared with illegal sources, the limited amount of information we have about the latter is shocking. Table 2.1 displays the approximate number of people who use various opioids, and the rest of the section walks through the sources and limitations of these figures.

For insights about the number of people filling opioid prescriptions and the amounts dispensed, the Centers for Disease Control and Prevention (CDC) relies on IQVIA pharmacy claims data which cover approximately 92 percent of all retail pharmacy prescriptions

TABLE 2.1

Number of People Using Opioids in the United States

Type of Opioid Users	Year	Approximate Number of People	Source
People filling an opioid analgesic prescription at a pharmacy in the past year	2018	> 50 million	CDC, 2019
People who self-report using prescription opioids in any way a doctor did not direct them to use it in the past year	2019	> 10 million	SAMHSA, 2020d
People who used heroin on more than three days in the past month	2016	2 million	Midgette et al., 2019
People receiving methadone or buprenorphine for OUD at some point in the past year	2019	1 million to 1.5 million	Krawczyk et al., 2022; SAMHSA, 2020d; SAMHSA, 2020b; Stein et al., 2021
People using illegally produced synthetic opioids	2022	N/A	N/A

NOTE: N/A = not available. Rows are not mutually exclusive.

in the country (CDC, 2019). These data suggest that in 2018, nearly 50 million individuals (approximately 15 percent of the population) filled at least one prescription for codeine, fentanyl, hydrocodone, hydromorphone, methadone, morphine, oxycodone, oxymorphone, propoxyphene, tapentadol, tramadol, or buprenorphine (CDC, 2019). This figure does not include buprenorphine formulations prescribed for treatment of OUD, methadone dispensed through opioid treatment programs, or opioids dispensed or administered in a hospital or other health care setting. Of the 168 million opioid prescriptions filled in 2018, almost 43 percent of them were for 30 or more days (CDC, 2019).

There is no official estimate of the number of people currently receiving opioids to treat OUD, but the figure is greater than 1 million. Survey data from the NSDUH suggest that 637,000 individuals would self-report receiving methadone treatment and 747,000 buprenorphine treatment in 2019 (SAMHSA, 2020a).[1] Using IQVIA data, Stein et al., 2021, found that for the 2017 to 2018 period there were approximately 1.25 million buprenorphine treatment episodes for OUD from 2017 to 2018 for 911,284 unique patients.

Of course, some of these medications are diverted to individuals without prescriptions, but data on diversion are sparse. The NSDUH reports that more than 9 million people "mis-

---

[1] The National Survey of Substance Abuse Treatment Services is an annual survey of substance use treatment programs. In March 29, 2019, there were approximately 409,000 and 168,000 individuals receiving methadone and buprenorphine for OUD, respectively (SAMHSA, 2020b). This is a point-in-time estimate, so the actual number of individuals receiving these medications for OUD throughout the year will be higher.

used" opioids in 2019, but misuse is an umbrella term that is not terribly helpful.[2] It includes those with OUD who obtained opioids in the illegal market as well those who may have had them prescribed for a root canal but used them to treat a sprained ankle. In sum, it is not a very informative estimate (further discussed in Chapter Six).

When it comes to estimating the number of individuals in the United States using heroin, illegally produced synthetic opioids, or both, the country is largely flying blind. It is common to see estimates of people who use heroin; however, these are usually based on the NSDUH data, which seriously undercounts the number of people who use heroin (Kilmer et al., 2014). NSDUH captures less than 15 percent of those who use heroin on a daily to near daily basis (Reuter, Caulkins, and Midgette, 2021).

The Office of National Drug Control Policy (ONDCP) regularly produces more-comprehensive estimates in their *What America's Users Spend on Illicit Drugs* series, but the most-recent estimates only extend through 2016 (Midgette et al., 2019). For 2016, it was estimated that roughly 2.3 million people used heroin on four or more days in the previous month, and of these, about 1.5 million used heroin daily or nearly daily; however, there is substantial uncertainty surrounding these estimates. It is unclear how the number of people using heroin has fluctuated since 2016, although the number of overdose deaths involving heroin slightly decreased from 2016 through 2020 (CDC, 2021c).

We know even less about the number of individuals using illegally produced synthetic opioids like fentanyl. Although fentanyl is increasingly being mixed into heroin, albeit to a much greater extent in some parts of the country than others (Pardo et al., 2019), it is incorrect to assume those using fentanyl are just a subset of the heroin-using population. Synthetic opioids are also being inserted into counterfeit prescription pills, and there are reports of these drugs being mixed (perhaps inadvertently) into other drugs like cocaine. Some markets are emerging where people are seeking illegally produced fentanyl, not heroin (Morales et al., 2019).[3] As of 2020, more than 84 percent of the U.S. population lives in states where deaths involving synthetic opioids exceed deaths involving heroin or prescription opioids.[4]

---

[2] The NSDUH question used to measure "misuse" asks, "Have you used any prescription pain reliever in any way a doctor did not direct you to use it?" and includes this prompt:

> The next question asks about using prescription pain relievers in any way a doctor did not direct you to use them. When you answer these questions, please think only about your use of the drug in any way a doctor did not direct you to use it, including:
> - Using it without a prescription of your own
> - Using it in greater amounts, more often, or longer than you were told to take it
> - Using it in any other way a doctor did not direct you to use it. (SAMHSA, 2020d)

[3] Chapter Seven offers insights about the amount of illegally produced fentanyl consumed in the United States.

[4] Calculating this ratio is not necessarily clear because many that overdose as a result of synthetic opioids may also have heroin or prescription opioids in their system. However, as of 2020, the vast majority of states are experiencing more overdose deaths involving synthetic opioids than the combined total of deaths involving heroin or prescription opioids.

A large share of PWUO initiated opioid use not with fentanyl or heroin but with a prescription opioid analgesic that was legitimately prescribed or diverted (Cerdá et al., 2015; Cicero et al., 2014; Jones, 2013; Kolodny et al., 2015; Novak et al., 2016; Pardo et al., 2019; Pollini et al., 2011). Using self-reported data from the NSDUH, Jones, 2013, reported that the share of people using heroin who had used prescription opioids nonmedically in the year prior to heroin initiation rose from 64 percent of respondents in 2002 to 2004 to 83 percent in 2008 to 2010. Historically, those who started using heroin in the 1960s or 1970s initiated opioids with heroin, but that is less true for the newer generation of heroin users (e.g., see Cicero et al., 2014; Novak et al., 2016).[5]

How Does the Rate of Opioid Prescriptions in the United States Compare with That of Other Developed Countries?

The consumption of prescription opioids has increased globally over the past 25 years, and the United States has consistently outpaced every other country (Duff et al., 2021).[6] Expressed as morphine milligram equivalents (MME) per capita (a metric used to account for the potency of different opioids), the volume of U.S. opioid prescriptions quadrupled from 180 MME per capita in 1999 to 782 MME per capita in 2010 (Guy et al., 2017). Since the early 2010s, opioid prescription rates in the United States have been declining, in parallel with increasing awareness of the risks associated with opioids and implementation of policies to reduce harms associated with OUD (Helmerhorst et al., 2017; Ho, 2019). After plateauing between 2010 and 2012, U.S. consumption of prescribed opioids decreased from 790 MME per capita to 366 MME per capita (Aitken et al., 2020)—still nearly double what it had traditionally been. A similar decrease appears when the prescription rate is expressed as the number of prescriptions per 100 persons, which decreased 13 percent between 2012 and 2015 (Guy et al., 2017) and more than 40 percent between 2012 and 2019 (CDC, 2020).

---

[5] Only limited insights are available regarding the age of people with OUD when they started using opioids. According to 2019 NSDUH data, 15 percent (confidence interval [CI]: 6 to 34 percent) of individuals with heroin use disorder first used heroin when they were less than 18 years old, 41 percent (CI: 26 to 59 percent) first used when they were 18 to 24 years old, and 38 percent (CI: 22 to 57 percent) first used when they were 25 to 34 years old. Only 5 percent (CI: 2 to 13 percent) of individuals with heroin use disorder reported first using when they were 35 or older. Among individuals reporting both a heroin and pain reliever use disorder, the reported ages of first use of heroin were as follows: 21 percent were less than 18 years old (CI: 7 to 47 percent), 27 percent were 18 to 24 years old (CI: 12 to 49 percent), 41 percent were 25 to 34 years old (CI: 24 to 60 percent), and 12 percent were 35 years and older (CI: 4 to 28 percent). Using analysis at Substance Abuse and Mental Health Data Archive [SAMHDA], undated-a, using key variables: "UDPYHRPNR Rc-Heroin And/or Pain Reliever Dependence Or Abuse - Pst Yr" and "IRHERAGE Heroin Age of First Use" recoded into the age categories shown here. No information is available from NSDUH regarding the age of first use-disorder diagnosis.

[6] A paper by Jayawardana et al. (2021) is an exception to findings reported in most studies in that it found the United States to have higher rates than most comparator countries but not the highest rates in the world.

But even after recent decreases, the U.S. opioid prescription rate continues to be notably higher than in other countries (Organisation for Economic Co-operation and Development [OECD], 2019). In 2015, the per capita amount of opioids prescribed in the United States was almost four times higher than that in Europe (Schuchat, Houry, and Guy, 2017) and almost double the next highest country. These figures account for only prescribed opioids (which may have been diverted); they do not include consumption in MME of such illegally produced opioids as heroin.

Figure 2.1 shows the total consumption of prescription opioids in Group of Seven (G7) countries. According to Duff et al., 2021,

> The opioids included in the total are hydrocodone, oxycodone, morphine, methadone, dextropropoxyphene, dihydrocodeine, diphenoxylate, ethylmorphine, pethidine, pholcodine, tilidine, hydromorphone, and fentanyl. Defined daily doses (DDD) are "the assumed average maintenance dose per day" for an opioid used for "its main indication in adults," according to the World Health Organization. DDDs are commonly used as a standard measure of drug use in national and international comparison studies at the population level because one DDD per day is implied. DDDs do not necessarily reflect the prescribed therapeutic dose, which is based on individual patient characteristics (age, weight, etc.).

FIGURE 2.1

Total Prescription Opioid Consumption for G7 Countries: Defined Daily Doses per 1 Million Inhabitants, 1964–2018

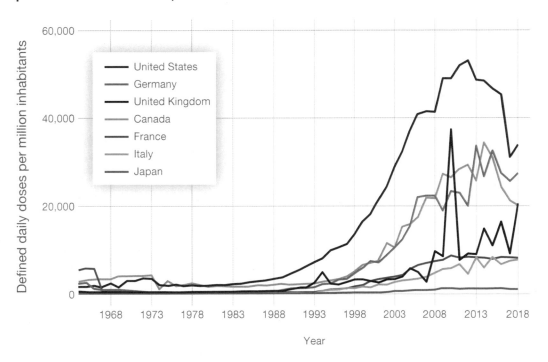

SOURCE: Adapted from Duff et al., 2021, p. 5, using data provided to the Congressional Research Service by the International Narcotics Control Board (August 2020).

Differences between the United States and other countries in opioid prescribing have also been described in studies examining particular medical contexts. For instance, Ladha et al., 2019, compared opioid prescribing in Sweden, the United States, and Canada in patients following four types of surgical procedures. They found that the share of patients filling prescriptions was seven times lower in Sweden than in North America. Furthermore, patients in the United States received the highest mean dose of opioids. Similarly, a comparative study of opioid prescribing by dentists in 2016 found that opioids accounted for a 37-times higher proportion of dental prescriptions in the United States than in England (Suda et al., 2019).

There continue to be substantial differences in prescribing rates even within the United States (see Figure 2.2), with differences in demographics (e.g., larger proportions of men and unemployed people), access to care, and health care supply among possible explanatory factors (Griffith et al., 2021).[7] Although the national opioid prescription rate had decreased by 2019 to 46.7 per 100 persons, five percent of U.S. counties reported rates higher than 100, and the prescribing rate in the highest-reporting counties was six times the national average (CDC, 2020). The differences across states have narrowed, with the largest declines in prescribing recorded among states that had previously had the highest rates of prescription opioid use (Aitken et al., 2020).

FIGURE 2.2

U.S. Opioid Prescribing Rates, 2020

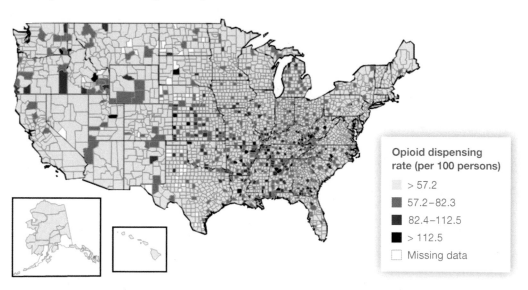

SOURCE: CDC, 2022a.

---

[7] See also Chapter Twelve for a discussion on the relationship between prescribing rates and employment indicators.

What Share of People Who Use Opioids Transition to Opioid Use Disorder?

The answer depends largely on the type of opioid being used and what is included in the denominator: Everyone who has ever used an opioid? Those who have used in the past few years? Those who have used them daily for at least 90 days? In some cases, there may be no tangible connection between the first use of opioids and meeting clinical criteria for an OUD; for example, someone who used opioids as prescribed as a teenager may become addicted to heroin in their late twenties.

First consider data on the proportion of people using or misusing prescription opioids who escalate to OUD. The vast majority of Americans prescribed opioid analgesics suffer no ill effects, let alone develop an OUD. However, the rates become much higher when the prescription is for chronic pain treated at home. One systematic review focused on chronic non-cancer pain patients who were using prescription opioids found that 8 percent to 12 percent were documented as suffering from opioid "addiction," although the 95-percent confidence interval (CI) was quite wide (3 to 17 percent; Vowles et al., 2015).[8] It is unclear what share of these individuals may have had an OUD before presenting with chronic pain and having opioids prescribed, but regardless of whether the prescription opioids caused the OUD or were "merely" being prescribed to someone with OUD, such rates are concerning.

A more recent study focused on those who were *opioid naïve* in Massachusetts—a term used to define those with "no opioid prescriptions or evidence of OUD in the six months prior to the index prescription"—found that among those who received a prescription for opioids in 2011, only 1 percent of them were diagnosed with OUD within one year. Within four years, the OUD rate had increased to about 5 percent (Burke et al., 2020).

Although 5 percent may not seem like a lot, we need to account for the flow of opioid naïve people who are prescribed an opioid each year to an OUD diagnosis. If 20 percent of those prescribed an opioid each year are opioid naïve as defined by Burke et al., 2020 (about 12 million; likely a lower bound), this would mean that about 600,000 people would suffer from an OUD within four years. And an annual flow into OUD of 150,000 per year coupled with an average dwell time in that state of 10 to 20 years implies an increase of 1.5 to 3 million more people with OUD than there would otherwise be in steady state.

Similar to other studies, Burke et al., 2020, found that those who had longer opioid therapy (defined as 90 or more days) were more likely to be subsequently diagnosed with OUD (Bohnert et al., 2011; Edlund et al., 2014; Moreno et al., 2019). Using claims data, Edlund and colleagues, 2014, examined more than 500,000 adults with a chronic noncancer pain diagnosis who had no similar diagnosis in the prior six months and no reported opioid use or OUD in the prior six months. Overall, they found that "[d]uration of opioid therapy was more

---

[8] The authors defined an *addiction* as a "[p]attern of continued use with experience of, or demonstrated potential for, harm '(e.g., impaired control over drug use, compulsive use, continued use despite harm, and craving).'"

important than daily dose in determining OUD risk." (For more on the evidence about using opioids to treat chronic noncancer pain, see Chapter Five.)

Now consider data on the proportion of people using heroin who develop OUD at some point. With respect to heroin, an old but frequently cited study by Anthony, Warner, and Kessler, 1994, that was based on a general household population survey reported that 23 percent of those who *tried* heroin eventually met clinical criteria for heroin dependence within 10 years. In the tobacco literature, people are usually only counted as ever smokers if they have smoked on 100 or more occasions. If we apply that kind of thinking to this context, then the share of people who had used heroin on more than 100 occasions and later met criteria instead for dependence would be much higher than the 23 percent cited above (which refers to people who ever tried heroin, i.e., even only once).

Furthermore, there are multiple reasons to believe that even this 23 percent figure is too low. First, this is based on a general population survey, and as noted earlier, such surveys do a poor job of capturing people who frequently use heroin. Second, because the survey was retrospective, it did not include people who may have used heroin and died before taking the survey.

It is also unclear whether the research from Anthony, Warner, and Kessler, 1994, which was based on heroin use in the 1980s and early 1990s, still applies today. Although the purity-adjusted price of heroin tends to be higher than other street drugs like cocaine and methamphetamine (Midgette et al., 2019), the inflation-adjusted price for heroin has dropped dramatically—from about $3,000 per pure gram at the retail level in the early 1980s to closer to $500 in 2012 (ONDCP, 2016). Because it is cheaper to maintain a heroin habit today than it was 30 years ago, the probability today could be higher. Likewise, the purity of heroin then was much lower than it is today (ONDCP, 2016). It is unfortunate that such analyses as Anthony, Warner, and Kessler, 1994, are not regularly updated.

It might make more sense to examine those who used more than once (for example, occasional users) to assess addiction rates; however, those data are scarce. There are people who use heroin, other opioids, or both on a regular basis who do not run into any problems (see, e.g., Hart, 2021; Kaplan, 1983), but we are not aware of any systematic efforts to follow people who use heroin regularly to see how many subsequently meet clinical criteria for an OUD.

How Many People Currently Suffer from Opioid Use Disorder?

This number is even harder to establish than the number of PWUO. It is common to see estimates that there are about 2 million people suffering from OUD in the United States (see, e.g., McCance-Katz, Houry, and Collins, 2017; National Safety Council, undated; National Institute on Drug Abuse, 2021). However, this figure is largely based on the aforementioned NSDUH data, which do not capture most heavy users of illegally produced opioids (Reuter, Caulkins, and Midgette, 2021). For that matter, general population surveys even undercount use of legal drugs like alcohol, so it probably also undercounts OUD from prescription opioids. Thus, the figures from NSDUH should be considered a very low estimate. To help put this in perspective, the best estimates available suggest there were approximately 1.5 million people who used heroin on a daily or near daily basis in 2016 (Midgette et al., 2019), and the vast majority of them likely meet clinical criteria for OUD.[9] There are many other people with OUD who do not use heroin (further discussed next) either because they do not use heroin at all (e.g., they use prescription opioids instead) or because they are temporarily not using even though they have used heroin in the past (e.g., people who use heroin with OUD who are currently incarcerated or are in treatment and are abstinent).

A study measuring the prevalence of OUD in Massachusetts using a capture-recapture analysis with rich Chapter 55 data (discussed more in Chapter Fourteen) found "that the total population prevalence of OUD in Massachusetts reached 4.60% in 2015, nearly 4 times higher than current national prevalence estimates" (Barocas et al., 2018). Of course, Massachusetts may not be representative of the rest of the country, but this discrepancy is consistent with other evidence suggesting NSDUH misses a large share of those with OUD.

Using this estimate from Massachusetts and combining it with data from NSDUH, Keyes et al., 2022, estimated that the number of people aged 12 and older with OUD in 2019 was 7.6 million. Keyes et al., 2022, also used mortality data to generate a separate OUD figure, and after correcting these data to account for the fact that the probability of a drug poisoning death given OUD has changed with the onset of synthetic opioids, they estimate that there were 6.7 million people with OUD in 2019 (Keyes et al., 2022).

We can also gain some *rough* insights into the scope of OUD by looking at Medicaid enrollees. Medicaid provides health coverage to low-income individuals and other populations, such as some people with disabilities. As of January 2021, Medicaid covered nearly 74 million individuals (which we discuss further in Chapter Five on medical care, Chapter Four on SUD treatment, and Chapter Eleven on income support and homeless services) (Medicaid.gov, 2021). Some individuals are dually eligible for both Medicaid and Medicare (the health insurance program for those 65 and older, which may cover some costs that Medicaid does not), but most of the Medicaid population are nondual eligible (Medicaid.gov, undated).

A recent analysis focused on nondual Medicaid enrollees aged 12 to 64 in 11 states.[10] The analysis found that 5 percent of this population received an OUD diagnosis in 2018 (527,983 of 10,585,790; The Medicaid Outcomes Distributed Research Network [MODRN] et al., 2021). There are reasons to believe that this rate could be too high (e.g., doctors may diagnose OUD if patients are dependent on prescription opioids, even if they do not meet criteria for

---

[9] According to the 2019 NSDUH, of the 186,000 people reporting heroin use on 20 or more days in the past month, 94 percent met clinical criteria for a heroin use disorder (SAMHSA, 2020c).

[10] Delaware, Kentucky, Maryland, Maine, Michigan, North Carolina, Ohio, Pennsylvania, Virginia, West Virginia, and Wisconsin.

an OUD diagnosis; Lagisetty et al., 2021) or too low (e.g., the rate only includes those with a claim for OUD; if OUD is unrecognized by the medical system, it is not counted).[11]

MODRN et al., 2021, reported that the 11 states included in the study covered 22 percent of the Medicaid population in the country, but this 22 percent likely includes dual and non-dual enrollees.[12] If one believes this 22 percent rate is a reasonable approximation for the nondual population and the 5 percent OUD figure is accurate, applying these figures to the national population of nondual Medicaid enrollees suggests that the number of individuals receiving an OUD diagnosis in just this population *alone* would be close to 2.4 million (5 percent × 10,585,790/22 percent). Of course, a more sophisticated analysis would account for how these 11 states differ from others (e.g., in terms of Medicaid populations and levels of opioid use).[13] The analysis would also incorporate the uncertainty around these estimates. However, this rough calculation helps us appreciate how many of the current estimates of OUD are likely too low.

There are reasons to believe that the OUD rate for the Medicaid population may be higher than it is for the rest of the population (e.g., OUD can create financial difficulties and employment problems that lead some people to eventually enroll in Medicaid). If one assumed that the entire population of the United States aged 12 to 64 years (about 206 million in 2018) had an OUD rate that was 2 percent instead of the 5 percent in the Medicaid population in these 11 states,[14] there would be more than 4 million people in this age group with OUD (206 million × 2 percent)—more than twice the figure that is routinely reported for the entire country.

What Are the Characteristics of Those with Opioid Use Disorder and Those Who Receive Treatment?

Because we do not know exactly how many people suffer from OUD nationally, it is difficult to describe the characteristics of this population or know what share are currently receiving treatment. We do have some information on subpopulations (e.g., NSDUH respondents,

---

[11] There are also reasons to believe that the dual-eligible population (who are excluded from this analysis) may be more likely to have an OUD (e.g., many Medicare recipients with OUD have comorbid mental health disorders that can make them eligible for Medicaid). Thus, the 5 percent figure may be a low estimate for the full Medicaid population.

[12] The authors note that "[t]hese states accounted for 16.3 million (22%) Medicaid enrollees" (MODRN et al., 2021, p. 155). But the calculations focus on 10.6 million nondual enrollees, possibly suggesting that about one-third of the Medicaid enrollees were dually enrolled. We are not aware of any estimates that distinguish the number of dual and nondual enrollees in every state, which presents challenges for making projections to the rest of the country.

[13] These 11 states accounted for six of the top ten states in terms of opioid overdoses in 2018.

[14] Among 2019 NSDUH respondents insured by Medicaid/CHIP, 0.5 percent reported OUD; the comparable figure for those not covered by Medicaid/CHIP was 1.3 percent. Applying this ratio (0.5/1.3) to the 5 percent figure yields 2 percent.

Medicaid enrollees, those entering substance use treatment) and some states have comprehensive data-collection efforts (e.g., Massachusetts, Maryland).

All these sources have major limitations (some described in the box at the beginning of this chapter), and they do not cover mutually exclusive populations. However, together they can help us understand the basic contours of the population of those with OUD. Next, we discuss what is known about that population, drawing on NSDUH, TEDS, and the aforementioned study of Medicaid enrollees with OUD in 11 states. We highlight some of the major takeaways; more details appear in the additional data provided at the end of this chapter (see Tables 2.5, 2.6, and 2.7).

Treatment Episode Data Set

Historically, most individuals who meet clinical criteria for an SUD eventually quit without formal treatment (Robins et al., 2010). Of course, that does not mean that treatment would not have reduced the duration of the SUD, or that the harms caused by the SUD were any less consequential for that individual, their loved ones, or their community.

Primary Opioid Used

Heroin and other opiates were the primary substance for roughly one-third of all drug and alcohol admissions in TEDS, and admissions for heroin were much larger than they were for other opiates in 2018 (502,845 and 144,337, respectively). As in the NSDUH data, those presenting for heroin were more than 60 percent male, but there is more gender balance then for other opioids.

Previous Treatment Episodes

Those presenting with heroin as their primary drug were much more likely to have had a previous treatment episode (75 percent versus 58 percent), with twice as many heroin users having three or more previous episodes compared with those presenting for other opioids.

Types of Treatment and Referrals

The majority of treatment episodes for both heroin and other opiates were outpatient, and both categories of users had pretty similar rates of medication treatment for OUD. More than 50 percent of treatment referrals were from individuals, including family members, friends, and self-referrals. The criminal legal system referred 13 percent of individuals receiving treatment for heroin and 16 percent of those receiving treatment for other opioids, but this may underestimate the role of criminal legal pressure (e.g., family members threatening to report PWUO for stealing from them if users do not enter treatment).

Medicaid

Data from studies of Medicaid enrollees only cover a portion of those with OUD; hence, we need to be careful about generalizing to the entire population with OUD. That said, a few details stand out from the previously discussed study by MODRN et al., 2021, examining the nondual population in 11 states. First, the share of enrollees with OUD increased by roughly 50 percent from 2014 to 2018 (from 3.3 percent to 5 percent). Second, about 50 percent of individuals with OUD also had another SUD and about 60 percent had a comorbid mental health condition. Third, similar to other studies (e.g., Lagisetty et al., 2019), the authors found that Black enrollees with OUD had lower use of medications than White enrollees (this disparity is further discussed in Chapter Four).

National Survey on Drug Use and Health

NSDUH reports the characteristics of those who met clinical criteria for OUD based on their self-reported responses to the survey in 2019, separated into those with disorders for heroin, pain relievers, or both. NSDUH reports percentages and CIs, but the uncertainty around these figures is much larger than what is reported, given the issues with sampling and honest reporting (Harrison et al., 2007; Reuter, Caulkins, and Midgette, 2021).

Types of Opioid Use Disorders

As mentioned, NSDUH badly underestimates the number of people with OUD. For 2019, NSDUH estimates there were only 1.7 million individuals aged 12 and older with an OUD, which is clearly too low. However, it is still interesting to look at the composition of that group, and it is very heavily dominated by those who are dependent on prescription pain relievers: Users of only heroin accounted for 267,000 of the total, users of only pain relievers for 1,253,000, and users of both heroin and pain relievers for 180,000. The number of people with a disorder involving only pain relievers is nearly five times higher than it is for people with an OUD reporting only heroin use, but we should not put too much stock in that figure given the inability of NSDUH to capture heavy heroin users.

Race and Ethnicity

More than 70 percent of those self-reporting OUD in the NSDUH were non-Hispanic White people, which is greater than their share of the overall population. Table 2.2 presents weighted counts for the three groups with the highest rates of OUD (non-Hispanic White, non-Hispanic Black, and Hispanic) and the number of people in each of these groups covered by the survey. The OUD rate for non-Hispanic White people was 724 per 100,000; rates for non-Hispanic Black and Hispanic people were 526 and 348, respectively. We know that the raw numbers of those with OUD in NSDUH are too low, but the per capita rates may yield some information; however, it is unclear whether those with OUD not covered by NSDUH follow a similar racial/ethnic distribution.

Age

Those with OUD for pain relievers only were more likely to be 50 years or older than were those with an OUD for heroin. Nearly half of those meeting clinical criteria for an OUD for both heroin and pain relievers were in the 26 to 34 years old category.

TABLE 2.2

Per Capita Opioid Use Disorder Rates, by Race/Ethnicity, for Three Groups with Highest Prevalence Rates (2019 NSDUH, rounded)

Race/Ethnic Group	Number with Opioid Use Disorder in 2019 NSDUH	Total Population Covered by NSDUH	Opioid Use Disorder Rate per 100,000 Population
Black, non-Hispanic	175,000	33,253,000	526
Hispanic	165,000	47,466,000	348
White, non-Hispanic	1,235,000	170,641,000	724

SOURCES: OUD population: SAMHDA, undated-e; NSDUH population: SAMHSA, 2020c.

Education, Employment, and Medicaid Status

NSDUH also collects information on education, employment, and Medicaid status. Those with an OUD for pain relievers (with and without heroin) were much more likely to have more than a high school education than those with an OUD for heroin alone. Roughly 40 percent of those with OUD are working, and these rates were fairly similar across groups. With respect to Medicaid, those with OUD for heroin were more likely to be covered by Medicaid than those with OUD for pain relievers only.[15]

Opioid Use Disorder Treatment

When considering treatment utilization in the past year, it is important to remember that those in a jail and prison at the time of the survey are not included in the NSDUH sampling frame. Among those responding to the survey and meeting clinical criteria for OUD, about 40 percent of those who have OUD for heroin only participated in treatment compared with about 20 percent for those with OUD for pain relievers.[16] In terms of those receiving medication treatment for OUD, those using heroin had much higher rates than those who only used prescription opioids.[17]

---

[15] Future work could combine these NSDUH data with the Medicaid analysis from MODRN et al., 2021, and other data sources to generate more-detailed estimates of the number of people with OUD in the country.

[16] The NSDUH question asks, "How long has it been since you were last in treatment or counseling for your alcohol or drug use, not counting cigarettes?"

[17] The number of people reporting buprenorphine use in the past year was much higher for all the groups compared with those reporting past year medication treatment. It is unknown what share of these individuals are using it to address withdrawal symptoms, for its euphoric effects (likely depending on formulation), or for some other reason. A growing body of research suggests that diverted buprenorphine is being used by those with OUD to address withdrawal (Allen and Harocopos, 2016; Cicero, Ellis, and Chilcoat, 2018). Although it may not be prescribed to these individuals and show up as a formal treatment episode, that does not mean those individuals are not using the buprenorphine to help manage their OUD.

Involvement with the Criminal Legal System

Finally, those with a heroin-related OUD were much more likely to report having been arrested or being on probation compared with those with solely an analgesic-related OUD. This is not surprising because those using analgesics have higher incomes and options for obtaining these substances other than the illegal market. There is also strong literature linking heroin use with property crime (see, e.g., Pacula et al., 2013).

Concluding Thoughts

Because we do not have reliable estimates of the number of people with OUD, it is difficult to determine what share are only using prescription opioids versus heroin and other illegally produced opioids; it is also hard to pin down their characteristics. Although NSDUH suggests most with OUD are only using prescription opioids, those with OUD involving heroin were nearly twice as likely to have received treatment for OUD in the past year. This is somewhat consistent with the TEDS data which suggest that primary admissions involving heroin far exceed those involving prescription opioids, and those admitted for heroin were more likely to have previous episodes.

There are many possible explanations for this difference, including the following: (1) It may be harder to abstain from heroin; (2) people who use heroin are more likely to become involved in the criminal legal system and so be referred or mandated to treatment; and (3) those using heroin may have longer drug use histories and may have had more time to enter treatment.

But as noted earlier, the NSDUH data are not very useful for understanding the characteristics of those with OUD, and the TEDS data are becoming less useful for assessing OUD treatment episodes as more people are receiving buprenorphine treatment for OUD outside the specialty treatment sector covered by TEDS. Combining these data sources with detailed analyses of insurance claims data and those filling prescriptions for buprenorphine could help us better understand the characteristics of this population and how it is changing—especially in the age of illegally produced synthetic opioids.

Who Is Dying from Opioid-Involved Overdoses and How Has This Changed?

The text for this section was produced for this volume and some of it appears in Commission on Combating Synthetic Opioid Trafficking, 2022.

Drug overdose deaths involving opioids have increased annually since the beginning of the 21st century. In the span of 20 years, the United States has seen a nearly seven-fold increase in the per capita death rate involving opioid overdoses, from nearly three per 100,000 in 2000 to more than 20 per 100,000 in 2020 (see Figure 2.3). Since 2016, opioid overdose death rates

FIGURE 2.3

U.S. Opioid-Involved Overdose Deaths, 2000–2020

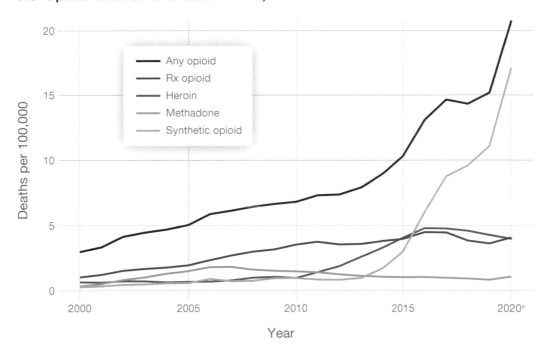

SOURCE: Overdose death data come from National Vital Statistics System MCOD data (CDC, 2021c) and data shared with RAND researchers under a data use agreement.
[a] Death counts for 2020 are provisional and subject to change.

have surpassed fatalities for every other form of accidental death, including those involving firearms or motor vehicles (CDC, 2016; CDC, 2021b; National Highway Traffic Safety Administration, 2020).

Yet this increase does not adequately convey the sheer magnitude of deaths. Nearly 560,000 U.S. residents have died from an opioid-involved overdose just since 2000. Today, the annual number of deaths involving opioids is 50 percent higher than the number of people who died from HIV/AIDS at its peak in the mid-1990s (CDC, 2013; CDC, 2022b).

However, it is important to recognize that many deaths that involved opioids also involved other substances. Indeed, many who died with fentanyl and cocaine in their bodies may not even have been aware that they were ingesting an opioid because the illegal supply chains sometimes mix fentanyl into other drugs. Figure 2.4 displays the total number of overdose deaths from 2000 to 2020 for specific drugs and whether synthetic opioids were also recorded. More than half of all deaths involving cocaine or heroin also mention synthetic opioids other than methadone (largely fentanyl). Deaths involving psychostimulants (e.g., methamphetamine) have steadily increased over the past decade and those also involving synthetic opioids account for an increasing share of the total.

FIGURE 2.4

U.S. Drug Overdose Deaths Involving Synthetic Opioids, 2000–2020

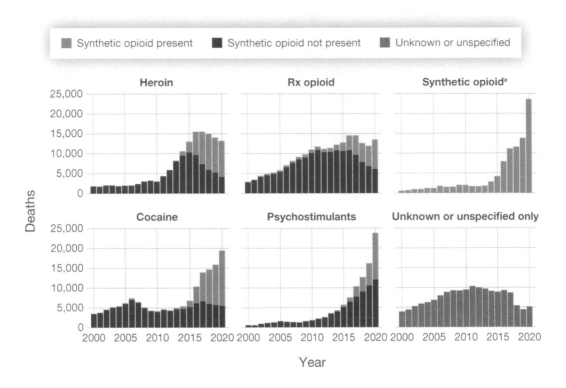

SOURCE: Author analysis of overdose death data from National Vital Statistics System MCOD data (CDC, 2021c) and data shared with RAND researchers under a data use agreement.

[a] Excludes cocaine, heroin, Rx opioid, and psychostimulant deaths from synthetic opioids.

But overdose death totals or trends over time often gloss over details about *who* is dying from *what*. The remainder of this section describes changes in opioid-involved overdose deaths over time by several characteristics: sex, race/ethnicity, age, educational attainment, marital status, urbanicity, and census region. We use mortality data from the CDC and demographic data from the U.S. Census Bureau to calculate per capita death rates from 2000 through 2020 (the latest year for which we have individual death records that permit examining trends across the population). We show trends for specific overdose ICD-10 codes, including heroin (T40.1), semisynthetic opioids (most commonly prescription opioids, T40.2), methadone (T40.3), and synthetic opioids excluding opioids (T40.4). We also include deaths involving any opioid, which includes the four T-codes listed, along with opium (T40.0) and unspecified narcotic (T40.6). The counts for each type of opioid are not mutually exclusive (i.e., if synthetic opioids and heroin were recorded for a particular death, that death is included in the rates for synthetic opioids and heroin) and are based on the raw data provided by the CDC (i.e., no attempt is made to adjust these figures for possible underreporting).

Sex

There have been long-standing disparities in drug use, related outcomes, and responses by sex (Correa-de-Araujo et al., 2005; Grella and Joshi, 1999; Schuler et al., 2018). Opioids are no different: Men typically report higher rates of problematic opioid use and adverse outcomes, especially those related to illegally sourced opioids, like heroin (Marsh et al., 2018; Serdarevic, Striley, and Cottler, 2017). In contrast, women often obtain and fill opioid pain reliever prescriptions at higher rates than men (Marsh et al., 2018; Schieber et al., 2020). In terms of overdose deaths, Figure 2.5 shows the per capita rates of overdose deaths over time for both populations. Rates for both groups increased over this period, but unevenly.

Men continue to and have always had higher overdose death rates than women across all categories of opioids, although that disparity has narrowed. In 2000, the male overdose death rate involving opioids was about 2.8 times that of women. By 2020, the gap had slightly narrowed to 2.5 times. Over this period, overdose deaths involving prescription opioids in women grew by a factor of 5.0, whereas death rates for men increased by a factor of 3.5. Heroin overdose deaths never overtook those of prescription opioids in the female population, but that cannot be said for men. By 2013, men were dying at higher rates from heroin than from prescription opioids.

FIGURE 2.5

U.S. Opioid-Involved Overdose Deaths, by Sex, 2000–2020

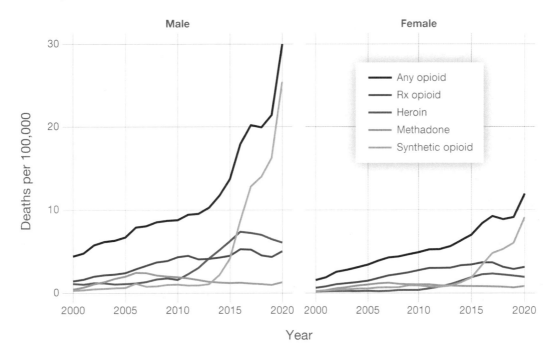

SOURCE: Data shared with RAND researchers under a data use agreement. Overdose death data come from National Vital Statistics System MCOD data and sex population data come from CDC Bridged-Race population estimates (CDC, 2021c).

The biggest spike in overdose deaths over time comes from synthetic opioids. Both sexes reported similar overdose death rates in 2000, around 0.2 to 0.3 per 100,000, but by 2020, that number had grown to 9.12 and 25.4 per 100,000 for women and men, respectively. By 2016, synthetic opioid overdoses overtook heroin related overdoses for both populations. Men are now dying from synthetic opioids at rates 2.8 times that for women. This difference is partially related to the nature of sourcing: Men are more likely to source opioids from the illicit market where illegally manufactured fentanyl is increasingly present (Pardo et al., 2019; Marsh et al., 2018).

Race/Ethnicity

Using CDC mortality and population data, we calculated race/ethnicity death rates across the six categories shown in Figure 2.6. The public health literature has noted racial disparities in how causes of death are recorded, which we cannot account for here (Cooper, Yuan, and Rimm, 1997; Tucker et al., 2007).

Across all groups, death rates for non-Hispanic White people and non-Hispanic Black people were the highest. Overdose death rates have increased for other racial and ethnic groups since 2015, but that trend is largely related to the encroachment of illegally supplied synthetic opioids in drug markets.

In 2000, rates of opioid-involved overdose deaths among non-Hispanic White and non-Hispanic Black populations were similar—around 3.4 per 100,000. However, over time prescription overdose deaths in the non-Hispanic White population increased. The non-Hispanic Black population never experienced the prescription overdose death burden that affected the non-Hispanic White population, although rates of overdoses involving these drugs did increase among the latter population. Some researchers have attributed some of this disparity to long-standing structural inequities and racial biases in health care provision and access to pain treatment in the United States (Goyal et al., 2015; Pletcher et al., 2008; Singhal, Tien, and Hsia, 2016). However, the issues of such structural inequities, racial biases, and systemic racism are important problems in the U.S. health care system that go well beyond the opioids and pain management.

Among non-Hispanic Black people, heroin overdose deaths increased over time. Most of those deaths were older non-Hispanic Black men who began to use heroin decades earlier (Jalal et al., 2018). Heroin deaths only overtook prescription opioids in the non-Hispanic White population starting in 2018. Disparities in opioid-involved overdoses between non-Hispanic White and Black populations grew over time until the emergence of illegally manufactured synthetic opioids.

The introduction of potent synthetic opioids like fentanyl to drug markets is now affecting stimulant users and non-White populations in diverging ways (Lippold et al., 2019). Recent studies have documented racial disparities in opioid-involved overdose deaths nationally, showing that non-Hispanic Black people are now dying from synthetic opioids at greater rates than White people (Furr-Holden et al., 2021). In 2018, overdose deaths involving any

FIGURE 2.6

U.S. Opioid-Involved Overdose Deaths, by Race/Ethnicity, 2000–2020

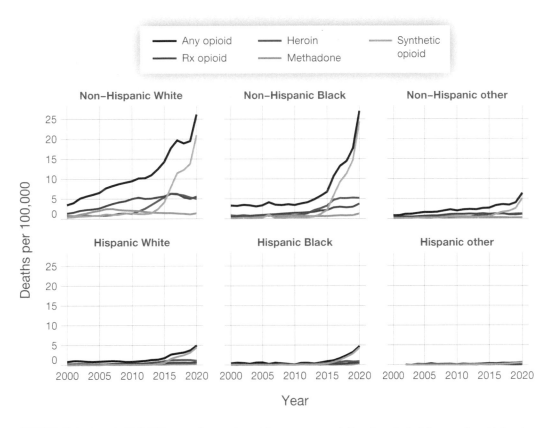

SOURCE: Data shared with RAND researchers under a data use agreement. Overdose death data come from National Vital Statistics System MCOD data, and race and ethnicity data come from CDC Bridged-Race population estimates (CDC, 2021c).

opioid declined in the non-Hispanic White population but continued to accelerate in the Black population. Today, a greater share of opioid-involved overdoses in Black populations (both Hispanic and non-Hispanic) are the result of synthetic opioids.

Age

Opioid-involved overdose deaths also vary by age (see Figure 2.7). These deaths are least common for those under 20 or above 61 years of age, and highest for those aged 31 to 40. The CDC also notes that increases across all age groups have been both substantial and significant (Hedegaard, Miniño, and Warner, 2020).

Heroin-involved overdose deaths are more common and appear earlier in the period for younger age groups, with the exception of those under 20. Prescription opioid overdose deaths were more common in populations over the age of 40. Synthetic opioid overdoses rose

FIGURE 2.7

U.S. Opioid-Involved Overdose Deaths, by Age Group, 2000–2020

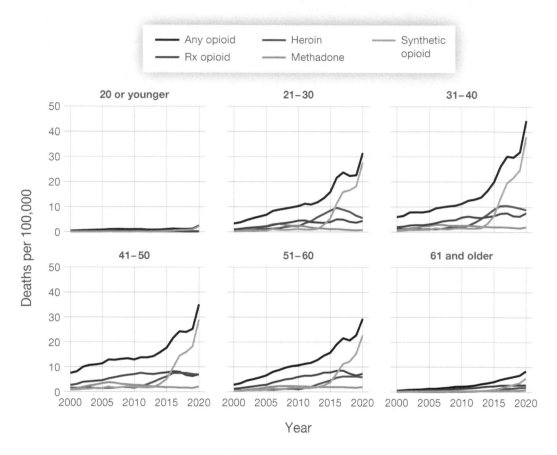

SOURCE: Overdose death data come from National Vital Statistics System MCOD data (CDC, 2021c) and data shared with RAND researchers under a data use agreement.

simultaneously across all age groups and have continued to rise, but the increase was sharpest in age groups from 21 to 60 years.

The vast majority of overdose deaths are individuals in the middle-aged brackets, from 20 to 60. Deaths in these age groups are of great concern given the years of potential lives lost, and the effects on families and whole communities. The Economic Council of Advisers for the White House estimated that the overdose crisis in 2017 cost the U.S. economy some $500 billion (Ropero-Miller and Speaker, 2019).[18] The vast majority of that cost was attrib-

---

[18] The majority of those economic costs derive from lost productivity from loss of life. Here, measures assume that decedents would have been economically active for the remainder of their expected life. Those costs are then summed to a single year rather than amortized over the life span of remaining years of life. Needless to say, these total costs are inflated relative to one's expected life span and economic or productive activity.

uted to lost productivity in people 25 to 55 years old, the most economically active and productive age range.

Educational Attainment

Using census estimates of educational attainment for those aged 25 and older, we have calculated the per capita rates of opioid-involved overdoses by four levels of education (see Figure 2.8). Decedents younger than 25 have been removed from these plots. Education attainment correlates with other important outcomes, such as earning potential and other health indicators (Conti, Heckman, and Urzua, 2010).

There is a clear pattern in overdose death rates. Those with some high school or less report the highest opioid overdose death rates throughout the period, but disparities across groups grew over time. In 2000, death rates involving any opioid were higher in those with lower education attainment, but the difference between those without a high school degree and those with a college degree differed only by a factor of 4.6. By 2020, the opioid overdose death rate for those with less than a high school degree neared 57 per 100,000, outpacing those with a college degree by a factor of 10.5. By 2020, those with some college reported opioid-involved death rates of about 22.7 per 100,000. In contrast, those with a college degree reported overdose death rates at 5.4 per 100,000.

In 2015, heroin overdoses overtook prescription opioids in groups with a high school degree or less; deaths involving synthetic opioids later surpassed heroin overdoses. In contrast, heroin-involved overdoses never surpassed prescription opioid deaths among those who had completed college or had some college education. By the end of the series, deaths involving synthetic opioids surpassed deaths involving either heroin or prescription opioids.

Marital Status

Using census estimates of marital status for those aged 15 and over, we can calculate death rates across four groups (see Figure 2.9). We have removed decedents younger than 15 from the plots. There is some literature about the protective effects of marriage on crime and health (e.g., Lillard and Panis, 1996). Opioid overdose death rates are highest for the divorced population, followed by those who were never married or single. Married populations had the lowest rates of overdose, hovering around 5 per 100,000 throughout the period.

However, we can see variations in deaths by drug class. Divorced populations were dying at greater rates from prescription opioids than from other opioids, until illegally sourced synthetic opioids arrived on the scene. In contrast, initially the never married or single population died predominantly from prescription opioid overdoses, but in 2013, deaths involving heroin overtook prescription opioids.

FIGURE 2.8

U.S. Opioid-Involved Overdose Deaths, by Educational Attainment, 2000–2020

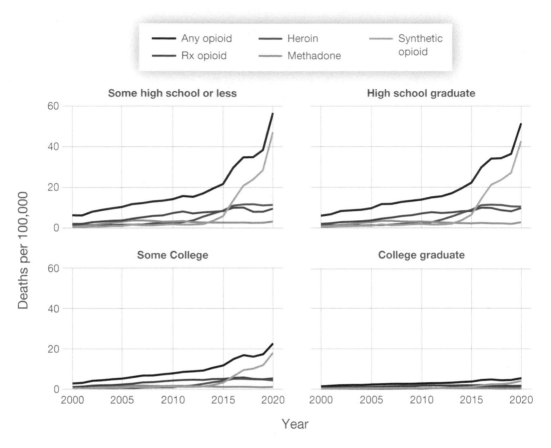

SOURCE: Data shared with RAND researchers under a data use agreement. Overdose death data come from National Vital Statistics System MCOD data, and educational attainment data come from the U.S. Census and are for those aged 25 and older (CDC, 2021c). Deaths for those under 25 years of age have been dropped.

Urbanicity

We can also examine opioid-involved overdose death trends across degree of urbanicity, using the core-based statistical area (CBSA) designation for the six different statistical areas shown in Figure 2.10, as defined by the federal government. More densely populated areas, including large central metros, large fringe metros, and medium metro areas report the highest shares of opioid-involved overdose deaths per capita. Yet there is substantial variation. More rural areas report higher rates of prescription opioid overdose deaths as noted by others (Jalal et al., 2018), sometimes approaching 5 per 100,000 for some years. Deaths involving prescription opioids have trended downward, with steepest declines in more rural areas.

Heroin overdose deaths increased for all six designated areas but surpassed prescriptions only for more densely populated areas. In short, heroin overdoses were more common in

FIGURE 2.9

U.S. Opioid-Involved Overdose Deaths, by Marital Status, 2000–2020

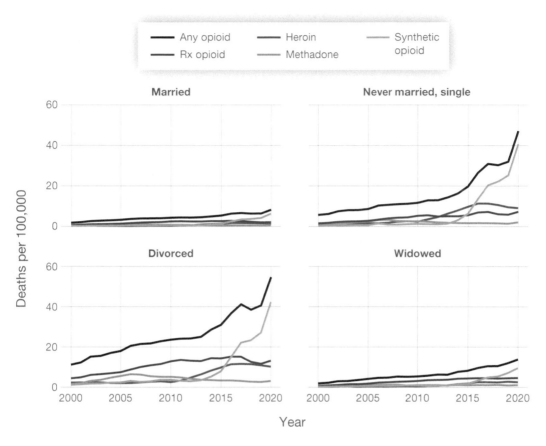

SOURCE: Data shared with RAND researchers under a data use agreement. Overdose death data come from National Vital Statistics System MCOD data, and marital status data come from the U.S. Census for those aged 15 and older (CDC, 2021c). Deaths for those under 15 years of age have been dropped.

more populated areas, whereas prescription opioid overdoses were more common in rural areas. Synthetic opioid overdose deaths were greater in dense regions as well, especially toward the end of the period, when rates were close to 12.5 per 100,000. That said, after 2016, deaths involving synthetic opioids outpaced those for heroin or prescription opioids across all six designations.

Synthetic opioid overdoses were more common than heroin in more rural areas, especially up through 2010. These overdoses may be related to prescription fentanyl, not illegally sourced fentanyl; the latter really began to increase around 2014 (Pardo et al., 2019). There is a noticeable spike in synthetic opioid overdose deaths in the large central metro designation in 2006—which more than doubled from the previous year—likely associated with a prior outbreak of illegally sourced fentanyl affecting major heroin and cocaine markets in parts of Chicago, Detroit, and Philadelphia (Pardo et al., 2019).

FIGURE 2.10

U.S. Opioid-Involved Overdose Deaths, by CBSA Designation, 2000–2020

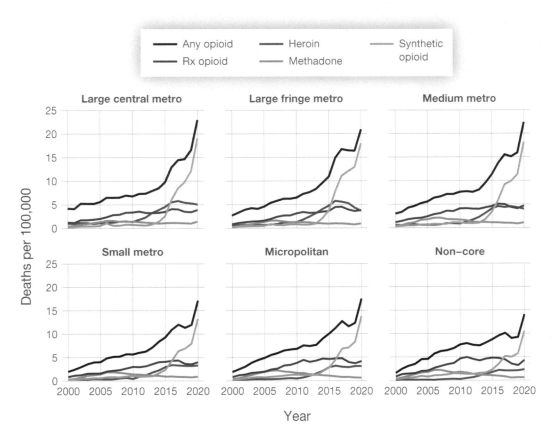

SOURCE: Data shared with RAND researchers under a data use agreement. Overdose death data come from National Vital Statistics System MCOD data and CBSA status data come from the U.S. Census (CDC, 2021c).

Census Region

Using census region designations,[19] we can also observe important geographic variation in opioid-involved overdose fatalities (Figure 2.11). What is most clear is that the rise in synthetic opioid overdose deaths around 2014 are most prevalent in the Northeast and the North Central regions. The South and West report rises, with the West only at the very end of the time series and at much lower rates than the Northeast and North Central regions. The Northeast

---

[19] State designations by region are as follows: Northeast: Connecticut, Massachusetts, Maine, New Hampshire, New Jersey, New York, Pennsylvania, Rhode Island, and Vermont; South: Alabama, Arkansas, District of Columbia, Delaware, Florida, Georgia, Kentucky, Louisiana, Maryland, Mississippi, North Carolina, Oklahoma, South Carolina, Tennessee, Texas, Virginia, and West Virginia; North Central: Iowa, Illinois, Indiana, Kansas, Michigan, Minnesota, Missouri, North Dakota, Nebraska, Ohio, South Dakota, and Wisconsin; and West: Alaska, Arizona, California, Colorado, Hawaii, Idaho, Montana, New Mexico, Nevada, Oregon, Utah, Washington, and Wyoming.

FIGURE 2.11

U.S. Opioid-Involved Overdose Deaths, by Census Region, 2000–2020

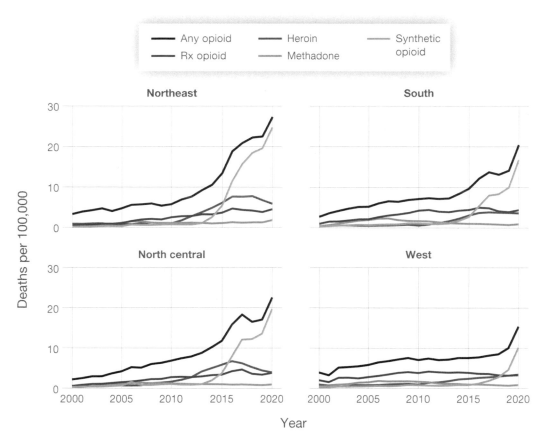

SOURCE: Data shared with RAND researchers under a data use agreement. Overdose death data come from National Vital Statistics System MCOD data, and region population status data come from CDC Bridged-Race population estimates (CDC, 2021c).

is particularly of note given that synthetic opioid death rates never slowed since they started rising in late 2013. There was a considerable slowing of deaths involving synthetic opioids in the North Central and South for 2018, which some have noted may be because of the departure of extremely potent synthetic opioids, such as carfentanil, from some markets (Jalal and Burke, 2021).

There is a similar geographic pattern for heroin overdose deaths overtaking prescription opioid overdose deaths in the Northeast and North Central regions, which was not the case for the South and West. Deaths involving heroin in the Northeast and North Central have declined starting in 2016, perhaps because of its partial replacement by fentanyl in illicit markets. In contrast, the death rates involving prescription drugs were higher in the South and West through much of the series, although the West never saw death rates at or above 5 per 100,000, which was reached in all other regions at some point. With the exception of the

West, prescription opioid overdose death rates rose substantially, by a factor of three or four from 2000 to 2019. The West saw fairly steady death rates, rising from 2 to 3.2 per 100,000 from 2000 to 2019. In terms of all opioid-involved overdoses, there is also a similar rise across regions, with the West reporting the smallest growth over the 20-year period as deaths doubled per capita from 4 to 10 per 100,000. All other regions saw a six- or seven-fold increase in opioid-involved death rates.

What Is the Scope of Other Health Harms Related to Opioid Use, Including Nonfatal Overdose?

The vast majority individuals who use opioids in a clinically appropriate way benefit from them and do not experience any harms. That said, opioid use can lead to health harms beyond fatal overdose or those related to having an SUD for some individuals. Some of these other harms are generally associated with long-term use, including those related to injecting drugs, aggravated mental health conditions, and deaths from other causes (e.g., suicide, injury). Others can be associated with long- or short-term use, including impaired driving and nonfatal overdoses.[20] Nonfatal overdoses, even if reversed by emergency services, may be associated with other brain and body injuries (Voronkov, Cocchiaro, and Stock, 2021; Zibbell et al., 2019). This section provides a brief overview of some of these harms and pays special attention to what is known about the scope of nonfatal overdoses in the United States. For additional information on the benefits of opioid use, see Chapter Five.

Harms Beyond Overdose and Addiction

In addition to overdose and addiction, there are other sources of harm related to opioid use. This is particularly true for injection opioid use, which includes risk of blood-borne disease transmission, such as hepatitis C virus and HIV, but also other soft-tissue damage and infections (e.g., endocarditis). For example, acute hepatitis C infection rates more than doubled from 2004 to 2014, with more than 80 percent of cases in 2014 with risk factor data involving injection drug use (Zibbell et al., 2018). Subsequent analyses found that similar to the increase in overdose deaths (Alpert, Powell, and Pacula, 2018), much of the increase in hepatitis C was associated with the reformulation of OxyContin and the subsequent increase in injection drug use (Powell, Alpert, and Pacula, 2019). Skin and soft-tissue infections related to injection opioid use more than doubled from 1993 to 2010 nationwide (Ciccarone et al., 2016), a period before the greatest increase in injection drug use, and state studies have found that drug use-associated infective endocarditis and associated heart surgery increased 200 percent or more from 2013 to 2017 (Meisner et al., 2020; Schranz et al., 2019). OUD may also

---

[20] For insights about the association between opioid use and traffic safety, see Gomes et al., 2013, and Governors Highway Safety Association, 2018.

be associated with other forms of premature death (e.g., suicide), addiction, and comorbid mental health disorders (Degenhardt et al., 2019; Imtiaz et al., 2014).

These and other potential harms are discussed in the forthcoming chapters, including the consequences for family members and those who live with someone with OUD. But readers must not forget about the medical benefits that can come from using opioids for prescribed purposes (further addressed in Chapters Four and Five). The United States could be doing much more to reduce the harms associated with opioid use, but it could also be doing a better job at making sure pain patients are receiving the appropriate treatments they need.

Nonfatal Overdoses

Although tens of thousands of opioid overdose fatalities occur each year, this is just a fraction of the total number of overdoses. Although data are poor, in the United States, there appear to be at least about ten nonfatal heroin overdoses for every fatal overdose, and somewhat fewer for opioids overall.[21] However, there are major limitations to calculating those ratios. Data collection systems for nonfatal overdoses are not national because of privacy concerns, funding limitations, and other shortcomings involving a generally fractured health care system. Additionally, nonfatal overdoses are not always recorded or reported, unless they are attended to by first responders or treated in an emergency department (ED).

Using federal public health data systems, such the Healthcare Cost and Utilization Project (HCUP) and the CDC's Overdose Data Action Program, the CDC estimates national nonfatal overdose totals and rates for recent years. Nevertheless, national public health data obscure many of the details surrounding these figures.[22] For example, these data provide only annual changes in rates per 100,000 ED visits rather than the year-specific rate or total number of events in the general population (Liu et al., 2020). The CDC's 2017 estimates were the last that reported figures for national rates of ED events.

Since 2018, the number reported is the year-over-year change in the number of ED events, making it impossible to estimate the ratio of nonfatal overdoses to fatal overdoses (CDC, 2021a; Liu et al., 2020). Per the 2018 to 2019 report, the rates of nonfatal overdoses involving opioids have increased significantly across all demographic strata. There was a 9.7 percent relative increase in total opioid-involved nonfatal overdose events reported in EDs from 2018 to 2019 (Liu et al., 2020). This was higher for men (10.7 percent) than for women (7.1 percent) but still significant within each group over time. Those aged 35 to 44 (15.2 percent) and living in urban areas (13.6 percent) had the largest year-over-year increase. These are percentage changes in the rates per 100,000 ED events; they do not reflect ED events in the general

---

[21] ONDCP has noted the importance of creating a national tracking system for nonfatal drug overdoses (Gupta and Holtgrave, 2022).

[22] Although it is possible to get more-detailed information on nonfatal overdoses with dates and zip codes, these data need to be purchased; thus, this limits how often they are used to examine nonfatal overdoses (and other opioid-related harms that are not fatal).

public. In 2017, there were nearly 1 million estimated drug overdoses treated in EDs; of those, 30 percent involved opioids (Liu et al., 2020).

Table 2.3 shows 2017 CDC estimates of nonfatal overdoses involving heroin or any opioid juxtaposed to fatal overdoses for the same categories, stratified across a few demographic groups. We have omitted nonheroin opioids because of imprecision in determining the opioid in question.

To examine the ratio of reported nonfatal to fatal overdoses, we show death counts and ratios for 2017 across the same groups, then divide nonfatal overdose rates by fatal overdose rates to obtain a ratio of how many estimated nonfatal overdose ED events occur per fatal overdose events. This estimated ratio is likely a lower bound given that an unknown share of nonfatal overdose events are not treated in EDs but instead by passersby, intimates, first responders (without subsequent transport to ED), or in other ways that may not be captured by official data-collection systems.

In 2017, men, individuals between the ages of 20 and 34, and those living in medium metro and micropolitan areas had the highest rates of nonfatal overdoses involving opioids. This trend generally holds in fatal overdoses involving any opioid, but with higher fatality rates in those aged 25 to 44 and those living in large fringe metro areas.

In terms of heroin, we see a similar pattern for nonfatal overdoses, with men reporting higher rates than women. Those aged 25 to 34 report the greatest frequency of nonfatal heroin overdoses. However, the most rural areas (e.g., noncore) reported the highest frequency of nonfatal heroin-involved overdoses.

Issues of precision confound some of this analysis: These are rates in the general population and not in the estimated user base. Currently, prevalence estimates of heroin use are substantially biased and unreliable given the inadequacy of household surveys that overlook institutionalized populations like jails, which may include chronic heroin-using populations (Reuter, Caulkins, and Midgette, 2021). Although we compare rates in the general population, a more precise measure would attempt to estimate the rates of fatal and nonfatal overdose in the respective populations that use opioids or heroin.

In terms of geographic variation in census regions for fatal and nonfatal overdoses, we see a similar pattern as described earlier with rates highest in the Northeast and North Central regions, but lowest in the West. There is also a similar pattern in which the ratio of nonfatal to fatal heroin overdoses is higher than that for any opioid in all U.S. Census regions with the exception of the West, which reports the same ratio for heroin and other opioids. However, the ratio of nonfatal to fatal overdoses across regions differs considerably and in hard-to-explain ways. For example, the Northeast has slightly lower nonfatal to fatal ratios for either heroin or any opioid than the South, yet this region experiences much higher rates for either category.

Comparing the rates of nonfatal and fatal overdoses within drug categories in the general population suggests that there are about 6.4 nonfatal overdoses for each fatal overdose that involves any opioid. The estimate of 30 nonfatal events to a fatal overdose cited earlier seems quite high in light of this ratio, unless only one in five nonfatal overdoses are treated in

TABLE 2.3
National Nonfatal and Fatal Opioid-Involved Overdose Counts and Rates per 100,000 Individuals, 2017

| | Nonfatal Overdose ED Events | | | | Fatal Overdose | | | | Ratio of Nonfatal to Fatal | |
| | Any Opioid | | Heroin | | Any Opioid | | Heroin | | | |
	Count	Rate	Count	Rate	Count	Rate	Count	Rate	Any Opioid	Heroin
All	305,623	93.0	154,626	48.6	47,600	14.5	15,482	4.9	6.4	10.0
Sex										
Male	182,169	112.6	106,466	66.7	32,337	20.0	11,596	7.3	5.6	9.2
Female	123,428	73.1	48,146	30.5	15,263	9.0	3,886	2.5	8.1	12.4
Age group										
0–14	3,721	6.1	87	0.1	79	0.1	4	0.0	47.1	21.8
15–19	7,541	35.7	2,437	11.5	507	2.4	140	0.7	14.9	17.4
20–24	31,865	144.1	21,326	96.4	3,587	16.2	1,314	5.9	8.9	16.2
25–34	94,915	209.3	65,445	144.3	13,181	29.1	4,890	10.8	7.2	13.4
35–44	54,223	132.7	30,972	75.8	11,159	27.3	3,713	9.1	4.9	8.3
45–54	44,533	105.1	19,612	46.3	10,207	24.1	3,043	7.2	4.4	6.4
55–64	41,246	98.2	12,027	28.6	7,153	17.0	2,005	4.8	5.8	6.0
≥ 65	27,579	54.2	2,720	5.3	1,724	3.4	368	0.7	16.0	7.4
Census region										
Northeast	63,742	113	38,797	70.5	11,784	20.9	4,310	7.8	5.4	9.0
North Central	86,002	129.2	50,004	77.0	12,483	18.8	4,228	6.5	6.9	11.8
South	110,478	88.6	50,278	42.0	16,999	13.6	4,776	4.0	6.5	10.5

Table 2.3—Continued

	Nonfatal Overdose ED Events				Fatal Overdose				Ratio of Nonfatal to Fatal	
	Any Opioid		Heroin		Any Opioid		Heroin			
	Count	Rate	Count	Rate	Count	Rate	Count	Rate	Any Opioid	Heroin
West	45,402	56.1	15,547	19.7	6,334	7.8	2,168	2.7	7.2	7.2
County urbanization										
Large central metro	86,882	81.8	45,025	42.5	14,518	13.7	5,820	5.5	6.0	7.7
Large fringe metro	74,211	94.0	41,175	54.2	13,594	17.2	4,526	6.0	5.5	9.1
Medium metro	74,709	111.4	37,316	57.8	10,561	15.7	2,973	4.6	7.1	12.6
Small metro	25,296	86.5	11,031	40.1	3,462	11.8	801	2.9	7.3	13.8
Micropolitan	26,256	100.4	12,330	50.8	1,905	7.3	390	1.6	13.8	31.6
Noncore	13,414	74.5	4,475	28.9	3,560	19.8	972	6.3	3.8	4.6

NOTE: National nonfatal overdose ED events are estimated by the CDC using HCUP data from 36 states and the District of Columbia. Fatal counts come from the National Vital Statistics System MCOD records (CDC, 2021c). We use the same population estimates from the CDC to calculate death rates across stratified groups and by drug. Given that not all nonfatal overdoses are recorded in official data systems, the figures shown here are likely lower-bound estimates.

EDs. The number of naloxone administration events for suspected drug overdoses handled by emergency medical services (EMS) has risen by 75 percent from 2012 to 2016, amounting to more than 100,000 events, but it is unclear how many of those were transferred to and recorded in EDs (Cash et al., 2018).

Table 2.3 shows a 10 to 1 ratio of nonfatal to fatal overdoses involving heroin. The narrower ratio of nonfatal to fatal overdoses for any opioid may reflect the fact that those figures include prescription opioids, whose dosing is more consistent than heroin, and in a larger population than for heroin. Across all strata, the ratio of nonfatal to fatal heroin overdoses is higher than the ratio of nonfatal to fatal overdoses involving any opioid. In the general population, men reported fewer nonfatal overdoses than fatal overdoses when compared with women, perhaps reflective of the higher death rates for men.

It is difficult to interpret these ratios for other demographic groups, but lower ratios by age groups may suggest that those aged 35 to 44 may be less likely to survive a heroin overdose compared with those aged 25 to 34. Similarly, those living in major urban areas and remote rural areas report the narrowest ratios of nonfatal to fatal heroin overdoses, which may reflect limits in emergency services available to reverse fatal overdoses. These trends generally hold for ratios of nonfatal to fatal overdoses involving any opioid.

The earlier discussion focused on ratios of nonfatal to fatal overdoses in the general population. Other research has attempted to determine this ratio within individuals over time to better understand the risks that opioids pose to users. Using Medicaid data from 2001 to 2007, one longitudinal study of enrollees between 18 to 64 examined risks and causes of death 12 months after a nonfatal opioid overdose. The study found that substance use–related deaths were the most common cause of death for this group (26.2 percent) (Olfson et al., 2018). The all-cause standardized mortality ratio (SMR) was 24.2 but highest for deaths involving drugs (SMR 132.1). This was higher for women than men (drug-involved SMR of 153.4 to 115.7) and those aged 18 to 34 (SMR of 148.1).

In another study, authors using the same Medicaid data over the same period estimated that the rate of repeat overdose during the first 12 months after a patient's first nonfatal overdose was 29,500 per 100,000 person-years, and that the rate of fatal overdoses over the first 12 months was 1,154 per 100,000 person-years (Olfson et al., 2018). Controlling for demographics, the hazard ratio of a fatal overdose in this population was higher for those whose initial reported overdose was for heroin compared with those whose first overdose involved prescription opioids (Olfson et al., 2018). Authors concluded that "Adults treated for opioid overdose frequently have repeated opioid overdoses in the following year" (Olfson et al., 2018). However, their findings may be specific to Medicaid enrollees and not generalizable to the broader opioid-using population.

Another study examined opioid prescribing and treatment outcomes after an overdose event, using data from 2000 to 2012 in a private insurer database. Authors found that of the 2,848 patients in the database, 90 percent of patients continued to receive an opioid prescription after an overdose event. About 7 percent of the sample reported a repeated overdose event, and the risk of repeated overdose was greater for those receiving higher doses (Larochelle et al., 2016). However, this study was limited to patients receiving pain medications.

The CDC examined recent EMS naloxone administration data for 2012 to 2016 from the National Emergency Medical Services Information System (Cash et al., 2018). These data showed that suspected overdoses rose from nearly 37,000 events in 2012 to more than 100,000 in 2016. These are suspected events in which naloxone was administered, and EMS data do not confirm the drug in question. The total number of naloxone administrations rose from 92,000 in 2012 to nearly 210,000 in 2016. In 2016, men contributed to more than 60 percent of events, and those aged 25 to 34 were involved with nearly one-quarter of events. White individuals accounted for 72 percent of naloxone EMS events, while Black individuals accounted for more than 20 percent (Cash et al., 2018). Data beyond 2017 were unavailable but would likely show rising counts. It is unknown how many of these events were transferred to EDs, but EMS services handled several hundred thousand naloxone administration events each year.

Finally, individuals, even if successfully revived, can experience long-term harms of an opioid overdose. The most common of harms include injuries to the head or body from falling while unconscious, but others, such as burns, assaults, neuropathy, temporary paralysis, and long-term limb damage, can also occur (Warner-Smith, Darke, and Day, 2002; Zibbell et al., 2019). In effect, some segment of those who survive an opioid overdose or have it reversed with naloxone may live with lifelong injuries should their overdose result in some physical injury.

What Do We Know About the Families of Those with Opioid Use Disorder?

We devote Chapter Three to the families and households of those with OUD, but it is useful to draw attention to some of the insights here. According to the 2019 NSDUH, about 80 percent of those self-reporting enough problems to meet the clinical criteria for OUD reported having other family household members older than 18 years, a proportion similar to that of families without a member who meets clinical criteria for OUD (see Table 2.8). That means that most of the time when someone suffers from OUD, there is at least one other adult who may be negatively affected.

Likewise, approximately one-third of respondents with OUD reported having at least one child in their household. The proportion of respondents who reported having children in their household was nearly twice as large (59 percent) for individuals meeting the criteria for both heroin and pain reliever OUD; however, the large CI around this figure suggests that we should not put too much stock in this insight (see Table 2.9).

Here is a rough calculation to help us think about the scale of family members affected by OUD. If one believed there were about 4 million people with OUD and that these NSDUH figures about household composition apply to those not covered by the survey, this would suggest that *at a minimum* there are on the order of 4.5 million family members living with someone who has been diagnosed with OUD.[23] This rough calculation assumes that those with OUD living with an adult family member and those living with a child have no more than one of each in the household. If those with OUD who had adult family members in the household lived with an average of two adults, that would push this number of family household members potentially affected by a relative's OUD closer to 8 million.[24] Of course, the harms experienced by these family household members will vary depending on several factors (e.g., presence of adults without SUD, duration and severity of OUD, if the OUD is in remission or the individual is currently impaired), but the total suffering experienced by these family members is an important and often neglected cost (see Chapter Three). And it would be even larger if one considers the effects that OUD could have on family members outside the household and nonfamily members who live in the household.

The majority of NSDUH respondents with an OUD for heroin have never been married, and only about one in seven is currently married (see Table 2.10). The proportion of individuals with only a pain reliever OUD who reported being currently married was notably higher (about a third), though still lower than the proportion of respondents without an OUD (49 percent).

Small local studies offer additional insights into families of people with OUD and how they are affected (see Chapter Three); however, there are questions about the generalizability of these results.

How Many Arrests Can Be Linked to Opioids Each Year?

As will become clear in the subsequent chapters, involvement with the criminal legal system has implications for many components of the opioid ecosystem. When thinking about these interactions, it can be useful to distinguish between (1) opioid-specific arrests (e.g., possession or sales), (2) arrests for crimes related to opioid use (e.g., property crimes) or supply (e.g., robberies and violence associated with street-level markets), and (3) all other arrests that are unrelated to opioid use or supply. This section focuses on the first two.

This section focuses on data from 2019. The Federal Bureau of Investigation (FBI) is in the process of changing how it generates national totals for arrests and crimes (FBI, 2018), and the latest data available about arrests for specific types of drugs across the country (as of October 2022) are for 2019.

Historically, the main data source for national-level arrest data from state and local departments has been the FBI's annual *Crime in the United States* series, which is based on the FBI's Uniform Crime Reports' (UCR's) Summary Reporting System (SRS). The SRS data were collected from most police departments across the country, and then adjustments are made to

---

[23] 4.5M = 4M × ~80% + 4M × ~33%.

[24] 7.7M = 4M × ~80% × 2 + 4M × ~33%.

account for missing or questionable data. For our purposes, there are two major limits to using the SRS data. First, heroin and cocaine arrests are reported together in one combined sum; in addition, it is unclear how many arrests in the "[s]ynthetic or manufactured drugs" category include opioids. Second, the FBI's hierarchy rule for the SRS means that only the most serious charge is included in their arrest figures. Thus, someone arrested for heroin possession and armed robbery would not be included in the drug arrest totals. This suggests that the actual drug arrest totals from the SRS underestimate the total number of drug arrests.

For roughly 30 years, the FBI has also been collecting more-detailed information about reported crimes and arrests through the National Incident-Based Reporting System (NIBRS). NIBRS provides information about all the arrest charges involved with a police incident, and, if drugs were involved, it lists up to three specific substances. Over time, an increasing number of police departments have participated in NIBRS, and for 2019, it covered approximately 147 million U.S. inhabitants (FBI, 2020b). With the discontinuation of the SRS, NIBRS will now be the primary data system for generating national totals.

The 2019 *Crime in the United States* report, which is based on the SRS, indicates that there were 1,558,862 drug arrests in the United States, of which "heroin or cocaine and their derivatives" accounted for 23.8 percent of—or about 371,000—arrests. There were also roughly 89,000 arrests for "synthetic or manufactured drugs." Although the 2019 NIBRS data are incomplete, we can use this data set to get a rough idea of what share of cocaine and heroin arrests are attributable to heroin. It is much more difficult to isolate opioids from the "synthetic or manufactured drugs" group.

Table 2.4 reports the number of arrests involving cocaine/crack or heroin in the 2019 NIBRS. Although NIBRS allows us to learn about the specific drugs involved, these numbers do not represent national totals. The entries in the first row, which include the counts for cocaine and heroin regardless of whether there were other arrest charges, are somewhat larger for cocaine (heroin: 53,027; cocaine: 67,007). The entries in the second row, which include incidents in which only a drug offense was reported (i.e., no other arrest charges), are also higher for cocaine (heroin: 45,321; cocaine: 60,533).[25] Thus, for jurisdictions covered by NIBRS in 2019, roughly 43 percent of arrests involving heroin or cocaine included heroin.

Whether this 43 percent figure applies to jurisdictions not covered by NIBRS is unknown. But if it did, it would suggest that approximately 160,000 (371,000 × 43 percent) of the arrests in the "heroin or cocaine and their derivatives" group include heroin. Acknowledging that the 160,000 figure excludes arrests for other opioids, undercounts drug arrests because of the hierarchy rule, and does not account for federal opioid arrests (Drug Enforcement Administration [DEA] domestic arrests for all drugs in 2019 were almost 29,000) (DEA, undated), it would not be unreasonable to assume that there were on the order of 200,000 to 300,000

---

[25] The incident was considered involving drug charges only if (1) variable V20061 equaled 351 or 352, and if (2) variables V20062 and V20063 both had values less than zero.

TABLE 2.4

Comparing Heroin and Cocaine Mentions in NIBRS, 2019

Measure	A. Any Heroin	B. Any Cocaine	C. Heroin (%)[a]
Any drug mention in arrestee file	53,027	67,007	44.2
Arrests only involving drugs	45,321	60,533	42.8

SOURCE: Authors' calculations using data from the Bureau of Justice Statistics, 2022, for 147 million U.S. inhabitants.

[a] The numerator is from Column A. The denominator is based on total incidents involving heroin or cocaine, including the small share of incidents involving both substances.

opioid-specific arrests nationwide in the United States in 2019, including for production, distribution, and sale, not just possession.[26]

But these arrests are only a subset of the criminal justice interactions associated with opioid demand and supply. In particular, there is strong evidence linking frequent illegal heroin use with property crimes (see, e.g., Bennett, Holloway, and Farrington, 2008; Pacula et al., 2013; Smart and Reuter, 2022). In a classic study, Ball, Shaffer, and Nurco, 1983, observed that in their sample of 243 heroin "addicts" (their term), there were alternating periods of high and low rates of property crime offending corresponding to the times that the subjects were or were not using heroin often. Furthermore, those involved with distribution are sometimes robbed and may engage in violence, e.g., to settle disputes (Goldstein, 1985). Indeed, it is such "systemic violence" by drug suppliers that is often considered to be the greatest crime problem related to drug use in a prohibitionist regime, especially when considering the violence in Mexico and other trafficking countries. Reliable figures on the prevalence of the property crimes related to opioid use are unavailable, especially for those with OUD who only use prescription opioids.[27]

Some people with OUD do not commit any crimes, while others may commit multiple crimes per day to maintain their habit. To get a sense of the order of magnitude for arrests linked to opioids beyond those related to possession and sales, we offer the following thought experiment using round numbers: If one assumed that there were on the order of 4 million people with OUD (which is plausible, and possibly low) and that each of them, on average, committed two property crimes per year to help sustain their habit, that would be 8 million property crimes. This may seem like a lot, but data from the National Crime Victimization Survey (NCVS) suggest that, in 2019, there were on the order of 12 million property crime victimizations involving those living in households (Morgan and Truman, 2020). This is a

---

[26] In 2019, there were 1.56 million drug arrests made by state and local authorities, approximately 371,000 involved "heroin or cocaine and their derivatives," and about 80 percent of these were for possession (See Table 2.11). The charge is influenced by the weight of drugs seized or believed to be involved, and some individuals arrested for possession are actually involved in distribution. There are also some individuals arrested for distribution-related charges who are only engaging in those activities to obtain free or discounted drugs (e.g., those who hold the drugs for the dealers on the streets) (FBI, 2020a).

[27] For more on the uncertainty surrounding these figures and the problems with "drug attribution factors" for crime, see Pacula et al., 2013, and Caulkins and Kleiman, 2014.

massive underestimate of all property crime because it excludes all thefts from retail businesses and other populations not covered by the NCVS (e.g., those who are unhoused).

We know that about one-third of the property victimizations reported in the NCVS are reported to the police (Morgan and Thompson, 2022) and, of the share of property crimes reported to the police, about 17 percent are cleared (which means that it leads to an arrest, the person is charged with the commission of a crime, or the defendant is turned over to the court for prosecution) (FBI, 2020b). If we multiplied the 8 million crimes by 33 percent and 17 percent, we generated approximately 450,000 arrests for property crimes.

This figure obviously would be higher if we assumed more than an *average* of two property crimes per year per person with OUD that were linked to opioid use. It also excludes any arrests related to robbery, impaired driving, victimization of people who use drugs (including sexual assault), prostitution, and other crimes that may be related to opioid intoxication. Furthermore, it excludes any arrests for crimes committed by those producing and supplying opioids (e.g., violent conflicts over turf, weapons-related crimes associated with weapons the person would not have owned but for their involvement in distribution).

The rough analyses in this section suggest that arrests for opioid-specific offenses (i.e., possession and sales) might be in the range of 200,000 to 300,000 annually; arrests for other crimes related to opioid use and sales could be multiple times that amount. It is plausible that opioids could be involved with on the order of 1 million arrests in the United States each year, and possibly more.[28]

One could easily quibble with some of the assumptions underlying these back-of-the-envelope calculations, but it would not change the bottom line: Opioid-specific arrests account for only a fraction of the total arrests linked to opioids.

---

[28] Here is another way to think about this: As noted earlier, NSDUH misses the vast majority of people who frequently use heroin and illegally manufactured fentanyl (Reuter, Caulkins, and Midgette, 2021). But for the 1.7 million people meeting criteria for OUD in NSDUH, about 20 percent of them reported being arrested and booked in the previous year (Table 2.5). The rate for those with OUD using heroin was closer to 45 percent (Table 2.5). We do not know what share of these individuals were arrested for crimes related to opioid use, but if one thought that it was half, that would suggest that there were roughly 170,000 people in NSDUH arrested for crimes related to opioids (1.7M × 20 percent × 50 percent). Note that this is the number of people, not the number of arrests; people could generate multiple arrests over the year. Reuter, Caulkins, and Midgette (2021) estimate that NSDUH misses about 1.5 million people who use heroin on a daily and near-daily basis (the vast majority of whom likely meet criteria for OUD; 94 percent, see footnote 8). If we applied a similar calculation (which assumes that the arrest rate for those with heroin use disorder in NSDUH is similar to that of those with heroin use disorder not covered by NSDUH), we would generate an additional 317,000 people arrested for crime related to opioids (1.5M × 94 percent × 50 percent × 45 percent). There is a lot of uncertainty surrounding these calculations, but if we believe that there were approximately 500,000 people arrested for crimes related to opioids, and some were arrested multiple times for crimes related to their opioid use, the rough calculation suggesting that there could be on the order of 1 million arrests linked to opioids does not seem unreasonable—especially since this calculation excludes crimes related to opioid supply by those who do not have an OUD.

For Those with Opioid Use Disorder Who Are Justice Involved, What Share of Their Arrests Are for Drug Law Violations Versus Other Crimes?

As noted earlier, the vast majority the arrests involving opioids are not for drug law violations. This raises a related, but different question: For those with OUD who are justice involved, what share of their arrests are for drug law violations compared with other crimes? This is an important parameter (among others; see Chapter Six) when thinking about the consequences of changing drug laws, whether it be expunging or sealing certain offenses or deprioritizing or decriminalizing drug possession offenses.

There is no national data set that provides an answer to this question. Although not related to opioids, an analysis using state criminal history data about cannabis offenses is insightful. An article published in the *New York Times* about expungement related to cannabis offenses in New York State found that even after expunging these offenses, about 85 percent of these individuals would still have a criminal record because of other crimes (Paybarah, 2019).[29] Given that heavy opioid use has a much stronger association with criminal activity than heavy cannabis use (Pacula et al., 2013), one could imagine this figure being even larger for those with OUD.

This implication that people with OUD who are justice involved typically have criminal histories involving nondrug law offenses is also consistent with the early qualitative research in this space; however, there are always questions about representativeness cohort studies and we cannot assume that people who regularly use opioids suffer from OUD. The previously cited Ball, Shaffer, and Nurco, 1983, study of 243 male opiate "addicts" (their term, and it was mostly heroin) in Baltimore, Maryland, found via criminal history database searches that this cohort had an average of 3.7 drug possession arrests, 1.5 violent crime arrests, and 8.7 nondrug arrests (mostly theft). Another early study focused on 356 people actively using heroin in Miami, Florida, found that men and women in the sample self-reported a median number of previous arrests of 3.5 and 2.6 (Inciardi, 1979). The median number of arrests for drug law offenses was 1.4 and 0.8, suggesting a large share of their previous arrests were for nondrug offenses.[30]

---

[29] A quote from the *New York Times* correction to the article reads as follows:

> About 160,000 people with low-level marijuana convictions in New York will see those convictions cleared from their record. And of that number, 10,872 in New York City and 13,537 in the rest of the state, will have no criminal records after their marijuana convictions are cleared. The remaining approximately 136,000 people will still have criminal records because of other convictions. (Paybarah, 2019)

[30] It is unclear whether the total arrest figures for Miami are lower because the author only presented the median (instead of the mean, which is more sensitive to outliers); because people were not as accurate with their self-reports (Ball, Shaffer, and Nurco, 1983, examined criminal records); because of the sample composition (active users versus those from a treatment-based sample); or because of something else.

More recently, a retrospective analysis was conducted of 907 people who fatally overdosed in Philadelphia, Pennsylvania, in 2016 (most involving opioids).[31] The analysis found that one-third had no contact with the Philadelphia criminal legal system (Shefner et al., 2020). Of the two-thirds who did have contact before they died, they had accumulated 3,926 arrests: "1,128 (28.7%) were for drugs, 1,062 (27.1%) property, 738 (18.8%) violent, 475 (12.1%) public disorder and 523 (17%) other putative offenses" (p. 3). The mean (median) number of arrests for these individuals was 6.6 (5.0). Although we do not know what share of those who were involved with the criminal justice system had an arrest for drugs (some people may have been arrested for drug offenses more than once) versus other crimes, among people in this cohort who overdosed and likely had an OUD, more than two-thirds had arrests for nondrug law violations.

Of course, not all crime committed by those with OUD can be attributed to substance use; however, this insight can improve analyses of the impact of efforts to change drug possession laws and/or expunge or seal criminal records related to drug offenses. These issues are further discussed in Chapter Six.

Improving the Data Infrastructure for Describing People Who Use Opioids, Their Families, and Drug Markets

Much of this section is reproduced from Pardo et al., 2019.

Our answers to the preceding questions make it abundantly clear that we lack critical information about the number of people with OUD, those using illegally produced opioids, or both; likewise, we lack information about the number of family members who are exposed to harms from that use. This creates challenges for efficiently allocating resources to help PWUO and their families, monitoring changes in these markets, and conducting rigorous program and policy evaluations.

The HIV/AIDS crisis prompted large-scale investments in new data and monitoring systems, such as the National HIV Behavioral Surveillance (NHBS) system. The overdose crisis, which now kills more than HIV/AIDS did at its peak, has not elicited any comparable investment in data infrastructure. The failure is particularly severe on the supply side (further discussed in Chapter Seven).

Here we offer four ideas that would help us better answer some of the preceding questions about PWUO and generate many other insights.

---

[31] "According to the agency [CDC], 719 Philadelphians died of drug overdoses in 2016. There were 907 drug deaths in the city that year, recorded by Philadelphia's Department of Public Health, mostly linked to opioids" (Eichel and Pharis, 2018).

Getting Serious About Wastewater Testing to Track Drug Consumption, Including Synthetic Opioids

New approaches to measuring drug consumption might be needed in the United States, especially because many fentanyl analogs and other synthetic opioids enter and exit markets quickly. Users themselves might not know that they consumed a synthetic opioid, let alone be able to point to which compound was supplied. Wastewater testing is another way to monitor the spread of new psychoactive substances and to measure consumption (Castiglioni, 2016). This technique—used commonly in Europe and many other places around the world, but to a much lesser extent in the United States—can supplement traditional epidemiological drug indicators (such as prevalence rates or overdoses). Indeed, for many purposes it is superior to traditional indicators. For example, wastewater analysis in Washington State found sharp increases in cannabis consumption after legalization (Burgard et al., 2019). In Oregon, it showed that higher concentrations of drug metabolites were found in municipalities that reported higher rates of drug use (Banta-Green et al., 2009).

Cities in Europe have been developing and deploying this technique for decades, with demonstrated success in delivering near-real-time and high-frequency information about shifting use patterns (Castiglioni, 2016). For example, results from one wastewater examination of eight cities in Europe found high correlations between results from tested water samples and various indicators of local drug markets, including the sales of pharmaceuticals and illicit drug seizure records (Baz-Lomba et al., 2016). A 2018 report from Australia found that fentanyl consumption, though low to begin with, might have doubled outside capital city jurisdictions from April 2017 to April 2018 (Australian Criminal Intelligence Commission, 2018).

Resurrecting Some Version of the Arrestee Drug Abuse Monitoring Program

The Arrestee Drug Abuse Monitoring (ADAM) program collected rich drug market data (including urinalysis results) from thousands of individuals arrested and jailed for any offense. In the early 2000s, ADAM covered more than 40 counties (almost exclusively urban), and there were plans to expand the program to 75 counties. The program was cut in 2003. A much smaller version was brought back in 2007, only to be eliminated after 2013. Although the ADAM program did not test for fentanyl and novel synthetic opioids, it would not have been hard to incorporate these tests.

As with wastewater testing, ADAM's biological testing could serve as an early-warning and monitoring system. One could also imagine modules that ask people who use heroin, sell it, or both about their experiences and decisions around fentanyl and other synthetic opioids. Multiple researchers (Kilmer et al., 2014; Midgette et al., 2019) and the President's Commission on Combating Drug Addiction and the Opioid Crisis (Christie et al., 2017) have called for the resurrection of some version of the ADAM program. Even at its peak, ADAM cost about one-fifth of what is spent each year on the NSDUH, which is not very useful for understanding heroin and illegal opioid markets (Caulkins et al., 2015; Reuter, Caulkins, and Midgette, 2021). It seems like a wise investment to use a small percentage of the billions of dollars devoted to reducing opioid overdoses to reconstitute ADAM.

Introducing a Community Behavioral Surveillance Program Focused on People Who Use Drugs

One option to generate knowledge on local drug markets and collect insights from PWUO is to introduce a community-based behavioral surveillance program.[32] Such a program could engage with individuals who are neither in treatment nor subject to criminal justice supervision, thus addressing a major information gap. One such model that could be adapted for individuals who use opioids is the NHBS system. Begun in 2003 by the CDC, the NHBS consists of regular waves of surveys of different populations at increased risk of HIV; the surveys collect data on a variety of topics, including such behavioral risk factors as sexual behavior and drug use, and use and engagement with services. The program is implemented in 22 project areas with high levels of HIV prevalence and is currently in its sixth cycle. To recruit participants among people who inject drugs, the program uses respondent-driven sampling, whereby a small number of initial participants are identified by service providers and local health departments, and these initial respondents are then asked to recruit their peers until the sample quotas are met (CDC, 2021d). A similar principle, perhaps involving such low-threshold facilities as syringe service programs, could be applied in the context of PWUO.

Validating the NSDUH and Adding Questions Specific to Synthetic Opioid Use and Consequences of Opioid Use on Families

Because it seems likely that NSDUH will continue to play a major role in policy discussions and evaluations on drug-related matters, we need to know whether it is accurate. To our knowledge, the last time the NSDUH was validated was in 2000–2001 (Harrison et al., 2007). In that study, a sample of respondents aged 12 to 25 were asked to submit a urine sample, hair sample, or both after completing the survey (and were offered $25 for doing so), and nearly 90 percent provided at least one specimen. Validation need not happen annually, but incorporating a regular validity test into a survey that costs approximately $50 million a year seems

---

[32] This effort should build on and collaborate with the National Drug Early Warning System, which incorporates real-time surveillance to detect early signals of potential drug epidemics. Our new system implements an expanded Early Warning Network that utilizes novel surveillance methods and harmonizes and disseminates data in a rapid and timely manner. By focusing on leading indicators, the resulting system is more responsive than reactive. Ongoing data collection provides an integrated and comprehensive characterization of drug use and availability by synthesizing traditional, indirect sources with new, direct sources of data, as well as on-the-ground epidemiologic investigations within high-priority areas of concern. (National Drug Early Warning System, undated-b)

For more information, see National Drug Early Warning System, undated-a.

like a wise investment—especially as we seek more information about illegally produced fentanyl that respondents may not know they are consuming.

Adding questions to the NSDUH about the use—both known and suspected—of illegally produced synthetic opioids would provide additional information if there are not already plans to add such questions. Asking respondents using illegal drugs—especially heroin, counterfeit pills, cocaine, and methamphetamine—about the perceived risk of the product being mixed with fentanyl could also yield useful insights about the saturation of fentanyl in certain markets. Detailed questions about quantity consumed and spending would also be immensely helpful. It would also be astute to add a market module that focuses on the amount of opioids obtained during the most recent or typical transaction; whether the respondent paid for them, and if so, how much; and whether they resold or gave any opioids away. NSDUH already incorporates a market module about cannabis and includes some questions about where people got their opioids, so there is a precedent for collecting this type of information from respondents.

Finally, NSDUH could add questions to learn more about how families are affected by a relative's opioid use, SUD, or both. Indeed, getting a better sense of how many people have been negatively affected and how they have been affected would be immensely helpful for understanding the full social costs of SUD. Because opioids also benefit millions of Americans, learning more about the benefits of treatment of pain of an individual or family member, whether with opioids or a non-opioid modality, would also produce useful information.

Additional Data

This section provides additional figures and tables pertaining to the discussion presented in this chapter. Figure 2.12 shows changes in opioid consumption in OECD countries in the 2010s.

Table 2.5 provides information on the characteristics of those who reported having an OUD in the past year in NSDUH.

Table 2.6 shows selected characteristics of individuals admitted to treatment, as captured by TEDS.

Table 2.7 shows data on the characteristics of OUD treatment enrollees covered by Medicaid, as reported by MODRN et al., 2021.

Table 2.8 presents NSDUH data on the composition of households with an individual reporting past year OUD.

Table 2.9 presents NSDUH data on the presence and number of children in households with an individual reporting past year OUD.

Table 2.10 presents NSDUH data on the composition of households with an individual reporting past year OUD.

Table 2.11 presents data on arrests for drug violations, as recorded by UCR.

FIGURE 2.12

Mean Availability of Analgesic Opioids in OECD Countries, 2011–2013 and 2014–2016

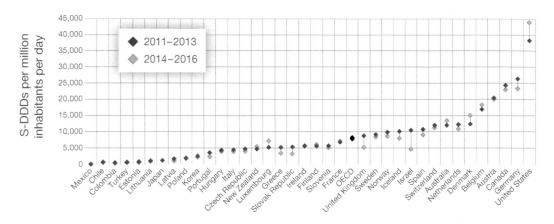

SOURCE: Adapted from OECD, 2019, p. 15.

NOTE: OECD = Organisation for Economic Co-operation and Development; S-DDD = defined daily doses for statistical purposes. "Analgesic opioids include codeine, dextropropoxyphene, dihydrocodeine, fentanyl, hydrocodone, hydromorphone, morphine, ketobemidone, oxycodone, pethidine, tilidine and trimeperidine. It does NOT include illicit opioids" (OECD, 2019, p. 15).

TABLE 2.5

Characteristics of Those with Self-Reported Past-Year Opioid Use Disorder in NSDUH, 2019

	Any Opioid Use Disorder	Heroin Only	Pain Relievers Only	Heroin and Pain Relievers
N (weighted)	1,700,870	267,312	1,253,326	180,232
Age				
12–17	5.3% (3.6%–7.7%)	0.0%	7.1% (4.8%–10.4%)	0.0%
18–25	13.2% (9.7%–17.8%)	13.1% (7.0%–23.5%)	13.1% (9.4%–17.9%)	14.4% (7.3%–26.3%)
26–34	25.5% (19.3%–32.9%)	34.4% (17.9%–55.8%)	20.1% (14.6%–27.2%)	49.8% (30.7%–68.9%)
35–49	30.2% (24.7%–36.4%)	32.6% (19.3%–49.5%)	29.2% (22.1%–37.6%)	33.7% (17.3%–55.2%)
50+	25.80% (17.1%–36.9%)	19.84% (8.1%–41.0%)	30.46% (19.8%–43.8%)	2.23% (0.4%–11.3%)
Sex				
Male	54.1% (46.49%–61.50%)	65.0% (48.55%–78.51%)	53.2% (43.83%–62.27%)	44.4% (25.58%–64.91%)
Female	45.9% (38.5%–53.5%)	35.0% (21.5%–51.5%)	46.9% (37.7%–56.2%)	55.6% (35.1%–74.4%)
Race/Ethnicity				
White, NH	72.6% (65.5%–78.7%)	72.2% (55.2%–84.6%)	71.0% (62.7%–78.2%)	83.9% (55.0%–95.7%)
Black, NH	10.3% (6.6%–15.8%)	13.3% (4.8%–31.7%)	10.8% (6.8%–16.9%)	2.2% (0.4%–11.3%)
Hispanic	9.7% (6.7%–13.8%)	10.5% (3.9%–25.2%)	9.1% (5.5%–14.9%)	12.5% (2.2%–46.9%)
Native American, NH	0.9% (0.3%–2.3%)	0.3% (0.0%–1.9%)	1.1% (0.4%–3.1%)	0.0%
Native Hawaii, NH	0.3% (0.1%–0.9%)	0.0%	0.3% (0.1%–1.2%)	0.0%
Asian, NH	3.4% (1.0%–10.8%)	0.0%	4.7% (1.4%–14.1%)	0.0%
Two or more races, NH	2.9% (1.1%–7.0%)	3.7% (0.5%–21.7%)	2.9% (1.0%–8.1%)	1.4% (0.2%–9.3%)
Education status				
Less than high school	11.1% (7.6%–15.9%)	21.9% (10.1%–41.2%)	8.6% (5.1%–14.1%)	12.1% (4.5%–28.8%)
High school graduate	27.5% (22.1%–33.7%)	55.1% (37.6%–71.5%)	22.0% (16.1%–29.2%)	25.0% (10.5%–48.7%)

Table 2.5—Continued

	Any Opioid Use Disorder	Heroin Only	Pain Relievers Only	Heroin and Pain Relievers
Some college	39.5% (31.4%–48.3%)	21.4% (11.5%–36.3%)	40.6% (30.7%–51.2%)	59.5% (38.6%–77.5%)
College graduate	16.6% (10.6%–25.2%)	1.6% (0.2%–10.9%)	21.8% (13.8%–32.6%)	3.3% (0.4%–21.1%)
12–17 year olds	5.3% (3.6%–7.7%)	0.0%	7.1% (4.8%–10.4%)	0.0%
Employment				
Employed full-time	38.4% (31.6%–45.8%)	32.7% (18.3%–51.3%)	40.7% (32.8%–49.1%)	31.2% (14.8%–54.3%)
Employed part-time	10.0% (7.3%–13.6%)	5.1% (1.8%–13.7%)	11.2% (8.0%–15.5%)	8.8% (2.8%–24.3%)
Unemployed	12.8% (8.6%–18.5%)	11.0% (5.4%–21.2%)	10.2% (6.5%–15.8%)	32.8% (16.3%–54.9%)
Not in the labor force or other	37.5% (29.7%–46.0%)	51.1% (32.2%–69.7%)	36.1% (27.0%–46.4%)	27.3% (12.5%–49.7%)
12–14 year olds	1.3% (0.7%–2.5%)	0.0%	1.8% (0.9%–3.4%)	0.0%
Family income				
Less than $20,000	29.7% (21.8%–38.9%)	50.8% (33.7%–67.7%)	24.3% (16.0%–35.0%)	36.1% (19.5%–57.0%)
$20,000–$49,999	31.1% (24.0%–39.2%)	15.2% (7.9%–27.3%)	34.3% (26.9%–42.5%)	32.2% (14.7%–56.7%)
$50,000–$74,999	15.5% (11.0%–21.6%)	11.3% (4.3%–26.8%)	17.3% (11.7%–24.8%)	9.9% (3.4%–25.4%)
$75,000 or more	23.7% (15.9%–33.9%)	22.7% (9.4%–45.6%)	24.2% (15.2%–36.4%)	21.9% (8.8%–44.8%)
Covered by Medicaid or CHIP	36.2% (29.0%–44.1%)	44.3% (28.8%–60.9%)	32.0% (23.7%–41.7%)	53.2% (31.7%–73.5%)
Treatment history				
Any SUD treatment, lifetime	53.8% (46.4%–61.1%)	75.7% (57.9%–87.7%)	43.2% (35.1%–51.7%)	95.3% (84.3%–98.7%)
Any SUD treatment, past year	27.7% (22.3%–33.9%)	42.4% (28.0%–58.2%)	18.0% (11.9%–26.4%)	73.5% (52.7%–87.3%)
Received MOUD, past year	17.3% (12.5%–23.5%)	24.9% (14.3%–39.7%)	10.1% (5.9%–16.8%)	55.7% (34.7%–74.9%)

Table 2.5—Continued

	Any Opioid Use Disorder	Heroin Only	Pain Relievers Only	Heroin and Pain Relievers
Any buprenorphine use, past year	37.1% (29.5%–45.4%)	52.7% (33.3%–71.4%)	27.8% (20.6%–36.4%)	78.8% (55.3%–91.8%)
Any methadone use, past year	14.4% (10.1%–20.1%)	13.1% (6.3%–25.2%)	10.2% (5.6%–18.1%)	45.3% (27.2%–64.7%)
Criminal legal system				
Ever arrested and booked	53.7% (46.0%–61.3%)	84.6% (69.6%–92.9%)	43.7% (35.6%–52.2%)	78.4% (57.5%–90.7%)
Arrested and booked, past year	19.9% (14.1%–27.4%)	43.5% (25.6%–63.2%)	10.8% (6.7%–16.9%)	47.0% (26.2%–68.9%)
On probation, past year	14.7% (10.1%–20.9%)	26.4% (13.8%–44.6%)	10.5% (6.3%–17.1%)	26.7% (10.9%–52.2%)

SOURCE: Using analysis at SAMHDA, undated-a, using key variable "UDPYHRPNR Rc-Heroin And/or Pain Reliever Dependence Or Abuse - Pst Yr."

NOTES: CHIP = Children's Health Insurance Program; MOUD = medications for opioid use disorder; NH = non-Hispanic. 95-percent CIs in parentheses. Dependence and addiction (i.e., OUD) are different concepts, but in the NSDUH, *dependence* is capturing a disorder, not referring to someone who is simply dependent on opioids. Responses coded as "Don't know," "Refused," "Blank," and legitimate skips (where appropriate) omitted from analysis.

TABLE 2.6

Substance Use Treatment Admissions from TEDS, by Primary Drug, 2018

	Heroin	Other Opioids, Including Synthetics
N	502,845	144,337
Gender		
Male	63.9%	52.4%
Female	36.1%	47.2%
Unknown	0.0%	0.4%
Age		
12–17 years	0.1%	0.3%
18–25 years	13.2%	12.0%
26–35 years	42.0%	44.3%
35–50 years	29.4%	31.1%
51+	15.5%	12.2%
Race		
White	69.9%	79.3%
Black or African-American	16.4%	9.0%

Table 2.6—Continued

	Heroin	Other Opioids, Including Synthetics
American Indian or Alaska Native	1.1%	1.5%
Asian or Native Hawaiian or Other Pacific Islander	0.7%	0.6%
Other	8.2%	3.3%
Unknown	3.7%	6.2%
Ethnicity		
Hispanic or Latino	13.6%	8.4%
Not Hispanic or Latino	84.0%	85.7%
Unknown	2.4%	5.9%
Employment status		
Full-time	10.8%	17.7%
Part-time	4.9%	7.3%
Unemployed	35.0%	35.4%
Not in labor force	38.5%	29.3%
Missing or unknown	10.8%	10.3%
Prior treatment episodes		
None	25.2%	42.1%
One	16.8%	20.5%
Two	13.0%	11.5%
Three or more	34.6%	17.8%
Missing/unknown	10.5%	8.1%
Current treatment service or setting		
Detox	24.3%	13.4%
Outpatient	59.0%	74.8%
Rehab or residential	16.7%	11.8%
Medication for OUD		
Yes	39.8%	37.2%
No	55.7%	56.4%
Missing/unknown	4.5%	6.5%
Referral source		
Individual (includes self-referral)	58.8%	52.9%
Alcohol or drug use care provider	13.4%	7.8%

Table 2.6—Continued

	Heroin	Other Opioids, Including Synthetics
Other health care provider	4.3%	7.6%
School (educational)	0.0%	0.1%
Employer or EAP	0.2%	0.3%
Other community referral	7.9%	13.0%
Court or criminal justice referral or DUI or DWI	13.3%	16.1%

SOURCE: This analysis is based on administrative data reported by states to TEDS through April 1, 2021.

NOTES: DUI = driving under the influence; DWI = driving while intoxicated; EAP = Employee Assistance Program. These totals are slightly different from those produced in summary tables by the Center for Behavioral Health Statistics and Quality, SAMHSA, TEDS (SAMHSA, 2020e). Excludes 3,000 observations for methadone as primary substance.

TABLE 2.7

Characteristics of Medicaid Enrollees with Opioid Use Disorder

	2014	2015	2016	2017	2018
Total (N)[a]	8,737,082	10,032,720	10,437,883	10,599,340	10,585,790
Total with OUD (n)	290,628	385,012	462,586	506,429	527,983
Percentage with OUD	3.3	3.8	4.4	4.8	5.0
Age					
12–20	8,921 (3.1%)	9,930 (2.6%)	10,229 (2.2%)	9,319 (1.8%)	8,070 (1.5%)
21–34	141,074 (48.5%)	183,174 (47.6%)	210,981 (45.6%)	221,593 (43.8%)	220,198 (41.7%)
35–44	68,912 (23.7%)	95,630 (24.8%)	120,522 (26.1%)	139,766 (27.6%)	155,131 (29.4%)
45–54	47,490 (16.3%)	62,997 (16.4%)	77,703 (16.8%)	85,465 (16.9%)	89,317 (16.9%)
55–64	24,231 (8.3%)	33,281 (8.6%)	43,151 (9.3%)	50,286 (9.9%)	55,267 (10.5%)
Sex					
Female	156,862 (54.0%)	202,433 (52.6%)	240,409 (52.0%)	260,500 (51.4%)	270,489 (51.2%)
Male	133,765 (46.0%)	182,579 (47.4%)	222,177 (48.0%)	245,929 (48.6%)	257,494 (48.8%)
Race/ethnicity					
Non-Hispanic White	220,709 (75.9%)	293,380 (76.2%)	351,510 (76.0%)	385,197 (76.1%)	402,043 (76.1%)
Non-Hispanic Black	42,452 (14.6%)	52,835 (13.7%)	64,587 (14.0%)	70,723 (14.0%)	73,096 (13.8%)

Table 2.7—Continued

	2014	2015	2016	2017	2018
Hispanic	7,701 (2.6%)	10.310 (2.7%)	13,019 (2.8%)	14,244 (2.8%)	15,388 (2.9%)
Other/unknown[b]	19,766 (6.8%)	28,487 (7.4%)	33,470 (7.2%)	36,265 (7.2%)	37,456 (7.1%)
Eligibility group					
Nondisabled adults	112,267 (38.6%)	105,764 (27.5%)	117,878 (25.5%)	126,364 (25.0%)	130,298 (24.7%)
Expansion adults[c]	79,313 (27.3%)	166,489 (43.2%)	219,792 (47.5%)	252,786 (49.9%)	267,783 (50.7%)
Disabled adults	71,045 (24.4%)	80,282 (20.9%)	85,759 (18.5%)	87,963 (17.4%)	92,170 (17.5%)
Pregnant women	19.155 (6.6%)	22,539 (5.9%)	29,016 (6.3%)	30,175 (6.0%)	29,731 (5.6%)
Youth	8,848 (3.0%)	9,938 (2.6%)	10,141 (2.2%)	9,141 (1.8%)	8,001 (1.5%)
Any other SUD[d]	147,245 (50.7%)	200,830 (52.2%)	230,570 (49.8%)	253,464 (50.0%)	267,417 (50.6%)
Any mental health condition[d]	182,727 (62.9%)	241,825 (62.8%)	288,552 (62.4%)	315,463 (62.3%)	330,995 (62.7%)
Location of residence	289,515	383,801	461,330	505,155	526,730
Urban	218,757 (75.6%)	286,055 (74.5%)	342,801 (74.3%)	374,247 (74.1%)	387,053 (73.5%)
Rural	70,758 (24.4%)	97,746 (25.5%)	118,529 (25.7%)	130,908 (25.9%)	139,677 (26.5%)

SOURCE: Adapted from MODRN et al., 2021.

NOTES: Table notes are adapted from MODRN et al., 2021.

[a] This study includes all full-benefit, non–dual-eligible Medicaid enrollees aged 12 through 64 with any enrollment in the calendar year in the 11 state Medicaid programs discussed in MODRN et al., 2021.

[b] *Other* includes Native Hawaiian, Pacific Islander, American Indian, Alaska Native, and Asian racial/ethnic groups.

[c] *Expansion adults* are enrollees who are newly eligible under the Affordable Care Act in a Medicaid expansion adopted during the study period of MODRN et al., 2021.

[d] Mental health conditions and other SUDs were defined using any claim with one or more *International Classification of Diseases, Ninth Revision (ICD-9)* or *ICD-10* diagnosis codes listed in eTable 2 in Supplement 1 of MODRN et al., 2021.

TABLE 2.8

Other Adult Family Members in a Household

Other Adult Family Members	Opioid Use Disorder					Past Year Heroin Use or Pain Reliever Misuse				
	Any Opioid Use Disorder	Heroin	Pain Reliever	Heroin and Pain Reliever	Neither	Heroin or Pain Reliever	Heroin	Pain Reliever	Heroin and Pain Reliever	Neither
Yes	77.5% (70.9%–83.0%)	69.8% (50.1%–84.2%)	77.6% (70.6%–83.3%)	88.3% (75.9%–94.8%)	81.3% (80.7%–81.8%)	78.2% (75.1%–81.0%)	65.7% (43.9%–82.4%)	78.7% (75.6%–81.5%)	78.4% (67.2%–86.5%)	81.4% (80.8%–81.9%)
No	22.5% (17.0%–29.1%)	30.2% (15.8%–49.9%)	22.4% (16.7%–29.4%)	11.7% (5.2%–24.1%)	18.7% (18.2%–19.3%)	21.8% (19.0%–24.9%)	34.3% (17.6%–56.1%)	21.3% (18.6%–24.4%)	21.6% (13.5%–32.8%)	18.6% (18.1%–19.2%)

SOURCE: SAMHDA, undated-b.
NOTE: Responses coded as "Unknown" removed from analysis.

TABLE 2.9

Number of Children in a Household (people with and without past-year opioid dependence)

Number of Children	Opioid Use Disorder					Past Year Heroin Use or Prescription Opioid Misuse				
	Any Opioid Use Disorder	Heroin	Pain Reliever	Heroin and Pain Reliever	Neither	Heroin or Pain Reliever	Heroin	Pain Reliever	Heroin and Pain Reliever	Neither
0	64.2% (57.0%–70.8%)	70.5% (53.8%–83.0%)	66.1% (58.8%–72.7%)	41.4% (23.1%–62.5%)	58.4% (57.7%–59.1%)	58.4% (55.6%–61.2%)	90.2% (79.0%–95.7%)	57.6% (54.5%–60.7%)	47.8% (32.8%–63.3%)	58.4% (57.8%–59.1%)
1	16.7% (12.2%–22.5%)	8.6% (3.6%–18.9%)	14.8% (10.6%–20.3%)	42.3% (22.4%–65.1%)	16.6% (16.1%–17.0%)	18.2% (16.2%–20.3%)	5.5% (2.1%–13.1%)	18.4% (16.5%–20.6%)	23.5% (13.2%–38.2%)	16.5% (16.0%–17.0%)
2	10.4% (7.1%–15.1%)	16.6% (7.3%–33.6%)	9.6% (6.4%–14.3%)	6.5% (1.9%–20.0%)	14.9% (14.5%–15.4%)	13.3% (11.2%–15.7%)	3.7% (0.7%–17.0%)	13.5% (11.3%–16.0%)	17.1% (9.0%–30.3%)	15.0% (14.5%–15.4%)
3 or more	8.7% (5.7%–13.1%)	4.4% (1.0%–17.3%)	9.5% (5.9%–15.0%)	9.7% (2.4%–32.4%)	10.1% (9.8%–10.5%)	10.2% (8.2%–12.5%)	0.6% (0.1%–2.6%)	10.5% (8.4%–12.9%)	11.5% (5.2%–23.6%)	10.1% (9.8%–10.5%)

SOURCE: SAMHDA, undated-c.

TABLE 2.10

Marriage Status of People With or Without Opioid Dependence and With or Without Past-Year Heroin Use or Pain Reliever Misuse

Status	Opioid Use Disorder					Past Year Heroin Use or Pain Reliever Misuse				
	Any Opioid Use Disorder	Heroin	Pain Reliever	Heroin and Pain Reliever	Neither	Heroin or Pain Reliever	Heroin	Pain Reliever	Heroin and Pain Reliever	Neither
Never married	48.7% (41.8%–55.6%)	64.6% (44.3%–80.7%)	43.4% (35.6%–51.6%)	61.0% (38.6%–79.6%)	32.4% (31.8%–33.0%)	47.4% (44.5%–50.3%)	64.8% (43.0%–81.7%)	46.2% (43.2%–49.2%)	61.5% (49.2%–72.5%)	31.9% (31.3%–32.5%)
Now married	30.7% (23.2%–39.3%)	15.2% (6.9%–30.3%)	36.5% (26.7%–47.6%)	13.8% (4.6%–34.8%)	48.6% (47.7%–49.4%)	33.4% (30.3%–36.7%)	10.2% (4.1%–23.5%)	35.1% (31.7%–38.7%)	13.7% (6.1%–27.8%)	49.0% (48.2%–49.9%)
Divorced or separated	18.9% (13.3%–26.0%)	20.3% (8.6%–40.7%)	19.2% (13.0%–27.6%)	14.2% (5.7%–31.5%)	13.1% (12.5%–13.7%)	15.6% (13.7%–17.8%)	25.0% (11.1%–47.3%)	15.3% (13.4%–17.4%)	15.7% (9.1%–25.7%)	13.1% (12.5%–13.7%)
Widowed	1.8% (0.5%–6.9%)	0.0%	0.9% (0.3%–3.1%)	10.9% (1.6%–48.9%)	5.9% (5.7%–6.2%)	3.6% (2.2%–5.7%)	0.0%	3.5% (2.0%–5.9%)	9.2% (2.8%–26.1%)	6.0% (5.7%–6.3%)

SOURCE: SAMHDA, undated-d.

NOTE: Responses coded as "Legitimate skip" (respondent 14 years old or younger) omitted from analysis.

TABLE 2.11

Uniform Crime Reports Arrests for Drug Violations in the United States, 2019

Drug Abuse Violations	United States Total (%)	Northeast (%)	Midwest (%)	South (%)	West (%)
Total[a]	100.0	100.0	100.0	100.0	100.0
Sale or manufacturing					
Total	13.3	15.8	12.2	15.8	9.6
Heroin or cocaine and their derivatives	4.2	8.0	2.6	4.3	3.2
Marijuana	2.9	4.5	3.6	3.3	1.4
Synthetic or manufactured drugs	1.7	1.1	0.8	3.4	0.4
Other dangerous nonnarcotic drugs	4.4	2.2	5.3	4.7	4.6
Possession					
Total	86.7	84.2	87.8	84.2	90.4
Heroin or cocaine and their derivatives	19.6	17.4	12.9	14.2	30.7
Marijuana	32.1	48.2	40.4	39.4	11.3
Synthetic or manufactured drugs	4.0	3.4	4.7	5.3	2.4
Other dangerous nonnarcotic drugs	31.0	15.2	29.7	25.3	46.0

[a] Because of rounding, the percentages may not add to 100.0.

Abbreviations

ADAM	Arrestee Drug Abuse Monitoring
AIDS	acquired immunodeficiency syndrome
CBSA	core-based statistical area
CDC	Centers for Disease Control and Prevention
CI	confidence interval
COVID-19	coronavirus disease 2019
DEA	Drug Enforcement Administration
ED	emergency department
EMS	emergency medical services
FBI	Federal Bureau of Investigation
G7	Group of Seven
HCUP	Healthcare Cost and Utilization Project
HIV	human immunodeficiency virus
ICD-10	International Classification of Diseases, tenth revision
MCOD	multiple cause of death
MME	morphine milligram equivalents
MODRN	Medicaid Outcomes Distributed Research Network
NCVS	National Crime Victimization Survey
NHBS	National HIV Behavioral Surveillance
NIBRS	National Incident-Based Reporting System
NSDUH	National Survey on Drug Use and Health
ONDCP	Office of National Drug Control Policy
OUD	opioid use disorder
PWUO	people who use opioids
SAMHSA	Substance Abuse and Mental Health Services Administration
SRS	Summary Reporting System
SUD	substance use disorder
TEDS	Treatment Episode Data Set
UCR	Uniform Crime Reports

References

Aitken, M., M. Kleinrock, A. Campbell, and E. Munoz, *Prescription Opioid Trends in the United States: Measuring and Understanding Progress in the Opioid Crisis*, IQVIA Institute for Human Data Science, December 2020.

Allen, Bennett, and Alex Harocopos, "Non-Prescribed Buprenorphine in New York City: Motivations for Use, Practices of Diversion, and Experiences of Stigma," *Journal of Substance Abuse Treatment*, Vol. 70, 2016, pp. 81–86.

Alpert, Abby, David Powell, and Rosalie Liccardo Pacula, "Supply-Side Drug Policy in the Presence of Substitutes: Evidence from the Introduction of Abuse-Deterrent Opioids," *American Economic Journal*, Vol. 10, No. 4, 2018.

Anthony, James C., Lynn A. Warner, and Ronald C. Kessler, "Comparative Epidemiology of Dependence on Tobacco, Alcohol, Controlled Substances, and Inhalants: Basic Findings from the National Comorbidity Survey," *Experimental and Clinical Psychopharmacology*, Vol. 2, No. 3, 1994, pp. 244–268.

Australian Criminal Intelligence Commission, *National Wastewater Drug Monitoring Program: Report 6*, Canberra, Australia, December 2018.

Ball, John C., John W. Shaffer, and David N. Nurco, "The Day to-Day Criminality of Heroin Addicts in Baltimore—A Study in the Continuity of Offence Rates," *Drug and Alcohol Dependence*, Vol. 12, No. 2, 1983, pp. 119–142.

Banta-Green, Caleb J., Jennifer A. Field, Aurea C. Chiaia, Daniel L. Sudakin, Laura Power, and Luc de Montigny, "The Spatial Epidemiology of Cocaine, Methamphetamine and 3,4-methylenedioxymethamphetamine (MDMA) Use: A Demonstration Using a Population Measure of Community Drug Load Derived from Municipal Wastewater," *Addiction*, Vol. 104, No. 11, 2009, pp. 1874–1880.

Barocas, Joshua A., Laura F. White, Jianing Wang, Alexander Y. Walley, Marc R. LaRochelle, Dana Bernson, Thomas Land, Jake R. Morgan, Jeffrey H. Samet, and Benjamin P. Linas, "Estimated Prevalence of Opioid Use Disorder in Massachusetts, 2011–2015: A Capture–Recapture Analysis," *American Journal of Public Health*, Vol. 108, No. 12, December 2018, pp. 1675–1681.

Baz-Lomba, Jose Antonio, Stefania Salvatore, Emma Gracia-Lor, Richard Bade, Sara Castiglioni, Erika Castrignanò, Ana Causanilles, Felix Hernandez, Barbara Kasprzyk-Hordern, Juliet Kinyua, et al., "Comparison of Pharmaceutical, Illicit Drug, Alcohol, Nicotine and Caffeine Levels in Wastewater with Sale, Seizure and Consumption Data for 8 European Cities," *BMC Public Health*, Vol. 16, No. 1035, 2016.

Bennett, Trevor, Katy Holloway, and David Farrington, "The Statistical Association Between Drug Misuse and Crime: A Meta-Analysis," *Aggression and Violent Behavior*, Vol. 13, No. 2, 2008, pp. 107–118.

Bohnert, Amy S., Marcia Valenstein, Matthew J. Bair, Dara Ganoczy, John F. McCarthy, Mark A. Ilgen, and Frederic C. Blow, "Association Between Opioid Prescribing Patterns and Opioid Overdose-Related Deaths," *JAMA*, Vol. 305, No. 13, 2011, pp. 1315–1321.

Bureau of Justice Statistics, *National Incident-Based Reporting System, 2019: Extract Files*, Inter-University Consortium for Political and Social Research, October 4, 2022. As of November 6, 2022:
https://doi.org/10.3886/ICPSR38565.v1

Burgard, Daniel A., Jason Williams, Danielle Westerman, Rosie Rushing, Riley Carpenter, Addison LaRock, Jane Sadetsky, Jackson Clarke, Heather Fryhle, Melissa Pellman, and Caleb J. Banta-Green, "Using Wastewater-Based Analysis to Monitor the Effects of Legalized Retail Sales on Cannabis Consumption in Washington State, USA," *Addiction*, Vol. 114, No. 9, 2019, pp. 1582–1590.

Burke, Laura G., Xiner Zhou, Katherine L. Boyle, E. John Orav, Dana Bernson, Maria-Elena Hood, Thomas Land, Monica Bharel, and Austin B. Frakt, "Trends in Opioid Use Disorder and Overdose Among Opioid-Naive Individuals Receiving an Opioid Prescription in Massachusetts from 2011 to 2014," *Addiction*, Vol. 115, No. 3, 2020, pp. 493–504.

Cash, Rebecca E., Jeremiah Kinsman, Remle P. Crowe, Madison K. Rivard, Mark Faul, and Ashish R. Panchal, "Naloxone Administration Frequency During Emergency Medical Service Events—United States, 2012–2016," *Morbidity and Mortality Weekly Report*, Vol. 67, No. 31, 2018, pp. 850–853.

Castiglioni, Sara, ed., *Assessing Illicit Drugs in Wastewater: Advances in Wastewater-Based Drug Epidemiology*, Luxembourg: European Monitoring Centre for Drugs and Drug Addiction, 2016.

Caulkins, Jonathan P., Beau Kilmer, Peter H. Reuter, and Greg Midgette, "Cocaine's Fall and Marijuana's Rise: Questions and Insights Based on New Estimates of Consumption and Expenditures in U.S. Drug Markets," *Addiction*, Vol. 110, No. 5, 2015, pp. 728–736.

Caulkins, Jonathan P., and Mark A. R. Kleiman, *How Much Crime Is Drug-Related? History, Limitations, and Potential Improvements of Estimation Methods*, Washington, D.C., April 2014.

CDC—*See* Centers for Disease Control and Prevention.

Centers for Disease Control and Prevention, *HIV Surveillance Report*, Vol. 23, Atlanta, Ga., February 2013.

Centers for Disease Control and Prevention, "Motor Vehicle Crash Deaths: How Is the US Doing?" webpage, updated July 6, 2016. As of August 2, 2021:
https://www.cdc.gov/vitalsigns/motor-vehicle-safety/index.html

Centers for Disease Control and Prevention, *Annual Surveillance Report of Drug-Related Risks and Outcomes: United States, 2019*, Atlanta, Ga., 2019.

Centers for Disease Control and Prevention, "U.S. Opioid Dispensing Rate Maps," webpage, updated 2020. As of August 2, 2021:
https://www.cdc.gov/drugoverdose/rxrate-maps/index.html

Centers for Disease Control and Prevention, "DOSE Dashboard: Nonfatal Overdoses Data," webpage, 2021a. As of August 2, 2021:
https://www.cdc.gov/drugoverdose/nonfatal/all-opioids.html

Centers for Disease Control and Prevention, "Fast Facts: Firearm Violence Prevention," webpage, 2021b. As of August 2, 2021:
https://www.cdc.gov/violenceprevention/firearms/fastfact.html

Centers for Disease Control and Prevention, "National Center for Health Statistics: Provisional Drug Overdose Death Counts," webpage, 2021c. As of August 2, 2021:
https://www.cdc.gov/nchs/nvss/vsrr/drug-overdose-data.htm

Centers for Disease Control and Prevention, "National HIV Behavioral Surveillance (NHBS)," webpage, 2021d. As of August 14, 2021:
https://www.cdc.gov/hiv/statistics/systems/nhbs/index.html

Centers for Disease Control and Prevention, "U.S. County Opioid Dispensing Rates, 2020," webpage, last updated January 21, 2022a. As of June 15, 2022: https://www.cdc.gov/drugoverdose/rxrate-maps/county2020.html

Centers for Disease Control and Prevention, "NVSS Vital Statistics Rapid Release Provisional Drug Overdose Death Counts," webpage, updated February 9, 2022b. As of June 15, 2022: https://www.cdc.gov/nchs/nvss/vsrr/drug-overdose-data.htm

Cerdá, Magdalena, Julian Santaella, Brandon D. L. Marshall, June H. Kim, and Silvia S. Martins, "Nonmedical Prescription Opioid Use in Childhood and Early Adolescence Predicts Transitions to Heroin Use in Young Adulthood: A National Study," *Journal of Pediatrics*, Vol. 167, No. 3, 2015, pp. 605–612.

Christie, Chris, Charlie Baker, Roy Cooper, Patrick J. Kennedy, Bertha Madras, and Pam Bondi, *The President's Commission on Combating Drug Addiction and the Opioid Crisis*, Washington, D.C.: U.S. Government Printing Office, November 1, 2017.

Ciccarone, Daniel, George Jay Unick, Jenny K. Cohen, Sarah G. Mars, and Daniel Rosenblum, "Nationwide Increase in Hospitalizations for Heroin-Related Soft Tissue Infections: Associations with Structural Market Conditions," *Drug and Alcohol Dependence*, Vol. 163, 2016, pp. 126–133.

Cicero, Theodore J., Matthew S. Ellis, and Howard D. Chilcoat, "Understanding the Use of Diverted Buprenorphine," *Drug and Alcohol Dependence*, Vol. 193, 2018, pp. 117–123.

Cicero, Theodore J., Matthew S. Ellis, Hilary L. Surratt, and Steven P. Kurtz, "The Changing Face of Heroin Use in the United States: A Retrospective Analysis of the Past 50 Years," *JAMA Psychiatry*, Vol. 71, No. 7, 2014, pp. 821–826.

Commission on Combating Synthetic Opioid Trafficking, *Commission on Combating Synthetic Opioid Trafficking: Final Report*, Washington, D.C., February 2022.

Conti, Gabriella, James Heckman, and Sergio Urzua, "The Education-Health Gradient," *American Economic Review*, Vol. 100, No. 2, May 2010, pp. 234–238.

Cooper, G. S., Z. Yuan, A. A. Rimm, "Racial Disparity in the Incidence and Case-Fatality of Colorectal Cancer: Analysis of 329 United States Counties," *Cancer Epidemiology and Prevention Biomarkers*, Vol. 6, No. 4, 1997, pp. 283–285.

Correa-de-Araujo, Rosaly, G. Edward Miller, Jessica S. Banthin, and Yen Trinh, "Gender Differences in Drug Use and Expenditures in a Privately Insured Population of Older Adults," *Journal of Women's Health*, Vol. 14, No. 1, 2005, pp. 73–81.

DEA—*See* Drug Enforcement Administration.

Degenhardt, Louisa, Jason Grebely, Jack Stone, Matthew Hickman, Peter Vickerman, Brandon D. L. Marshall, Julie Bruneau, Frederick L. Altice, Graeme Henderson, Afarin Rahimi-Movaghar, and Sarah Larney, "Global Patterns of Opioid Use and Dependence: Harms to Populations, Interventions, and Future Action," *The Lancet*, Vol. 394, No. 10208, 2019, pp. 1560–1579.

Drug Enforcement Administration, "Domestic Arrests," webpage, undated. As of September 2, 2022: https://www.dea.gov/data-and-statistics/domestic-arrests

Duff, Johnathan H., Sara M. Tharakan, Carla Y. Davis-Castro, Ada S. Cornell, and Paul D. Romero, *Consumption of Prescription Opioids for Pain: A Comparison of Opioid Use in the United States and Other Countries*, Washington, D.C.: Congressional Research Service, R46805, June 2, 2021.

Edlund, Mark J., Bradley C. Martin, Joan E. Russo, Andrea DeVries, Jennifer Brennan Braden, and Mark D. Sullivan, "The Role of Opioid Prescription in Incident Opioid Abuse and Dependence Among Individuals with Chronic Non-Cancer Pain: The Role of Opioid Prescription," *Clinical Journal of Pain*, Vol. 30, No. 7, 2014, pp. 557–564.

Eichel, Larry, and Meagan Pharis, *Philadelphia's Drug Overdose Death Rate Among Highest in Nation*, Philadelphia, Pa.: PEW Charitable Trusts, February 15, 2018.

FBI—*See* Federal Bureau of Investigation.

Federal Bureau of Investigation, *30 Questions and Answers About NIBRS Transition*, Uniform Crime Reporting Program, National Incident-Based Reporting System, October 2018.

Federal Bureau of Investigation, "Crime in the United States 2019: Clearances," webpage, fall 2020a. As of November 16, 2021: https://ucr.fbi.gov/crime-in-the-u.s/2019/crime-in-the-u.s.-2019/topic-pages/clearances

Federal Bureau of Investigation, "FBI Releases 2019 NIBRS Crime Data," press release, December 9, 2020b.

Furr-Holden, Debra, Adam J. Milam, Ling Wang, and Richard Sadler, "African Americans Now Outpace Whites in Opioid-Involved Overdose Deaths: A Comparison of Temporal Trends from 1999 to 2018," *Addiction*, Vol. 116, No. 3, 2021, pp. 677–683.

Goldstein, Paul J., "The Drugs/Violence Nexus: A Tripartite Conceptual Framework," *Journal of Drug Issues*, Vol. 15, No. 4, 1985, pp. 493–506.

Gomes, Tara, Donald A. Redelmeier, David N. Juurlink, Irfan A. Dhalla, Ximena Camacho, and Muhammad M. Mamdani, "Opioid Dose and Risk of Road Trauma in Canada: A Population-Based Study," *JAMA Internal Medicine*, Vol. 173, No. 3, 2013, pp. 196–201.

Governors Highway Safety Association, *Drug-Impaired Driving: Marijuana and Opioids Raise Critical Issues for States*, Washington, D.C., 2018.

Goyal, Monika K., Nathan Kuppermann, Sean D. Cleary, Stephen J. Teach, and James M. Chamberlain, "Racial Disparities in Pain Management of Children with Appendicitis in Emergency Departments," *JAMA Pediatrics*, Vol. 169, No. 11, 2015, pp. 996–1002.

Grella, Christine E., and Vandana Joshi, "Gender Differences in Drug Treatment Careers Among Clients in the National Drug Abuse Treatment Outcome Study," *American Journal of Drug and Alcohol Abuse*, Vol. 25, No. 3, 1999, pp. 385–406.

Griffith, Kvein N., Yevgeniy Feyman, Samantha G. Auty, Erika L. Crable, and Timothy W. Levengood, "Implications of County-Level Variation in US Opioid Distribution," *Drug and Alcohol Dependence*, Vol. 219, 2021.

Gupta, Rahul, and David R. Holtgrave, "A National Tracking System for Nonfatal Drug Overdoses," *JAMA*, Vol. 328, No. 3, 2022, pp. 239–240.

Guy, Gery P., Jr., Kun Zhang, Michele K. Bohm, Jan Losby, Brian Lewis, Randall Young, Louise B. Murphy, and Deborah Dowell, "Vital Signs: Changes in Opioid Prescribing in the United States, 2006–2015," *Morbidity and Mortality Weekly Report*, Vol. 66, No. 26, 2017, pp. 697–704.

Harrison, Lana Debra, Steven S. Martin, Tihomir Enev, and Deborah Harrington, *Comparing Drug Testing and Self-Report of Drug Use Among Youths and Young Adults in the General Population*, Rockville, Md.: Substance Abuse and Mental Health Services Administration, Office of Applied Studies, 2007.

Hart, Carl L., *Drug Use for Grown-Ups: Chasing Liberty in the Land of Fear*, New York: Penguin Press, 2021.

Hedegaard, Holly, Arialdi M. Miniño, and Margaret Warner, "Drug Overdose Deaths in the United States, 1999–2018," NCHS Data Brief, No. 394, December 2020.

Helmerhorst, G. T. T., T. Teunis, S. J. Janssen, and D. Ring, "An Epidemic of the Use, Misuse and Overdose of Opioids and Deaths Due to Overdose, in the United States and Canada: Is Europe Next?" *Bone & Joint Journal*, Vol. 99, No. 7, 2017, pp. 856–864.

Ho, Jessica Y., "The Contemporary American Drug Overdose Epidemic in International Perspective," *Population and Development Review*, Vol. 45, No. 1, March 2019, pp. 7–40.

Imtiaz, Sameer, Kevin D. Shield, Benedikt Fischer, and Jürgen Rehm, "Harms of Prescription Opioid Use in the United States," *Substance Abuse Treatment, Prevention, and Policy*, Vol. 9, No. 1, 2014.

Inciardi, J. A., "Heroin Use and Street Crime," *Crime & Delinquency*, Vol. 25, No. 3, July 1979, pp. 335–346.

Jalal, Hawre, Jeanine M. Buchanich, Mark S. Roberts, Lauren C. Balmert, Kun Zhang, and Donald S. Burke, "Changing Dynamics of the Drug Overdose Epidemic in the United States from 1979 through 2016," *Science*, Vol. 361, No. 6408, 2018.

Jalal, Hawre, and Donald S. Burke, "Carfentanil and the Rise and Fall of Overdose Deaths in the United States," *Addiction*, Vol. 116, No. 6, 2021, pp. 1593–1599.

Jayawardana, Sahan, Rebecca Forman, Charlotte Johnston-Webber, Allen Campbell, Stefano Berterame, Cees de Joncheere, Murray Aitken, and Elias Mossialos, "Global Consumption of Prescription Opioid Analgesics Between 2009–2019: A Country-Level Observational Study," *eClinicalMedicine*, Vol. 42, December 2021.

Jones, Christopher M., "Heroin Use and Heroin Use Risk Behaviors Among Nonmedical Users of Prescription Opioid Pain Relievers–United States, 2002–2004 and 2008–2010," *Drug and Alcohol Dependence*, Vol. 132, No. 1–2, 2013, pp. 95–100.

Kaplan, John, *The Hardest Drug: Heroin and Public Policy*, Chicago, Ill.: University of Chicago Press, 1983.

Keyes, Katherine M., Caroline Rutherford, Ava Hamilton, Joshua A. Barocas, Kitty H. Gelberg, Peter P. Mueller, Daniel J. Feaster, Nabila El-Bassel, and Magdalena Cerdá, "What Is the Prevalence of and Trend in Opioid Use Disorder in the United States from 2010 to 2019? Using Multiplier Approaches to Estimate Prevalence for an Unknown Population Size," *Drug and Alcohol Dependence Reports*, Vol. 3, June 2022.

Kilmer, Beau, Susan M. Sohler Everingham, Jonathan P. Caulkins, Gregory Midgette, Rosalie Liccardo Pacula, Peter Reuter, Rachel M. Burns, Bing Han, and Russell Lundberg, *What America's Users Spend on Illegal Drugs, 2000–2010*, Santa Monica, Calif.: RAND Corporation, RR-534-ONDCP, 2014. As of August 20, 2019:
https://www.rand.org/pubs/research_reports/RR534.html

Kolodny, Andrew, David T. Courtwright, Catherine S. Hwang, Peter Kreiner, John L. Eadie, Thomas W. Clark, and G. Caleb Alexander, "The Prescription Opioid and Heroin Crisis: A Public Health Approach to an Epidemic of Addiction," *Annual Review of Public Health*, Vol. 36, 2015, pp. 559–574.

Krawczyk, Noa, Bianca D. Rivera, Victoria Jent, Katherine M. Keyes, Christopher M. Jones, and Magdalena Cerdá, "Has the Treatment Gap for Opioid Use Disorder Narrowed in the U.S.? A Yearly Assessment from 2010 to 2019," *International Journal of Drug Policy*, August 4, 2022.

Ladha, Karim S., Mark D. Neuman, Gabriella Broms, Jennifer Bethell, Brian T. Bateman, Duminda N. Wijeysundera, Max Bell, Linn Hallqvist, Tobias Svensson, Craig W. Newcomb, Colleen M. Brensinger, Lakisha J. Gaskins, and Hannah Wunsch, "Opioid Prescribing After Surgery in the United States, Canada, and Sweden," *JAMA*, Vol. 2, No. 9, 2019.

Lagisetty, Pooja, Claire Garpestad, Angela Larkin, Colin Macleod, Derek Antoku, Stephanie Slat, Jennifer Thomas, Victoria Powell, Amy S. B. Bohnert, and Lewei A. Lin, "Identifying Individuals with Opioid Use Disorder: Validity of International Classification of Diseases Diagnostic Codes for Opioid Use, Dependence and Abuse," *Drug and Alcohol Dependence*, Vol. 221, 2021.

Lagisetty, Pooja A., Ryan Ross, Amy Bohnert, Michael Clay, and Donovan T. Maust, "Buprenorphine Treatment Divide by Race/Ethnicity and Payment," *JAMA Psychiatry*, Vol. 76, No. 9, 2019, pp. 979–981.

Larochelle, Marc R., Jane M. Liebschutz, Fang Zhang, Dennis Ross-Degnan, and J. Frank Wharam, "Opioid Prescribing After Nonfatal Overdose and Association with Repeated Overdose: A Cohort Study," *Annals of Internal Medicine*, Vol. 164, No. 1, 2016.

Lillard, Lee A., and Constantijn W. A. Panis, "Marital Status and Mortality: The Role of Health," *Demography*, Vol. 33, No. 3, 1996, pp. 313–327.

Lippold, Kumiko M., Christopher M. Jones, Emily O'Malley Olsen, and Brett P. Giroir, "Racial/ Ethnic and Age Group Differences in Opioid and Synthetic Opioid–Involved Overdose Deaths Among Adults Aged ≥18 Years in Metropolitan Areas—United States, 2015–2017," *Morbidity and Mortality Weekly Report*, Vol. 68, No. 43, 2019, pp. 967–973.

Liu, Stephen, Lawrence Scholl, Brooke Hoots, and Puja Seth, "Nonfatal Drug and Polydrug Overdoses Treated in Emergency Departments—29 States, 2018–2019," *Morbidity and Mortality Weekly Report*, Vol. 69, No. 34, 2020, pp. 1149–1155.

Marsh, Jeanne C., Keunhye Park, Yu-An Lin, and Cliff Bersamira, "Gender Differences in Trends for Heroin Use and Nonmedical Prescription Opioid Use, 2007–2014," *Journal of Substance Abuse Treatment*, Vol. 87, 2018, pp. 79–85.

McCance-Katz, Elinore, Debra Houry, and Francis Collins, "Testimony on Addressing the Opioid Crisis in America: Prevention, Treatment, and Recovery Before the Senate Subcommittee," testimony before the Senate Appropriations Subcommittee on Labor, Health and Human Services, Education and Related Agencies, December 5, 2017.

Medicaid.gov, "Dual-Eligible Enrollment," webpage, undated. As of August 14, 2021: https://www.medicaid.gov/dual-eligible-enrollment/index.html

Medicaid.gov, "February 2021 Medicaid and CHIP Enrollment Data Highlights," webpage, 2021. As of August 2, 2021: https://www.medicaid.gov/medicaid/program-information/medicaid-and-chip-enrollment-data/report-highlights/index.html

The Medicaid Outcomes Distributed Research Network, Julie M. Donohue, Marian P. Jarlenski, Joo Yeon Kim, Lu Tang, Katherine Ahrens, Lindsay Allen, Anna Austin, Andrew J. Barnes, Marguerite Burns, et al., "Use of Medications for Treatment of Opioid Use Disorder Among US Medicaid Enrollees in 11 States, 2014–2018," *JAMA*, Vol. 326, No. 2, 2021, pp. 154–164.

Meisner, Jessica A., Judith Anesi, Xinwei Chen, and David Grande, "Changes in Infective Endocarditis Admissions in Pennsylvania During the Opioid Epidemic," *Clinical Infectious Diseases*, Vol. 71, No. 7, 2020, pp. 1664–1670.

Midgette, Gregory, Steven Davenport, Jonathan P. Caulkins, and Beau Kilmer, *What America's Users Spend on Illegal Drugs, 2006–2016*, Santa Monica, Calif.: RAND Corporation, RR-3140-ONDCP, 2019. As of August 20, 2019:
https://www.rand.org/pubs/research_reports/RR3140.html

MODRN—*See* The Medicaid Outcomes Distributed Research Network.

Morales, Kenneth B., Ju Nyeong Park, Jennifer L. Glick, Saba Rouhani, Traci C. Green, and Susan G. Sherman, "Preference for Drugs Containing Fentanyl from a Cross-Sectional Survey of People Who Use Illicit Opioids in Three United States Cities," *Drug and Alcohol Dependence*, Vol. 204, 2019.

Moreno, Jessica L., Sarah E. Wakeman, Matthew S. Duprey, Russell J. Roberts, Jared S. Jacobson, and John W. Devlin, "Predictors for 30-Day and 90-Day Hospital Readmission Among Patients with Opioid Use Disorder," *Journal of Addiction Medicine*, Vol. 13, No. 4, 2019, pp. 306–313.

Morgan, Rachel E., and Alexandra Thompson, *The Nation's Two Crime Measures, 2011–2020*, Washington, D.C.: U.S. Department of Justice, Office of Justice Programs, Bureau of Justice Statistics, February 2022.

Morgan, Rachel E., and Jennifer L. Truman, *Criminal Victimization, 2019*, Washington, D.C.: U.S. Department of Justice, Office of Justice Programs, Bureau of Justice Statistics, September 2020.

National Drug Early Warning System, homepage, undated-a. As of May 25, 2022:
https://ndews.org/

National Drug Early Warning System, "About NDEWS," undated-b. As of May 25, 2022:
https://ndews.org/about/

National Highway Traffic Safety Administration, "Early Estimates of 2019 Motor Vehicle Traffic Data Show Reduced Fatalities for Third Consecutive Year," press release, May 5, 2020. As of August 2, 2021:
https://www.nhtsa.gov/press-releases/early-estimates-2019-motor-vehicle-traffic-data-show-reduced-fatalities-third

National Institute on Drug Abuse, "Opioid Overdose Crisis," March 11, 2021. As of August 2, 2021:
https://www.drugabuse.gov/drug-topics/opioids/opioid-overdose-crisis

National Safety Council, "Addressing the Opioid Crisis," webpage, undated. As of August 2, 2021:
https://www.nsc.org/home-safety/safety-topics/opioids

Novak, Scott P., Ricky Bluthenthal, Lynn Wenger, Daniel Chu, and Alex H. Kral, "Initiation of Heroin and Prescription Opioid Pain Relievers by Birth Cohort," *American Journal of Public Health*, Vol. 106, No. 2, 2016, pp. 298–300.

OECD—*See* Organisation for Economic Co-operation and Development.

Office of National Drug Control Policy, *National Drug Control Strategy: Data Supplement 2016*, Washington, D.C., 2016.

Olfson, Mark, Stephen Crystal, Melanie Wall, Shuai Wang, Shang-Min Liu, and Carlos Blanco, "Causes of Death After Nonfatal Opioid Overdose," *JAMA Psychiatry*, Vol. 75, No. 8, 2018, pp. 820–827.

ONDCP—*See* Office of National Drug Control Policy.

Organisation for Economic Co-operation and Development, *Addressing Problematic Opioid Use in OECD Countries*, Paris: OECD Health Policy Studies, 2019.

Pacula, R. L., R. Lundberg, J. P. Caulkins, B. Kilmer, S. Greathouse, T. Fain, and P. Steinberg, *Improving the Measurement of Drug-Related Crime*, Washington, D.C.: Office of National Drug Control Policy, Executive Office of the President, October 2013.

Pardo, Bryce, Jirka Taylor, Jonathan P. Caulkins, Beau Kilmer, Peter Reuter, and Bradley D. Stein, *The Future of Fentanyl and Other Synthetic Opioids*, Santa Monica, Calif.: RAND Corporation, RR-3117-RC, 2019. As of May 25, 2022: https://www.rand.org/pubs/research_reports/RR3117.html

Paybarah, Azi, "About 160,000 People in New York to See Their Marijuana Convictions Disappear," *New York Times*, August 28, 2019.

Pletcher, Mark J., Stefan G. Kertesz, Michael A. Kohn, and Ralph Gonzales, "Trends in Opioid Prescribing by Race/Ethnicity for Patients Seeking Care in US Emergency Departments," *JAMA*, Vol. 299, No. 1, 2008, pp. 70–78.

Pollini, Robin A., Caleb J. Banta-Green, Jazmine Cuevas-Mota, Mitcheal Metzner, Eyasu Teshale, and Richard S. Garfein, "Problematic Use of Prescription-Type Opioids Prior to Heroin Use Among Young Heroin Injectors," *Substance Abuse and Rehabilitation*, Vol. 2, No. 1, 2011, pp. 173–180.

Powell, David, Abby Alpert, and Rosalie L. Pacula, "A Transitioning Epidemic: How the Opioid Crisis Is Driving the Rise in Hepatitis C," *Health Affairs*, Vol. 38, No. 2, 2019, pp. 287–294.

Reuter, Peter, Jonathan P. Caulkins, and Greg Midgette, "Heroin Use Cannot Be Measured Adequately with a General Population Survey," *Addiction*, Vol. 116, No. 10, 2021, pp. 2600–2609.

Robins, Lee N., John E. Helzer, Michie Hesselbrock, and Eric Wish, "Vietnam Veterans Three Years After Vietnam: How Our Study Changed Our View of Heroin," *American Journal on Addictions*, Vol. 19. No. 3, 2010, pp. 203–211.

Ropero-Miller, Jeri D., and Paul J. Speaker, "The Hidden Costs of the Opioid Crisis and the Implications for Financial Management in the Public Sector," *Forensic Science International: Synergy*, Vol. 1, 2019, pp. 227–238.

Ruhm, Christopher J., "Corrected US Opioid-Involved Drug Poisoning Deaths and Mortality Rates, 1999–2015," *Addiction*, Vol. 113, No. 7, 2018, pp. 1339–1344.

Saloner, Brendan, and Benjamin Lê Cook, "Blacks and Hispanics Are Less Likely Than Whites to Complete Addiction Treatment, Largely Due to Socioeconomic Factors," *Health Affairs*, Vol. 32, No. 1, 2013, pp. 135–145.

SAMHDA—*See* Substance Abuse and Mental Health Data Archive.

SAMHSA—*See* Substance Abuse and Mental Health Services Administration.

Schieber, Lyna Z., Gery P. Guy, Jr., Puja Seth, and Jan L. Losby, "Variation in Adult Outpatient Opioid Prescription Dispensing by Age and Sex—United States, 2008–2018," *Morbidity and Mortality Weekly Report*, Vol. 69, No. 11, 2020, pp. 298–302.

Schranz, Asher J., Aaron Fleischauer, Vivian H. Chu, Li-Tzy Wu, and David L. Rosen, "Trends in Drug Use-Associated Infective Endocarditis and Heart Valve Surgery, 2007 to 2017: A Study of Statewide Discharge Data," *Annals of Internal Medicine*, Vol. 170, No. 1, 2019, pp. 31–40.

Schuchat, Anne, Debra Houry, and Gery P. Guy, "New Data on Opioid Use and Prescribing in the United States," *JAMA*, Vol. 318, No. 5, 2017, pp. 425–426.

Schuler, Megan S., Cara E. Rice, Rebecca J. Evans-Polce, and Rebecca L. Collins, "Disparities in Substance Use Behaviors and Disorders Among Adult Sexual Minorities by Age, Gender, and Sexual Identity," *Drug and Alcohol Dependence*, Vol. 189, 2018, pp. 139–146.

Serdarevic, Mirsada, Catherine W. Striley, and Linda B. Cottler, "Gender Differences in Prescription Opioid Use," *Current Opinion in Psychiatry*, Vol. 30, No. 4, 2017, pp. 238–246.

Shefner, Ruth T., Jason S. Sloan, Kayla R. Sandler, and Evan D. Anderson, "Missed Opportunities: Arrest and Court Touchpoints for Individuals Who Fatally Overdosed in Philadelphia in 2016," *International Journal of Drug Policy*, Vol. 78, April 2020.

Singhal, Astha, Yu-Yu Tien, and Renee Y. Hsia, "Racial-Ethnic Disparities in Opioid Prescriptions at Emergency Department Visits for Conditions Commonly Associated with Prescription Drug Abuse," *PLoS ONE*, Vol. 11, No. 8, 2016.

Smart, Rosanna, and Peter Reuter, "Does Heroin-Assisted Treatment Reduce Crime? A Review of Randomized-Controlled Trials," *Addiction*, Vol. 117, No. 3, 2022, pp. 518–531.

Stein, Bradley D., Christopher M. Jones, Rosanna Smart, Flora Sheng, and Mark Sorbero, "Patient, Prescriber, and Community Factors Associated with Filled Naloxone Prescriptions Among Patients Receiving Buprenorphine 2017–18," *Drug and Alcohol Dependence*, Vol. 221, 2021.

Substance Abuse and Mental Health Data Archive, "National Survey on Drug Use and Health, 2019: Crosstab Creator," webpage, undated-a. As of May 25, 2022:
https://pdas.samhsa.gov/#/survey/NSDUH-2019-DS0001

Substance Abuse and Mental Health Data Archive, "National Survey on Drug Use and Health, 2019, Crosstab Creator: Family in HH 18 or Older and Heroin and/or Pain Reliever Dependence or Abuse—Pst Yr," webpage, undated-b. As of June 15, 2022:
https://pdas.samhsa.gov/#/survey/NSDUH-2019-DS0001/crosstab/?column=UDPYHRPNR&results_received=true&row=EDFAM18&run_chisq=false&weight=ANALWT_C

Substance Abuse and Mental Health Data Archive, "National Survey on Drug Use and Health, 2019, Crosstab Creator: Kids Aged < 18 in HH and Heroin and/or Pain Reliever Dependence or Abuse—Pst Yr," webpage, undated-c. As of June 15, 2022:
https://pdas.samhsa.gov/#/survey/NSDUH-2019-DS0001?column=UDPYHRPNR&results_received=true&row=IRKI17_2&run_chisq=false&weight=ANALWT_C

Substance Abuse and Mental Health Data Archive, "National Survey on Drug Use and Health, 2019, Crosstab Creator: Marital Status and Heroin and/or Pain Reliever Dependence or Abuse—Pst Yr," webpage, undated-d. As of June 15, 2022:
https://pdas.samhsa.gov/#/survey/NSDUH-2019-DS0001?column=UDPYHRPNR&recodes=IRMARIT_RECODE%7C1%3DMarried%262%3DWidowed%263%3DDivorced+or+Separated%264%3DNever+been+married&results_received=true&row=IRMARIT_RECODE&run_chisq=false&weight=ANALWT_C

Substance Abuse and Mental Health Data Archive, "National Survey on Drug Use and Health, 2019, Crosstab Creator: Opioid Dependence or Abuse—Past Year and Race/Hispanicity" webpage, undated-e. As of June 15, 2022:
https://pdas.samhsa.gov/#/survey/NSDUH-2019-DS0001?column=NEWRACE2&results_received=true&row=UDPYOPI&run_chisq=false&weight=ANALWT_C

Substance Abuse and Mental Health Services Administration, "2020 National Survey of Drug Use and Health (NSDUH) Releases," webpage, undated-a. As of June 15, 2022:
https://www.samhsa.gov/data/release/2020-national-survey-drug-use-and-health-nsduh-releases

Substance Abuse and Mental Health Services Administration, "National Survey on Drug Use and Health (NSDUH)," webpage, undated-b. As of June 15, 2022: https://www.samhsa.gov/data/data-we-collect/nsduh-national-survey-drug-use-and-health

Substance Abuse and Mental Health Services Administration, "State Data Tables and Reports from the 2019–2020 NSDUH," webpage, undated-c. As of June 15, 2022: https://www.samhsa.gov/data/nsduh/state-reports-NSDUH-2020

Substance Abuse and Mental Health Services Administration, *Key Substance Use and Mental Health Indicators in the United States: Results from the 2019 National Survey on Drug Use and Health*, Rockville, Md.: Center for Behavioral Health Statistics and Quality, 2020a.

Substance Abuse and Mental Health Services Administration, *National Survey of Substance Abuse Treatment Services (N-SSATS): 2019, Data on Substance Abuse Treatment Facilities*, Rockville, Md., August 20, 2020b.

Substance Abuse and Mental Health Services Administration, "2019 NSDUH Detailed Tables," webpage, September 11, 2020c. As of June 15, 2022: https://www.samhsa.gov/data/report/2019-nsduh-detailed-tables

Substance Abuse and Mental Health Services Administration, *2019 National Survey on Drug Use and Health: Public Use File Codebook*, Rockville, Md.: Center for Behavioral Health Statistics and Quality, October 20, 2020d.

Substance Abuse and Mental Health Services Administration, *Treatment Episode Data Set (TEDS): 2018 Admissions to and Discharges from Publicly-Funded Substance Use Treatment*, Rockville, Md., October 30, 2020e.

Substance Abuse and Mental Health Services Administration, *Key Substance Use and Mental Health Indicators in the United States: Results from the 2020 National Survey on Drug Use and Health*, Rockville, Md.: Center for Behavioral Health Statistics and Quality, October 2021.

Suda, Katie J., Michael J. Durkin, Gregory S. Calip, Walid F. Gellad, Hajwa Kim, Peter B. Lockhart, Susan A. Rowan, and Martin H. Thornhill, "Comparison of Opioid Prescribing by Dentists in the United States and England," *JAMA*, Vol. 2, No. 5, 2019.

Tucker, Myra J., Cynthia J. Berg, William M. Callaghan, and Jason Hsia, "The Black–White Disparity in Pregnancy-Related Mortality from 5 Conditions: Differences in Prevalence and Case-Fatality Rates," *American Journal of Public Health*, Vol. 97, No. 2, 2007, pp. 247–251.

Voronkov, Michael, Benjamin Cocchiaro, and Jeffry B. Stock, "Does a Hypoxic Injury from a Non-Fatal Overdose Lead to an Alzheimer Disease?" *Neurochemistry International*, Vol. 143, February 2021.

Votaw, Victoria R., Katie Witkiewitz, Linda Valeri, Olivera Bogunovic, and R. Kathryn McHugh, "Nonmedical Prescription Sedative/Tranquilizer Use in Alcohol and Opioid Use Disorders," *Addictive Behaviors*, Vol. 88, January 2019, pp. 48–55.

Vowles, Kevin E., Mindy L. McEntee, Peter Siyahhan Julnes, Tessa Frohe, John P. Ney, and David N. van der Goes, "Rates of Opioid Misuse, Abuse, and Addiction in Chronic Pain: A Systematic Review and Data Synthesis," *Pain*, Vol. 156, No. 4, 2015, pp. 569–576.

Warner-Smith, Matthew, Shane Darke, and Carolyn Day, "Morbidity Associated with Non-Fatal Heroin Overdose, *Addiction*, Vol. 97, No. 8, August 2002, pp. 963–967.

Wu, Li-Tzy, He Zhu, and Marvin S. Swartz, "Treatment Utilization Among Persons with Opioid Use Disorder in the United States," *Drug and Alcohol Dependence*, Vol. 169, December 2016, pp. 117–127.

Zibbell, Jon E., Alice K. Asher, Rajiv C. Patel, Ben Kupronis, Kashif Iqbal, John W. Ward, and Deborah Holtzman, "Increases in Acute Hepatitis C Virus Infection Related to a Growing Opioid Epidemic and Associated Injection Drug Use, United States, 2004 to 2014," *American Journal of Public Health*, Vol. 108, No. 2, 2018, pp. 175–181.

Zibbell, Jon, Jennifer Howard, Sarah Duhart Clarke, Abigail Ferrell, and Sarita L. Karon, *Non-Fatal Opioid Overdose and Associated Health Outcomes: Final Summary Report*, Washington, D.C.: RTI International, September 3, 2019.

CHAPTER THREE

Family Members of Individuals with Opioid Use Disorder

Rosalie Liccardo Pacula, Sierra Smucker, Jonathan P. Caulkins, Beau Kilmer, Bradley D. Stein, and Jirka Taylor

Introduction

Although media and policy attention understandably focuses on individuals who overdose, suffer from opioid use disorder (OUD), or both, their families and others who are close to them are also important stakeholders and their needs have often received less attention. That relative neglect influences our understanding of the problem and artificially narrows the range of policy responses that are discussed.

Family members of people with OUD are deeply impacted. Children, in particular, are known to suffer a variety of harms (Barnard and McKeganey, 2004). Recent reports show a more than doubling of children entering the foster care system and large numbers of children placed with relative caregivers because of parental substance use including OUD (Meinhofer and Anglero-Diaz, 2019; National Conference of State Legislatures, 2019; Patrick et al., 2019), a rise in neonatal opioid withdrawal syndrome (Patrick et al., 2012), and a dramatic increase in the number of children currently living with an adult with OUD (Bullinger and Wing, 2019; Mihalec-Adkins et al., 2020). These outcomes generate identifiable financial costs, such as administrative and personnel costs within and payments made by the child welfare system, medical care, or the income support and homeless services system. Children also suffer emotional and psychological harms because of neglect (and in some cases abuse), displacement, trauma, and grief. Those harms are important in the moment, and can sometimes have repercussions well into the future, including risk of developing OUD (Haggerty et al., 2008) or difficulties in school (National Association for Children of Addiction, 2018).

It is not just children that are impacted, however. Adult family members likewise can endure enormous strain in the course of living with and/or caring for a loved one suffering from OUD, with family broadly construed to include biological relatives, relatives via marriage, and long-term significant others and friends. The costs of caring for the family member suffering from OUD can include financial support for daily activities (transportation, food, child or elder supervision) and/or longer-term costs like health care, treatment, legal issues, and those associated with unemployment or underemployment. They can also include costs of relatives caring for children instead of parents who may be in treatment or incarcerated. In addition, there are emotional and psychological costs caused by concern about the welfare of the loved one, persistent worry about their risk of overdose, and the emotional burden of ongoing spells of relapse.

For multiple reasons, costs imposed on family members are often overlooked or understated (Birnbaum et al., 2011; Maclean et al., 2020; White et al., 2009; Wittenberg et al., 2016). First, most calculations of cost take an agency not a societal perspective, e.g., focusing on budgetary costs. Second, many estimates focus only on current costs, ignoring the fact that adverse effects of present family dysfunction continue to accumulate over long periods of time. Third, many of the costs imposed on family members are what economists call *intangible costs*, such as pain and suffering, that are difficult to quantify but nonetheless real.

In this chapter, we offer three insights that should feature more prominently in policy discussions about opioids, but that are also applicable to other drugs such as alcohol and methamphetamines:

1. Family members of individuals with OUD often suffer financial, emotional, and sometimes mental and physical health burdens because of that OUD.
2. OUD's harms to society are often intermediated through effects on family.
3. Family members can play an integral role in helping individuals with OUD remain in treatment or sustain recovery; however, there may also be times when family members may also act as barriers to recovery and change.

We then discuss some policy options targeted at helping and empowering these family members.

How Are Families Affected by Opioids?

Family Members of Individuals with Opioid Use Disorder Often Suffer Financial, Emotional, and Sometimes Mental and Physical Health Burdens Because of That Opioid Use Disorder

Family members can suffer because of their loved one's use, and this suffering extends well beyond the financial, health care, and caregiving costs. They do not just take on the various costs the way a banker takes on a house or car loan; they are emotionally vested in the success and/or failure of the individual with the OUD. Likewise, when they are cheated, lied to, stolen from, or abused by a loved one with OUD, there can be an extra angst beyond that of being victimized by a stranger (Dorius et al., 2020). As such, they experience their own suffering caused by the stress, anxiety, worry, and fear of living through these events. Given the magnitude of the ongoing opioid crisis, even the most dramatic events, such as the death of a family member or a close friend, have touched a considerable number of individuals. A national poll in 2018 found that one in eight adults have had a family member or close friend die from opioids (The Associated Press–NORC Center for Public Affairs Research [AP-NORC], 2018), and a 2019 poll targeting Philadelphia residents found that nearly 30 percent of respondents personally knew someone who had died from opioids in this heavily stricken area (Eichel and Pharis, 2019). Furthermore, these impacts are accentuated among families in communities facing long-standing underresourcing and structural disadvantages, including communities in rural areas and communities of minority populations (Drake et al., 2020; El-Bassel et al., 2021).

Although this may seem obvious once stated, its implications are often insufficiently considered. As John Donne observed, no individual is an island; parents, grandparents, children, siblings, and extended family members may have emotional, financial, and legal connections with the individual suffering from OUD (Winstanley, 2020). For example, approximately 550,000 children currently live with an adult with an OUD (Bullinger and Wing, 2019). If individuals suffering from OUD cannot take care of their children, other family members commonly step in and help, incurring various costs associated with the parental duties the alternative caregiver now needs to do (e.g., time away from work, cost of groceries or transportation, lost time with their own family members). Similarly, family members may take care of responsibilities for the individual with OUD when that person is impaired because of drug use, in treatment, hospitalized because of an overdose, incarcerated, or serving some other community supervision violation. Family members may also pay unpaid bills because the individual with OUD spent their limited funds purchasing drugs or could not work. These costs can be incurred repeatedly by family members, because of the chronic relapsing nature of the disease (McLellan, 2002) and because addiction *careers* can be long. Families can also experience material losses if their relatives with OUD do not pay back loans made to them by their family members or if they steal from family members (Adam and Kitt-Lewis, 2020; Maina et al., 2021; Ólafsdóttir, Orjasniemi, and Hrafnsdóttir, 2020). Elsewhere, families can be left financially worse off if one earner is unable to keep their job because of their substance use (Daley, 2013; Ólafsdóttir, Orjasniemi, and Hrafnsdóttir, 2020). Financial impacts may be particularly challenging for grandparents who find themselves assuming new caretaking responsibilities that they did not plan for, especially if they are on a fixed income (Stanik, 2020). For instance, in a study by Davis et al., 2020, grandparents taking care of grandchildren because of parents' OUD reported deferring their downsizing plans, taking on new mortgages, and incurring new costs by trying to move to more child-friendly, and pricier, communities with good schools. Along similar lines, Stanik, 2020, found in a survey of grandparents caring for their grandchildren (of whom one fifth indicated parental drug use as the reason) that 32 percent of respondents either delayed retirement or were forced to go back to work.

Family members can also suffer intangible costs through a variety of mechanisms. They can experience stress created by the unpredictable behavior of the loved one, which often requires vigilance on the part of family members (Adam and Kitt-Lewis, 2020; Johnson,

Worth, and Brookover, 2019). Family members assume new caregiving and other responsibilities for their relative who suffers from OUD, which can lead to poorer physical and
psychosocial outcomes for caregivers (Huhn and Dunn, 2020). Grandparents taking care of
their grandchildren or children taking care of their younger siblings may see their well-being
affected (Davis et al., 2020; Dolbin-McNab and O'Connell, 2021; Johnson et al., 2019; Lander,
Howsare, and Byrne, 2013). Relatedly, family members frequently experience fear and concern regarding the loved one's survival and well-being (Daley, 2013).

Compounding these stressors may be societal stigma, which can contribute to families'
feelings of guilt and shame, and barriers to accessing services that might offer support to the
loved one (Adam and Kitt-Lewis, 2020; Dolbin-MacNab and O'Connell, 2021). This is especially true where family members try to navigate the challenging and unfamiliar landscape of
OUD service provision in search of options for their loved ones (Adam and Kitt-Lewis, 2020).

Furthermore, families with individuals suffering from OUD may see a disruption in
family functioning, marked by elevated rates of tension and conflict and by breakdowns in
mutual trust (Adam and Kitt-Lewis, 2020; Davis et al., 2020; Ellis et al., 2020). In some cases,
the result may be family breakups, spurred by separation, divorce, or child removal (Daley,
2013; Ólafsdóttir, Orjasniemi, and Hrafnsdóttir, 2020). Moreover, the time family members
devote to the individual with OUD or to other new responsibilities cannot be spent on other
things. This has serious implications for caregivers' ability to attend to other necessities of
life and balance their caregiving with other responsibilities and interests that they may have
(Maina et al., 2021; Wittenberg et al., 2016). For instance, grandparents having to care for
their grandchildren can feel increasingly isolated as the new responsibilities may prevent
socializing with their friends (Davis et al., 2020; Stanik, 2020).

In the introduction chapter, we offered a vignette on Doug, whose wife has suffered from
OUD and, as is the case with most people who use opioids, has had difficulty finding a treatment program that worked for her. In this vignette, it is easy to spot the tangible financial
cost of repeated episodes of treatment and lost wages to cover care for the children, but additional intangible costs are also imposed on the family. For example, there is the worry about
the mental and physical well-being of Doug's wife, Marie, felt by Doug and the children.
Overdoses can generate sleepless nights for family members, wondering what they could have
done differently, wondering what they can do or say to help their loved one, worrying about
whether treatment will work this time and, if so, how long will it take. (From the child's perspective: Will Mommy come home? Will she be the same when she comes home? Was it my
fault she had to go away? Will this happen again? How can I help Mommy?)

There are also psychological strains placed on the family with Doug's unpaid leave from
his business to care for children while Marie is in treatment and the risk of losing current
and future customers, the financial strain of having to cover these unexpected treatment
expenses, and the possible cost of prolonged child care needs if the treatment is not successful. The financial and emotional stress may cause Doug to be more short-tempered with the
kids, leading to additional stress. The intangible costs on the children include extended sepa-

ration from their mother (Feder, Letourneau, Brook, 2019; Lester and Lagasse, 2010) and the prolonged exposure of living in a stressed household.

These adverse childhood experiences can result in or contribute to a variety of short- and long-term mental health problems for the children, such as anxiety and depression; it can also increase the risk for behavior problems, including early substance use (Romanowicz et al., 2019; Stulac et al., 2019; Winstanley and Stover, 2019) and worse academic performance (Conradt et al., 2019). The stress can be cyclical and ongoing as the patient suffering with OUD experiences recurrent episodes of substance use and treatment and recovery (see Chapter Ten on Child Welfare for an in-depth discussion of impacts on children).

This vignette brings attention to different types of financial and emotional costs: the strain of trying to manage the family while temporarily missing the loved one and the worry that exists while someone is in treatment and recovery; the emotional duress of wondering whether there was anything else they could do to help the loved one; the dread of what to expect if the person falls out of recovery, and so on. Although studies have examined aspects of these intangible costs (e.g., Copello, Templeton, and Powell, 2010; Maclean et al., 2020; McCollister, French, and Fang, 2010; Nicosia et al., 2009), estimates of their magnitude are highly variable because there is not a consensus regarding the best method for valuing them.

How Do Families Interact with the Opioid Ecosystem?

Opioid Use Disorder's Harms to Society Are Often Intermediated Through Effects on Family

Harms suffered by families matter to policy planners who seek to maximize societal welfare, because families are part of society. But there are not moats and walls around families, insulating the rest of society from their misfortune. When family members are harmed, it can have ramifications for their community and society more generally. In other words, the public externalities of the opioid crisis can be mediated by outcomes suffered by family members but still fall beyond the inner circle of the family.

There are several ways this can happen. First, health insurance and other mechanisms for spreading risk can transfer costs from family members to a broader group. For example, if a person with OUD physically harms a family member (Ghertner and Ali, 2021), and that person receives medical care, much of that cost may be paid by insurance or government programs (e.g., Medicaid). Some conditions even spread physically, not just via insurance. To give a concrete example, undiagnosed hepatitis C and/or HIV in an individual suffering from OUD subsequently contracted by a spouse or sexual partner has the potential to infect both additional sex partners (Conrad et al., 2015; Liang and Ward, 2018) and infants (Patrick et al., 2017). It can also require medical treatment (Conrad et al., 2015; Liang and Ward, 2018). Thus, this example demonstrates both types of mechanisms of how harms incurred by family members spill over to society—disease transmission *and* risk-sharing arrangements.

Second, the public can bear the short- and long-term impacts of children born with neonatal opioid withdrawal syndrome to and raised by parents with an OUD. Caring for an infant exposed to opioids in utero and born with neonatal opioid withdrawal syndrome (also discussed in Chapter Five on medical care) can be costly; recent estimates find that Medicaid-financed births impacted by neonatal opioid withdrawal syndrome cost taxpayers more than $460 million in hospital costs in 2014 (Winkelman et al., 2018). Babies born with neonatal opioid withdrawal syndrome may also be at risk for longer term behavioral problems (Davis and Templer, 1988; Hans, 1996; Ornoy et al., 2001; Romanowicz et al., 2019), attention deficits (Davis and Templer, 1988; Slinning, 2004), and lower cognition (Nygaard et al., 2015). A recent study, using Pennsylvania as a case study, sought to quantify the cost of neonatal opioid withdrawal syndrome on the education system. It estimated that the state paid annually approximately $500,000 in 2017 dollars for special education services to a one-year cohort of children born with neonatal opioid withdrawal syndrome associated with maternal use of prescription opioids (Morgan and Wang, 2019). Further exacerbating these consequences is the fact that parents with OUD may be less emotionally available to their newly born and more likely to express frustration and anger (Daley, 2013). Parental OUD also carries the risk of child mistreatment and placement in foster care, which can lead to substantial societal costs (Barth et al., 2006).

As these children get older, psychological trauma, neglect, or abuse that a child experiences at home because of a parent's OUD can put the child at risk for mental health and substance use problems, thereby increasing the risk of similar behaviors with their own children, and perpetuating a cycle of addiction (Egeland, Jacobvitz, and Sroufe, 1988; Jääskeläinen et al., 2016; Normile, Hanlon, and Eichner, 2018; Romanowicz et al., 2019). The intergenerational nature of substance use underlines the importance of considering the impact of OUD on family members, especially children, when designing policy interventions aimed at reducing short- and long-term costs of opioid misuse.

These examples represent just a few of the ways that harms to family impose broader costs on the communities in which those family members live. Importantly, in many cases, the costs are imposed intergenerationally, making them difficult to measure. At the same time, it is important to recognize that as families absorb costs stemming from the loved ones' OUD, they shield the society, or more precisely the public purse, from realizing the full costs of OUD. For instance, in at least some situations where family members assume unpaid caregiver responsibilities, these responsibilities would, in the absence of the family intervention, be taken up by some other public service. Thus, while costs imposed on families are an inseparable component of the societal costs of OUD, they often act to mitigate the impact of OUD on public finances.

Family Members Can Play an Integral Role at Helping Individuals with Opioid Use Disorder Remain in Treatment or Sustain Recovery; However, There Also Might Be Times When Family Members Can Act as Barriers to Recovery and Change

Family members can serve as key agents acting on behalf of the individual suffering from OUD, as agents of responsibility or agents of change. They can also, conversely, be barriers to recovery and change.

On the one hand, family members can play a critical role in encouraging and supporting individuals with OUD to seek, engage, and remain in treatment (Ellis et al., 2020; Jalali et al., 2020). They may be quicker to recognize the warning signs of substance misuse than the misusing individual, who may be unwilling or unable to recognize symptoms of dependence or associated impairment (Meyers and Wolfe, 2004; Osilla et al., 2016; Osilla et al., 2018; Smith and Meyers, 2007). Family members are also highly motivated to help their loved ones stop using substances (Fleming, 2016; Halford and Osgarby, 1993; Thomas and Agar, 1993). In one study of natural recovery, 23 of 50 subjects cited "external pressures or ultimatums exerted by significant others—usually family, friends, or spouses" as motivating them to quit (Toneatto et al., 1999, p. 264).

Many twelve-step and comparable programs encourage the involvement of family members. Al-anon and Alateen's primary focus is on providing support to family members, and treatment programs and the juvenile legal system may also routinely involve family in efforts to manage minors' substance use disorder problems (Lochman and van den Steenhoven, 2002; Ozechowski and Liddle, 2000). There are also family-oriented treatment programs that can benefit parents and pregnant women (Kameg, 2021), and for many individuals, maintaining established relationships with family members, such as retaining custody of children, or reuniting with children who have been removed can serve as motivation to successfully complete treatment (Casey Family Programs, 2019). Including family members or incorporating family therapy alongside other types of treatment, such as methadone, can improve adherence to treatments (Anton et al., 1981; Fals-Stewart and O'Farrell, 2003; Stanton and Shadish, 1997).

Beyond applying pressure and directly participating in treatment, family members can also contribute by providing stable housing and financial support while an individual is in treatment and transporting an individual to and from treatment sessions.

Family members are also in a position to reduce harms stemming from the loved one's opioid use. Family members may be the first to witness an opioid overdose and thus be the ones calling for emergency medical help. As discussed in the medical care, harm reduction, and first responders chapters (Chapters Five, Eight, and Nine, respectively), family members can often administer naloxone obtained from opioid education and naloxone distribution programs or from the pharmacy, which has become a more common occurrence with the proliferation of such programs and state policies supporting pharmacy distribution of naloxone (Haffajee, Cherney, and Smart, 2020; Kerensky and Walley, 2017). In some localities, after a medical emergency that has involved first responders is over, family members can also interact with first responders, get more naloxone, and obtain information on various service options for their loved ones. This can happen as part of a naloxone leave-behind program (Scharf et al., 2021) or as part of various post-overdose outreach programs organized by local agencies (Wagner et al., 2019). These programs can in turn enhance the role families can play in encouraging their loved ones to enter treatment and access other forms of support.

However, family members can also help perpetuate an individual's substance use disorder. This can occur when family members minimize an individual's substance related symptoms or impairment. In the case of treatment for OUD, family members may be against an individual receiving medication treatment (Matusow et al., 2013; Myers, Fakier, and Louw, 2009). Furthermore, in some cases an individual's treatment and recovery can be complicated by the ongoing substance use of a family member, a particular challenge when the individual in recovery commonly misused drugs with a family member who is still misusing (Cavacuiti, 2004; Hedges, 2012).

When we leave families out of the policy assessments, or neglect their role in sustaining recovery, we risk reducing the viability of a successful approach for tackling the problem and helping people reach a point of sustained recovery. Families are active agents in these complex trajectories, and their role is often neglected. When policy solutions emphasize increasing access to treatment but forget the supportive role families play during treatment and recovery, it makes it harder to achieve the intended goals.

Other Considerations and Policy Options

While tangible costs of treating OUD are important, family members also bear intangible costs associated with informal caregiving and importantly, psychological costs of anxiety, stress and trauma. Furthermore, many costs experienced by family members are not just one-time costs. People with OUD often cycle through multiple rounds of misuse followed by periods of abstinence, possibly because of treatment, and then relapse (McLellan, 2002). That means families also cycle through phases of greater and lesser anxiety, stress, and strain (Adam and Kitt-Lewis, 2020). The resulting psychological and emotional impact on family members may be more than additive. A loved one experiencing repeated cycles of improvement and relapse can lead to more intense and disproportionate growth in emotional and psychological costs for the family members (McFarlane, 2010).

Consider this simple thought experiment, which closely follows one proposed by Kleiman, 1999: What is the average person's willingness to pay to avoid having a family member struggle with OUD for a year? We are unaware of anyone who has yet tried to estimate the number, but suppose for the sake of argument it is $10,000. If one believed there were approximately 4 million Americans struggling with OUD and they, on average, have two family members willing to pay that amount, then families' collective willingness to pay to avoid that

OUD is 4 million × 2 × $10,000 = $80 billion per year.[1] That is not a small figure, even compared with the total of all societal costs that are reflected in standard assessments, such as one estimate by Altarum, 2018, which projected the total burden of opioid crisis in the United States to be near $200 billion in 2020.

Given the tremendous costs experienced by many families, one might ask whether these families should be directly compensated in some form, perhaps from settlements of the state opioid litigation lawsuits. However, consideration of such compensation raises questions about whether society should consider compensating families who experience similar financial and psychological costs from a variety of other severe or chronic disorders, such as cancer, gunshot wounds, major depression, or morbid obesity. Some might argue for such compensation only for families of those with OUD because of the special role the pharmaceutical industry played in contributing to the opioid crisis and the profits generated from those activities. However, a similar argument could be made for many other disorders, including those mentioned previously. As a result, discussions of compensation to family members of individuals with an OUD belong to a much larger discussion and are beyond the scope of this chapter.

But even those reluctant to write checks to compensate family members have no excuse for ignoring those costs altogether, as sometimes happens. Costs to family may get lost when analysts take a Western, individualistic view of society and focus on the person suffering with OUD, and not on the risks and harm to the rest of the family. The full burden of this crisis will only be reduced if and when society also addresses the costs imposed directly on family members and indirectly on their local communities. How do we do this? We offer here three considerations. Some have been tried but not fully evaluated, so we are not endorsing the specific ideas. Rather, we offer them as illustrations of the feasibility of developing responses that embrace the entire family as the stakeholder—not just the patient suffering with OUD. The considerations are as follows:

1. Empower family members to play a more active role in supporting their loved one to engage in treatment and ongoing recovery.
2. Provide resources to help family members prepare for the non–treatment-related challenges associated with OUD, including psychological stress and anxiety and possibly responding to overdoses.
3. Do a better job monitoring the needs of family members living with or caring for a loved one suffering from OUD.

The first approach would be to enhance family members' ability to support their loved one obtaining and engaging in treatment and ongoing recovery (Daley et al., 2018; Kumar et al., 2021; Nayak et al., 2021). This could occur at multiple stages throughout the treatment cycle, and potentially include developing and disseminating

---

[1] For more on the uncertainty surrounding estimates of people with OUD, see Chapter Two.

- information to allow family members to identify indicators of substance misuse or addiction
- tools and information to support family members intervening with a family member with a substance use disorder
- tools that allow family members to identify high-quality treatment programs for individuals with substance use disorders
- interventions that increase the involvement of family members in supporting treatment, including payment coupons and/or daycare assistance
- information for family members about how to support an individual in recovery (who may or may not be in treatment).

Of course, efforts to help families get their loved one into treatment will depend on there being adequate treatment available. Unfortunately, in most parts of the country, there continues to be an inadequate supply of treatment options for individuals with substance use disorders, along with persistent concerns about their quality. This is particularly the case in rural communities and communities of minority populations where overdose rates are climbing. Federal efforts have been focused on enhancing the availability of effective treatment, particularly the availability of buprenorphine, which has resulted in a substantial increase in the number of practitioners who can prescribe buprenorphine for OUD (McBain et al., 2020). These efforts could be enhanced by additional steps to increase the number of providers who have obtained the minimal education required to prescribe buprenorphine, but should be complemented by efforts to more broadly increase the substance use disorder treatment workforce (Haffajee, Cherney, and Smart, 2020; Stein, 2019).

Efforts could also be taken to expand treatment options that directly involve families (American Association for Marriage and Family Therapy [AAMFT], 2018; Dopp et al., 2022; Seibert et al., 2019). One example would be family-based comprehensive treatment programs—specialized programs that enable the family to stay together. They often provide substance use disorder treatment, therapy, parenting skills training, life skills training, and job readiness education along with professional staff who ensure the safety of children while their parents and families achieve sobriety and recovery (Wilder Research and Volunteers of America, 2019). Another would be programs that directly involve spouses in treatment. Programs such as Community Reinforcement and Family Training (CRAFT) were developed to teach significant others how to engage a treatment-resistant loved one into treatment through positive communication and other behavioral strategies (Archer et al., 2020; Meyers and Wolfe, 2004; Smith and Meyers, 2007) and has been adapted for OUD (Osilla et al., 2020). CRAFT is listed on the Substance Abuse and Mental Health Services Administration's National Registry of Evidence-Based Programs and Practices and has been adapted for a variety of disadvantaged populations (Substance Abuse and Mental Health Services Administration, 2013).

In addition, family members could receive greater support in navigating across multiple systems to orientate themselves in the complex landscape of existing service provision, which many families are unlikely to be familiar with (Adam and Kitt-Lewis, 2020). This is not dissimilar to the needs of individuals with OUD themselves and could help ensure (1) that there is a plan for appropriate services for family members and their close ones with OUD and (2) that families develop relationships and linkages with corresponding agencies.

A second opportunity is to better prepare families of those with OUD for the many non-treatment challenges that they will face (Adam and Kitt-Lewis, 2020; Bagley et al., 2021; Crowley and Miller, 2020). Additional resources could be devoted to helping family members deal with their stress (Daley et al., 2018; Davis et al., 2020). Many treatment facilities offer support groups for family members of individuals receiving treatment for OUD. These programs could be subsidized and expanded and could go beyond support groups to offering concrete, tangible services like respite care. However, families do not only feel stress when the person with OUD is in treatment; efforts could be made to expand support programs for family members of those with OUD, irrespective of whether they are in treatment or recovery or active stage. The very fact that support for family members has often been connected to the person with OUD's treatment is symptomatic of the way family members' needs are neglected. Arguably, caring for someone with active addiction might be recognized as a situation requiring monitoring and potential intervention. In some cases, the stress and demands and the resulting problems mean that they could be considered as patients in their own right, not just as family of a patient.

Another mechanism that can address concerns about close ones' well-being is providing families with naloxone and training about how to use it (Adams, 2018; Bagley et al., 2021). This is especially important when individuals with OUD return from residential treatment or incarceration. Because tolerance is often lower after an extended period of abstinence, these returnees face a much greater risk of overdose (see, e.g., Binswanger et al., 2007).

Furthermore, given our increased understanding of the lifelong consequences of adverse childhood experiences, we need to develop, evaluate, and disseminate more and better programs that help children raised in a household with a parent with a substance use disorder. These programs could be delivered in OUD treatment settings, alongside parents receiving treatment. But given the large number of households with children in which a parent is suffering from a substance use disorder (Lipari and Van Horn, 2017), such programs could also be offered in schools and other settings, particularly in communities with higher rates of substance use disorder. It is also important to continue to provide such services to children if a parent with OUD dies. The impact of having a parent with OUD will not diminish in the event of their death, and in many cases may be compounded from the grief associated with the loss.

Finally, there is a pressing need to collect data on the needs of family members. Any survey that asks respondents, "Have you misused opioids in the last year?" could likewise ask, "Has anyone in your family misused opioids in the last year?" There could also be questions such as, "Has a family member stolen or borrowed from you without repaying because of their OUD?" or "Has someone's OUD been a financial burden on you at any time over this last year?" Similarly, just as doctors can do screening, brief intervention, and referral to treatment for SUD, doctors could do screening, brief intervention, and referral to services for having a family member with OUD.

In summary, the harms associated with the opioid crisis extend beyond those experienced by people who use opioids. This chapter discusses three insights about families' role in the opioid crisis that do not receive enough attention: (1) Family members of individuals with OUD often suffer financial, emotional, and sometimes physical burdens because of that OUD; (2) OUD's harms to society are often intermediated through effects on family; and (3) family members can play an integral role at helping individuals with OUD seek and remain in treatment; however, there may also be times when family members may also act as barriers to recovery and change. Furthermore, while what we have stated in this chapter applies to OUD, these insights may be generalizable to individuals suffering from substance use disorder more broadly.

References

AAMFT—*See* American Association for Marriage and Family Therapy.

Adam, Marianne, and Erin Kitt-Lewis, "Family Members Lived Experience with an Opioid Addicted Loved One," *Journal of Addictive Diseases*, Vol. 38, No. 4, 2020, pp. 475–481.

Adams, Jerome M., "Increasing Naloxone Awareness and Use: The Role of Health Care Practitioners," *JAMA*, Vol. 319, No. 20, 2018, pp. 2073–2074.

Altarum, "Economic Toll of Opioid Crisis in U.S. Exceeded $1 Trillion Since 2001," February 13, 2018. As of May 25, 2022:
https://altarum.org/news/economic-toll-opioid-crisis-us-exceeded-1-trillion-2001

American Association for Marriage and Family Therapy, "Helping Families Overcome Opioid Addiction," *Family Therapy Magazine*, Vol. 17, No. 4, 2018.

Anton, Raymond F., Izola Hogan, Behnaz Jalali, Charles Riordan, and Herbert D. Kleber, "Multiple Family Therapy and Naltrexone in the Treatment of Opiate Dependence," *Drug and Alcohol Dependence*, Vol. 8, No. 2, 1981, pp. 157–168.

AP-NORC—*See* The Associated Press–NORC Center for Public Affairs Research.

The Associated Press–NORC Center for Public Affairs Research, *Americans Recognize the Growing Problem of Opioid Addiction*, Chicago, Ill., Issue Brief, April 2018.

Archer, Marc, Hannah Harwood, Sharon Stevelink, Laura Rafferty, and Neil Greenberg, "Community Reinforcement and Family Training and Rates of Treatment Entry: A Systematic Review," *Addiction*, Vol. 115, No. 6, June 2020, pp. 1024–1037.

Bagley, Sarah M., Alicia S. Ventura, Karen E. Lasser, and Fred Muench, "Engaging the Family in the Care of Young Adults with Substance Use Disorders," *Pediatrics*, Vol. 147, Suppl. 2, 2021, pp. S215–S219.

Barnard, Mairna, and Neil McKeganey, "The Impact of Parental Problem Drug Use on Children: What Is the Problem and What Can Be Done to Help?" *Addiction*, Vol. 99, No. 5, 2004, pp. 552–559.

Barth, Richard P., Chung Kwon Lee, Judith Wildfire, and Shenyang Guo, "A Comparison of the Governmental Costs of Long-Term Foster Care and Adoption," *Social Service Review*, Vol. 80, No. 1, 2006, pp. 127–158.

Binswanger, Ingrid A., Marc F. Stern, Richard A. Deyo, Patrick J. Heagerty, Allen Cheadle, Joann G. Elmore, and Thomas D. Koepsell, "Release from Prison—A High Risk of Death for Former Inmates," *New England Journal of Medicine*, Vol. 356, No. 2, 2007, pp. 157–165.

Birnbaum, Howard G., Alan G. White, Matt Schiller, Tracy Waldman, Jody M. Cleveland, and Carl L. Roland, "Societal Costs of Prescription Opioid Abuse, Dependence, and Misuse in the United States," *Pain Medicine*, Vol. 12, No. 4, April 2011, pp. 657–667.

Bullinger, Lindsey Rose, and Coady Wing, "How Many Children Live with Adults with Opioid Use Disorder?" *Children and Youth Services Review*, Vol. 104, 2019.

Casey Family Programs, *How Can Family-Based Residential Treatment Programs Help Reduce Substance Use and Improve Child Welfare Outcomes?* Seattle, Wash., August 2019.

Cavacuiti, Chris A., "You, Me . . . and Drugs—A Love Triangle: Important Considerations When Both Members of a Couple Are Abusing Substances," *Substance Use & Misuse*, Vol. 39, No. 4, 2004, pp. 645–656.

Conrad, Caitlin, Heather M. Bradley, Dita Broz, Swamy Buddha, Erika L. Chapman, Romeo R. Galang, Daniel Hillman, John Hon, Karen W. Hoover, Monita R. Patel, et al., "Community Outbreak of HIV Infection Linked to Injection Drug Use of Oxymorphone—Indiana, 2015," *Morbidity and Mortality Weekly Report*, Vol. 64, No. 16, 2015, pp. 443–444.

Conradt, Elisabeth, Tess Flannery, Judy L. Aschner, Robert D. Annett, Lisa A. Croen, Cristiane S. Duarte, Alexander M. Friedman, Constance Guille, Monique M. Hedderson, Julie A. Hofheimer, et al., "Prenatal Opioid Exposure: Neurodevelopmental Consequences and Future Research Priorities," *Pediatrics*, Vol. 144, No. 3, 2019.

Copello, Alex G., Lorna Templeton, and Jane E. Powell, "The Impact of Addiction on the Family: Estimates of Prevalence and Costs," *Drugs: Education, Prevention, and Policy*, Vol. 17, Suppl. 1, 2010, pp. 63–74.

Crowley, Jenny L., and Laura E. Miller, "How People with Opioid Use Disorder Communicatively Experience Family: A Family Systems Approach," *Journal of Family Communication*, Vol. 20, No. 4, 2020, pp. 298–312.

Daley, Dennis C., "Family and Social Aspects of Substance Use Disorders and Treatment," *Journal of Food and Drug Analysis*, Vol. 21, No. 4, 2013, pp. S73–S76.

Daley, Dennis C., Erin Smith, Daniel Balogh, and Jodi Toscaloni, "Forgotten But Not Gone: The Impact of the Opioid Epidemic and Other Substance Use Disorders on Families and Children," *Commonwealth*, Vol. 20, No. 2–3, 2018.

Davis, Donald D., and Donald I. Templer, "Neurobehavioral Functioning in Children Exposed to Narcotics in Utero," *Addictive Behaviors*, Vol. 13, No. 3, 1988, pp. 275–283.

Davis, Margot Trotter, Marji Erikson Warfield, Janet Boguslaw, Dakota Roundtree-Swain, and Gretchen Kellogg, "Parenting a 6-Year Old Is Not What I Planned in Retirement: Trauma and Stress Among Grandparents Due to the Opioid Crisis," *Journal of Gerontological Social Work*, Vol. 63, No. 4, 2020, pp. 295–315.

Dolbin-MacNab, Megan L., and Lyn M. O'Connell, "Grandfamilies and the Opioid Epidemic: A Systemic Perspective and Future Priorities," *Clinical Child and Family Psychology Review*, Vol. 24, No. 2, 2021, pp. 207–223.

Dopp, Alex R., Jennifer K. Manuel, Joshua Breslau, Barbara Lodge, Brian Hurley, Courtney Kase, and Karen Chan Osilla, "Value of Family Involvement in Substance Use Disorder Treatment: Aligning Clinical and Financing Priorities," *Journal of Substance Use and Addiction Treatment*, Vol. 132, January 2022.

Dorius, Cassandra, Shawn Dorius, Heather Rouse, Elizabeth Richey, Elizabeth Talbert, Kelsey Van Selous, and Darien Bahe, *Substance Use Among Iowa Families: An Intergenerational Mixed Method Approach for Informing Policy and Practice*, Iowa Department of Public Health, 2020.

Drake, Jasmine, Creaque Charles, Jennifer W. Bourgeois, Elycia S. Daniel, and Melissa Kwende, "Exploring the Impact of the Opioid Epidemic in Black and Hispanic Communities in the United States," *Drug Science, Policy and Law*, Vol. 6, 2020.

Egeland, Byron, Deborah Jacobvitz, and L. Alan Sroufe, "Breaking the Cycle of Abuse," *Child Development*, Vol. 59, No. 4, August 1988, pp. 1080–1088.

Eichel, Larry, and Meagan Pharis, Poll Shows Impact of Opioid Crisis on Philadelphians and Their Neighborhoods, Philadelphia, Pa.: PEW Charitable Trusts, August 6, 2019.

El-Bassel, Nabila, Steven Shoptaw, David Goodman-Meza, and Hiromi Ono, "Addressing Long Overdue Social and Structural Determinants of the Opioid Epidemic," *Drug and Alcohol Dependence*, Vol. 222, 2021.

Ellis, Jennifer D., Stella M. Resko, Suzanne Brown, Elizabeth Agius, Rachel Kollin, and Viktor Burlaka, "Correlates of Expressed Emotion Among Family Members of Individuals Who Sought Treatment for Opioid Use," *Journal of Nervous and Mental Disease*, Vol. 208, No. 11, 2020, pp. 870–875.

Fals-Stewart, William, and Timothy J. O'Farrell, "Behavioral Family Counseling and Naltrexone for Male Opioid-Dependent Patients," *Journal of Consulting and Clinical Psychology*, Vol. 71, No. 3, 2003, pp. 432–442.

Feder, Kenneth A., Elizabeth J. Letourneau, and Jody Brook, "Children in the Opioid Epidemic: Addressing the Next Generation's Public Health Crisis," *Pediatrics*, Vol. 143, No. 1, 2019.

Fleming, C. J. Eubanks, "Do as I Say, Not as I Do? An Examination of the Relationship Between Partner Behaviors and Help Seeking for Alcohol Related Issues," *Substance Use & Misuse*, Vol. 51, No. 9, 2016, pp. 1185–1194.

Ghertner, Robin, and Mir M. Ali, *Treatment for Opioid Use Disorder May Reduce Substantiated Cases of Child Abuse and Neglect*, Washington, D.C.: U.S. Department of Health and Human Services, Office of the Assistant Secretary for Planning and Evaluation, January 2021.

Haffajee, Rebecca L., Samantha Cherney, and Rosanna Smart, "Legal Requirements and Recommendations to Prescribe Naloxone," *Drug and Alcohol Dependence*, Vol. 209, 2020.

Haggerty, Kevin P., Martie Skinner, Charles B. Fleming, Randy R. Gainey, and Richard F. Catalano, "Long-Term Effects of the Focus on Families Project on Substance Use Disorders Among Children of Parents in Methadone Treatment," *Addiction*, Vol. 103, No. 12, 2008, pp. 2008–2016.

Halford, W. Kim, and Sue M. Osgarby, "Alcohol Abuse Clients Presenting with Marital Problems," *Journal of Family Psychology*, Vol. 6, No. 3, 1993, pp. 245–254.

Hans, S. L., "Prenatal Drug Exposure: Behavioral Functioning in Late Childhood and Adolescence," *NIDA Research Monographs*, Vol. 164, 1996, pp. 261–276.

Hedges, Kristin E., "A Family Affair: Contextual Accounts from Addicted Youth Growing Up in Substance Using Families," *Journal of Youth Studies*, Vol. 15, No. 3, 2012, pp. 257–272.

Huhn, Andrew S., and Kelly E. Dunn, "Challenges for Women Entering Treatment for Opioid Use Disorder," *Current Psychiatry Reports*, Vol. 22, No. 12, 2020, pp. 1–10.

Jääskeläinen, Marke, Marja Holmila, Irma-Leena Notkola, and Kirsimarja Raitasalo, "Mental Disorders and Harmful Substance Use in Children of Substance Abusing Parents: A Longitudinal Register-Based Study on a Complete Birth Cohort Born in 1991," *Drug and Alcohol Review*, Vol. 35, No. 6, November 2016, pp. 728–740.

Jalali, Mohammad S., Michael Botticelli, Rachael C. Hwang, Howard K. Koh, and R. Kathryn McHugh, "The Opioid Crisis: A Contextual, Social-Ecological Framework," *Health Research Policy and Systems*, Vol. 18, No. 87, 2020, pp. 1–9.

Johnson, Kaprea F., Allison Worth, and Dana Brookover, "Families Facing the Opioid Crisis: Content and Frame Analysis of YouTube Videos," *Family Journal*, Vol. 27, No. 2, 2019, pp. 209–220.

Kameg, Brayden N., "Modernizing Perinatal Substance Use Management," *Policy, Politics, & Nursing Practice*, Vol. 22, No. 2, 2021, pp. 146–155.

Kerensky, Todd, and Alexander Y. Walley, "Opioid Overdose Prevention and Naloxone Rescue Kits: What We Know and What We Don't Know," *Addiction Science & Clinical Practice*, Vol. 12, No. 4, 2017, pp. 1–7.

Kleiman, M. A., "'Economic Cost' Measurements, Damage Minimization and Drug Abuse Control Policy," *Addiction*, Vol. 94, No. 5, 1999, pp. 638–641.

Kumar, Navin, William Oles, Benjamin A. Howell, Kamila Janmohamed, Selena T. Lee, Patrick G. O'Connor, and Marcus Alexander, "The Role of Social Network Support in Treatment Outcomes for Medication for Opioid Use Disorder: A Systematic Review," *Journal of Substance Abuse Treatment*, Vol. 127, 2021.

Lander, Laura, Janie Howsare, and Marilyn Byrne, "The Impact of Substance Use Disorders on Families and Children: From Theory to Practice," *Social Work in Public Health*, Vol. 28, No. 3–4, 2013, pp. 194–205.

Lester, Barry M., and Linda L. Lagasse, "Children of Addicted Women," *Journal of Addictive Diseases*, Vol. 29, No. 2, 2010, pp. 259–276.

Liang, T. Jake, and John W. Ward, "Hepatitis C in Injection-Drug Users—A Hidden Danger of the Opioid Epidemic," *New England Journal of Medicine*, Vol. 378, No. 13, 2018, pp. 1169–1171.

Lipari, Rachel N., and Struther L. Van Horn, *Children Living with Parents Who Have a Substance Use Disorder*, Washington, D.C.: Substance Abuse and Mental Health Services Administration, August 24, 2017.

Lochman, John E., and Antoinette van den Steenhoven, "Family-Based Approaches to Substance Abuse Prevention," *Journal of Primary Prevention*, Vol. 23, No. 1, 2002, pp. 49–114.

Maclean, Johanna C., Justine Mallatt, Christopher J., Ruhm, and Kosali Simon, *Economic Studies on the Opioid Crisis: A Review*, Cambridge, Mass.: National Bureau of Economic Research, Working Paper, No. 28067, 2020.

Maina, Geoffrey, Marcella Ogenchuk, Taryn Phaneuf, and Abukari Kwame, "'I Can't Live Like That': The Experience of Caregiver Stress of Caring for a Relative with Substance Use Disorder," *Substance Abuse Treatment, Prevention, and Policy*, Vol. 16, No. 11, 2021.

Matusow, Harlan, Samuel L. Dickman, Josiah D. Rich, Chunki Fong, Dora M. Dumont, Carolyn Hardin, Douglas Marlowe, and Andrew Rosenblum, "Medication Assisted Treatment in US Drug Courts: Results from a Nationwide Survey of Availability, Barriers and Attitudes," *Journal of Substance Abuse Treatment*, Vol. 44, No. 5, 2013, pp. 473–480.

McBain, Ryan K., Andrew Dick, Mark Sorbero, and Bradley D. Stein, "Growth and Distribution of Buprenorphine-Waivered Providers in the United States, 2007–2017," *Annals of Internal Medicine*, Vol. 172, No. 7, 2020, pp. 504–506.

McCollister, Kathryn E., Michael T. French, and Hai Fang, "The Cost of Crime to Society: New Crime-Specific Estimates for Policy and Program Evaluation," *Drug and Alcohol Dependence*, Vol. 108, No. 1–2, 2010, pp. 98–109.

McFarlane, Alexander C., "The Long-Term Costs of Traumatic Stress: Intertwined Physical and Psychological Consequences," *World Psychiatry*, Vol. 9, No. 1, 2010, pp. 3–10.

McLellan, A. Thomas, "Have We Evaluated Addiction Treatment Correctly? Implications from a Chronic Care Perspective," *Addiction*, Vol. 97, No. 3, 2002, pp. 249–252.

Meinhofer, Angélica, and Yohanis Angleró-Díaz, "Trends in Foster Care Entry Among Children Removed from Their Homes Because of Parental Drug Use, 2000 to 2017," *JAMA Pediatrics*, Vol. 173, No. 9, 2019, pp. 881–883.

Meyers, Robert J., and Brenda L. Wolfe, *Get Your Loved One Sober: Alternatives to Nagging, Pleading, and Threatening*, Center City, Minn.: Hazelden, 2004.

Mihalec-Adkins, Brittany Paige, Elizabeth Coppola, Denise A. Hines, Sarah Verbiest, and Shelley MacDermid Wadsworth, *Juggling Child Protection and the Opioid Epidemic: Lessons from Family Impact Seminars*, National Council on Family Relations, Policy Brief, Vol. 5, No. 2, 2020.

Morgan, Paul L., and Yangyang Wang, "The Opioid Epidemic, Neonatal Abstinence Syndrome, and Estimated Costs for Special Education Services," *American Journal of Managed Care*, Vol. 25, Suppl. 13, July 2019, pp. s264–s269.

Myers, B., N. Fakier, and J. Louw, "Stigma, Treatment Beliefs, and Substance Abuse Treatment Use in Historically Disadvantaged Communities," *African Journal of Psychiatry*, Vol. 12, No. 3, 2009.

National Association for Children of Addiction, *Children Impacted by Addiction: A Toolkit for Educators*, Kensington, Md., 2018.

National Conference of State Legislatures, "The Child Welfare Placement Continuum: What's Best for Children?" webpage, November 3, 2019. As of November 6, 2020: https://www.ncsl.org/research/human-services/the-child-welfare-placement-continuum-what-s-best-for-children.aspx

Nayak, Sandeep M., Andrew S. Huhn, Cecilia L. Bergeria, Eric C. Strain, and Kelly E. Dunn, "Familial Perceptions of Appropriate Treatment Types and Goals for a Family Member Who Has Opioid Use Disorder," *Drug and Alcohol Dependence*, Vol. 221, 2021.

Nicosia, Nancy, Rosalie Liccardo Pacula, Beau Kilmer, Russell Lundberg, and James Chiesa, *The Economic Cost of Methamphetamine Use in the United States, 2005*, Santa Monica, Calif.: RAND Corporation, MG-829-MPF/NIDA, 2009. As of May 25, 2022: https://www.rand.org/pubs/monographs/MG829.html

Normile, Becky, Carrie Hanlon, and Hannah Eichner, *State Strategies to Meet the Needs of Young Children and Families Affected by the Opioid Crisis*, Washington, D.C.: National Academy for State Health Policy, 2018.

Nygaard, Egil, Vibeke Moe, Kari Slinning, and Kristine B. Walhovd, "Longitudinal Cognitive Development of Children Born to Mothers with Opioid and Polysubstance Use," *Pediatric Research*, Vol. 78, No. 3, 2015, pp. 330–335.

Ólafsdóttir, Jóna, Tarja Orjasniemi, and Steinunn Hrafnsdóttir, "Psychosocial Distress, Physical Illness, and Social Behaviour of Close Relatives to People with Substance Use Disorders," *Journal of Social Work Practice in the Addictions*, Vol. 20, No. 2, 2020, pp. 136–154.

Ornoy, Asher, Jacob Segal, Rachel Bar-Hamburger, and Charles Greenbaum, "Developmental Outcome of School-Age Children Born to Mothers with Heroin Dependency: Importance of Environmental Factors," *Developmental Medicine and Child Neurology*, Vol. 43, No. 10, 2001, pp. 668–675.

Osilla, Karen Chan, Kirsten Becker, Liisa Ecola, Brian Hurley, Jennifer K. Manuel, Allison Ober, Susan M. Paddock, and Katherine E. Watkins, "Study Design to Evaluate a Group-Based Therapy for Support Persons of Adults on Buprenorphine/Naloxone," *Addiction Science and Clinical Practice*, Vol. 15, No. 25, 2020.

Osilla, Karen Chan, Eric R. Pedersen, Anagha Tolpadi, Stefanie Stern Howard, Jessica L. Phillips, and Kristie L. Gore, "The Feasibility of a Web-Intervention for Military Veteran Spouses Concerned About Their Partner's Alcohol Misuse," *Journal of Behavioral Health Services and Research*, Vol. 45, No. 1, 2016, pp. 57–73.

Osilla, Karen Chan, Thomas E. Trail, Eric R. Pedersen, Kristie L. Gore, Anagha Tolpadi, and Lindsey M. Rodriguez, "Efficacy of a Web-Based Intervention for Concerned Spouses of Service Members and Veterans with Alcohol Misuse," *Journal of Marital and Family Therapy*, Vol. 44, No. 2, 2018, pp. 292–306.

Ozechowski, Timothy J., and Howard A. Liddle, "Family-Based Therapy for Adolescent Drug Abuse: Knowns and Unknowns," *Clinical Child and Family Psychology Review*, Vol. 3, No. 4, 2000, pp. 269–298.

Patrick, Stephen W., Audrey M. Bauer, Michael D. Warren, Timothy F. Jones, and Carolyn Wester, "Hepatitis C Virus Infection Among Women Giving Birth—Tennessee and United States, 2009–2014," *Morbidity and Mortality Weekly Report*, Vol. 66, No. 18, 2017, pp. 470–473.

Patrick, Stephen W., Richard G. Frank, Elizabeth McNeer, and Bradley D. Stein, "Improving the Child Welfare System to Respond to the Needs of Substance-Exposed Infants," *Hospital Pediatrics*, Vol. 9, No. 8, 2019, pp. 651–654.

Patrick, Stephen W., Robert E. Schumacher, Brian D. Benneyworth, Elizabeth E. Krans, Jennifer M. McAllister, and Matthew M. Davis, "Neonatal Abstinence Syndrome and Associated Health Care Expenditures: United States, 2000–2009," *JAMA*, Vol. 307, No. 18, 2012, pp. 1934–1940.

Romanowicz, Magdalena, Jennifer L. Vande Voort, Julia Shekunov, Tyler S. Oesterle, Nuria J. Thusius, Teresa A. Rummans, Paul E. Croarkin, Victor M. Karpyak, Brian A. Lynch, and Kathryn M. Schak, "The Effects of Parental Opioid Use on the Parent-Child Relationship and Children's Developmental and Behavioral Outcomes: A Systematic Review of Published Reports," *Child and Adolescent Psychiatry and Mental Health*, Vol. 13, 2019.

Scharf, Becca M., David J. Sabat, James M. Brothers, Asa M. Margolis, and Matthew J. Levy, "Best Practices for A Novel EMS-Based Naloxone Leave Behind Program," *Prehospital Emergency Care*, Vol. 25, No. 3, 2021, pp. 418–426.

Seibert, Julie, Holly Stockdale, Rose Feinberg, Erin Dobbins, Elysha Theis, and Sarita L. Karon, *State Policy Levers for Expanding Family-Centered Medication-Assisted Treatment*, Washington, D.C.: Office of the Assistance Secretary for Planning and Evaluation, 2019.

Slinning, K., "Foster Placed Children Prenatally Exposed to Poly-Substances—Attention-Related Problems at Ages 2 and 4 1/2," *European Child & Adolescent Psychiatry*, Vol. 13, No. 1, 2004, pp. 19–27.

Smith, Jane Ellen, and Robert J. Meyers, *Motivating Substance Abusers to Enter Treatment: Working with Family Members*, New York: The Guilford Press, 2007.

Stanik, Christine, *Collateral Damage of the Opioid Crisis: Grandparents Raising Grandchildren— What They Need and How to Help*, Ann Arbor, Mich.: Altarum, 2020.

Stanton, M. D., and W. R. Shadish, "Outcome, Attrition, and Family–Couples Treatment for Drug Abuse: A Meta-Analysis and Review of the Controlled, Comparative Studies," *Psychological Bulletin*, Vol. 122, No. 2, 1997, pp. 170–191.

Stein, Bradley D., *Addressing the U.S. Opioid Crisis: Using an Integrated Systems-Based Approach*, Santa Monica, Calif.: RAND Corporation, CT-520, 2019. As of June 15, 2022: https://www.rand.org/pubs/testimonies/CT520.html

Stulac, Sara, Megan Bair-Merritt, Elisha M. Wachman, Marilyn Augustyn, Carey Howard, Namrata Madoor, and Eileen Costello, "Children and Families of the Opioid Epidemic: Under the Radar," *Current Problems in Pediatric and Adolescent Health Care*, Vol. 49, No. 8, 2019.

Substance Abuse and Mental Health Services Administration, *Community Reinforcement and Family Training (CRAFT) Intervention Summary*, Washington, D.C., 2013.

Thomas, Edwin J., and Richard D. Agar, "Unilateral Family Therapy with the Spouses of Uncooperative Alcohol Abusers," in Timothy J. O'Farrell, ed., *Treating Alcohol Problems: Marital and Family Interventions*, New York: Guilford Press, 1993, pp. 3–33.

Toneatto, Tony, Linda C. Sobell, Mark B. Sobell, and Eric Rubel, "Natural Recovery from Cocaine Dependence," *Psychology of Addictive Behaviors*, Vol. 13, No. 4, 1999, pp. 259–268.

Wagner, Karla D., Robert W. Harding, Richard Kelley, Brian Labus, Silvia R. Verdugo, Elizabeth Copulsky, Jeanette M. Bowles, Maria Luisa Mittal, and Peter J. Davidson, "Post-Overdose Interventions Triggered by Calling 911: Centering the Perspectives of People Who Use Drugs (PWUDs)," *PLoS One*, Vol. 14, No. 10, 2019.

White, Alan G., Howard G. Birnbaum, Dov B. Rothman, and Nathaniel Katz, "Development of a Budget-Impact Model to Quantify Potential Cost Savings from Prescription Opioids Designed to Deter Abuse or Ease of Extraction," *Applied Health Economics and Health Policy*, Vol. 7, No. 1, 2009, pp. 61–70.

Wilder Research and Volunteers of America, *Family-Based Residential Treatment: Directory of Residential Substance Use Disorder Treatment Programs for Parents with Children*, St. Paul, Minn., March 2019, updated July 2019.

Winkelman, Tyler N. A., Nicole Villapiano, Katy B. Kozhimannil, Matthew M. Davis, and Stephen W. Patrick, "Incidence and Costs of Neonatal Abstinence Syndrome Among Infants with Medicaid: 2004–2014," *Pediatrics*, Vol. 141, No. 4, 2018.

Winstanley, Erin L., "The Bell Tolls for Thee and Thine: Compassion Fatigue and the Overdose Epidemic," *International Journal of Drug Policy*, Vol. 85, 2020.

Winstanley, Erin L., and Amanda N. Stover, "The Impact of the Opioid Epidemic on Children and Adolescents," *Clinical Therapeutics*, Vol. 41. No. 9, 2019, pp. 1655–1662.

Wittenberg, Eve, Jeremy W. Bray, Brandon Aden, Achamyeleh Gebremariam, Bohdan Nosyk, and Bruce R. Schackman, "Measuring Benefits of Opioid Misuse Treatment for Economic Evaluation: Health-Related Quality of Life of Opioid-Dependent Individuals and Their Spouses as Assessed by a Sample of the US Population," *Addiction*, Vol. 111, No. 4, 2016, pp. 675–684.

CHAPTER FOUR

Specialty Treatment System for Opioid Use Disorders

Bradley D. Stein, Martin Y. Iguchi, Karen Osilla, Jirka Taylor

Overview

The primary objective of the substance use disorder (SUD) specialty treatment system is to assist individuals in their attempts to reduce or stop use of substances and to decrease associated harms of SUDs; in this chapter, we focus on individuals living with an opioid use disorder (OUD). Given the chronic, relapsing nature of SUDs and common challenges to seeking and obtaining treatment, the system involves a variety of activities over the course of the disorder, including successfully identifying at-risk individuals, engaging individuals in treatment, providing evidence-supported treatment, and keeping individuals in treatment long enough for it to be effective. The SUD specialty treatment system also often plays an important role in monitoring and supporting patients who are in remission, along with reengaging individuals who have relapsed.

The primary care system has taken a more active role in treating OUD. Buprenorphine and specialty substance use providers are playing an important supportive role in telehealth systems, providing expert advice in what has been described as a *hub-and-spoke* approach. Thus, for example, the specialty treatment system might serve as an important backbone for inexperienced buprenorphine providers via remote consultations in the prescribing and management of buprenorphine for patients living with an OUD.

Key Interactions with Other Components of the Ecosystem

The SUD specialty treatment system is closely linked with the **medical care system** described in the following chapter on multiple dimensions. Individuals with OUDs have high rates of both physical health and mental health comorbidities that, if untreated, can significantly complicate treatment of OUD and increase rates of OUD-related morbidity and mortality. Increasing numbers of individuals with OUD are being treated by providers in the traditional medical system, most commonly with formulations of buprenorphine and buprenorphine and naloxone indicated for treatment of OUD (hereafter BUP), a medication treatment for OUD that is one of the most-effective treatments available. The SUD specialty treatment system is also closely linked to the medical care system with respect to insurance and how services are paid for; commercial and public insurers oversee many factors that influence treatment, including but not limited to reimbursement rates for OUD treatment services; the nature of services that are covered; requirements for prior authorizations; levels of care; treatment episode and lifetime treatment caps; provider credentialing; and SUD treatment networks.

The SUD specialty treatment system is also closely linked with the **criminal legal system.** Increasingly, the criminal legal system is pursuing opportunities to divert individuals with OUD from jails to treatment. Drug courts—and later, family drug courts—were introduced in 1989, growing to more than 3,500 in 2021 (U.S. Department of Justice, Office of Justice Programs, 2021). These are increasingly used as tools to connect individuals and families to effective treatment and potentially to divert some individuals from incarceration. Prearrest diversion strategies, such as Law Enforcement Assisted Diversion (LEAD) and the Police Assisted Addiction and Recovery Initiative (PAARI), are being adopted in communities around the country (The Police Assisted Addiction and Recovery Initiative, undated; Saloner et al., 2018). Such strategies connect individuals with SUDs to community-based treatment, diverting them from more-extensive involvement in the justice system.

However, in many of these drug courts, individuals are denied access to the most-effective medication treatments for OUD (Matusow et al., 2013). Furthermore, approximately half of incarcerated individuals have an SUD, and according to a classic 2007 study in the state of Washington, incarcerated individuals have an elevated risk of death in first two weeks after release; fatal overdoses are the most common cause of those deaths. As a result, the SUD specialty treatment system is increasingly involved in efforts to initiate medications for OUD (MOUD) before prisoners are released and connect newly released prisoners to treatment programs in their communities (Moore et al., 2019); connection to treatment is likely to substantially reduce the risk of overdose, relapse following release, and potentially the risk of reoffending (Kinlock et al., 2009; Malta et al., 2019; Mattick et al., 2009).

Links between the SUD specialty treatment system and the **illegal supply system** are weaker and less direct, in no small part because methadone prescribed to treat OUD, as opposed to prescriptions for chronic pain, has traditionally been required to be taken on-site, limiting diversion; most overdoses from methadone are of methadone diverted from pain treatment, not MOUD (Reuter, 2009). Medication to treat OUD such as BUP and methadone can be diverted for illicit use. However, the amount of methadone diverted for illicit use from treatment for OUD is quite modest compared with other diverted opioids. BUP, or the most commonly used formulation known as Suboxone® (BUP and naloxone) is also diverted, but Suboxone® is used primarily to self-treat OUD or prevent the onset of opioid withdrawal symptoms: The blended naloxone component remains inert unless injected, resulting in severe opioid withdrawal.

In many locations, the SUD specialty treatment system and the **child welfare system** are closely linked in efforts to provide treatment to the many adults living with OUD involved in the child welfare system. These efforts include but are not limited to comprehensive family-based treatment programs—specialized programs that enable the family to stay together. The programs often provide SUD treatment, therapy, parenting skills training, life skills, and job readiness education, supported by professional staff who ensure the safety of children while their parents and families achieve abstinence from opioids and recovery (Wilder Research and Volunteers of America, 2019). Efforts also include family drug courts, in which parents who have SUDs receive supports and must participate in services as a condition of retaining custody of their children.

The SUD specialty treatment system also interacts in multiple ways with the **employment system**. Effective treatment for individuals with OUD and their family members is often critical to enabling such individuals to remain employed and productive. Employers also greatly influence health insurance benefit design, which directly affects the generosity of insurance benefits that cover specialty SUD treatment among commercially insured populations.

There are also several areas in which the interactions are currently modest, but greater interactions might significantly improve outcomes. For example, many individuals with OUD also experience housing insecurity and homelessness, with rates of 33 percent in some populations (Iheanacho, Stefanovics, and Rosenheck, 2018), and housing insecurity is associated with poorer outcomes for individuals receiving OUD treatment. There are also multiple dimensions on which the specialty SUD treatment system overlaps with homeless service agencies and housing. Another potential opportunity lies with first responders (Elliott, Bennett, and Wolfson-Stofko, 2019), who often interact with individuals not currently engaged in treatment who have overdosed and are at higher risk of subsequent overdose (Bagley et al., 2019; Kelty and Hulse, 2017; Olfson et al., 2018). Several communities now have programs in which first responders are working to link individuals with opioid problems to treatment services (Formica et al., 2018; Streisel et al., 2019; Wagner et al., 2010). Several preliminary studies suggest that simple interventions provided by first responders may provide an opportunity to increase subsequent treatment engagement for those individuals (Langabeer et al., 2020), although the effectiveness of such approaches has yet to be evaluated.

Policy Opportunities and Considerations

Given that the SUD specialty treatment system is not extensive or robust enough to address the unmet need for treatment for OUD, policymakers should continue to expand access to effective treatment by supporting the development of networks linking buprenorphine-prescribing primary care providers (PCPs) and SUD treatment experts. The latter, working in specialty clinics, can give PCPs clinical support, consultation, and an option for the timely referral of more-complicated patients who require greater clinical expertise that is likely to result in improved outcomes (Watkins et al., 2017b). These approaches, first used on a wide scale in Vermont and New Mexico, are now being implemented in several states (Dahlhamer et al., 2018). These models contain many of the elements of collaborative care models used to improve treatment for depression, which have been successfully implemented in multiple large health systems (Katzelnick and Williams, 2015).

Policymakers should also continue to enhance efforts to increase effective treatment for individuals involved in the criminal legal system, including increasing access to MOUD among incarcerated individuals (Bandara et al., 2021) and facilitating access to treatment for individuals being released from incarceration (Kennedy-Hendricks et al., 2021).

Many individuals who misuse opioids remain disengaged from the treatment system because of a variety of factors, including stigmatization and criminalization. Locating and engaging those with OUD requires understanding hidden populations and how best to reach them and encourage them to get treatment, other services, or both.

Introduction

Effective specialty treatment for individuals with opioid and other drug-related problems is a critical component of the nation's response to the opioid crisis. This section provides an overview of the SUD specialty treatment system for individuals experiencing opioid and other drug-related problems, describes how the approach to treatment has evolved, and discusses some of the more common ways in which the treatment system interacts with other components of the ecosystem.

The SUD specialty treatment system comprises multiple levels of care, including outpatient and intensive outpatient services, opioid treatment programs dispensing methadone, partial hospital and residential treatment, and inpatient services.[1] It also comprises many different types of providers, including physicians with specialized expertise in providing treatment for SUDs, such as OUD; other health care and mental health clinicians, such as psychologists, social workers, and licensed clinicians; certified addiction counselors, or individuals who have received a certificate in the treatment of SUDs; and peer navigators, or individuals with lived experience. Because OUD is often chronic and characterized by relapse, the SUD cascade of care framework (Socías, Volkow, and Wood, 2016; Williams et al., 2018) is drawn from the HIV treatment cascade framework (Kay et al., 2016), which recognizes the importance of multiple sequential steps in the care of an individual with an OUD; therefore, this approach is an appropriate way to view the treatment process. The SUD system may be involved with many of these steps, including conducting outreach and diagnosis, engaging in treatment, providing effective treatment, retaining individuals in care during active treatment long enough for it to be effective, offering evidence-based treatments, preventing remission and relapse, and quickly reengaging individuals who have relapsed in treatment. Providing treatment to an individual with an OUD and other SUDs may span multiple levels of care, including residential treatment, partial hospital treatment, intensive outpatient services, and more-traditional outpatient services. In many cases, individuals would receive these services after receiving detoxification services, i.e., services designed to enable an individual who is physically dependent on opioids to undergo withdrawal more safely and comfortably. However, unlike in some other countries (Sumnall and Brotherhood, 2012), detoxification, which is intended to facilitate a medically safe withdrawal but not to change behaviors related to opioid misuse, is not commonly considered in the United States to be an effective treatment for OUD, and in many cases, individuals receiving detoxification are not successfully transitioned to treatment services following detoxification (Stein, Orlando, and Sturm, 2000; Stein, Kogan, and Sorbero, 2009). Relapse after detoxification often occurs rapidly; many studies report relapse rates as high as 82 percent, and 50 percent of people relapsed by week three,

---

[1] SUD and alcohol use disorder are two distinct diagnoses according to the *Diagnostic and Statistical Manual of Mental Disorders*. Unless noted otherwise, when this report uses the term *SUD*, it refers to drugs other than alcohol and tobacco.

whether they were using ultra-rapid detoxification (anesthesia-supported detox) or standard inpatient detox (Bradley et al., 1989; O'Connor, 2005).

Today, the SUD system is commonly considered part of the health care system, although it is considered separately in this report given its importance in the treatment of OUD. Historically, however, SUDs in the United States were diagnosed and treated separately, whereas some other countries, e.g., European Union (EU) member states, made concerted effort to integrate SUD treatment into the larger health care system (European Monitoring Centre for Drugs and Drug Addiction [EMCDDA], 2011). Furthermore, in contrast to what often occurs in the United States, in other high-income countries, such as EU member states, SUD treatment is typically complemented by a suite of programs and interventions addressing the psychosocial needs of people who use drug and assisting them not only with the management and/or cessation of use but also with their social reintegration and do not include substantial numbers of for-profit providers (EMCDDA, 2017; Sumnall and Brotherhood, 2012).[2] In addition, this broader service provision is generally delivered in an environment with a comprehensive social safety net and higher levels of public social spending than in the United States (d'Agostino, Pieroni, and Scarlato, 2020; Hälg, Potrafke, and Sturm, 2020). For that reason, caution is required when thinking about transferrable lessons from other countries regarding possible treatment interventions. For instance, there is strong evidence from clinical trials that prescribing heroin as a form of medication treatment can lead to a variety of positive outcomes (see a review by Smart, 2018). However, this evidence comes from clinical trials conducted in countries with stronger wraparound and other social service provision than the United States so, while this is certainly not an argument against a U.S.-based trial, a question remains about the extent to which similar results could be expected from usual clinical practice in the United States.

It used to be the case that nonspecialty medical providers did not commonly treat SUD in the United States (Substance Abuse and Mental Health Services Administration [SAMHSA], 2016c). A separation increased in the 1970s when SUDs were often viewed as social problems to be addressed through civil or criminal legal interventions (SAMHSA, 2016c; White, 1998) and the dispensation of methadone. Methadone was the first medication approved for the treatment of OUD, through specialty opioid treatment programs that were distinct and separate from the medical system. In recent years, the SUD system has become more integrated with the medical system. Prior to the 1970s, the specialty SUD treatment system in the United States was relatively modest, but in the 1970s there was a major federal effort to expand treatment for SUD (SAMHSA, 2016b) and methadone was approved as the first medication treatment for OUD (Ali et al., 2017). However, the historical separation of SUD treatment from the rest of health care has likely contributed to lingering challenges to improving delivery of SUD services, including inadequate training for clinicians in health care training programs

---

[2] That said, there is substantial variation in the universe of service providers across countries, and it is possible to identify areas with relatively high representation of for-profit organizations. For instance, nearly half of residential treatment facilities in Sweden are for-profit (EMCDDA, 2014).

in identifying and treating SUD (D'Amico et al., 2005; Miller et al., 2001; O'Connor, Nyquist, and McLellan, 2011). Until the 2008 Mental Health Parity Addiction Equity Act and the 2010 Affordable Care Act (ACA), treatment for SUD has generally not been included as a covered health benefit in insurance (Humphreys and Frank, 2014).

System Components and How They Interact with Opioids

The goal of the SUD specialty system is to provide services in the least restrictive and least intensive setting that can safely and effectively treat individuals with OUD, given the severity of their illness and comorbidities, without creating an appreciable risk of diversion. SUD specialty services can be provided along a continuum of care reflecting a range of intensity, including inpatient services, high- and low-intensity residential services, partial hospital and intensive outpatient services, and more-traditional outpatient services (Figure 4.1). Individuals often move along the continuum of care as the severity of their illness waxes and wanes, and the criteria developed by the American Society of Addiction Medicine are often used to identify the level of care most appropriate for a patient at a given time (Mee-Lee et al., 2013).

OUD Treatment

Central to the effective treatment of OUD in the specialty SUD treatment system was the U.S. Food and Drug Administration's (FDA's) approval in 1972 of methadone, a full *mu*-opioid receptor agonist, for the maintenance treatment of individuals with OUD. That is, as an agonist, methadone triggers more or less the same neuroreceptors in the brain as does heroin, but oral formulations enter the brain with less speed, so individuals with OUD do not experience the intense high that they seek. Furthermore, methadone has a much longer half-life and requires only one dose per day, so people maintained on methadone experience a *normalized* state (without the rapid onset and withdrawal associated with commonly misused opioids) and develop a receptor-level tolerance to the drug that protects them from overdose and significantly diminishes the high from other consumed opioids. This combination of factors allows for relatively normal, productive lives, particularly when combined with effective psychosocial supports.

Initially, the idea of *substitution treatment*, or treating OUD with another opioid, was highly controversial. To understand how this form of treatment can help, it is sometimes useful to think about tobacco smokers. Most smokers are addicted to nicotine, but that SUD does not prevent individuals from functioning in normal life roles. Use of Nicorette, nicotine gum, or even vaping substitutes an addictive but much less harmful substance for another. However, one needs to be careful when referring to MOUD-like methadone or buprenorphine as substitutes for heroin and fentanyl. Technically, yes, the initial goal is for PWUO to substitute one opioid with another, and in the past this was even referred to as *opioid substitution therapy* or *opioid agonist therapy*. But this does not mean that the goal of MOUD is to substitute or trade one addiction or SUD for another. *Addiction* is best characterized as con-

FIGURE 4.1

SUD Treatment System and Its Interactions

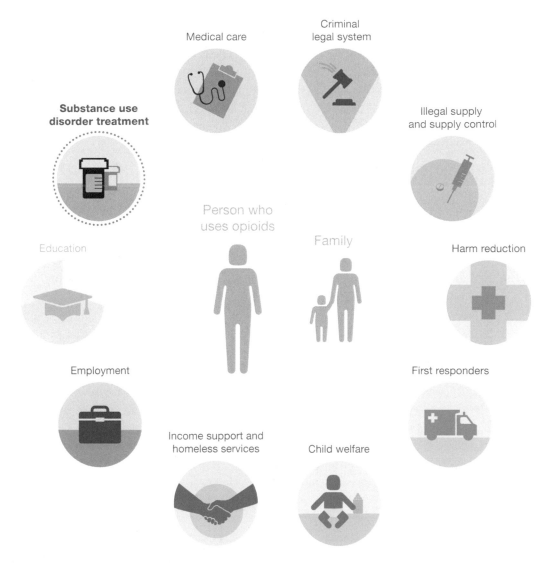

tinued use despite harmful consequences—which is different from being physically dependent on a drug (e.g., many of those with diabetes are dependent on insulin treatment, but not
addicted). When someone transitions to MOUD, they often will initially remain physically
dependent on opioids, but the goal is to make sure that they are no longer addicted to opioids.

Essential to opioid agonist therapy is the fact that—rather surprisingly—chronic use of
opioids is not unhealthy in terms of organ damage. Smoking or drinking alcohol heavily
cause long-term health harm (e.g., lung cancer and cirrhosis of the liver). Heroin and methadone are not like that. They are dangerous in terms of acute health harms; overdose is a very
real risk. But if one does not overdose, they are not particularly damaging drugs, although

they can have cardiotoxic effects (Alinejad et al., 2015). Most of the health harms that chronic heroin users suffer come from (1) injecting with nonsterile equipment, leading to such blood-borne infections as HIV, hepatitis B, hepatitis C, and soft-tissue injuries; (2) impurities in the heroin; (3) use of other drugs; (4) poor lifestyle choices leading to or exacerbating poverty; and (5) criminal legal involvement.

This approval of methadone changed the treatment landscape for individuals with OUD, adding a pharmacological treatment option to the nonpharmacological treatments that had been available until that point. Dispensed only through licensed OUD treatment programs, commonly referred to as *methadone clinics*, methadone was a more effective treatment for OUD than many of the nonpharmacological treatments commonly provided (Mattick et al., 2009). In addition, methadone clinics provided counseling and often case management services to patients, allowing clinics to address many of the psychosocial challenges experienced by many individuals with OUD. The restriction to clinics was driven in no small part by recognition that there is high demand for diverted methadone in illegal drug markets. Studies have shown an association between diversion of methadone from pain treatment and overdose deaths (Jones et al., 2016).[3] This is seen in plots over time in overdose deaths from methadone. They increased with the expansion of methadone's use in treating pain, not so much in proportion to methadone's use in treating OUD.

However, there remain many barriers to accessing methadone treatment. Opioid treatment programs, the only licensed providers of methadone to treat OUD, are located predominantly in urban areas (Center for Substance Abuse Treatment, 2006; Clark et al., 2011), and the programs commonly require patients to take methadone at the clinic daily to limit diversion; this limits easy availability of methadone for many individuals who are unable or unwilling to come to the clinic daily. Opioid treatment programs have a limited number of treatment slots, and there is often greater demand for treatment slots than there are available slots. Facility waiting lists can often be weeks long; in addition, the requirement to attend the clinic daily for most individuals can serve as a barrier, particularly for individuals who have full-time jobs or are caring for young children (Andrews et al., 2013; Center for Substance Abuse Treatment, 2006; Clark et al., 2011; Gryczynski et al., 2011; Rosenblum et al., 2011; Sigmon, 2014). And historically, methadone services have been funded primarily by Medicaid or state block grants, although in recent years Medicare has begun to reimburse for methadone treatment of OUD (Centers for Medicare & Medicaid Services [CMS], undated). As a result, even among individuals interested in receiving treatment for their OUD, the majority of individuals with OUDs historically have not, and continue not to, receive methadone (American Methadone Treatment Association, 1998; O'Brien, 2008).

The 2002 approval of BUP, a partial *mu*-opioid receptor agonist and kappa-opioid receptor antagonist, for OUD therapy was welcomed as an opportunity to increase access to treatment for many individuals (Ducharme and Abraham, 2008; O'Brien, 2008). BUP has

---

[3]   Research on relaxations of take-home rules during the coronavirus disease 2019 (COVID-19) pandemic generally found no association with overdose deaths (Jones et al., 2022).

an advantage over methadone in that it only partially occupies the *mu* receptor, preventing opioid overdose from occurring. BUP also has an advantage over methadone in that dosing can be increased, allowing those in treatment to avoid daily visits to the clinic. More recently, a monthly injectable form of BUP was approved for treatment of OUD, creating additional flexibility in administering to patients. Furthermore, withdrawal from BUP is relatively mild. BUP is indicated for the treatment of OUD alone and in combination with naloxone (Suboxone®). The Drug Addiction Treatment Act of 2000 allows physicians who were board certified in addiction medicine or psychiatry or who completed an approved course or were waivered from the special registration requirements in the Controlled Substances Act to prescribe medications such as BUP outside opioid treatment programs for up to 30 patients at any one time (S. 2634, 2000). The Office of National Drug Control Policy Reauthorization Act of 2006 modified restrictions to grant approval for treating up to 100 patients at a time to office-based physicians who had been waivered for at least a year, were currently treating patients with BUP, and had applied for the higher patient limit (Pub. L. 109-469, 2006). Waivered physicians increased the supply of available MOUD, particularly for individuals who would not or could not attend opioid treatment programs for geographical, ideological, or practical considerations (Clark et al., 2011; Fiellin and O'Connor, 2002; Oliva et al., 2011). More recently, in July 2016, the U.S. Department of Health and Human Services allowed certain waivered physicians who were qualified to treat 100 patients with OUD with BUP to obtain a 275-patient limit (SAMHSA, 2016a). The Comprehensive Addiction and Recovery Act of 2016 permitted physician assistants and nurse practitioners to obtain a waiver to prescribe BUP after completing certain training requirements (Jones and McCance-Katz, 2019).[4]

These changes substantially enhanced options for persons living with OUD. The number and geographic distribution of waivered physicians grew substantially (Dick et al., 2015), more SUD treatment facilities used BUP (SAMHSA, Center for Behavioral Health Statistics and Quality, 2013), and more BUP was dispensed (Stein et al., 2015). The past decade has seen a substantial increase in the number of waivered clinicians qualified to prescribe BUP, increasing from 3.80 to 17.29 per 100,000 persons from 2007 to 2017. More than 25 percent of waivered physicians have been certified to treat more than 30 patients with OUD with BUP (McBain et al., 2020). There are approximately 100,000 waivered clinicians as of July 2021 (SAMHSA, 2021b), largely made up of primary care physicians, psychiatrists, physician assistants, and nurse practitioners (Stein et al., 2021), yet the total number of BUP-waivered physicians is still estimated to be only approximately 5 percent of U.S. physicians and a relatively small proportion of physician assistants and nurse practitioners (Davis and Samuels, 2021; Olfson et al., 2020).

Many BUP-prescribing clinicians provide office-based treatment separate from the specialty SUD system, while others practice within such settings or with support from or connections to SUD experts through models such as hub-and-spoke, Project Extension for Community Healthcare Outcomes (ECHO), or collaborative care models discussed more

---

[4] After this volume went to press, legislation eliminated the requirement for the waiver.

extensively in the medical chapter. Given the magnitude of the population with an unmet need for MOUD treatment and the insufficient capacity of MOUD treatment availability, efforts are needed to expand effective treatment capacity in both the general medical system and the specialty system, with the expectation that BUP prescribers in the general medical system are likely to be better prepared to effectively treat individuals with less severe OUD and less complicated clinical presentations, and specialty providers will likely be serving individuals with more severe or complicated clinical presentations.

To provide context, if one believes that there are roughly 4 million individuals in the United States with OUD (see Chapter Two), and if each of these 100,000 clinicians treated 40 patients with OUD, there would be sufficient BUP treatment capacity for all individuals with OUD. In fact, it would likely be more than sufficient given that some individuals with OUD are receiving methadone treatment, doing well with nonpharmacological treatment, or not currently seeking treatment. Alternatively, if each of the estimated 489,000 active primary care physicians and 55,878 active psychiatrists were to treat eight individuals with OUD with buprenorphine, it would also provide sufficient capacity for the estimated 4 million individuals with OUD (Kaiser Family Foundation, 2021). Of course, such a back-of-the-envelope calculation does not take into account many factors that limit the availability of BUP beyond just requiring a waivered clinician to prescribe it. Not all clinicians are practicing in appropriate settings to provide such treatment, many likely already have full caseloads, and there are moderately low levels of interest and high levels of stigma among primary care physician in prescribing BUP (Stone et al., 2021). Furthermore, many clinicians waivered to prescribe BUP do not prescribe it at all (Thomas et al., 2017), and the majority of clinicians who do prescribe BUP to treat OUD treat relatively few patients (Duncan et al., 2020; Stein et al., 2016)—and often treat them for relatively short periods of time (Stein et al., 2021). There is poor access in more-rural counties (Andrilla et al., 2019), and rural patients often need to travel long distances for treatment (Lister et al., 2020). Many BUP prescribers do not accept insurance (Beetham et al. 2019; Patrick et al., 2020), and in a recent study from Texas, more than half of pharmacies did not have BUP on-hand to dispense (Hill et al., 2021).

Naltrexone is an opioid antagonist, meaning that it blocks opioids from occupying *mu*-opioid receptors, and extended-release (injectable) naltrexone is the third medication approved by the FDA to treat OUD. Naltrexone, which is nonaddictive and cannot result in overdose, is available as both daily pills and monthly injections. It can be prescribed by any individual licensed to prescribe medications, although it is used less commonly than either methadone or BUP as patients are more reluctant to initiate it, treatment adherence tends to be poor, and opioid use after naltrexone is more likely to result in overdose as naltrexone treatment participants do not develop tolerance to opioids. Furthermore, both BUP and methadone have been shown to decrease mortality among individuals with OUD (Larochelle et al., 2018; Ma et al., 2019; Santo et al., 2021; Vakkalanka et al., 2021), while decreased mortality is not something that has been associated with naltrexone.

A brief overview is useful to understanding some of the strengths and limitations of each of the agents. Because methadone and BUP are agonists or partial agonists with long half-lives that occupy the *mu*-opioid receptor site, they are medications that can be taken once a day to decrease opioid craving and withdrawal symptoms and thereby stabilize someone's life compared with taking a short-acting agonist, such as heroin. Full agonists, such as methadone, can produce respiratory depression and overdose if the dose is too high or if the drug is consumed with other substances that have sedative properties, such as alcohol, barbiturates, benzodiazepines, sleep aids, or muscle relaxants. Although it is safer than more-potent opioids, methadone can be a dangerous drug that commonly requires monitoring for safe use. Partial agonists, such as BUP, are much less likely to result in opioid overdose, as the partial agonist properties do not allow opioid receptor activation to the point of respiratory depression; however, when mixed with medications with sedative properties, BUP can result in respiratory depression and overdose (Park et al., 2020; Reynaud et al., 1998).

As agonists, both methadone and BUP have the possibility of generating a mild high, and the perception of the high can be enhanced by consuming other substances combined to blend the highs (Iguchi et al., 1993; Votaw et al., 2019); this is enhanced further by injecting the crushed powder form of either treatment formulation. Injection use is deterred, however, by the use of a viscous syrupy mixture in (generally observed) oral dosing of methadone and by the presence of naloxone in the buprenorphine and naloxone formulation. In stark contrast, naltrexone is a *mu*-opioid receptor antagonist that efficiently occupies the *mu*-opioid receptor without activation, effectively blocking opioids from activating the opioid receptor and any associated adverse outcomes.

Nonpharmacological Interventions

Although medication treatment for OUD on its own can be effective for some individuals, many individuals can benefit from concurrent nonpharmacological interventions. Behavioral interventions, such as contingency management (CM), motivational interviewing, and cognitive behavioral therapy have all been shown to be effective tools for adjunctive treatment of OUD and for reducing use of commonly used non-opioid substances while enrolled in medication treatment for OUD. However, nonpharmacological treatment, such as what is commonly referred to as *abstinence-based treatment*, often does not include such therapeutic approaches, and the nonpharmacological SUD services commonly provided that do not include these approaches do not have empirical support (Madras et al., 2020).

Contingency Management

CM is an effective, evidence-based approach for decreasing use of licit and illicit substances of use. CM, in essence, pays people to stop using drugs. As currently used in medication treatment for OUD programs, CM involves delivery of an incentive (e.g., cash, vouchers exchangeable for goods or services [Higgins et al., 1991], or clinic privileges) (Iguchi et al., 1988; Stitzer et al., 1993), contingent on demonstration of a prespecified target behavior or behaviors (e.g., providing a urine sample demonstrating abstinence, attending a counseling session, or meeting a treatment plan goal). The intent is to increase the probability that the target behavior will occur more frequently. Urine-verified abstinence is the most common target behavior, and vouchers exchangeable for goods or services are the most commonly used incentives in the many randomized controlled trials (RCTs) that use CM to reduce substance use in medication treatment for OUD programs. More than 100 RCTs (Davis et al., 2016; Prendergast et al., 2006) and seven meta-analyses demonstrate CM's effectiveness (Ainscough et al., 2017; Benishek et al., 2014; Dutra et al., 2008; Griffith et al., 2000; Lussier et al., 2006; Prendergast et al., 2006).

However, despite numerous demonstrations of effectiveness, CM is not commonly used in medication treatment for OUD programs. Oft-cited reasons include a lack of staff time to monitor the CM protocol over time and across numerous participants, stigma, a reluctance to pay for abstinence (Scott et al., 2021), a lack of resources or sources to pay for the contingencies (Ryan-Pettes, Devoto, and DeFulio, 2020), and a lack of evidence for longer-term efficacy. There are also philosophical issues regarding the use of CM because some clinicians feel that such behavioral approaches as CM do not address the underlying causes of addiction. For others who view addiction as a physiologic illness, CM makes it seem that an SUD is something that a patient can "choose to stop" (Petry et al., 2017). Indeed, CM does show that even people with SUD have some control over their behavior, even if they do not have control over the underlying condition. People can exercise control over their choices even when they cannot simply choose to undo the changes to their brain wrought by long-term drug use.

Many of these issues (other than stigma and a reluctance to pay for abstinence) appear to have been well addressed in the literature (Ginley et al., 2021). The problem of staff time and monitoring requirements might be partially overcome by using digital applications (apps) as demonstrated in nonmedication treatment for OUD settings and in studies of non-opioid SUDs. For example, Campbell and colleagues computerized a CM protocol to facilitate participant reward calculations, but the intervention still involved considerable staff time to collect and test the urine drug samples and to deliver the incentives (Campbell et al., 2014; Campbell et al., 2012). Reynolds and colleagues used a personal computer camera to record use of a breath carbon monoxide monitor in a CM study to promote smoking abstinence (Reynolds et al., 2015), while Alessi and Petry texted participants when it was time to provide a video recording of their breath alcohol test—using a smartphone application and camera to monitor testing and results (Alessi and Petry, 2013). Several mobile phone technologies have also been developed and are in various stages of implementation for delivery of CM in methadone treatment. For example, Metrebian and colleagues describe a mobile-phone-delivered CM intervention for reinforcing adherence to supervised medication consumption (Metrebian et al., 2021).

Motivational Interviewing and Cognitive Behavioral Therapies

There are also a variety of nonpharmacological approaches, such as motivational interviewing and cognitive behavioral therapies, that have been found to be effective in individuals with SUDs, although the evidence base specifically with respect to OUD is still evolving (DiClemente et al., 2017). Motivational interviewing is a directive counseling approach intended to support individuals in changing behavior by exploring and resolving ambivalence in a wide variety of situations and has been used to help individuals both decrease substance misuse and engage in treatment (Osilla et al., 2018; Otiashvili et al., 2012; Smedslund et al., 2011). Cognitive-behavioral approaches, in which a therapist works with a patient to examine the relationship between thoughts, feelings, and behaviors, have been shown to be effective in a wide variety of mental health disorders; these approaches have also shown promise in decreasing drug use and increasing retention in treatment (Barry et al., 2019; Moore et al., 2016; Nunes et al., 2006).

Opioid Use Disorder Treatment and the Family

At all levels of treatment and with all types of interventions, the specialty OUD treatment system commonly focuses on the individuals with the disorder; however, involving family can be an important but underappreciated component of treatment (Lodge, 2022). Family can be an important catalyst for engaging and keeping patients engaged in substance use treatment (Hunt and Azrin, 1973; Kirby et al., 1999; Meyers et al., 1998). Family members are more likely to recognize warning signs of substance misuse compared with the affected individual, who may not recognize or admit symptoms (Kaufmann, 1999; Sobell and Sobell, 1993). Family members also tend to be highly motivated and typically want to help the individual reduce their substance use, seek to improve their relationship with the individual being treated, and also want to alleviate their own difficulties associated with the family member's substance use (Halford and Osgarby, 1993; Thomas and Agar, 1993). Furthermore, many family members also struggle with OUD; unless all are engaged in treatment at the same time, these individuals may serve as a catalyst for use by the family members who are in treatment for OUD (Riehman et al., 2003; Willems et al., 1997). As a result, experts argue that the base of treatment needs to be broadened to see the family as a legitimate unit for intervention (Carroll et al., 2001; Stanton and Shadish, 1997). Involvement of family is not just to help the person with OUD. Family members also suffer from the OUD of their loved one and are in need of receiving services for their own benefit as well (Stulac et al., 2019).

Although some facilities are moving in this direction, many SUD treatment facilities still minimize or limit contact with family members. Sharing information with family members (and other medical providers) is further complicated by confidentiality restrictions, which have consistently been stricter for SUD treatment than for other health care issues.

It is important to note, however, that in some cases family members can perpetuate an individual's substance misuse when they knowingly or unknowingly facilitate use, fail to recognize or reinforce the patient's steps toward recovery, or are a barrier to the patient's accessing effective treatments (Stuart, 1969; Weiss, Hope, and Patterson, 1973). Furthermore, family members often have concerns about individuals using pharmacotherapies long term and the safety of opioid agonist therapies. In fact, a common barrier to medication treatment for OUD retention is the assumption by both patients and families that medication treatment is "simply trading one addiction for another," but as noted earlier, this is not the case (National Institute on Drug Abuse, 2018a). Dependence is not the same as addiction.

Key Interactions with Other Components of the Ecosystem

In this section, we describe the strong and direct interactions between the SUD specialty treatment system and three other elements of the ecosystem: medical care, criminal legal system, and illegal supply.

Opioid Use Disorder Treatment System and Medical Care

There are extensive interactions between the larger health care system and the system providing OUD treatment. PCPs play a critical role in the treatment of individuals with OUD that extends far beyond treatment of the OUD.

Identification and Referral from Medical Care

OUD often goes unrecognized by individuals with an OUD who do not see their drug use as a problem, and as a result individuals do not seek treatment and are reluctant to go to treatment even when suggested by others. Even when those individuals begin to recognize their drug use is causing problems, there often is a delay in seeking and receiving treatment. The health care system plays a critical role in identifying individuals with OUD and referring them for treatment. There are a variety of ways in which health care providers may identify individuals with, or at risk of, an OUD, engage them in a discussion about their disorder, refer them to treatment, and encourage them to become engaged in treatment. Physical health and mental health clinicians are aware of clinical factors, such as chronic pain or comorbid mental health disorders, that can place an individual at increased risk for an OUD, and in many cases clinicians monitor such individuals for signs of misuse of prescription opioid analgesics or illegal opioids. A patient may also present to the health care system following an overdose, or with clinical conditions common in individuals with OUD, such as HIV, Hepatitis C, and infective endocarditis (Schwetz et al., 2019). In some cases family members may also raise concerns about opioid misuse with an individual's clinicians.

In all of these cases, physical health care and mental health professionals can play an important role, exploring opioid misuse with the individual, making a diagnosis of OUD when appropriate, and either initiating treatment or referring the individual to the specialty system and supporting their engagement in care. Emergency departments can also have a particularly important role to play as they represent an opportunity to engage individuals at a moment in crisis in treatment. Emergency departments can increase the likelihood that an individual will engage in treatment for OUD by initiating treatment with BUP and providing direct links to ongoing treatment (Bernstein and D'Onofrio, 2017; D'Onofrio et al., 2015; Duber et al., 2018), as recommended by recent consensus recommendations (Hawk et al., 2021). More recently, there has been increased interest in efforts to initiate BUP treatment in emergency departments, subsequently connecting those individuals to specialty care for ongoing medication treatment for OUD. There has also been increased interest in efforts to initiate BUP while individuals are hospital inpatients (Priest et al., 2020; Priest, Englander, and McCarty, 2020; Wakeman et al., 2017). There have also been increasing efforts to increase

PCPs' routine screening of patients for OUD (Wakeman et al., 2017; Wakeman et al., 2019), although the impact of such efforts is unclear in the absence of concurrent efforts to increase treatment capacity in the primary care or specialty treatment system. Also, targeted screening efforts focused on populations at higher risk for developing OUD, such as individuals receiving chronic opioids, those with a prior history of a non-opioid SUD, or those with a mental health disorder, would likely have higher rates of detection with lower rates of false positives.

Treatment of Opioid Use Disorder in Medical Care

FDA approval of BUP and subsequent regulatory changes provided physicians, nurse practitioners, and physician assistants with an opportunity to provide MOUD. A majority of BUP prescribers are not addiction specialists (Rosenblatt et al., 2015). Office-based treatment expanded substantially with BUP's approval for expanded prescription authority (Stein et al., 2018; Stein et al., 2015), greatly increasing the number of individuals receiving effective OUD treatment. However, a great majority of PCPs appear reluctant to prescribe BUP. Factors that appear to dissuade clinicians from its use include concerns about its efficacy, uncertainty about how best to use it, lack of confidence in an ability to manage OUD patients in a primary care setting, lack of availability of counseling to complement MOUD, stigma regarding the treatment of individuals with OUD, lack of understanding regarding the effectiveness of BUP, and adequacy of reimbursement (Cioe et al., 2020; Huhn and Dunn, 2017; McGinty et al., 2020; Stone et al., 2021).

The specialty SUD system can play a significant role in addressing many of the concerns of PCPs and nonaddiction specialists by offering consultation and additional support to BUP prescribers. The ACA motivated statewide experimentation to support primary care physicians and other clinicians in their decision to provide BUP—beyond traditional practice-based models, e.g., office-based opioid therapy or clinic-based medication treatment for OUD programs providing methadone. New systems-based models, such as hub-and-spoke (e.g., Vermont), Project ECHO in New Mexico, Medicaid home health models, and collaborative models of care (e.g., Maryland), are described by Korthuis and colleagues (Korthuis et al., 2017). The system-based models commonly seek to facilitate the recruitment of new medical providers while also improving care for individuals with OUD.

For example, ACA (section 2703) allowed for creation of specialty health homes that provide comprehensive treatment services. In Vermont, the health homes are organized in *hubs* (regional centers for treating individuals with more-complex or severe OUD) and *spokes* (health centers or primary care offices serving as medical homes for individuals with less-complicated or severe OUD, or individuals who had already been started on and were stable on BUP). Methadone is provided only in opioid treatment programs serving as hubs, while BUP and naltrexone are prescribed in both hubs and spokes. The hubs provide a central intake, along with mental health and other specialty care services. Initial evaluations of the hub and spoke (medical home) model in Vermont indicate that the approach was successful: waitlist numbers decreased over time, numbers enrolled in OUD treatment increased, and the number of BUP providers doubled (Brooklyn and Sigmon, 2017).

In New Mexico, Project ECHO links PCPs in rural areas with university-affiliated OUD treatment experts, offering provider education and support via an internet-based audio and video communications platform (Komaromy et al., 2016). The ECHO model also emphasizes screening of patients and counseling with behavioral therapies.

These innovations in OUD treatment delivery have involved novel funding and billing models, supported greater coordination of care delivery and clinician education, and resulted in greatly improved service delivery. Many of these approaches are consistent with the chronic care framework for treating individuals with other chronic illnesses, and use many of the approaches that are well established in collaborative care models. Collaborative care models commonly involve a series of elements in a population management–based approach. In addition to consultation with experts in SUD treatment, the models often involve a registry, measurement-based care, and care coordinators. They also often use motivational approaches to enhance engagement in treatment (Osilla et al., 2016; Watkins et al., 2017a). Such approaches have been shown to be more effective than usual care in increasing access to treatment and decreasing drug use (Watkins et al., 2017b). We are unaware of rigorous evaluations assessing the extent to which these models improve quality of care. There is, however, emerging evidence that PCPs deliver care at quality levels that are comparable with that of specialists (Gertner et al., 2020).

Treatment of Comorbid Disorders Common in Individuals with Opioid Use Disorder

Individuals receiving OUD treatment in the SUD system can often have that treatment complicated by comorbid physical and mental health disorders. Effective communication between systems is critical to ensure that OUD and comorbid disorders are effectively treated, and collaborative care studies are underway to evaluate this (Harris et al., 2021; Meredith et al., 2021). Mental health disorders, such as major depression, bipolar disorder, and PTSD are common in individuals who misuse opioids and in those with OUD; unless these mental health disorders can be effectively treated, it can be far more difficult to effectively treat OUD. But effective treatment of these disorders can enhance the likelihood that an individual with OUD will stay in recovery.

As described in Chapter Five, medical providers often treat a variety of physical health disorders that are more common in individuals misusing opioids. These include blood-borne infectious diseases, such as HIV and Hepatitis C, and infectious endocarditis. Effective treatment of individuals with OUD decreases rates of these physical health comorbidities, as do several harm reduction strategies, such as syringe exchange programs. However, given the high rates of opioid misuse among individuals with mental health disorders (Novak et al., 2019; Rogers et al., 2019), effective treatment of comorbid mental health disorders is likely to decrease the rates of opioid misuse and rates of OUD.

Appropriate Management of Pain in Individuals Receiving Treatment for Opioid Use Disorder

Many individuals with OUD receiving treatment in the specialty SUD system also experience significant pain, both acutely because of trauma or procedures and chronically. In some cases, continued prescribing of opioid analgesics to these individuals is clinically appropriate to better manage their pain, and numerous anecdotal reports suggest that if pain is insufficiently treated, individuals will turn to illicit opioids. However, treatment of their pain should be done thoughtfully by prescribers fully aware of the OUD diagnosis.

Medical providers can complicate treatment of individuals with OUD by continuing to prescribe opioid analgesics without being aware that those individuals are receiving OUD treatment, and both opioid analgesics for treating pain and MOUD for treating OUD trigger some of the same brain receptors. Systems such as prescription drug monitoring programs (PDMPs) can alert prescribers to individuals prescribed opioid analgesics, but medical providers are often unaware of individuals who are receiving treatment for SUD. Specifically, some PDMPs provide information about individuals filling prescriptions for BUP, but PDMPs do not contain information about individuals receiving methadone for OUD treatment that is dispensed by an opioid treatment program. Coordinating treatment of individuals with OUD can be further complicated by confidentiality rules governing the sharing of information about the treatment of SUDs; these restrictions involve not only the Health Insurance Portability and Accountability Act but also 42 C.F.R. Part 2. These rules can often serve as a barrier to accessing needed health care information and effective coordination of care for individuals receiving treatment for SUD by multiple providers. Effective treatment for pain of individuals receiving treatment for OUD from the SUD system requires effective communication between clinicians.

Insurance and Opioid Use Disorder Specialty Treatment

For a long time, many SUD specialty services were not covered by insurance. In 2008, the Mental Health Parity Addiction Equity Act and the ACA increased coverage of treatment for SUD (Humphreys and Frank, 2014). For many individuals, however, inability to pay for SUD treatment remains a significant barrier to care (Ali et al., 2016; McKenna, 2017), and medical insurance is critical for supporting effective treatment. Even for those with insurance, they may still experience barriers to treatment because of the need for prior authorization for certain treatments, co-pays, and limited networks of providers.

As recently as 2008, the majority of funding for SUD treatment services came from public sources, with commercial insurance responsible for less than a quarter of funding (Levit et al., 2008). The majority of SUD specialty care was provided in nonprofit or government-owned facilities (Andrews et al., 2015; SAMHSA, 2009), many of which did not accept Medicaid or commercial insurance (SAMHSA, 2009). As a result, approximately one-third of individuals receiving SUD specialty care received services that were not covered by insurance (SAMHSA, 2010). However, in light of the high costs associated with the opioid crisis, starting in the early 2000s, many states started including coverage of methadone and BUP for Medicaid enrollees (Burns et al., 2016; Ducharme and Abraham, 2008). Today, Medicaid covers methadone and BUP treatment for most enrollees with OUD (Rinaldo and Rinaldo, 2013). Many states have also activated reimbursement codes for screening, brief interventions, and referrals to treatment (Humphreys and Frank, 2014), providing reimbursement for efforts to identify Medicaid enrollees with OUD and refer them to treatment. Furthermore, the expansion of service provision by for-profit entities might have contributed to decreases in the quality of care. To illustrate, according to National Survey of Substance Abuse Treatment Services data, the share of treatment facilities run by private, for-profit operators increased from 30 percent in the 2010 survey to 41 percent in the 2020 iteration (SAMHSA, 2021a). Existing evidence indicates that for-profit providers are less likely to offer comprehensive services (Bachhuber, Southern, and Cunningham, 2014) and more likely to engage in problematic recruitment practices (Beetham et al., 2021).

Opioid Use Disorder Treatment System and the Criminal Legal System

Diversion and Deflection Programs

Opioid misuse and OUD increase the risk of involvement with the criminal legal system (Brinkley-Rubinstein et al., 2018b), and many individuals with opioid misuse and OUD engage in criminal activity, much of it low-level, but not all. As a result, an increasing number of criminal legal agencies are implementing strategies such as LEAD and The Police Assisted Addiction and Recovery Initiative (PAARI) (PAARI, undated; Saloner et al., 2018) to divert and deflect individuals from the criminal legal system by responding before arrest, sentencing, and incarceration (for a discussion of these programs' origins and relevant terminology, see Chapter Six). The diversion or deflection does not need to be linked to a drug-related offense. For instance, LEAD covers violations "driven by unmet behavioral health needs" (LEAD, undated). Moreover, in some deflection programs, such as post-overdose outreach programs (discussed in Chapter Nine) or self-referral programs (discussed more next), law enforcement agencies are helping connect individuals with SUDs to community-based treatment without any underlying violation—the connection is either initiated by the person with OUD or their close ones, or it is initiated by the police as a welfare check.

Clients, officers, treatment staff, and the public generally support these programs (Center for Technology and Behavioral Health, 2018; Ormsby, 2018; Reichert et al., 2017; Schiff et al., 2017). Police officers believe that they are addressing a community need, improving community relations, and offering such services at low cost to municipalities (Reichert, 2017). Although there is a paucity of empirical research on the effectiveness of such programs, initial findings are promising. Preliminary studies suggest that such approaches may decrease subsequent involvement in the criminal legal system and reduce legal costs, although further research is needed (Collins, Lonczak, and Clifasefi, 2017). Still, many questions regarding diversion and deflection programs so far remain unanswered. For instance, given the proliferation of various models of diversion and deflection, how successful are various pathways in achieving positive public health and public safety outcomes? Are some models more suitable for certain contexts? More broadly, do diversion and deflection programs produce any negative outcomes at the system level?

Drug courts and family drug courts continue to be seen as having the potential to connect individuals and families to treatment, potentially diverting some individuals—generally those with arrests or convictions for nonviolent crimes—from incarceration (Longshore et al., 2001; Turner et al., 2002). Drug courts commonly use drug testing and require treatment, although in many cases treatment for OUD does not involve or permit medications for treatment of OUD. Drug court participants who do not complete treatment or other designated programs may have to serve the sentence that they would have received if they had not entered the drug court program, and judges play a critical role in drug courts by requiring participants to come to court on a regular basis and publicly praising their successes in court.

The treatment options available to those in such courts can vary widely. Despite medication treatment for OUD being viewed as the most effective treatment, MOUD is not offered or supported by many drug courts (Krawczyk et al., 2017; Matusow et al., 2013). Although we are unaware of studies of drug using outcomes specifically in individuals with OUD involved in drug courts, studies of drug courts in the broader population suggest that they can reduce drug use and criminal legal system recidivism for some individuals (Mitchell et al., 2012) but have little effect on employment, schooling, or community service outcomes (Roman, 2013). Very little evidence exists on treatment quality in drug court programs and associate measures such as treatment utilization or overdose (Joudrey et al., 2021). Drug courts are further discussed in Chapter Six.

Substance Use Disorder Specialty Treatment System and Criminal Legal System

The SUD specialty system interacts in multiple ways with the criminal legal system. Approximately half of incarcerated individuals have an SUD of one sort or another, and according to an estimate by the National Academies of Sciences, Engineering, and Medicine, 2019, about 15 percent have OUD. According to a classic 2007 study in Washington State, incarcerated individuals have 12 times the risk of death in the first two weeks after release (Binswanger et al., 2007), and fatal overdoses are the most common cause of those deaths. Medication treatment for OUD accompanied by counseling is the most effective treatment for incarcerated individuals with OUD (Moore et al., 2019), but officials in the criminal legal system often simply—and incorrectly—view medication treatment for OUD as substituting one addiction for another (Csete and Catania, 2013), and instead refer individuals with OUD to drug free treatment settings. Additional barriers to providing medication treatment to incarcerated individuals includes security concerns and concerns about diversion, belief in abstinence-based approaches, insufficient resources, and state and local regulations (Belenko, Hiller, and Hamilton, 2013).

For those recently released from incarceration, seeking help in an already overwhelmed treatment system is particularly challenging. But beginning medication for OUD before prisoners are released and connecting newly released prisoners to treatment programs in their communities can help (Moore et al., 2019). Although offering medication treatment to inmates is not yet widespread (Nunn et al., 2009; Vestal, 2016), such effective interventions are now routine in such places as Rhode Island (Green et al., 2018), and increasingly communities around the country are trying different ways to treat incarcerated individuals before release or initiating treatment just after they are released (Bronson et al., 2017). Such approaches have been shown to decrease risk of OD, crime, and other harms (Hedrich et al., 2012; Moore et al., 2019), but they require both sufficient treatment capacity for individuals to continue treatment upon their release and a system that ensures that individuals can successfully engage in such treatment upon release.

Treating Incarcerated Individuals and Connecting Them to Treatment upon Release

As discussed earlier, incarcerated individuals have an elevated risk of death in the first two weeks after release (Binswanger et al., 2007), and fatal overdoses are the most common cause of those deaths, with deaths from suicide and homicide (combined) coming in a close second. Some of this may be related to resuming opioid use at dosing levels used prior to institutional entry, resulting in OD as prior levels of opioid tolerance at the receptor level are reset to much lower levels of opioid tolerance. Initiating individuals who are incarcerated on treatment for OUD that can be continued following release, particularly with medications, and connecting newly released prisoners to treatment programs in their communities is likely to substantially reduce the risk of overdose and relapse following release and potentially the risk of reoffending (Moore et al., 2019). Most European countries offer MOUD in prisons (Montanari et al., 2021), as does Canada, though with gaps in provision (College of Family Physicians of Canada, 2019). In the United States, although offering medication treatment to inmates is not yet widespread (Nunn et al., 2009; Vestal, 2016), such interventions are now routine in places such as Rhode Island (Green et al., 2018), and increasingly communities around the country are trying different ways to treat incarcerated individuals either before or just after they are released (Bronson et al., 2017). Although the empirical evidence examining the effectiveness of such approaches is still evolving (Moore et al., 2019), early studies show an increase in rates of treatment engagement following discharge and a decreased risk of illicit drug use, overdose, crime, and other harms (Brinkley-Rubinstein et al., 2018a; Gordon et al., 2017; Hedrich et al., 2012; Moore et al., 2019). For instance, in a randomized trial in Rhode Island, 12 months after discharge, participants who were receiving methadone maintenance therapy at release were significantly less likely to report injecting and overdosing in the past 12 months than those not receiving methadone. They were also significantly less likely to report heroin use (Brinkley-Rubinstein et al., 2018a). Similarly, a systematic review and meta-analysis of trials on methadone provision during incarceration found that it was significantly associated with higher treatment engagement (odds ratio [OR] 8.69) and reductions in illicit opioid use (OR 0.22) and injecting (OR 0.26). The meta-analysis did not find a significant effect on recidivism, although some individual non-RCT studies included in the review did (Moore et al., 2019). However, relatively few correctional institutions offer such treatments (National Sheriffs' Association and National Commission on Correctional Health Care, 2018; Nunn et al., 2009; Vestal, 2016).

Opioid Use Disorder Treatment System and Illegal Supply

To a large extent, the demand for illicitly obtained opioids is driven by individuals with OUD; thus, unmet need for treatment for OUD is likely to sustain the demand for these drugs. Conversely, engaging individuals in effective treatment is likely to decrease the demand for illegal opioids.

The other arena in which the SUD treatment system and illegal supply are most likely to interact is with the diversion of BUP and methadone, medications commonly used in the SUD system for the treatment of OUD. Methadone is dispensed in opioid treatment programs to treat OUD and can also be prescribed by physicians to treat pain. Opioid treatment programs that dispense methadone must provide behavioral counseling, and patients must undergo urinalysis and supervised daily dosing (although some patients may obtain take-home doses under certain conditions) (McBournie et al., 2019). Local jurisdictions may also impose additional regulatory or zoning restrictions on where fixed sites that offer methadone to treat OUD can be located and how they may operate (Sigmon, 2014). Although diverted methadone can be used for its euphoric effects, studies suggest that it is also commonly used for self-medication for withdrawal or self-detoxification (Rettig and Yarmolinsky, 1995; Spunt et al., 1986). Diverted BUP is also most commonly used for self-medication for withdrawal or self-detoxification and may decrease the likelihood of fatal overdose (Carlson et al., 2020); as a result, multiple jurisdictions have chosen to no longer make arrests or press charges for individuals with diverted BUP (del Pozo, Krasner, and George, 2020).[5]

Opioid Use Disorder Treatment System and the Education System

According to 2017 data from the nationally representative Monitoring the Future survey, 4.2 percent of 12th graders reported having used "narcotics other than heroin" (i.e., prescription opioids [National Institute on Drug Abuse, 2018b]) not under a doctor's orders in the past year. With respect to heroin, 0.7 percent of high school seniors reported ever having used and 0.4 percent reported use in the preceding 12 months (Miech et al., 2017); a thoughtful, comprehensive approach in schools can help (1) identify students misusing opioids and (2) support the students and their families in getting the student into treatment when needed (Council on School Health and Committee on Substance Abuse, 2007; American Academy of Pediatrics, 2007). It is likely more common however, that educational institutions respond to student drug use with disciplinary actions. Public school districts and institutions of higher education have authority to regulate and impose consequences for student behavior—including

---

[5] Note that gaps in our knowledge remain with respect to the effects of liberalizing access to medication used in OUD treatment. It is worth pointing out that, in a small number of countries, the medications used for the treatment of OUD—not heroin—are the most common substances identified in drug-related deaths.

but not limited to illegal drug-related behavior—that is detrimental to the education process or threatens the safety of other students, staff, or school property. Many states have laws that require schools to involve state or local law enforcement when certain crimes are committed on campuses and impose minimum consequences for certain types of offenses; illegal drug-related offenses are often on those lists.

However, there are relatively few direct interactions between the SUD specialty system and the education system. Exceptions are Recovery High Schools, educational settings designed to support students in recovery from SUDs (Moberg, Finch, and Lindsley, 2014). Collegiate recovery communities serve a similar role for college students, recognizing the need for living arrangements that can support recovery. A recent systematic review concluded, however, that at this time there is insufficient evidence to determine if such Recovery High Schools or collegiate recovery communities are effective in reducing rates of relapse or improving outcomes (Hennessy et al., 2018).

Opioid Use Disorder Treatment System and Income Support and Homeless Services

Individuals with OUD for whom the disorder is a contributing factor material to their disability determination are denied Social Security disability insurance (U.S. Government Accountability Office [GAO], 2020). However, while OUD is likely present in many individuals applying for Social Security disability insurance (Wu et al., 2020), OUD is seldom a key factor in determining eligibility decisions (GAO, 2020, p. 21).

With respect to Temporary Assistance for Needy Families (TANF), there is little accurate data on rates of OUD because of underreporting of substance use by individuals across all income levels, and concern among lower income individuals that they may lose their welfare benefits if they reveal an SUD. Many state welfare offices rely on recipients' self-disclosure of SUD concerns versus using a comprehensive screening tool, but TANF agencies screen and refer far fewer individuals to treatment than prevalence rates would imply (Radel, Joyce, and Wulff, 2011) and few OUD programs tailor their assessment, treatment, prevention, or recovery services specifically to TANF recipients' needs (Germain, 2018).

A second area in which (1) the SUD specialty system and (2) income support and homeless services interact is with respect to housing. Federal policies allow housing agencies to prohibit people who have histories of past drug use or who are considered at risk of engaging in illegal drug use from receiving housing assistance. Specifically, the U.S. Department of Housing and Urban Development requires that all public housing agencies (PHAs) establish lifetime bans on the admission to the Public Housing and Housing Choice Voucher (Tenant-Based Section 8) programs for individuals found to have manufactured or produced methamphetamine, which presents the risk of fires or explosions, on the premises of federally assisted housing (U.S. Department of Housing and Urban Development [HUD], 2013). In addition, PHAs must also prohibit admission if (1) the PHA determines that any household member is engaged in illegal drug use; (2) the PHA has reasonable cause to believe that a household member's illegal drug use, alcohol use, or pattern of drug or alcohol use may threaten the health, safety, or right to peaceful enjoyment of the premises by other residents; or (3) a household member of the applicant was evicted from federally assisted housing for drug-related criminal activity in the past three years (HUD, 2013; Iguchi et al., 2002).

Such laws are intended to decrease drug use and drug markets in public housing, which can be associated with criminal activity and negatively affect the life of public housing residents. However, as a result of these policies, a single failed drug test that occurs during an individual's participation in treatment can result in eviction from public housing (Curtis, Garlington, and Schottenfeld, 2013; Local Progress, 2019) because federal policies allow housing agencies to prohibit people who have histories of past drug use or who are considered at risk of engaging in illegal drug use from receiving housing assistance (HUD, 2013). This creates a challenge for housing officials and policymakers, who need to balance the interests of the residents of public housing while also addressing the needs of individuals with SUDs. For these individuals, stable housing is significantly associated with better outcomes after detox and housing instability is associated with worse outcomes (Saloner and Lê Cook, 2013; Timko et al., 2016).

Opioid Use Disorder Treatment System and the Child Welfare System

The worsening opioid crisis, with many parents struggling with OUD, is contributing to an increase in the number of children who are involved with the child welfare system and placed in foster care (Kohomban, Rodriguez, and Haskins, 2018). Communities experiencing more-severe harms from the opioid crisis have higher rates of entry of children into foster care (Radel et al., 2018).

However, there are several obstacles that the child welfare system and SUD treatment system must face in order to effectively meet this challenge. Efforts to ensure children can safely remain in their parents' custody can often be enhanced if parents with OUD are able to receive the most effective treatment, but there are many barriers to this occurring. Parents involved in child welfare may fear that if they reveal misuse of opioids, such as when seeking treatment, they could lose custody of their child, particularly if they are not currently in treatment (Falletta et al., 2018; Roberts and Pies, 2011; Winstanley and Stover, 2019). The assessments of parents by child welfare workers are often cursory, inconsistent, and lag behind placement decisions (Radel et al., 2018), hampering timely identification of parents who might benefit from OUD treatment. Parents encouraged by child welfare workers to seek treatment often have inadequate access to treatment, or they may only be able to get services that do not match their needs. Some child welfare professionals and judges remain skeptical about MOUD, viewing it as "trading one drug addiction for another," and in some cases are concerned about diversion and misuse (Radel et al., 2018). MOUD has been associated with greater odds of parents retaining custody of their children (Hall et al., 2016), likely because of both the effectiveness of MOUD and the fact that parents motivated to receive MOUD are also more motivated to retain custody of their children. But because of barriers such as these, parents involved in the child welfare system in some communities often do not receive the most effective treatment for OUD.

Punitive state policies regarding drug use among pregnant women, whereby substance use during pregnancy is criminalized, considered grounds for civil commitment, or considered child abuse can also potentially result in the unintended consequence of more infants being born physically dependent on opioids (*neonatal abstinence syndrome* or *neonatal opioid withdrawal syndrome*).[6] Infants born with neonatal opioid withdrawal syndrome represented 7.3 per 1,000 births in hospitals in 2017, or about 28,000—an 82 percent increase from 2010 (Hirai et al., 2021). As a result, in many locations children may become involved in the child welfare system soon after birth. In situations in which a pregnant woman is misusing opioids, referral to effective treatment is a better alternative, but it appears that state policies supporting such treatment currently have little effect (Faherty et al., 2019). The lack of effect of these policies in increasing rates of treatment among pregnant women is likely the result of fewer available treatment slots for pregnant women, difficulties pregnant women have in getting appointments, and other barriers faced by pregnant women in accessing treatment (Patrick et al., 2020).

The lack of family-friendly treatment can also serve as a barrier for parents involved in the child welfare system to receive effective treatment for their OUD because many residential treatment programs do not allow children, forcing parents to decide between treatment and their children while receiving residential service. Some specialized programs, which are often residential, enable the family to stay together, and often provide SUD treatment, therapy, parenting skills training, life skills, and job readiness education with the support of professional staff who ensure the safety of children while their parents and families achieve sobriety and recovery (Wilder Research and Volunteers of America, 2019). Such programs allow parents to enter treatment without giving up custody of their children and enhance the willingness of parents with OUD to engage in effective treatment.

Historically, welfare system regulations collided with this approach: the system could only pay for a child's care if the child were separated from their parents but not when a child accompanied a parent to residential treatment. The Comprehensive Addiction and Recovery Act and the Families First Act contains provisions to help keep families involved in the child welfare system together while providing effective treatment to parents struggling with addiction, and family drug courts often try to use such programs to keep families together and support parents in receiving effective treatment (Zhang et al., 2019). However, such programs remain in short supply because of their intensity and cost (Radel et al., 2018).

Sober treatment and recovery teams are another approach being used by the child welfare system in situations in which a young child is involved with the welfare system and substance misuse by at least one parent is a child safety risk factor (California Evidence-Based Clearinghouse for Child Welfare, 2020). These intensive programs pair child welfare workers

---

[6] We prefer the term *neonatal opioid withdrawal syndrome*.

with peer-support individuals and are designed to facilitate parents' rapid access and ongoing engagement with SUD care, enabling the child to be safely cared for at home. Preliminary pre-post studies are encouraging (Hall et al., 2015; Huebner, Willauer, and Posze, 2012; Huebner et al., 2015), but we are unaware of more-rigorous research examining the effectiveness of such programs.

Opioid Use Disorder Treatment System and First Responders

First responders interact with the SUD specialty system in that they can facilitate and enhance engagement in specialty treatment following a nonfatal overdose. Individuals surviving a nonfatal overdose are at increased risk of a subsequent overdose (Bagley et al., 2019; Kelty and Hulse, 2017; Olfson et al., 2018), and first responders interacting with such individuals can potentially increase the likelihood that they access and stay engaged in specialty treatment (Langabeer et al., 2020). However, many individuals who survive a nonfatal overdose do not engage in treatment (Larochelle et al., 2018; Koyawala et al., 2019). As a result, several communities have introduced post-overdose outreach programs, often including first responders, that aim to engage overdose survivors (Formica et al., 2018; Streisel et al., 2019; Wagner et al., 2019). In other communities, individuals with OUD can come to fire stations where emergency medical services are based and ask for help with accessing services without any fear of criminal liability or other negative repercussions (Sacco, Unick, and Gray, 2018). The effectiveness of such post-overdose outreach programs or efforts involving first responders has not yet been rigorously evaluated.

Opioid Use Disorder Treatment System and Employment

One area in which the SUD treatment system interacts with the employment system is in the availability and generosity of employer-sponsored health insurance, which is the dominant source of health care financing for nonelderly adults. Prior to the Mental Health Parity and Addiction Equity Act (2008) and ACA (2010), coverage of mental health and substance use treatment in private insurance (including employer-sponsored health insurance) was often limited compared with public insurance. Even today, commercially insured individuals may face a variety of barriers to getting effective treatment for their OUD, including limited provider networks, insufficient coverage, low reimbursement, inadequate networks, prior authorizations, and duration limits. Prior authorizations have been shown to decrease the use of high BUP in Medicaid enrollees (Clark et al., 2014) and removal of prior authorization policies was associated with greater BUP use among Medicare beneficiaries (Mark, Parish, and Zarkin, 2020). Furthermore, stigma, including stigma related to employment prospects, remains a widely reported reason for privately insured individuals with SUDs to not seek treatment (Ali et al., 2017) or to pay cash rather than use insurance, because of concerns about employers becoming aware of treatment for SUD. This may be a particularly important issue for certain industries in which misuse of opioids or a history of treatment can create barriers to obtaining a job or being allowed to do particular activities.

The SUD treatment system and employment system also intersect with respect to the SUD system's treatment workforce. A long-standing challenge faced by the system has been an insufficient number of individuals trained and certified to provide SUD specialty services (Hoge et al., 2009), a challenge exacerbated by the low wages provided for frontline SUD workers.

Opioid Use Disorder Treatment System and Harm Reduction and Community-Initiated Interventions

The SUD treatment system and broader harm reduction and community engagement efforts intersect regarding the need to engage hidden populations. Many individuals with SUD remain disengaged from the treatment system because of a variety of factors, including lack of interest in treatment, efforts to conceal their drug use, and reluctance to seek treatment because of societal stigmatization of SUD and criminalization of illegal drug use (Crapanzano et al., 2019; Hammarlund et al., 2018). Locating and engaging them requires an understanding of hidden populations and how best to reach out to them. In many cases, other parts of the ecosystem will play an important role in such efforts.[7]

To address these challenges, there have been increasing efforts to facilitate better linkages between specialty SUD treatment and harm reduction programs, such as syringe service programs. Existing evidence demonstrates that, in addition to mitigating harms of opioid use and providing information about existing treatment options, syringe service programs can effectively facilitate individuals' engagement with treatment services and help them maintain the engagement (Hagan et al., 2000; Heimer, 1998; Strathdee et al., 1999). In newer developments, some syringe service programs have even become locations where people who use opioids can begin receiving medication treatment, with the possibility of transferring to a more traditional provider later on (Hood et al., 2020). Other harm reduction programs, such as supervised consumption sites (SCSs), can provide the same treatment linkage function. In fact, some, though not all, SCSs implemented in other countries are located with treatment providers (Strang and Taylor, 2018). Relatedly, the first two sanctioned SCSs in the United States opened in New York City in late 2021, and other cities and states have signaled interest in following suit (Mann, 2021).

---

[7] It is also important to understand that risk of overdose is not limited to individuals who misuse opioids. Individuals receiving opioids for clinical reasons are also at risk of overdose (Kolodny et al., 2015), and, in the past, an estimated 60 percent of opioid overdose deaths were thought to occur in individuals provided prescriptions consistent with prescribing guidelines provided by medical boards (Manchikanti et al., 2012). This was particularly true for those who were prescribed opioids for chronic, nonmalignant pain (Paulozzi, Budnitz, and Xi, 2006).

Policy Opportunities and Considerations

Much has been written about the many ways in which the SUD treatment system could be improved for the treatment of OUD. These include efforts to increase funding for SUD treatment services, expand and enhance the skills of the SUD treatment workforce, increase the use of interventions that are most effective for OUD, such as medication treatment, identify facilities providing higher quality services, and direct patients and families to those facilities. These changes would be likely to enhance the availability and quality of specialty services available to individuals with OUD. However, given the nature of the opioid ecosystem in the United States, the number of individuals with OUD, and the fact that many individuals with OUD have no contact with the SUD treatment system, the SUD specialty treatment system is not and likely never will be extensive or robust enough to address the unmet need for treatment for OUD. Therefore, policymakers should consider policies that involve both the SUD system and other interacting systems as they consider responses to the opioid crisis because such policies have the potential to increase access to OUD treatment for individuals being served by other systems and to help such individuals be more successfully engaged in treatment, ultimately decreasing a variety of harms associated with OUD.

The medical system is one in which there are multiple opportunities to address OUD. One of the most prominent is ensuring parity of coverage for OUD and adequate reimbursement for OUD treatment in both the private and commercial insurance markets. This would likely increase the availability of OUD treatment services and provide additional resources that could be used to increase the quality of those services. An additional opportunity comes from supporting the development of networks linking PCPs and SUD treatment experts. Such models should be tailored to the needs of the community and the existing capacity and expertise available in the primary care and SUD treatment system. Such models are similar to the collaborative care models that are used in large health systems in the treatment of depression (Katzelnick and Williams, 2015). In these models, SUD treatment experts often provide PCPs with training in treating SUD, clinical support, consultation, and an option for the timely referral of more-complicated patients. There is also a care manager or care coordinator, who commonly serves as a link between the patient and other members of the care team, and a registry to facilitate the monitoring of patients' clinical status and engagement with services. Studies of such models in the treatment of individuals with OUD are encouraging (Setodji et al., 2018; Watkins et al., 2017b), and versions containing several of these elements, such as the hub-and-spoke model, have now been implemented in multiple states after being modified to meet the local needs of those communities (Dahlhamer et al., 2018).

Another important opportunity to address the opioid crisis lies at the intersection of the SUD treatment system and the criminal legal system. There have been several positive initiatives to better integrate the criminal legal system and the SUD treatment system, including multiple initiatives to divert or deflect individuals from the criminal legal system who might be better served in the SUD system, efforts to provide effective OUD treatment to incarcerated individuals, and efforts to link individuals being released from incarceration to effective services in the SUD treatment system. Linking individuals involved with the criminal legal system with treatment services can lead to benefits not only for people with OUD but also for the wider society, for instance via reductions in crime and its societal costs and impacts on victims and families. However, there remain multiple ways that such efforts could be improved and enhanced. Treatment options provided to individuals being diverted or deflected from the criminal legal system for OUD treatment should be offered a full spectrum of available treatments, including the gold standard treatment: medication. Decreasing barriers to effective treatment for individuals being released from incarceration includes ensuring individuals have insurance coverage to pay for SUD treatment. In many states, individuals being incarcerated have their Medicaid eligibility suspended, or in some cases terminated. Section 1905(a)(A) of the Social Security Act excludes federal Medicaid funding for medical care provided to "inmates of a public institution" (National Association of Counties, 2017). It often takes a substantial period of time for Medicaid to be reinstated when incarcerated individuals are released, and this poses a significant barrier to initiation of treatment for their SUD. To address this, the U.S. Department of Health and Human Services issued guidance strongly recommending that states suspend, rather than terminate, Medicaid benefits while individuals are in jail or prison (Pew Charitable Trusts, 2016). As of May 2016, 31 states and the District of Columbia had policies to suspend coverage. Fifteen states suspended coverage for a specific period, such as the first 30 days or the first year of incarceration. An additional 16 states plus the District of Columbia suspended coverage for the full duration of time spent in correctional facilities. Of concern is the fact that 19 states terminated Medicaid coverage, including states who had expanded Medicaid under the ACA. To address this situation, a bipartisan and bicameral legislative proposal (the Humane Correctional Health Care Act) was introduced in Congress in May 2021 to end the exclusion of incarcerated individuals from Medicaid, which would ensure continuous Medicaid coverage for people in jails and prisons (Choi, 2021).

Opportunities to lower barriers and enhance access and engagement in effective SUD treatment also exist in the (1) child welfare and (2) income support and homeless services systems. Expanding the availability of family friendly treatment options could decrease the barriers to care for child welfare–involved families, who often must decide between continuing to care for their child or receiving treatment for their SUDs. Similarly, expanding OUD treatment integration with the housing first model could enhance the successful treatment of individuals with unstable housing and decrease concerns among individuals in public housing that a relapse could cost them and their family their home. More broadly, community-initiated interventions spanning multiple systems and bringing together diverse stakeholders can work to engage individuals with OUD who are currently not in treatment or involved in the criminal legal system. Such interventions can also mobilize support for comprehensive community-based efforts (Palombi et al., 2019). Such systems could draw on community resources and various forms of lay advocates as disparate as churches (Castillo et al., 2019) or barber shops (Luque, Ross, and Gwede, 2014), which have been shown as potentially effective in helping address other physical and mental health needs.

Abbreviations

ACA	Affordable Care Act
BUP	buprenorphine
CM	contingency management
ECHO	Extension for Community Healthcare Outcomes
FDA	U.S. Food and Drug Administration
HIV	human immunodeficiency virus
LEAD	Law Enforcement Assisted Diversion
MOUD	medications for opioid use disorder
OUD	opioid use disorder
PAARI	Police Assisted Addiction and Recovery Initiative
PCP	primary care provider
RCT	randomized controlled trial
SAMHSA	Substance Abuse and Mental Health Services Administration
SUD	substance use disorder

References

Ainscough, Tom S., Ann McNeill, John Strang, Robert Calder, and Leonie S. Brose, "Contingency Management Interventions for Non-Prescribed Drug Use During Treatment for Opiate Addiction: A Systematic Review and Meta-Analysis," *Drug and Alcohol Dependence*, Vol. 178, 2017, pp. 318–339.

Alessi, Sheila M., and Nancy M. Petry, "A Randomized Study of Cellphone Technology to Reinforce Alcohol Abstinence in the Natural Environment," *Addiction*, Vol. 108, No. 5, 2013, pp. 900–909.

Ali, Mir M., Jie Chen, Ryan Mutter, Priscilla Novak, and Karoline Mortensen, "The ACA's Dependent Coverage Expansion and Out-of-Pocket Spending by Young Adults with Behavioral Health Conditions," *Psychiatric Services*, Vol. 67, No. 9, 2016, pp. 977–982.

Ali, Shahid, Barira Tahir, Shagufta Jabeen, and Madeeha Malik, "Methadone Treatment of Opiate Addiction: A Systematic Review of Comparative Studies," *Innovations in Clinical Neuroscience*, Vol. 14, No. 7–8, 2017, pp. 7–19.

Alinejad, Samira, Toba Kazemi, Nasim Zamani, Robert S. Hoffman, and Omid Mehrpour, "A Systematic Review of the Cardiotoxicity of Methadone," *EXCLI Journal*, Vol. 14, 2015, pp. 577–600.

American Academy of Pediatrics, *Pediatrics*, Vol. 120, No. 6, December 2007.

American Methadone Treatment Association, *1998 Methadone Maintenance Program and Patient Census in the U.S.*, New York, 1998.

Andrews, Christina, Amanda Abraham, Colleen M. Grogan, Harold A. Pollack, Clifford Bersamira, Keith Humphreys, and Peter Friedmann, "Despite Resources from the ACA, Most States Do Little To Help Addiction Treatment Programs Implement Health Care Reform," *Health Affairs*, Vol. 34, No. 5, 2015, pp. 828–835.

Andrews, Christina M., Hee-Choon Shin, Jeanne C. Marsh, and Dingcai Cao, "Client and Program Characteristics Associated with Wait Time to Substance Abuse Treatment Entry," *American Journal of Drug and Alcohol Abuse*, Vol. 39, No. 1, 2013, pp. 61–68.

Andrilla, C. Holly A., Tessa E. Moore, Davis G. Patterson, and Eric H. Larson, "Geographic Distribution of Providers with a DEA Waiver to Prescribe Buprenorphine for the Treatment of Opioid Use Disorder: A 5-Year Update," *Journal of Rural Health*, Vol. 35, No. 1, 2019, pp. 108–112.

Bachhuber, Marcus A., William N. Southern, and Chinazo O. Cunningham, "Profiting and Providing Less Care: Comprehensive Services at For-Profit, Nonprofit, and Public Opioid Treatment Programs in the United States," *Medical Care*, Vol. 52, No. 5, 2014, 428.

Bagley, Sarah M., Samantha F. Schoenberger, Katherine M. Waye, and Alexander Y. Walley, "A Scoping Review of Post Opioid-Overdose Interventions," *Preventive Medicine*, Vol. 128, 2019.

Bandara, Sachini, Alene Kennedy-Hendricks, Sydney Merritt, Colleen L. Barry, and Brendan Saloner, "Methadone and Buprenorphine Treatment in United States Jails and Prisons: Lessons from Early Adopters," *Addiction*, Vol. 116, No. 12, 2021, pp. 3473–3481.

Barry, Declan T., Mark Beitel, Christopher J. Cutter, David A. Fiellin, Robert D. Kerns, Brent A. Moore, Lindsay Oberleitner, Lynn M. Madden, Christopher Liong, Joel Ginn, and Richard S. Schottenfeld, "An Evaluation of the Feasibility, Acceptability, and Preliminary Efficacy of Cognitive-Behavioral Therapy for Opioid Use Disorder and Chronic Pain," *Drug and Alcohol Dependence*, Vol. 194, 2019, pp. 460–467.

Beetham, Tamara, Brendan Saloner, Marema Gaye, Sarah E. Wakeman, Richard G. Frank, and Michael Lawrence Barnett, "Admission Practices and Cost of Care for Opioid Use Disorder at Residential Addiction Treatment Programs in the US," *Health Affairs*, Vol. 40, No. 2, 2021, pp. 317–325.

Beetham, Tamara, Brendan Saloner, Sarah E. Wakeman, Marema Gaye, and Michael L. Barnett, "Access to Office-Based Buprenorphine Treatment in Areas with High Rates of Opioid-Related Mortality: An Audit Study," *Annals of Internal Medicine*, Vol. 171, No. 1, 2019.

Belenko, Steven, Matthew Hiller, and Leah Hamilton, "Treating Substance Use Disorders in the Criminal Justice System," *Current Psychiatry Reports*, Vol 15, No. 11, 2013.

Benishek, Lois A., Karen L. Dugosh, Kim C. Kirby, Jason Matejkowski, Nicolle T. Clements, Brittany L. Seymour, and David S. Festinger, "Prize-Based Contingency Management for the Treatment of Substance Abusers: A Meta-Analysis," *Addiction*, Vol. 109, No. 9, 2014, pp. 1426–1436.

Bernstein, Steven L., and Gail D'Onofrio, "Screening, Treatment Initiation, and Referral for Substance Use Disorders," *Addiction Science and Clinical Practice*, Vol. 12, No. 1, 2017.

Binswanger, Ingrid A., Marc F. Stern, Richard A. Deyo, Patrick J. Heagerty, Allen Cheadle, Joann G. Elmore, and Thomas D. Koepsell, "Release from Prison—A High Risk of Death for Former Inmates," *New England Journal of Medicine*, Vol. 356, No. 2, 2007, pp. 157–165.

Bradley, Brendan P., Grania Phillips, Lynete Green, and Michael Gossop, "Circumstances Surrounding the Initial Lapse to Opiate Use Following Detoxification," *British Journal of Psychiatry*, Vol. 154, No. 3, 1989, pp. 354–359.

Brinkley-Rubinstein, Lauren, Michelle McKenzie, Alexandria Macmadu, Sarah Larney, Nickolas Zaller, Emily Dauria, and Josiah Rich, "A Randomized, Open Label Trial of Methadone Continuation Versus Forced Withdrawal in a Combined US Prison and Jail: Findings at 12 Months Post-Release," *Drug and Alcohol Dependence*, Vol. 184, 2018a, pp. 57–63.

Brinkley-Rubinstein, Lauren, Nickolas Zaller, Sarah Martino, David H. Cloud, Erin McCauley, Andrew Heise, and David Seal, "Criminal Justice Continuum for Opioid Users at Risk of Overdose," *Addictive Behaviors*, Vol. 86, 2018b, pp. 104–110.

Bronson, Jennifer, Jessica Stroop, Stephanie Zimmer, and Marcus Berzofsky, *Drug Use, Dependence, and Abuse Among State Prisoners and Jail Inmates, 2007–2009*, Washington, D.C.: Bureau of Justice Statistics, June 2017.

Brooklyn, John R., and Stacey C. Sigmon, "Vermont Hub-and-Spoke Model of Care for Opioid Use Disorder: Development, Implementation, and Impact," *Journal of Addictive Medicine*, Vol. 11, No. 4, 2017, pp. 286–292.

Burns, Rachel M., Rosalie L. Pacula, Sebastian Bauhoff, Adam J. Gordon, Hollie Hendrikson, Douglas L. Leslie, and Bradley D. Stein, "Policies Related to Opioid Agonist Therapy for Opioid Use Disorders: The Evolution of State Policies from 2004 to 2013," *Substance Abuse*, Vol. 37, No. 1, 2016, pp. 63–69.

California Evidence-Based Clearinghouse for Child Welfare, "Sobriety Treatment and Recovery Teams (START)," webpage, April 2020. As of May 25, 2022:
https://www.cebc4cw.org/program/sobriety-treatment-and-recovery-teams/

Campbell, Aimee N. C., Edward V. Nunes, Abigail G. Matthews, Maxine Stitzer, Gloria M. Miele, Daniel Polsky, Eva Turrigiano, Scott Walters, Erin A. McClure, Tiffany L. Kyle et al., "Internet-Delivered Treatment for Substance Abuse: A Multisite Randomized Controlled Trial," *American Journal of Psychiatry*, Vol. 171, No. 6, 2014, pp. 683–690.

Campbell, Aimee N. C., Edward V. Nunes, Gloria M. Miele, Abigail Matthews, Daniel Polsky, Udi E. Ghitza, Eva Turrigiano, Genie L. Bailey, Paul VanVeldhuisem, and Rita Chapdelaine, "Design and Methodological Considerations of an Effectiveness Trial of a Computer-Assisted Intervention: An Example from the NIDA Clinical Trials Network," *Contemporary Clinical Trials*, Vol. 33, No. 2, 2012, pp. 386–395.

Carlson, Robert G., Raminta Daniulaityte, Sydney M. Silverstein, Ramzi W. Nahhas, and Silvia S. Martins, "Unintentional Drug Overdose: Is More Frequent Use of Non-Prescribed Buprenorphine Associated with Lower Risk of Overdose?" *International Journal of Drug Policy*, Vol. 79, 2020.

Carroll, K. M., S. A. Ball, C. Nich, P. G. O'Connor, D. A. Eagan, T. L. Frankforter, E. G. Triffleman, J. Shi, and B. J. Rounsaville, "Targeting Behavioral Therapies to Enhance Naltrexone Treatment of Opioid Dependence: Efficacy of Contingency Management and Significant Other Involvement," *Archives of General Psychiatry*, Vol. 58, No. 8, 2001, pp. 755–761.

Castillo, Enrico G., Roya Ijadi-Maghsoodi, Sonya Shadravan, Elizabeth Moore, Michael O. Mensah, III, Mary Docherty, Maria Gabriela Aguilera Nunez, Nicolás Barcelo, Nichole Goodsmith, Laura E. Halpin, et al., "Community Interventions to Promote Mental Health and Social Equity," *Current Psychiatry Reports*, Vol. 21, No. 5, 2019.

Center for Substance Abuse Treatment, *The Determinations Report: A Report on the Physician Waiver Program Established by the Drug Addiction Treatment Act of 2000 ("DATA")*, Rockville, Md.: Substance Abuse and Mental Health Services Administration, March 30, 2006.

Center for Technology and Behavioral Health, "Safe Station: A Systematic Evaluation of a Novel Community-Based Model to Tackle the Opioid Crisis," webpage, 2018. As of May 25, 2022:
https://www.c4tbh.org/active-project/safe-station-systematic-evaluation-novel-community-based-model-tackle-opioid-crisis/

Centers for Medicare & Medicaid Services, "Opioid Treatment Programs," webpage, undated. As of October 1, 2021:
https://www.cms.gov/Center/Provider-Type/Opioid-Treatment-Program-Center

Choi, Joseph, "Bipartisan Group of Lawmakers Reintroduces Bill to Give Inmates Medicaid Access," *The Hill*, May 25, 2021.

Cioe, Katharine, Breanne Biondi, Rebecca Easly, Amanda Simard, Xiao Zheng, and Sandra A. Springer, "A Systematic Review of Patients' and Providers' Perspectives of Medications for Treatment of Opioid Use Disorder," *Journal of Substance Abuse Treatment*, Vol. 119, 2020.

Clark, Robin E., Jeffrey D. Baxter, Bruce A. Barton, Gideon Aweh, Elizabeth O'Connell, and William H. Fisher, "The Impact of Prior Authorization on Buprenorphine Dose, Relapse Rates, and Cost for Massachusetts Medicaid Beneficiaries with Opioid Dependence," *Health Services Research*, Vol. 49, No. 6, 2014, pp. 1964–1979.

Clark, Robin E., Mihail Samnaliev, Jeffrey D. Baxter, and Gary Y. Leung, "The Evidence Doesn't Justify Steps by State Medicaid Programs to Restrict Opioid Addiction Treatment with Buprenorphine," *Health Affairs, Vol. 30, No. 8,* 2011, pp. 1425–1433.

CMS—*See* Centers for Medicare & Medicaid Services.

Code of Federal Regulations, Title 42, Public Health; Chapter I, Public Health Service, Department of Health and Human Services; Subchapter A, General Provisions; Part 2, Confidentiality of Substance Use Disorder Patient Records.

College of Family Physicians of Canada, *Position Statement on Access to Opioid Agonist Treatment in Detention*, Mississauga, Ontario, November 2019.

Collins, Susan E., Heather S. Lonczak, and Seema L. Clifasefi, "Seattle's Law Enforcement Assisted Diversion (LEAD): Program Effects on Recidivism Outcomes," *Evaluation and Program Planning*, Vol. 64, 2017, pp. 49–56.

Council on School Health and Committee on Substance Abuse, "The Role of Schools in Combating Illicit Substance Abuse," *Pediatrics*, Vol. 120, No. 6, 2007, pp. 1379–1384.

Crapanzano, Kathleen A., Rebecca Hammarlund, Bilal Ahmad, Natalie Hunsinger, and Rumneet Kullar, "The Association Between Perceived Stigma and Substance Use Disorder Treatment Outcomes: A Review," *Substance Abuse and Rehabilitation*, Vol. 10, No. 1–12, 2019.

Csete, Joanne, and Holly Catania, "Methadone Treatment Providers' Views of Drug Court Policy and Practice: A Case Study of New York State," *Harm Reduction Journal*, Vol. 10, No. 1, 2013.

Curtis, Marah A., Sarah Garlington, and Lisa S. Schottenfeld, "Alcohol, Drug, and Criminal History Restrictions in Public Housing," *Cityscape*, Vol. 15, No. 3, 2013, pp. 37–52.

D'Agostino, Giorgio, Luca Pieroni, and Margherita Scarlato, "Social Transfers and Income Inequality in OECD Countries," *Structural Change and Economic Dynamics*, Vol. 52, 2020, pp. 313–327.

Dahlhamer, James, Jacqueline Lucas, Carla Zelaya, Richard Nahin, Sean Mackey, Lynn DeBar, Robert Kerns, Michael Von Korff, Linda Porter, and Charles Helmick, "Prevalence of Chronic Pain and High-Impact Chronic Pain Among Adults—United States, 2016," *Morbidity and Mortality Weekly Report*, Vol. 67, No. 36, 2018, pp. 1001–1006.

d'Amico, Elizabeth J., Susan M. Paddock, Audrey Burnam, and Fuan-Yue Kung, "Identification of and Guidance for Problem Drinking by General Medical Providers: Results from a National Survey," *Medical Care*, Vol. 43, No. 3, 2005, pp. 229–236.

Davis, Corey S., and Elizabeth A. Samuels, "Continuing Increased Access to Buprenorphine in the United States via Telemedicine After COVID-19," *International Journal on Drug Policy*, Vol. 93, 2021.

Davis, Danielle R., Allison N. Kurti, Joan M. Skelly, Ryan Redner, Thomas J. White, and Stephen T. Higgins, "A Review of the Literature on Contingency Management in the Treatment of Substance Use Disorders, 2009–2014," *Preventive Medicine*, Vol. 92, 2016, pp. 36–46.

Del Pozo, Brandon, Lawrence S. Krasner, and Sarah F. George, "Decriminalization of Diverted Buprenorphine in Burlington, Vermont and Philadelphia: An Intervention to Reduce Opioid Overdose Deaths," *Journal of Law, Medicine & Ethics*, Vol. 48, No. 2, 2020, pp. 373–375.

Dick, Andrew W., Rosalie L. Pacula, Adam J. Gordon, Mark Sorbero, Rachel M. Burns, Douglas Leslie, and Bradley D. Stein, "Growth in Buprenorphine Waivers for Physicians Increased Potential Access to Opioid Agonist Treatment, 2002–2011," *Health Affairs*, Vol. 34, No. 6, 2015, pp. 1028–1034.

DiClemente, Carlo C., Catherine M. Corno, Meagan M. Graydon, Alicia E. Wiprovnick, and Daniel J. Knoblach, "Motivational Interviewing, Enhancement, and Brief Interventions Over the Last Decade: A Review of Reviews of Efficacy and Effectiveness," *Psychology of Addictive Behaviors*, Vol. 31, No. 8, 2017, pp. 862–887.

D'Onofrio, Gail, Patrick G. O'Connor, Michael V, Pantalon, Marek C. Chawarski, Susan H. Busch, Patricia H. Owens, Steven L. Bernstein, and David A. Fiellin, "Emergency Department-Initiated Buprenorphine/Naloxone Treatment for Opioid Dependence: A Randomized Clinical Trial," *JAMA*, Vol. 313, No. 16, 2015, pp. 1636–1644.

Duber, Herbert C., Isabel A. Barata, Eric Cioè-Peña, Stephne Y. Liang, Eric Ketcham, Wendy Macias-Konstantopoulos, Shawn A. Ryan, Mark Stavros, and Lauren K. Whiteside, "Identification, Management, and Transition of Care for Patients with Opioid Use Disorder in the Emergency Department," *Annals of Emergency Medicine*, Vol. 72, No. 4, 2018, pp. 420–431.

Ducharme, Lori J., and Amanda J. Abraham, "State Policy Influence on the Early Diffusion of Buprenorphine in Community Treatment Programs," *Substance Abuse Treatment, Prevention, and Policy*, Vol. 3, No. 1, 2008, pp. 17–27.

Duncan, Alexandra, Jared Anderman, Travis Deseran, Ian Reynolds, and Bradley Stein, "Monthly Patient Volumes of Buprenorphine-Waivered Clinicians in the US," *JAMA Network Open*, Vol. 3, No. 8, 2020.

Dutra, Lissa, Georgia Stathopoulou, Shawnee L. Basden, Teresa M. Leyro, Mark B. Powers, and Michael W. Otto, "A Meta-Analytic Review of Psychosocial Interventions for Substance Use Disorders," *American Journal of Psychiatry*, Vol. 165, No. 2, 2008, pp. 179–187.

Elliott, Luther, Alex S. Bennett, and Brett Wolfson-Stofko, "Life After Opioid-Involved Overdose: Survivor Narratives and Their Implications for ER/ED Interventions," *Addiction*, Vol. 114, No. 8, August 2019, pp. 1379–1386.

EMCDDA—*See* European Monitoring Centre for Drugs and Drug Addiction.

European Monitoring Centre for Drugs and Drug Addiction, *Guidelines for the Treatment of Drug Dependence: A European Perspective*, Luxembourg: Publications Office of the European Union, November 2011.

European Monitoring Centre for Drugs and Drug Addiction, *Residential Treatment for Drug Use in Europe*, Luxembourg: Publications Office of the European Union, 2014.

European Monitoring Centre for Drugs and Drug Addiction, *Health and Social Responses to Drug Problems: A European Guide*, Luxembourg: Publications Office of the European Union, 2017.

European Monitoring Centre for Drugs and Drug Addiction, *Denmark Country Drug Report 2019*, Luxembourg: Publications Office of the European Union, 2019a.

European Monitoring Centre for Drugs and Drug Addiction, *Finland Country Drug Report 2019*, Luxembourg: Publications Office of the European Union, 2019b.

Faherty, Laura J., Ashley M. Kranz, Joshua Russell-Fritch, Stephen W. Patrick, Jonathan Cantor, and Bradley D. Stein, "Association of Punitive and Reporting State Policies Related to Substance Use in Pregnancy with Rates of Neonatal Abstinence Syndrome," *JAMA*, Vol. 2, 2019.

Falletta, Lynn, Kelsey Hamilton, Rebecca Fischbein, Julie Aultman, Beth Kinney, and Deric Kenne, "Perceptions of Child Protective Services Among Pregnant or Recently Pregnant, Opioid-Using Women in Substance Abuse Treatment," *Child Abuse & Neglect*, Vol. 79, 2018, pp. 125–135.

Fiellin, David A., and Patrick G. O'Connor, "Clinical Practice. Office-Based Treatment of Opioid-Dependent Patients," *New England Journal of Medicine*, Vol. 347, No. 11, 2002, pp. 817–823.

Formica, Scott W., Robert Apsler, Lindsay Wilkins, Sarah Ruiz, Brittni Reilly, and Alexander Y. Walley, "Post Opioid Overdose Outreach by Public Health and Public Safety Agencies: Exploration of Emerging Programs in Massachusetts," *International Journal of Drug Policy*, Vol. 54, 2018, pp. 43–50.

GAO—*See* U.S. Government Accountability Office.

Germain, Justin, *Opioid Use Disorder, Treatment, and Barriers to Employment Among TANF Recipients*, Washington, D.C.: Office of Family Assistance, Administration for Children and Families, U.S. Department of Health and Human Services, February 2018.

Gertner, Alex K., Allison G. Robertson, Byron J. Powell, Hendree Jones, Pam Silberman, and Marisa Elena Domino, "Primary Care Providers and Specialists Deliver Comparable Buprenorphine Treatment Quality," *Health Affairs*, Vol. 39, No. 8, 2020, pp. 1395–1404.

Ginley, Meredith K., Rory A. Pfund, Carla J. Rash, and Kristyn Zajac, "Long-Term Efficacy of Contingency Management Treatment Based on Objective Indicators of Abstinence from Illicit Substance Use Up to 1 Year Following Treatment: A Meta-Analysis," *Journal of Consulting and Clinical Psychology*, Vol. 89, No. 1, 2021, pp. 58–71.

Gordon, Michael S., Timothy W. Kinlock, Robert P. Schwartz, Kevin E. O'Grady, Terrence T. Fitzgerald, and Frank J. Vocci, "A Randomized Clinical Trial of Buprenorphine for Prisoners: Findings at 12-Months Post-Release," *Drug and Alcohol Dependence*, Vol. 172, 2017, pp. 34–42.

Green, Traci C., Jennifer Clarke, Lauren Brinkley-Rubinstein, Brandon D. L., Marshall, Nicole Alexander-Scott, Rebecca Boss, and Josiah D. Rich, "Postincarceration Fatal Overdoses After Implementing Medications for Addiction Treatment in a Statewide Correctional System," *JAMA Psychiatry*, Vol. 75, No. 4, 2018, pp. 405–407.

Griffith, J. D., G. A. Rowan-Szal, R. R. Roark, and D. D. Simpson, "Contingency Management in Outpatient Methadone Treatment: A Meta-Analysis," *Drug and Alcohol Dependence*, Vol. 58, No. 1–2, 2000, pp. 55–66.

Gryczynski, Jan, Robert P. Schwartz, David S. Salkever, Shannon Gwin Mitchell, and Jerome H. Jaffe, "Patterns in Admission Delays to Outpatient Methadone Treatment in the United States," *Journal of Substance Abuse Treatment*, Vol. 41, No. 4, 2011, pp. 431–439.

Hagan, Holly, James P. McGough, Hanne Thiede, Sharon Hopkins, Jeffrey Duchin, and E. Russell Alexander, "Reduced Injection Frequency and Increased Entry and Retention in Drug Treatment Associated with Needle-Exchange Participation in Seattle Drug Injectors," *Journal of Substance Abuse Treatment*, Vol. 19, No. 3, 2000, pp. 247–252.

Halford, W. Kim, and Sue M. Osgarby, "Alcohol Abuse Clients Presenting with Marital Problems," *Journal of Family Psychology*, Vol. 6, No. 3, 1993, pp. 245–254.

Hälg, Florian, Kiklas Potrafke, and Jan-Egbert Sturm, *Determinants of Social Expenditure in OECD Countries*, Zurich: KOF Swiss Economic Institute, Working Paper No. 475, 2020.

Hall, Martin T., Ruth A. Huebner, Jeanelle S. Sears, Lynn Posze, Tina Willauer, and Janell Oliver, "Sobriety Treatment and Recovery Teams in Rural Appalachia: Implementation and Outcomes," *Child Welfare*, Vol. 94, No. 4, 2015, pp. 119–138.

Hall, Martin T., Jordan Wilfong, Ruth A. Huebner, Lynn Posze, and Tina Willauer, "Medication-Assisted Treatment Improves Child Permanency Outcomes for Opioid-Using Families in the Child Welfare System," *Journal of Substance Abuse Treatment*, Vol. 71, 2016, pp. 63–67.

Hammarlund, R., K. A. Crapanzano, L. Luce, L. Mulligan, and K. M. Ward, "Review of the Effects of Self-Stigma and Perceived Social Stigma on the Treatment-Seeking Decisions of Individuals with Drug- and Alcohol-Use Disorders," *Substance Abuse and Rehabilitation*, Vol. 9, 2018, pp. 115–136.

Harris, Rebecca Arden, David S. Mandell, Kyle M. Kampman, Yuhua Bao, Kristen Campbell, Zuleyha Cidav, Donna M. Coviello, Rachel French, Cecilia Livesey, Margaret Lowenstein, et al., "Collaborative Care in the Treatment of Opioid Use Disorder and Mental Health Conditions in Primary Care: A Clinical Study Protocol," *Contemporary Clinical Trials*, Vol. 103, April 2021.

Hawk, Kathryn, Jason Hoppe, Eric Ketcham, Alexis LaPietra, Aimee Moulin, Lewis Nelson, Evan Schwarz, Sam Shahid, Donald Stader, Michael P. Wilson, and Gail D'Onofrio, "Consensus Recommendations on the Treatment of Opioid Use Disorder in the Emergency Department," *Annals of Emergency Medicine*, 2021.

Hedrich, Dagmar, Paula Alves, Michael Farrell, Heino Stöver, Lars Møller, and Soraya Mayet, "The Effectiveness of Opioid Maintenance Treatment in Prison Settings: A Systematic Review," *Addiction*, Vol. 107, No. 3, 2012, pp. 501–517.

Heimer, Robert, "Can Syringe Exchange Serve as a Conduit to Substance Abuse Treatment?" *Journal of Substance Abuse Treatment*, Vol. 15, No. 3, 1998, pp. 183–191.

Hennessy, Emily A., Emily E. Tanner-Smith, Andrew J. Finch, Nila Sathe, and Shannon Kugley, "Recovery Schools for Improving Behavioral and Academic Outcomes Among Students in Recovery from Substance Use Disorders: A Systematic Review," *Campbell Systematic Reviews*, Vol. 14, No. 1, 2018.

Higgins, S. T., D. D. Delaney, A. J. Budney, W. K. Bickel, J. R. Hughes, F. Foerg, and J. W. Fenwick, "A Behavioral Approach to Achieving Initial Cocaine Abstinence," *American Journal of Psychiatry*, Vol. 148, No. 9, 1991, pp. 1218–1224.

Hill, Lucas G., Lindsey J. Loera, Kirk E. Evoy, Mandy L. Renfro, Sorina B. Torrez, Claire M. Zagorski, Joshua C. Perez, Shaun M. Jones, and Kelly R. Reveles, "Availability of Buprenorphine/ Naloxone Films and Naloxone Nasal Spray in Community Pharmacies in Texas, USA," *Addiction*, Vol. 116, No. 6, 2021, pp. 1505–1511.

Hirai, Ashley H., Jean Y. Ko, Pamela L. Owens, Carol Stocks, and Stephen W. Patrick, "Neonatal Abstinence Syndrome and Maternal Opioid-Related Diagnoses in the US, 2010–2017," *JAMA*, Vol. 325, No. 2, 2021, pp. 146–155.

Hoge, Michael A., John A. Morris, Gail W. Stuart, Leighton Y. Huey, Sue Bergeson, Michael T. Flaherty, Oscar Morgan, Janice Peterson, Allen S. Daniels, Manuel Paris, and Kappy Madenwald, "A National Action Plan for Workforce Development in Behavioral Health," *Psychiatric Services*, Vol. 60, No. 7, 2009, pp. 883–887.

Hood, Julia E., Caleb J. Banta-Green, Jeffrey S. Duchin, Joseph Breuner, Wendy Dell, Brad Finegood, Sara N. Glick, Malin Hamblin, Shayla Holcomb, Darla Mosse, Thea Oliphant-Wells, and Mi-Hyun Mia Shim, "Engaging an Unstably Housed Population with Low-Barrier Buprenorphine Treatment at a Syringe Services Program: Lessons Learned from Seattle, Washington," *Substance Abuse*, Vol. 41, No. 3, 2020, pp. 356–364.

HUD—*See* U.S. Department of Housing and Urban Development.

Huebner, Ruth A., Tina Willauer, and Lynn Posze, "The Impact of Sobriety Treatment and Recovery Teams (START) on Family Outcomes," *Families in Society-the Journal of Contemporary Social Services*, Vol. 93, No. 3, 2012, pp. 196–203.

Huebner, Ruth A., Tina Willauer, Lynn Posze, Martin T. Hall, and Janell Oliver, "Application of the Evaluation Framework for Program Improvement of START," *Journal of Public Child Welfare*, Vol. 9, No. 1, 2015, pp. 42–64.

Huhn, Andrew S., and Kelly E. Dunn, "Why Aren't Physicians Prescribing More Buprenorphine?" *Journal of Substance Abuse Treatment*, Vol. 78, 2017.

Humphreys, Keith, and Richard G. Frank, "The Affordable Care Act Will Revolutionize Care for Substance Use Disorders in the United States," *Addiction*, Vol. 109, No. 12, 2014, pp. 1957–1958.

Hunt, George M., and N. H. Azrin, "A Community-Reinforcement Approach to Alcoholism," *Behaviour Research and Therapy*, Vol. 11, No. 1, 1973, pp. 91–104.

Iguchi, Martin Y., Leonard Handelsman, Warren K. Bickel, and Roland R. Griffiths, "Benzodiazepine and Sedative Use/Abuse by Methadone Maintenance Clients," *Drug and Alcohol Dependence*, Vol. 32, No. 3, 1993, pp. 257–266.

Iguchi, Martin Y., Jennifer A. London, Nell Griffith Forge, Laura Hickman, Terry Fain, and Kara Riehman, "Elements of Well-Being Affected by Criminalizing the Drug User," *Public Health Reports*, Vol. 117, Suppl. 1, 2002, pp. S146–S150.

Iguchi, Martin Y., Maxine L. Stitzer, George E. Bigelow, and Ira A. Liebson, "Contingency Management in Methadone Maintenance: Effects of Reinforcing and Aversive Consequences on Illicit Polydrug Use," *Drug and Alcohol Dependence*, Vol. 22, No. 1–2, 1988.

Iheanacho, Theddeus, Elina Stefanovics, and Robert Rosenheck, "Opioid Use Disorder and Homelessness in the Veterans Health Administration: The Challenge of Multimorbidity," *Journal of Opioid Management*, Vol. 14, No. 3, 2018, pp. 171–182.

Jones, Christopher M., Grant T. Baldwin, Teresa Manocchio, Jessica O. White, and Karin A. Mack, "Trends in Methadone Distribution for Pain Treatment, Methadone Diversion, and Overdose Deaths—United States, 2002–2014," *Morbidity and Mortality Weekly Report*, Vol. 65, No. 26, July 8, 2016, pp. 667–671.

Jones, Christopher M., Wilson M. Compton, Beth Han, Grant Baldwin, and Nora D. Volkow, "Methadone-Involved Overdose Deaths in the US Before and After Federal Policy Changes Expanding Take-Home Methadone Doses from Opioid Treatment Programs," *JAMA Psychiatry*, Vol. 79, No. 9, 2022, pp. 932–934.

Jones, Christopher M., and Elinore F. McCance-Katz, "Characteristics and Prescribing Practices of Clinicians Recently Waivered to Prescribe Buprenorphine for the Treatment of Opioid Use Disorder," *Addiction*, Vol. 114, No. 3, 2019, pp. 471–482.

Joudrey, Paul J., Benjamin A. Howell, Kate Nyhan, Ali Moravej, Molly Doernberg, Joseph S. Ross, and Emily A. Wang, "Reporting of Substance Use Treatment Quality in United States Adult Drug Courts," *International Journal of Drug Policy*, Vol. 90, 2021.

Kaiser Family Foundation, "State Health Facts: Professionally Active Specialist Physicians by Field," webpage, 2021. As of July 21, 2021:
https://www.kff.org/other/state-indicator/physicians-by-specialty-area

Katzelnick, David J., and Mark D. Williams, "Large-Scale Dissemination of Collaborative Care and Implications for Psychiatry," *Psychiatric Services*, Vol. 66, No. 9, 2015, pp. 904–906.

Kaufmann, M., "Recognizing the Signs and Symptoms of Distress," *Ontario Medical Review*, Vol. 66, No. 5, 1999, pp. 46–47.

Kay, Emma Sophia, D. Scott Batey, and Michael J. Mugavero, "The HIV Treatment Cascade and Care Continuum: Updates, Goals, and Recommendations for the Future," *AIDS Research and Therapy*, Vol. 13, No. 1, 2016, pp. 1–7.

Kelty, Erin, and Gary Hulse, "Fatal and Non-Fatal Opioid Overdose in Opioid Dependent Patients Treated with Methadone, Buprenorphine or Implant Naltrexone," *International Journal of Drug Policy*, Vol. 46, 2017, pp. 54–60.

Kennedy-Hendricks, Alene, Sachini Bandara, Sydney Merritt, Colleen L. Barry, and Brendan Saloner, "Structural and Organizational Factors Shaping Access to Medication Treatment for Opioid Use Disorder in Community Supervision," *Drug and Alcohol Dependence*, Vol. 226, 2021.

Kinlock, Timothy W., Michael S. Gordon, Robert P. Schwartz, Terrence T. Fitzgerald, and Kevin E. O'Grady, "A Randomized Clinical Trial of Methadone Maintenance for Prisoners: Results at 12 Months Postrelease," *Journal of Substance Abuse Treatment*, Vol. 37, No. 3, 2009, pp. 277–285.

Kirby, Kimberly C., Douglas B. Marlowe, David S. Festinger, Kerry A. Garvey, and Vincent La Monaca, "Community Reinforcement Training for Family and Significant Others of Drug Abusers: A Unilateral Intervention to Increase Treatment Entry of Drug Users," *Drug and Alcohol Dependence*, Vol. 56, No. 1, 1999, pp. 85–96.

Kohomban, Jeremy, Jennifer Rodriguez, and Ron Haskins, *The Foster Care System Was Unprepared for the Last Drug Epidemic—Let's Not Repeat History*, Washington, D.C.: Brookings Institution, 2018.

Kolodny, Andrew, David T. Courtwright, Catherine S. Hwang, Peter Kreiner, John L. Eadie, Thomas W. Clark, and G. Caleb Alexander, "The Prescription Opioid and Heroin Crisis: A Public Health Approach to an Epidemic of Addiction," *Annual Review of Public Health*, Vol. 36, 2015, pp. 559–574.

Komaromy, Miriam, Dan Duhigg, Adam Metcalf, Cristina Carlson, Summers Kalishman, Leslie Hayes, Tom Burke, Karla Thornton, and Sanjeev Arora, "Project ECHO (Extension for Community Healthcare Outcomes): A New Model for Educating Primary Care Providers About Treatment of Substance Use Disorders," *Substance Abuse*, Vol. 37, No. 1, 2016, pp. 20–24.

Korthuis, P. Todd, Dennis McCarty, Melissa Weimer, Christina Bougatsos, Ian Blazina, Bernadette Zakher, Sara Grusing, Beth Devine, and Roger Chou, "Primary Care–Based Models for the Treatment of Opioid Use Disorder: A Scoping Review," *Annals of Internal Medicine*, Vol. 166, No. 4, 2017, pp. 268–278.

Koyawala, Neel, Rachel Landis, Colleen L. Barry, Bradley D. Stein, and Brendan Saloner, "Changes in Outpatient Services and Medication Use Following a Non-Fatal Opioid Overdose in the West Virginia Medicaid Program," *Journal of General Internal Medicine*, Vol. 34, No. 6, 2019, pp. 789–791.

Krawczyk, Noa, Caroline E. Picher, Kenneth A. Feder, and Brendan Saloner, "Only One in Twenty Justice-Referred Adults in Specialty Treatment for Opioid Use Receive Methadone or Buprenorphine," *Health Affairs*, Vol. 36, No. 12, 2017, pp. 2046–2053.

Langabeer, James, Tiffany Champagne-Langabeer, Samuel D. Luber, Samuel J. Prater, Angela Stotts, Katherine Kirages, Andrea Yatsco, and Kimberly A. Chambers, "Outreach to People Who Survive Opioid Overdose: Linkage and Retention in Treatment," *Journal of Substance Abuse Treatment*, Vol. 111, 2020, pp. 11–15.

Larochelle, Marc R., Dana Bernson, Thomas Land, Thomas J. Stopka, Na Wang, Ziming Xuan, Sarah M. Bagley, Jane M. Liebschutz, and Alexander Y. Walley, "Medication for Opioid Use Disorder After Nonfatal Opioid Overdose and Association with Mortality: A Cohort Study," *Annals of Internal Medicine*, Vol. 169, No. 3, 2018, pp. 137–145.

Law Enforcement Assisted Diversion National Support Bureau, "What is LEAD?" webpage, undated. As of October 27, 2021:
https://www.leadbureau.org/about-lead

LEAD—*See* Law Enforcement Assisted Diversion.

Levit, Katharine R., Cheryl A. Kassed, Rosanna M. Coffey, Tami L. Mark, David R. McKusick, Edward C. King, Rita Vandivort-Warren, Jeffrey A. Buck, Katheryn Ryan, and Elizabeth Stranges, *Projections of National Expenditures for Mental Health Services and Substance Abuse Treatment: 2004–2014*, Rockville, Md.: Substance Abuse and Mental Health Services Administration, 2008.

Lister, Jamey J., Addie Weaver, Jennifer D. Ellis, Joseph A. Himle, and David M. Ledgerwood, "A Systematic Review of Rural-Specific Barriers to Medication Treatment for Opioid Use Disorder in the United States," *American Journal of Drug and Alcohol Abuse*, Vol. 46, No. 3, 2020, pp. 273–288.

Local Progress, "Ending Drug-Related Evictions in Public Housing," policy brief, Washington, D.C., 2019.

Lodge, Barbara Straus, "A Call for Kindness, Connection, and Science," *Journal of Substance Use and Addiction Treatment*, Vol. 141, October 2022.

Longshore, Douglas, Susan Turner, Suzanne Wenzel, Andrew Morral, Adele Harrell, Duane McBride, Elizabeth Deschenes, and Martin Iguchi, "Drug Courts: A Conceptual Framework," *Journal of Drug Issues*, Vol. 31, No. 1, 2001, pp. 7–25.

Luque, John S., Levi Ross, and Clement K. Gwede, "Qualitative Systematic Review of Barber-Administered Health Education, Promotion, Screening and Outreach Programs in African-American Communities," *Journal of Community Health*, Vol. 39, No. 1, 2014, pp. 181–190.

Lussier, Jennifer Plebani, Sarah H. Heil, Joan A. Mongeon, Gary J. Badger, and Stephen T. Higgins, "A Meta-Analysis of Voucher-Based Reinforcement Therapy for Substance Use Disorders," *Addiction*, Vol. 101, No. 2, 2006, pp. 192–203.

Ma, Jun, Yan-Ping Bao, Ru-Jia Wang, Meng-Fan Su, Mo-Xuan Liu, Jin-Qiao Li, Louisa Degenhardt, Michael Farrell, Frederic C. Blow, Mark Ilgen, Jie Shi, and Lin Lu, "Effects of Medication-Assisted Treatment on Mortality Among Opioids Users: A Systematic Review and Meta-Analysis," *Molecular Psychiatry*, Vol. 24, No. 12, 2019, pp. 1868–1883.

Madras, Bertha K., N. Jia Ahmad, Jenny Wen, and Joshua Sharfstein, "Improving Access to Evidence-Based Medical Treatment for Opioid Use Disorder: Strategies to Address Key Barriers Within the Treatment System," *National Academy of Medicine Perspectives*, 2020.

Malta, Monica, Thepikaa Varatharajan, Cayley Russell, Michelle Pang, Sarah Bonato, and Benedikt Fischer, "Opioid-Related Treatment, Interventions, and Outcomes Among Incarcerated Persons: A Systematic Review," *PloS Medicine*, Vol. 16, No. 12, 2019.

Manchikanti, Laxmaiah, Standiford Helm, II, Bert Fellows, Jeffrey W. Janata, Vidyasagar Pampati, Jay S. Grider, and Mark V. Boswell, "Opioid Epidemic in the United States," *Pain Physician*, Vol. 15, Suppl. 3, 2012, pp. ES9–ES38.

Mann, Brian, "New York City Allows the Nation's 1st Supervised Consumption Sites for Illegal Drugs," NPR, November 30, 2021.

Mark, Tami L., William J. Parish, and Gary A. Zarkin, "Association of Formulary Prior Authorization Policies with Buprenorphine-Naloxone Prescriptions and Hospital and Emergency Department Use Among Medicare Beneficiaries," *JAMA Network Open*, Vol. 3, No. 4, 2020.

Mattick, Richard P., Courtney Breen, Jo Kimber, and Marina Davoli, "Methadone Maintenance Therapy Versus No Opioid Replacement Therapy for Opioid Dependence," *Cochrane Database of Systematic Reviews*, Vol. 3, 2009.

Matusow, Harlan, Samuel L. Dickman, Josiah D. Rich, Chunki Fong, Dora M. Dumont, Carolyn Hardin, Douglas Marlowe, and Andrew Rosenblum, "Medication Assisted Treatment in US Drug Courts: Results from a Nationwide Survey of Availability, Barriers and Attitudes," *Journal of Substance Abuse Treatment*, Vol. 44, No. 5, 2013, pp. 473–480.

McBain, Ryan K., Andrew Dick, Mark Sorbero, and Bradley D. Stein, "Growth and Distribution of Buprenorphine-Waivered Providers in the United States, 2007–2017," *Annals of Internal Medicine*, Vol. 172, No. 7, 2020, pp. 504–506.

McBournie, Alaina, Alexandra Duncan, Elizabeth Connolly, and Josh Rising, "Methadone Barriers Persist, Despite Decades of Evidence," *Health Affairs Blog*, September 23, 2019. As of November 5, 2020:
https://www.healthaffairs.org/do/10.1377/hblog20190920.981503/full/

McGinty, Emma E., Elizabeth M. Stone, Alene Kennedy-Hendricks, Marcus A. Bachhuber, and Colleen L. Barry, "Medication for Opioid Use Disorder: A National Survey of Primary Care Physicians," *Annals of Internal Medicine*, Vol. 173, No. 2, 2020, pp. 160–162.

McKenna, Ryan M., "Treatment Use, Sources of Payment, and Financial Barriers to Treatment Among Individuals with Opioid Use Disorder Following the National Implementation of the ACA," *Drug and Alcohol Dependence*, Vol. 179, 2017, pp. 87–92.

Mee-Lee, David, Gerald D. Shulman, Marc Fishman, David R. Gastfriend, and Michael M. Miller, eds., *The ASAM Criteria: Treatment Criteria for Addictive, Substance-Related, and Co-Occurring Conditions*, 3rd ed., Chevy Chase, Md.: American Society of Addiction Medicine, 2013.

Meredith, Lisa S., Miriam S. Komaromy, Matthew Cefalu, Cristina Murray-Krezan, Kimberly Page, Karen Chan Osilla, Alex R. Dopp. Isabel Leamon, Lina Tarhuni, Grace Hindmarch, et al., "Design of CLARO (Collaboration Leading to Addiction Treatment and Recovery from Other Stresses): A Randomized Trial of Collaborative Care for Opioid Use Disorder and Co-Occurring Depression and/or Posttraumatic Stress Disorder," *Contemporary Clinical Trials*, Vol. 104, May 2021.

Metrebian, N., E. Carr, K. Goldsmith, T. Weaver, S. Pilling, J. Shearer, K. Woolston-Thomas, B. Tas, C. Cooper, C. A. Getty, et al., "Mobile Telephone Delivered Contingency Management for Encouraging Adherence to Supervised Methadone Consumption: Feasibility Study for an RCT of Clinical and Cost-Effectiveness (TIES)," *Pilot and Feasibility Studies*, Vol. 7, No. 14, 2021.

Meyers, Robert J., William R. Miller, Dina E. Hill, and J. Scott Tonigan, "Community Reinforcement and Family Training (CRAFT): Engaging Unmotivated Drug Users in Treatment," *Journal of Substance Abuse*, Vol. 10, No. 3, 1998, pp. 291–308.

Miech, Richard A., Lloyd D. Johnston, Patrick M. O'Malley, Jerald G. Bachman, John E. Schulenberg, and Megan E. Patrick, *Monitoring the Future National Survey Results on Drug Use, 1975–2017: Vol. I, Secondary School Students*, Ann Arbor, Mich.: Institute for Social Research, University of Michigan, 2017.

Miller, N. S., L. M. Sheppard, C. C. Colenda, and J. Magen, "Why Physicians Are Unprepared to Treat Patients Who Have Alcohol- and Drug-Related Disorders," *Academic Medicine*, Vol. 76, No. 5, 2001, pp. 410–418.

Mitchell, Ojmarrh, David B. Wilson, Amy Eggers, and Doris L. MacKenzie, "Assessing the Effectiveness of Drug Courts on Recidivism: A eta-Analytic Review of Traditional and Non-Traditional Drug Courts," *Journal of Criminal Justice*, Vol. 40, No. 1, 2012, pp. 60–71.

Moberg, D. Paul, Andrew J. Finch, and Stephanie M. Lindsley, "Recovery High Schools: Students and Responsive Academic and Therapeutic Services," *Peabody Journal of Education*, Vol. 89, No. 2, 2014, pp. 165–182.

Montanari, Linda, Luis Royuela, Ines Hasselberg, and Liesbeth Vandam, *Prison and Drugs in Europe*, Luxembourg: European Monitoring Centre for Drugs and Drug Addiction, Publications Office of the European Union, 2021.

Moore, Brent A., David A. Fiellin, Christopher J. Cutter, Frank D. Buono, Declan T. Barry, Lynn E. Fiellin, Patrick G. O'Connor, and Richard S. Schottenfeld, "Cognitive Behavioral Therapy Improves Treatment Outcomes for Prescription Opioid Users in Primary Care Buprenorphine Treatment," *Journal of Substance Abuse Treatment*, Vol. 71, 2016, pp. 54–57.

Moore, Kelly E., Walter Roberts, Holly H. Reid, Kathryn M. Z. Smith, Lindsay M. S. Oberleitner, and Sherry A. McKee, "Effectiveness of Medication Assisted Treatment for Opioid Use in Prison and Jail Settings: A Meta-Analysis and Systematic Review," *Journal of Substance Abuse Treatment*, Vol. 99, 2019, pp. 32–43.

National Academies of Sciences, Engineering, and Medicine, *Medications for Opioid Use Disorder Save Lives*, Washington, D.C.: National Academies Press, 2019.

National Association of Counties, *Medicaid Coverage and County Jails: Understanding Challenges and Opportunities for Improving Health Outcomes for Justice-Involved Individuals*, Washington, D.C., February 2017.

National Institute on Drug Abuse, *Medications to Treat Opioid Use Disorder Research Report*, Washington, D.C.: U.S. Department of Health and Human Services, June 2018a.

National Institute on Drug Abuse, "Teens Using Vaping Devices in Record Numbers," news release, December 17, 2018b.

National Sheriffs' Association and National Commission on Correctional Health Care, *Jail-Based Medication-Assisted Treatment: Promising Practices, Guidelines, and Resources for the Field*, 2018.

Novak, Priscilla, Kenneth A. Feder, Mir M. Ali, and Jie Chen, "Behavioral Health Treatment Utilization Among Individuals with Co-Occurring Opioid Use Disorder and Mental Illness: Evidence from a National Survey," *Journal of Substance Abuse Treatment*, Vol. 98, 2019, pp. 47–52.

Nunes, Edward V., Jami L. Rothenberg, Maria A. Sullivan, Kenneth M. Carpenter, and Herbert D. Kleber, "Behavioral Therapy to Augment Oral Naltrexone for Opioid Dependence: A Ceiling on Effectiveness?" *The American Journal of Drug and Alcohol Abuse*, Vol. 32, No. 4, 2006, pp. 503–517.

Nunn, Amy, Nickolas Zaller, Samuel Dickman, Catherine Trimbur, Ank Nijhawan, and Josiah D. Rich, "Methadone and Buprenorphine Prescribing and Referral Practices in US Prison Systems: Results from a Nationwide Survey," *Drug and Alcohol Dependence*, Vol. 105, No. 1–2, 2009, pp. 83–88.

O'Brien, Charles P., "A 50-Year-Old Woman Addicted to Heroin: Review of Treatment of Heroin Addiction," *JAMA*, Vol. 300, No. 3, 2008, pp. 314–321.

O'Connor, Patrick G., "Methods of Detoxification and Their Role in Treating Patients with Opioid Dependence," *JAMA*, Vol. 294, No. 8, 2005, pp. 961–963.

O'Connor, Patrick G., Julie G. Nyquist, and A. Thomas McLellan, "Integrating Addiction Medicine into Graduate Medical Education in Primary Care: The Time Has Come," *Annals of Internal Medicine*, Vol. 154, No. 1, 2011, pp. 56–59.

Olfson, Mark, Melanie Wall, Shuai Wang, Stephen Crystal, and Carlos Blanco, "Risks of Fatal Opioid Overdose During the First Year Following Nonfatal Overdose," *Drug and Alcohol Dependence*, Vol. 190, 2018, pp. 112–119.

Olfson, Mark, Victoria (Shu) Zhang, Michael Schoenbaum, and Marissa King, "Trends in Buprenorphine Treatment in the United States, 2009–2018," *JAMA*, Vol. 323, No. 3, 2020, pp. 276–277.

Oliva, Elizabeth M., Natalya C. Maisel, Adam J. Gordon, and Alex H. S. Harris, "Barriers to Use of Pharmacotherapy for Addiction Disorders and How to Overcome Them," *Current Psychiatry Reports*, Vol. 13, No. 5, 2011, pp. 374–381.

Ormsby, David, "Poll: 69% Back Illinois Law Pushing Drug Treatment Over Arrest," *Chicago Tribune*, November 27, 2018.

Osilla, Karen Chan, Elizabeth J. D'Amico, Mimi Lind, Allison J. Ober, and Katherine E. Watkins, *Brief Treatment for Substance Use Disorders: A Guide for Behavioral Health Providers*, Santa Monica, Calif.: Santa Monica, TL-147-NIDA, 2016. As of May 25, 2022: http://www.rand.org/pubs/tools/TL147.html

Osilla, Karen Chan, Katherine E. Watkins, Elizabeth J. D'Amico, Colleen M. McCullough, and Allison J. Ober, "Effects of Motivational Interviewing Fidelity on Substance Use Treatment Engagement in Primary Care," *Journal of Substance Abuse Treatment*, Vol. 87, 2018, pp. 64–69.

Otiashvili, David, Irma Kirtadze, Kevin E. O'Grady, and Hendrée E. Jones, "Drug Use and HIV Risk Outcomes in Opioid-Injecting Men in the Republic of Georgia: Behavioral Treatment + Naltrexone Compared to Usual Care," *Drug and Alcohol Dependence*, Vol. 120, No. 1, 2012, pp. 14–21.

PAARI—*See* The Police Assisted Addiction and Recovery Initiative.

Palombi, Laura, Michelle Olivarez, Laura Bennett, and Amanda N. Hawthorne, "Community Forums to Address the Opioid Crisis: An Effective Grassroots Approach to Rural Community Engagement," *Substance Abuse: Research and Treatment*, Vol. 13, 2019.

Park, Tae Woo, Marc R. Larochelle, Richard Saitz, Na Wang, Dana Bernson, and Alexander Y. Walley, "Associations Between Prescribed Benzodiazepines, Overdose Death and Buprenorphine Discontinuation Among People Receiving Buprenorphine," *Addiction*, Vol. 115, No. 5, 2020, pp. 924–932.

Patrick, Stephen W., Michael R. Richards, William D. Dupont, Elizabeth McNeer, Melinda B. Buntin, Peter R. Martin, Matthew M. Davis, Corey S. Davis, Katherine E. Hartmann, Ashley A. Leech, Kim S. Lovell, Bradley D. Stein, and William O. Cooper, "Association of Pregnancy and Insurance Status with Treatment Access for Opioid Use Disorder," *JAMA*, Vol. 3, No. 8, 2020.

Paulozzi, Leonard J., Daniel S. Budnitz, and Yongli Xi, "Increasing Deaths from Opioid Analgesics in the United States," *Pharmacoepidemiology and Drug Safety*, Vol. 15, No. 9, 2006, pp. 618–627.

Petry, Nancy M., Sheila M. Alessi, Todd A. Olmstead, Carla J. Rash, and Kristyn Zajac, "Contingency Management Treatment for Substance Use Disorders: How Far Has It Come, and Where Does It Need to Go?" *Psychology of Addictive Behaviors*, Vol. 31, No. 8, 2017, pp. 897–906.

Pew Charitable Trusts, *How and When Medicaid Covers People Under Correctional Supervision*, Philadelphia, Pa., Issue Brief, 2016.

The Police Assisted Addiction and Recovery Initiative, homepage, undated. As of May 25, 2022: https://paariusa.org/

Prendergast, Michael, Deborah Podus, John Finney, Lisa Greenwell, and John Roll, "Contingency Management for Treatment of Substance Use Disorders: A Meta-Analysis," *Addiction*, Vol. 101, No. 11, 2006, pp. 1546–1560.

Priest, Kelsey C., Honora Englander, and Dennis McCarty, "'Now Hospital Leaders Are Paying Attention': A Qualitative Study of Internal and External Factors Influencing Addiction Consult Services," *Journal of Substance Abuse Treatment*, Vol. 110, March 2020, pp. 59–65.

Priest, Kelsey C., Travis I. Lovejoy, Honora Englander, Sarah Shull, and Dennis McCarty, "Opioid Agonist Therapy During Hospitalization Within the Veterans Health Administration: a Pragmatic Retrospective Cohort Analysis," *Journal of General Internal Medicine*, Vol. 35, 2020, pp. 2365–2374.

Public Law 109-469, Office of National Drug Control Policy Reauthorization Act of 2006, December 29, 2006.

Radel, Laura, Melinda Baldwin, Gilbert Crouse, Robin Ghertner, and Annette Waters, *Substance Use, the Opioid Epidemic, and the Child Welfare System: Key Findings from a Mixed Methods Study*, Washington, D.C.: U.S. Department of Health and Human Services, Office of the Assistant Secretary for Planning and Evaluation, March 7, 2018.

Radel, Laura, Kristen Joyce, and Carli Wulff, *Drug Testing Welfare Recipients: Recent Proposals and Continuing Controversies*, Washington, D.C.: U.S. Department of Health and Human Services, Office of the Assistant Secretary for Planning and Evaluation, October 2011.

Reichert, J., *Fighting the Opioid Crisis Through Substance Use Disorder Treatment: A Study of a Police Program Model in Illinois*, Chicago, Ill., September 2017.

Reichert, Jessica, Lily Gleicher, Lynne Mock, Sharyn Adams, and Kimberly Lopez, *Police-Led Referrals to Treatment for Substance Use Disorders in Rural Illinois: An Examination of the Safe Passage Initiative*, Chicago, Ill.: Illinois Criminal Justice Information Authority, 2017.

Rettig, R. A., and A. Yarmolinsky, eds., "Chapter 7: Treatment Standards and Optimal Treatment," *Federal Regulation of Methadone Treatment*, Washington, D.C.: National Academies Press, 1995.

Reuter, Peter, "The Unintended Consequences of Drug Policies," in Franz Trautman, Beau Kilmer, and Paul Turnbull, eds., *Further Insights into Aspects of the Illicit EU Drugs Market*, Luxembourg: Publications Office of the European Union, 2009.

Reynaud, Michel, Georges Petit, Denis Potard, and Pascal Courty, "Six Deaths Linked to Concomitant Use of Buprenorphine and Benzodiazepines," *Addiction*, Vol. 93, No. 9, 1998, pp. 1385–1392.

Reynolds, Brady, Millie Harris, Stacey A. Slone, Brent J. Shelton, Jesse Dallery, William Stoops, and Russell Lewis, "A Feasibility Study of Home-Based Contingency Management with Adolescent Smokers of Rural Appalachia," *Experimental and Clinical Psychopharmacology*, Vol. 23, No. 6, 2015, pp. 486–493.

Riehman, Kara S., Martin Y. Iguchi, Michelle Zeller, and Andrew R. Morral, "The Influence of Partner Drug Use and Relationship Power on Treatment Engagement," *Drug and Alcohol Dependence*, Vol. 70, No. 1, 2003.

Rinaldo, Suzanne Gelber, and David W. Rinaldo, "Availability Without Accessibility? State Medicaid Coverage and Authorization Requirements for Opioid Dependence Medications," in *Advancing Access to Addiction Medications: Implications for Opioid Addiction Treatment*, Chevy Chase, Md.: American Society of Addiction Medicine, 2013, pp. 9–60.

Roberts, Sarah C. M., and Cheri Pies, "Complex Calculations: How Drug Use During Pregnancy Becomes a Barrier to Prenatal Care," *Maternal and Child Health Journal*, Vol. 15, No. 3, 2011, pp. 333–341.

Rogers, Andrew H., Brooke Y. Kauffman, Jafar Bakhshaie, R. Kathryn McHugh, Joseph W. Ditre, and Michael J. Zvolensky, "Anxiety Sensitivity and Opioid Misuse Among Opioid-Using Adults with Chronic Pain," *American Journal of Drug and Alcohol Abuse*, Vol. 45, No. 5, 2019, pp. 470–478.

Roman, John, "Cost-Benefit Analysis of Criminal Justice Reforms," *NIJ Journal*, Vol. 272, 2013, pp. 31–38.

Rosenblatt, Roger A., C. Holly A. Andrilla, Mary Catlin, and Eric H. Larson, "Geographic and Specialty Distribution of US Physicians Trained to Treat Opioid Use Disorder," *Annals of Family Medicine*, Vol. 13, No. 1, 2015, pp. 23–26.

Rosenblum, Andrew, Charles M. Cleland, Chunki Fong, Deborah J. Kayman, Barbara Tempalski, and Mark Parrino, "Distance Traveled and Cross-State Commuting to Opioid Treatment Programs in the United States," *Journal of Environmental and Public Health*, 2011.

Ryan-Pettes, Stacy R., Amanda Devoto, and Anthony DeFulio, "Acceptability and Willingness to Pay for Contingency Management Interventions Among Parents of Young Adults with Problematic Opioid Use," *Drug and Alcohol Dependence*, Vol. 206, 2020.

Sacco, Paul, G. Jay Unick, and Christina Gray, "Enhancing Treatment Access Through 'Safe Stations,'" *Journal of Social Work Practice in the Addictions*, Vol. 18, No. 4, 2018, pp. 458–464.

Saloner, Brendan, Anika Alvanzo, Amanda Latimore, Joshua Sharfstein, Susan Sherman, and Daniel Webster, *Ten Standards of Care: Policing and the Opioid Crisis*, Washington, D.C.: Police Executive Research Forum, 2018.

Saloner, Brendan, and Benjamin Lê Cook, "Blacks and Hispanics Are Less Likely Than Whites to Complete Addiction Treatment, Largely Due to Socioeconomic Factors," *Health Affairs*, Vol. 32, No. 1, 2013, pp. 135–145.

SAMHSA—*See* Substance Abuse and Mental Health Services Administration.

Santo, Thomas, Jr., Brodie Clark, Matt Hickman, Jason Grebely, Gabrielle Campbell, Luis Sordo, Aileen Chen, Lucy Thi Tran, Chrianna Bharat, Prianka Padmanathan, et al., "Association of Opioid Agonist Treatment with All-Cause Mortality and Specific Causes of Death Among People with Opioid Dependence: A Systematic Review and Meta-Analysis," *JAMA Psychiatry*, Vol. 78, No. 9, 2021, pp. 979–993.

Schiff, Davida M., Mari-Lynn Drainoni, Zoe M. Weinstein, Lisa Chan, Megan Bair-Merritt, and David Rosenbloom, "A Police-Led Addiction Treatment Referral Program in Gloucester, MA: Implementation and Participants' Experiences," *Journal of Substance Abuse Treatment*, Vol. 82, 2017, pp. 41–47.

Schwetz, Tara A., Thomas Calder, Elana Rosenthal, Sarah Kattakuzhy, and Anthony S. Fauci, "Opioids and Infectious Diseases: A Converging Public Health Crisis," *Journal of Infectious Diseases*, Vol. 220, No. 3, 2019, pp. 346–349.

Scott, Kelli, Cara M. Murphy, Kimberly Yap, Samantha Moul, Linda Hurley, and Sara J. Becker, "Health Professional Stigma as a Barrier to Contingency Management Implementation in Opioid Treatment Programs," *Translational Issues in Psychological Science*, Vol. 7, No. 2, 2021, pp. 166–176.

Setodji, Claude M., Katherine E. Watkins, Sarah B. Hunter, Colleen McCullough, Bradley D. Stein, Karen Chan Osilla, and Allison J. Ober, "Initiation and Engagement as Mechanisms for Change Caused by Collaborative Care in Opioid and Alcohol Use Disorders," *Drug and Alcohol Dependence*, Vol. 192, 2018, pp. 67–73.

Sigmon, Stacey C., "Access to Treatment for Opioid Dependence in Rural America: Challenges and Future Directions," *JAMA Psychiatry*, Vol. 71, No. 4, 2014, pp. 359–360.

Smart, Rosanna, *Evidence on the Effectiveness of Heroin-Assisted Treatment*, Santa Monica, Calif.: RAND Corporation, WR-1263-RC, 2018. As of May 25, 2022: https://www.rand.org/pubs/working_papers/WR1263.html

Smedslund, Geir, Rigmor C. Berg, Karianne T Hammerstrøm, Asbjørn Steiro, Kari A. Leiknes, Helene M. Dahl, and Kjetil Karlsen, "Motivational Interviewing for Substance Abuse," *Campbell Systematic Reviews*, Vol. 7, No. 1, 2011.

Sobell, Mark B., and Linda C. Sobell, *Problem Drinkers: Guided Self-Change Treatment*, New York: Guilford Press, 1993.

Socías, M. Eugenia, Nora Volkow, and Evan Wood, "Adopting the 'Cascade of Care' Framework: An Opportunity to Close the Implementation Gap in Addiction Care?" *Addiction*, Vol. 111, No. 12, 2016, pp. 2079–2081.

Spunt, Barry, Dana E. Hunt, Douglas S. Lipton, and Douglas S. Goldsmith, "Methadone Diversion: A New Look," *Journal of Drug Issues*, Vol. 16, No. 4, 1986, pp. 569–583.

Stanton, M. D., and W. R. Shadish, "Outcome, Attrition, and Family–Couples Treatment for Drug Abuse: A Meta-Analysis and Review of the Controlled, Comparative Studies," *Psychological Bulletin*, Vol. 122, No. 2, 1997, pp. 170–191.

Stein, Bradley D., Andrew W. Dick, Mark Sorbero, Adam J. Gordon, Rachel M. Burns, Douglas L. Leslie, and Rosalie Liccardo Pacula, "A Population-Based Examination of Trends and Disparities in Medication Treatment for Opioid Use Disorders Among Medicaid Enrollees," *Substance Abuse*, Vol. 39, No. 4, 2018, pp. 419–425.

Stein, Bradley D., Jane N. Kogan, and Mark Sorbero, "Substance Abuse Detoxification and Residential Treatment Among Medicaid Enrolled Adults: Rates and Duration of Subsequent Treatment," *Drug and Alcohol Dependence*, Vol. 104, No. 1–2, 2009, pp. 100–106.

Stein, Bradley, Maria Orlando, and Roland Sturm, "The Effect of Copayments on Drug and Alcohol Treatment Following Inpatient Detoxification Under Managed Care," *Psychiatric Services*, Vol. 51, No. 2, 2000, pp. 195–198.

Stein, Bradley D., Rosalie Liccardo Pacula, Adam J. Gordon, Rachel M. Burns, Douglas L. Leslie, Mark J. Sorbero, Sebastian Bauhoff, Todd W. Mandell, and Andrew W. Dick, "Where Is Buprenorphine Dispensed to Treat Opioid Use Disorders? The Role of Private Offices, Opioid Treatment Programs, and Substance Abuse Treatment Facilities in Urban and Rural Counties," *Milbank Quarterly*, Vol. 93, No. 3, 2015, pp. 561–583.

Stein, Bradley D., Brendan Saloner, Megan S. Schuler, Jill Gurvey, Mark Sorbero, and Adam J. Gordon, "Concentration of Patient Care Among Buprenorphine-Prescribing Clinicians in the US," *JAMA*, Vol. 325, No. 21, 2021, pp. 2206–2208.

Stein, Bradley D., Mark Sorbero, Andrew W. Dick, Rosalie Liccardo Pacula, Rachel M. Burns, Adam J. Gordon, "Physician Capacity to Treat Opioid Use Disorder with Buprenorphine-Assisted Treatment," *JAMA*, Vol. 316, No. 11, 2016, pp. 1211–1212.

Stitzer, Maxine L., Martin Y. Iguchi, Michael Kidorf, and George E. Bigelow, "Contingency Management in Methadone Treatment: The Case for Positive Incentives," *National Institute on Drug Abuse Research Monographs*, Vol. 137, 1993.

Stone, Elizabeth M., Alene Kennedy-Hendricks, Colleen L. Barry, Marcus A. Bachhuber, and Emma E. McGinty, "The Role of Stigma in U.S. Primary Care Physicians' Treatment of Opioid Use Disorder," *Drug and Alcohol Dependence*, Vol. 221, 2021.

Strang, Lucy, and Jirka Taylor, *Heroin-Assisted Treatment and Supervised Drug Consumption Sites: Experience from Four Countries*, Santa Monica, Calif.: RAND Corporation, WR-1262-RC, 2018. As of May 25, 2022:
https://www.rand.org/pubs/working_papers/WR1262.html

Strathdee, Steffanie A., David D. Celentano, Nina Shah, Cynthia Lyles, Veronica A. Stambolis, Grace Macalino, Kenrad Nelson, and David Vlahov, "Needle-Exchange Attendance and Health Care Utilization Promote Entry into Detoxification," *Journal of Urban Health*, Vol. 76, No. 4, 1999, pp. 448–460.

Streisel, Shannon, Christy Visher, Daniel O'Connell, and Steven S. Martin, "Using Law Enforcement to Improve Treatment Initiation and Recovery," *Federal Probation Journal*, Vol. 83, No. 2, 2019.

Stuart, R. B. "Operant-Interpersonal Treatment for Marital Discord," *Journal of Consulting and Clinical Psychology*, Vol. 33, No. 6, 1969, pp. 675–682.

Stulac, Sara, Megan Bair-Merritt, Elisha M. Wachman, Marilyn Augustyn, Carey Howard, Namrata Madoor, and Eileen Costello, "Children and Families of the Opioid Epidemic: Under the Radar," *Current Problems in Pediatric and Adolescent Health Care*, Vol. 49, No. 8, 2019.

Substance Abuse and Mental Health Services Administration, *Treatment Episode Data Sets (TEDS): 1997–2007—National Admissions to Substance Abuse Treatment Services*, Rockville, Md., 2009.

Substance Abuse and Mental Health Services Administration, *Results from the 2009 National Survey on Drug Use and Health: Detailed Tables*, Rockville, Md., 2010.

Substance Abuse and Mental Health Services Administration, "Medication Assisted Treatment for Opioid Use Disorders," *Federal Register*, Vol. 81, 2016a, pp. 44711–44739.

Substance Abuse and Mental Health Services Administration, *Facing Addiction in America: The Surgeon General's Report on Alcohol, Drugs, and Health*, Washington, D.C.: U.S. Department of Health and Human Services, November 2016b.

Substance Abuse and Mental Health Services Administration, "Chapter 6: Health Care Systems and Substance Use Disorders," in *Facing Addiction in America: The Surgeon General's Report on Alcohol, Drugs, and Health*, Washington, D.C.: U.S. Department of Health and Human Services, November 2016c, pp. 6-1–6-45.

Substance Abuse and Mental Health Services Administration, *National Survey of Substance Abuse Treatment Services (N-SSATS): 2020—Data on Substance Abuse Treatment Facilities*, Rockville, Md., 2021a.

Substance Abuse and Mental Health Services Administration, "Practitioner and Program Data," webpage, February 2, 2021b. As of August 5, 2021:
https://www.samhsa.gov/medication-assisted-treatment/practitioner-resources/
DATA-program-data

Substance Abuse and Mental Health Services Administration, Center for Behavioral Health Statistics and Quality, *The N-SSATS Report: Trends in the Use of Methadone and Buprenorphine at Substance Abuse Treatment Facilities: 2003 to 2011*, Rockville, Md., 2013.

Sumnall, Harry, and Angelina Brotherhood, *Social Reintegration and Employment: Evidence and Interventions for Drug Users in Treatments*, Luxembourg: Publications Office of the European Union, European Monitoring Centre for Drugs and Drug Addiction, 2012.

Thomas, Cindy Parks, Erin Doyle, Peter W. Kreiner, Christopher M. Jones, Joel Dubenitz, Alexis Horan, and Bradley D. Stein, "Prescribing Patterns of Buprenorphine Waivered Physicians," *Drug and Alcohol Dependence*, Vol. 181, 2017, pp. 213–218.

Thomas, Edwin J., and Richard D. Agar, "Unilateral Family Therapy with the Spouses of Uncooperative Alcohol Abusers," in Timothy J. O'Farrell, ed., *Treating Alcohol Problems: Marital and Family Interventions*, New York: Guilford Press, 1993, pp. 3–33.

Timko, C., N. R. Schultz, J. Britt, and M. A. Cucciare, "Transitioning from Detoxification to Substance Use Disorder Treatment: Facilitators and Barriers," *Journal of Substance Abuse Treatment*, Vol. 70, 2016, pp. 64–72.

Turner, Susan, Douglas Longshore, Suzanne Wenzel, Elizabeth Deschenes, Peter Greenwood, Terry Fain, Adele Harrell, Andrew Morral, Faye Taxman, Martin Iguchi, Judith Greene, and Duane McBride, "A Decade of Drug Treatment Court Research," *Substance Use & Misuse*, Vol. 37, No. 12–13, 2002, pp. 1489–1527.

U.S. Department of Housing and Urban Development, *Admissions/Eviction Policies for Public Housing/Voucher Lease Holders*, Washington, D.C., May 3, 2013.

U.S. Department of Justice, Office of Justice Programs, *Drug Courts*, Washington, D.C., August 2021.

U.S. Government Accountability Office, *Social Security Disability: Action Needed to Help Agency Staff Understand and Follow Policies Related to Prescription Opioid Misuse*, Washington, D.C., GAO-20-120, January 2020.

U.S. Senate, Drug Addiction Treatment Act of 2000, Bill 2634, July 27, 2000.

Vakkalanka, Priyanka, Brian C. Lund, Stephan Arndt, William Field, Mary Charlton, Marcia M. Ward, and Ryan M. Carnahan, "Association Between Buprenorphine for Opioid Use Disorder and Mortality Risk," *American Journal of Preventive Medicine*, Vol. 61, No. 3, 2021, pp. 418–427.

Vestal, Christine, "At Rikers Island, a Legacy of Medication-Assisted Opioid Treatment," *Stateline*, Pew Charitable Trusts Blog, May 23, 2016. As of May 25, 2022: https://www.pewtrusts.org/en/research-and-analysis/blogs/stateline/2016/05/23/ at-rikers-island-a-legacy-of-medication-assisted-opioid-treatment

Votaw, Victoria R., Rachel Geyer, Maya M. Rieselbach, and R. Kathryn McHugh, "The Epidemiology of Benzodiazepine Misuse: A Systematic Review," *Drug and Alcohol Dependence*, Vol. 200, 2019, pp. 95–114.

Wagner, Karla D., Robert W. Harding, Richard Kelley, Brian Labus, Silvia R. Verdugo, Elizabeth Copulsky, Jeanette M. Bowles, Maria Luisa Mittal, and Peter J. Davidson, "Post-Overdose Interventions Triggered by Calling 911: Centering the Perspectives of People Who Use Drugs (PWUDs)," *PLoS One*, Vol. 14, No. 10, 2019.

Wagner, Karla D., Thomas W. Valente, Mark Casanova, Susan M. Partovi, Brett M. Mendenhall, James H. Hundley, Mario Gonzalez, and Jennifer B. Unger, "Evaluation of an Overdose Prevention and Response Training Programme for Injection Drug Users in the Skid Row Area of Los Angeles, CA," *International Journal of Drug Policy*, Vol. 21, No. 3, 2010, pp. 186–193.

Wakeman, Sarah E., Joshua P. Metlay, Yuchiao Chang, Grace E. Herman, and Nancy A. Rigotti, "Inpatient Addiction Consultation for Hospitalized Patients Increases Post-Discharge Abstinence and Reduces Addiction Severity," *Journal of General Internal Medicine*, Vol. 32, No. 8, 2017, pp. 909–916.

Wakeman, Sarah E., Nancy A. Rigotti, Yuchiao Chang, Grace E. Herman, Ann Erwin, Susan Regan, and Joshua P. Metlay, "Effect of Integrating Substance Use Disorder Treatment into Primary Care on Inpatient and Emergency Department Utilization," *Journal of General Internal Medicine*, Vol. 34, No. 6, 2019, pp. 871–877.

Watkins, Katherine E., Allison J. Ober, Karen Lamp, Mimi Lind, Allison Diamant, Karen Chan Osilla, Keith Heinzerling, Sarah B. Hunter, Harold Alan Pincus, "Implementing the Chronic Care Model for Opioid and Alcohol Use Disorders in Primary Care," *Progress in Community Health Partnerships*, Vol. 11, No. 4, 2017a, pp. 397–407.

Watkins, Katherine E., Allison J. Ober, Karen Lamp, Mimi Lind, Claude Setodji, Karen Chan Osilla, Sarah B. Hunter, Colleen M. McCullough, Kirsten Becker, Praise O. Iyiewuare, et al., "Collaborative Care for Opioid and Alcohol Use Disorders in Primary Care: The SUMMIT Randomized Clinical Trial," *JAMA Internal Medicine*, Vol. 177, 2017b, pp. 1480–1488.

Weiss, Robert L., Hyman Hope, and Gerald R. Patterson, "A Framework for Conceptualizing Marital Conflict: A Technology for Altering It, Some Data for Evaluating It," in L. A. Hamerlynck, L. Handy, and E. Mash, eds., *Behavior Change: Methodology, Concepts, and Practice*, Champaign, Ill.: Research Press, 1973, pp. 390–342.

White, William L., *Slaying the Dragon: The History of Addiction Treatment and Recovery in America*, Bloomington, Ill.: Chestnut Health Systems/Lighthouse Institute, 1998.

Wilder Research and Volunteers of America, *Family-Based Residential Treatment: Directory of Residential Substance Use Disorder Treatment Programs for Parents with Children*, St. Paul, Minn., March 2019, updated July 2019.

Willems, Johannes C. E. W., Martin Y. Iguchi, Victor Lidz, and Donald A. Bux, "Change in Drug-Using Networks of Injecting Drug Users During Methadone Treatment: A Pilot Study Using Snowball Recruitment and Intensive Interviews," *Substance Use & Misuse*, Vol. 32, No. 11, 1997, pp. 1539–1554.

Williams, Arthur Robin, Edward V. Nunes, Adam Bisaga, Harold A. Pincus, Kimberly A. Johnson, Aimee N. Campbell, Remien H. Remien, Stephen Crystal, Peter D. Friedmann, Frances R. Levin, and Mark Olfson, "Developing an Opioid Use Disorder Treatment Cascade: A Review of Quality Measures," *Journal of Substance Abuse Treatment*, Vol. 91, 2018, pp. 57–68.

Winstanley, Erin L., and Amanda N. Stover, "The Impact of the Opioid Epidemic on Children and Adolescents," *Clinical Therapeutics*, Vol. 41. No. 9, 2019, pp. 1655–1662.

Wu, April Yanyuan, Peter Mariani, Jia Pu, and Andrew Hurwitz, *A New Approach to Analyzing Opioid Use Among SSDI Applicants*, Washington, D.C.: Mathematica Policy Research, 2020.

Zhang, Saijun, Hui Huang, Qi Wu, Yong Li, and Meirong Liu, "The Impacts of Family Treatment Drug Court on Child Welfare Core Outcomes: A Meta-Analysis," *Child Abuse and Neglect*, Vol. 88, 2019.

CHAPTER FIVE

Medical Care

Tisamarie B. Sherry[1]

Overview

The medical care system is a critical component of the opioid ecosystem. It both *contributes* to the opioid crisis, by shaping opioid treatment for pain and other risk factors for opioid use disorder (OUD), and *mitigates* it as a major setting in which OUD and its complications are treated. This chapter describes the numerous interactions between the medical care system and the opioid crisis. These include the following:

- **Pain management:** The medical care system is the main setting in which severe pain is treated. Pain management approaches are influenced by characteristics of health care providers (e.g., training, specialty, preferences), health care delivery organizations, insurer policies, and the medical education and licensing systems.
- **Addressing the misuse of prescription opioid analgesics:** The medical care system has been central to many efforts to limit opioid misuse. Health care delivery organizations have developed clinical guidelines promoting safer opioid prescribing practices, shaped by guidance from professional societies and state and national public health agencies, along with clinical interventions to prevent opioid misuse and diversion (e.g., electronic health record defaults, clinical decision support). Insurers have used utilization management tools and provider oversight to encourage safer prescribing. Pharmacies aim to prevent opioid misuse by verifying prescriptions, educating patients, and implementing opioid take-back and safe disposal initiatives to reduce the risk of diversion. State governments have shaped many of these activities through regulatory efforts, such as prescription drug monitoring programs (PDMPs), and legislation limiting the dose or duration of opioid therapy for acute pain.

---

[1] This chapter was conceived of and drafted when Dr. Sherry was employed at the RAND Corporation, and the findings and views in this chapter do not necessarily reflect the official views or policy of her current employer, the U.S. Department of Health and Human Services, or the U.S. government.

- **Treatment of OUD:** Treatment of OUD has increasingly expanded beyond the specialty addiction treatment system to involve the general medical care system. Medications for OUD (MOUD) can be provided in emergency departments, inpatient hospital units, and primary care settings; medications are being expanded to additional care settings frequented by patients with OUD (e.g., prenatal care). The medical education and licensing systems influence OUD diagnosis and treatment by training providers to recognize OUD and provide evidence-based care, while insurers influence the use of such treatments through benefit and formulary design. Finally, both state governments and the federal government influence the capacity of health care professionals to prescribe MOUD through scope-of-practice laws and federal regulations governing buprenorphine (e.g., the Drug Addiction Treatment Act [DATA] waiver), respectively.[2]
- **Prevention and treatment of common complications and comorbidities associated with opioid misuse:** The medical care system is the primary setting in which complications and comorbidities of opioid misuse are managed, notably infectious complications of injection heroin and synthetic opioid use (e.g., HIV, hepatitis B [HBV], and hepatitis C [HCV], soft-tissue infections, endocarditis) and such common comorbidities as non-opioid substance use disorders (SUDs) and psychiatric disorders. The medical care system also addresses the family and intergenerational impacts of the opioid crisis, including neonatal opioid withdrawal syndrome (NOWS) and other physical and mental health conditions that are prevalent among children whose parents misuse opioids. Finally, the medical care system supports certain harm reduction initiatives and overdose prevention (e.g., prescribing naloxone).

Key Interactions with Other Components of the Ecosystem

The medical care system interacts with nearly every other component of the opioid ecosystem. In particular, it interacts with the **specialty addiction treatment system** by extending treatment capacity for OUD and other SUDs; it interacts with the **criminal legal system** by providing medical care in correctional settings to the estimated 15 percent of inmates with OUD (Baillargeon et al., 2009; James and Glaze, 2006; Leshner and Mancher, 2019b) and in the especially vulnerable postincarceration period, when opioid overdose is among the leading causes of death (Binswanger et al., 2013). In some states, law enforcement partners with state health agencies on initiatives to limit opioid misuse (e.g., PDMPs, drug treatment courts). Conversely, activities of the medical care and criminal legal systems can sometimes be in conflict. For example, policies that criminalize or otherwise punish substance use during pregnancy might discourage women with OUD from seeking prenatal care or OUD treatment.

The medical care system and **illegal opioid supply** have important and complex interactions. On the one hand, the overprescribing of opioid analgesics in health care settings con-

---

[2] After this volume went to press, legislation eliminated the requirement for the waiver.

tributes to opioid dependence, misuse, and diversion. On the other hand, there are concerns that some efforts to limit opioid prescribing and prevent the misuse of opioids prescribed by clinicians in the medical care system might have had the unintended consequence of shifting demand toward illegal opioids.

The medical care system interacts with **first responders** by caring for the approximately 300,000 individuals brought to emergency departments annually following nonfatal opioid overdoses (Vivolo-Kantor et al., 2020); with the **harm reduction and community-initiated interventions component** through harm reduction initiatives, such as naloxone prescribing and distribution, which contributed to a doubling in pharmacy-based naloxone dispensing between 2017 and 2018 alone (Guy et al., 2019); and with **income support and homeless services** by connecting patients with needed services, notably housing. Among children who have suffered maltreatment as a result of their parents' struggles with opioid misuse, the medical care system plays a role in identifying these harms and involving **child welfare services**.

Interactions also occur with the **employment system**: The medical care system evaluates the eligibility of individuals for workers' compensation or disability insurance benefits. At the same time, many of these individuals are on long-term opioid therapy for pain, and opioid overprescribing in health care settings can contribute to patients' opioid dependence and declining work-related functioning.

Policy Opportunities and Considerations

Given its central role in the opioid crisis and interactions with other components of the opioid ecosystem, the medical care system presents numerous policy opportunities for mitigating the crisis. Several such opportunities are highlighted in this section.

Balancing the Goals of Effective Pain Treatment and Prevention of Opioid Misuse

Opioid prescribing rates have fallen in the United States in recent years in the face of growing concerns about the risks of using opioids to treat pain, but they are still very high compared with rates in other countries. It is hoped that limiting the use of opioid analgesics to treat pain can reduce the flow of people into both prescription and illegal opioid misuse. However, there are also concerns about potential negative unintended consequences of limiting the prescribing of opioids, including the undertreatment of pain, withdrawal and depression resulting from abrupt tapering of long-term opioid therapy, barriers to general medical care among patients on chronic opioid therapy, and possibly even shifting demand toward the illegal opioid market. Therefore, a critical policy challenge facing the medical care system— and involving the illegal supply system—is how to prevent opioid misuse while still ensuring high-quality pain care. This will likely require changes in medical training on pain care, policies to expand the capacity of health care organizations to provide non-opioid evidence-based pain treatment, and policies to reduce financial barriers to such treatment. It will also require efforts by both the medical care and illegal supply systems to systematically monitor for and share data on negative unintended consequences of policies to limit opioid analgesic prescribing.

Expanding Access to OUD Treatment

Given capacity constraints in the specialty addiction treatment system, the medical care system presents a critical yet underutilized opportunity to expand access to MOUD. Scaling up OUD treatment will require reforms to medical training to better equip providers to treat OUD; prioritization of OUD treatment by health care organizations, including delivery reforms and clinical innovations to facilitate the broader use of MOUD in a variety of general medical care settings; efforts by professional societies and public health agencies to establish standards for high-quality OUD treatment and to monitor performance; and action by payers to reduce financial barriers to MOUD. It will also be important for state and federal agencies and lawmakers to continuously reevaluate the appropriateness of the additional restrictions placed on the use of certain medications to treat OUD (e.g., the DATA 2000 waiver for buprenorphine). Many of these policies can be advanced through increased collaboration between the specialty addiction treatment and medical care systems (e.g., Vermont's Hub-and-Spoke system) and collaborative care models (e.g., Massachusetts's nurse care manager program).

Interagency Collaboration and Care Integration

Individuals with OUD often face other physical and mental health challenges and social and economic vulnerabilities. A growing literature has demonstrated that such individuals benefit from integrating OUD treatment with other medical, psychiatric, and social services tailored to their needs, spanning other components discussed in this report. The medical care system currently connects individuals with OUD to services across these systems—but there is significant room to integrate care more effectively. This will require cross-systems collaboration, data-sharing across organizations, and flexible financing models to facilitate integrated service provision. Promising examples of cross-systems collaboration for integrated OUD care include the Rikers Island Key Extended Entry Program (which involves medical care, criminal legal system, and specialty addiction treatment components); the Vermont Children and Recovering Mothers Collaborative (which involves medical care, specialty addiction treatment, education, and child welfare systems); and Oregon's Housing Choice model (which involves medical care, specialty addiction treatment, income support and homelessness services, and employment systems).

Introduction

The medical care system is a central component of the opioid ecosystem. It both *contributes* to the opioid crisis, by shaping opioid treatment for pain and other risk factors for the development of OUD, and *mitigates* it as a major setting in which OUD and its complications are treated. This chapter describes the role of the medical care system in the opioid ecosystem, including its important linkages with other aspects of the ecosystem. The chapter is organized as follows. This chapter begins by describing the four activities of the medical care system with respect to the opioid crisis. For each of these activities, the chapter then presents discussion of the relevant components of the medical care system and how they interact to influence opioid-related outcomes for individuals and families. Next, the chapter explores how the medical system interacts with other key elements of the opioid ecosystem (see Figure 5.1). It concludes with a discussion of policy opportunities to strengthen the role of the medical care system in mitigating the opioid crisis, as well as challenges that will need to be overcome to do so.

System Components and How They Interact with Opioids

Activities of the Medical Care System in the Context of the Opioid Crisis

The medical care system has four principal activities with respect to the opioid crisis:

- manage acute and chronic pain
- address diversion and misuse of prescription opioids
- treat OUD
- prevent and treat common complications and comorbidities associated with opioid misuse.

Pain Management

The medical care system is the main setting in which severe acute and chronic pain are treated. Providers treating pain must balance the goals of effective pain relief that improves functioning and quality of life with the safety profile of different pain treatment modalities and the risks of diversion (Owen et al., 2018; Rosenblum et al., 2008). There is growing evidence that opioids have limited efficacy in treating chronic noncancer pain: In the Strategies for Prescribing Analgesics Comparative Effectiveness trial, for example, opioids were not superior to non-opioid treatments in improving pain-related functioning among veterans with chronic back or arthritis pain (Krebs et al., 2018). Therefore, given the known adverse effects of opioids, providers are increasingly encouraged to prescribe non-opioid therapies for pain when appropriate (Dowell, Haegerich, and Chou, 2016), particularly for chronic pain. Decreasing the utilization of opioids in individuals for whom adequate pain management can be achieved through non-opioid approaches, and decreasing the amount of opioids needed to

FIGURE 5.1

The Medical Care System and Its Interactions

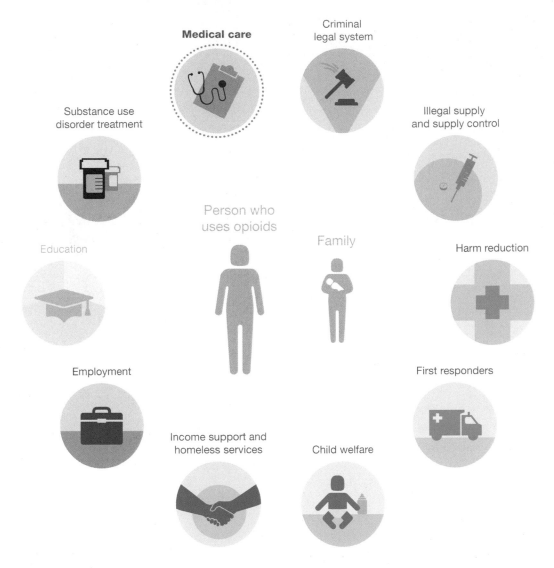

manage pain through the concurrent use of non-opioid pain management approaches, can result in prescribing fewer opioids while not compromising patient care. This can reduce the number of individuals exposed to opioids who might go on to misuse and dependence and can decrease the supply of opioids that can be diverted for misuse. Access to a variety of non-opioid pain therapies—particularly nonpharmacological treatments—depends on whether such therapies are offered by health care delivery organizations and the extent to which they are covered by payers (National Association of Attorneys General, 2017). Although non-opioid therapy for pain is preferable when possible, there are some clinical scenarios in which treatment with opioid analgesics is appropriate, so providers have been called on to maintain access to prescription opioids for this subset of patients (Kroenke et al., 2019).

Addressing the Misuse of Prescription Opioid Analgesics

The medical care system is central to many efforts to reduce the misuse of opioid pain medications. The majority of individuals who are prescribed opioids for pain do not develop opioid misuse (Minozzi, Amato, and Davoli, 2013), but certain patient and prescription characteristics (e.g., male sex, younger age, mental health or SUD history, higher opioid doses, longer opioid treatment duration) increase this risk (Campbell et al., 2020; Cragg et al., 2019; Voon, Karamouzian, and Kerr, 2017). Numerous policy initiatives and health care delivery reforms have sought to educate both providers and patients about the appropriate use of opioids, reduce risky or inappropriate opioid prescribing by providers, and prevent and monitor for care-seeking patterns that can indicate opioid misuse or diversion (e.g., "doctor shopping") (Haegerich et al., 2019; Mauri, Townsend, and Haffajee, 2020).

Treatment of OUD

Although OUD treatment is an essential health service, access to evidence-based therapies has historically been limited in the general medical care system (Lapham et al., 2020). Efforts to expand the availability of MOUD in general medical care settings (e.g., initiatives to increase the number of physicians with DATA 2000 waivers) and improve its affordability (e.g., expanded insurance coverage of MOUD) have increased access to these therapies (Jones et al., 2015; Sandoe, Fry, and Frank, 2018). As a result, treatment for OUD has increasingly shifted from specialty behavioral health settings into mainstream medical care settings, such as primary care (Korthuis et al., 2017; Lagisetty et al., 2017), prenatal care, emergency rooms (D'Onofrio et al., 2015; D'Onofrio et al., 2017), and even inpatient hospital settings (Liebschutz et al., 2014; Suzuki, 2016; Trowbridge et al., 2017). Medical providers can initiate and continue MOUD, link patients to other providers offering evidence-based treatments, and offer harm reduction (e.g., naloxone distribution) (Korthuis et al., 2017). Despite these changes, the availability of OUD treatment in general medical settings remains insufficient to meet demand (Jones and McCance-Katz, 2019).

Prevention and Treatment of Common Complications and Comorbidities Associated with Opioid Diversion and Misuse

The medical care system is the primary setting in which complications, comorbidities, and other harms of opioid misuse are managed. Individuals who are dependent on opioids may have their detoxification overseen by the medical system, which can enhance safety and decrease discomfort associated with opioid withdrawal. Infectious complications of injection heroin and synthetic opioid use include HCV, HIV, endocarditis, and skin and soft-tissue infections (Springer, Korthuis, and Del Rio, 2018), all of which are treated in the general medical care system. OUD frequently is comorbid with other mental health disorders and SUDs. These conditions can be managed in primary care settings, although more-severe and more-complex manifestations may warrant treatment in specialty behavioral health settings (Brooner et al., 1997; Griffin et al., 2014; Saunders et al., 2015). Finally, complications of opioid misuse may be experienced not only by individuals who misuse opioids but also by their family members. For example, infants born to women who misuse opioids are at risk of NOWS (Ko et al., 2016; Winkelman et al., 2018), and children whose parents misuse opioids have an increased risk of physical and mental health problems (Anda et al., 2006). Therefore, the medical system also addresses the intergenerational and family complications of opioid misuse in adult, obstetric, and pediatric health care settings.

Components of the Medical Care System

The U.S. medical care system is complex, comprises many individual and often poorly coordinated actors, and includes components that interact with and affect individuals who use opioids through a variety of avenues. Health care providers, for example, interact directly with individuals who use opioids; medical schools and state medical boards influence individuals through their impacts on health care providers; and insurers interact with patients both directly through coverage decisions and indirectly through restrictions placed on providers.

Components Relevant to Pain Management

Health Care Providers

Frontline health care providers are the interface between patients and the rest of the medical care system, and their opioid treatment patterns have been the subject of much research and scrutiny.

Providers who can **legally prescribe opioids** to treat pain include physicians, dentists, and physician-extenders with prescribing authority—depending on the state, this can include physician assistants, nurse practitioners, registered pharmacists, and other practitioners (Drug Enforcement Administration [DEA], 2019). Among physicians, numerous specialties care for patients with pain. Opioid prescribing rates vary markedly across specialties, and primary care physicians, surgeons, pain medicine specialists, and physical medicine and rehabilitation specialists account for a substantial share of opioid prescriptions (Levy et al., 2015; Weiner et al., 2018). The majority of chronic pain management occurs in primary care settings (Institute of Medicine, 2011), but pain specialists (typically anesthesiologists with additional subspecialty training in pain management) have a consultative role in the management of patients with especially severe pain or complex comorbidities (Owen et al., 2018). Oncologists and palliative care physicians may use opioids to treat severe pain associated with cancer and end-of-life care.

Providers who **do not prescribe opioids but may distribute them or monitor their use** include pharmacists,[3] nurses, home health providers, and nonphysician staff in long-term care facilities or hospice.

---

[3] Pharmacists have opioid prescribing authority in some states.

A final category of providers involved in pain care is those who **exclusively offer non-opioid, or even nonpharmacological, pain therapies**—this group includes physical therapists; occupational therapists; pain psychologists; acupuncturists; chiropractors; massage therapists; and specialists in yoga, mindfulness, or meditation (Institute of Medicine, 2011). Some of these nonpharmacological services and interventions (e.g., acupuncture, meditation, yoga) are considered complementary and alternative medicine services and are typically offered outside traditional medical settings (Institute of Medicine, 2011).

Pain care, like many other types of medical care, has traditionally been siloed, with limited coordination between different provider types (Polacek et al., 2020). Increasingly, however, it has been recognized that interdisciplinary pain management teams, in which different types of providers collaborate to provide coordinated and multimodal treatment, might hold promise for improving the quality of chronic pain management (Institute of Medicine, 2011), and there is emerging evidence that they might safely reduce opioid prescribing specifically (Seal et al., 2017).

Providers' attitudes toward different pain management strategies—and opioid analgesics in particular—have undergone significant changes in recent years. Between the mid-1990s and the mid-2010s, the intensity of pain treatment increased and prescription opioid use rose more than threefold (Guy et al., 2017). These changes were prompted by concerns about the undertreatment of pain and calls by professional societies to improve pain assessment and management (e.g., the American Pain Society's "Pain as a Fifth Vital Sign" campaign) (Tompkins, Hobelmann, and Compton, 2017) and were subsequently reinforced by policies and practices promulgated by health care delivery organizations and regulatory bodies (e.g., the Joint Commission's standards for pain management) (Baker, 2017; Mularski et al., 2006).

Current clinical guidelines discourage the use of opioid analgesics for managing acute or chronic pain in most circumstances (Dowell, Haegerich, and Chou, 2016). This shift in the medical community's approach to pain management has been prompted by accumulating evidence on the limited efficacy of opioids in treating chronic pain (Krebs et al., 2018), together with a growing appreciation of the risks and potential harms of prescription opioids, particularly when used long term (Baldini, Von Korff, and Lin, 2012). As a result, the rate of opioid prescriptions in the United States has fallen considerably—although it is still the highest in the world (Duff et al., 2021; Suda et al., 2019). Between 2012 and 2017, the rate of initial opioid prescriptions to opioid-naive[4] commercially insured adults fell 50 percent (Zhu et al., 2019); during this same period, the overall monthly opioid prescribing rate fell 35 percent (Bohnert, Guy, and Losby, 2018). Declining rates of opioid prescriptions have generally been viewed as a policy success because prescription opioid exposure—and, in particular, chronic use—can lead to misuse, overdose, dependence, and OUD (Martell et al., 2007; Volkow and McLellan, 2016; Vowles et al., 2015). Among individuals with chronic pain who are treated with prescription opioids, meta-analyses estimate rates of opioid misuse ranging from 5 to

---

[4] The term *opioid-naive* describes individuals with "no opioid prescriptions or evidence of OUD in the six months prior to the index prescription" (Burke et al., 2020, p. 495).

24 percent (Martell et al., 2007) and rates of opioid addiction ranging from 8 to 12 percent (Vowles et al., 2015).

Excess opioid prescribing can also increase the supply of diverted prescriptions, placing others at risk (Han et al., 2017). In a study that used commercial claims data to identify individuals with diagnoses of opioid misuse but no opioid prescriptions prior to their diagnoses, 50 percent of these individuals had a family member who had previously received an opioid prescription (Shei et al., 2015). Reducing unnecessary exposure to prescription opioids can reduce the frequency of these negative downstream consequences and prevent many people from developing OUD over the longer term. Modeling studies also estimate that reducing opioid prescriptions for both acute and chronic pain can reduce opioid overdose deaths over a ten-year horizon because of a decrease in the incidence of OUD (Pitt, Humphreys, and Brandeau, 2018).

A key consideration, however, involves the manner in which such reductions in opioid prescribing are achieved and the goal of avoiding negative unintended consequences for individuals with chronic pain. Health care providers, patients, and advocacy groups have voiced concerns that growing "opioid hesitancy" might result in inadequate access to pain treatment for individuals with severe, disabling pain for whom other therapies have not been effective (Hoffman, 2018; Kertesz, 2017). There are also concerns that more-restrictive opioid prescribing policies might disproportionately harm patients from minority racial and ethnic groups, who are already less likely to receive opioids for pain and more likely to experience discontinuation of long-term opioid treatment (Burgess et al., 2014; Gaither et al., 2018; Phan et al., 2021; Singhal, Tien, and Hsia, 2016). There is limited but accumulating evidence on the ways in which individuals with pain might experience harm as a result of more-restrictive opioid prescribing practices, especially patients with chronic pain on long-term opioid therapy, who are at increased risk of adverse health outcomes if opioid therapy is abruptly discontinued or tapered too quickly (Mark and Parish, 2019; Oliva et al., 2020). A large study of individuals with commercial insurance or Medicare Advantage who were prescribed opioids between 2008 and 2017 found that dose tapering has become more common since 2016, including tapering at rates that exceed those recommended by guidelines from the Centers for Disease Control and Prevention (CDC) (Fenton et al., 2019). Similarly, a study of Medicaid beneficiaries in Vermont who received chronic high-dose opioid analgesic therapy between 2013 and 2017 found that more than 50 percent of patients who discontinued opioid treatment did so suddenly. This study also highlighted the potential risks of rapid discontinuation: 49 percent of patients who discontinued opioid treatment had an opioid-related emergency department or hospital visit, but the probability of these adverse events decreased by 7 percent with each additional week that dose tapering was extended (Mark and Parish, 2019). A national study of patients receiving care from the Veterans Health Administration found that all patients who were exposed to opioids had an increased risk of death because of overdose or suicide after stopping opioids and that the risk increased with the length of time an individual had been treated with opioids (Oliva et al., 2020).

There is concern that, in addition to their impacts on opioid prescribing patterns, restrictive prescribing policies and stigmatizing attitudes among clinicians with respect to caring for individuals with SUDs may serve as a barrier to care for patients with chronic pain more broadly (Kennedy-Hendricks et al., 2016; Stone et al., 2021). In a survey of members of the North Carolina medical board, 13 percent had stopped accepting new patients on chronic opioid therapy for pain (North Carolina Medical Board, 2018). In an audit study in Michigan, 40 percent of primary care clinics that were contacted declined new patients receiving opioids for pain (Lagisetty et al., 2019). Although evidence is still emerging, concerns about possible unintended consequences of restricting access to prescription opioids have been sufficient to prompt the authors of the CDC's 2016 opioid prescribing guideline to issue a clarification reminding clinicians of the need for flexibility and attention to individual patients' circumstances when applying the guideline and of the harm that can result from abrupt tapers, discontinuation of long-term opioid treatment, or dismissal from care (Dowell, Haegerich, and Chou, 2019).

Much of the policy discussion about health care providers' opioid prescribing practices has focused on the risks and benefits of opioid treatment for chronic noncancer pain. However, research has also highlighted the need to examine the ways in which acute pain treatment practices might influence opioid misuse and dependence. Studies have identified a higher risk of developing chronic opioid use among opioid-naive individuals who receive opioids for acute pain management in a hospital setting, compared with individuals who do not receive opioids (Calcaterra et al., 2016; Donohue et al., 2019). In addition, there is limited research on how to optimally balance the risks and benefits of opioid treatment for pain among patients with serious illnesses, such as advanced cancer, including those with comorbid substance misuse or SUD (Jones and Merlin, 2021; Merlin et al., 2020). Such patients are typically excluded from guidelines for opioid prescribing, but there are concerns that the guidelines intended to address noncancer pain might be misapplied to this population (Jairam et al., 2021; Tyson et al., 2021). On the other hand, as treatments for cancers and other serious illnesses have advanced and survivorship has improved, there is a need to understand the longer-term consequences of opioid treatment for pain in serious illness and how an understanding of these consequences can inform safe pain management (Jairam et al., 2020; Jones et al., 2021; Salz et al., 2021).

Health Care Delivery Organizations

Health care delivery organizations that offer pain treatment include physician groups, hospitals, long-term care facilities, hospice providers and health systems, and specialty pain management clinics and organizations providing wraparound health care services, such as home health care or case management. Health care organizations influence individuals' pain care experiences through numerous channels, including the specific pain management therapies that they offer, the providers that they employ or with whom they contract for services, and the policies and clinical processes that they adopt toward pain management (Polacek et al., 2020). Health care organizations directly influence providers' approaches to pain management through clinical guidelines, technologies, and workflows (e.g., opioid treatment agreements, opioid patient registries, clinical decision support, interdisciplinary pain management teams) (Haegerich et al., 2019); they also influence pain treatment indirectly through the overall practice environment. For example, productivity demands (e.g., patient panel size requirements, appointment length restrictions), reimbursement policies (e.g., bonuses based on patient satisfaction scores), and the availability of case management services for patients with complex medical and psychosocial needs might indirectly influence the delivery of pain care (Polacek et al., 2020; Zgierska, Miller, and Rabago, 2012).

Among health care organizations, a subset of specialty pain clinics referred to as "pill mills" have received significant attention in the context of the opioid crisis—the role of these care settings is discussed in the section titled "Components Relevant to Prescription Opioid Misuse." However, it is important to understand that a great deal of prescription opioid diversion comes from prescriptions written elsewhere in the health care system, such as the overprescribing of opioids for individuals undergoing procedures (Suda et al., 2020; Thiels et al., 2017), not just from pill mills.

Insurers

Through coverage decisions, insurers can directly influence the pain treatments that patients receive. Patient costs for pharmacological treatments, such as opioids, are generally less than patient costs for nonpharmacological treatments and require less patient time, and the latter are more likely to be subject to prior authorization requirements (Goertz and George, 2018; Heyward et al., 2018; Bonakdar, Palanker, and Sweeney, 2019). As a result, patients often face lower out-of-pocket costs for pharmacological pain treatments, which might influence their therapy choices (Becker et al., 2017).

Insurers also influence pain care indirectly through their interactions with providers. As the risks of prescription opioid analgesics have become better understood, many insurers have launched opioid stewardship programs that aim to limit inappropriate or unsafe prescribing (Mauri, Townsend, and Haffajee, 2020); examples of such initiatives are described in "Components Relevant to Prescription Opioid Misuse." Although efforts to improve the safety of pain treatment are important, at the same time, limits on opioid prescribing may conflict with the more fundamental economic trade-offs created by prevailing reimbursement models. Fee-for-service reimbursement, which is still the dominant model by which insurers pay health care providers for their services, financially rewards providers for seeing larger numbers of patients within a given period. This could, in turn, disproportionately incentivize the use of pain management strategies that are less time-intensive, such as pharmacological treatments. It could also create barriers to the use of certain promising models of chronic pain management, such as multidisciplinary team–based care, which typically involve some case management or care coordination services that might not be reimbursed under traditional fee-for-service models.

Although the relationships between insurers, patients, and providers and the incentives they create surrounding opioid use are common to all payer types, it is important to note that there also exist important variations between major payer categories (i.e., Medicare, Medicaid, the Veterans' Health Administration, and commercial insurers) in their approaches to financing pain treatments, such as opioids. These variations are more pronounced when one is comparing approaches to opioid stewardship, so they will be discussed in "Components Relevant to Prescription Opioid Misuse."

The Pharmaceutical Industry

Historically, manufacturers of prescription opioid analgesics have played a significant role in influencing pain management strategies, primarily through their interactions with physicians and their efforts to influence prescribing behavior but also by funding pain management advocacy organizations (DeShazo et al., 2018). The history of OxyContin's marketing illustrates these channels of influence. OxyContin was introduced by Purdue Pharma in 1996 and was aggressively marketed to physicians through invitations to all-expenses-paid pain management symposia; the distribution of promotional literature to physicians; the recruitment and training of physicians, pharmacists, and nurses to participate in Purdue's national speaker bureau; the deployment of a large pharmaceutical sales representative force to directly target physicians treating large numbers of patients with pain; and the distribution of branded promotional items to prescribers (Kelvey, 2018). In all of these promotional activities, a consistent marketing message was that OxyContin carried a low risk of addiction—an unsupported claim that misrepresented the scientific literature on the risks of opioid dependence (Van Zee, 2009).

Although physicians were the primary targets of Purdue Pharma's OxyContin marketing activities, the company also directly promoted the drug to patients through the distribution of marketing brochures and videotapes touting OxyContin's effectiveness for pain and through literature on its corporate website (Schulte, 2018). In addition, the company provided "starter coupons" that allowed patients to receive a limited-duration first time prescription of OxyContin free of charge (U.S. General Accounting Office, 2003).

The marketing of OxyContin was, in several ways, unprecedented in its scope and intensity, and Purdue's misleading tactics prompted thousands of lawsuits, ultimately leading to convictions on federal criminal charges and large fines (Associated Press, 2021; U.S. Department of Justice, 2020). But the tactics employed were not unique to this specific drug or company. Similar coupon programs have been used by manufacturers of Avinza and Kadian, other brand-name opioids (Huskamp et al., 2018), and illegal marketing activities resulted in the convictions of the leadership of Insys and, ultimately, the company's bankruptcy (Dyer, 2019). As the risks of OxyContin became more apparent, and in response to increased regulatory and legal scrutiny of its marketing activities, Purdue Pharma significantly curtailed marketing of this drug within the United States—while shifting attention to markets in other countries (Randazzo and Hopkins, 2019; Ryan, Girion, and Glover, 2016). The channels and tactics through which it was able to influence physicians and patients, however, have been and can still be used by other companies in the United States that seek to promote a specific pain therapy.

Components Relevant to Prescription Opioid Misuse

Many of the medical system components involved in pain management are also involved in efforts to limit prescription opioid misuse (e.g., providers, health care organizations, insurers). This section describes how these components influence prescription opioid misuse specifically.

Health Care Providers

The risk of prescription opioid misuse increases with increased medical exposure to opioid analgesics, especially at higher doses and longer durations of therapy (Bonnie, Ford, and Phillips, 2017). Therefore, health care providers directly influence the risk of opioid misuse through their prescribing practices. There is tremendous heterogeneity in prescribing practices, and a substantial number of providers continue to issue opioid prescriptions at doses and durations in excess of those recommended under the 2016 CDC guidelines (Zhu et al., 2019). Moreover, although overall prescription opioid use has declined, U.S. health care providers still prescribe opioids at a significantly higher rate than their counterparts in other countries, despite similar pain prevalence (see Chapter Two for further details) (Guy et al., 2017). Prescribing excess amounts of opioids not only increases an individual's risk of opioid misuse but can also pose a risk to family members and others if unused pills are diverted (Han et al., 2017).

The risk of prescription opioid misuse is also influenced by *patient factors*: Adolescents and young adults, patients with mental health disorders, and patients with personal histories of SUD are all at elevated risk (Han et al., 2017; Hu et al., 2017; Klimas et al., 2019). Health care providers have a critical role in screening for and, where possible, modifying these risk factors through medical interventions (e.g., treatment for mental health disorders and SUD).

Health Care Delivery Organizations

Physician groups, hospitals, and health systems are increasingly working to limit prescription opioid misuse through a variety of strategies that primarily target health care providers, although some directly engage patients (Haegerich et al., 2019). For example, a growing number of clinics and health systems require patients on chronic opioid therapy to pledge via "pain management contracts" that they will use their medications only as intended (Substance Abuse and Mental Health Services Administration, 2011).

Strategies targeting health care providers can be classified as *primary prevention efforts*, which attempt to limit opioid misuse by limiting excess exposure to opioids among patients and others (indirectly via diversion), and *secondary prevention efforts*, which attempt to promptly identify and address patients' opioid misuse. Examples of primary prevention efforts include provider education, development and dissemination of clinical guidelines for pain management, auditing of providers' opioid prescribing practices, opioid stewardship programs, clinical decision support systems, multidisciplinary team–based pain care, adoption of electronic prescribing of controlled substances, and default opioid prescription doses or durations in electronic health records (Haegerich et al., 2019). Examples of secondary prevention efforts include efforts to monitor for opioid misuse and policies stipulating how patients on chronic opioid therapy should be monitored for misuse (e.g., mandating urine drug testing, frequency of visits) (Anderson et al., 2015; Turner et al., 2014). A systematic review of policies to limit prescription opioid misuse found moderate-quality evidence that clinical health system interventions as a group (specifically, multidisciplinary team approaches to pain management, brief motivational interviewing to reduce opioid misuse, patient education, electronic health record clinical decision support and opioid prescription defaults, provider auditing and feedback, and health system policies targeting opioid dose reduction or risk mitigation) are effective in improving the safety of opioid prescribing (Haegerich et al., 2019). Such interventions are highly varied, and, although there is insufficient evidence to recommend any single such intervention over others, electronic health record–based clinical decision support tools and interventions that alert providers to higher-risk patients (e.g., through patient registries or unsolicited PDMP reports) might hold particular promise (Anderson et al., 2015; Gugelmann et al., 2013; Patel et al., 2018; Young, Kreiner, and Panas, 2018; Zaman et al., 2018).

In contrast to the efforts just described, there remain pill mills, which prescribe or dispense opioids in excessive amounts, for inappropriate reasons, or both (Rigg, March, and Inciardi, 2010). In recent years, policy efforts to regulate pill mills have reduced their footprint and impact on prescription opioid misuse (Brighthaupt et al., 2019; Rutkow et al., 2015). Yet it is important to recognize that, historically, these clinics have been an important contributor to excess opioid analgesics circulating in the community, which have been a substantial contributor to inappropriate opioid use, though one of many sources.

Pharmacies

Pharmacies interact directly with patients to limit prescription opioid misuse in several ways. First, clinical pharmacists can discuss with patients how to safely and appropriately use prescription opioids. Second, pharmacies can take back and dispose of unused opioid analgesics, thereby reducing the risk of diversion. Third, pharmacists can identify opioid prescriptions that are potentially unsafe (e.g., because of high doses or co-prescribing with benzodiazepines) and either review them with the prescribing physicians or decline to dispense the medications. Fourth, pharmacists can screen for opioid misuse and can refuse to dispense prescriptions if they have concerns about misuse or diversion (Bach and Hartung, 2019). Finally, particularly with the advent of PDMPs, pharmacists can identify signs of possible opioid misuse, such as doctor shopping or attempts to fill overlapping prescriptions (Hartung et al., 2018).

Insurers

Insurers have increasingly become engaged in opioid stewardship efforts in an attempt to limit prescription opioid misuse. Such efforts may involve utilization management techniques that deny approval or require prior authorization for opioid prescriptions with characteristics that increase the risk of adverse outcomes, such as high doses, overlapping prescriptions, or a long days' supply or long-acting formulations for acute pain. Other utilization management techniques include requiring "stepped therapy" for pain, whereby opioids will not be approved unless non-opioid pain therapies are tried first; auditing high-volume prescribers; limiting pharmacy mail orders; and "locking in" patients to specific providers or pharmacies (García et al., 2016; Haegerich et al., 2019; Mauri, Townsend, and Haffajee, 2020). Two reviews of the effects of policies to limit opioid prescribing found moderate-quality evidence in support of these initiatives by insurers (Haegerich et al., 2019; Mauri, Townsend, and Haffajee, 2020).

A recent study of utilization management techniques among a sample of state Medicaid, Medicare Advantage, and commercial plans found that while certain techniques were commonly used for opioid prescriptions (e.g., 30-day quantity limits), others were less widespread (e.g., prior authorization, stepped therapy requirements) (Lin et al., 2018). Opioid analgesic use is especially prevalent among older Medicare beneficiaries; one in three Medicare Part D enrollees received an opioid prescription in 2016 (U.S. Department of Health and Human Services, Office of Inspector General, 2017). Recognizing this, the Centers for Medicare & Medicaid Services introduced opioid stewardship policies targeting pharmacists, such as safety alerts, and permitted Part D plans to adopt utilization management techniques, such as provider and pharmacy lock-ins (Brandt, 2019). Efforts by Medicare and other payers to restrict prescription opioid use, however, have not been accompanied by an easing of utilization management techniques for non-opioid analgesics that could be possible substitutes for pain management (Lin et al., 2018).

Components Relevant to the Treatment of OUD

MOUD, with buprenorphine, methadone, or extended-release naltrexone (XR-NTX), is the cornerstone of evidence-based treatment for OUD (Leshner and Mancher, 2019a; Substance Abuse and Mental Health Services Administration, 2020). In addition, novel medications to treat OUD are being investigated (Rasmussen, White, and Acri, 2019). Treatment of OUD in the specialty addiction treatment system is reviewed in detail in Chapter Four. The following subsections briefly discuss the components of the medical care system that are relevant to the treatment of OUD.

Health Care Providers

Buprenorphine can be prescribed to treat OUD only by clinicians with DATA 2000 waivers.[5] Physicians who obtain a DATA 2000 waiver may prescribe buprenorphine to limited numbers of patients and are eligible over time to increase their patient limits (Stein et al., 2016). In almost all states, multiple nonphysician providers are also eligible to obtain waivers (Sandoe, Fry, and Frank, 2018). The supply of addiction treatment specialists is limited, and the large number of U.S. adults living with OUD greatly exceeds the capacity of specialty addiction treatment facilities (Jones et al., 2015). Increasing attention has therefore been devoted to expanding OUD treatment capacity in general medical care settings, by encouraging, in particular, primary care physicians, emergency medicine physicians, and hospitalists to obtain buprenorphine waivers and initiate MOUD. Pregnant women may receive OUD treatment

---

[5] After this volume went to press, legislation eliminated the requirement for the waiver.

from primary care physicians or addiction treatment specialists, although obstetricians have increasingly been encouraged to offer MOUD as part of prenatal care (Tiako et al., 2020). Several Medicaid managed care organizations have even offered financial incentives to providers to obtain DATA 2000 waivers (Barrett et al., 2017; Schulman, 2018).

The total number of physicians with buprenorphine waivers is still estimated to be only approximately 5 percent of U.S. physicians and a relatively small proportion of physician assistants and nurse practitioners (Davis and Samuels, 2021; Olfson et al., 2020). To encourage additional providers to prescribe buprenorphine for OUD, in April 2021, the U.S. Department of Health and Human Services (HHS) issued updated buprenorphine practice guidelines that aimed to reduce the administrative burden of obtaining a waiver. The new practice guidelines allow eligible providers to treat up to 30 patients while exempting them from both the training requirements and the requirement to attest to the provision of psychosocial services that were previously conditions of receiving a waiver (U.S. Department of Health and Human Services, 2021). It is not yet known to what extent this policy change will encourage additional providers to obtain waivers and expand access to MOUD—notably, even among providers who have waivers, many are not prescribing close to their patient limits (Haffajee, Bohnert, and Lagisetty, 2018; Stein et al., 2016).

Office-based health care providers are not permitted to prescribe methadone for the treatment of OUD—by law, when methadone is used for this indication, it must be dispensed in federally certified, specialty opioid treatment programs or in the inpatient hospital setting (Substance Abuse and Mental Health Services Administration, undated). Office-based providers can, however, prescribe methadone for the treatment of chronic pain (Sandoe, Fry, and Frank, 2018).

XR-NTX is not a scheduled medication, so it can be prescribed by any clinician with prescribing authority—but uptake has been low for multiple reasons, including because patients must abstain from all opioids for one week prior to XR-NTX initiation to avoid precipitating acute withdrawal (Andraka-Christou and Capone, 2018; Jarvis et al., 2018; Volkow and Blanco, 2020).

Beyond providers who can prescribe MOUD, in many promising models for integrating OUD treatment into general medical care settings, case managers are employed to support care coordination activities (Alford et al., 2011). Case managers are typically nurses, social workers, or behavioral health specialists.

Pharmaceutical Industry

The pharmaceutical industry has a key role in developing and manufacturing medications to treat OUD. At present, there are three U.S. Food and Drug Administration (FDA)–approved MOUD: buprenorphine, methadone, and injectable naltrexone. Several formulations of buprenorphine are approved for the treatment of OUD, including a once-monthly injectable formulation that was approved in 2017 (FDA, 2017). Although these agents represent the most-effective OUD treatment modalities currently available in the United States, each has disadvantages, and not all patients achieve satisfactory responses (Volkow, 2018), indicating a need for ongoing development and the adoption of efficacious treatments. Researchers and policymakers have noted that, despite the considerable need for effective OUD treatments, the U.S. pharmaceutical industry has invested relatively little in the development of novel treatments beyond these three approved medications (National Academies of Sciences, Engineering, and Medicine, 2018). They have hypothesized that stigma and other structural barriers to OUD treatment uptake (e.g., requirements for DATA 2000 waivers, restriction of methadone treatment for OUD to specialty facilities) may dampen incentives for research and development of new pharmacotherapies. In an attempt to spur further innovation, the National Institutes of Health has partnered with various pharmaceutical companies to facilitate the development of novel MOUD and improved formulations of existing treatments (Volkow and Collins, 2017). There are also MOUD that are used in other countries but not in the United States, such as heroin or hydromorphone (further discussed in Chapter Eight and Kilmer et al., 2018).

Insurers

Coverage for MOUD is limited among both private and public insurers. A study examining coverage of opioid analgesics and MOUD by plans in the Health Insurance Marketplace exchanges in 2017 found that 14 percent of plans did not cover any formulation of buprenorphine/naloxone, and plans were more likely to require prior authorization for MOUD than for short-acting opioid analgesics (Huskamp et al., 2018). Such prior authorization requirements impose additional administrative burdens on health care providers that are viewed as a barrier to providing MOUD (Andraka-Christou and Capone, 2018; Burns, 2017; Kermack et al., 2017). Beyond medication coverage, inadequate reimbursement from public and private payers for physician services related to MOUD has been cited by providers as a reason why they are hesitant to offer these medications (Chou et al., 2016; Haffajee, Bohnert, and Lagisetty, 2018; Huhn and Dunn, 2017).

Conversely, insurers—and state Medicaid programs in particular—can be an effective vehicle for expanding access to MOUD in the general medical care system. From 2008 to 2011, counties in states where Medicaid reimbursed providers for office-based treatment with buprenorphine had 20 percent more physicians with buprenorphine waivers per capita than states without such support (Stein et al., 2015). Innovative Medicaid financing models can also facilitate the integration of OUD treatment into general medical care settings by supporting key treatment program elements that are otherwise not commonly reimbursed by insurance, such as case management—the Medicaid Health Home state option, discussed further in a later section, is one such example (Clemans-Cope et al., 2017).

Components Relevant to the Prevention and Treatment of Common Complications and Comorbidities Associated with Opioid Misuse

Common medical complications of opioid misuse include infectious complications of injection heroin and synthetic opioid use, such as HIV, HCV, HBV, endocarditis, and skin and soft-tissue infections (Springer, Korthuis, and Del Rio, 2018). Untreated viral hepatitis may over time result in cirrhosis of the liver and hepatocellular carcinoma. Common behavioral health comorbidities include anxiety and mood disorders, posttraumatic stress disorder, serious mental illness (e.g., schizophrenia, bipolar disorder), and non-opioid SUDs (Brooner et al., 1997). Both medical and psychiatric complications and comorbidities of opioid misuse are managed primarily in the general medical care system, while more-serious mental illness may be managed in specialty mental health treatment settings. The medical care system also has an important role in preventing and treating the most serious consequence of opioid misuse—overdose. Finally, medical complications and adverse sequelae of opioid misuse may be experienced not only by the individuals misusing opioids but also by their family members. Examples of such "intergenerational complications" include NOWS, which may be experienced by neonates whose mothers misuse opioids or receive MOUD during pregnancy (Winkelman et al., 2018), and other physical and mental health problems experienced by children whose parents misuse opioids (Feder, Letourneau, and Brook, 2019; Ornoy et al., 2001; Patrick et al., 2019). Intergenerational and family complications are also managed in part by the medical care system.

The medical complications and comorbidities associated with opioid misuse are costly, and their burden has been increasing. A study in North Carolina, for example, found that the average cost for each hospitalization for endocarditis related to injection drug use was more than $50,000, and the total costs of hospitalizations for drug use–associated endocarditis increased 18-fold between 2010 and 2015 (Fleischauer et al., 2017). Average hospital costs per admission for individuals who inject drugs are nearly double those for hospitalized individuals who do not use drugs (Gray et al., 2018; Rapoport et al., 2021). Total health care costs associated with OUD were estimated to be $35 billion in 2017 (Florence, Luo, and Rice, 2021).

Health Care Providers

Milder infectious complications of injection use, such as skin and soft-tissue infections, are typically managed by primary care or emergency room physicians. More-serious blood-borne infections, such as HIV, HCV, and HBV, can also be managed by primary care physicians, although consultation with infectious disease specialists is also recommended, and serious joint infections may require management by orthopedic surgeons. Individuals with long-standing, untreated HCV are at risk of cirrhosis of the liver, kidney dysfunction, and hepatocellular carcinoma, which are treated by gastroenterologists and hepatologists, nephrologists, and oncologists, respectively. Finally, infective endocarditis is initially treated in the inpatient setting by a multidisciplinary team that usually involves infectious disease and cardiovascular medicine specialists, but it may also involve cardiothoracic surgeons in cases in which valve damage is sufficiently severe to warrant surgical repair. Addiction medicine or psychiatry consultation may also be sought in the inpatient setting to connect patients with OUD treatment during the hospital stay and following discharge.

Some psychiatric comorbidities, such as anxiety and mood disorders, can be treated by primary care physicians, while more-severe mental illness, or a complex trauma history, may warrant treatment by psychiatrists in specialty mental health settings.

NOWS and pediatric physical and mental health conditions experienced by children whose parents misuse opioids are treated by pediatricians. Severe child and adolescent mental health disorders warrant consultation with child and adolescent psychiatrists and behavioral health specialists, although the critical shortage of such specialists contributes to significant barriers to accessing care for these conditions. Notably, pediatric health care providers may also screen for and identify parental opioid misuse during children's medical encounters and assist parents in connecting with adult treatment resources (Dubowitz, 2014).

Insurers

Insurers influence the treatment of the complications and comorbidities of opioid misuse through benefit design and coverage decisions. Medications to treat HIV, and HCV in particular, can be very costly, and coverage might be restricted (Trooskin, Reynolds, and Kostman, 2015; Zamani-Hank, 2016). State and federal efforts to assure parity in the coverage of treatments for medical and psychiatric disorders have reduced financial barriers to behavioral health treatments; still, because of the limited supply of mental health professionals, patients are more likely to go out of network for behavioral health care than for other services—and typically incur additional costs in doing so (Benson and Song, 2020). Therefore, through their coverage decisions and provider networks, insurers heavily influence financial barriers to the treatment of medical and psychiatric comorbidities of OUD.

Medicaid in particular is an important source of insurance coverage for pregnant women who misuse opioids and for children in families affected by opioid misuse (together with the Children's Health Insurance Program) (Martin, Hamilton, and Osterman, 2018; Winkelman et al., 2018). State Medicaid policies and benefit design, therefore, have considerable potential to influence the care of these populations. In recognition of this, multiple states have considered expanding postpartum Medicaid eligibility for pregnant women to facilitate ongoing access to essential health services, including treatment for opioid misuse and its complications (Eckert, 2020).

Cross-Cutting Components of the Medical Care System

Finally, there are additional components of the medical care system that fundamentally shape care delivery and have a broader influence over multiple aspects of the opioid crisis.

Health Care Delivery Organizations

Although this chapter has already described some ways in which health care delivery organizations affect specific aspects of the opioid crisis, it is important to also acknowledge that such organizations shape medical care more generally in ways that could indirectly influence the opioid crisis. Health care delivery organizations make hiring and payment decisions, structure medical teams, provide health care infrastructure (e.g., information technology), manage the daily practice and operations of health care providers, and create an organizational culture. Through all of these channels, they may influence how providers approach patients with medically and socially complex histories—including the subset of patients with OUD. They may also influence patients' experiences with medical care and stigma, which can in turn affect care-seeking for pain, OUD, and its complications and comorbidities.

Payment Reform

Although the predominant model of reimbursement for medical care remains the fee-for-service model, a growing number of insurers and health systems are moving toward value-based payment. Under the fee-for-service model, health care providers are reimbursed for each service they render to a patient. In contrast, under value-based payment models, providers typically receive a fixed payment for each patient that is intended to cover all of that person's medical care, typically on an annual basis and risk-adjusted to account for medical complexity. To discourage under-provision of care, payments are often adjusted based on quality performance. Mixed payment models that incorporate both fee-for-service elements and elements of value-based payment (e.g., a pay-for-performance model) also exist.

It is uncertain how the shift toward value-based payment might influence the treatment of pain or OUD. On the one hand, patients with chronic pain or OUD, or both, could be more costly to manage than other patients; if risk adjustment is inadequate to offset these increased costs, value-based payment could disincentivize providers from accepting these patients. Moreover, there are currently limited performance metrics to assess the quality of pain care or OUD treatment (Saloner, Stoller, and Alexander, 2018; Thomas et al., 2018; Williams et al., 2018). There are efforts underway to develop such measures, but a key concern is whether more-punitive quality metrics (e.g., penalties for patients on high-dose opioid analgesic therapy, penalties for patients who experience overdoses or other OUD-related complications) might have unintended negative consequences by again disincentivizing providers from accepting such patients.

On the other hand, value-based payment could potentially mitigate several of the current challenges in improving care for pain and OUD under the fee-for-service model. Moving away from fee-for-service payments could better align incentives to provide noninterventional and nonpharmacological pain treatments with the evidence base for these treatments. It could also allow more-generous reimbursement for behavioral treatments for pain. Payment that is tied to patients rather than services could also facilitate more-innovative and more-multidisciplinary models of care, as described in the section titled "Health Care Delivery Reform," and finance wraparound services and case management. Finally, well-designed performance measures can be helpful in improving the quality of both pain and OUD care (Williams et al., 2018). Current evidence of the impact of value-based payment arrangements on the opioid crisis is extremely limited, but it is emerging; in 2021, the Centers for Medicare and Medicaid Innovation launched the "Value in Opioid Use Disorder Treatment" demonstration program, which will evaluate the impacts of performance incentives and receipt of additional care management fees on opioid-related outcomes (Centers for Medicare & Medicaid Services, 2021). Such payment reforms merit further study.

Health Care Delivery Reform

The patchwork of different insurers, health systems, and providers that make up the U.S. medical care system contributes to significant fragmentation of care and challenges in care coordination (Enthoven, 2009). The lack of integrated medical records across health systems exacerbates the challenge of care coordination. Care fragmentation has special relevance to the opioid crisis. It exacerbates the challenge of identifying patient care-seeking patterns that are suggestive of opioid misuse (e.g., doctor shopping, emergency room shopping, obtaining overlapping opioid prescriptions or misusing other controlled substances), and it creates difficulties in coordinating treatment of the medical and psychiatric comorbidities of opioid misuse across multiple providers and settings (Meyer and Clancy, 2019; Moyo et al., 2019). In particular, care fragmentation during pregnancy and in the postnatal period poses a significant challenge for the management of opioid misuse in this especially vulnerable population (Uchitel et al., 2019). During pregnancy, many women receive care from obstetricians or midwives rather than their primary care providers, but they might not regularly follow up with their obstetricians after birth.

In recognition of this challenge, a growing number of health care delivery reform initiatives seek to improve care access, integration, and coordination, especially for medically and socially complex populations, such as individuals with chronic pain, OUD, or both. These care models have varying designs, and some incorporate elements of value-based payment, as described earlier.

The Medicaid Health Home State Plan Option is one notable example. This optional state program that was implemented under the Affordable Care Act aims to improve the quality of care for Medicaid beneficiaries with multiple chronic medical conditions—including behavioral health conditions, such as OUD—by using federal funds as a source of enhanced and flexible funding to subsidize the cost of establishing and operating patient-centered medical homes that provide integrated behavioral health services and case management. Several states, including Maryland, Rhode Island, and Vermont, have adopted the Health Home option with the explicit goal of integrating OUD treatment and primary care (Clemans-Cope et al., 2017). In these states, participating practices receive a per-member-per-month Health Home payment based on prospective staffing needs that they may use to fund MOUD services. Practices have some flexibility in how the funds can be allocated and may use them to finance activities that are not traditionally reimbursed, such as case management.

Several other notable examples of delivery reform initiatives that integrate specialty addiction treatment into general medical care settings are described in the section titled "Key Interactions with Other Components of the Ecosystem."

Medical Training

Medical school curricula, residency programs, and other health professional educational training programs commonly devote little time to teaching pain management and to training providers in the identification and evidence-based treatment of OUD (Loeser and Schatman, 2017; Mezei, Murinson, and Johns Hopkins Pain Curriculum Development Team; Tesema et al., 2018; Yanni et al., 2010).[6] As a result, many physicians entering clinical practice feel ill prepared to manage patients with chronic pain or OUD, despite the high and growing prevalence of these conditions. This lack of training and preparedness likely contributes to the

---

[6] After this report went to press, legislation introduced requirements for education of opioid prescribers.

significant practice variations observed in the use of opioid analgesics and in the hesitancy of providers to obtain waivers to prescribe buprenorphine.[7]

Organizations that oversee accreditation of medical schools and residency training programs (e.g., Association of American Medical Colleges, Accreditation Council for Graduate Medical Education) can shape education and training requirements, and specialty certification boards (e.g., American Board of Internal Medicine, American Board of Emergency Medicine) can further influence education and training by determining what specific knowledge is required for certification in a particular field.

Continuing medical education (CME) activities offer an opportunity for health care providers to supplement and expand their knowledge of pain management and OUD treatment. CME activities are required by states as a condition of licensure, by specialty boards as a condition of certification, and sometimes by health care delivery organizations as a condition of credentialing. Some states have explicitly required that physicians obtain CME related to pain management and OUD (Mauri, Townsend, and Haffajee, 2020).

Stigma

Stigma against patients with SUD, including OUD, has long been pervasive in the medical care system. Stigma arises from the belief that OUD is a personal moral failing rather than a complex chronic illness (McGinty and Barry, 2020). An analysis of a 2014 survey that asked primary care providers (PCPs) about their beliefs about prescription OUD found that 74.4 percent agreed with the statement "some people lack self-discipline to use prescription pain medications without becoming addicted," and 89 percent felt that individuals with prescription OUD were responsible for addressing the problem (Kennedy-Hendricks et al., 2016). In addition, 79.3 percent of PCPs were unwilling to have people with prescription OUD marry into their families, 76.6 percent were unwilling to work closely with people with prescription OUD at their jobs, 66.4 percent believed that people with prescription OUD were more dangerous than the general population, and 64.1 percent felt that employers should be allowed to deny employment to individuals with this condition. These findings illustrate how prevalent negative and stigmatizing attitudes toward OUD are, even among medical professionals. Stigma against OUD has far-reaching negative consequences for both individuals with OUD and the medical care system that treats them: It can prevent individuals from seeking treatment, impede recovery, decrease access to care, contribute to lower-quality medical care for individuals with OUD, and lead to insufficient investment in OUD treatment in general medical settings (Ashford et al., 2019; Kimmel et al., 2021; McGinty and Barry, 2020). Other recent surveys of health care providers have found, for example, that 13.5 percent of physicians without waivers expressed a lack of belief in opioid agonist therapy and that PCPs reporting greater stigma against OUD were substantially less likely to prescribe MOUD (Huhn and Dunn, 2017; Stone et al., 2021).

---

[7] After this volume went to press, legislation eliminated the requirement for the waiver.

Individuals with chronic pain also encounter stigma in the medical care system. Stigma may arise from disbelief or dismissiveness by health care providers of patients' experiences of chronic pain because of the lack of identifiable pathology or because of its persistence beyond the time frame of typical acute pain processes (De Ruddere and Craig, 2016; Waugh, Byrne, and Nicholas, 2014). As in the case of OUD, stigma toward patients with chronic pain can have negative effects on their medical care, such as through inaccurate assessment of the severity and functional impairment associated with chronic pain and its undertreatment (de C. Williams, 2016).

Given the clear harms associated with stigma toward individuals with chronic pain or OUD, there is increasing recognition of the importance of reducing stigma in the medical care system. There is also a growing evidence base that has identified effective interventions to combat stigma in health care settings—including education and contact-based training (Livingston et al., 2012)—but these are not yet widely implemented. There is a need for coordination and investment in disseminating and scaling up effective interventions to reduce stigma.

Government Regulatory Bodies

Numerous regulatory bodies at both the state and federal levels influence the medical care system in ways that are relevant to the opioid crisis.

At the state level, state medical licensing boards determine which physicians may practice in the state, investigate providers alleged of wrongdoing, and take disciplinary actions when deemed necessary. State medical boards also evaluate physicians who are reported to have misused controlled substances or to have developed SUD, determine what rehabilitative or disciplinary action is warranted, and determine whether and when these physicians may resume clinical practice (Ross, 2003). State departments of public health typically issue state-controlled substance registrations, which are required by many states in addition to the federal DEA registration to prescribe controlled substances. State departments of public health also typically administer (or coadminister with law enforcement) PDMPs,[8] and they are responsible for creating and enforcing other regulations related to issues of public health concern, such as OUD.

At the federal level, relevant regulatory bodies include the DEA, FDA, Centers for Medicare & Medicaid Services (CMS), and CDC. The DEA licenses providers to prescribe controlled substances and enforces laws and regulations related to controlled substances in the United States. The FDA approves medications for medical use and oversees ongoing monitoring of drug safety. CMS directly influences benefit design and reimbursement policies in Medicare and Medicaid, which can have ripple effects across other insurers. Finally, the CDC conducts research and develops guidelines that inform medical care for pain and OUD; the

---

[8] PDMPs may also be managed by other state agencies (e.g., boards of pharmacy) and in some states are coadministered with law enforcement.

most prominent example is its 2016 guideline on the use of prescription opioids for pain management (Dowell, Haegerich, and Chou, 2016).

Key Interactions with Other Components of the Ecosystem

SUD Treatment

Excess and inappropriate prescribing of opioid analgesics has been a powerful driver of the prevalence of OUD (Kolodny et al., 2015). As opioid prescribing has fallen, the contribution of opioid analgesics to the inflow of individuals developing OUD has declined, and the majority of overdose deaths now involve illegal opioids, such as heroin and fentanyl (Dasgupta, Beletsky, and Ciccarone, 2018). However, the medical use of opioids continues to be one factor contributing to the flow of additional people developing OUD, even if at a lower rate than at its peak. Inappropriate pain treatment, therefore, increases the demand for specialty addiction treatment. It is hoped that the more recent emphasis on safer opioid prescribing practices might reduce the inflow of individuals developing OUD.

Medical providers also play an important role in treating comorbid disorders that are common in individuals with OUD being treated in the SUD system, including infectious disorders and comorbid mental health disorders. And, as discussed earlier, insurers play a critical role in determining what services are going to be provided in the SUD system.

The most important interaction between the medical care system and the specialty addiction treatment system is their joint role as OUD treatment providers. The physician specialty addiction treatment workforce is quite small—as of 2019, it was estimated that there were only 3,000 U.S. physicians who were board certified in either addiction medicine or addiction psychiatry (Ryan, 2020), and the availability of specialty SUD treatment care more broadly is limited (Hoge et al., 2013). The medical care system extends treatment capacity for OUD and comorbid SUD by providing evidence-based therapies in primary care (Watkins et al., 2017), emergency department, and hospital settings (D'Onofrio et al., 2015; D'Onofrio et al., 2017; Liebschutz et al., 2014; Suzuki, 2016; Trowbridge et al., 2017), in particular buprenorphine via the DATA 2000 waiver, as described earlier. Specialty treatment providers, in turn, may support the provision of OUD treatment in the medical care system through provider education, consultation, and acceptance of referrals of more-complex patients who might initially be identified in general medical care settings but require specialized treatment. Some promising models of collaboration between the medical care and specialty addiction treatment systems to expand access to OUD treatment are as follows:

- Collaborative care models: Collaborative care models represent an evidence-based approach to integrating OUD treatment into primary care (Watkins et al., 2017). Core elements of collaborative care include team-based care (with enhanced access to specialist consultation and case management), population health management, use of a patient registry, measurement-guided care, and evidence-based care that is based on treatment protocols. The Massachusetts nurse care manager program is an example of a successful collaborative care model that has been used to integrate OUD treatment into primary care settings (Alford et al., 2011).

- Hub-and-spoke models: Hub-and-spoke models aim to (1) enhance access to specialty consultation providers ("hubs") so that MOUD can be provided by a larger number of providers in primary care and other nonspecialty settings ("spokes") and (2) match patients to the appropriate treatment settings based on their needs. Hub providers provide consultation to spoke providers, and patients at spoke sites who encounter difficulties with their treatment can be referred to hub sites as needed. Vermont's hub-and-spoke model is the best-known example, and evaluations of the model found that it was associated with an expansion of treatment capacity, a decrease in waiting times, and a decrease in total health care costs for individuals with OUD (Brooklyn and Sigmon, 2017; Krantz, 2014; Nordstrom et al., 2016).

- Project ECHO (Extension for Community Healthcare Outcomes): Project ECHO is a telementoring program that connects specialists with multiple community providers via video conference to train and mentor these providers in caring for patients with complex illnesses. Originally developed for the treatment of HCV, the model has since been extended to train community providers in the evaluation and treatment of other conditions, including OUD (Arora et al., 2007; Chaple et al., 2018; Covell et al., 2015; Komaromy et al., 2016; Komaromy et al., 2018; Project ECHO, 2014).

Illegal Supply

Overprescribing of opioid analgesics by physicians increases the overall supply of prescription opioids. Through diversion, these medications can then be resold in illicit drug markets, thereby increasing the illicit drug supply. In addition, some individuals who develop opioid dependence and addiction from exposure to prescription opioids subsequently transition to misusing heroin and fentanyl because of cost, accessibility, or potency (Cerda et al., 2015; Victor et al., 2017). Overprescribing of opioid analgesics has therefore increased both the supply and the demand for illegal opioids (Dasgupta, Beletsky, and Ciccarone, 2018).

At the same time, there have also been growing concerns about whether measures to *restrict* legal access to prescription opioids might have the unintended consequence of leading individuals who misuse these drugs to seek opioids in illicit drug markets. So, restricting prescription opioids can be expected to create short-term harm and long-term benefits. The short-term harm is increased substitution toward illicit opioids by people who already have OUD. The long-term benefit is reducing the flow of people into the state of having OUD. For example, several research studies documented a positive association between the presence of a PDMP in a particular area and local rates of heroin poisonings (Delcher et al., 2016; Meinhofer, 2018), and, in qualitative studies of both individuals who misuse opioids and state agency officials who oversee PDMPs, interviews suggest that decreased access to prescription opioids might contribute to some individuals' decisions to use heroin and synthetic opioids

(Mars et al., 2014; Yuanhong Lai et al., 2019). Overall, however, the available evidence from existing studies on the relationships between the presence of PDMPs and prescribing rates, prescription opioid misuse, and opioid-related mortality remains mixed; some studies have shown significant effects, and others have found little evidence of association (Stein et al., 2022). Differences across states with respect to policy definitions and implementation are a likely contributor to inconsistencies in findings across existing studies (Horwitz et al., 2021; Pacula, Smart, and Stein, 2020). Rigorous empirical research about the effects of policies to limit prescription opioid use remains a priority.

In contrast, there is stronger evidence that the reformulation of OxyContin to a tamper-resistant version resulted in increased heroin use and subsequent HCV infections and overdose deaths, as individuals who were previously crushing OxyContin for euphoric effects found it more difficult to do so after the reformulation and switched to using heroin (Alpert, Powell, and Pacula, 2018; Pacula and Powell, 2018). The impacts of policies targeting prescription opioid misuse on the illegal opioid market are therefore variable, and their causal impacts are not completely understood. Further complicating an understanding of these relationships are the differing time horizons of the interactions between opioid prescribing and illegal supply: Restricting opioid prescribing or reformulating opioids to create tamper-resistant versions could result in short-term harms if individuals using prescription opioids substitute with illegal opioids, but it could also create long-term benefits if such measures reduce the inflow of individuals developing OUD.

Finally, as described earlier, the medical care system is the major setting in which the infectious complications of illicit injection opioids (e.g., heroin, fentanyl) and their long-term sequelae are treated, and it is also among the major settings in which overdoses are managed.

Criminal Legal System

Inappropriate opioid prescribing in the medical care system that leads to OUD can, for some, ultimately result in involvement with the criminal legal system because of affected individuals turning to illegal activities to purchase opioids through illicit markets, or because of the numerous other destabilizing effects of untreated OUD on peoples' lives (Prince and Wald, 2018; Yatsco et al., 2020). It is estimated that 15 percent of inmates in correctional settings have OUD, although not all or even most are there because of drug law violations (see Chapter Two; and James and Glaze, 2006).

The medical care system can also provide essential health services, including OUD treatment to incarcerated individuals in correctional settings. MOUD has been successfully integrated into jail systems in New York City, New Jersey, and San Francisco and in state prison systems in Connecticut and Rhode Island (Fiscella, Wakeman, and Beletsky, 2018). For formerly incarcerated individuals, contact with the medical care system in the days and weeks immediately after release is critically important because this represents a particularly vulnerable period during which opioid overdose is among the leading causes of death (Binswanger et al., 2013). Successful MOUD programs in correctional settings typically work to establish linkages with MOUD providers in the community to facilitate continuity of care upon release (Fiscella, Wakeman, and Beletsky, 2018; Friedmann et al., 2012). Although these model programs represent a promising step forward, it is important to recognize that only a small minority of correctional institutions offer MOUD (Wakeman and Rich, 2015), in part because of the considerable challenges that administering MOUD creates for those institutions, particularly jails. Recently incarcerated individuals with OUD continue to experience substantial barriers to accessing treatment after release, whether in the specialty addiction treatment system or in the general medical care system (Bunting et al., 2018). An important policy opportunity to facilitate access to medical care following release from correctional settings lies in reforming how Medicaid eligibility is treated during and immediately following incarceration. As of this writing, a majority of states suspend rather than terminate Medicaid eligibility for enrollees who become incarcerated; suspension allows faster resumption of Medicaid services following release, and CMS has encouraged all states to adopt this policy (Pew Charitable Trusts, 2020). A smaller but substantial share of states have gone a step further, implementing automated and integrated data systems to facilitate reinstatement of Medicaid enrollment following release (Kaiser Family Foundation, 2019).

Finally, the medical care and criminal legal systems might partner together to implement policies designed to limit opioid misuse or facilitate its earlier detection, with the goal of preventing adverse health- and justice-related outcomes. PDMPs are one example of such collaboration: In some states, these databases are jointly administered and consulted by public health officials, health care providers, and law enforcement (Grecu, Dave, and Saffer, 2019). Conversely, activities of these two systems can, at times, be in conflict and detrimental to individuals who misuse opioids. Policies that criminalize or otherwise punish substance use in pregnancy are one such example. There are concerns that, among pregnant women struggling with opioid misuse, such policies might discourage women from seeking prenatal care or OUD treatment—and enactment of these policies is associated with a higher incidence of NOWS (Faherty et al., 2019; Patrick et al., 2017).

First Responders

Approximately 300,000 individuals are brought to emergency departments annually, often by first responders, following nonfatal opioid overdoses (Vivolo-Kantor et al., 2020). The medical care system then attempts to medically stabilize these individuals and provides a window of opportunity to help connect them with treatment in the community or even to initiate treatment in the emergency department itself. Emerging evidence suggests that emergency department initiation of buprenorphine with referral to community-based treatment settings results in higher rates of treatment engagement and decreased illicit opioid use compared with referrals to community settings alone (Busch et al., 2017; D'Onofrio et al., 2015; D'Onofrio et al., 2017; Korthuis et al., 2017).

Harm Reduction and Community-Initiated Interventions

The medical care system is a growing partner in harm reduction initiatives, such as naloxone prescribing and distribution. For example, many policies that aim to expand access to naloxone for overdose reversal have operated in part through the medical care system: Third-party prescription laws allow health care providers to prescribe naloxone to individuals who are not at risk of overdose themselves but might be in a position to assist others who are; prescriber immunity provisions aim to incentivize naloxone prescribing by conferring civil or criminal immunity; and standing order policies allow pharmacists to dispense naloxone to individuals at risk of overdose without person-specific prescriptions (Mauri, Townsend, and Haffajee, 2020). Pharmacy-based naloxone dispensing doubled between 2017 and 2018 alone. In addition, harm reduction programs, such as syringe service programs and safe consumption sites, can serve as settings to provide low-barrier medical care and treatment for OUD (Des Jarlais et al., 2015; Strang and Taylor, 2018).

Income Support and Homeless Services

The medical care system may serve as an important point of access and referral to numerous social service systems that benefit individuals and families affected by opioid misuse, including housing, income support, nutritional support, and legal services (Andermann, 2018). However, health care providers and delivery organizations vary greatly in the extent to which they systematically screen patients for social service needs, connect them with the appropriate agencies, and assist them in navigating the process of demonstrating eligibility for benefits (Alley et al., 2016). In many communities, there are efforts to enroll eligible clients of social service programs in Medicaid, enhancing their ability to receive medical care and care for OUD (Andermann, 2018).

Child Welfare

Pediatric health care providers play a critical role in identifying children who have suffered maltreatment and other harms as a result of their parents' struggles with opioid misuse and in referring affected families to child welfare services. Harms to children may be identified when children are brought to medical practices or emergency departments for the evaluation of specific problems, and medical providers can play an important role in identifying and treating children with posttraumatic stress disorder or other mental health disorders resulting from childhood traumatic event exposure (Dubowitz, 2002). Some pediatric practices also systematically screen families during well-child visits to identify risk factors for child maltreatment, such as parental substance misuse, and proactively connect families with appropriate resources to prevent harms to children and child welfare involvement. One such model program is the Safe Environment for Every Kid intervention, which trains pediatric primary care providers to identify parental substance misuse and other child maltreatment risk factors, provide motivational interviewing to engage parents in addressing substance misuse, and then connect parents with community resources for ongoing care (Dubowitz, 2014).

Employment

The medical care system interacts with the employment system in the context of the opioid crisis. Pain is a leading reason why workers exit the labor force (Center on Budget and Policy Priorities, 2019; Krueger, 2017). Although pain-related medical conditions are clearly negatively associated with labor outcomes, the contribution of opioid analgesic therapy to work and disability outcomes is debated and remains uncertain. Regions with high levels of opioid analgesic prescribing tend to have higher unemployment (Krueger, 2017), which has raised questions about whether opioid overprescribing in health care settings might contribute to patients' declining work-related functioning. Existing research on this subject has yielded mixed findings, and whether opioids have a causal impact on employment outcomes remains uncertain (Currie, Jin, and Schnell, 2018; Harris et al., 2020). There is also emerging evidence that negative economic shocks and low economic opportunity and mobility might increase opioid misuse and related harms (i.e., the concept of "deaths of despair") (Venkataramani et al., 2020).

Among workers who experience chronic pain, health care providers and employer-sponsored insurance plans are key components of the medical care system that influence the pain care they receive. For patients with high-impact chronic pain that limits their work-related functioning, health care providers can evaluate their eligibility for workers' compensation and disability insurance benefits.

Policy Opportunities and Considerations

In the past two decades, as awareness of the magnitude of the opioid crisis has grown, and as understanding of the medical care system's contributions to this crisis has deepened, numerous policy initiatives have been implemented to mitigate the opioid crisis by operating wholly or in part through the medical care system. There have been some markers of success: Opioid analgesic prescribing has fallen, although prescribing still remains very high by historical and international standards (Schuchat, Houry, and Guy, 2017), and the availability of OUD treatment in general medical care settings has increased, though it still lags that in many peer countries. There remains a great deal of work to do to better address the opioid crisis through the medical care system. This final section summarizes several policy opportunities and considerations. Special attention is paid to how these policies might involve or influence other components of the opioid ecosystem. The policy opportunities described in this section are intended not to represent an exhaustive list of strategies that the medical care system should undertake to mitigate the opioid crisis, but rather to highlight several key priorities.

Balancing the Goals of Effective Pain Treatment and Prevention of Opioid Misuse

Opioid prescribing rates have fallen in the United States in recent years in the face of growing concerns about the risks of using opioids to treat pain and as a result of policy efforts by governments, payers, and health care organizations to improve opioid prescribing safety (Zhu et al., 2019). It is hoped that limiting the use of opioid analgesics to treat pain can reduce the incidence of both prescription and illegal opioid misuse and their harmful consequences.

It has always been apparent, however, that lowering opioid prescribing rates is just one of many measures that are necessary for achieving high-quality chronic pain treatment and opioid misuse prevention. Chronic pain remains among the most prevalent and disabling medical conditions in the United States (Dahlhamer et al., 2018), and, although reliance on opioids to treat pain has decreased, efforts to identify and improve access to effective and safe substitute therapies have been inadequate.

A key policy opportunity for the medical care system, therefore, is to improve access to effective and safe pain treatment that balances the need for opioid analgesic therapy in some circumstances with measures to prevent opioid misuse. This will require investments in the development and testing of novel pharmacological and nonpharmacological pain treatment modalities; better education on pain care at every stage of medical training, including through CME; investments by health care organizations to increase their capacity to provide non-opioid evidence-based pain treatment; and policies by payers that both incentivize and reward such investments by providers and reduce financial barriers to non-opioid treatment for patients.

Importantly, balancing effective pain care with patient safety and the risk of diversion involves an appreciation of the interactions between the medical care and illegal supply systems. There is a need for additional research to better understand how commonly and under what circumstances prescription opioids continue to be diverted and how efforts to limit opioid analgesic prescribing might shift demand toward illegal supply. Achieving this, in turn, requires investments in systematic data collection, integration, and sharing related to illicit drug markets, pain treatment, and opioid-related harms.

Expanding Access to OUD Treatment

Because the high and growing demand for OUD treatment has overwhelmed the capacity of the specialty addiction treatment system, the medical care system presents an underutilized opportunity to expand access to MOUD. Efforts to scale up access to OUD treatment in general medical care settings are growing but require further investment and support.

HHS's recent relaxation of the requirements for obtaining a buprenorphine waiver aims to reduce barriers to MOUD provision among providers in general medical care settings, but to what extent this policy change will improve treatment access is not yet known.[9] Advocates and certain lawmakers argue that the DATA 2000 waiver requirement should be removed altogether to further increase the capacity of nonspecialists to treat OUD. They also argue that doing so would lessen the stigma related to OUD treatment by removing a regulation related to prescribing that is unique to a medication used to treat OUD. It is unlikely, however, that repeal of the waiver alone will meaningfully increase the supply of providers willing

---

[9] After this volume went to press, legislation eliminated the requirement for the waiver.

to provide MOUD. Many providers with waivers treat substantially fewer than the maximum number of patients permitted. Moreover, OUD recognition and treatment have been largely neglected by medical school and residency curricula, so the extent to which a larger number of providers would feel comfortable prescribing MOUD and the quality of care they might provide are uncertain.

With or without the DATA 2000 waiver requirement, several other investments and initiatives are required from the medical care system to expand access to MOUD. All of these aim to shift *attitudes* toward viewing MOUD as an essential, mainstream health service akin to any other medical service and to establish the *expectation* that MOUD must be available in any health care setting. Such initiatives include the incorporation of education and training on providing MOUD into core medical school and residency curricula; financial incentives; clinical innovations; efforts by professional societies and public health agencies to establish standards for high-quality OUD treatment and to monitor and incentivize performance improvement; and actions by payers to reduce financial barriers to MOUD.

In addition to expanding access to buprenorphine in general medical care settings, some health care providers and advocates have argued for decreasing restrictions on the use of methadone for OUD in primary care and other general medical settings, noting that this strategy has been used successfully in other countries (McBournie et al., 2019). Along similar lines, relaxations on methadone dispensation rules were introduced during the coronavirus disease 2019 pandemic in the United States, and available research suggests that they did not lead to an increase in methadone overdoses (Brothers, Viera, and Heimer, 2021). All of the aforementioned policy opportunities require close collaboration between the specialty addiction treatment and medical care systems, with the former providing education, expert consultation, and care for more-complex patients. Several models of successful collaboration between these sectors that are described in this chapter (e.g., Vermont's hub-and-spoke system, Massachusetts's nurse care manager program) provide possible blueprints for how to implement and scale up initiatives.

Interagency Collaboration and Care Integration

Individuals with chronic pain, OUD, or both often face other physical and mental health challenges, in addition to social and economic vulnerabilities, such as unstable housing and employment. A growing body of literature has demonstrated that such individuals benefit from integrating their pain and OUD treatment with other medical, psychiatric, and social services that are tailored to their needs and span other system components discussed in this report. Despite the existence of potential benefits, these patients commonly encounter difficulties with accessing necessary medical, behavioral health, and social services.

The medical care system is a potential point of entry not only for physical health care but also for treatment for comorbid behavioral health conditions (e.g., OUD) and referral to other social service agencies (e.g., nutritional supports, housing assistance). Although there is growing recognition of the need for the medical care system to screen for vulnerabilities in social determinants of health among high-risk individuals (i.e., those with chronic pain,

OUD, or both), there is wide variation in the implementation of this practice—and even wider variation in how health care organizations respond to this information and to what extent they attempt to connect high-risk individuals with recommended social services. Therefore, investments by health care organizations, payers, and state and federal agencies to support universal screening for social service needs, referral, patient navigation (through the health care system), and care coordination through the medical care system present a policy opportunity to bridge gaps in care.

Although the medical care system can serve as a focal point for such efforts to connect individuals to social services, a more ambitious strategy could involve the development of truly integrated health and social service models that screen for vulnerabilities in social determinants of health at any point of entry (e.g., medical care system, specialty addiction treatment system, child welfare, criminal legal), tailor services to individual needs, and provide integrated services in the setting that is most convenient for the patient. Many promising examples of such cross-systems collaboration target parents with OUD and their children (e.g., the Vermont Children and Recovering Mothers Collaborative, which integrates medical care, specialty addiction treatment, counseling, parenting education, and consultation for child welfare [Meyer et al., 2012; Meyer et al., 2015]); intensive case management (case managers embedded in SUD treatment programs, child welfare agencies, or general medical care settings assist parents who have SUD with care coordination and clinical and social service needs [Dauber et al., 2012; Ryan et al., 2008; Ryan et al., 2017]); and family drug treatment courts (specialized courts that monitor treatment for parents with SUD with pending child abuse or neglect cases, provide SUD treatment and wraparound services, and coordinate with child welfare and health care providers [Green et al., 2007; Ogbonnaya and Keeney, 2018]). Promising examples of cross-systems collaboration targeting adults more generally include the Rikers Island Key Extended Entry Program, which integrates medical and specialty addiction care into criminal justice settings (Farahmand, Modesto-Lowe, and Chaplin, 2017), and Oregon's Housing Choice model, which integrates the medical care, specialty addiction treatment, social services, and employment systems (Pfefferle, Karon, and Wyant, 2019).

Such integrated models require cross-systems collaboration; data-sharing across agencies and partner organizations; and flexible financing models to facilitate integrated service provision (Marsh and Smith, 2011). All of these components, in turn, requires engagement from relevant state and local agencies, particularly state Medicaid programs.

Abbreviations

CDC	Centers for Disease Control and Prevention
CME	continuing medical education
CMS	Centers for Medicare & Medicaid Services
DATA	Drug Addiction Treatment Act
DEA	Drug Enforcement Administration
FDA	U.S. Food and Drug Administration
HBV	hepatitis B
HCV	hepatitis C
HHS	U.S. Department of Health and Human Services
HIV	human immunodeficiency virus
MOUD	medications for opioid use disorder
NOWS	neonatal opioid withdrawal syndrome
OUD	opioid use disorder
PDMP	prescription drug monitoring program
SUD	substance use disorder
XR-NTX	extended-release naltrexone

References

Alford, Daniel P., Colleen T. LaBelle, Natalie Kretsch, Alexis Bergeron, Michael Winter, Michael Botticelli, and Jeffrey H. Samet, "Collaborative Care of Opioid-Addicted Patients in Primary Care Using Buprenorphine: Five-Year Experience," *Archives of Internal Medicine*, Vol. 171, No. 5, 2011, pp. 425–431.

Alley, Dawn E., Chisara N. Asomugha, Patrick H. Conway, and Darshak M. Sanghavi, "Accountable Health Communities—Addressing Social Needs Through Medicare and Medicaid," *New England Journal of Medicine*, Vol. 374, No. 1, 2016, pp. 8–11.

Alpert, Abby, David Powell, and Rosalie Liccardo Pacula, "Supply-Side Drug Policy in the Presence of Substitutes: Evidence from the Introduction of Abuse-Deterrent Opioids," *American Economic Journal*, Vol. 10, No. 4, 2018.

Anda, Robert F., Vincent J. Felitti, J. Douglas Bremner, John D. Walker, Charles Whitfield, Bruce D. Perry, Shanta R. Dube, and Wayne H. Giles, "The Enduring Effects of Abuse and Related Adverse Experiences in Childhood: A Convergence of Evidence from Neurobiology and Epidemiology," *European Archives of Psychiatry and Clinical Neuroscience*, Vol. 256, No. 3, April 2006, pp. 174–186.

Andermann, Anne, "Screening for Social Determinants of Health in Clinical Care: Moving from the Margins to the Mainstream," *Public Health Reviews*, Vol. 39, No. 19, 2018.

Anderson, Daren, Ianita Zlateva, Khushbu Khatri, and Nicholas Ciaburri, "Using Health Information Technology to Improve Adherence to Opioid Prescribing Guidelines in Primary Care," *Clinical Journal of Pain*, Vol. 31, No. 6, 2015, pp. 573–579.

Andraka-Christou, Barbara, and Matthew J. Capone, "A Qualitative Study Comparing Physician-Reported Barriers to Treating Addiction Using Buprenorphine and Extended-Release Naltrexone in U.S. Office-Based Practices," *International Journal on Drug Policy*, Vol. 54, 2018, pp. 9–17.

Arora, Sanjeev, Cynthia M. A. Geppert, Summers Kalishman, Denise Dion, Frank Pullara, Barbara Bjeletich, Gary Simpson, Dale C. Alverson, Lori B. Moore, Dave Kuhl, and Joseph V. Scaletti, "Academic Health Center Management of Chronic Diseases Through Knowledge Networks: Project ECHO," *Academic Medicine*, Vol. 82, No. 2, 2007, pp. 154–160.

Ashford, Robert D., Austin M. Brown, Brent Canode, Jessica McDaniel, and Brenda Curtis, "A Mixed-Methods Exploration of the Role and Impact of Stigma and Advocacy on Substance Use Disorder Recovery," *Alcoholism Treatment Quarterly*, Vol. 37, No. 4, 2019, pp. 462–480.

Associated Press, "Multiple States Agree to $4.5B Deal with Sackler Family in Purdue Pharma Opioid Lawsuit," *NBC News*, July 8, 2021.

Bach, Paxton, and Daniel Hartung, "Leveraging the Role of Community Pharmacists in the Prevention, Surveillance, and Treatment of Opioid Use Disorders," *Addiction Science & Clinical Practice*, Vol. 14, No. 30, 2019.

Baillargeon, Jacques, Thomas P. Giordano, Josiah D. Rich, Z. Helen Wu, Katherine Wells, Brad H. Pollock, and David P. Paar, "Accessing Antiretroviral Therapy Following Release from Prison," *JAMA*, Vol. 301, 2009, pp. 848–857.

Baker, David W., "History of The Joint Commission's Pain Standards: Lessons for Today's Prescription Opioid Epidemic," *JAMA*, Vol. 317, No. 11, 2017, pp. 1117–1118.

Baldini, AnGee, Michael Von Korff, and Elizabeth H. B. Lin, "A Review of Potential Adverse Effects of Long-Term Opioid Therapy: A Practitioner's Guide," *Primary Care Companion for CNS Disorders*, Vol. 14, No. 3, 2012.

Barrett, Joshua, Mingjie Li, Brigitta Spaeth-Rublee, and Harold Pincus, "Value-Based Payment as Part of a Broader Strategy to Address Opioid Addiction Crisis," *Health Affairs Blog*, December 1, 2017. As of May 25, 2022: https://www.healthaffairs.org/do/10.1377/forefront.20171130.772229

Becker, William C., Lindsey Dorflinger, Sara N. Edmond, Leila Islam, Alicia A. Heapy, and Liana Fraenkel, "Barriers and Facilitators to Use of Non-Pharmacological Treatments in Chronic Pain," *BMC Family Practice*, Vol. 18, No. 41, 2017.

Benson, Nicole M., and Zirui Song, "Prices and Cost Sharing in Network vs. out of Network for Behavioral Health, 2007–2017," *Health Affairs*, Vol. 39, No. 7, July 2020, pp. 1210–1218.

Binswanger, Ingrid A., Patrick J. Blatchford, Shane R. Mueller, and Marc F. Stern, "Mortality After Prison Release: Opioid Overdose and Other Causes of Death, Risk Factors, and Time Trends from 1999 to 2009," *Annals of Internal Medicine*, Vol. 159, No. 9, 2013, pp. 592–600.

Bohnert, Amy S. B., Gery P. Guy, Jr., and Jan L. Losby, "Opioid Prescribing in the United States Before and After the Centers for Disease Control and Prevention's 2016 Opioid Guideline," *Annals of Internal Medicine*, Vol. 169, No. 6, 2018, pp. 367–375.

Bonakdar, Robert, Dania Palanker, and Megan M. Sweeney, "Analysis of State Insurance Coverage for Nonpharmacologic Treatment of Low Back Pain as Recommended by the American College of Physicians Guidelines," *Global Advances in Health and Medicine*, Vol. 8, 2019.

Bonnie, Richard J., Morgan A. Ford, and Jonathan K. Phillips, eds., *Pain Management and the Opioid Epidemic: Balancing Societal and Individual Benefits and Risks of Prescription Opioid Use*, Washington, D.C.: National Academies Press, 2017.

Brandt, Kimberly, "New Part D Policies Address Opioid Epidemic," Centers for Medicare and Medicaid Services blog, March 28, 2019. As of November 5, 2020: https://www.cms.gov/blog/new-part-d-policies-address-opioid-epidemic

Brighthaupt, S. C., E. M. Stone, L. Rutkow, and E. E. McGinty, "Effect of Pill Mill Laws on Opioid Overdose Deaths in Ohio and Tennessee: A Mixed-Methods Case Study," *Preventive Medicine*, Vol. 126, 2019.

Brooklyn, John R., and Stacey C. Sigmon, "Vermont Hub-and-Spoke Model of Care for Opioid Use Disorder: Development, Implementation, and Impact," *Journal of Addictive Medicine*, Vol. 11, No. 4, 2017, pp. 286–292.

Brooner, Robert K., Van L. King, Michael Kidorf, Chester W. Schmidt Jr., George E. Bigelow, "Psychiatric and Substance Use Comorbidity Among Treatment-Seeking Opioid Abusers," *Archives of General Psychiatry*, Vol. 54, No. 1, 1997, pp. 71–80.

Brothers, Sarah, Adam Viera, and Robert Heimer, "Changes in Methadone Program Practices and Fatal Methadone Overdose Rates in Connecticut During COVID-19," Journal of Substance Abuse Treatment, Vol. 131, 2021.

Bunting, Amanda M., Carrie B. Oser, Michele Staton, Katherine S. Eddens, and Hannah Knudsen, "Clinician Identified Barriers to Treatment for Individuals in Appalachia with Opioid Use Disorder Following Release from Prison: A Social Ecological Approach," *Addiction Science & Clinical Practice*, Vol. 13, No. 23, 2018.

Burgess, Diana J., David B. Nelson, Amy A. Gravely, Matthew J. Bair, Robert D. Kerns, Diana M. Higgins, Michelle van Ryn, Melissa Farmer, and Melissa R. Partin, "Racial Differences in Prescription of Opioid Analgesics for Chronic Noncancer Pain in a National Sample of Veterans," *Journal of Pain*, Vol. 15, No. 4, 2014, pp. 447–455.

Burke, Laura G., Xiner Zhou, Katherine L. Boyle, E. John Orav, Dana Bernson, Maria-Elena Hood, Thomas Land, Monica Bharel, and Austin B. Frakt, "Trends in Opioid Use Disorder and Overdose Among Opioid-Naive Individuals Receiving an Opioid Prescription in Massachusetts from 2011 to 2014," *Addiction*, Vol. 115, No. 3, March 2020, pp. 493–504.

Burns, Joseph, "Are Insurers' Prior Authorization Rules Killing Opioid Addicts?" *Managed Care*, Vol. 26, No. 4, 2017.

Busch, Susan H., David A. Fiellin, Marek C. Chawarski, Patricia H. Owens, Michael V. Pantalon, Kathryn Hawk, Steven L. Bernstein, Patrick G. O'Connor, Gail D'Onofrio, "Cost-Effectiveness of Emergency Department-Initiated Treatment for Opioid Dependence," *Addiction*, Vol. 112, No. 11, 2017, pp. 2002–2010.

Calcaterra, Susuan L., Traci E. Yamashita, Sung-Joon Min, Angela Keniston, Joseph W. Frank, and Ingrid A. Binswanger, "Opioid Prescribing at Hospital Discharge Contributes to Chronic Opioid Use," *Journal of General Internal Medicine*, Vol. 31, No. 5, 2016, pp. 478–485.

Campbell, Gabrielle, Firouzeh Noghrehchi, Suzanne Nielsen, Phillip Clare, Raimondo Bruno, Nicholas Lintzeris, Milton Cohen, Fiona Blyth, Wayne Hall, Briony Larance, et al., "Risk Factors for Indicators of Opioid-Related Harms Amongst People Living with Chronic Non-Cancer Pain: Findings from a 5-Year Prospective Cohort Study," *EClinicalMedicine*, Vol. 28, 2020.

Center on Budget and Policy Priorities, *Chart Book: Social Security Disability Insurance*, Washington, D.C., September 6, 2019.

Centers for Medicare & Medicaid Services, "Value in Opioid Use Disorder Treatment Demonstration Program," webpage, updated November 5, 2021. As of December 16, 2021: https://innovation.cms.gov/innovation-models/value-in-treatment-demonstration

Cerdá, Magdalena, Julian Santaella, Brandon D. L. Marshall, June H. Kim, and Silvia S. Martins, "Nonmedical Prescription Opioid Use in Childhood and Early Adolescence Predicts Transitions to Heroin Use in Young Adulthood: A National Study," *Journal of Pediatrics*, Vol. 167, No. 3, 2015, pp. 605–612.

Chaple, Michael J., Thomas E. Freese, Beth A. Rutkowski, Laurie Krom, Andrew S. Kurtz, James A. Peck, Paul Warren, and Susan Garrett, "Using ECHO Clinics to Promote Capacity Building in Clinical Supervision," *American Journal of Preventive Medicine*, Vol. 54, No. 6, 2018, pp. S275–S80.

Chou, R., P. Todd Korthuis, Melissa Weimer, Christina Bougatsos, Ian Blazina, Bernadette Zakher, Sara Grusing, Beth Devine, and Dennis McCarty, *Medication-Assisted Treatment Models of Care for Opioid Use Disorder in Primary Care Settings*, Rockville, Md.: Agency for Healthcare Research and Quality, Technical Brief No. 28, December 2016.

Clemans-Cope, Lisa, Jane B. Wishner, Eva H. Allen, Nicole Lallemand, Marni Epstein, and Brenda C. Spillman, "Experiences of Three States Implementing the Medicaid Health Home Model to Address Opioid Use Disorder—Case Studies in Maryland, Rhode Island, and Vermont," *Journal of Substance Abuse Treatment*, Vol. 83, 2017, pp. 27–35.

Covell, Nancy H., Forrest P. Foster, Paul J. Margolies, Luis O. Lopez, and Lisa B. Dixon, "Using Distance Technologies to Facilitate a Learning Collaborative to Implement Stagewise Treatment," *Psychiatric Services*, Vol. 66, 2015, pp. 645–648.

Cragg, Amber, Jeffrey P. Hau, Stephanie A. Woo, Sophie A. Kitchen, Christine Liu, Mary M. Doyle-Waters, and Corinne M. Hohl, "Risk Factors for Misuse of Prescribed Opioids: A Systematic Review and Meta-Analysis," *Annals of Emergency Medicine*, Vol. 74, No. 5, 2019, pp. 634–646.

Currie, Janet, Jonas Y. Jin, and Molly Schnell, *U.S. Employment and Opioids: Is There a Connection?* Cambridge, Mass.: National Bureau of Economic Research, Working Paper No. 24440, 2018.

Dahlhamer, James, Jacqueline Lucas, Carla Zelaya, Richard Nahin, Sean Mackey, Lynn DeBar, Robert Kerns, Michael Von Korff, Linda Porter, and Charles Helmick, "Prevalence of Chronic Pain and High-Impact Chronic Pain Among Adults—United States, 2016," *Morbidity and Mortality Weekly Report*, Vol. 67, No. 36, 2018, pp. 1001–1006.

Dasgupta, Nabarun, Leo Beletsky, and Daniel Ciccarone, "Opioid Crisis: No Easy Fix to Its Social and Economic Determinants," *American Journal of Public Health*, Vol. 108, 2018, pp. 182–186.

Dauber, Sarah, Charles Neighbors, Chris Dasaro, Annetee Riordan, and Jon Morgenstern, "Impact of Intensive Case Management on Child Welfare System Involvement for Substance-Dependent Parenting Women on Public Assistance," *Child and Youth Services Review*, Vol. 34, No. 7, 2012, pp. 1359–1366.

Davis, Corey S., and Elizabeth A. Samuels, "Continuing Increased Access to Buprenorphine in the United States via Telemedicine After COVID-19," *International Journal on Drug Policy*, Vol. 93, 2021.

de C. Williams, Amanda C., "Defeating the Stigma of Chronic Pain," *Pain*, Vol. 157, No. 8, 2016, pp. 1581–1582.

DEA—*See* Drug Enforcement Administration.

Delcher, Chris, Yanning Wang, Alexander C. Wagenaar, Bruce A. Goldberger, Robert L. Cook, and Mildred M. Maldonado-Molina, "Prescription and Illicit Opioid Deaths and the Prescription Drug Monitoring Program in Florida," *American Journal of Public Health*, Vol. 106, 2016.

De Ruddere, Lies, and Kenneth D. Craig, "Understanding Stigma and Chronic Pain: A-State-of-the-Art Review," *Pain*, Vol. 157, No. 8, 2016, pp. 1607–1610.

DeShazo, Richard D., McKenzie Johnson, Ike Eriator, and Kathryn Rodenmeyer, "Backstories on the US Opioid Epidemic. Good Intentions Gone Bad, an Industry Gone Rogue, and Watch Dogs Gone to Sleep," *American Journal of Medicine*, Vol. 131, No. 6, June 1, 2018, pp. 595–601.

Des Jarlais, Don C., Ann Nugent, Alisa Solberg, Jonathan Feelemyer, Jonathan Mermin, and Deborah Holtzman, "Syringe Service Programs for Persons Who Inject Drugs in Urban, Suburban, and Rural Areas—United States, 2013," *Morbidity and Mortality Weekly Report*, Vol. 64, No. 48, 2015, pp. 1337–1341.

D'Onofrio, Gail, Marek C. Chawarski, Patrick G. O'Connor, Michael V. Pantalon, Susan H. Busch, Patricia H. Owens, Kathryn Hawk, Steven L. Bernstein, and David A. Fiellin, "Emergency Department-Initiated Buprenorphine for Opioid Dependence with Continuation in Primary Care: Outcomes During and After Intervention," *Journal of General Internal Medicine*, Vol. 32, No. 6, 2017, pp. 660–666.

D'Onofrio, Gail, Patrick G. O'Connor, Michael V, Pantalon, Marek C. Chawarski, Susan H. Busch, Patricia H. Owens, Steven L. Bernstein, and David A. Fiellin, "Emergency Department-Initiated Buprenorphine/Naloxone Treatment for Opioid Dependence: A Randomized Clinical Trial," *JAMA*, Vol. 313, No. 16, 2015, pp. 1636–1644.

Donohue, Julie M., Jason N. Kennedy, Christopher W. Seymour, Timothy D. Girard, Wei-Hsuan Lo-Ciganic, Catharine H. Kim, Oscar C. Marroquin, Patience Moyo, Chung-Chou Chang, and Derek C. Angus, "Patterns of Opioid Administration Among Opioid-Naive Inpatients and Associations with Postdischarge Opioid Use: A Cohort Study," *Annals of Internal Medicine*, Vol. 171, No. 2, 2019, pp. 81–90.

Dowell, Deborah, Tamara M. Haegerich, and Roger Chou, "CDC Guideline for Prescribing Opioids for Chronic Pain—United States, 2016," *JAMA*, Vol. 315, No. 15, 2016, pp. 1624–1645.

Dowell, Deborah, Tamara Haegerich, and Roger Chou, "No Shortcuts to Safer Opioid Prescribing," *New England Journal of Medicine*, Vol. 380, 2019, pp. 2285–2287.

Drug Enforcement Administration, "Mid-Level Practitioners Authorization by State," webpage, 2019. As of May 25, 2022:
https://www.deadiversion.usdoj.gov/drugreg/practioners/index.html

Dubowitz, Howard, "Preventing Child Neglect and Physical Abuse: A Role for Pediatricians," *Pediatrics in Review*, Vol. 23, No. 6, 2002, pp. 191–196.

Dubowitz, Howard, "The Safe Environment for Every Kid (SEEK) Model: Helping Promote Children's Health, Development, and Safety—SEEK Offers a Practical Model for Enhancing Pediatric Primary Care," *Child Abuse and Neglect*, Vol. 38, No. 11, 2014, pp. 1725–1733.

Duff, Johnathan H., Sara M. Tharakan, Carla Y. Davis-Castro, Ada S. Cornell, and Paul D. Romero, *Consumption of Prescription Opioids for Pain: A Comparison of Opioid Use in the United States and Other Countries*, Washington, D.C.: Congressional Research Service, R46805, June 2, 2021.

Dyer, Owen, "Insys and Mallinckrodt Settle Allegations of Paying Doctors to Prescribe Drugs," *BMJ*, Vol. 365, 2019, pp. 1–2.

Eckert, Emily, "It's Past Time to Provide Continuous Medicaid Coverage for One Year Postpartum," *Health Affairs Blog*, February 6, 2020. As of November 5, 2020: https://www.healthaffairs.org/do/10.1377/hblog20200203.639479/full/

Enthoven, Alain C., "Integrated Delivery Systems: The Cure for Fragmentation," *American Journal of Managed Care*, Vol. 15, Suppl. 10, December 2009, pp. S284–S290.

Faherty, Laura J., Ashley M. Kranz, Joshua Russell-Fritch, Stephen W. Patrick, Jonathan Cantor, and Bradley D. Stein, "Association of Punitive and Reporting State Policies Related to Substance Use in Pregnancy with Rates of Neonatal Abstinence Syndrome," *JAMA*, Vol. 2, 2019.

Farahmand, Pantea, Vania Modesto-Lowe, and Margaret M. Chaplin, "Prescribing Opioid Replacement Therapy in U.S. Correctional Settings," *Journal of the American Academy of Psychiatry and the Law*, Vol. 45, No. 4, 2017, pp. 472–477.

FDA—*See* U.S. Food and Drug Administration.

Feder, Kenneth A., Elizabeth J. Letourneau, and Jody Brook, "Children in the Opioid Epidemic: Addressing the Next Generation's Public Health Crisis," *Pediatrics*, Vol. 143, No. 1, 2019.

Fenton, Joshua J., Alicia L. Agnoli, Guibo Xing, Lillian Hang, Aylin E. Altan, Daniel J. Tancredi, Anthony Jerant, and Elizabeth Magnan, "Trends and Rapidity of Dose Tapering Among Patients Prescribed Long-Term Opioid Therapy, 2008–2017," *JAMA*, Vol. 2, No. 11, 2019.

Fiscella, Kevin, Sarah E. Wakeman, and Leo Beletsky, "Implementing Opioid Agonist Treatment in Correctional Facilities," *JAMA Internal Medicine*, Vol. 178, No. 9, 2018, pp. 1153–1154.

Fleischauer, Aaron T., Laura Ruhl, Sarah Rhea, and Erin Barnes, "Hospitalizations for Endocarditis and Associated Health Care Costs Among Persons with Diagnosed Drug Dependence—North Carolina, 2010–2015," *Morbidity and Mortality Weekly Report*, Vol. 66, No. 22, 2017, pp. 569–573.

Florence, Curtis, Feijun Luo, and Ketra Rice, "The Economic Burden of Opioid Use Disorder and Fatal Opioid Overdose in the United States, 2017," *Drug and Alcohol Dependence*, Vol. 218, 2021.

Friedmann, Peter D., Randall Hoskinson, Michael Gordon, Robert Schwartz, Timothy Kinlock, Kevin Knight, Patrick M Flynn, Wayne N. Welsh, Lynda A. R. Stein, Stanley Sacks, et al., "Medication-Assisted Treatment in Criminal Justice Agencies Affiliated with the Criminal Justice-Drug Abuse Treatment Studies (CJ-DATS): Availability, Barriers, and Intentions," *Substance Abuse*, Vol. 33, No. 1, 2012, pp. 9–18.

Gaither, Julie R., Kirsha Gordon, Stephen Crystal, E. Jennifer Edelman, Robert D. Kerns, Amy C. Justice, David A. Fiellin, and William C. Becker, "Racial Disparities in Discontinuation of Long-Term Opioid Therapy Following Illicit Drug Use Among Black and White Patients," *Drug and Alcohol Dependence*, Vol. 192, 2018, pp. 371–376.

García, Macarena C., Anton B. Dodek, Tom Kowalski, John Fallon, Scott H. Lee, Michael F. Iademarco, John Auerbach, and Michele K. Bohm, "Declines in Opioid Prescribing After a Private Insurer Policy Change—Massachusetts, 2011–2015," *Morbidity and Mortality Weekly Report*, Vol. 65, No. 41, 2016, pp. 1125–1131.

Goertz, Christine M., and Steven Z. George, "Insurer Coverage of Nonpharmacological Treatments for Low Back Pain—Time for a Change," *JAMA*, Vol. 1, No. 6, 2018.

Gray, Megan E., Elizabeth T. Rogawski McQuade, W. Michael Scheld, and Rebecca Dillingham, "Rising Rates of Injection Drug Use Associated Infective Endocarditis in Virginia with Missed Opportunities for Addiction Treatment Referral: A Retrospective Cohort Study," *BMC Infectious Diseases*, Vol. 18, No. 1, 2018.

Grecu, Anca M., Dhaval M. Dave, and Henry Saffer, "Mandatory Access Prescription Drug Monitoring Programs and Prescription Drug Abuse," *Journal of Policy Analysis and Management*, Vol. 38, No. 1, 2019, pp. 181–209.

Green, Beth L., Carrie Furrer, Sonia Worcel, Scott Burrus, and Michael W. Finigan, "How Effective Are Family Treatment Drug Courts? Outcomes from a Four-Site National Study," *Child Maltreatment*, Vol. 12, No. 1, 2007, pp. 43–59.

Griffin, Margaret L., Dorian R. Dodd, Jennifer S. Potter, Lindsay S. Rice, William Dickinson, Steven Sparenborg, and Roger D. Weiss, "Baseline Characteristics and Treatment Outcomes in Prescription Opioid Dependent Patients With and Without Co-Occurring Psychiatric Disorder, *American Journal of Drug and Alcohol Abuse*, Vol. 40, No. 2, 2014, pp. 157–162.

Gugelmann, Hallam, Frances S. Shofer, Zachary F. Meisel, and Jeanmarie Perrone, "Multidisciplinary Intervention Decreases the Use of Opioid Medication Discharge Packs from 2 Urban EDs," *American Journal of Emergency Medicine*, Vol. 31, No. 9, 2013, pp. 1343–1348.

Guy, Gery P., Jr., Tamara M. Haegerich, Mary E. Evans, Jan L. Losby, Randall Young, and Christopher M. Jones, "Vital Signs: Pharmacy-Based Naloxone Dispensing—United States, 2012–2018," *Morbidity and Mortality Weekly Report*, Vol. 68, 2019, pp. 679–686.

Guy, Gery P., Jr., Kun Zhang, Michele K. Bohm, Jan Losby, Brian Lewis, Randall Young, Louise B. Murphy, and Deborah Dowell, "Vital Signs: Changes in Opioid Prescribing in the United States, 2006–2015," *Morbidity and Mortality Weekly Report*, Vol. 66, No. 26, 2017, pp. 697–704.

Haegerich, Tamara M., Christopher M. Jones, Pierre-Olivier Cote, Amber Robinson, and Lindsey Ross, "Evidence for State, Community and Systems-Level Prevention Strategies to Address the Opioid Crisis," *Drug and Alcohol Dependence*, Vol. 204, 2019.

Haffajee, Rebecca L., Amy S. B. Bohnert, and Pooja A. Lagisetty, "Policy Pathways to Address Provider Workforce Barriers to Buprenorphine Treatment," *American Journal of Preventive Medicine*, Vol. 54, No. 6, Suppl. 3, 2018, pp. S230–S242.

Han, Beth, Wilson M. Compton, Carlos Blanco, Elizabeth Crane, Jinhee Lee, and Christopher M. Jones, "Prescription Opioid Use, Misuse, and Use Disorders in U.S. Adults: 2015 National Survey on Drug Use and Health," *Annals of Internal Medicine*, Vol. 167, 2017, pp. 293–301.

Harris, Matthew C., Lawrence M. Kessler, Matthew N. Murray, and Beth Glenn, "Prescription Opioids and Labor Market Pains: The Effect of Schedule II Opioids on Labor Force Participation and Unemployment," *Journal of Human Resources*, Vol. 55, No. 4, Fall 2020, pp. 1319–1364.

Hartung, Daniel M., Jennifer Hall, Sarah N. Haverly, David Cameron, Lindsey Alley, Christi Hildebran, Nicole O'Kane, and Deborah Cohen, "Pharmacists' Role in Opioid Safety: A Focus Group Investigation," *Pain Medicine*, Vol. 19, No. 9, 2018, pp.1799–1806.

Heyward, James, Christopher M. Jones, Wilson M. Compton, Dora H. Lin, Jan L. Losby, Irene B. Murimi, Grant T. Baldwin, Jeromie M. Ballreich, David A. Thomas, Mark C. Bicket, et al., "Coverage of Nonpharmacologic Treatments for Low Back Pain Among US Public and Private Insurers," *JAMA*, Vol. 1, No. 6, 2018.

Hoffman, Jan, "Medicare Is Cracking Down on Opioids. Doctors Fear Pain Patients Will Suffer," *New York Times*, March 27, 2018.

Hoge, Michael A., Gail W. Stuart, John Morris, Michael T. Flaherty, Manuel Paris, Jr., and Eric Goplerud, "Mental Health and Addiction Workforce Development: Federal Leadership Is Needed to Address the Growing Crisis," *Health Affairs*, Vol. 32, No. 11, 2013, pp. 2005–2012.

Horwitz, Jill R., Corey Davis, Lynn McClelland, Rebecca Fordon, and Ellen Meara, "The Importance of Data Source in Prescription Drug Monitoring Program Research," *Health Services Research*, Vol. 56, No. 2, 2021, pp. 268–274.

Hu, Mei-chun, Pamela Griesler, Melanie Wall, and Denise B. Kandel, "Age-Related Patterns in Nonmedical Prescription Opioid Use and Disorder in the US Population at Ages 12–34 from 2002 to 2014," *Drug Alcohol and Dependence*, Vol. 177, 2017, pp. 237–243.

Huhn, Andrew S., and Kelly E. Dunn, "Why Aren't Physicians Prescribing More Buprenorphine?" *Journal of Substance Abuse Treatment*, Vol. 78, 2017.

Huskamp, Haiden A., Lauren E. Riedel, Colleen L. Barry, and Alisa B. Busch, "Coverage of Medications That Treat Opioid Use Disorder and Opioids for Pain Management in Marketplace Plans, 2017," *Medical Care*, Vol. 56, No. 6, June 2018, pp. 505–509.

Institute of Medicine, "Chapter 3: Care of People with Pain," *Relieving Pain in America: A Blueprint for Transforming Prevention, Care, Education, and Research*, Washington, D.C.: National Academies Press, 2011, pp. 113–178.

Jairam, Vikram, Daniel X. Yang, Saamir Pasha, Pamela R. Soulos, Cary P. Gross, James B. Yu, and Henry S. Park, "Temporal Trends in Opioid Prescribing Patterns Among Oncologists in the Medicare Population," *Journal of the National Cancer Institute*, Vol. 113, No. 3, 2021, pp. 274–281.

Jairam, Vikram, Daniel X. Yang, Vivek Verma, James B. Yu, and Henry S. Park, "National Patterns in Prescription Opioid Use and Misuse Among Cancer Survivors in the United States," *JAMA*, Vol. 3, No. 8, 2020.

James, Doris J., and Lauren E. Glaze, *Mental Health Problems of Prison and Jail Inmates*, Washington, D.C.: U.S. Department of Justice, Office of Justice Programs, Bureau of Justice Statistics, September 2006.

Jarvis, Brantley P., August F. Holtyn, Shrinidhi Subramaniam, D. Andrew Tompkins, Emmanuel A. Oga, George E. Bigelow, and Kenneth Silverman, "Extended-Release Injectable Naltrexone for Opioid Use Disorder: A Systematic Review," *Addiction*, Vol. 113, No. 7, 2018, pp. 1188–1209.

Jones, Christopher M., Melinda Campopiano, Grant Baldwin, and Elinore McCance-Katz, "National and State Treatment Need and Capacity for Opioid Agonist Medication-Assisted Treatment," *American Journal of Public Health*, Vol. 105, No. 8, 2015, pp. e55–e63.

Jones, Christopher M., and Elinore F. McCance-Katz, "Co-Occurring Substance Use and Mental Disorders Among Adults with Opioid Use Disorder," *Drug and Alcohol Dependence*, Vol. 197, 2019, pp. 78–82.

Jones, Katie Fitzgerald, Mei R. Fu, Jessica S. Merlin, Judith A. Paice, Rachelle Bernacki, Christopher Lee, and Lisa J. Wood, "Exploring Factors Associated with Long-Term Opioid Therapy in Cancer Survivors: An Integrative Review," *Journal of Pain and Symptom Management*, Vol. 61, No. 2, 2021, pp. 395–415.

Jones, Katie Fitzgerald, and Jessica S. Merlin, "Approaches to Opioid Prescribing in Cancer Survivors: Lessons Learned from the General Literature," *Cancer*, Vol. 128, No. 3, 2021, pp. 449–455.

Kaiser Family Foundation, "States Reporting Corrections-Related Medicaid Enrollment Policies in Place for Prisons or Jails," webpage, 2019. As of November 5, 2020:
https://www.kff.org/medicaid/state-indicator/
states-reporting-corrections-related-medicaid-enrollment-policies-in-place-for-prisons-or-jails

Kelvey, Jon, "How Advertising Shaped the First Opioid Epidemic: And What It Can Teach Us About the Second," *Smithsonian Magazine* online, April 3, 2018. As of May 25, 2022: https://www.smithsonianmag.com/science-nature/ how-advertising-shaped-first-opioid-epidemic-180968444/

Kennedy-Hendricks, Alene, Susan H. Busch, Emma E. McGinty, Marcus A. Bachhuber, Jeff Niederdeppe, Sarah E. Gollust, Daniel W. Webster, David A. Fiellin, and Colleen L. Barry, "Primary Care Physicians' Perspectives on the Prescription Opioid Epidemic," *Drug and Alcohol Dependence*, Vol. 165, 2016, pp. 61–70.

Kermack, Andrea, Mara Flannery, Babak Tofighi, Jennifer McNeely, and Joshua D. Lee, "Buprenorphine Prescribing Practice Trends and Attitudes Among New York Providers," *Journal of Substance Abuse Treatment*, Vol. 74, 2017.

Kertesz, Stefan G., "Turning the Tide or Riptide? The Changing Opioid Epidemic," *Substance Abuse*, Vol. 38, No. 1, 2017, pp. 3–8.

Kilmer, Beau, Jirka Taylor, Jonathan P. Caulkins, Pam A. Mueller, Allison J. Ober, Bryce Pardo, Rosanna Smart, Lucy Strang, and Peter H. Reuter, *Considering Heroin-Assisted Treatment and Supervised Drug Consumption Sites in the United States*, Santa Monica, Calif.: RAND Corporation, RR-2693-RC, 2018. As of May 25, 2022: https://www.rand.org/pubs/research_reports/RR2693.html

Kimmel, Simeon D., Sophie Rosenmoss, Benjamin Bearnot, Marc Larochelle, and Alexander Y. Walley, "Rejection of Patients with Opioid Use Disorder Referred for Post-Acute Medical Care Before and After an Anti-Discrimination Settlement in Massachusetts," *Journal of Addiction Medicine*, Vol. 15, No. 1, 2021, pp. 20–26.

Klimas, Jan, Lauren Gorfinkel, Nadia Fairbairn, Laura Amato, Keith Ahamad, Seonaid Nolan, David L. Simel, and Evan Wood, "Strategies to Identify Patient Risks of Prescription Opioid Addiction When Initiating Opioids for Pain: A Systematic Review," *JAMA*, Vol. 2, No. 5, 2019.

Ko, Jean Y., Stephen W. Patrick, Van T. Tong, Roshni Patel, Jennifer N. Lind, Wanda D. Barfield, "Incidence of Neonatal Abstinence Syndrome—28 States, 1999–2013," *Morbidity and Mortality Weekly Report*, Vol. 65, No. 31, 2016, pp. 799–802.

Kolodny, Andrew, David T. Courtwright, Catherine S. Hwang, Peter Kreiner, John L. Eadie, Thomas W. Clark, and G. Caleb Alexander, "The Prescription Opioid and Heroin Crisis: A Public Health Approach to an Epidemic of Addiction," *Annual Review of Public Health*, Vol. 36, 2015, pp. 559–574.

Komaromy, Miriam, Venice Ceballos, Andrea Zurawski, Thomas Bodenheimer, David H. Thom, and Sanjeev Arora, "Extension for Community Healthcare Outcomes (ECHO): A New Model for Community Health Worker Training and Support," *Journal of Public Health Policy*, Vol. 39, 2018, pp. 203–216.

Komaromy, Miriam, Dan Duhigg, Adam Metcalf, Cristina Carlson, Summers Kalishman, Leslie Hayes, Tom Burke, Karla Thornton, and Sanjeev Arora, "Project ECHO (Extension for Community Healthcare Outcomes): A New Model for Educating Primary Care Providers About Treatment of Substance Use Disorders," *Substance Abuse*, Vol. 37, No. 1, 2016, pp. 20–24.

Korthuis, P. Todd, Dennis McCarty, Melissa Weimer, Christina Bougatsos, Ian Blazina, Bernadette Zakher, Sara Grusing, Beth Devine, and Roger Chou, "Primary Care–Based Models for the Treatment of Opioid Use Disorder: A Scoping Review," *Annals of Internal Medicine*, Vol. 166, No. 4, 2017, pp. 268–278.

Krantz, Laura, "Opiate Addiction Treatment Hubs Save Money, State Says," VTDigger, March 20, 2014. As of May 25, 2022: https://vtdigger.org/2014/03/20/addiction-treatment-hubs-save-money-state-says/

Krebs, Erin E., Amy Gravely, Sean Nugent, Agnes C. Jensen, Beth DeRonne, Elizabeth S. Goldsmith, Kurt Kroenke, Matthew J. Bair, and Siamak Noorbaloochi, "Effect of Opioid vs Nonopioid Medications on Pain-Related Function in Patients with Chronic Back Pain or Hip or Knee Osteoarthritis Pain: The SPACE Randomized Clinical Trial," *JAMA*, Vol. 319, No. 9, 2018, pp. 872–882.

Kroenke, Kurt, Daniel P. Alford, Charles Argoff, Bernard Canlas, Edward Covington, Joseph W. Frank, Karl J. Haake, Steven Hanling, W. Michael Hooten, and Stefan G. Kertesz, "Challenges with Implementing the Centers for Disease Control and Prevention Opioid Guideline: A Consensus Panel Report," *Pain Medicine*, Vol. 20, No. 4, 2019, pp. 724–735.

Krueger, Alan B., "Where Have All the Workers Gone? An Inquiry into the Decline of the U.S. Labor Force Participation Rate," *Brookings Papers on Economic Activity*, Fall 2017.

Lagisetty, Pooja, Nathaniel Healy, Claire Garpestad, Mary Jannausch, Renuka Tipirneni, and Amy S. B. Bohnert, "Access to Primary Care Clinics for Patients with Chronic Pain Receiving Opioids," *JAMA*, Vol. 2, No. 7, 2019.

Lagisetty, Pooja, Katarzyna Klasa, Christopher Bush, Michele Heisler, Vineet Chopra, and Amy Bohnert, "Primary Care Models for Treating Opioid Use Disorders: What Actually Works? A Systematic Review," *PLoS One*, Vol. 12, 2017.

Lapham, Gwen, Denise M. Boudreau, Eric A. Johnson, Jennifer F. Bobb, Abigail G. Matthews, Jennifer McCormack, David Liu, Jeffrey H. Samet, Andrew J. Saxon, Cynthia I. Campbell, et al., "Prevalence and Treatment of Opioid Use Disorders Among Primary Care Patients in Six Health Systems," *Drug and Alcohol Dependence*, Vol. 207, 2020.

Leshner, Alan I., and Michelle Mancher, eds., "The Effectiveness of Medication-Based Treatment for Opioid Use Disorder," *Medications for Opioid Use Disorder Save Lives*, Washington, D.C.: National Academies Press, 2019a, pp. 33–62.

Leshner, Alan I., and Michelle Mancher, eds., *Medications for Opioid Use Disorder Save Lives*, Washington, D.C.: National Academies Press, 2019b.

Levy, Benjamin, Leonard Paulozzi, Karin A. Mack, and Christopher M. Jones, "Trends in Opioid Analgesic-Prescribing Rates by Specialty, U.S., 2007–2012," *American Journal of Preventive Medicine*, Vol. 49, No. 3, 2015, pp. 409–413.

Liebschutz, Jane M., Denise Crooks, Debra Herman, Bradley Anderson, Judith Tsui, Lidia Z. Meshesha, Shernaz Dossabhoy, and Michael Stein, "Buprenorphine Treatment for Hospitalized, Opioid-Dependent Patients: A Randomized Clinical Trial," *JAMA Internal Medicine*, Vol. 174, No. 8, 2014, pp. 1369–1376.

Lin, Dora H., Christopher M. Jones, Wilson M. Compton, James Heyward, Jan L. Losby, Irene B. Murimi, Grant T. Baldwin, Jeromie M. Ballreich, David A. Thomas, Mark Bicket, et al., "Prescription Drug Coverage for Treatment of Low Back Pain Among US Medicaid, Medicare Advantage, and Commercial Insurers," *JAMA*, Vol. 1, No. 2, 2018.

Livingston, James D., Teresa Milne, Mei Lan Fang, and Erica Amari, "The Effectiveness of Interventions for Reducing Stigma Related to Substance Use Disorders: A Systematic Review," *Addiction*, Vol. 107, No. 1, 2012, pp. 39–50.

Loeser, John D., and Michael E. Schatman, "Chronic Pain Management in Medical Education: A Disastrous Omission," *Postgraduate Medicine*, Vol. 129, No. 3, 2017, pp. 332–335.

Mark, Tami L., and William Parish, "Opioid Medication Discontinuation and Risk of Adverse Opioid-Related Health Care Events," *Journal of Substance Abuse Treatment*, Vol. 103, 2019, pp. 58–63.

Mars, Sarah G., Philippe Bourgois, George Karandinos, Fernando Montero, and Daniel Ciccarone, "'Every "Never" I Ever Said Came True': Transitions from Opioid Pills to Heroin Injecting," *International Journal of Drug Policy*, Vol. 25, No. 2, 2014, pp. 257–266.

Marsh, Jeanne C., and Brenda D. Smith, "Integrated Substance Abuse and Child Welfare Services for Women: A Progress Review," *Children and Youth Services Review*, Vol. 33, No. 3, 2011, pp. 466–472.

Martell, Bridgett A., Patrick G. O'Connor, Robert D. Kerns, William C. Becker, Knashawn H. Morales, Thomas R. Kosten, and David A. Fiellin, "Systematic Review: Opioid Treatment for Chronic Back Pain—Prevalence, Efficacy, and Association with Addiction," *Annals of Internal Medicine*, Vol. 146, No. 2, 2007, pp. 116–127.

Martin, Joyce A., Brady E. Hamilton, and Michelle J. K. Osterman, *Births in the United States, 2017*, National Center for Health Statistics Data Brief No. 318, August 2018.

Mauri, Amanda I., Tarlise N. Townsend, and Rebecca L. Haffajee, "The Association of State Opioid Misuse Prevention Policies with Patient- and Provider-Related Outcomes: A Scoping Review," *Milbank Quarterly*, Vol. 98, No. 1, 2020, pp. 57–105.

McBournie, Alaina, Alexandra Duncan, Elizabeth Connolly, and Josh Rising, "Methadone Barriers Persist, Despite Decades of Evidence," *Health Affairs Blog*, September 23, 2019. As of November 5, 2020:
https://www.healthaffairs.org/do/10.1377/hblog20190920.981503/full/

McGinty, Emma E., and Colleen L. Barry, "Stigma Reduction to Combat the Addiction Crisis—Developing an Evidence Base," *New England Journal of Medicine*, Vol. 382, No. 14, 2020, pp. 1291–1292.

Meinhofer, Angelica, "Prescription Drug Monitoring Programs: The Role of Asymmetric Information on Drug Availability and Abuse," *American Journal of Health Economics*, Vol. 4, 2018, pp. 504–526.

Merlin, Jessica S., Sarah R. Young, Robert Arnold, Hailey W. Bulls, Julie Childers, Lynn Gauthier, Karleen F. Giannitrapani, Dio Kavalieratos, Yael Schenker, J. Deanna Wilson, and Jane M. Liebschutz, "Managing Opioids, Including Misuse and Addiction, in Patients with Serious Illness in Ambulatory Palliative Care: A Qualitative Study," *American Journal of Hospice and Palliative Medicine*, Vol. 37, No. 7, 2020, pp. 507–513.

Meyer, Laurence J., and Carolyn M. Clancy, "Care Fragmentation and Prescription Opioids," *Annals of Internal Medicine*, Vol. 170, No. 7, 2019, pp. 497–498.

Meyer, Marjorie, Anna Benvenuto, Diantha Howard, Anne Johnston, Dawn Plante, Jerilyn Metayer, and Todd Mandell, "Development of a Substance Abuse Program for Opioid-Dependent Nonurban Pregnant Women Improves Outcome," *Journal of Addiction Medicine*, Vol. 6, No. 2, 2012, pp. 124–130.

Meyer, Marjorie, Anne M. Johnston, Abigail M. Crocker, and Sarah H. Heil, "Methadone and Buprenorphine for Opioid Dependence During Pregnancy: A Retrospective Cohort Study," *Journal of Addiction Medicine*, Vol. 9, No. 2, 2015, pp. 81–86.

Mezei, Lina, Beth B. Murinson, and the Johns Hopkins Pain Curriculum Development Team, "Pain Education in North American Medical Schools," *Journal of Pain*, Vol. 12, 2011, pp. 1199–1208.

Minozzi, Silvia, Laura Amato, and Marina Davoli, "Development of Dependence Following Treatment with Opioid Analgesics for Pain Relief: A Systematic Review," *Addiction*, Vol. 108, No. 4, 2013, pp. 688–698.

Moyo, Patience, Xinhua Zhao, Carolyn T. Thorpe, Joshua M. Thorpe, Florentina E. Sileanu, John P. Cashy, Jennifer A. Hale, Maria K. Mor, Thomas R. Radomski, Julie M. Donohue, et al., "Dual Receipt of Prescription Opioids From the Department of Veterans Affairs and Medicare Part D and Prescription Opioid Overdose Death Among Veterans: A Nested Case-Control Study," *Annals of Internal Medicine*, Vol. 170, No. 7, 2019, pp. 433–442.

Mularski, Richard A., Foy White-Chu, Devorah Overbay, Lois Miller, Steven M. Asch, and Linda Ganzini, "Measuring Pain as the 5th Vital Sign Does Not Improve Quality of Pain Management," *Journal of General Internal Medicine*, Vol. 21, No. 6, 2006, pp. 607–612.

National Academies of Sciences, Engineering, and Medicine, *Medication-Assisted Treatment for Opioid Use Disorder: Proceedings of a Workshop—in Brief*, Washington, D.C., November 2018.

National Association of Attorneys General, "Letter to America's Health Insurance Plans Re: Prescription Opioid Epidemic," Washington, D.C., September 18, 2017.

Nordstrom, Benjamin R., Elizabeth C. Saunders, Bethany McLeman, Andrea Meier, Haiyi Xie, Chantal Lambert-Harris, Beth Tanzman, John Brooklyn, Gregory King, Nels Kloster, et al., "Using a Learning Collaborative Strategy with Office-Based Practices to Increase Access and Improve Quality of Care for Patients with Opioid Use Disorders," *Journal of Addiction Medicine*, Vol. 10, No. 2, 2016, pp. 117–123.

North Carolina Medical Board, *North Carolina Medical Board Licensee Survey Results*, Raleigh, N.C., July 2018.

Ogbonnaya, Ijeoma Nwabuzor, and Annie J. Keeney, "A Systematic Review of the Effectiveness of Interagency and Cross-System Collaborations in the United States to Improve Child Welfare Outcomes," *Children and Youth Services Review*, Vol. 94, 2018, pp. 225–245.

Olfson, Mark, Victoria (Shu) Zhang, Michael Schoenbaum, and Marissa King, "Trends in Buprenorphine Treatment in the United States, 2009–2018," *JAMA*, Vol. 323, No. 3, 2020, pp. 276–277.

Oliva, Elizabeth M., Thomas Bowe, Ajay Manhapra, Stefan Kertesz, Jennifer M. Hah, Patricia Henderson, Amy Robinson, Meenah Paik, Friedhelm Sandbrink, Adam J. Gordon, and Jodie A. Trafton, "Associations Between Stopping Prescriptions for Opioids, Length of Opioid Treatment, and Overdose or Suicide Deaths in US Veterans: Observational Evaluation," *BMJ*, Vol. 368, 2020.

Ornoy, Asher, Jacob Segal, Rachel Bar-Hamburger, and Charles Greenbaum, "Developmental Outcome of School-Age Children Born to Mothers with Heroin Dependency: Importance of Environmental Factors," *Developmental Medicine and Child Neurology*, Vol. 43, No. 10, 2001, pp. 668–675.

Owen, Graves T., Brian M. Bruel, C. M. Schade, Maxim S. Eckmann, Erik C. Hustak, and Mitchell P. Engle, "Evidence-Based Pain Medicine for Primary Care Physicians," *Baylor University Medical Center Proceedings*, Vol. 31, No. 1, 2018, pp. 37–47.

Pacula, Rosalie Liccardo, and David Powell, "A Supply-Side Perspective on the Opioid Crisis," *Journal of Policy Analysis and Management*, Vol. 37, No. 2, Spring 2018, pp. 438–446.

Pacula, Rosalie Liccardo, Rosanna Smart, and Bradley Stein, *Pitfalls and Potholes: Data Issues to Consider When Analyzing State Opioid Policies, September 14, 2020*, Santa Monica, Calif.: RAND Corporation, PT-A921-1, 2020. As of April 9, 2021: https://www.rand.org/pubs/presentations/PTA921-1.html

Patel, Shardool, Jan M. Carmichael, Janice M. Taylor, Mark Bounthavong, and Diana T. Higgins, "Evaluating the Impact of a Clinical Decision Support Tool to Reduce Chronic Opioid Dose and Decrease Risk Classification in a Veteran Population," *Annals of Pharmacotherapy*, Vol. 52, No. 4, 2018, pp. 325–331.

Patrick, Stephen W., Richard G. Frank, Elizabeth McNeer, and Bradley D. Stein, "Improving the Child Welfare System to Respond to the Needs of Substance-Exposed Infants," *Hospital Pediatrics*, Vol. 9, No. 8, 2019, pp. 651–654.

Patrick, Stephen W., Davida M. Schiff, Sheryl A. Ryan, Joanna Quigley, Pamela K. Gonzalez, and Leslie R. Walker, "A Public Health Response to Opioid Use in Pregnancy," *Pediatrics*, Vol. 139, No. 3, 2017.

Pew Charitable Trusts, *Opioid Use Disorder Treatment in Jails and Prisons*, Philadelphia, Pa., Issue Brief, April 2020.

Pfefferle, Susan G., Samantha S. Karon, and Brandy Wyant, *Choice Matters: Housing Models That May Promote Recovery for Individuals and Families Facing Opioid Use Disorder*, Washington, D.C.: U.S. Department of Health and Human Services, Office of the Assistant Secretary for Planning and Evaluation, June 2019.

Phan, Michael T., Daniel M. Tomaszewski, Cody Arbuckle, Sun Yang, Candice Donaldson, Michelle Fortier, Brooke Jenkins, Erik Linstead, and Zeev Kain, "Racial and Ethnic Disparities in Opioid Use for Adolescents at US Emergency Departments," *BMC Pediatrics*, Vol. 21, No. 252, 2021.

Pitt, Allison L., Keith Humphreys, and Margaret L. Brandeau, "Modeling Health Benefits and Harms of Public Policy Responses to the US Opioid Epidemic," *American Journal of Public Health*, Vol. 108, No. 10, 2018, pp. 1394–1400.

Polacek, Cate, Roni Christopher, Michelle Mann, Margarita Udall, Terri Craig, Michael Deminski, and Nila A. Sathe, "Healthcare Professionals' Perceptions of Challenges to Chronic Pain Management," *American Journal of Managed Care*, Vol. 26, No. 4, 2020, pp. e135–e139.

Prince, Jonathan D., and Claudia Wald, "Risk of Criminal Justice System Involvement Among People with Co-Occurring Severe Mental Illness and Substance Use Disorder," *International Journal of Law and Psychiatry*, Vol. 58, 2018.

Project ECHO, *ECHO Access Opioid Use Disorder Treatment Guideline: Opioid Abuse and Addiction Management Protocol*, Albuquerque, N.M., 2014.

Randazzo, Sara, and Jared S. Hopkins, "OxyContin-Maker Owner Maligned Opioid Addicts, Suit Says," *Wall Street Journal*, March 29, 2019.

Rasmussen, Kurt, David A. White, and Jane B. Acri, "NIDA's Medication Development Priorities in Response to the Opioid Crisis: Ten Most Wanted," *Neuropsychopharmacology*, Vol. 44, No. 4, 2019, pp. 657–659.

Rigg, Khary K., Samantha J. March, and James A. Inciardi, "Prescription Drug Abuse and Diversion: Role of the Pain Clinic," *Journal of Drug Issues*, Vol. 40, 2010, pp. 681–702.

Rapoport, Alison B., Danielle R. Fine, Jennifer M. Manne-Goehler, Shoshana J. Herzig, and Christopher F. Rowley, "High Inpatient Health Care Utilization and Charges Associated with Injection Drug Use–Related Infections: A Cohort Study, 2012–2015," *Open Forum Infectious Diseases*, Vol. 8, No. 3, March 2021.

Rosenblum, Andrew, Lisa A. Marsch, Herman Joseph, and Russell K. Portenoy, "Opioids and the Treatment of Chronic Pain: Controversies, Current Status, and Future Directions," *Experimental and Clinical Psychopharmacology*, Vol. 16, No. 5, 2008, pp. 405–416.

Ross, Stephen, "Identifying an Impaired Physician," *AMA Journal of Ethics*, Vol. 5, No. 12, 2003, pp. 420–422.

Rutkow, Lainie, Hsien-Yen Chang, Matthew Daubresse, Daniel W. Webster, Elizabeth A. Stuart, and G. Caleb Alexander, "Effect of Florida's Prescription Drug Monitoring Program and Pill Mill Laws on Opioid Prescribing and Use," *JAMA Internal Medicine*, Vol. 175, No. 10, 2015, pp. 1642–1649.

Ryan, Harriet, Lisa Girion, and Scott Glover, "OxyContin Goes Global—'We're Only Just Getting Started,'" *Los Angeles Times*, December 18, 2016.

Ryan, Joseph P., Sam Choi, Jun Sung Hong, Pedro Hernandez, Christopher R. Larrison, "Recovery Coaches and Substance Exposed Births: An Experiment in Child Welfare," *Child Abuse & Neglect*, Vol. 32, No. 11, 2008, pp. 1072–1079.

Ryan, Joseph P., Brian E. Perron, Andrew Moore, Bryan G. Victor, and Keunhye Park, "Timing Matters: A Randomized Control Trial of Recovery Coaches in Foster Care," *Journal of Substance Abuse Treatment*, Vol. 77, 2017, pp. 178–184.

Ryan, Shawn, "Combatting an Epidemic: Legislation to Help Patients with Substance Use Disorders," testimony of the American Society of Addiction Medicine before the U.S. House Committee on Energy and Commerce, Health Subcommittee, March 3, 2020.

Saloner, Brendan, Kenneth B. Stoller, and G. Caleb Alexander, "Moving Addiction Care to the Mainstream—Improving the Quality of Buprenorphine Treatment," *New England Journal of Medicine*, Vol. 379, 2018, pp. 4–6.

Salz, Talya, Akriti Mishra Meza, Renee L. Gennarelli, Allison Lipitz-Snyderman, Natalie Moryl, Kathryn Ries Tringale, Denise M. Boudreau, Anuja Kriplani, Sankeerth Jinna, and Deborah Korenstein, "Safety of Opioid Prescribing Among Older Cancer Survivors," *Cancer*, Vol. 128, No. 3, 2021.

Sandoe, Emma, Carrie E. Fry, and Richard G. Frank, "Policy Levers That States Can Use to Improve Opioid Addiction Treatment and Address the Opioid Epidemic," *Health Affairs Blog*, October 2, 2018. As of November 5, 2020:
https://www.healthaffairs.org/do/10.1377/hblog20180927.51221/full/

Saunders, Elizabeth C., Mark P. McGovern, Chantal Lambert-Harris, Andrea Meier, Bethany McLeman, and Haiyi Xie, "The Impact of Addiction Medications on Treatment Outcomes for Persons with Co-Occurring PTSD and Opioid Use Disorders," *American Journal of Addiction*, Vol. 24, No. 8, 2015, pp. 722–731.

Schuchat, Anne, Debra Houry, and Gery P. Guy, "New Data on Opioid Use and Prescribing in the United States," *JAMA*, Vol. 318, No. 5, 2017, pp. 425–426.

Schulman, Meryl, "Encouraging Substance Use Disorder Treatment in Primary Care Through Value-Based Payment Strategies," *Center for Health Care Strategies Blog*, June 2018. As of May 25, 2022:
https://www.chcs.org/encouraging-substance-use-disorder-treatment-in-primary-care-through-value-based-payment-strategies/

Schulte, Fred, "Purdue Pharma's Sales Pitch Downplayed Risks of Opioid Addiction," Kaiser Health News, August 17, 2018.

Seal, Karen, William Becker, Jennifer Tighe, Yongmei Li, and Tessa Rife, "Managing Chronic Pain in Primary Care: It Really Does Take a Village," *Journal of General Internal Medicine*, Vol. 32, No. 8, 2017, pp. 931–934.

Shei, Amie, J. Bradford Rice, Noam Y. Kirson, Katharine Bodnar, Howard G. Birnbaum, Pamela Holly, and Rami Ben-Joseph, "Sources of Prescription Opioids Among Diagnosed Opioid Abusers," *Current Medical Research and Opinion*, Vol. 31, No. 4, 2015, pp. 779–784.

Singhal, Astha, Yu-Yu Tien, and Renee Y. Hsia, "Racial-Ethnic Disparities in Opioid Prescriptions at Emergency Department Visits for Conditions Commonly Associated with Prescription Drug Abuse," *PLoS ONE*, Vol. 11, No. 8, 2016.

Springer, Sandra A., P. Todd Korthuis, and Carlos Del Rio, "Integrating Treatment at the Intersection of Opioid Use Disorder and Infectious Disease Epidemics in Medical Settings: A Call for Action After a National Academies of Sciences, Engineering, and Medicine Workshop," *Annals of Internal Medicine*, Vol. 169, No. 5, 2018, pp. 335–336.

Stein, Bradley D., Adam J. Gordon, Andrew W. Dick, Rachel M. Burns, Rosalie Liccardo Pacula, Carrie M. Farmer, Douglas L. Leslie, and Mark Sorbero, "Supply of Buprenorphine Waivered Physicians: The Influence of State Policies," *Journal of Substance Abuse Treatment*, Vol. 48, 2015, pp. 104–111.

Stein, Bradley D., Flora Sheng, Erin A. Taylor, Andrew W. Dick, Mark Sorbero, and Rosalie Liccardo Pacula, "The Effect of State Policies on Rates of High-Risk Prescribing of an Initial Opioid Analgesic," *Drug and Alcohol Dependence*, Vol. 231, February 1, 2022, pp. 1–10.

Stein, Bradley D., Mark Sorbero, Andrew W. Dick, Rosalie Liccardo Pacula, Rachel M. Burns, and Adam J. Gordon, "Physician Capacity to Treat Opioid Use Disorder with Buprenorphine-Assisted Treatment," *JAMA*, Vol. 316, No. 11, 2016, pp. 1211–1212.

Stone, Elizabeth M., Alene Kennedy-Hendricks, Colleen L. Barry, Marcus A. Bachhuber, and Emma E. McGinty, "The Role of Stigma in U.S. Primary Care Physicians' Treatment of Opioid Use Disorder," *Drug and Alcohol Dependence*, Vol. 221, 2021.

Strang, Lucy, and Jirka Taylor, *Heroin-Assisted Treatment and Supervised Drug Consumption Sites: Experience from Four Countries*, Santa Monica, Calif.: RAND Corporation, WR-1262-RC, 2018. As of May 25, 2022:
https://www.rand.org/pubs/working_papers/WR1262.html

Substance Abuse and Mental Health Services Administration, "Certification of Opioid Treatment Programs (OTPs)," webpage, undated. As of December 16, 2021:
https://www.samhsa.gov/medication-assisted-treatment/
become-accredited-opioid-treatment-program

Substance Abuse and Mental Health Services Administration, *Managing Chronic Pain in Adults with or in Recovery from Substance Use Disorders*, Rockville, Md., Treatment Improvement Protocol 54, 2011.

Substance Abuse and Mental Health Services Administration, *Medications for Opioid Use Disorder*, Rockville, Md., Treatment Improvement Protocol 63, 2020.

Suda, Katie J., Michael J. Durkin, Gregory S. Calip, Walid F. Gellad, Hajwa Kim, Peter B. Lockhart, Susan A. Rowan, and Martin H. Thornhill, "Comparison of Opioid Prescribing by Dentists in the United States and England," *JAMA*, Vol. 2, No. 5, 2019.

Suda, Katie J., Jifang Zhou, Susan A. Rowan, Jessica C. McGregor, Rosanne I. Perez, Charlesnika T. Evans, Walid F. Gellad, and Gregory S. Calip, "Overprescribing of Opioids to Adults by Dentists in the U.S., 2011–2015," *American Journal of Preventive Medicine*, Vol. 58, No. 4, 2020, pp. 473–486.

Suzuki, Joji, "Medication-Assisted Treatment for Hospitalized Patients with Intravenous-Drug-Use Related Infective Endocarditis," *American Journal on Addictions*, Vol. 25, No. 3, 2016, pp. 191–194.

Tesema, Lello, Jeffrey Marshall, Rachel Hathaway, Christina Pham, Camille Clarke, Genevieve Bergeron, James Yeh, Michael Soliman, and Danny McCormick, "Training in Office-Based Opioid Treatment with Buprenorphine in US Residency Programs: A National Survey of Residency Program Directors," *Substance Abuse*, Vol. 39, 2018, pp. 434–440.

Thiels, Cornelius, Stephanie Anderson, Daniel S. Ubl, Kristine T. Hanson, Whitney J. Bergquist, Richard J. Gray, Halena Gazelka, Robert R. Cima, and Elizabeth B. Habermann, "Wide Variation and Overprescription of Opioids After Elective Surgery," *Annals of Surgery*, Vol. 266, No. 4, 2017, pp. 564–573.

Thomas, Cindy Parks, Grant A. Ritter, Alex A. Harris, Deborah Garnick, Kenneth I. Freedman, and Barbara Herbert, "Applying American Society of Addiction Medicine Performance Measures in Commercial Health Insurance and Services Data," *Journal of Addiction Medicine*, Vol. 12, No. 4, 2018, pp. 287–294.

Tiako, Nguemeni, Max Jordan, Jennifer Culhane, and Zachary F. Meisel, "Geographic Distribution of Medicaid-Claimant OB-GYNs Approved to Prescribe Buprenorphine for Opioid Use Disorder," *Obstetrics & Gynecology*, Vol. 135, 2020, p. 53S.

Tompkins, D. Andrew, J. Greg Hobelmann, and Peggy Compton, "Providing Chronic Pain Management in the 'Fifth Vital Sign' Era: Historical and Treatment Perspectives on a Modern-Day Medical Dilemma," *Drug and Alcohol Dependence*, Vol. 173, Suppl. 1, 2017, pp. S11–S21.

Trooskin, Stacey B., Helen Reynolds, and Jay R. Kostman, "Access to Costly New Hepatitis C Drugs: Medicine, Money, and Advocacy," *Clinical Infectious Diseases*, Vol. 61, No. 12, 2015, pp. 1825–1830.

Trowbridge, Paul, Zoe M. Weinstein, Todd Kerensky, Payel Roy, Danny Regan, Jeffrey H. Samet, and Alexander Y. Walley, "Addiction Consultation Services—Linking Hospitalized Patients to Outpatient Addiction Treatment," *Journal of Substance Abuse Treatment*, Vol. 79, August 2017.

Turner, Judith A., Kathleen Saunders, Susan M. Shortreed, Suzanne E. Rapp, Stephen Thielke, Linda LeResche, Kim M. Riddell, and Michael Von Korff, "Chronic Opioid Therapy Risk Reduction Initiative: Impact on Urine Drug Testing Rates and Results," *Journal of General Internal Medicine*, Vol. 29, No. 2, 2014, pp. 305–311.

Tyson, Dinorah Martinez, Melody N. Chavez, Paige Lake, Ana Gutierrez, Peggie Sherry, Khary K. Rigg, Victoria K. Marshall, Heather Henderson, Barbara Lubrano di Ciccone, Sahana Rajasekhara, and Smitha Pabbathi, "Perceptions of Prescription Opioid Medication Within the Context of Cancer Survivorship and the Opioid Epidemic," *Journal of Cancer Survivorship*, Vol. 15, No. 4, 2021, pp. 585–596.

Uchitel, Julie, Scott E. Hadland, Sudha R. Raman, Mark B. McClellan, and Charlene A. Wong, "The Opioid Epidemic: A Needed Focus on Adolescents and Young Adults," *Health Affairs Blog*, November 21, 2019. As of November 5, 2020: https://www.healthaffairs.org/do/10.1377/hblog20191115.977344/full/

U.S. Department of Health and Human Services, "HHS Releases New Buprenorphine Practice Guidelines, Expanding Access to Treatment for Opioid Use Disorder," news release April 27, 2021.

U.S. Department of Health and Human Services, Office of Inspector General, *Opioids in Medicare Part D: Concerns About Extreme Use and Questionable Prescribing*, Washington, D.C., Data Brief No. OEI-02-17-00250, July 2017.

U.S. Department of Justice, "Opioid Manufacturer Purdue Pharma Pleads Guilty to Fraud and Kickback Conspiracies," press release, November 24, 2020.

U.S. Food and Drug Administration, "FDA Approves First Once-Monthly Buprenorphine Injection, A Medication-Assisted Treatment Option for Opioid Use Disorder," press release, November 30, 2017.

U.S. General Accounting Office, *Prescription Drugs: OxyContin Abuse and Diversion and Efforts to Address the Problem*, Washington, D.C., GAO-04-110, December 2003.

Van Zee, Art, "The Promotion and Marketing of OxyContin: Commercial Triumph, Public Health Tragedy," *American Journal of Public Health*, Vol. 99, No. 2, 2009, pp. 221–227.

Venkataramani, Atheendar S., Elizabeth F. Bair, Rourke L. O'Brien, and Alexander C. Tsai, "Association Between Automotive Assembly Plant Closures and Opioid Overdose Mortality in the United States: A Difference-in-Differences Analysis," *JAMA Internal Medicine*, Vol. 180, No. 2, 2020, pp. 254–262.

Victor, Grant A., Robert Walker, Jennifer Cole, and T. K. Logan, "Opioid Analgesics and Heroin: Examining Drug Misuse Trends Among a Sample of Drug Treatment Clients in Kentucky," *International Journal of Drug Policy*, Vol. 46, 2017.

Vivolo-Kantor, Alana M., Brooke E. Hoots, Lawrence Scholl, Cassandra Pickens, Douglas R. Roehler, Amy Board, Desiree Mustaquim, Herschel Smith IV, Stephanie Snodgrass, and Stephen Liu, "Nonfatal Drug Overdoses Treated in Emergency Departments—United States, 2016–2017," *Morbidity and Mortality Weekly Report*, Vol. 69, 2020, pp. 371–376.

Volkow, Nora D., "Medications for Opioid Use Disorder: Bridging the Gap in Care," *Lancet*, Vol. 391, No. 10118, 2018, pp. 285–287.

Volkow, Nora D., and Carlos Blanco, "Medications for Opioid Use Disorders: Clinical and Pharmacological Considerations," *Journal of Clinical Investigation*, Vol. 130, No. 1, 2020, pp. 10–13.

Volkow, Nora D., and Francis S. Collins, "The Role of Science in Addressing the Opioid Crisis," *New England Journal of Medicine*, Vol. 377, 2017, pp. 391–394.

Volkow, Nora D., and A. Thomas McLellan, "Opioid Abuse in Chronic Pain—Misconceptions and Mitigation Strategies," *New England Journal of Medicine*, Vol. 374, No. 13, 2016, pp. 1253–1263.

Voon, Pauline, Mohammad Karamouzian, and Thomas Kerr, "Chronic Pain and Opioid Misuse: A Review of Reviews," *Substance Abuse Treatment, Prevention, and Policy*, Vol. 12, No. 36, 2017.

Vowles, Kevin E., Mindy L. McEntee, Peter Siyahhan Julnes, Tessa Frohe, John P. Ney, and David N. van der Goes, "Rates of Opioid Misuse, Abuse, and Addiction in Chronic Pain: A Systematic Review and Data Synthesis," *Pain*, Vol. 156, No. 4, 2015, pp. 569–576.

Wakeman, Sarah E., and Josiah D. Rich, "Addiction Treatment Within U.S. Correctional Facilities: Bridging the Gap Between Current Practice and Evidence-Based Care," *Journal of Addictive Diseases*, Vol. 34, 2015, pp. 220–225.

Watkins, Katherine E., Allison J. Ober, Karen Lamp, Mimi Lind, Claude Setodji, Karen Chan Osilla, Sarah B. Hunter, Colleen M. McCullough, Kirsten Becker, Praise O. Iyiewuare, et al., "Collaborative Care for Opioid and Alcohol Use Disorders in Primary Care: The SUMMIT Randomized Clinical Trial," *JAMA Internal Medicine*, Vol. 177, 2017, pp. 1480–1488.

Waugh, Olivia C., Donald G. Byrne, and Michael K. Nicholas, "Internalized Stigma in People Living with Chronic Pain," *Journal of Pain*, Vol. 15, No. 5, 2014.

Weiner, Scott G., Olesya Baker, Ann F. Rodgers, Chad Garner, Lewis S. Nelson, Peter W. Kreiner, and Jeremiah D. Schuur, "Opioid Prescriptions by Specialty in Ohio, 2010–2014," *Pain Medicine*, Vol. 19, No. 5, 2018, pp. 978–989.

Williams, Arthur Robin, Edward V. Nunes, Adam Bisaga, Harold A. Pincus, Kimberly A. Johnson, Aimee N. Campbell, Remien H. Remien, Stephen Crystal, Peter D. Friedmann, Frances R. Levin, and Mark Olfson, "Developing an Opioid Use Disorder Treatment Cascade: A Review of Quality Measures," *Journal of Substance Abuse Treatment*, Vol. 91, 2018, pp. 57–68.

Winkelman, Tyler N. A., Nicole Villapiano, Katy B. Kozhimannil, Matthew M. Davis, and Stephen W. Patrick, "Incidence and Costs of Neonatal Abstinence Syndrome Among Infants with Medicaid: 2004–2014," *Pediatrics*, Vol. 141, No. 4, 2018.

Yanni, Leanne M., Jessica L. McKinney-Ketchum, Sarah B. Harrington, Christine Huynh, Saad Amin, Robin Matsuyama, Patrick Coyne, Betty A. Johnson, Mark Fagan, and Linda Garufi-Clark, "Preparation, Confidence, and Attitudes About Chronic Noncancer Pain in Graduate Medical Education," *Journal of Graduate Medical Education*, Vol. 2, 2010, pp. 260–268.

Yatsco, Andrea J., Rachel D. Garza, Tiffany Champagne-Langabeer, and James R. Langabeer, "Alternatives to Arrest for Illicit Opioid Use: A Joint Criminal Justice and Healthcare Treatment Collaboration," *Substance Abuse: Research and Treatment*, Vol. 14, 2020.

Young, Leonard D., Peter W. Kreiner, and Lee Panas, "Unsolicited Reporting to Prescribers of Opioid Analgesics by a State Prescription Drug Monitoring Program: An Observational Study with Matched Comparison Group," *Pain Medicine*, Vol. 19, No. 7, 2018, pp. 1396–1407.

Yuanhong Lai, Alden, Katherine C. Smith, Jon S. Vernick, Corey S. Davis, G. Caleb Alexander, and Lainie Rutkow, "Perceived Unintended Consequences of Prescription Drug Monitoring Programs," *Substance Use and Misuse*, Vol. 54, 2019, pp. 345–349.

Zaman, Tauheed, Tessa L. Rife, Steven L. Batki, and David L. Pennington, "An Electronic Intervention to Improve Safety for Pain Patients Co-Prescribed Chronic Opioids and Benzodiazepines," *Substance Abuse*, Vol. 39, No. 4, 2018, pp. 441–448.

Zamani-Hank, Yasamean, "The Affordable Care Act and the Burden of High Cost Sharing and Utilization Management Restrictions on Access to HIV Medications for People Living with HIV/AIDS," *Population Health Management*, Vol. 19, No. 4, August 2016, pp. 272–278.

Zgierska, Aleksandra, Michael Miller, and David Rabago, "Patient Satisfaction, Prescription Drug Abuse, and Potential Unintended Consequences," *JAMA*, Vol. 307, No. 13, 2012, pp. 1377–1378.

Zhu, Wenjia, Michael E. Chernew, Tisamarie Sherry, and Nicole Maestas, "Initial Opioid Prescriptions Among U.S. Commercially Insured Patients, 2012–2017," *New England Journal of Medicine*, Vol. 380, 2019, pp. 1043–1052.

CHAPTER SIX

Criminal Legal System

Beau Kilmer

Overview

Laws and criminal legal agencies influence the supply and demand of opioids, along with the harms associated with using them. These laws and agencies can also influence the extent to which some people with opioid use disorder (OUD) and suppliers engage in criminal activity. The key components in this system are local, state, and federal laws; law enforcement agencies; lawyers and courts, corrections agencies (including community supervision); police and correction officials' unions; and the private and nonprofit organizations that support these institutions. Although each plays a different role, there are at least six activities (sometimes overlapping, sometimes contradictory) that many of these entities are trying to achieve with respect to opioids: (1) protect public safety and reduce burdens associated with crimes involving or related to opioid use and trafficking; (2) foster social disapproval (i.e., stigma) around the nonmedical use and selling of these drugs; (3) provide victims of crimes related to opioid use (e.g., violent crimes related to selling, property crimes related to consumption) with a sense of justice; (4) reduce supply by fighting the diversion of prescription opioids and the availability of illegally produced opioids; (5) reduce demand for drugs via deterrence, price inflation, reductions in availability, and referral of individuals to treatment and other services; and (6) reverse overdoses and get those who have overdosed the medical attention they need.

Some of these actions produce negative consequences, especially for people of color. As with many other types of crime, racial and ethnic inequities in drug arrests are well documented, and these have downstream effects throughout the adjudication and sentencing processes.

As noted in Chapter One, the early phases of the opioid crisis did not heavily involve criminal legal agencies. Most of the supply was diverted from prescribed drugs; there were no major trafficking organizations, little street violence, and few open-air drug markets focused on prescription opioids. It was largely after individuals who become addicted to prescription opioids began to trade down to buy illegal opioids that the demands on criminal legal agencies began to grow. Circa 2019, there were on the order of 200,000 to 300,000 annual arrests that are specific to opioids and likely multiple times that number that are related to opioids but not specific to drugs (e.g., property crimes committed to obtain money for drugs). These crimes impose burdens on these systems, and they can also impose costs—including trauma and sometimes violence—on victims. Related to this, Chapter Two makes clear that individuals with OUD who are involved with the criminal legal system often have extensive criminal records involving offenses other than drug violations.

Key Interactions with Other Components of the Ecosystem

The criminal legal system is directly involved in efforts to **control supply**. Although diverted prescription opioids, heroin, and even illegally produced synthetic opioids like fentanyl have posed challenges to law enforcement for decades, the mass production of potent, cheap synthetic opioids in China and Mexico has created new problems.

Criminal legal agencies have a large effect on admissions to **specialty treatment programs** via referrals, diversion or deflection programs, and sentencing; however, this does not mean that individuals with OUD—especially those who are incarcerated—always receive high-quality treatment. That said, jail- and prison-based health systems have made serious efforts in recent years to increase access to medications for opioid use disorder (MOUD).

Beyond prison health care systems, interactions with the criminal legal system can influence utilization of **health care** services in other ways. Community corrections agencies often make referrals for physical and mental health conditions, but whether individuals receive treatment for the conditions for which they are referred is another story. States have historically terminated or suspended Medicaid benefits once individuals are incarcerated, creating barriers to receiving care once they are released.

Local law enforcement officers often serve as **first responders** to overdoses, administering naloxone and sometimes taking individuals to medical facilities. They also sometimes provide security for other first responders. But whether someone reports an overdose can be influenced by the legal environment. Many jurisdictions have passed Good Samaritan laws that can offer some protection from being arrested for people who report overdoses. Some states have passed drug homicide laws, which punish those who shared or supplied drugs to individuals who overdosed and died.

Having a criminal record has implications for many other parts of the opioid ecosystem. Depending on the state, it can make some individuals ineligible for certain **services and programs** (e.g., public housing, nutritional assistance), and those who are incarcerated can have their access to Medicaid suspended or terminated.

The risk of being arrested also has implications for **harm reduction programs,** such as syringe service programs and drug content testing. The fear and stigma associated with criminalization can drive people who use drugs away from these programs (and other services), and many jurisdictions do not allow them.

There are also federal legal barriers to some harm reduction programs. For example, supervised consumption sites (SCSs) violate the "crack house statute" of the Controlled Substances Act (CSA). Various officials from the U.S. Department of Justice (DOJ) have written memoranda (e.g., U.S. Attorney's Office, District of Vermont, 2017) or op-eds (Lelling, 2019; Rosenstein, 2018) making this argument, and the U.S. Attorney for the Eastern District of Pennsylvania filed a preemptive injunction asking a federal judge to declare that Safehouse—the proposed supervised consumption site in Philadelphia—was in violation of the CSA. Although a federal judge ruled against the government, the case was subsequently overturned by the U.S. Court of Appeals (*United States v. Safehouse*, 2021), and the U.S. Supreme Court declined to hear the appeal. Despite the federal prohibition, two SCSs opened in New York City in November 2021, and, as of October 2022, the DOJ has not acted against these facilities or people who operate and use them.

Policy Opportunities and Considerations

Criminal legal agencies can do more to make sure that high-quality treatment for OUD is available for individuals who are incarcerated—during incarceration and once they leave. Progress is being made on this front, but there is still much more work to do. More can also be done to increase access to treatment *before* these individuals are incarcerated or even arrested. (See Chapters Four and Five.)

Many probationers with OUD are not referred for methadone treatment for a variety of reasons, such as court orders, department policies, concerns about overdose risk, knowledge and understanding of medication treatment of OUD, concerns about long-term use, lack of access to opioid treatment programs that dispense methadone for OUD, or some combination of these factors. Many of these barriers can be addressed by changing local policies and practices, but in some places, it will be necessary to educate those working in the criminal legal system about the benefits of these treatments, including the research documenting that MOUD decreases criminal activity. This does not mean that there is not a role for abstinence-based treatments, but MOUD should be available as an option for justice-involved individuals. Changing the law so that Medicaid benefits are not terminated as a result of incarceration could also help increase access to treatment and other health services.

Because the collateral consequences associated with having a criminal record for a drug offense have ripple effects throughout many parts of the opioid ecosystem, they should be reconsidered. One approach for addressing these consequences could be to consider changing drug possession laws or how they are enforced, or both. For example, one possibility would be for local jurisdictions to make enforcing the law against drug possession the lowest priority for law enforcement. (Some jurisdictions did this years ago with cannabis, and others are now doing so with psychedelics.) Another option, which has been implemented in some other countries and recently in Oregon, is decriminalizing the possession of heroin and other drugs. Doing so would reduce the penalties and associated consequences, but it would not necessarily reduce police interactions. These approaches all have pros, cons, and potential unintended consequences, so cautious jurisdictions implementing them might want to consider sunset clauses.

Many established harm reduction initiatives essentially operate at the discretion of local law enforcement agencies. For example, even if such programs are legally sanctioned, police, in theory, could arrest individuals seeking to test their drugs for possession or could follow those leaving a syringe service program. As a result, local law enforcement agencies play a critical role in determining access to these public health services. Making clear that individuals will not be arrested or convicted for patronizing or working at these programs would not only send a signal to people who use drugs; it could also send a signal to others that people who use drugs are valuable members of the community.

The federal government could also make it easier for local jurisdictions to experiment with harm reduction programs. For example, with SCSs, this could be done by amending the CSA to explicitly allow them or passing a budget rider prohibiting federal funds from being used to enforce the law against these programs; however, it is unclear whether bills to do either would make it through Congress. Another approach would be for the DOJ to use its prosecutorial discretion to make it low priority to target pilot supervised consumption site programs where certain criteria are met, such as having a signed memorandum of understanding among local health, safety, and community organizations and an independent evaluation.

Introduction

Laws and criminal legal agencies influence the supply and demand of opioids, along with the harms associated with producing, distributing, selling, and using them. The key components in this system are local, state, and federal laws; law enforcement agencies; lawyers and courts; corrections agencies (including community supervision); unions; and the private and non-profit organizations that support these institutions (e.g., drug-testing companies). Although each plays a different role, there are at least six activities (sometimes overlapping, sometimes contradictory) that many of these entities are trying to achieve with respect to opioids:

1. protect public safety and reduce burdens associated with crimes involving or related to opioid use and trafficking
2. foster social disapproval (i.e., stigma) around the nonmedical use and selling of these drugs
3. provide victims of crimes related to opioid use (e.g., violent crimes related to selling, property crimes related to consumption) with a sense of justice
4. reduce supply by fighting the diversion of prescription opioids and the availability of illegally produced opioids
5. reduce demand via deterrence, price inflation, reductions in availability, and referral of individuals to treatment and other services
6. reverse overdoses and get those who have overdosed the medical attention they need.

Some of these actions can also produce negative consequences, especially for people of color. As with many other types of crime, racial and ethnic inequities in drug arrests are well documented (see, e.g., Koch, Lee, and Lee, 2016; Mitchell and Caudy, 2015), and these have downstream effects throughout the adjudication and sentencing processes.

The opioid crisis has imposed burdens on these criminal legal agencies, especially on local law enforcement agents, who often serve as first responders to drug overdoses and address crimes related to opioid use. U.S. national data systems make it difficult to isolate the number of opioid-related arrests, but, as noted earlier, the research team estimates that there are on the order of 200,000 to 300,000 arrests annually for opioid possession or supply, and multiple times that number related to crimes committed to obtain money for opioids and crimes related to drug supply (see Chapter Two). These crimes impose burdens on these systems, and they also impose costs—including trauma and sometimes violence—on victims. When researchers attempt to estimate the social costs of substance use, crime is typically one of the largest components (see e.g., National Drug Intelligence Center, 2011; Nicosia et al., 2009).

This chapter begins with an overview of components of the criminal legal system, followed by a discussion about how they interact with many other components of the opioid ecosystem (Figure 6.1). It concludes with a discussion about policy considerations and opportunities.

FIGURE 6.1

The Criminal Legal System and Its Interactions

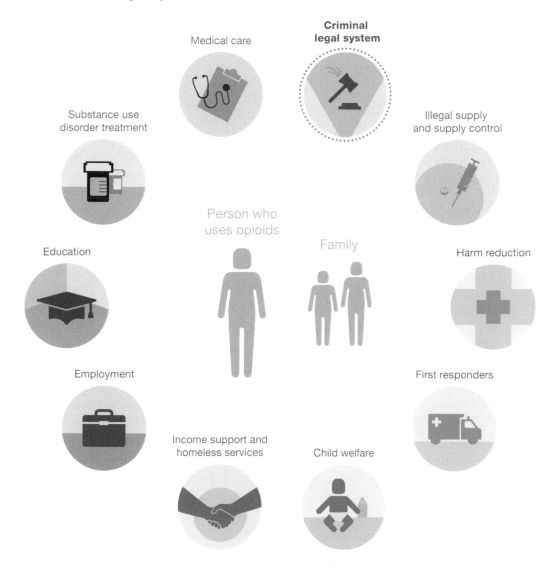

System Components and How They Interact with Opioids

This section largely describes the various entities within the criminal legal component of the opioid ecosystem that influence the demand for opioids and the harms related to illegal opioid use. The roles these entities play in controlling the supply of legally and illegally produced opioids are primarily discussed in the next chapter. Their influence is not equal and is shaped by local conditions (e.g., types of opioids used in the community, who is supplying them, availability of treatment and harm reduction services). These entities are also not independent, in the sense that laws can influence various actors in the system, and these actors can influence the laws and how they are enforced.

Laws

There are both federal and state laws that prohibit the production, distribution, and possession of opioids for nonprescribed purposes. Federal laws are largely rooted in the CSA, and many state laws are also based on this act. The recommended sentences for these offenses vary across jurisdictions, and, in some cases—primarily for suppliers, not those arrested for possession—individuals can be subject to mandatory minimum sentences. In recent years, more states have also applied "drug-induced homicide" laws, which impose severe penalties on those who supplied drugs that led to overdose deaths (Beletsky, 2019).

In November 2020, Oregon voters passed a ballot initiative to decriminalize the possession of small amounts of controlled substances and provide funding for services for people who use drugs (Measure 110, or M-110; further discussed in the "What Have We Learned from Oregon's Measure 110 So Far?" box). By making the unlawful possession of such drugs as methamphetamine and fentanyl noncriminal offenses, M-110 offers a historic change to the U.S. drug policy landscape. Although multiple countries in Europe and Latin America have decriminalized the unlawful possession of all drugs for personal use (see the next box, about Portugal, the country that receives the most attention), Oregon is the first U.S. state to implement this approach. The impacts of M-110 on criminal legal agencies and outcomes are theoretically ambiguous; much will depend on implementation and further refinement through legislation; funding decisions (the measure will allocate additional resources for treatment, harm reduction, and other services); policing practices; and the effect that the law has on drug consumption, drug selling, and other drug-related crimes. Despite the uncertainty, a similar bill was proposed in Massachusetts, and recent history of changes in cannabis laws suggests that it is likely that other states will consider related initiatives.

The U.S. experience with possession decriminalization has largely been with cannabis. Before reviewing the evidence on these efforts, we must note that we cannot assume that decriminalizing drugs other than cannabis will yield similar results. Although cannabis can be harmful for some people who use it, it has a much lower harm profile and risk of substance use disorder than many other drugs (Anthony, Warner, and Kessler, 1994; Nutt, King, and Phillips, 2010) and is not linked as much to crime compared with other drugs, such as heroin (e.g., see Pacula et al., 2013).

About a dozen U.S. states decriminalized possession of small amounts of cannabis in the 1970s. The evidence on these early efforts is mixed, and research led by RAND identified a major reason for the discrepancies: Many of these studies did not consistently define *decriminalization*. Pacula, Chriqui, and King, 2003, note that "[d]ecriminalized states are not uniquely identifiable based on statutory law as has been presumed by researchers over the past twenty years" (p. 26). Multistate studies of more-recent cannabis decriminalization efforts have found that it leads to large reductions in cannabis possession arrests (Grucza

What Have We Learned from Oregon's Measure 110 So Far?

As noted, M-110 does much more than decriminalize the unlawful possession of a controlled substance (PCS) for personal use. As of February 1, 2021, individuals cited by police for PCS can either pay a fine (maximum of $100) or undergo a substance use screening. Although referrals may be made to substance use disorder treatment and other services, individuals are not required to use these services. M-110 also allocates funding for these screenings and services for people who use drugs. Roughly $30 million in M-110 funds was released in 2021 (but not all of it was spent), and closer to $270 million is expected to be released in 2022 (Green, 2022).

Thus, for the first year after implementation, the major change was the decriminalization of PCS. Although M-110 authorized the creation of more than a dozen brick-and-mortar "Addiction and Recovery Centers"[a] throughout the state, they were not in operation when the law changed. Individuals cited by the police who wished to undergo screening could call a statewide hotline; however, very few people called this number. It was reported that in the first nine months following implementation, only 51 people called the hotline and completed screening (Crombie, 2021). There are also reports that some law enforcement officials have simply avoided citing some individuals for PCS because they believed that there were no services available for them (VanderHart, 2021). We do not know the extent to which this is a widespread belief or occurrence.

There was a drop in criminal arrests for drug possession after M-110 went into effect, but this was preceded by a large decline attributable to coronavirus disease 2019 (COVID-19). In 2019, fingerprinted arrests for PCS throughout the state hovered around 1,000–1,400 per month. In 2020, the number of these arrests hovered between 400 and 800 per month, and by July 2021 these arrests had dropped closer to 200 (Tallan and Officer, 2021). The Oregon Criminal Justice Commission cautions against attributing the entire decline to M-110, because of COVID-19, but notes that non-PCS arrests rebounded while PCS arrests continued to decline (Tallan and Officer, 2021).

Some individuals who use drugs get arrested for nondrug violations (e.g., property crimes), especially those individuals who use most frequently (see Chapter Two). How decriminalization affects the frequency of these offenses and whether they are cleared (i.e., an arrest is made after a crime is reported) remains to be seen. It will also be interesting to see what happens to arrests for drug dealing. On the one hand, it is now much easier for dealers to carry amounts that are under the threshold, making it harder for police and prosecutors to convict them for selling. On the other hand, some police officers may have previously charged low-level dealers with possession to make sure that they are not burdened with felony convictions. If there are no longer consequences for possessing small amounts of drugs, these individuals might just get charged with dealing.

It also remains to be seen whether M-110 leads to an increase in the *utilization* of such services as substance use disorder treatment. Much will depend on what services get funded in which parts of the state and the characteristics of those individuals who get cited for PCS. It also depends on where the funding for these services is coming from. A large share is supposed to come from cannabis tax revenues, which were already being used to fund some services in some parts of the state.

Evaluations of M-110 (and related efforts) should include strong qualitative components involving people who use drugs, law enforcement, and service providers to learn more about harder-to-measure outcomes related to stigma, discretion, and potential unintended consequences.

---

[a] These have been renamed *Behavioral Health Resource Networks* (BHRNs). Oregon's website notes:

A BHRN is an entity or group of entities working together to provide substance use services in Oregon. They serve people with substance use disorders or harmful substance use. At least one BHRN must be established in every county and Tribal area. Services provided by the BHRNs must be free of charge to the client. BHRNs must bill insurance for services where possible before using grant funds. Each BHRN must provide trauma-informed, culturally specific and linguistically responsive services. Services include but are not limited to:

- Screening for health and social service needs.
- Screening and referral for substance use disorder.
- Access to an individualized intervention plan.
- Case management.
- Low-barrier substance use disorder treatment.
- Harm reduction services.
- Peer-supported services.
- Housing.
- Mobile and virtual outreach.
- Referral to appropriate outside services. (Oregon Health Authority, 2022)

---

et al., 2018; Plunk et al., 2019), and one of these studies found that it had no effect on youth cannabis prevalence rates (Grucza et al., 2018).

A study of California's 2011 law to decriminalize cannabis possession found that past-month use among California 12th-graders increased from 24 percent to 29 percent from 2011 to 2012, leading the authors to argue that "these results provide empirical evidence to support concerns that decriminalization may be a risk factor for future increases in youth marijuana use and acceptance" (Miech et al., 2015). However, more-recent work by Midgette and Reuter, 2020, challenges this finding; the authors contend that other factors could have influenced this change, that there was no increase for 8th- and 10th-grade students, and that arguably better data suggest that prevalence was trending upward prior to decriminalization and continued afterward.

Studies exploring the effect of cannabis decriminalization or legalization on crime clearance rates in the United States are rare. The limited research toward this end has focused on legalization in Colorado and Washington and has yielded mixed results. Although there is evidence demonstrating a positive impact of legalization on crime clearance rates in these two states (Makin et al., 2019), another study with a more robust approach found no meaningful changes in crime clearance rates in the two states following legalization (Jorgensen and Harper, 2020). In addition to there being differences by state, we might expect that the effect of decriminalizing low-level possession of methamphetamine, fentanyl, and other drugs, as was done in Oregon, could differ from the effect of cannabis policy changes for myriad reasons.

There are laws on the books in the United States that are focused on reducing harm from use. For example, more than 30 states explicitly allow syringe service programs (sometimes referred to as needle exchange programs or syringe distribution programs; Law Atlas, 2019), and most states have passed Good Samaritan laws, which provide legal protections to individuals who report overdoses to authorities. Although fentanyl testing strips (and related technologies) are considered illegal drug paraphernalia in many states, they are being used in an increasing number of jurisdictions.

There are also federal legal barriers to some harm reduction programs. For example, SCSs violate the "crack house statute" of the CSA (Public Law 91-513, 1971, § 856(a)(2)). Various DOJ officials have written memoranda (e.g., U.S. Attorney's Office, District of Vermont, 2017) or op-eds (Lelling, 2019; Rosenstein, 2018) making this argument, and the U.S. Attorney for the Eastern District of Pennsylvania filed a preemptive injunction asking a federal judge to declare that Safehouse—the proposed supervised consumption site in Philadelphia—was in violation of the CSA. Although a federal judge ruled against the government, the case was subsequently overturned by the U.S. Court of Appeals (*United States v. Safehouse*, 2021), and the U.S. Supreme Court declined to hear the appeal. Despite the federal prohibition, two SCSs opened in New York City in November 2021, and, as of October 2022, the DOJ has not acted against these facilities or people who operate and use them.

Almost all cases related to opioids sold in the illegal market are handled in criminal courts. However, pharmaceutical companies can also be seen as supplying opioids that they knew or should have known were being diverted to illegal markets, and an increasing number of individuals, local governments, and state governments have filed civil lawsuits against pharmaceutical companies that produce medical opioids, along with distributors and retailers. Although the early cases largely focused on allegations related to design defect, negligent distribution, failure to warn, and fraud, the more recent cases also claim unjust enrichment, public nuisance, negligence, and violations of the CSA; Federal Food, Drug, and Cosmetic Act; and Racketeer Influenced and Corrupt Organizations Act (Haffajee, Kilmer, and Helland, 2022). There have been several well-publicized settlements and others that are likely pending, including a $26 billion settlement with AmerisourceBergen, Cardinal Health, McKesson, and Johnson and Johnson (Mann, 2021). There was a separate agreement with Purdue Pharma for $6 billion (Mann and Bebinger, 2022).

It would be incorrect to assume that criminal laws only cover those individuals possessing or selling illegally produced drugs and civil laws only cover those supplying pharmaceutical drugs. There have been criminal convictions against some pharmaceutical company executives (e.g., Lopez, 2019; U.S. Attorney's Office, District of Massachusetts, 2019), and civil forfeiture of the assets of individuals arrested for suppling illegal drugs is common.

Learning from Portugal

In the 1990s, Portuguese policymakers faced a public health emergency in the form of high rates of HIV transmission via injection drug use, mostly of heroin. A government-appointed commission developed 13 guidelines that became the basis of a new national drug strategy that stressed humanism, pragmatism, and participation (European Monitoring Centre for Drugs and Drug Addiction, 2011). One of those 13 guidelines was decriminalization of drug possession for personal use. The overall Portuguese reform is sometimes simplistically (incorrectly) described as decriminalization (and is sometimes confused with legalization). In reality, decriminalization was one part of a comprehensive suite of reforms that included a large increase in funding for substance use treatment and outreach services.

Drug use is still prohibited, but the new strategy robustly funded an innovative system of "dissuasion commissions," known as CDTs (for "Commission for the Dissuasion of Drug Abuse"). When an individual is found to possess up to ten days' worth of any drug without evidence indicating participation in sales or supply, the drugs are seized and the case is transferred to the nearest CDT. The three-member commission meets with the individual to assess their drug-taking habits and determines the most appropriate course of action. Most interventions involve cannabis rather than opioids and result in provisional suspension of the sentence. Fifteen percent involve referral to treatment, and 14 percent involve punitive ruling, such as warnings, fines, banning from certain places or from meeting certain people, obligation to attend drug education classes, and removal of professional or firearm licenses (European Monitoring Centre for Drugs and Drug Addiction, 2011). Although it is a topic of much debate, we are not aware of any peer-reviewed empirical evidence about what happens to those who are referred to treatment but do not enter. University of Kent scholar Alex Stevens, who has been researching Portugal for more than 15 years, has said that his discussions with several CDTs suggest that punishment is not applied to those who do not enter treatment (Stevens, 2022).

The suite of innovations appears to have produced favorable results. HIV transmission rates and drug-induced deaths declined, and self-reported use did not change substantially (Hughes and Stevens, 2010; Laqueur, 2015), but it is hard to parse out what caused what (or to what extent regression to the mean might describe some of the decrease). Furthermore, decriminalization largely formalized what was already happening. In most cases, prosecutors were already waiving sanctions for possession of small amounts of drugs; few users were convicted or serving time for drug possession even before decriminalization (Laqueur, 2015). Yet Laqueur (2015) notes that arrests for possession fell and were replaced with citations. Decriminalization might have been necessary to allow CDTs and other social services to operate legally and with greater reach within an administrative environment.

> In sum, the Portuguese example is an interesting case of a dramatic innovation in response to a public health crisis brought on by heroin that might serve as an inspiration for parallel innovation in the United States, but characterizing it as either decriminalization or legalization alone would not be accurate.
>
> ---
>
> SOURCE: Largely reproduced from Pardo et al., 2019b.

Law Enforcement

Approximately 18,000 law enforcement agencies are tasked with enforcing drug laws, mostly at the state and local levels. Although federal agencies typically focus on the larger producers and traffickers, this is not an absolute rule; there are instances of federal agencies making low-level sales arrests to obtain information or in special locations (e.g., in national parks). Conversely, some state and local agencies make high-level arrests and seizures, particularly those in regional distribution hubs, such as New York City. However, the typical priority for local police is targeting local wholesalers and keeping retail distribution from becoming flagrant and disrupting communities. There is also a wealth of evidence linking heavy heroin use with property crime (see, e.g., Pacula et al., 2013), and the vast majority of these cases are handled by state and local agencies.

State Police, Sheriffs, and Local Police Departments

As is noted in Chapter Two, there were on the order of 200,000–300,000 arrests for opioid-specific offenses circa 2019, and the vast majority of these were made by state and local law enforcement agencies. There are many more arrests linked to opioid use and sales (e.g., property crimes, violence associated with street-level markets) that are also mostly handled by nonfederal entities. These agencies sometimes collaborate on multijurisdictional investigations, including efforts led by the High Intensity Drug Trafficking Areas (funded by the White House Office of National Drug Control Policy) or other federal task forces.

However, when it comes to opioids, law enforcement agencies do more than conduct investigations and make arrests for drug-involved crimes. As mentioned earlier, state and local police often serve as first responders to overdoses, and they often participate in drug prevention efforts and prescription drug "take-back programs." There are also several law enforcement programs that are intended to help get people into treatment, including an increasing number of deflection programs that target the period after law enforcement finds someone using or possessing drugs but before that person is cited or booked.

Federal Agencies

Most of the federal agencies involved in drug law enforcement focus on supply control, which is described in more detail in the next chapter. The Drug Enforcement Administration (DEA) is the lead federal law enforcement body addressing crime related to illegal drugs. There are nearly 5,000 DEA special agents spread across 239 domestic offices and 92 foreign offices, and there are approximately another 5,000 employees in supporting roles (DEA, undated-a). In 2020, the DEA made more than 26,000 domestic arrests for all drugs, not just opioids (DEA, undated-b). Specific to opioids, the DEA has implemented a program known as the 360 Strategy, which uses a three-pronged approach to combating heroin and opioid use encompassing law enforcement coordination, diversion control, and community outreach (DEA, undated-c).

U.S. Customs and Border Protection (CBP) is a federal law enforcement agency that serves as the primary border control organization of the United States. CBP detects and apprehends individuals suspected of engaging in illegal activities, such as drug smuggling, often collaborating with other federal agencies and foreign governments. In addition, CBP operates within major international mail facilities to inspect parcels for illegal drugs and other prohibited goods (Pardo et al., 2019a).

Members of the U.S. military sometimes assist in counternarcotics efforts in other countries, and the U.S. Coast Guard plays a role in seizing heroin and other drugs being smuggled to the United States.

Lawyers and the Courts
Prosecutors

Similar to law enforcement agencies, there are prosecutors at the local, state, and federal levels who handle opioid-involved cases. The lead prosecutor positions at the local and state levels are often elected positions; at the federal level, the U.S. Attorney General is appointed by the President and confirmed by the Senate. The lead prosecutors then choose the other prosecutors who handle the bulk of the cases.

Prosecutors have a tremendous amount of discretion; they decide whether a case is pursued, what the charges are, and whether a plea bargain is offered, and they make recommendations to judges about bail and the sentence of an individual if that person is convicted. They can use this leverage to extract information from a defendant that can be used for other cases, sometimes agreeing to pursue a lesser charge or lower penalty if the person agrees to provide information or serve as an informant.

Some prosecutors have used their discretion to specifically address harms associated with drug prohibition. These individuals have made choices about cases and implemented programs intended to reduce incarceration and other negative consequences (e.g., risk of deportation) that are associated with drug offenses. Although this approach is consistent with many candidates who have run or been portrayed as "progressive prosecutors" (Davis, 2018–2019), prosecutorial efforts intended to reduce drug-related incarceration go back at least three decades. Before she was the U.S. Attorney General, Janet Reno was the lead prosecutor for Miami-Dade County and is credited with helping create the first drug court that was intended to reduce incarceration for individuals with drug problems and get them into treatment. Although drug courts (discussed in the section titled "Problem-Solving Courts") have come under fire from those seeking to liberalize drug laws (see, e.g., Drug Policy Alliance, 2011), they were designed as a progressive alternative to incarceration.

Defense Attorneys

People who are arrested for crimes can either hire their own attorneys or have attorneys appointed if they cannot afford representation. Those who are indigent are typically represented by public defenders or lawyers appointed by the court. Although the traditional public defense model emphasizes criminal representation and courtroom advocacy, there is an emerging "holistic" approach—involving public defenders working in teams to address each case (and not just cases involving drugs) along with the underlying circumstances (e.g., substance use disorder, housing instability)—that has yielded encouraging results (Anderson, Buenaventura, and Heaton, 2019).

Criminal Courts

Although a person who is charged with an offense is entitled to have their case heard before a jury of their peers, very few cases are resolved that way. The majority of criminal cases end with a plea bargain, in which the defendant admits guilt to an offense, typically in return for a lower sentence than what could be ordered if the person were found guilty by a judge (Devers, 2011); this approach saves the prosecutor and the defense attorney a lot of time, but it might not always be in the best interest of the defendant. Some defendants waive the right to a jury and let a judge decide on the matter.

One legal strategy is to take the case in front of a jury and hope that the jurors will acquit the defendant because they do not agree with the law, even if they think the person is guilty. This phenomenon, known as *jury nullification*, is not common, but it played a role in some of the early cases against people who were operating syringe service programs (Burris et al., 1996) and has been raised as a potential strategy for defending people who seek to operate SCSs (Burris et al., 2009).[1]

Problem-Solving Courts

This section was originally published in Kilmer, Caulkins, et al., 2018.

Problem-solving courts are intended to address defendants' underlying issues, which are believed to contribute to their criminal behavior. There are more than 3,000 problem-solving courts operating throughout the United States, and about half are drug courts (or drug treatment courts, as some are called); however, many defendants in other problem-solving courts also have substance-related issues.

A problem-solving court is typically not a separate building or courtroom; rather, it is a docket with a dedicated judge who meets with defendants on a regular basis and closely

---

[1] Some have argued that this approach should also be used to help address racial disparities in the legal system (see, e.g., Butler, 1995).

monitors their progress. The judge is usually in regular contact with treatment providers, defense attorneys, prosecutors, court coordinators, and other service providers. Their meetings often occur in the judge's chambers before the defendant's progress is publicly discussed in the courtroom. The collaboration among these offices with very different missions might serve as a model for interactions among the different components of the opioid ecosystem, not just those in the legal system.

Family Courts

Unlike problem-solving courts, which address criminal law violations, family courts abide by civil laws and address such issues as divorce and child custody. The judges in these cases strive to keep children with their parents, typically severing parental custody as a last resort. The opioid crisis has affected family courts in many parts of the United States, and some of these courts do not have the resources to adequately address substance use issues (Tabashneck, 2018). Thus, some jurisdictions have implemented family drug courts, which seek to resolve the underlying substance use issue while keeping the family unit intact.

Corrections

On any given day, there are approximately 6 million people under correctional supervision in the United States, most being supervised by probation or parole departments in the community (Minton, Beatty, and Zeng, 2021). Although racial and ethnic disparities across prison, jail, probation, and parole populations are declining (Sabol, Johnson, and Caccavale, 2019), they still exist. It is difficult to determine what share of individuals being supervised were engaging in opioid-involved crimes, but there is strong evidence to suggest that the share increased dramatically in the 2010s (e.g., Congressional Research Service, 2019).

Jails and Prisons

On any given day in 2020, there were roughly 1.75 million people incarcerated, a figure that has been declining for several years and fell further because of COVID-19 (Carson, 2021; Minton, Beatty, and Zeng, 2021). The pre-COVID-19 number of admissions to jail or prison each year is in the ballpark of 10 million, with jail accounting for the vast majority. The average stay in jail is about 25 days (Zeng, 2020),[2] and many people in jail are being held while awaiting trial rather than after conviction. The racial disparities in incarceration rates are large; Black Americans are jailed at more than three times the rate of White and Hispanic Americans (465 per 100,000; 133 and 134, respectively; Minton, Beatty, and Zeng, 2021). For prison, the incarceration rate for Black people is more than five times the rate for White people (938 versus 183 per 100,000; Carson, 2021). This disparity is a characteristic of the

---

[2] Zeng also notes how the length of stay varies by the size of the jail: "Smaller jails had higher weekly inmate-turnover rates and shorter lengths of stay than larger jails. On average, jails with an ADP [average daily population] of 2,500 or more inmates held inmates about twice as long (34 days) as jails with an ADP of less than 100 inmates (15 days)" (p. 8).

criminal legal system overall and is not specific to drug-related crimes; the rate of racial disproportionality is lower than average for drug offenses relative to other crimes and is highest for violent crimes.[3]

Between 2010 and 2019 (prior to COVID-19), the jail incarceration rate decreased for Black and Hispanic individuals (–2.4 percent and –3.1 percent) and increased for White people (1.1 percent). For prison, the changes were much more dramatic. There were reductions for all three groups, but they were much more pronounced for Black and Hispanic individuals: Black (–26.9 percent), Hispanic (–19.5 percent), White (–13.7 percent). Since 2000, there has been a large increase in rural jail population rates, while the rates for other, larger geographic areas have remained stable or declined (Vera Institute of Justice, 2018). It has been argued that opioid problems in rural communities have contributed to this increase (see, e.g., Levin and Haugen, 2018), and this is consisted with more-rural areas reporting higher rates of prescription opioid overdose deaths (Jalal et al., 2018; also see Chapter Two).

Although there has been enormous concern and frustration over racial disparities in incarceration rates, there has also been progress in that regard, particularly with respect to incarceration for drug law violations. Figure 6.2 displays the estimated number of sentenced prisoners under state jurisdiction for drug offenses at year-end in 2010 and 2019, by race/ethnicity (Carson, 2021; Carson and Sabol, 2012). The declines for non-Hispanic Black and Hispanic individuals were very large (54 percent and 35 percent, respectively), especially compared with the decline seen for non-Hispanic White people (8 percent). In 2010, there were approximately 36,000 *more* non-Hispanic Black people in state prisons for drug offenses than non-Hispanic White people, but this soon changed. By 2019, there were approximately 16,000 *fewer* non-Hispanic Black people in state prisons for drug offenses compared with non-Hispanic White people. There are multiple hypotheses for changes in racial disparities with respect to drug offenses, such as decreasing punitiveness, reductions in racial bias, and legal or policy changes (e.g., see Light, 2022). But these reductions in racial disparities are also consistent with the fact that the opioid problem was more entrenched among the non-Hispanic White population for most of the past 25 years. Now that the racial dynamics have changed, at least with respect to opioid overdose deaths largely involving illegally manufactured synthetic opioids (see Chapters One and Two), it remains to be seen what this will mean for disparities in arrests and incarceration.

For individuals incarcerated in state prisons at the end of 2019, the number (percentage) whose most serious offense was for drugs—all drugs including opioids but excluding alcohol—was 171,300 (14 percent), of which 46,700 (4 percent) had drug possession as their

---

[3] According to 2019 Uniform Crime Reporting data from almost 11,000 police agencies (covering about 230 million people), there were 748,874 drug arrests for White people and 274,670 for Black people, generating a ratio of 2.72:1 (Table 43A). Given that there are approximately five times as many White people as Black people, this represents a disparity when focused on population. The corresponding ratios for all, violent, and property arrests are 2.61, 1.62:1, and 2.24:1, respectively. These values are even further away from the 5:1 population ratio, suggesting that there are larger racial disparities for nondrug crimes (Federal Bureau of Investigation, undated).

most serious offenses (Carson, 2021). The corresponding figure for federal prisoners was 67,438 (47 percent), and, although this is not broken down by possession versus other offenses (Carson, 2021), the vast majority of federal drug cases involve supply. Official national figures for jail inmates are unavailable, but the Sentencing Project (2021) estimated that the number was close to 184,000 in 2017. In addition, some individuals were incarcerated for violating conditions on community supervision related to drugs (e.g., a positive drug test).

For those in prison in 2016, data from the Bureau of Justice Statistics (BJS) survey of prisoners show that almost 50 percent of them met diagnostic criteria for substance use disorders in the year before entering prison, although the BJS report does not allow us to estimate what share had OUD (Maruschak, Bronson, and Alper, 2021). However, BJS does provide drug-specific prevalence rates for lifetime use, in the month before the arrest, and at the time of the arrest. For heroin, the figures were 20 percent, 8 percent, and 5 percent, respectively. For prescription drugs used in a way not prescribed by a doctor (not specific to opioids), the rates were 34 percent, 16 percent, and 9 percent. These figures are not mutually exclusive (i.e., people could have been using both heroin and prescription drugs), and one cannot assume that, just because someone was using a drug at the time of the arrest, that drug was the reason for the arrest.

BJS also compared the self-reported rates of use in the month before arrest for 2004 and 2016 (Maruschak, Bronson, and Alper, 2021). For state prisoners, the rate for heroin increased from 6.1 percent to 8.2 percent and the rate for prescription drugs increased from 9.6 percent to 16.3 percent; both increases were statistically significant at the 95-percent confidence

FIGURE 6.2

Estimated Number of Sentenced Prisoners Under State Jurisdiction for Drug Offenses in 2010 and 2019, by Race/Ethnicity

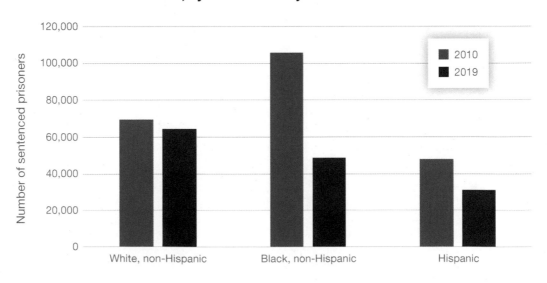

SOURCES: Carson, 2021; Carson and Sabol, 2012.

level. For federal prisoners, the change was not statistically significant for heroin (4.3 percent versus 3.9 percent) but was statistically significant for prescription drugs (7.9 percent to 12.9 percent).

BJS reports the share of prison inmates with substance use disorders who received treatment while incarcerated (Table 6.1). Treatment figures are not mutually exclusive, because individuals could receive multiple types of treatment, but approximately 20 percent of state prisoners received residential treatment, counseling, detoxification, or MOUD. The figure for federal prison was closer to 30 percent. The 1-percent figure for MOUD is not surprising given that this was for 2016, and the number is likely higher today given the progression of the opioid problem and the increasing number of facilities offering this type of treatment; however, there is much more work to be done to increase MOUD access for inmates (Pew Charitable Trusts, 2020).

Probation and Parole

Most individuals subject to correctional supervision live in their communities. On any given day in 2020, there were approximately 3 million people on probation and another 860,000 on parole (Kaeble, 2021). Probation supervision is typically in lieu of or in addition to a jail sentence, whereas parole supervises individuals who have been released from prison. As a condition of remaining in the community, these individuals are subject to various restrictions. Conditions can vary dramatically depending on the jurisdiction and the individual's criminal history and need for services; they range from abstaining from alcohol and other drugs to complying with curfews to attending drug treatment. Noncompliance with these conditions can lead to revocation of probation or parole and the individual serving the remainder of the sentence behind bars; however, the sanctions for these violations are usually not transparent and often seem arbitrary to those being supervised (Kleiman, 2009). Most revocations are attributable to violations of conditions of probation or parole (e.g., positive drug tests) and not the commission of a new crime (Hicks et al., 2020; Rodriguez and Webb, 2007).

For people leaving incarceration and entering the community, parole and probation officers can play an important role in connecting them with medical and social services; however, many of these officers have extremely large caseloads and tend to focus their time and effort on those individuals with the most-serious criminal histories. Furthermore, in many rural areas, service availability is sparse. This is especially problematic for people with OUD, who are at much greater risk of overdose in the first few weeks after they leave jail or prison (e.g., Binswanger et al., 2007).

Some individuals leaving incarceration will spend time in halfway houses before being allowed to fully reenter society. Wong and colleagues (2019) note that there is no singular definition of a halfway house but argue that they generally include "(a) temporary housing, (b) provided in a community-based residential facility (as an alternative to closed custody), (c) using around the clock supervision, and (d) offering services to assist with the difficult transition from incarceration to the community" (p. 1020). In the context of parole, these

TABLE 6.1

Alcohol or Drug Treatment Among State and Federal Prisoners Who Met the Criteria for Substance Use Disorder, 2016

Treatment	State Prisoners		Federal Prisoners	
	Percentage	Standard Error	Percentage	Standard Error
Any treatment program since admission[a]	33.1%	1.62%	46.2%	2.84%
Alcohol use only	3.1%	0.40%	3.3%	0.72%
Drug use only	7.4%	0.55%	9.8%	1.56%
Alcohol and drug use	22.6%	1.14%	32.9%	2.60%
Type of treatment program since admission				
Treatment[b]	19.7%	1.30%	28.4%	2.56%
Residential facility or unit	12.1%	1.20%	14.7%	2.59%
Counseling by a professional	10.1%	0.57%	17.9%	1.83%
Detoxification unit	1.7%	0.21%	1.6%	0.39%
Maintenance drug	0.9%	0.15%	1.1%	0.38%
Other programs[b]	32.7%	1.24%	41.4%	2.76%
Self-help group or peer counseling	27.0%	1.10%	25.0%	1.96%
Education program	23.5%	1.07%	36.8%	2.74%
Estimated number of prisoners who met the criteria for substance use disorder	397,500	15,700	31,600	2,400

SOURCE: Adapted from Maruschak, Bronson, and Alper, 2021.

[a] Details might not sum to totals because prisoners may have reported that they received treatment but not that it was for alcohol use only, drug use only, or alcohol and drug use.

[b] Details might not sum to totals because prisoners could report participating in more than one type of treatment or program.

houses can be used as part of early release, a form of prerelease supervision, or a back-end diversion program to remand those who violated parole (Rydberg and Nader, 2017).

Other Actors

The criminal legal system includes many other actors and organizations that can influence laws and policies that can affect people who use opioids:

- **Unions.** The unions of law enforcement and corrections officers play a large role in criminal legal policy. They often take positions on legislation and ballot initiatives, and their endorsements for political offices are highly sought after. These groups often oppose efforts intended to liberalize drug laws.

- **Private companies.** The criminal legal response to opioids is not limited to government agencies and employees. There are for-profit entities that work with the agencies in many capacities, ranging from companies that provide services in public prisons or jails to private prisons (which account for a very small share of total inmates) to companies that conduct drug testing.
- **Nonprofit organizations.** There are also many nonprofit organizations that provide many of the same services as private companies, such as OUD treatment and drug-testing services. Nonprofit organizations may also contract with corrections agencies to provide other services, such as mental health services.

Key Interactions with Other Components of the Ecosystem

Illegal Supply and Supply Control

The criminal legal system seeks to reduce illegal supply. Although diverted prescription opioids and heroin have posed challenges to law enforcement for decades, the mass production of potent, cheap synthetic opioids outside the United States has created new problems. Efforts are made to reduce their supply via many levers, including international agreements, precursor control laws, intelligence-sharing, eradication, seizure, and arrest.[4]

To help prevent diversion and monitor supply of legally produced opioids, the DEA sets the aggregate production quota to meet legal demand and tracks the manufacture and distribution of these drugs through its Automated Reports and Consolidated Ordering System.

All states have now implemented prescription drug monitoring programs (PDMPs) that make it easier for health officials to track an individual's prescription drug history. This information can be useful for making treatment decisions and assessing an individual's risk of misuse or diversion. Some states allow law enforcement agencies to access PDMP information to assist in criminal investigations. These states vary in the minimum standard that law enforcement must meet before it can access this information (Boustead, 2021). For example, some require probable cause, some require a subpoena, and others limit access depending on the type of investigation (Figure 6.3). The DOJ's Bureau of Justice Assistance (BJA) notes:

> In several states, drug courts and correctional supervision agencies (e.g., probation, parole) also access and use PDMPs to support cases they are adjudicating. The information is used to track a participant's acquisition of controlled substances and his or her adherence to court-ordered treatment or terms for release. (BJA, 2015, p. 8)

Law enforcement access to medical information has raised a series of privacy concerns, which must be balanced against the insights these data provide to support efforts to reduce

---

[4] For plant-based drugs, efforts are often made to incentivize farmers to grow alternative crops; in the past, the United States has helped fund these efforts in both Afghanistan and Colombia.

diversion. More research is needed to examine the extent to which fear of being detected in a PDMP might drive some individuals to the illegal market for opioids. For additional discussion about PDMPs, see Chapter Seven.

Substance Use Disorder Treatment

The primary goal of substance use disorder treatment programs is to treat individuals' substance use disorder and reduce drug consumption. These programs can also help individuals obtain other services needed to stabilize their lives and help them with recovery. Chapter Five provides more information about the different types of programs, but, with respect to opioids, there is a tension between programs that use medications (e.g., methadone, buprenorphine) to treat individuals with OUD and those that are abstinence based and forbid the use of any treatment medications. Although some contend that abstinence-based programs are just another approach to facilitating recovery, others argue that some abstinence-based programs perpetuate and foster stigma against the use of these medications. There have also been concerns about abstinence-based programs requiring individuals to discontinue buprenorphine or methadone treatment to obtain services. This tension is especially evident in discussions about the role of criminal legal agencies in getting people with substance use disorders into treatment.

Criminal legal agencies have a large effect on admissions to specialty treatment programs via referrals, diversion or deflection programs, and sentencing; however, this does not mean that people with OUD—especially those who are incarcerated—always receive high-quality treatment. That said, jail- and prison-based health systems have made serious efforts in recent years to increase access to methadone and buprenorphine treatment for OUD (see Chapter Four; Pew Charitable Trusts, 2020).

There are many pathways for justice-involved individuals to enter substance use treatment. Individuals may choose to enter after being referred or may be pressured to enter in lieu of incarceration. Although most individuals referred from criminal legal agencies for treatment have substance use disorders, some do not. There are cases in which people have been sent to treatment in error (e.g., the criminal legal agency did not perform an adequate screening) and people who would have been charged with distribution lied about having substance use disorders, perhaps to avoid more-severe sentences. The latter also may happen for those arrested for possession.

Although the specialty treatment sector accounts for a decreasing share of treatment episodes for people with OUD, specialty treatment admissions involving criminal legal referrals in which the primary drugs were opioids increased from roughly 70,000 in 2010 to 100,000 in 2017 (Substance Abuse and Mental Health Services Administration [SAMHSA], 2014; SAMHSA, 2019). Of course, this is likely an underestimate, as some individuals whose referrals were classified as self-referrals may have also entered treatment because of interactions with the criminal legal system.

FIGURE 6.3

State Policies Regarding Law Enforcement Access to Prescription Drug Monitoring Program Data, 2010–2017

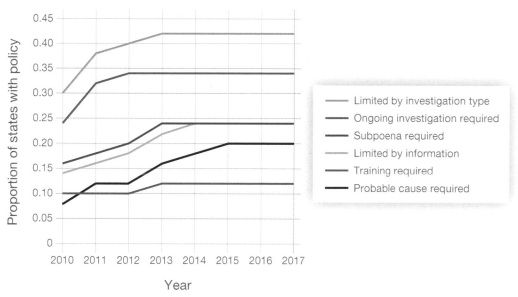

SOURCE: Adapted from Boustead, 2021, p. 236.

Opioid Use Disorder Treatment in the Community

Referrals to treatment can happen throughout the criminal legal process, and an increasing number of jurisdictions have implemented diversion programs where police officers can send those they believe have problems with drugs (even if they were not caught with drugs) *instead* of booking these individuals or giving them summons to appear in court. This section begins with these programs and then describes more-common approaches, such as problem-solving courts.

Police Deflection

Diversion programs, which attempt to get individuals who have been arrested for drugs and those arrested with drug problems into treatment, have been around for nearly 50 years. (For example, Treatment Alternatives for Safe Communities was a program from the Nixon administration.) These programs tend to focus on the period after someone has been arrested and booked or cited and often, but not always, before they are convicted. However, there is a growing focus on getting individuals into substance use treatment and other services before they are booked, cited, or arrested. These efforts are typically referred to as *deflection*, although there is some ambiguity about the label. For example, the well-known Law Enforcement Assisted Diversion (LEAD) program is better thought of as deflection than as a traditional diversion program. In addition, many programs referred to as *pre-arrest diversion* are better thought of as deflection programs (see the "Deflection Terminology" box).

Deflection Terminology

A recent national survey of deflection programs conducted by NORC at the University of Chicago and the Center for Health and Justice at Treatment Alternatives for Safe Communities offered the following clarifying note on terminology:

Deflection and pre-arrest diversion are two sides of the same coin—i.e., they are complementary practices of a systems approach at the intersection of first responders, SUD [substance use disorder] and MHD [mental health disorder] treatment, recovery support, and community. These two practices, always taken together as a single coin, are simply referred to as the "field of deflection." . . .

Deflection is the practice by which law enforcement or other first responders (i.e., fire and EMS [emergency medical services]) connect individuals to community-based treatment and/or services when arrest would not have been necessary or permitted, or *in lieu of taking no action* when issues of addiction, mental health, and/or other need are present. Deflection is performed without fear by the individual that if they do not "accept the deflection" they will subsequently be arrested.

Pre-arrest diversion is the practice by which law enforcement officers connect individuals who otherwise would have been eligible for criminal charges to community-based treatment and/or services in lieu of arrest, thereby *diverting* them from the justice system into the community. Some pre-arrest diversion programs have policies that mandate holding charges in abeyance until treatment or other requirements, such as restitution or community service, are completed, at which time the charges are dropped. Although pre-arrest diversion is facilitated by justice system stakeholders (usually police and sheriffs but sometimes prosecutors or a local government agency . . .), clients are diverted to community-based services. (NORC at the University of Chicago and Center for Health and Justice at Treatment Alternatives for Safe Communities, 2021, emphasis in original)

The aim of deflection programs is to connect individuals with substance use disorders or mental health disorders to community-based treatment instead of traditional enforcement. Deflection programs have expanded organically into various "pathways," including "self-referral," "active outreach," "naloxone-plus," "officer prevention," and "officer intervention" (Charlier and Reichert, 2020, pp. 2–3). The pathways are differentiated by (1) how individuals are identified for deflection, (2) the type of outreach done by police officers, and (3) whether the threat of arrest is present. (For more, see Table 6.2.)

Overall, most of the research on these programs has been descriptive, and their impact has not been carefully studied. A recent review of the literature on diversion and deflection programs for people who use drugs found that most of the research was focused on postbooking programs (Lindquist-Grantz et al., 2021, p. 494). Of the 31 studies evaluated, only two focused on prebooking programs, and another two focused on both pre- and postbooking. Given the heterogeneity in programs, populations, and study designs considered, the authors

TABLE 6.2

Example Programs, Locations, and Model Activity, by Pathway

Pathway	Program	Location	Model
Self-Referral	Police Assisted Addiction and Recovery Initiative (PAARI) Angel Program	Gloucester, Massachusetts	Walk-in model: Individuals approach police for assistance in accessing treatment
Officer Prevention	LEAD	Seattle, Washington	Police officers exercise discretion and divert individuals to treatment during their normal patrols or calls for services
Officer Prevention and Intervention	Stop, Triage, Engage, Educate, and Rehabilitate (STEER)	Montgomery County, Maryland	If an arrest takes place, charges can be held in abeyance if the participant accepts the referral to treatment
Naloxone Plus	Quick Response Team (QRT)	Colerain Township, Ohio	Reactive outreach after responding to a nonfatal overdose
Active Outreach	Drug Abuse Response Team (DART)	Lucas County, Ohio	Proactive outreach is conducted with known opioid users to engage them in treatment

SOURCE: Adapted from Charlier and Reichert, 2020.

NOTE: For more on these programs, see City of Cuyahoga Falls, undated; LEAD King County, undated; Lucas County Sheriff's Office, homepage, undated; and Police Assisted Addiction and Recovery Initiative, "About Us," webpage, undated.

concluded that "this review did not produce definitive conclusions about the effectiveness of substance use diversion programs, but this may be due in part to variations in how programs are implemented and the methodological limitations of studies conducted to date."

The LEAD program, which started in Seattle in 2011 and is now operating in nearly 40 U.S. counties (LEAD National Support Bureau, undated), receives a lot of attention in deflection discussions. As noted by Collins, Lonczak, and Clifasefi, 2019, p. 203, LEAD largely focuses on people who use drugs who are suspected by police of drug and prostitution offenses and includes the following components:

> First, after arrest and prior to booking, potential participants were offered a one-time diversion from the criminal justice and legal systems to the LEAD program. Next, officers introduced interested individuals to a case manager who conducted an informed consent process and began provision of time-unlimited, harm-reduction-oriented case management. Harm-reduction case management entailed a low-barrier approach to connecting participants to services fulfilling participants' stated goals and basic needs (e.g., shelter; food; clothing; housing; vocational services; medical, psychiatric or substance-use treatment). Participants were not required to attain abstinence or attend treatment or any other services to maintain standing in the program. Finally, the prosecuting attorney's office, program leads, and case managers engaged in higher-level coordination of subsequent legal system involvement to maximize LEAD participants' and community health and safety.

A study of Seattle's program in its early years focused on 318 people suspected of low-level drug and prostitution activity in downtown Seattle between 2011 and 2014; 203 were receiving LEAD, and 115 were going through the criminal legal system "as usual" (Collins, Lonczak, and Clifasefi, 2017). The researchers found that participation in LEAD led to "58% lower odds of arrest and 39% lower odds of being charged with a felony over the longer term" (p. 49). A follow-up analysis suggested that LEAD reduced incarceration and legal costs for participants (Collins, Lonczak, and Clifasefi, 2019); however, questions remain about how much of this effect can be causally attributed to the program.[5]

In a more recent study, Malm, Perrone, and Magaña (2020) examined LEAD programs in Los Angeles and San Francisco.[6] The authors were unable to conduct an outcome analysis for Los Angeles because of missing data, but the cost analysis for San Francisco showed that LEAD "reduced average yearly criminal justice system utilization and associated costs over system-as-usual comparisons" (p. 122).[7] The results from Seattle and San Francisco are encouraging, but more work needs to be done to isolate the causal effect of LEAD. Jurisdictions adopting these programs should consider robust evaluation strategies before the programs are implemented.

Prosecutor-Led Diversion

In recent years, a growing number of prosecutors have established pretrial diversion programs—either *prefiling* (before charges are filed with the court) or *postfiling* (after the court process begins but before a disposition) (Labriola et al., 2018). Participating defendants must complete assigned treatment, services, or other diversion requirements. If they do, the

---

[5] Collins, Lonczak, and Clifasefi, 2017, report that "police officer shifts were randomized to be either LEAD or control shifts, and eligible individuals were allocated to those conditions if they were arrested during the respective shifts" (p. 50). However, this randomization was not used to estimate the causal effect of the program. Other individuals made it to the LEAD condition via "social contacts" with police officers, which could introduce bias into the analysis. The authors also report changes to the sample during the evaluation:

> Finally, after the evaluation began, operational partners recognized that there was a limited number of potential participants in the originally planned catchment area. Over time, most of these individuals were approached for LEAD involvement, which left a dwindling number of individuals available for inclusion in the control group. Thus, to accommodate the need for an adequate and comparable control group, control areas (in addition to control shifts) were added to the evaluation. (p. 50)

For an outcome study focused on only those individuals participating in LEAD (i.e., no control group), see Clifasefi, Lonczak, and Collins, 2017.

[6] The report includes extensive process evaluations that will be of interest to those considering adoption of LEAD or related programs. An analysis of Albany's LEAD program by Worden and McLean, 2018, will also be of interest.

[7] The authors used propensity score matching to evaluate the program, an approach that is the subject of much debate in the methodological literature (see, e.g., King and Nielsen, 2019; Peikes, Moreno, and Orzol, 2008; and Smith and Todd, 2001). Malm, Perrone, and Magaña, 2020, note that "while these techniques are not foolproof, they are commonly used in the social sciences to increase confidence in field evaluations" (p. 121).

charges are typically dismissed. In other words, pretrial diversion prevents defendants from progressing through other parts of the criminal legal ecosystem (specifically probation or jail, or both).

Collaborative or Problem-Solving Courts

This section was largely reproduced from Kilmer, Caulkins, et al., 2018.

Most of the empirical research on problem-solving courts focuses on drug courts, which debuted in Miami in 1989 and subsequently proliferated throughout the United States. Eligibility criteria for drug courts vary dramatically from one jurisdiction to the next but typically focus on arrests for nonviolent crimes committed by drug-involved persons who do not have extensive criminal records. Judges play a critical role in drug courts by requiring participants to come to court on a regular basis and providing them with public praise when it is earned.

Drug courts employ frequent alcohol and other drug testing and sometimes apply immediate but small sanctions on those who test positive or miss tests. Drug court participants who do not complete treatment or other designated programs may have to serve the sentences that they would have received if they had not entered the drug court program.

Although dozens of drug court evaluations have been published, few have used experimental designs. Studies that simply rely on matched controls do not allow selection effects to be ruled out; that is, participants who choose to enter drug courts (or participants selected by judges for these programs) may have other characteristics that are positively correlated with the evaluation outcomes (e.g., probability of rearrest). A meta-analysis of the literature that accounts for the varying methodological rigor of these studies concluded that "the average effect of participation is analogous to a drop in recidivism from 50% to 38% [about a 25-percent drop]; and, these effects last up to three years" (Mitchell et al., 2012, p. 60).

A meta-analysis that focused on incarceration as the outcome of interest found that "the typical drug court yields small to moderate reductions in the use of jail and prison incarceration when measured as a discrete sanction, but also that they deliver no significant advantage toward reducing the aggregate number of jail or prison days incarcerated" (Sevigny, Fuleihan, and Ferdik, 2013, p. 423). The authors hypothesize that the lower incarceration rates might be offset by the longer sentences imposed on drug court participants who do not comply with the program.

Of course, reducing rearrest and incarceration are not the only goals; drug courts also seek to reduce substance use and help participants achieve healthier lives. The National Institute of Justice's Multisite Adult Drug Court Evaluation, which looked beyond traditional criminal legal outcomes, found that drug courts reduced drug use and criminal offenses but did not have a statistically significant effect on employment, schooling, or community service outcomes (Roman, 2013).

The National Institute of Justice's evaluation included a rigorous cost-benefit analysis, which showed that drug courts produce about $1.50 in benefits for every $1.00 in costs. The analysis also noted that

> Drug courts prevent many petty crimes and a few serious crimes. In fact, the CBA [cost-benefit analysis] results showed that those few serious crimes drive much of the drug court effect; if we remove those outliers, the benefits of drug courts barely exceed the cost. This finding suggests that although drug courts may reduce recidivism among many types of persons convicted of a crime, drug courts that target persons committing serious crimes with a high need for substance abuse treatment will produce the most effective interventions and a maximum return on investment. (Roman, 2013)

This point is consistent with a common criticism that some drug courts exclude individuals with violent histories and others who might be in serious need of treatment and close monitoring (Sevigny, Pollack, and Reuter, 2013).

Another criticism is that many drug courts prioritize abstinence-only treatment programs and do not offer MOUD. In response, in 2015, federal funding for drug courts was made conditional upon not prohibiting the use of these medications (Nordstrom and Marlowe, 2016). Not all drug courts receive federal funding, however, so this did not completely solve the problem. Furthermore, some drug courts operate in places where access to MOUD is limited.

Opioid Use Disorder Treatment in Prisons and Jails

This section is reproduced from Kilmer, 2020.

Efforts targeting justice-involved individuals with OUD are particularly important, as the risk of overdose is much higher immediately after individuals leave jail or prison because their tolerances are lower (see, e.g., Binswanger et al., 2007). The risk is likely even higher in places that are swamped with illegally produced synthetic opioids. One strategy for increasing the probability that incarcerated individuals enter treatment after they are released is to provide them with treatment for OUD while they are incarcerated. A recently published meta-analysis reported that individuals who received methadone while incarcerated were more likely than those who did not receive methadone to engage in community-based substance use treatment (Moore et al., 2019). Another recent systematic review by Sugarman et al. (2020) concluded that "evidence supports medication treatment administered throughout the period of criminal justice involvement as an effective method of improving post-release outcomes in individuals with criminal justice involvement" (p. 1).

There are a host of barriers to this continuity of care, besides the fact that treatment access is limited in many communities. Most importantly, the vast majority of correctional institutions do not offer MOUD to all inmates (Nunn et al., 2009; Vestal, 2018). There are laws requiring correctional institutions to provide these treatments to expectant mothers with OUD, and some facilities use these drugs to detox individuals undergoing withdrawal when they are first incarcerated, but that is only for a short period. Thus, most incarcerated individuals with OUD are denied access to MOUD. But change is happening in this space; for example, the governor of New York recently signed a bill requiring that MOUD be available to incarcerated individuals (New York State Senate, 2021).

There are several possible reasons for the denial of evidence-based MOUD. Some decisionmakers still view methadone and buprenorphine as simply switching one addiction for another and contend that abstinence-based treatment is the only approach, an argument that is not unique to the correctional setting. However, this argument does not account for the fact that MOUD have very different harm profiles from illegally produced opioids and do not commonly produce the high that individuals receive from commonly misused opioids. Another concern is that providing a highly sought-after and valued drug within a penal institution creates administrative and logistical challenges, as well as risks of diversion and of corruption of staff. Supervising the use of medications and reducing diversion does require staff and training, and some locations argue that they do not have the resources.[8]

Additional Thoughts on Prioritization of and Coercion to Substance Use Disorder Treatment

Given the lack of treatment access in many parts of the United States, there are questions about the ways in which scarce services should be allocated. This is somewhat less relevant for people with OUD given the strong evidence that many individuals can do well receiving medications alone, particularly after their symptoms have been stabilized, so the notion of treatment beds or "slots" is less applicable; however, there are some individuals who seek treatment for OUD in a residential facility or structured outpatient program. When scarcity is an issue, should admissions be purely on a first-come, first-served basis, or should other criteria be considered? If so, which criteria? These questions raise ethical and legal issues that we do not address here but highlight the triage issue as something that confronts funding agencies, health officials, and treatment providers.

There is also a long-standing debate about whether people with substance use disorders who are involved in the legal system should be coerced to enter treatment as an alternative to incarceration or some other sanction (see, e.g., Farabee, Prendergast, and Anglin, 1998; McSweeney et al., 2007; and Seddon, 2007).[9] This is how most drug courts work, and, as noted earlier, whether they are "successful" depends on how success is defined; research suggests that they can reduce recidivism for some participants and are cost-beneficial from a societal perspective (largely driven by a reduction in a small number of serious crimes), but they do not appear to reduce overall incarceration days because many individuals violate program rules, do not complete the program, or both. This coercion occurs in other parts of the criminal legal system as well (e.g., "If you do not enter treatment, we will run your case through the

---

[8] For insights about how to administer these substances in correctional settings, see SAMHSA, 2019.

[9] Werb et al., 2016, p. 2, reviews the evidence on compulsory drug treatment, which the authors argue is different from coerced treatment:

> Compulsory drug treatment can be defined as the mandatory enrollment of individuals, who are often but not necessarily drug-dependent, in a drug treatment program . . . . Compulsory treatment is distinct from coerced treatment, wherein individuals are provided with a choice, however narrow, to avoid treatment (Bright and Martire, 2012). Perhaps the most widely known example of coerced treatment is the drug treatment court model.

traditional adjudication process"). Judges in many states can also civilly commit individuals to treatment if their drug use imposes a high likelihood of serious harm (Christopher et al., 2015).

The considerations surrounding coercion can be even more complex if the mandated treatment is abstinence based (Rafful et al., 2018). Although the risk of overdose after a period of abstinence has always been an issue, whether the period of abstinence was caused by incarceration, treatment, or another factor, it is especially salient given how dangerous and unpredictable street drug markets are today. This raises a question about whether the cumulative risk of fatal overdose for a person who uses opioids is higher by allowing that person to remain in the community or by forcing them to abstain for a fixed period. Although forced abstention could lead to long-term recovery for some people, many others will likely resume opioid consumption with a lower tolerance. Of course, the likelihood of either recovery or resumption of drug use will be shaped by multiple factors, such as the availability of treatment, and the type of treatment available, in both settings; the probability that the individual is using alone; the availability of naloxone; and the saturation of synthetic opioids in the local drug market. In the era of fentanyl, the decision to coerce abstinence is more complex, requiring much more thought about the services available to individuals during and after coercion, as well as a better understanding of the drug markets in which these individuals are participating.

Medical Care

Although the OUD treatment system is an important part of the medical system, criminal legal institutions interact with other parts of the medical system in important ways when it comes to opioids. Individuals with OUD who interact with the criminal legal system often have infections (e.g., hepatitis C, HIV) and other health issues that need to be addressed (Winetsky et al., 2020; further discussed in Chapter Five). But medical care is not just about treating the acute conditions; it has also been argued that more attention needs to be paid to addressing the social determinants of health for justice-involved individuals with OUD (Sugarman et al., 2020; further addressed in Chapters Eight, Eleven, and Twelve).

Arrest and Prosecution of Opioid Prescribers, Distributors, and Manufacturers

An earlier section of this chapter highlights some of the criminal legal actions intended to reduce the diversion of controlled substances. Although the criminal cases against pill mills that helped flood the United States with prescription opioids have received a lot of attention, it has been challenging to isolate the effects of pain management clinic laws from other policy interventions (e.g., the implementation of PDMPs) because many of these efforts happened roughly around the same time and may have had interaction effects (Schuler et al., 2020).[10]

In addition, as noted earlier, individuals and governments have also pursued legal action against prescribers, distributors, and manufacturers via the civil courts. These cases have led to some large settlements that can influence many parts of the opioid ecosystem; however, there is much debate about how these funds should be spent (Haffajee and Stein, 2019). Should this money be spent to compensate the victims and their families, to prevent future diversion and misuse, or some combination?

Incarceration and Medicaid Eligibility

Medicaid, which is jointly funded by federal and state governments, provides health coverage to more than 75 million people, including low-income adults, children, and people with disabilities (Medicaid.gov, undated). The Medicaid and CHIP Payment and Access Commission (2018) notes that federal law prohibits states from using federal Medicaid funds to cover individuals residing in

- state or federal prisons, local jails, or detention facilities;
- federal residential reentry centers;
- residential mental health and substance use disorder treatment facilities for incarcerated individuals; or
- hospitals or nursing facilities that exclusively serve incarcerated individuals. (p. 3)

However, these Medicaid funds can be used to cover off-site hospitalizations lasting 24 hours or longer.

When someone who is on Medicaid is incarcerated for a drug law violation or anything else, most states suspend that person's Medicaid eligibility; however, as of 2019, nine states terminate eligibility during jail stays and eight states terminate it during prison sentences (Kaiser Family Foundation, 2019). Termination requires individuals to reenroll, and gaps in coverage can be detrimental; former White House Office of National Drug Control Policy Director Michael Botticelli argues that "immediate Medicaid coverage upon release 'can mean the difference between . . . life and death'" (Pew Charitable Trusts, 2016, quoting Hancock, 2016). Although some states work to reenroll inmates before they are released and have introduced multiple innovative programs to this end (Pew Charitable Trusts, 2020),

---

[10] Schuler and colleagues, 2020, p. 7, note:

> Of the 13 pain clinic studies, 8 (62 %) analyzed longitudinal data with a comparison group design, and the remaining 5 (38 %) used longitudinal data with no comparison group. Of the 8 studies with a comparison group design, 3 (38 %) did not account for differences between policy and comparison states, which may bias policy effect estimates. Furthermore, 9 studies (69 %) did not adjust for co-occurring policies. The majority (n = 7; 54 %) did not examine policy heterogeneity through more complex specifications of the policy variable, largely due to a preponderance of studies that only considered a single policy state (e.g., Florida, Texas). Notably, due to the near simultaneous enactment of Florida's PDMP and pain clinic laws, two studies strictly estimated the joint effect of both policies (Chang et al., 2016; 2018).

termination—and, to a lesser extent, suspension—creates barriers and can lead to delays in accessing OUD treatment and other health services.

Health Services After Incarceration

Relatedly, there have been efforts to facilitate faster engagement of individuals released from prisons with primary care providers, for instance through the work of Transitions Clinics (Shavit et al., 2017). Existing evidence from studies involving participants with chronic health issues (including OUD) suggests that such interventions can reduce subsequent emergency department utilization (Wang et al., 2012) and odds of reincarceration for technical violations of parole or probation conditions (Wang et al., 2019). Work is currently underway to examine whether similar benefits hold specifically for individuals on MOUD returning from prisons (Howell et al., 2021).

Changing Drug Laws to Allow Medical Cannabis

More than 35 states have passed laws to allow individuals to obtain cannabis products for medicinal purposes, and most of these states allow medical officials to recommend it for pain. This allows patients to use it as an adjunct or an alternative for opioids and other pain medications. There are also some states that allow medical cannabis to be used to help treat OUD.[11]

The extent to which these laws have reduced overall pain is unclear. Researchers have attempted to examine the effects of these laws on opioid-involved outcomes, and a review by Smart and Pacula, 2019, concluded:

> Studies assessing impacts on self-reported misuse and distribution of opioids show no impact of MCLs [medical cannabis laws], yet studies evaluating opioid-related adverse events and opioid prescribing show reductions. Opioid-related mortality, which early studies suggested was reduced by MCLs, now appears to be positively correlated with these policies and the adoption of RCLs [recreational cannabis laws]. The significant policy action being taken to combat the opioid crisis as well as the evolution of the types of opioids driving opioid-related harm likely contributes to the lack of robust findings for this outcome. (p. 659)

Education

There are some drug-specific interactions between the criminal legal and education systems, but they are not necessarily specific to opioids. Law enforcement agencies do participate in school-based drug prevention programs and assist with the investigation of students who are believed to be involved with opioids. In addition, there are correctional education programs, which have demonstrated some success (see, e.g., Bozick et al., 2018).

---

[11] For reviews of the evidence on the effectiveness of medical cannabis for addressing pain and other conditions, see National Academies of Sciences, Engineering, and Medicine, 2017, and Nugent et al., 2017.

Although it used to be the case that a drug conviction could make individuals ineligible for federal aid for postsecondary education, this restriction was removed in 2020.[12]

Employment

Having a criminal record negatively affects many labor market outcomes, including making individuals ineligible for various professional licenses (e.g., a barber's license in some states). As Apel and Ramakers, 2018, note in a recent review,

> Overall, there is remarkable consistency in the finding that incarceration is highly disruptive for certain aspects of the employment experience—even relative to other highly disadvantaged individuals and even in countries with far more liberal and humane justice systems, formerly incarcerated individuals experience a great deal of instability in the labor market. (p. 98)

Some jails and prisons offer education and work release programs to help with the transition, and parole and probation departments can refer individuals to education, employment, and treatment services. But these agencies also have the power to revoke community supervision—such as for a positive or missed drug test or other violations—which can take these individuals back out of the labor market.

Income Support and Homeless Services

Having a criminal record has implications for many other parts of the opioid ecosystem. Not only can drug arrests and convictions make it harder to get a job; they can also increase barriers to accessing social services, from public housing to income and food assistance.

Housing

Access to adequate housing can play an important role in helping people with OUD achieve and sustain recovery. People who have been convicted of drug offenses or other felonies are sometimes prohibited from living with other individuals who have been convicted of felonies, which can create housing challenges. Accounting for pre-prison living arrangements, being incarcerated leads to living in more-disadvantaged neighborhoods (Massoglia, Firebaugh, and Warner, 2013).

In response to the crack problem and associated violence in the late 1980s, a series of federal laws and regulations were implemented to reduce drug activity in public housing proj-

---

[12] Lovenheim and Owens, 2014, evaluated the Higher Education Act of 1998, which temporarily eliminated federal financial aid eligibility for students convicted of drug offenses in the previous two years, and found that this policy had little effect on deterring drug crimes and led to a "large decline in the fraction of drug offenders who enrolled in college within two years of graduating from high school, particularly for students living in urban areas" (p. 11). The authors argue that this delay likely lowered the lifetime earnings of these students.

ects. As Curtis, Garlington, and Schottenfeld (2013) note, many of these efforts did not even require a drug conviction—suspected use was often enough to lead to eviction:

> The Anti-Drug Abuse Act of 1988 required PHAs [public health authorities] to construct lease clauses allowing for the eviction of tenants who engaged in drug use or other behaviors that could threaten the safety of other tenants (Blanks, 2002–2004). The Quality Housing and Work Responsibility Act of 1998 supported PHAs' right to exclude applicants with a criminal history and use their discretion to determine which applicants were possible risks to the safety of the community. In addition, the Cranston-Gonzalez National Affordable Housing Act of 1990 (NAHA) imposed a mandatory 3-year ban on the readmission of tenants evicted for drug-related criminal activity. PHAs have the option of extending the ban beyond 3 years. The Housing Opportunity Program Extension Act of 1996 (HOPEA) further strengthened eviction rules and called on the National Crime Information Center and local police departments to provide PHAs with applicants' criminal records (Human Rights Watch, 2004; Mazerolle et al., 2000). Further, HOPEA allowed for PHAs to deny applicants who were believed to be using drugs or abusing alcohol or who were found to have a pattern of alcohol or drug use that might threaten the health or safety of other tenants. Several PHAs currently have drug-testing policies in their public housing programs (McCarty et al., 2012). Federal policies neither permit nor prohibit PHAs from testing residents or applicants for the presence of drugs. (p. 39)

The PHAs have a lot of discretion when it comes to evicting or preventing people who use drugs from obtaining public housing, and there appears to be considerable variation in these policies across the country despite the lack of hard numbers (Silva, 2015). We are not aware of any rigorous analyses that attempt to evaluate the social costs and benefits of these public housing policies.

Income and Food Assistance

At the same time that public housing was becoming less available to people who used drugs, so were certain welfare benefits. As part of the Personal Responsibility and Work Opportunity Reconciliation Act of 1996, states could impose lifetime bans on Temporary Assistance for Needy Families (TANF), or what is now known as the Supplemental Nutrition Assistance Program (SNAP), to people who had been convicted of drug felonies. Although 30 states chose to impose full bans on TANF when the law took effect in 1997, this number decreased to 17 in 2010 (Martin and Shannon, 2020). Today, only South Carolina has the full SNAP ban on the books (Polkey, 2019; Thompson and Burnside, 2019) (Figure 6.4).[13] About half the states in the United States impose some type of modified ban on these programs; examples include limiting bans to individuals who sell drugs or requiring drug testing (Polkey, 2019).

---

[13] Mauer and McCalmont, 2013, note, "Although states are minimally more lenient in allowing people to receive food stamps, SNAP restrictions generally mirror state TANF restrictions" (pp. 2–3).

The number of people affected by these full and modified bans is in the hundreds of thousands. In just the 12 states that still had full bans as of 2011, an estimated 180,000 women were ineligible for TANF because of the bans (Mauer and McCalmont, 2013). This number excludes family members of those were banned who would benefit from the programs. An analysis by Tuttle, 2019, of a modified food stamp ban on convicted drug traffickers in Florida showed that the ban increased the probability of returning to prison, "primarily driven by an increase in recidivism for financially motivated crimes (such as property crime and selling drugs)" (p. 303).

Child Welfare

A drug or other arrest, or even drug use, can flag child protective services to investigate a parent and possibly lead to a recommendation to revoke custody (Crowley et al., 2019). Child welfare workers try hard to keep the children of parents who use drugs out of the foster care system, but their primary is goal to protect the safety and welfare of the children. Ultimately, the decision about custody is made by a judge in a family court.

First Responders

As mentioned earlier, local law enforcement officers often serve as first responders to opioid overdoses, administering naloxone and sometimes taking individuals to medical facilities. There has been public debate about whether law enforcement officers responding to overdoses, as well as those addressing alleged crimes involving potent synthetic opioids, such as fentanyl, are at risk of overdosing if they touch or inhale fentanyl during the interactions. In 2017, the American College of Medical Toxicology and the American Academy of Clinical Toxicology noted:

> Fentanyl and its analogs are potent opioid receptor agonists, but the risk of clinically significant exposure to emergency responders is extremely low. To date, we have not seen reports of emergency responders developing signs or symptoms consistent with opioid toxicity from incidental contact with opioids. Incidental dermal absorption is unlikely to cause opioid toxicity. (American College of Medical Toxicology, undated)

Since then, there have been many more media reports of first responders being exposed to fentanyl, and some of these stories have gone viral (Siegel, 2022). These stories rarely, if ever, provide evidence that fentanyl intoxication led to the reported symptoms. The Centers for Disease Control and Prevention removed a video from its website after experts expressed concerns that the video, which was about the risks of fentanyl exposure to law enforcement officers, mischaracterized these risks (D'Ambrosio, 2022).

There have been media reports of law enforcement fatigue to responding to overdoses, especially when naloxone is administered on the same person multiple times (DeMio, 2017). At least one community in Ohio debated a "three strikes" policy, which would have required

FIGURE 6.4

Supplemental Nutrition Assistance Program Eligibility for Individuals Convicted of Drug Felonies

SOURCE: Adapted from Polkey, 2019.

people who use drugs to do community service before emergency responders would respond to a third overdose call, although it did not get implemented (Richter, 2017). In 2020, during the COVID-19 pandemic, there were reports of police departments in Indiana no longer administering naloxone because of the risk of COVID-19 infection (Blanchard, 2020).

There have been arguments that first responders to overdoses should not be law enforcement officers because that could deter people from calling for medical attention; however, in many communities—especially in rural areas—police are the only available entity to respond quickly to 911 calls. First responders other than police might want additional protection and support (because, for example, individuals who have overdosed are sometimes revived in an agitated state) (Neale and Strang, 2015).

Whether someone reports an overdose can be influenced by the legal environment. Most jurisdictions have passed Good Samaritan laws (National Conference of State Legislatures, 2017), and others have passed drug homicide laws. Good Samaritan laws are meant to help address the risk of arrest when police respond to an overdose, and while one study found that these laws reduce state-level overdose deaths (McClellan et al., 2018), two others found that they do not have a statistically significant effect on overdose deaths (Atkins, Durrance, and Kim, 2019; Rees et al., 2019). With the increased focus on reducing police contacts in the wake of the death of George Floyd, law enforcement's role in addressing opioids will likely become a more prominent topic of discussion.

Harm Reduction and Community-Initiated Interventions

Much of this section is reproduced from Kilmer, 2020.

Given the increased risk of overdose after a period of incarceration, an increasing number of jurisdictions are looking beyond improving treatment linkages and are training individuals in preventing overdoses and providing naloxone to individuals who are reentering the community (Horton et al., 2017; Zucker et al., 2015). This makes sense not only because some of these individuals will likely resume opioid consumption once they are back in the community (and might benefit from having naloxone nearby) but also because they might be interacting with others who are at risk of overdose. One randomized controlled trial in Scotland found that two-thirds of the naloxone administered as part of the trial was not used on the ex-prisoners who received the naloxone, leading to the study being stopped because the naloxone may have been administered to those in the control group (Parmar et al., 2017).[14]

Even in places where such harm reduction efforts as syringe service programs are legally allowed, fear and stigma associated with criminalization can drive some people who use drugs away from these programs (and other services) and can prevent other community members from implementing or staffing these efforts. These programs essentially operate at the discretion of local law enforcement, who could—if they wanted to—make it difficult or inconvenient for people who use drugs to access these services (e.g., arresting those seeking drug content testing for possession or following individuals after they leave syringe service programs).

There are also federal legal barriers to some harm reduction programs. For example, SCSs violate the "crack house statute" of the CSA (Public Law 91-513, § 856(a)(2)). Various DOJ officials have written memoranda (e.g., U.S. Attorney's Office, District of Vermont, 2017) or op-eds (Lelling, 2019; Rosenstein, 2018) making this argument, and the U.S. Attorney for the Eastern District of Pennsylvania filed a preemptive injunction asking a federal judge to declare that Safehouse—the proposed supervised consumption site in Philadelphia—was in violation of the CSA. Although a federal judge ruled against the government, the case was subsequently overturned by the U.S. Court of Appeals (*United States v. Safehouse*, 2021), and the U.S. Supreme Court declined to hear the appeal. Despite the federal prohibition, two SCSs opened in New York City in November 2021, and, as of October 2022, the DOJ has not taken action against these facilities or people who operate and use them.

---

[14] The authors note:

> The N-ALIVE [NALoxone InVEstigation] pilot trial stopped early because its own data, together with those from Scotland's National Naloxone Programme, were persuasive that approximately two-thirds of NOR [naloxone on release] administrations were not to the ex-prisoner for whom NOR was assigned. We had no means of knowing the identities of these other people: confounding of N-ALIVE's control group could have occurred. The N-ALIVE pilot trial ceased because individualized randomization to NOR cannot offer a clear-cut answer: other trial designs are required. (Parmar et al., 2017, p. 512).

Policy Opportunities and Considerations

Parts of this section are reproduced from Kilmer, 2020.

We conclude with some policy considerations involving various parts of the legal system but offer one meta comment about research and evaluation. Some of the ideas offered in this chapter (as well as in the other chapters) would be large departures from current practice and could have significant unintended consequences. It is critical that if jurisdictions decide to pilot some of these approaches, they think through how these approaches will be evaluated and which data need to be collected. But this standard should not apply just to new ideas. The massive rise in overdose deaths and addiction involving opioids shows that some of the current efforts to address drug problems are insufficient and that some might be counterproductive. The "business as usual" approach must also be subject to rigorous evaluation.

The policy opportunities discussed in this section largely focus on demand and harm reduction; policy opportunities that focus more on the supply side are discussed in Chapter Seven.

Reducing Barriers to Opioid Use Disorder Treatment for Justice-Involved Individuals (and Everyone Else)

Although some jurisdictions are making progress when it comes to increasing access to MOUD for justice-involved populations (see Chapter Four and Pew Charitable Trusts, 2020), and the National Institutes of Health should be applauded for allocating more than $150 million to the Justice Community Opioid Innovation Network to better understand which approaches are most effective, more can be done to make sure that inmates in jails and state prisons have access to MOUD during and after incarceration. Funding is one component, but this problem will not be solved by increasing resources alone.[15] As noted earlier, the tension between abstinence-based treatment and MOUD still exists in many criminal legal settings.

Most individuals involved in the criminal legal system live in their communities on probation or parole, and nearly one-third of adults on probation in 2010 were people who used illegal drugs (Feucht and Gfroerer, 2011). People who have been recently released from correctional facilities (many of whom are under some form of community supervision) are at an elevated risk of death from drug overdose.

Community corrections agencies could ensure that officers are trained and equipped with naloxone. Departments will need to consider budgeting for the acquisition of naloxone and providing storage and replacement policies; BJA reports that a naloxone spray kit costs law enforcement between $22 and $60 (BJA, National Training and Technical Assistance Center,

---

[15] Humphreys et al., 2022, makes the point that it is important to make sure that treatments that could make patients worse are not funded.

undated-b). A good source of information for community corrections agencies is BJA's online Naloxone Toolkit (BJA, National Training and Technical Assistance Center, undated-a).

In terms of treatment referral options, there are effective, federally approved MOUD, and the UNODC and WHO recommend opioid pharmacotherapy for treating opioid-dependent individuals under supervision. However, as mentioned earlier, many probationers are not referred for methadone treatment for a variety of reasons, such as court orders, department policies, concerns about overdose risk, gaps in knowledge and understanding of MOUD, concerns about long-term use, or some combination of these factors (Gryczynski et al., 2012; National Association of State Alcohol and Drug Abuse Directors, Inc., 2006; Nunn et al., 2009; Reichert and Gleicher, 2019).

To successfully connect individuals to treatment, community corrections departments cannot work alone. They need to coordinate with the treatment agencies and other health providers. Because these organizations have different mandates, structures, and cultures, a first step toward better coordination is for the organizations to develop relationships and understanding about one another's systems, processes, and protections for individuals. Criminal legal agencies should consider organizing meetings at varying ranks (e.g., executive, middle management, support staff, line officers) with treatment agency representatives and other key health providers (Capoccia et al., 2007; Edmonson, 2003; Lehman et al., 2009; Welsh et al., 2016). This could also help improve officers' knowledge of MOUD and start addressing their concerns. The next step is for organizations to engage in discussions about strategic planning activities (Welsh et al., 2016). There is some guidance about how community corrections agencies can go about implementing a recovery-oriented system of care (Heaps et al., 2009; SAMHSA, undated). In addition, to improve knowledge about OUD generally, senior staff could encourage staff at corrections agencies to take courses like the National Institute on Drug Abuse's (NIDA's) *Understanding Addiction: An Overview for Corrections Professionals* (available for continuing education credit) and refer to materials by the American Probation and Parole Association. NIDA (or other agencies) could consider developing a probation course for credit focused on educating probation officers on MOUD.

Addressing the Collateral Consequences of Being Arrested and Convicted

The consequences of being arrested and convicted extend well beyond the sentence imposed by the judge and can affect many parts of the opioid ecosystem. As noted earlier, a criminal record can make it harder to get a job or professional license, and, depending on where one lives, there are many additional consequences associated with being convicted (e.g., inability to access public housing, ineligibility for public benefits).

Most arrests of people with OUD are not for violations of drug laws; rather, most are for other crimes (see Chapter Two). However, some of the collateral consequences for the minority of offenses that are drug law violations could be changed by amending current laws, and other restrictions could be changed at the agency level. Jurisdictions considering this will have to decide which drug law offenses will be eligible (e.g., possession, possession with intent to distribute, sales involving amount under a certain threshold).

Another option is to allow certain offenses to be sealed or expunged and make the process automatic instead of requiring individuals to petition the court. States have different laws and definitions related to expungement and sealing, but, in general, the former focuses on eliminating the offense from all criminal records while the latter allows the offense to be seen only under certain circumstances. Some states allow individuals to have their records expunged if they have not been convicted of new offenses within a certain number of years; however, the onus is on the individuals to petition the court, and this process can be complicated and expensive. Governments could make this process easier by automatically sealing or expunging these offenses after a fixed period (e.g., two years after the conviction), and there are nonprofit organizations, such as Code for America, and many state-specific organizations that could help states and localities implement bulk sealings or expungements. Furthermore, lessons could be learned from two states—Pennsylvania and Utah—that have already implemented automatic expungement (Unified Judicial System of Pennsylvania, undated; Clean Slate Utah, undated). The overall effects of these efforts will likely depend on whether individuals have other offenses in their records,[16] but, given that some consequences are specific to drug offenses, sealing or expungement could make a meaningful difference to individuals with drug records and to their families.

Revisit Drug Possession and Drug-Induced Homicide Laws and Sentences

Because the collateral consequences associated with having a criminal record for a drug offense have ripple effects throughout many parts of the opioid ecosystem, they should be reconsidered. It would be disingenuous to refer to them as *unintended consequences*; these consequences are a feature, not a bug. One approach for addressing these consequences would be to consider changing drug possession laws or how they are enforced, or both. For example, one possibility would be for local jurisdictions to make enforcing the law against drug possession the lowest priority for law enforcement. (Some jurisdictions did this years ago with cannabis). Another option, which has been implemented in some other countries and recently in Oregon (see the text boxes about Portugal and Oregon), is decriminalizing the possession of heroin and other drugs. Doing so would reduce the penalties and associated consequences,

---

[16] We are not aware of any research on expungement of criminal records related to offenses involving opioids specifically, but an article in the *New York Times* about expungement related to cannabis offenses in New York state says that, even after expungement of these offenses, about 85 percent of individuals would still have criminal records because of other crimes:

> About 160,000 people with low-level marijuana convictions in New York will see those convictions cleared from their record. And of that number, 10,872 in New York City and 13,537 in the rest of the state, will have no criminal records after their marijuana convictions are cleared. The remaining approximately 136,000 people will still have criminal records because of other convictions. (Paybarah, 2019)

but it would not necessarily reduce police interactions. These approaches all have pros, cons, and potential unintended consequences, so cautious jurisdictions implementing them might want to consider sunset clauses.

As noted at the beginning of this section, robust evaluations should be built into efforts that involve significant changes to criminal laws and practices. Especially relevant to discussions of decriminalization is the hypothesis that it reduces stigma toward people who use drugs and drug use in general. This is very much an empirical question and one that could be addressed with research involving people who use drugs, law enforcement, other service providers, and the public. It will also require clear definitions of *stigma* that can be measured over time. Many other outcomes should be assessed, ranging from criminal legal outcomes (and whether they might differ by race and ethnicity) to treatment outcomes (e.g., uptake, type of treatment, duration). A criticism of decriminalization is that it will make it harder to make cases against retail sellers because retail sellers often possess amounts of drugs suitable for personal consumption and are rarely directly observed making sales, so some arrests of retail sellers are actually arrests for possession. Whether this happens, and the possible consequences, should also be included in evaluations.

For jurisdictions committed to incarcerating individuals convicted of drug possession, it is worth considering whether the typical sentence length is appropriate. There is tremendous variation in sentence length across the United States, but a study of state prisoners released in 2016 whose most serious offense was drug possession showed that the mean *time served* was 15 months (the median was ten months; Kaeble, 2018). The average *time sentenced* for these individuals was four years (Kaeble, 2018), and it is common for people to be released early and subject to community supervision. Many individuals convicted for drug possession serve time in local jails, and there is also the time an individual might spend in jail before trial; thus, a comprehensive assessment of incarceration cannot focus exclusively on prisons or what happens after conviction.

Finally, drug-induced homicide laws make little sense, especially in the era of synthetic opioids (Goulka et al., 2021). In many parts of the United States, individuals sharing or selling powdered opioids (and increasingly other substances, such as counterfeit pills) do not know whether these substances contain fentanyl, and, if so, how much. Levying additional sanctions on these individuals if someone overdoses and dies from a product they supplied is unlikely to create a deterrent effect. (Increasing the severity of sanctions is not a very effective way of producing deterrence, especially for individuals with substance use disorders; see, e.g., Chalfin and McCrary, 2017; Kleiman, 2009; National Research Council, 2014). Furthermore, doing so could create disincentives for those individuals who shared or sold the drug to call for help if they witness an overdose; if the person dies, they could face additional time behind bars. One could argue that the additional sanctions could give prosecutors more leverage in extracting information from individuals to go after others in the supply chain, but this contention presupposes that the maximum penalties for supplying by itself are too low to coerce compliance.

The Federal Government Could Make It Easier to Allow Local Experimentation with Supervised Consumption Sites and Other Harm Reduction Efforts

Parts of this section were previously published in Kilmer, 2020.

No one is arguing that SCSs alone will solve the opioid crisis, and it would be impossible to supervise all drug use (see the scaling discussion Chapter Eight), but there are some community leaders who argue that they might be able to help address some of the problems they confront. One federal option is to amend the CSA to explicitly allow SCSs and start funding demonstration programs. Of course, the law would have to be broad enough to make sure that the people who worked at these sites could not be sanctioned (e.g., lose the ability to prescribe drugs) and that those who entered with drugs would not be arrested. (Although the federal government usually does not make arrests for possessing small amounts of drugs for personal use, such arrests are still a possibility.)

Another option would be to pass a budget rider that prohibits federal funds from being used to enforce federal laws against individuals implementing, staffing, or using SCSs (Beletsky, personal communication).[17] A recent precedent with respect to the CSA was the budget rider that prohibited federal funds from being used to enforce federal law against those participating in state-legal medical cannabis programs. This approach would still leave the federal prohibition in place, and there would still be some risks for people who operate and work at these sites.

However, Congress does not have to pass legislation to reduce federal barriers to implementing SCSs. U.S. Attorneys have limited resources and discretion about the types of cases they pursue. They could simply decide not to enforce federal laws against people implementing, staffing, or using SCSs. They could also issue guidance about the types of cases that they will prioritize (Kilmer and Pardo, 2019).

For example, after the voters in Colorado and Washington passed cannabis legalization for nonmedical purposes in 2012, it was not clear what the federal government would do. The following year, the DOJ released a memorandum making it clear that cannabis activities in these states violated federal law but that, as long as the states had strict enforcement and regulatory systems and individuals participating in the markets did not violate eight explicit guidelines, the federal government would consider such activities a low enforcement priority. For better or worse, the Obama administration did not interfere. Although the Trump administration eventually repealed the memorandum, enforcement activities did not noticeably change.

The DOJ could take a similar approach to SCSs. It could publish guidance indicating that it is not "legalizing" SCSs but will not make it an enforcement priority to target sites that are consistent with state and local laws. Additional guidelines could be added, such as requiring

---

[17] Leo Beletsky, personal communication with Beau Kilmer, December 5, 2019.

that a memorandum of understanding be signed by local public health and public safety officials. The DOJ could also require that any sites that are opening have robust evaluation plans with credible control conditions and disinterested evaluators (e.g., the Government Accountability Office, or state equivalents). Although this type of guidance could always be overturned, it would allow local governments to experiment with interventions that might help reduce some of the harms associated with unsupervised consumption.

There is much to learn about the community-level outcomes associated with implementing SCSs. As noted in Chapter Eight, there is an unsanctioned supervised consumption site in the United States that has been studied (Davidson et al., 2021; Kral et al., 2020; Kral et al., 2021; Lambdin et al., 2022; Suen et al., 2022), and two sites opened in New York City in late 2021. Other jurisdictions seem poised to open their own, and now is the time to start collecting pre-implementation data and thinking critically about possible control jurisdictions for pilot studies. Although a randomized controlled trial at the individual level would likely raise ethical concerns, there are other research designs that could be implemented (Kilmer, Taylor, et al., 2018).

Abbreviations

BJA	Bureau of Justice Assistance
BJS	Bureau of Justice Statistics
CDT	Commission for the Dissuasion of Drug Abuse
COVID-19	coronavirus disease 2019
CSA	Controlled Substances Act
DEA	Drug Enforcement Administration
DOJ	U.S. Department of Justice
LEAD	Law Enforcement Assisted Diversion
M-110	Measure 110
MOUD	medications for opioid use disorder
OUD	opioid use disorder
PCS	possession of a controlled substance
PDMP	prescription drug monitoring program
PHA	public health authority
SAMHSA	Substance Abuse and Mental Health Services Administration
SCS	supervised consumption site
SNAP	Supplemental Nutrition Assistance Program
TANF	Temporary Assistance for Needy Families

References

American College of Medical Toxicology, *ACMT and AACT Position Statement: Preventing Occupational Fentanyl and Fentanyl Analog Exposure to Emergency Responders*, Phoenix, Ariz., undated.

Anderson, James M., Maya Buenaventura, and Paul Heaton, "The Effects of Holistic Defense on Criminal Justice Outcomes," *Harvard Law Review*, Vol. 132, No. 3, 2019.

Anthony, James C., Lynn A. Warner, and Ronald C. Kessler, "Comparative Epidemiology of Dependence on Tobacco, Alcohol, Controlled Substances, and Inhalants: Basic Findings from the National Comorbidity Survey," *Experimental and Clinical Psychopharmacology*, Vol. 2, No. 3, 1994, pp. 244–268.

Apel, R., and A. A. T. Ramakers, "Impact of Incarceration on Employment Prospects," in B. M. Huebner and N. A. Frost, eds., *Handbook on the Consequences of Sentencing and Punishment Decisions*, New York: Routledge, 2018, pp. 85–104.

Atkins, Danielle N., Christine Piette Durrance, and Yuna Kim, "Good Samaritan Harm Reduction Policy and Drug Overdose Deaths," *Health Services Research*, Vol. 54, No. 2, 2019, pp. 407–416.

Beletsky, Leo, "America's Favorite Antidote: Drug-Induced Homicide in the Age of the Overdose Crisis," *Utah Law Review*, Vol. 2019, No. 4, 2019, pp. 833–890.

Binswanger, Ingrid A., Marc F. Stern, Richard A. Deyo, Patrick J. Heagerty, Allen Cheadle, Joann G. Elmore, and Thomas D. Koepsell, "Release from Prison—A High Risk of Death for Former Inmates," *New England Journal of Medicine*, Vol. 356, No. 2, 2007, pp. 157–165.

BJA—*See* Bureau of Justice Assistance.

Blanchard, Sessi Kuwabara, "An Indiana Police Dept. No Longer Reversing Overdoses During Pandemic," *Filter*, April 9, 2020.

Blanks, Valerie, "An Examination of No-Fault Evictions: An Analysis of the *Department of Housing and Urban Development v. Rucker*," *National Black Law Journal*, Vol. 17, No. 2, 2002–2004, pp. 268–281.

Boustead, Anne E., "Privacy Protections and Law Enforcement Use of Prescription Drug Monitoring Databases," *Law & Policy*, Vol. 43, No. 3, 2021.

Bozick, Robert, Jennifer L. Steele, Lois M. Davis, and Susan Turner, "Does Providing Inmates with Education Improve Postrelease Outcomes? A Meta-Analysis of Correctional Education Programs in the United States," *Journal of Experimental Criminology*, Vol. 14, No. 3, 2018, pp. 389–428.

Bright, David A., and Kristy A. Martire, "Does Coerced Treatment of Substance-Using Offenders Lead to Improvements in Substance Use and Recidivism? A Review of the Treatment Efficacy Literature," *Australian Psychologist*, Vol. 48, No. 1, 2012, pp. 69–81.

Bureau of Justice Assistance, *Justice System Use of Prescription Drug Monitoring Programs: Overview and Recommendations for Addressing the Nation's Prescription Drug and Opioid Abuse Epidemic*, Washington, D.C.: U.S. Department of Justice, 2015.

Bureau of Justice Assistance, National Training and Technical Assistance Center, "Law Enforcement Naloxone Toolkit: Naloxone Background," webpage, undated-a. As of November 13, 2020:
https://bjatta.bja.ojp.gov/tools/naloxone/Naloxone-Background

Bureau of Justice Assistance, National Training and Technical Assistance Center, "Law Enforcement Naloxone Toolkit: What Are the Typical Costs of a Law Enforcement Overdose Response Program?" webpage, undated-b. As of September 9, 2021:
https://bjatta.bja.ojp.gov/naloxone/what-are-typical-costs-law-enforcement-overdose-response-program

Burris, Scott, Evan D. Anderson, Leo Beletsky, and Corey S. Davis, "Federalism, Policy Learning, and Local Innovation in Public Health: The Case of the Supervised Injection Facility," *St. Louis University Law Journal*, Vol. 53, 2009.

Burris, Scott, David Finucane, Heather Gallagher, and Joseph Grace, "The Legal Strategies Used in Operating Syringe Exchange Programs in the United States," *American Journal of Public Health*, Vol. 86, No. 8, 1996, pp. 1161–1166.

Butler, Paul, "Racially Based Jury Nullification: Black Power in the Criminal Justice System," *Yale Law Journal*, Vol. 105, No. 3, 1995, pp. 677–725.

Capoccia, V. A., F. Cotter, D. H. Gustafson, E. Cassidy, J. Ford, L. Madden, et al., "Making Slow Process Improvement Is Changing the Addiction Treatment Field," *Joint Commission Journal on Quality and Patient Safety*, Vol. 33, 2007, pp. 95–103.

Caputo, Gail A., *Intermediate Sanctions in Corrections*, Denton, Tex.: University of North Texas Press, 2004.

Carson, E. Ann, *Prisoners in 2020—Statistical Tables*, Washington, D.C.: Bureau of Justice Statistics, December 2021.

Carson, E. Ann, and William J. Sabol, *Prisoners in 2011*, Washington, D.C.: Bureau of Justice Statistics, December 2012.

Chalfin, Aaron, and Justin McCrary, "Criminal Deterrence: A Review of the Literature," *Journal of Economic Literature*, Vol. 55, No. 1, March 2017, pp. 5–48.

Chang, Hsien-Yen, Tatyana Lyapustina, Lainie Rutkow, Matthew Daubresse, Matt Richey, Mark Faul, Elizabeth A. Stuart, and G. Caleb Alexander, "Impact of Prescription Drug Monitoring Programs and Pill Mill Laws on High-Risk Opioid Prescribers: A Comparative Interrupted Time Series Analysis," *Drug and Alcohol Dependence*, Vol. 165, 2016.

Chang, Hsien-Yen, Irene Murimi, Mark Faul, Lainie Rutkow, and G. Caleb Alexander, "Impact of Florida's Prescription Drug Monitoring Program and Pill Mill Law on High-Risk Patients: A Comparative Interrupted Time Series Analysis," *Pharmacoepidemiology and Drug Safety*, Vol. 27, 2018, pp. 422–429.

Charlier, Jac, and Jessica Reichert, "Introduction: Deflection—Police-Led Responses to Behavioral Health Challenges," *Journal for Advancing Justice*, Vol. 3, 2020, pp. 1–13.

Christopher, Paul P., Debra A. Pinals, Taylor Stayton, Kellie Sanders, and Lester Blumberg, "Nature and Utilization of Civil Commitment for Substance Abuse in the United States," *Journal of the American Academy of Psychiatry and the Law Online*, Vol. 43, No. 3, 2015, pp. 313–320.

City of Cuyahoga Falls, "Quick Response Team," webpage, undated. As of June 21, 2022: https://www.cityofcf.com/services/quick-response-team

Clean Slate Utah, "About," webpage, undated. As of June 21, 2022: https://www.cleanslateutah.org/about

Clifasefi, Seema L., Heather S. Lonczak, and Susan E. Collins, "Seattle's Law Enforcement Assisted Diversion (LEAD) Program: Within-Subjects Changes on Housing, Employment, and Income/Benefits Outcomes and Associations with Recidivism," *Crime & Delinquency*, Vol. 63, No. 4, 2017, pp. 429–445.

Collins, Susan E., Heather S. Lonczak, and Seema L. Clifasefi, "Seattle's Law Enforcement Assisted Diversion (LEAD): Program Effects on Recidivism Outcomes," *Evaluation and Program Planning*, Vol. 64, 2017, pp. 49–56.

Collins, Susan E., Heather S. Lonczak, and Seema L. Clifasefi, "Seattle's Law Enforcement Assisted Diversion (LEAD): Program Effects on Criminal Justice and Legal System Utilization and Costs," *Journal of Experimental Criminology*, Vol. 15, 2019, pp. 201–211.

Congressional Research Service, *Heroin Trafficking in the United States*, Washington, D.C., 2019.

Crombie, Noelle, "Police Issue Few Tickets Under New Drug Decriminalization Law; Most People Ignore Court, Hotline," *The Oregonian*, last updated October 29, 2021.

Crowley, Daniel Max, Christian M. Connell, Damon Jones, and Michael W. Donovan, "Considering the Child Welfare System Burden from Opioid Misuse: Research Priorities for Estimating Public Costs. *American Journal of Managed Care*, Vol. 25, Suppl. 13, 2019, pp. S256–S263.

Curtis, Marah A., Sarah Garlington, and Lisa S. Schottenfeld, "Alcohol, Drug, and Criminal History Restrictions in Public Housing," *Cityscape*, Vol. 15, No. 3, 2013, pp. 37–52.

D'Ambrosio, Amanda, "CDC Nixes Misleading Video About Cops' Risk of Fentanyl Overdose," MedPage Today, July 14, 2022.

Davidson, Peter J., Barrot H. Lambdin, Erica N. Browne, Lynn D. Wenger, and Alex H. Kral, "Impact of an Unsanctioned Safe Consumption Site on Criminal Activity, 2010–2019," *Drug and Alcohol Dependence*, Vol. 220, March 2021, pp. 1–6.

Davis, Angela J., "The Progressive Prosecutor: An Imperative for Criminal Justice Reform," *Fordham Law Review Online*, Vol. 87, No. 3, 2018–2019, pp. 8–12.

DEA—*See* Drug Enforcement Administration.

DeMio, Terry, "More Victims of ODs: First Responders Suffer Compassion Fatigue," *Cincinnati Enquirer*, May 31, 2017.

Devers, Lindsey, *Plea and Charge Bargaining: Research Summary*, Washington, D.C.: Bureau of Justice Assistance, 2011.

Drug Enforcement Administration, "Divisions," webpage, undated-a. As of September 9, 2021:
https://www.dea.gov/divisions

Drug Enforcement Administration, "Domestic Arrests," webpage, undated-b. As of September 2, 2022:
https://www.dea.gov/data-and-statistics/domestic-arrests

Drug Enforcement Administration, "Operation Engage," webpage, undated-c. As of September 9, 2021:
https://www.dea.gov/divisions/360-strategy

Drug Policy Alliance, *Drug Courts Are Not the Answer: Toward a Health-Centered Approach to Drug Use*, Washington, D.C., 2011.

Edmonson, Amy C., "Speaking Up in the Operating Room: How Team Leaders Promote Learning in Interdisciplinary Action Teams," *Journal of Management Studies*, Vol. 40, No. 6, 2003, pp. 1419–1452.

European Monitoring Centre for Drugs and Drug Addiction, *Drug Policy Profiles: Portugal*, Luxembourg: Publications Office of the European Union, 2011.

Farabee, David, Michael Prendergast, and M. Douglas Anglin, "The Effectiveness of Coerced Treatment for Drug-Abusing Offenders," *Federal Probation*, Vol. 62, No. 1, 1998, pp. 3–10.

Federal Bureau of Investigation, "Crime in the United States 2019: Table 43—Arrests by Race and Ethnicity, 2019," webpage, undated. As of November 15, 2021:
https://ucr.fbi.gov/crime-in-the-u.s/2019/crime-in-the-u.s.-2019/tables/table-43

Feucht, Thomas E., and Joseph Gfroerer, *Mental and Substance Use Disorders Among Adult Men on Probation or Parole: Some Success Against a Persistent Challenge*, Rockville, Md.: Substance Abuse and Mental Health Services Administration, 2011.

Goulka, Jeremiah, Valena Elizabeth Beety, Alex Kreit, Anne Boustead, Justine Newman, and Leo Beletsky, *Drug-Induced Homicide Defense Toolkit (2021 edition)*, Ohio State Public Law Working Paper No. 467, 2021.

Green, Emily, "Few Obtain Treatment in First Year of Oregon Drug-Decriminalization Grants," OPB, February 14, 2022.

Grucza, Richard A., Mike Vuolo, Melissa J. Krauss, Andrew D. Plunk, Arpana Agrawal, Frank J. Chaloupka, and Laura J. Bierut, "Cannabis Decriminalization: A Study of Recent Policy Change in Five U.S. States," *International Journal of Drug Policy*, Vol. 59, September 2018, pp. 67–75.

Gryczynski, Jan, Timothy W. Kinlock, Sharon M. Kelly, Kevin E. O'Grady, Michael S. Gordon, and Robert P. Schwartz, "Opioid Agonist Maintenance for Probationers: Patient-Level Predictors of Treatment Retention, Drug Use, Crime," *Substance Abuse*, Vol. 33, No. 1, 2012, pp. 30–39.

Haffajee, Rebecca, Beau Kilmer, and Eric Helland, "Government Opioid Litigation: The Extent of Liability," *DePaul Law Review*, Vol. 70, No. 2, 2022, pp. 275–320.

Haffajee, Rebecca, and Bradley Stein, "Spending the Opioid Settlement Most Effectively," *Pittsburgh Post-Gazette*, December 19, 2019.

Hancock, Jay, "HHS Acts to Help More Ex-Inmates Get Medicaid," KHN news release, April 29, 2016. As of September 9, 2021:
https://khn.org/news/hhs-acts-to-help-more-ex-inmates-get-medicaid/

Heaps, Melody M., Arthur J. Lurigio, Pamela Rodriguez, Thomas Lyons, and Laura Brookes, "Recovery-Oriented Care for Drug-Abusing Offenders," *Addiction Science and Clinical Practice*, Vol. 5, No. 1, 2009, pp. 31–36.

Hicks, William D., Jefferson E. Holcomb, Melissa A. Alexander, and Tammatha A. Clodfelter, "Drug Testing and Community Supervision Outcomes," *Criminal Justice and Behavior*, Vol. 47, No. 4, 2020, pp. 419–436.

Horton, Meredith, Rebecca McDonald, Traci C. Green, Suzanne Nielsen, John Strang, Louisa Degenhardt, and Sarah Larney, "A Mapping Review of Take-Home Naloxone for People Released from Correctional Settings," *International Journal of Drug Policy*, Vol. 46, August 2017, pp. 7–16.

Howell, Benjamin A., Lisa Puglisi, Katie Clark, Carmen Albizu-Garcia, Evan Ashkin, Tyler Booth, Lauren Brinkley-Rubinstein, David A. Fiellin, Aaron D. Fox, Kathleen F. Maurer, et al., "The Transitions Clinic Network: Post Incarceration Addiction Treatment, Healthcare, and Social Support (TCN-PATHS): A Hybrid Type-1 Effectiveness Trial of Enhanced Primary Care to Improve Opioid Use Disorder Treatment Outcomes Following Release from Jail," *Journal of Substance Abuse Treatment*, Vol. 128, 2021.

Hughes, Caitlin Elizabeth, and Alex Stevens, "What Can We Learn from the Portuguese Decriminalization of Illicit Drugs?" *British Journal of Criminology*, Vol. 50, No. 6, 2010, pp. 999–1022.

Human Rights Watch, *No Second Chance: People with Criminal Records Denied Access to Public Housing*, 2004.

Humphreys, Keith, Chelsea L. Shover, Christina M. Andrews, Amy S. B. Bohnert, Margaret L. Brandeau, Jonathan P. Caulkins, Jonathan H. Chen, Mariano-Florentino Cuéllar, Yasmin L. Hurd, David N. Juurlink, et al., "Responding to the Opioid Crisis in North America and Beyond: Recommendations of the Stanford-*Lancet* Commission," *The Lancet*, Vol. 399, No. 10324, February 5, 2022, pp. 555–604.

Jalal, Hawre, Jeanine M. Buchanich, Mark S. Roberts, Lauren C. Balmert, Kun Zhang, and Donald S. Burke, "Changing Dynamics of the Drug Overdose Epidemic in the United States from 1979 Through 2016," *Science*, Vol. 361, No. 6408, 2018.

Jorgensen, Cody, and Alexis J. Harper, "Examining the Effects of Legalizing Marijuana in Colorado and Washington on Clearance Rates: A Quasi-Experimental Design," *Journal of Experimental Criminology*, Vol. 18, 2022, pp. 365–386.

Kaeble, Danielle, *Time Served in State Prison, 2016*, Washington, D.C.: Bureau of Justice Statistics, November 2018.

Kaeble, Danielle, *Probation and Parole in the United States, 2020*, Washington, D.C.: Bureau of Justice Statistics, December 2021.

Kaiser Family Foundation, "States Reporting Corrections-Related Medicaid Enrollment Policies in Place for Prisons or Jails," webpage, 2019. As of November 5, 2020:
https://www.kff.org/medicaid/state-indicator/
states-reporting-corrections-related-medicaid-enrollment-policies-in-place-for-prisons-or-jails

Kilmer, Beau, *Reducing Barriers and Getting Creative: 10 Federal Options to Increase Treatment Access for Opioid Use Disorder and Reduce Fatal Overdoses*, Washington, D.C.: Brookings Institution, June 2020.

Kilmer, Beau, and Bryce Pardo, "Addressing Federal Conflicts Over Supervised Drug Consumption Sites," *The Hill*, March 14, 2019.

Kilmer, Beau, Jonathan P. Caulkins, Robert L. DuPont, and Keith Humphreys, "Reducing Substance Use in Criminal Justice Populations," in Shannon C. Miller, David A. Fiellin, Richard N. Rosenthal, and Richard Saitz, eds., *The ASAM Principles of Addiction Medicine*, 6th ed., 2018, pp. 1768–1783.

Kilmer, Beau, Jirka Taylor, Jonathan P. Caulkins, Pam A. Mueller, Allison J. Ober, Bryce Pardo, Rosanna Smart, Lucy Strang, and Peter H. Reuter, *Considering Heroin-Assisted Treatment and Supervised Drug Consumption Sites in the United States*, Santa Monica, Calif.: RAND Corporation, RR-2693-RC, 2018. As of May 25, 2022:
https://www.rand.org/pubs/research_reports/RR2693.html

King, Gary, and Richard Nielsen, "Why Propensity Scores Should Not Be Used for Matching," *Political Analysis*, Vol. 27, No. 4, 2019, pp. 435–454.

Kleiman, Mark A. R., *When Brute Force Fails: How to Have Less Crime and Less Punishment*, Princeton, N.J.: Princeton University Press, 2009.

Koch, David W., Jaewon Lee, and Kyunghee Lee, "Coloring the War on Drugs: Arrest Disparities in Black, Brown, and White," *Race and Social Problems*, Vol. 8, No. 4, 2016, pp. 313–325.

Kral, Alex H., Barrot H. Lambdin, Lynn D. Wenger, and Pete J. Davidson, "Evaluation of an Unsanctioned Safe Consumption Site in the United States," letter to the editor, *New England Journal of Medicine*, Vol. 383, No. 6, August 6, 2020, pp. 589–590.

Kral, Alex H., Barrot H. Lambdin, Lynn D. Wenger, Erica N. Browne, Leslie W. Suen, and Peter J. Davidson, "Improved Syringe Disposal Practices Associated with Unsanctioned Safe Consumption Site Use: A Cohort Study of People Who Inject Drugs in the United States," *Drug and Alcohol Dependence*, Vol. 229, Part A, December 2021, pp. 1–6.

Labriola, Melissa M., Warren A. Reich, Robert C. Davis, Priscillia Hunt, Michael Rempel, and Samantha Cherney, *Prosecutor-Led Pretrial Diversion: Case Studies in Eleven Jurisdictions*, New York: Center for Court Innovation, April 2018. As of June 21, 2022:
https://www.rand.org/pubs/external_publications/EP67597.html

Lambdin, Barrot H., Peter J. Davidson, Erica N. Browne, Leslie W. Suen, Lynn D. Wenger, and Alex H. Kral, "Reduced Emergency Department Visits and Hospitalisation with Use of an Unsanctioned Safe Consumption Site for Injection Drug Use in the United States," *Journal of General Internal Medicine*, 2022.

Laqueur, Hannah, "Uses and Abuses of Drug Decriminalization in Portugal," *Law and Social Inquiry*, Vol. 40, No. 3, 2015, pp. 746–781.

Law Atlas, "Syringe Service Program Laws," webpage, updated August 1, 2019. As of September 9, 2021:
https://lawatlas.org/datasets/syringe-services-programs-laws

LEAD King County, homepage, undated. As of June 21, 2022:
https://leadkingcounty.org/

LEAD National Support Bureau, homepage, undated. As of September 9, 2021:
https://www.leadbureau.org/

Lehman, Wayne E. K., Bennett W. Fletcher, Harry K. Wexler, and Gerald Melnick, "Organizational Factors and Collaboration and Integration Activities in Criminal Justice and Drug Abuse Treatment Agencies," *Drug and Alcohol Dependence*, Vol. 103, Suppl. 1, 2009, pp. S65–S72.

Lelling, Andrew, "Safe Injection Sites Aren't Safe or Legal," *Boston Globe*, January 28, 2019.

Levin, Marc, and Michael Haugen, *Open Roads and Overflowing Jails: Addressing High Rates of Rural Pretrial Incarceration*, Right on Crime and Texas Public Policy Foundation, 2018.

Light, Michael T., "The Declining Significance of Race in Criminal Sentencing: Evidence from U.S. Federal Courts," *Social Forces*, Vol. 100, No. 3, March 2022, pp. 1110–1141.

Lindquist-Grantz, Robin, Peter Mallow, Leah Dean, Michelle Lydenberg, and Jennifer Chubinski, "Diversion Programs for Individuals Who Use Substances: A Review of the Literature," *Journal of Drug Issues*, Vol. 51, No. 3, July 2021, pp. 483–503.

Lopez, German, "Top Executives at Major Opioid Company Found Guilty of Criminal Racketeering," *Vox*, May 3, 2019. As of July 10, 2022:
https://www.vox.com/policy-and-politics/2019/5/3/18528123/
insys-fentanyl-trial-verdict-john-kapoor-opioid-epidemic

Lovenheim, Michael F., and Emily G. Owens, "Does Federal Financial Aid Affect College Enrollment? Evidence from Drug Offenders and the Higher Education Act of 1998," *Journal of Urban Economics*, Vol. 81, May 2014, pp. 1–13.

Lucas County Sheriff's Office, homepage, undated. As of June 21 2022:
https://lucascountysheriff.org/

Makin, David A., Dale W. Willits, Guangzhen Wu, Kathryn O. DuBois, Ruibin Lu, Mary K. Stohr, Wendy Koslicki, Duane Stanton, Craig Hemmens, John Snyder, and Nicholas P. Lovrich, "Marijuana Legalization and Crime Clearance Rates: Testing Proponent Assertions in Colorado and Washington State," *Police Quarterly*, Vol. 22, No. 1, March 2019, pp. 31–55.

Malm, Aili, Dina Perrone, and Erica Magaña, *Law Enforcement Assisted Diversion (LEAD) External Evaluation: Report to the California State Legislature*, Long Beach, Calif.: California State University Long Beach, 2020.

Mann, Brian, "State Attorneys General Reach a $26 Billion National Opioid Settlement," NPR, updated July 21, 2021.

Mann, Brian, and Martha Bebinger, "Purdue Pharma, Sacklers Reach $6 Billion Deal with State Attorneys General," NPR, March 3, 2022.

Martin, Brittany T., and Sarah K. S. Shannon, "State Variation in the Drug Felony Lifetime Ban on Temporary Assistance for Needy Families: Why the Modified Ban Matters," *Punishment & Society*, Vol. 22, No. 4, 2020, pp. 439–460.

Maruschak, Laura M., Jennifer Bronson, and Mariel Alper, *Alcohol and Drug Use and Treatment Reported by Prisoners: Survey of Prison Inmates, 2016*, Washington, D.C.: Bureau of Justice Statistics, July 2021.

Massoglia, Michael, Glenn Firebaugh, and Cody Warner, "Racial Variation in the Effect of Incarceration on Neighborhood Attainment," *American Sociological Review*, Vol. 78, No. 1, 2013, pp. 142–165.

Mauer, Marc, and Virginia McCalmont, *A Lifetime of Punishment: The Impact of the Felony Drug Ban on Welfare Benefits*, Washington, D.C.: The Sentencing Project, November 14, 2013.

Mazerolle, Lorraine G., Justin Ready, William Terrill, and Elin Waring, "Problem-Oriented Policing in Public Housing: The Jersey City Evaluation," *Justice Quarterly*, Vol. 17, No. 1, 2000, pp. 129–158.

McCarty, Maggie, Gene Falk, Randy A. Aussenberg, and David H. Carpenter, *Drug Testing and Crime-Related Restrictions in TANF, SNAP, and Housing Assistance*, Washington, D.C.: Congressional Research Service, 2012.

McClellan, Chandler, Barrot H. Lambdin, Mir M. Ali, Ryan Mutter, Corey S. Davis, Eliza Wheeler, Michael Pemberton, and Alex H. Kral, "Opioid-Overdose Laws Association with Opioid Use and Overdose Mortality," *Addictive Behaviors*, Vol. 86, 2018, pp. 90–95.

McSweeney, Tim, Alex Stevens, Neil Hunt, and Paul J. Turnbull, "Twisting Arms or a Helping Hand? Assessing the Impact of 'Coerced' and Comparable 'Voluntary' Drug Treatment Options," *British Journal of Criminology*, Vol. 47, No. 3, 2007, pp. 470–490.

Medicaid and CHIP Payment and Access Commission, *Medicaid and the Criminal Justice System*, Washington, D.C., July 2018.

Medicaid.gov, "Medicaid," webpage, undated. As of November 15, 2021: https://www.medicaid.gov/medicaid/index.html

Midgette, Greg, and Peter Reuter, "Has Cannabis Use Among Youth Increased After Changes in Its Legal Status? A Commentary on Use of Monitoring the Future for Analyses of Changes in State Cannabis Laws," *Prevention Science*, Vol. 21, 2020, pp. 137–145.

Miech, Richard A., Lloyd Johnston, Patrick M. O'Malley, Jerald G. Bachman, John Schulenberg, and Megan E. Patrick, "Trends in Use of Marijuana and Attitudes Toward Marijuana Among Youth Before and After Decriminalization: The Case of California 2007–2013," *International Journal of Drug Policy*, Vol. 26, No. 4, April 2015, pp. 336–344.

Minton, Todd D., Lauren G. Beatty, and Zhen Zeng, *Correctional Populations in the United States, 2019–Statistical Tables*, Washington, D.C.: U.S. Department of Justice, Office of Justice Programs, July 2021.

Mitchell, Ojmarrh, and Michael S. Caudy, "Examining Racial Disparities in Drug Arrests," *Justice Quarterly*, Vol. 32, 2015, pp. 288–313.

Mitchell, Ojmarrh, David B. Wilson, Amy Eggers, and Doris L. MacKenzie, "Assessing the Effectiveness of Drug Courts on Recidivism: A meta-Analytic Review of Traditional and Non-Traditional Drug Courts," *Journal of Criminal Justice*, Vol. 40, No. 1, 2012, pp. 60–71.

Moore, Kelly E., Walter Roberts, Holly H. Reid, Kathryn M. Z. Smith, Lindsay M. S. Oberleitner, and Sherry A. McKee, "Effectiveness of Medication Assisted Treatment for Opioid Use in Prison and Jail Settings: A Meta-Analysis and Systematic Review," *Journal of Substance Abuse Treatment*, Vol. 99, 2019, pp. 32–43.

National Academies of Sciences, Engineering, and Medicine, *The Health Effects of Cannabis and Cannabinoids: The Current State of Evidence and Recommendations for Research*, Washington, D.C.: The National Academies Press, 2017.

National Association of State Alcohol and Drug Abuse Directors, Inc., *Methadone Maintenance Treatment and the Criminal Justice System*, Washington, D.C., 2006.

National Conference of State Legislatures, "Drug Overdose Immunity and Good Samaritan Laws," webpage, June 5, 2017. As of November 15, 2021: https://www.ncsl.org/research/civil-and-criminal-justice/drug-overdose-immunity-good-samaritan-laws.aspx

National Drug Intelligence Center, *The Economic Impact of Illicit Drug Use on American Society*, Washington, D.C.: U.S. Department of Justice, April 2011.

National Research Council, *The Growth of Incarceration in the United States: Exploring Causes and Consequences*, Washington, D.C.: The National Academies Press, 2014.

Neale, Joanne, and John Strang, "Naloxone—Does Over-Antagonism Matter? Evidence of Iatrogenic Harm After Emergency Treatment of Heroin/Opioid Overdose," *Addiction*, Vol. 110, No. 10, October 2015, pp. 1644–1652.

New York State Senate, Senate Bill S1795, An Act to Amend the Correction Law, in Relation to the Establishment of a Program for the Use of Medication Assisted Treatment for Inmates; and to Amend the Mental Hygiene Law, in Relation to the Implementation of Substance Use Disorder Treatment and Transition Services in Jails, 2021.

Nicosia, Nancy, Rosalie Liccardo Pacula, Beau Kilmer, Russell Lundberg, and James Chiesa, *The Economic Cost of Methamphetamine Use in the United States, 2005*, Santa Monica, Calif.: RAND Corporation, MG-829-MPF/NIDA, 2009. As of May 25, 2022: https://www.rand.org/pubs/monographs/MG829.html

NORC at the University of Chicago and Center for Health and Justice at Treatment Alternatives for Safe Communities, *Report of the National Survey to Assess First Responder Deflection Programs in Response to the Opioid Crisis: Final Report*, Chicago, Ill., May 13, 2021.

Nordstrom, Benjamin R., and Douglas B. Marlowe, *Medication-Assisted Treatment for Opioid Use Disorders in Drug Courts*, Washington, D.C.: National Drug Court Institute, Drug Court Practitioner Fact Sheet, August 2016.

Nugent, Shannon M., Benjamin J. Morasco, Maya E. O'Neil, Michele Freeman, Allison Low, Karli Kondo, Camille Elven, Bernadette Zakher, Makalapua Motu'apuaka, Robin Paynter, and Devan Kansagara, "The Effects of Cannabis Among Adults with Chronic Pain and an Overview of General Harms: A Systematic Review," *Annals of Internal Medicine*, Vol. 167, No. 5, September 2017, pp. 319–331.

Nunn, Amy, Nickolas Zaller, Samuel Dickman, Catherine Trimbur, Ank Nijhawan, and Josiah D. Rich, "Methadone and Buprenorphine Prescribing and Referral Practices in US Prison Systems: Results from a Nationwide Survey," *Drug and Alcohol Dependence*, Vol. 105, No. 1–2, 2009, pp. 83–88.

Nutt, David J., Leslie A. King, and Lawrence D. Phillips, "Drug Harms in the UK: A Multicriteria Decision Analysis," *The Lancet*, Vol. 376, No. 9752, November 6, 2010, pp. 1558–1565.

Oregon Health Authority, "Drug Addiction Treatment and Recovery Act (Measure 110)," news release, June 9, 2022. As of June 21, 2022: https://www.oregon.gov/oha/hsd/amh/pages/measure110.aspx

Pacula, Rosalie Liccardo, Jamie F. Chriqui, and Joanna King, *Marijuana Decriminalization: What Does It Mean in the United States?* Washington, D.C.: National Bureau of Economic Research, Working Paper 96990, 2003.

Pacula, Rosalie Liccardo, Russell Lundberg, Jonathan P. Caulkins, Beau Kilmer, Sarah Greathouse, Terry Fain, and Paul Steinberg, *Improving the Measurement of Drug-Related Crime*, Washington, D.C.: Office of National Drug Control Policy, 2013.

Pardo, Bryce, Lois M. Davis, and Melinda Moore, *Characterization of the Synthetic Opioid Threat Profile to Inform Inspection and Detection Solutions*, Homeland Security Operational Analysis Center operated by the RAND Corporation, RR-2969-DHS, 2019a. As of May 25, 2022: https://www.rand.org/pubs/research_reports/RR2969.html

Pardo, Bryce, Jirka Taylor, Jonathan P. Caulkins, Beau Kilmer, Peter Reuter, and Bradley D. Stein, *The Future of Fentanyl and Other Synthetic Opioids*, Santa Monica, Calif.: RAND Corporation, RR-3117-RC, 2019b. As of May 25, 2022: https://www.rand.org/pubs/research_reports/RR3117.html

Parmar, Mahesh K. B., John Strang, Louise Choo, Angela M. Meade, and Sheila M. Bird, "Randomized Controlled Pilot Trial of Naloxone-on-Release to Prevent Post-Prison Opioid Overdose Deaths," *Addiction*, Vol. 112, No. 3, 2017, pp. 502–515.

Paybarah, Azi, "About 160,000 People in New York to See Their Marijuana Convictions Disappear," *New York Times*, updated August 29, 2019.

Peikes, Deborah N., Lorenzo Moreno, and Sean Michael Orzol, "Propensity Score Matching: A Note of Caution for Evaluators of Social Programs," *American Statistician*, Vol. 62, No. 3, 2008, pp. 222–231.

Pew Charitable Trusts, *How and When Medicaid Covers People Under Correctional Supervision*, Philadelphia, Pa., Issue Brief, 2016.

Pew Charitable Trusts, *Opioid Use Disorder Treatment in Jails and Prisons*, Philadelphia, Pa., Issue Brief, April 2020.

Plunk, Andrew D., Stephanie L. Peglow, Paul T. Harrell, and Richard A. Grucza, "Youth and Adult Arrests for Cannabis Possession After Decriminalization and Legalization of Cannabis," *JAMA Pediatrics*, Vol. 173, No. 8, June 17, 2019, pp. 763–769.

Police Assisted Addiction and Recovery Initiative, "About Us," webpage, undated. As of September 9, 2021: https://paariusa.org/

Polkey, Chesterfield, "Most States Have Ended SNAP Ban for Convicted Drug Felons," National Conference of State Legislatures blog, 2019. As of September 9, 2021: https://www.ncsl.org/blog/2019/07/30/most-states-have-ended-snap-ban-for-convicted-drug-felons.aspx

Public Law 91-513, Controlled Substances Act, 1971.

Rafful, Claudia, Ricardo Orozco, Gudelia Rangel, Peter Davidson, Dan Werb, Leo Beletsky, and Steffanie A. Strathdee, "Increased Non-Fatal Overdose Risk Associated with Involuntary Drug Treatment in a Longitudinal Study with People Who Inject Drugs," *Addiction*, Vol. 113, No. 6, June 2018, pp. 1056–1063.

Rees, Daniel I., Joseph J. Sabia, Laura M. Argys, Dhaval Dave, and Joshua Latshaw, "With a Little Help from My Friends: The Effects of Good Samaritan and Naloxone Access Laws on Opioid-Related Deaths," *Journal of Law and Economics*, Vol. 62, No. 1, 2019.

Reichert, Jessica, and Lily Gleicher, "Probation Clients' Barriers to Access and Use of Opioid Use Disorder Medications," *Health and Justice*, Vol. 7, No. 10, 2019.

Richter, Ed, "Middletown Councilman Drops Controversial '3-Strike' Narcan Proposal," *Journal-News*, July 19, 2017.

Rodriguez, Nancy, and Vincent J. Webb, "Probation Violations, Revocations, and Imprisonment: The Decisions of Probation Officers, Prosecutors, and Judges Pre- and Post-Mandatory Drug Treatment," *Criminal Justice Policy Review*, Vol. 18, No. 1, 2007, pp. 3–30.

Roman, John, "Cost-Benefit Analysis of Criminal Justice Reforms," *NIJ Journal*, Vol. 272, 2013, pp. 31–38.

Rosenstein, Rod J., "Fight Drug Abuse, Don't Subsidize It," *New York Times*, August 27, 2018.

Rydberg, Jason, and Elias Nader, "Halfway Houses and House Arrest," in O. Hayden Griffin and Vanessa H. Woodward, *Routledge Handbook of Corrections in the United States*, 2017.

Sabol, William J., Thaddeus L. Johnson, and Alexander Caccavale, *Trends in Correctional Control by Race and Sex*, Washington, D.C.: Council on Criminal Justice, December 2019.

SAMHSA—*See* Substance Abuse and Mental Health Services Administration.

Schuler, Megan S., Sara E. Heins, Rosanna Smart, Beth Ann Griffin, David Powell, Elizabeth A. Stuart, Bryce Pardo, Sierra Smucker, Stephen W. Patrick, Rosalie Liccardo Pacula, and Bradley D. Stein, "The State of the Science in Opioid Policy Research," *Drug and Alcohol Dependence*, Vol. 214, 2020.

Seddon, Toby, "Coerced Drug Treatment in the Criminal Justice System: Conceptual, Ethical and Criminological Issues," *Criminology & Criminal Justice*, Vol. 7, No. 3, 2007, pp. 269–286.

Seiter, Richard P., and Karen R. Kadela, "Prisoner Reentry: What Works, What Does Not, and What Is Promising," *Crime and Delinquency*, Vol. 49, No. 3, 2003, pp. 360–388.

The Sentencing Project, *Trends in U.S. Corrections*, Washington, D.C., 2021.

Sevigny, Eric L., Brian K. Fuleihan, and Frank Valentino Ferdik, "Do Drug Courts Reduce the Use of Incarceration? A Meta-Analysis," *Journal of Criminal Justice*, Vol. 41, No. 6, 2013, pp. 416–425.

Sevigny Eric L., Harold A. Pollack, and Peter Reuter, "Can Drug Courts Help to Reduce Prison and Jail Populations?" *Annals of the American Academy of Political and Social Science*, Vol. 647, No. 1, 2013, pp. 190–212.

Shavit, Shira, Jenerius A. Aminawung, Nathan Birnbaum, Scott Greenberg, Timothy Berthold, Amie Fishman, Susan H. Busch, and Emily A. Wang, "Transitions Clinic Network: Challenges and Lessons in Primary Care for People Released from Prison," *Health Affairs*, Vol. 36, No. 6, 2017, pp. 1006–1015.

Siegel, Zachary, "What's Really Going On in Those Police Fentanyl Exposure Videos?" *New York Times Magazine*, July 13, 2022.

Silva, Lahny R., "Collateral Damage: A Public Housing Consequence of the 'War on Drugs,'" *University of California Irvine Law Review*, Vol. 5, No. 4, 2015.

Smart, Rosanna, and Rosalie Liccardo Pacula, "Early Evidence of the Impact of Cannabis Legalization on Cannabis Use, Cannabis Use Disorder, and the Use of Other Substances: Findings from State Policy Evaluations," *American Journal of Drug and Alcohol Abuse*, Vol. 45, No. 6, 2019, pp. 644–663.

Smith, Jeffrey A., and Petra E. Todd, "Reconciling Conflicting Evidence on the Performance of Propensity-Score Matching Methods," *American Economic Review*, Vol. 91, No. 2, 2001, pp. 112–118.

Stevens, Alex [@AlexStevensKent], "I have asked question 3 to members of several CDTs. Answer: no punishment for not entering treatment," Twitter post, June 15, 2022. As of July 25, 2022:
https://twitter.com/AlexStevensKent/status/1537119923348054017

Substance Abuse and Mental Health Services Administration, *SAMHSA Technical Assistance Package ATR3: Collaborating with the Criminal Justice System*, Rockville, Md., undated.

Substance Abuse and Mental Health Services Administration, *Treatment Episode Data Set (TEDS) 2000–2010: National Admissions to Substance Abuse Treatment Services*, Rockville, Md., 2014.

Substance Abuse and Mental Health Services Administration, *Treatment Episode Data Set (TEDS) 2017: Admissions to and Discharges from Publicly-Funded Substance Use Treatment*, Rockville, Md., 2019.

Suen, Leslie W., Peter J. Davidson, Erica N. Browne, Barrot H. Lambdin, Lynn D. Wenger, and Alex H. Kral, "Effect of an Unsanctioned Safe Consumption Site in the United States on Syringe Sharing, Rushed Injections, and Isolated Injection Drug Use: A Longitudinal Cohort Analysis," *Journal of Acquired Immune Deficiency Syndrome*, Vol. 89, No. 2, February 2022, pp. 172–177.

Sugarman, Olivia K., Marcus A. Bachhuber, Ashley Wennerstrom, Todd Bruno, and Benjamin F. Springgate, "Interventions for Incarcerated Adults with Opioid Use Disorder in the United States: A Systematic Review with a Focus on Social Determinants of Health," *PLoS One*, Vol. 15, No. 1, 2020, pp. 1–14.

Tabashneck, Stephanie, "Family Drug Courts: Combatting the Opioid Epidemic," *Family Law Quarterly*, Vol. 52, No. 1, 2018, pp. 183–202.

Tallan, Katherine, and Kelly Officer, "Drug Possession Decriminalization and Ballot Measure 110," presentation, Oregon Criminal Justice Commission, November 5, 2021.

Thompson, Darrel, and Ashley Burnside, *No More Double Punishments: Lifting the Ban on SNAP and TANF for People with Prior Felony Drug Convictions*, Washington, D.C.: Center for Law and Social Policy, updated March 2019.

Tuttle, Cody, "Snapping Back: Food Stamp Bans and Criminal Recidivism," *American Economic Journal: Economic Policy*, Vol. 11, No. 2, 2019, pp. 301–327.

Unified Judicial System of Pennsylvania, "Clean Slate, Expungement and Limited Access," webpage, undated. As of June 21, 2022: https://www.pacourts.us/learn/learn-about-the-judicial-system/clean-slate-expungement-and-limited-access

United States v. Safehouse, No. 20-1422, 3d Cir. 2021.

U.S. Attorney's Office, District of Massachusetts, "Founder and Four Executives of Insys Therapeutics Convicted of Racketeering Conspiracy," press release, U.S. Department of Justice, May 2, 2019.

U.S. Attorney's Office, District of Vermont, "Statement of the U.S. Attorney's Office Concerning Proposed Injection Sites," December 13, 2017.

VanderHart, Dirk, "Oregon's Pioneering Drug Law Raises More Questions Than Answers in Early Months," OPB, October 27, 2021.

Vera Institute of Justice, *Overdose Deaths and Jail Incarceration: National Trends and Racial Disparities*, Brooklyn, N.Y., 2018.

Vestal, Christine, *New Momentum for Addiction Treatment Behind Bars*, Philadelphia, Pa.: Pew Charitable Trusts, April 4, 2018.

Wang, Emily A., Clemens S. Hong, Shira Shavit, Ronald Sanders, Eric Kessell, and Margot B. Kushel, "Engaging Individuals Recently Released from Prison into Primary Care: A Randomized Trial," *American Journal of Public Health*, Vol. 102, No. 9, 2012, pp. e22–e29.

Wang, Emily A., Hsiu-Jin Lin, Jenerius A. Aminawung, Susan H. Busch, Colleen Gallagher, Kathleen Maurer, Lisa Puglisi, Shira Shavit, and Linda Frisman, "Propensity-Matched Study of Enhanced Primary Care on Contact with the Criminal Justice System Among Individuals Recently Released from Prison to New Haven," *BMJ Open*, Vol. 9, No. 5, 2019.

Welsh, Wayne N., Hannah K. Knudsen, Kevin Knight, Lori Ducharme, Jennifer Pankow, Terry Urbine, Adrienne Lindsey, Sami Abdel-Salam, Jennifer Wood, Laura Monico, et al., "Effects of an Organizational Linkage Intervention on Inter-Organizational Service Coordination Between Probation/Parole Agencies and Community Treatment Providers," *Administration and Policy in Mental Health and Mental Health Services Research*, Vol. 43, 2016, pp. 105–121.

Werb, D., A. Kamarulzaman, M. C. Meacham, C. Rafful, B. Fischer, and S. A. Strathdee, "The Effectiveness of Compulsory Drug Treatment: A Systematic Review," *International Journal of Drug Policy*, Vol. 28, February 2016, pp. 1–9.

Winetsky, Daniel, Aaron Fox, Ank Nijhawan, and Josiah D. Rich, "Treating Opioid Use Disorder and Related Infectious Diseases in the Criminal Justice System," *Infectious Disease Clinics of North America*, Vol. 34, No. 3, September 2020, pp. 585–603.

Wong, Jennifer S., Jessica Bouchard, Kelsey Gushue, and Chelsey Lee, "Halfway Out: An Examination of the Effects of Halfway Houses on Criminal Recidivism," *International Journal of Offender Therapy and Comparative Criminology*, Vol. 63, No. 7, 2019, pp. 1018–1037.

Worden, Robert E., and Sarah J. McLean, "Discretion and Diversion in Albany's Lead Program," *Criminal Justice Policy Review*, Vol. 29, No. 6-7, 2018, pp. 584–610.

Zeng, Zhen, *Jail Inmates in 2018*, Washington, D.C.: U.S. Department of Justice, Office of Justice Programs, Bureau of Justice Statistics, March 2020.

Zucker, Howard, Anthony J. Annucci, Sharon Stancliff, and Holly Catania, "Overdose Prevention for Prisoners in New York: A Novel Program and Collaboration," *Harm Reduction Journal*, Vol. 12, No. 51, 2015.

CHAPTER SEVEN

Illegal Supply and Supply Control

Bryce Pardo, Beau Kilmer, and Jirka Taylor

Overview

Some of the material in this chapter was previously published in Pardo et al., 2019.

There are multiple entities that are involved in the illegal supply of opioids, ranging from multinational drug trafficking organizations to unscrupulous pain management clinics to patients who decide to give or sell their prescription opioids to others. Illegally produced synthetic opioids, such as fentanyl, most of which are manufactured outside the United States and are not of pharmaceutical origin, have diffused across illicit drug markets and, in some places, to dominate. The production of counterfeit prescription pills—some of which include illegally produced fentanyl—also poses a major risk.[1]

The shift to illegally produced synthetic opioids not only makes the use of illegally sourced opioids much more deadly, but their high potency and low production costs, which attract dealers, pose major challenges to supply reduction efforts. Although it is difficult to know how much illegally produced fentanyl is consumed in the United States, the amount is likely very small compared with most other drugs (in terms of pure weight, likely in the single-digit metric tons as of 2021).

There are also multiple entities that are involved in attempting to control the supply of opioids. For drugs that are legally produced by pharmaceutical companies, the Drug Enforcement Administration (DEA) and the Food and Drug Administration (FDA) regulate production and wholesale distribution. Medical officials ultimately determine who can get a prescription for these drugs, and most of these prescribers and dispensers act in good faith. The U.S. Department of Justice, state and local criminal justice agencies, and medical boards are often involved in addressing those prescribers who are breaking the law (e.g., knowingly overprescribing, engaging in payback schemes). Local law enforcement agencies typically take the lead in reducing the diversion of prescription pills that are being illegally distributed in street markets.

For illegally produced opioids like heroin and fentanyl, law enforcement agencies, the U.S. Postal Service, and some defense agencies are involved in trying to reduce supply and ultimately increase prices of these drugs at the retail level. But supply control efforts for synthetic opioids can

---

[1] The remainder of this chapter will refer to fentanyl and other synthetic opioids as *fentanyl*.

also involve negotiating with other countries to get those countries to better monitor or reduce the production and trafficking of these drugs and their precursors.

The efficacy of supply control depends on one's goals. Prohibition and a base level of enforcement surely increase retail prices. By the time a kilo of heroin leaves Mexico and ends up in New York City, the price jumps from roughly $20,000 to $50,000. (If one were to ship that same kilo via FedEx, it would cost closer to $100 to transport.) But once a retail market is established, increasing enforcement (in terms of arrests or prison sentences) yields diminishing returns and is not expected to make much of a difference in the price. At best, there might be temporary disruption, but it usually does not take long for established markets to adapt.

However, supply control can also be used to help reduce the harm surrounding drug markets (e.g., targeting the most-violent suppliers, trying to address open-air drug markets and the instability they cause by moving dealers indoors or toward delivery). Focused deterrence strategies have had some success in reducing overt retail markets, and some people have suggested using this approach to address harms caused by higher-level traffickers.

Key Interactions with Other Components of the Ecosystem

Illegal supply of opioids is closely linked with the **criminal legal system**. This is by design: Unlawful production and distribution of opioids are criminal offenses, often triggering law enforcement actions resulting in arrest, conviction, and incarceration. Individuals experiencing opioid use disorder (OUD) sometimes trade down to illegal opioids, including heroin and fentanyl, which can be cheaper than prescription opioids. Distribution of illegal drugs not only supplies chemicals that can harm health; it also spawns disorder, corruption, and considerable amounts of violence. Violence is associated with street-level markets and higher-level transactions in the United States, as well as in source and transshipment countries.

Sometimes prescription opioids are stolen from pharmacies or distribution trucks are hijacked, but the vast majority of diversion of prescription medication occurs after a licensed provider has written a prescription and that prescription is filled at a pharmacy. Hence, the multiple parts of the **medical care system** that deal with pain management are inextricably bound up in the supply of diverted opioids, including those that are then resold in illegal markets. Opioids are also used to treat OUD, which leads to some diversion, but not as much as from pain management. To reduce opportunities for diversion, the medical system has historically used the prescription system, which separates the prescriber from the dispenser. The DEA tracks the distribution of prescription opioids, and many states use triplicate prescription forms or tamper-resistant security prescription forms to prevent diversion of prescriptions to illegal markets. In the context of the opioid crisis, many jurisdictions in the United States have adopted additional policy responses to enhance how the prescription system guards against diversion or oversupply (e.g., prescription drug monitoring programs [PDMPs] and efforts to regulate pain clinics). The specific nature of access to prescription opioids means that some patients sometimes seek out additional medication (e.g., doctor shopping) and divert some share to the illegal market or to others. Even though some individuals who use heroin also sell small amounts to pay for their use, their dealing is limited by the quantities they can buy. Prior to the stricter monitoring and oversight of pain clinics, patients receiving prescriptions had much greater access to opioids.

These policies appear to have reduced some of the misuse and diversion of prescription opioids, but there are also reports that they have created access problems for some individuals with chronic pain (see Chapter One). Some experts have noted that these supply constraints have coincided with a marked increase in heroin use and overdose, suggesting that a segment of individuals with OUD switched to heroin after finding it difficult or more expensive to obtain prescription opioids. There is an issue of stocks and flows that must be considered: Any effort to reduce the diversion of prescription opioids must involve consideration of the possible effects of nudging the market toward more-harmful illegal alternatives.

The **OUD treatment system** has multiple effects on illegal supply. Effective treatment for those with OUD can reduce the demand for illegally sourced opioids, potentially affecting supplier behavior at the retail level (e.g., user-sellers might no longer need to sell). Because evidence-based treatment for OUD includes opioid agonists and partial agonists, such as methadone and buprenorphine, the OUD treatment system provides another possible avenue for diversion. However, increasing evidence suggests that individuals purchasing diverted medications for OUD (MOUD) are largely doing so for self-treatment and reduction of withdrawal, not necessarily to get intoxicated.

First responders now have more overdoses to respond to, reflecting the large expansion in the number of people with OUD and the increase in potency and unpredictability of doses and chemicals associated with the synthetic opioids that are becoming increasingly common in illegal drug markets. However, the probability that first responders are called for an illicit drug overdose can be influenced by the legal environment (e.g., the type of Good Samaritan law).

Synthetic opioid overdoses sometimes require multiple administrations of naloxone, imposing additional costs on the community-initiated intervention systems that often supply it to law enforcement and community organizations, although those costs are still small compared with the value of preventing a death.

Policy Opportunities and Considerations

Despite its large role in overdose deaths, a relatively small amount of illegally manufactured fentanyl is currently consumed in the United States. This poses massive challenges for those seeking to meaningfully reduce its supply. This does not mean that temporary disruptions in some markets are not possible, but it does raise questions about the cost-effectiveness of interventions—ranging from supply reduction to demand reduction to harm reduction—intended to reduce overdose deaths and addiction.

To reduce some of the illegal supply, criminal justice agencies would likely need to innovate, especially when it comes to fentanyl. Efforts could be made to target importers and distributors higher up the supply chain that are disproportionately contributing to overdose risk (e.g., those that mix fentanyl into non-opioids, those that handle potent analogs), who sometimes use the internet to obtain and distribute fentanyl. For example, the DEA or another federal agency could set up phony drug-selling websites the way the Dutch police did with major cryptomarket websites (Europol, 2018). Other law enforcement–operated counterfeit sites could promise—but not deliver—synthetic opioids, sending either nothing or inert powders. Even if purchasers do not face arrest, the failure of some sites to fulfill orders might stimulate general wariness of online procurement, reducing the demand for actual fentanyl sellers.

It is hard to determine how dealers would adapt to these supply-side efforts, but the fact that some of these individuals use the internet to transact sales might offer law enforcement unique opportunities. Of course, there will always be a large share of people who use opioids who are unable to obtain drugs online; thus, segments of the illegal market might rely on more-conventional means of transacting drugs.

Although reducing the illegal supply of opioids, particularly prescription opioids, is an important goal for many public safety and public health agencies, one must also consider what successful supply reduction means for other segments of the illegal market and components of the opioid ecosystem (e.g., medical care, substance use disorder treatment, harm reduction). This is especially important in the context of local efforts to disrupt the supply of opioid analgesics, which might lead some individuals to obtain opioids from the illegal market if treatment is not readily available. A fundamental matter is whether the prevention of initiation and escalation that could come from reduced illegal supply would more than offset these problems.

Emerging evidence suggests that people seeking diverted buprenorphine largely do so to manage withdrawal and for self-treatment. Many opioid compounds roughly serve as traditional substitutes in the economic sense. That is, individuals experiencing OUD and withdrawal might seek out any opioid to alleviate their suffering. This raises questions about the appropriate sanctions for illicitly possessing and distributing buprenorphine. Because buprenorphine's effect on the body plateaus at a certain point (because buprenorphine is a partial opioid agonist), the drug is much less likely than methadone to lead to overdose and other side effects, and evidence suggests that it is about as effective at treating OUD.

Unauthorized possession of buprenorphine is a criminal offense under state and federal laws. Some decisionmakers argue that this is too harsh, especially in places where availability of high-quality treatment is limited. For example, in 2019, prosecutors in Chittenden County, Vermont, announced that they would no longer charge individuals for illegally possessing the drug. Philadelphia adopted a similar approach in 2020. These efforts have yet to be evaluated, but they offer examples of a new policy approach at the intersection of criminal justice and public health. There is related discussion regarding the restrictive regulatory barriers to access for methadone, which have been relaxed during the coronavirus disease 2019 pandemic.

The illegal supply of fentanyl poses important challenges to public health surveillance efforts, and data limitations have implications for evaluating criminal justice efforts. Although substantial resources are devoted to research and monitoring with respect to health issues, much less effort is devoted to understanding the behavior of suppliers or measuring such fundamental parameters as prices and quantities. This issue can be addressed with some of the recommendations listed in Chapter Two (e.g., wastewater testing, reviving the Arrestee Drug Abuse Monitoring program), but also with more qualitative research of people who sell and supply these substances. There is also much more that could be done with the DEA's STARLIMS (formerly the System to Retrieve Information About Drug Evidence [STRIDE]) and National Forensic Laboratory Information System (NFLIS) data systems. In addition, investment in the analysis of crowd-sourced data sets (e.g., StreetRx) and online marketplaces (on the dark and surface webs), as well as interviewing convicted or incarcerated dealers and importers, could provide useful information about the supply of these substances and their precursors.

Introduction

The supply of opioids, especially the oversupply of prescription pain relievers beginning in the 1990s, was critical in laying the foundation for the current crisis (Kolodny et al., 2015). Before the spread of legally produced prescription opioid analgesics, heroin had long been the dominant illegal opioid, although its geographic scope was somewhat limited, with availability greatest in certain major urban areas (Musto, 2002). One way in which the spread of OUD involving prescription opioids changed illegal supply is that it gave drug traffickers an incentive to provide heroin to parts of the United States where there had not previously been a user base.

More recently, fentanyl and other potent synthetic opioids, most of which are illegally manufactured and not of pharmaceutical origin, have started to diffuse across illicit drug markets, initially in the eastern United States and western Canada, but now more broadly. All of these classes of opioids are illicitly supplied to drug markets; however, the nature of the production and distribution is different for each. This in turn shapes how the illegal supply of opioids affects people who use opioids and other components of the opioid ecosystem (see Figure 7.1).

Although most patients follow physicians' orders and take opioids as prescribed (Han et al., 2017), a proportion of patients and those around them may inappropriately or illegally divert medications to street markets (Khan et al., 2019; Substance Abuse and Mental Health Services Administration [SAMHSA], 2018). In 2020, roughly 50 million people filled at least one opioid prescription, totaling 143 *million* opioid prescriptions that equaled 110 *billion* morphine milligram equivalents (American Medical Association, 2021).[2] These figures include many different opioids, but if we think about this in terms of oxycodone, which has a morphine-equivalent dose (MED) of 1.5, the number would be 92.6 billion milligrams. Prices for oxycodone vary, but it is not uncommon to hear of people paying $1 per milligram in the illegal market. If one assumes a comparable price per MED for other prescription opioids in the illegal market, and if one assumes that even 10 percent of what is being prescribed is being diverted to the illegal market, the total amount spent on diverted prescription opioids comes to about $9 billion per year, or about a quarter of what was spent on heroin circa 2016 (Midgette et al., 2019). Diversion of prescription pain medications, unscrupulous prescriber practices (e.g., "pill mills"), and patients seeking and filling multiple prescriptions ("doctor shopping") have furthered the reach of prescription opioids (Betses and Brennan, 2013; Dhalla, Persaud, and Juurlink, 2011; Kennedy-Hendricks et al., 2016).

Although policies have attempted to reduce diversion and stem the flow of prescription opioid analgesics to patients, other opioids, such as heroin, have been substituted for prescription pills in some segments of the opioid-using population (Alpert, Powell, and Pacula, 2017; Cicero, Ellis, and Surratt, 2012). Heroin use indicators and drug seizures started to increase

---

[2] These numbers are down substantially from a peak in 2012 of 260 million prescriptions and nearly 240 billion morphine milligram–equivalent doses (American Medical Association, 2021).

FIGURE 7.1

The Illegal Supply System and Its Interactions

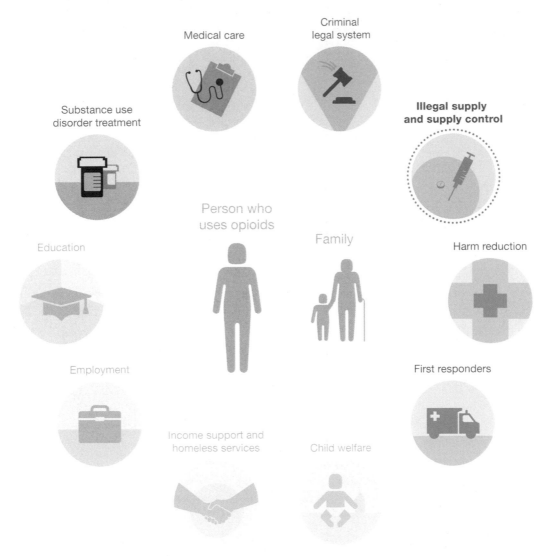

in some markets around 2010 (DEA, 2016b; DEA, 2019; Midgette et al., 2019), and many of the new heroin customers were individuals who were known to have previously misused prescription opioids. By late 2013, illicit fentanyl made its way into the heroin supply as adulterants. Since then, fentanyl have been pressed into counterfeit prescription tablets made to look like pharmaceutical-grade products, and law enforcement has encountered cocaine and methamphetamine that contain fentanyl during seizures (DEA, 2019).

The expansion of fentanyl across markets has been accompanied by a steep increase in overdoses, some of which are fatal. As displayed in Figure 2.3 in Chapter Two, between 2013 and 2020, the rate of overdose death records mentioning synthetic opioids jumped from 1 per

100,000 people to 17.8 per 100,000, which is more than quadruple the corresponding 2020 rates for overdoses involving heroin (4.4 per 100,000) or prescription opioids (4.0 per 100,000) (Hedegaard, Miniño, and Warner, 2020).

The number of people with OUD and the number of people using illegal opioids both increased substantially between the late 1990s and the time fentanyl arrived in the United States. These numbers may have increased further since then, but it appears that most of the rapid increase in deaths after fentanyl arrived comes from a higher rate of death per person-year lived with OUD, not so much from increases in the population with OUD.[3] The *emergence* of fentanyl is a supply-driven phenomenon (i.e., dealers are opting for cheaper and more-potent alternatives to other illegal opioids, specifically heroin and diverted prescription opioids, concealing them in bags sold as heroin or tablets made to look like genuine medications) and one that is still largely regionally concentrated for reasons that are not well understood.

In 2021, synthetic opioids (principally fentanyl) were involved in more than 80 percent of opioid-involved deaths and thus more than half of all drug overdose deaths. Synthetic opioids are now reported in 70 percent of overdoses involving heroin or cocaine (see Figure 7.2). The number of drug overdoses involving synthetic opioids, especially novel synthetics that are illegally manufactured, is undercounted, as some states do not accurately report underlying causes of death (Scholl et al., 2019). The supply of illegally manufactured opioids can generate additional harms (e.g., unregulated substances having unknown purity or consistency, people who use opioids coming into contact with criminal elements), and these opioids serve as ready substitutes for individuals with OUD that originated with prescription opioids.

The shift to illegally produced synthetic opioids not only makes the crisis much more deadly, but the high potency and low production costs of these opioids pose major challenges to supply control efforts. There is also some evidence to suggest that the purity-adjusted price for illegally manufactured fentanyl dropped dramatically from 2016 to 2021 in some segments of the market (Kilmer et al., 2022b).

Although it is currently impossible to know the amount of illegally produced synthetic opioids consumed in the United States (see Chapter Two), this amount is likely very small in terms of pure weight but very large in terms of morphine milligram equivalents. Using two different approaches, Kilmer et al., 2022a, argues that the total amount of pure illegally manufactured fentanyl used in the United States in 2021 was likely in the single-digit metric tons. For comparison, the most-recent figures for cocaine and heroin (2016) put pure consumption at roughly 150 and 50 pure metric tons, respectively (Midgette et al., 2019).

---

[3]   The extent to which fentanyl multiplies the death risk cannot be computed as just the ratio of the fentanyl death rate (17.8) divided by the older numbers for heroin or prescription opioids, because fentanyl produces those high national average death rates despite not yet being common everywhere in the United States. The actual "multiplier" to overdose deaths per person-year lived with OUD is likely even greater.

FIGURE 7.2

Drug-Involved Deaths in the United States by Synthetic Opioid Involvement, 2000–2020

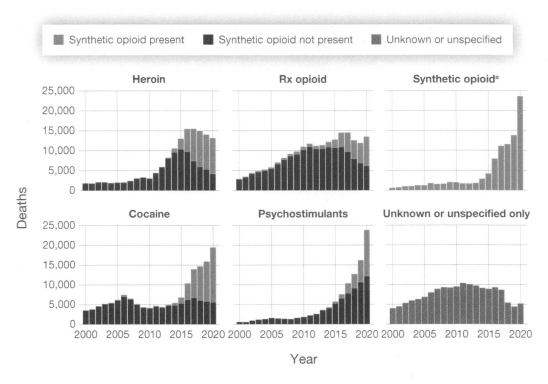

SOURCE: RAND analysis of Centers for Disease Control and Prevention (CDC) National Vital Statistics System Multiple Cause of Death data (CDC, 2021b).

[a] Excludes cocaine, heroin, prescription opioid, and psychostimulant deaths involving synthetic opioids.

System Components and How They Interact with Opioids

Opioids are necessary medications, especially for pain relief and anesthesia. However, they have the potential to generate adverse health events, such as overdose, and are liable to be misused. For more than 100 years, Western societies have used a set of rules, now known as the prescription and dispensing system, aimed at safeguarding patient health to avoid harms associated with iatrogenic addiction, unsupervised use, or excessive supply of medicines (Babor et al., 2010); see the box on the next page. Any unauthorized production, distribution, or use of opioids is generally seen as a violation and deemed illegal. For example, the diversion of prescription medications is illegal under federal and state law. There are also some opioids, such as heroin, that have no recognized medical application in the United States and are therefore banned outside narrow research exemptions.

For the purposes of understanding and defining the illegal supply of opioids, the distinction of whether an opioid has legal uses—and that there are rules associated with these uses—matters. Oxycodone and hydrocodone are manufactured and distributed by licensed and regulated companies, and most of the retail cost of these prescription medications is paid by public and private insurance. Even when these prescription opioids are diverted into illegal markets, the original manufacture was by a legal, regulated company. By contrast, outside limited research purposes, all of the heroin supplied and used in the United States is entirely illegal. It is produced, imported, trafficked, and sold illegally.

Fentanyl is more complicated. Fentanyl is a legal, regulated medication used to treat certain types of pain (e.g., through fentanyl pain patches) and as an anesthetic in invasive surgeries. There has long been diversion of medical fentanyl, to a degree that resulted in some deaths—numbers that used to seem substantial, even though they are now dwarfed by current totals. And the reason these totals are so large is because of the influx of wholly illegal fentanyl that is not manufactured or distributed by licensed companies (Gladden, Martinez, and Seth, 2016).

Drug Scheduling

Most national drug control laws are modeled after an international system of control established by three international treaties: the Single Convention on Narcotic Drugs of 1961 as Amended by the 1972 Protocol, the Convention on Psychotropic Substances of 1971, and the United Nations Convention Against Illicit Traffic in Narcotic Drugs and Psychotropic Substances of 1988. These treaties established a tiered system of controls, known as *schedules*, over drugs. In the United States, the federal Controlled Substances Act (CSA) lists drugs according to five schedules (I–V) based on three criteria (determined by the DEA and the FDA): their potential for abuse, their accepted medical uses, and their potential for addiction. States maintain their own drug schedules but, with a few exceptions (e.g., cannabis), mostly adhere to the federal scheduling regime (Braun, 1991).[a]

Drugs in Schedule I are strictly controlled, as they are categorized as having high potential for abuse and no accepted medical uses. Supply and use of Schedule I drugs, such as heroin, cannabis, and LSD, are permitted only for narrow research exemptions. Restrictions on prescribing, dispensing, or possessing drugs decline from Schedules II to V. Schedule II drugs are those deemed to have high abuse potential, which could lead to severe mental and physical addiction; drugs in this schedule include oxycodone, hydrocodone, and fentanyl. Schedule III drugs have medium abuse potential, which could lead to moderate physical addiction; these drugs include buprenorphine and dihydrocodeine. Schedule IV drugs have moderate abuse potential, which could result in moderate addiction; drugs include many benzodiazepines and tramadol. And Schedule V drugs have the lowest abuse potential, which could lead to mild physical or mental addiction; drugs include some cough suppressants that contain low amounts of codeine.

---

[a] We do not endorse the use of the word *abuse* because it is stigmatizing. However, given that *abuse* is the word that is used in the scheduling laws, we reluctantly use it in this section.

The illegal supply of opioids touches on many important elements of the opioid ecosystem, and in several ways. This has to do, in part, with the variations in how these opioids are produced and distributed. Pharmaceutical-grade prescription opioids are supplied in different ways than heroin, and different actors are involved in almost every stage of the supply chain. In turn, interventions aimed at reducing the illicit (i.e., unauthorized) supply of these substances can vary.

Production

Prescription Opioids

Schedule II–IV prescription opioids are produced by manufacturers that are licensed and regulated by the DEA and the FDA. This licensing and regulation covers the production of the pharmaceutical ingredients, as well as the manufacture of various formulations of prescription opioids. Both these regulatory agencies implement laws aimed at protecting patient and consumer health while creating a secure system to prevent diversion or excessive supply; most diversion of prescription opioids occurs after the prescriptions are filled, not from licensees. However, as recent opioid litigation cases have shown (Haffajee and Mello, 2017), that does not mean that licensed producers or distributors are always unaware that diversion is occurring. Some doctors or other licensees have knowingly violated the law; however, most of the time when doctors write prescriptions for pills that are then diverted, they are being perhaps naive or incautious, but not corrupt. In terms of production, federal law can determine which drugs are legal for licensees to produce and in what formulations, as well as how much they can manufacture. Any production beyond these limitations or outside the rules set forth would be unlawful.

Under the CSA, the DEA sets annual production caps (aggregate production quotas) for Schedule I and II drugs (Yeh, 2018). The CSA stipulates civil and criminal penalties for violations, including unlawful manufacture of controlled substances. To prevent unlawful diversion or production, the DEA requires licensees to maintain accurate records regarding production, inventories, and transfers. In recent years, the DEA, in part because of reductions in demand, has reduced aggregate production quotas for several Schedule II opioids that are commonly prescribed. In 2019, the DEA reduced the amount of many prescription opioids from the prior year by 10 percent based on numbers of prescriptions dispensed, manufacturer inventories, forecasts, and other factors (DEA, 2018a).

Under the Federal Food, Drug, and Cosmetic Act, the FDA regulates premarket approval of new drugs and market authorization of these medications. This law generally prohibits the introduction or dissemination of new drugs, including reformulations, without FDA approval. A drug manufacturer must first file a new drug application with the FDA while undertaking clinical trials to show that the new drug is both safe and effective. In 1995, Purdue Pharma developed a reformulation of controlled-release oxycodone (OxyContin), which many now consider to be a major contributor to increases in opioid prescribing (Staman, 2018). Likewise, if a medication that received approval is later found to be unsafe or liable to abuse, then the FDA can recall or withdraw that medication from the market. In 2017, the FDA determined that the potent painkiller Opana ER (oxymorphone), made by Endo Pharmaceuticals, was linked to misuse, and it was recalled (Staman, 2018).

Heroin

The supply of heroin to the United States has shifted over time. Historically, heroin was smuggled from Turkey or Southeast Asia. Over time, the U.S. market transitioned to powder heroin from Colombia, generally found east of the Mississippi River, and black and brown tar from Mexico, generally found out west. In recent years, Mexican tar and powder have displaced Colombian-sourced heroin (DEA, 2018b; Sacco and Bagalman, 2017). Although the sources of heroin and the actors involved in its supply might have changed, the basic architecture of the production chain is largely the same.

Heroin is derived from opium, which is extracted from the poppy plant. Illicit poppy cultivation in Mexico occurs mainly in remote regions in the Sierra Madre Occidental, concentrated near Sinaloa, Chihuahua, and Durango, and in the Sierra Madre del Sur in Guerrero and Oaxaca (United Nations [UN] Office on Drugs and Crime [UNODC], 2018). According to the UN, illicit crop cultivation is a large part of the economy in these remote communities. According to the U.S. government, the area of poppy cultivated rose from 11,000 hectares to about 42,000 hectares between 2013 and 2018, although estimates are subject to a variety of uncertainties. Likewise, the UN noted an increase according to satellite imagery over the same period (Office of National Drug Control Policy [ONDCP], 2019; UNODC, 2018), although more-recent estimates by the UN and the ONDCP indicated a notable decrease since the previously reported peaks (UNODC, 2021; The White House, 2021a), which might be the result of the market shifting from heroin to fentanyl.

Poppy farmers, who are often relatively poor, like other small-scale farmers who do not use much modern machinery or farming technology, extract opium latex from poppy pods to sell to regional drug trafficking organizations, who process the raw opium into heroin (Le Cour Grandmaison, Morris, and Smith, 2019). There are several grades of heroin, which is synthesized from morphine found in the raw opium. White powder heroin is the purest, while black tar is less pure and the least expensive grade to produce because several purification steps are skipped in the process (Congressional Research Service, 2019).

Fentanyl and Other Synthetic Opioids

Synthetic opioids are produced in a laboratory or chemical production process, not derived from the poppy or any other plant. For this reason, a small number of people are involved in its production, not thousands of farmers. Although fentanyl and several other synthetic opioids, such as tramadol and methadone, are used for legitimate medical purposes in treating pain or OUD, we focus here on the variety of illicitly manufactured synthetic opioids, of which fentanyl is most commonly reported in overdose mortality records and drug seizure data (Pardo et al., 2019; Spencer et al., 2019). These synthetic opioids can be manufactured in labs using chemical precursors, and most fentanyl-class drugs are many times more potent than heroin in terms of MED (Vardanyan and Hruby, 2014), meaning that a much smaller weight or quantity provides the same amount of stimulation of neuroreceptors in the brain. Some of these substances were researched for potential medical applications, and several, including fentanyl, sufentanil, remifentanil, and carfentanil, became useful in a variety of applications.

In addition to each of these chemicals in its classic form, there can be many variants that might produce comparable effects but can sometimes skirt laws that ban just the classic forms of these drugs. That is, the nature of these chemicals allows innovative chemists to alter the molecular structures of compounds in minor ways, designing wholly new substances (e.g., analogs). Sometimes these analogs are quite similar to the parent molecules; other times, their pharmacodynamics and harms are different and unknown.

Illicit production of fentanyl often occurs in unregulated, clandestine settings. Until recently, few individuals possessed the knowledge or inputs necessary to synthesize fentanyl. Since the late 1970s, the United States has witnessed a handful of short and generally localized fentanyl outbreaks, each tied to a single chemist (Pardo et al., 2019). Most of these clandestine laboratories were in the United States. However, in the mid-2000s, the first foreign clandestine lab linked to a fentanyl outbreak in the United States was discovered in Mexico (Coleman, 2007; Pardo et al., 2019).

The current wave of fentanyl is linked to foreign producers, including drug trafficking organizations in Mexico and underregulated pharmaceutical manufacturers in Asia (DEA, 2018b; O'Connor, 2017). Production in Mexico often occurs in clandestine labs in residential areas with precursors imported from China. According to U.S. federal law enforcement, seizures of fentanyl from Mexico are often of low purity (U.S. Customs and Border Protection [CBP], 2019). In contrast, seizures arriving from China to ports of entry, including mail processing and private consignment (e.g., DHL, FedEx) facilities, are smaller in weight but nearly pure (CBP, 2019). Seizures directly from China have declined substantially in recent years, in large part because of the Chinese government's extension of controls over all "fentanyl-related structures" (Commission on Combating Synthetic Opioid Trafficking, 2022). That said, illegal production has grown in Mexico (DEA, 2021).[4] Although China was implicated in the majority of fentanyl that arrived in the United States until recently, authorities in India have reported two seizures of fentanyl destined to North America in 2018 (Pardo and Reuter, 2019).

The manufacture of many fentanyl and other precursors is linked to China's large chemical and pharmaceutical sectors, although the scale of fentanyl production is tiny in dollar terms (at most a few tens of millions of dollars), so, from the industry's perspective, it would be an afterthought, not a noticeable source of revenue. This is because the industry in China

---

[4] The timing of the shift in seizures from direct shipments from China to products coming from Mexico across the southwestern border of the United States broadly coincided with China's introduction of generic control over fentanyl-related structures. One possible consequence of the scheduling decision was that most producers who had up to that point supplied fentanyl and fentanyl precursors (now controlled in China) directly to the United States switched to supplying precursor chemicals (which remained largely uncontrolled in China) to Mexico.

is large and faces minimal oversight, allowing a handful of chemical producers to continue to manufacture and distribute synthetic opioids or related precursor chemicals.

China is a leading exporter of active pharmaceutical ingredients and chemicals that can be used in the production of controlled substances (Pardo, 2018). In recent years, China's pharmaceutical industry counted some 5,000 manufacturers that produce more than 2,000 products, making the country the single largest exporter of active pharmaceutical ingredients in the world (World Health Organization, 2017). Regulatory gaps have led to a large increase in the number of unlicensed or "semi-legitimate" chemical manufacturers or distributors. There are reports that the use of shell facilities and weak oversight let some chemical and pharmaceutical manufacturers avoid scrutiny, allowing companies to produce and sell beyond their legal limits (O'Connor, 2016).

In China, and, to a lesser extent, India, producers of fentanyl—who often operate as legitimate chemical or pharmaceutical firms—can easily escape regulatory scrutiny and may endeavor to develop novel synthetic opioids or uncontrolled precursors that escape existing legal prohibitions.

In Mexico, drug trafficking organizations operate on an entirely different scale. Total Chinese revenues from participating in illegal fentanyl production are unknown but are probably on the order of low double-digit millions (Commission on Combating Synthetic Opioid Trafficking, 2022). Mexican drug trafficking organizations' total revenues from moving drugs into the United States are also unknown, but were estimated to be on the order of $10 billion circa 2010 (Kilmer et al., 2010). Thus, criminals in Mexico make perhaps 1,000 times as much from supplying drugs to the United States as do criminals in China, and of course China's economy is much larger than Mexico's. Drug trafficking to the United States is a significant economic activity in parts of Mexico, but not in China.

Criminals in Mexico are synthesizing fentanyl of lower purity in wholly clandestine settings. The extent to which clandestine manufacturing occurs in other parts of North America is unclear. U.S. law enforcement has reportedly not encountered a fentanyl synthesis lab in the United States since 2005 (Pardo et al., 2019); however, Canada has reported clandestine synthesis labs in recent years (Royal Canadian Mounted Police, 2021). Although fentanyl and heroin arrive in the United States from overseas, these substances are often diluted for distribution and retail sale to end users, although that might be changing as law enforcement increasingly seizes counterfeit tablets containing fentanyl that originate from Mexico.

Distribution and Sale

Prescription Opioids

Prescription opioids are distributed and sold through a system whose goal is to ensure responsible access to potentially harmful substances. Per federal law, this is designed to be a closed system and prevent unnecessary supply or diversion, or the supply of prescription medications to someone other than the person they were meant for. Typically, prescriptions are written by prescribers, such as doctors, for patients and are filled by dispensers, such as pharmacists. In this section, we examine the illicit distribution and sales of these substances, focusing on prescription opioids that are misused outside physician supervision or those that are diverted to illicit markets. Diversion of prescription opioids occurs through several mechanisms, including primarily through doctor or pharmacy shopping, pill mills, and prescription forgery, but also through robberies and thefts from pharmacies and distributors and pilfering from family, friends, and neighbors.

Doctor or pharmacy shopping occurs when a patient visits multiple prescribers or dispensers to obtain and fill multiple prescriptions for opioids (Peirce et al., 2012). The patient does so to circumvent prescription guidelines and limits in an effort to avoid alerting medical practitioners or authorities to suspicious or illegitimate prescription patterns. On the other hand, "pill mills" are doctors, clinics, and pharmacies that inappropriately prescribe and dispense prescription opioids (Sacco and Bagalman, 2017). These points of distribution generally serve as pain management clinics, which have sometimes operated under a minimal regulatory structure to prescribe or dispense large quantities of opioids (Centers for Disease Control and Prevention [CDC], Office for State, Tribal, Local and Territorial Support, 2012). Prescription forgery can include a patient or health care worker forging or altering a prescription, making it look legitimate when in fact it is not (Inciardi et al., 2007).

Thefts and robberies from pharmacies and distributors and pilfering from medicine cabinets are ways in which individuals directly obtain prescription opioids for unauthorized use without an attempt to game the prescription access system. The DEA tracks the number of thefts and robberies, which includes armed robberies, customer theft, employee pilferage, losses during transit, and break-ins. In recent years, the number of opioid doses lost or stolen has declined from a peak of 19.4 million units in 2011 to 9.1 million units in 2017 while the number of armed robberies has increased slightly, from 712 events in 2011 to 875 events in 2017 (DEA, 2018b). These figures might sound large, but they are actually very small compared with the total number of opioids diverted.

Whatever the method, diversion of legitimate prescription opioids to the illicit market is characterized by Inciardi and colleagues as

> a disorganized, for-profit industry. It is referred to here as "disorganized" because there are so many different players involved in the phenomenon, including: physicians, pharmacists, and other health care professionals; drug abusers, patients, students, street dealers, and white-collar criminals; and tourists, saloonkeepers, and all types of service personnel to name but a few. The range of diversion is so broad, furthermore, that answers as to what the major sources of diversion are really depend on who is asked. Federal agencies maintain that diverted drugs enter the illegal market primarily through "doctor shoppers," inappropriate prescribing practices by physicians, and improper dispensing by pharmacists. (Inciardi et al., 2007, p. 172)

Inciardi and colleagues' characterization of diversion as disorganized is largely accurate as it pertains to the distribution of opioids at points of dispensing and beyond. It is also important to stress what does not occur. There is next to no participation of violent organized crime groups in the diversion or distribution of prescription opioids, which makes their supply very different from that of traditional drugs of concern (e.g., heroin, cocaine) and might help explain why stemming that diversion was not always a high priority for law enforcement or the country more generally. The diversion of prescription opioids led to addictions and deaths of consumers of these opioids, but not to disorderly, flagrant street markets; homicides by drug trafficking organizations; or other threats to the public safety of bystanders.

However, the distribution of prescription opioid analgesics was known by some manufacturers and distributors and has been documented in legal cases. Recently, state and local governments have aggressively pursued legal actions, in the form of consolidated multidistrict litigation, against opioid manufacturers (e.g., Purdue Pharma and Johnson & Johnson), distributors (e.g., McKesson Corporation, AmerisourceBergen, and Cardinal Health), and retail pharmacies (e.g., Rite Aid and Walgreens) for their knowledge and role in the opioid crisis (Gluck, Hall, and Curfman, 2018; Haffajee and Mello, 2017). Some of these lawsuits for violating drug control or consumer safety laws were settled as early as 2004 (Haffajee and Mello, 2017). Several defendants named in ongoing suits have previously faced regulatory scrutiny, investigation, and fines for violating drug control laws by fulfilling shipments of prescription opioids that resulted in diversion.

Plaintiffs argue and media investigations show that distributors were complicit in the diversion of prescription opioids by failing to report suspicious bulk orders to pharmacies. In one case, distributors shipped some 40 million tablets over a five-year period to a rural county in West Virginia home to 96,000 residents (Barasch, 2018). Subsequently, *Washington Post* reporters analyzed the DEA's prescription control database (the Automation of Reports and Consolidated Orders System [ARCOS]) and documented the extent to which distributors supplied large amounts of pills to sparsely populated rural counties between 2006 and 2012 (Abelson et al., 2019). Another *Washington Post* article notes that, between 2006 and 2012, just 15 percent of pharmacies received almost 50 percent of all of the opioids distributed, and six distributors, including such companies as McKesson, Cardinal Health, and Amerisource-Bergen, distributed 75 percent of these pills (Higham et al., 2019). On the other hand, that concentration in the hands of a few distributors mostly just reflects that there are relatively few companies in that industry, and whatever any single company's knowledge of excess dispensing in one geographical location, the DEA—which had access to information from all of the distributors—had even better insight into that oversupply.

Industry actors were reporting shipments, as required under the law, but the DEA did not always intervene. Regulatory authorities, principally the DEA, did not stop all suspicious shipments, although some two dozen cases were adjudicated from 2006 to 2016, resulting in $500 million in fines (Higham et al., 2019). Enforcement efforts declined, especially after 2015. Reports by investigative journalists have documented coordinated efforts by distributors and producers to capture regulatory authorities by hiring former DEA employees and working with Congress to pass the Ensuring Patient Access and Effective Law Enforcement Act (Higham et al., 2019). The bill amended language in the CSA to effectively limit the DEA's ability to intervene by requiring authorities to first identify "an immediate threat of death, serious bodily harm, or abuse of a controlled substance due to a registrant's failure to maintain effective controls against diversion" before suspending a licensee's registration to distribute controlled substances (U.S. Senate, 2016).

Although excessive or unlawful distribution of prescription opioids is likely to have contributed to the oversupply of these substances, the fact remains that most prescription opioids were diverted after fulfillment of a prescription. The National Household Survey on Drug Use and Health (NSDUH)—which, admittedly, is enormously limited when it comes to studying all things related to OUD—has asked people who misuse prescription pain relievers where they obtained prescription opioids for their most recent misuse episodes. But here, we must exert extreme caution: *Misuse* includes cases in which an individual may have been prescribed opioids for a root canal and then, months later, took a few for a sprained ankle, as well as those in which an individual with OUD was doctor shopping and misleading prescribers about their need for opioids.

With Figure 7.3, we attempt to get at this distinction by looking at the source of pain relievers for last misuse by whether individuals met clinical criteria for OUD in the 2019 NSDUH. Although nearly 40 percent of individuals without OUD reported getting the pain relievers from friends or relatives for free, this share was closer to 20 percent for those with OUD. Of those with OUD, 33 percent bought the pain relievers from dealers, strangers, relatives, or friends, compared with only 12 percent of those without OUD (a difference of 21 per-

FIGURE 7.3

Source of Most Recent Misused Pain Reliever, by Opioid Use Disorder Status (2019 National Household Survey on Drug Use and Health)

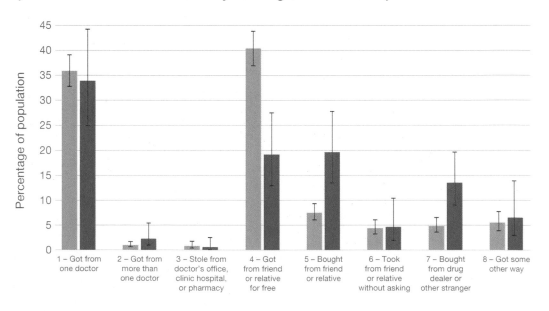

SOURCE: Substance Abuse and Mental Health Data Archive, undated.
NOTE: Blue bars represent individuals without OUD (*N* = 7,776,852); orange bars represent those with OUD (*N* = 1,367,034).

centage points). However, this perspective underestimates the OUD versus non-OUD difference in making these illegal purchases, because people who use opioids more frequently are more likely to buy from dealers. If we thought about this in terms of total use days (which are dominated by those with OUD), the difference between those with and without OUD who made illegal purchases would be much larger than 21 percentage points.

The methods of and reasons behind diversion may also vary by type of opioid. Although the diversion of prescription pain relievers is a noted problem that has contributed to the opioid crisis in the form of misuse, a much smaller share of individuals seek out opioids used for OUD treatment, including methadone and buprenorphine. In these cases, individuals with OUD might resort to diverted methadone or buprenorphine to avoid withdrawal symptoms if they are unable to obtain diverted prescription pain relievers (Harris and Rhodes, 2013; Monte et al., 2009). Diversion of buprenorphine is generally found to be higher in areas with high opioid prescribing prevalence, and, in one cross-sectional study of 51 individuals with OUD in New England, all but two were found to have used or sought out diverted buprenorphine to modulate withdrawal symptoms (Monte et al., 2009).[5] Some researchers have noted that inadequate access to controlled OUD medications is a potential risk factor for seeking out diverted buprenorphine or methadone (Lofwall and Walsh, 2014).

Heroin

Because heroin is a Schedule I substance, its distribution and supply outside narrow research exemptions is illegal. The vast majority of heroin is illegally imported from Mexico, mostly through transport across the southwestern border of the United States by privately owned vehicles at legal ports of entry, followed by concealment in legitimate goods on tractor trailers (DEA, 2018b). A smaller amount of heroin is seized at express consignment facilities at air ports of entry (DEA, 2017), and there also are exotic smuggling methods, such as tunnels and unmanned aerial vehicles, as well as drug couriers carrying it across the border on foot. According to the DEA, Mexican drug trafficking organizations control the importation and wholesale distribution of heroin until it reaches U.S. cities (DEA, 2018b). Local distribution and retail to consumers varies from city to city because local gangs and various other groups are often involved at this point in the supply chain.

Recent analysis suggests that the number of chronic heroin users has increased by almost 50 percent from 2006 to 2016, from about 1.6 million to 2.3 million individuals (Midgette et al., 2019), and both of these figures are much larger than the stable levels from before the big expansion in opioid prescribing (Rhodes et al., 2001). Similarly, the amount consumed has increased from an estimated 27 to 47 metric tons, while total national retail expenditures rose from $31 billion to $43 billion between 2006 and 2016 (Midgette et al., 2019). The slower rise in expenditures is due in large part to the declining price per pure gram since 2010, as shown in Figure 7.4.

---

[5] For more-recent insights on diversion of buprenorphine, see Butler et al., 2020; Daniulaityte et al., 2019; Silverstein et al., 2020; and Smith et al., 2020.

The DEA notes that heroin availability has been highest in the northeastern and Midwestern parts of the United States, although heroin availability was increasing across the country through 2016 (DEA, 2016a). Prices for retail purchases of heroin have fluctuated in recent years but remain at historic lows. At the same time, purity has risen since 2010, but it has stabilized at around 30 percent since 2012 (Figure 7.4). A declining purity-adjusted price likely results in greater consumption or initiation, while price spikes may reduce consumption because consumers of drugs, including heroin—like consumers of other goods—respond to changing prices (Gallet, 2014). Since 2013, the heroin supply in some parts of the country has started to become contaminated by fentanyl. In 2017, the DEA stated that "[f]entanyl will continue to make inroads into the U.S. heroin market and, in select areas, may eventually supplant heroin" (DEA, 2017, p. 55). That prediction has become true, with heroin having vanished almost entirely in some drug markets.

Fentanyl and Other Synthetic Opioids

Fentanyl is a Schedule II narcotic, and, since its reformulation into transdermal patches for treating pain in the 1990s, some prescribed fentanyl has been misused or diverted to illicit markets (Bianchi et al., 2005; Devine, Gutierrez, and Rogers, 2012). However, the vast majority of fentanyl reported in recent drug seizures is imported powders or counterfeit tablets that are illicitly manufactured (Commission on Combating Synthetic Opioid Trafficking, 2022).

FIGURE 7.4
Price and Purity of Heroin

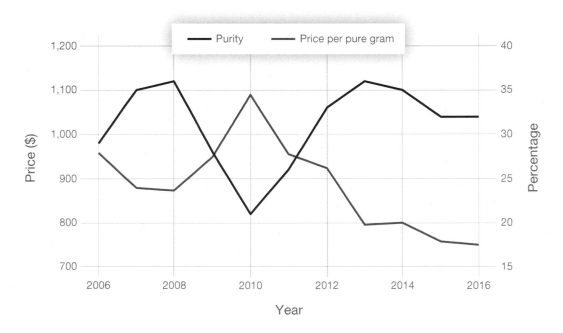

SOURCE: Midgette et al., 2019.

Many novel synthetic opioids and fentanyl analogs have been controlled by the DEA as Schedule I substances (the same schedule as heroin) because they have a high potential for abuse and no medically recognized application.[6] Since 2018, all "fentanyl-related substances"—i.e., chemicals that are structurally related to fentanyl—are scheduled as Schedule I substances. That designation has been temporarily renewed and, as of this writing (November 2021), is likely to be made permanent by statute. The emergence of this generic control on all fentanyl compounds was in response to the growing numbers of novel fentanyl analogs that were appearing each year. Since the initiation of the generic ban (which was followed a year later by a similar ban in China), the numbers of new fentanyl analogs have sharply declined (U.S. Government Accountability Office, 2021). That said, there have been reports of increases in the numbers of new, non-fentanyl synthetic opioids found in drug seizures and overdose reports (Shover et al., 2021).

Fentanyl can be lawfully distributed only under the provisions set forth by the CSA. Illegally manufactured fentanyl started to make its way into drug markets most recently in late 2013, first as adulterants in heroin. Somewhat later, fentanyl was found in counterfeit tablets made to look like pharmaceutical-grade prescription medications (Congressional Research Service, 2019), and there have been some law enforcement reports of fentanyl found in seizures of such stimulants as cocaine and methamphetamine (DEA, 2019), although the share of stimulants mixed with fentanyl remains very low according to other analyses (Park et al., 2021; Zibbell et al., 2019). Because fentanyl was first used as an adulterant and is now increasingly found as a substitute for heroin or other opioids (Pardo et al., 2019), its distribution patterns are somewhat similar to those of heroin at the retail level. In this case, drug dealers started selling heroin adulterated with fentanyl or counterfeit prescription opioid tablets containing fentanyl. Yet an examination of drug seizures and overdose mortality data shows that fentanyl may have supplanted heroin almost entirely in some places, such as New Hampshire (Pardo et al., 2019). An examination by the U.S. Synthetic Opioid Commission of state and local law enforcement seizure data shows a shift in acutely affected states in the eastern part of the United States (Commission on Combating Synthetic Opioid Trafficking, 2022). In this case, fentanyl is largely mixed with heroin, at least initially. Over time, fentanyl comes to dominate the market, as evidenced by declines in the number of seizures involving heroin or heroin mixed with fentanyl. This pattern is most apparent in states in New England and parts of Appalachia. Seizures of fentanyl remain largely concentrated in the east, with a few exceptions. In the western United States, most prominently in Arizona, there has been a rise in seizures of synthetic opioids unmixed with heroin (Figure 7.5).

According to federal law enforcement, up through part of 2019, fentanyl used to arrive in U.S. markets directly from Chinese manufacturers via the post, private couriers, or cargo

---

[6] As a stopgap measure, federal law enforcement, under the Federal Analogue Act, can prosecute people who knowingly supply uncontrolled substances that are chemically or pharmacologically similar to controlled substances. However, investigations of supply of analogs are resource intensive and have been challenged in court.

(e.g., UPS, FedEx); smuggled from Mexico; or smuggled from Canada after being pressed into counterfeit prescription pills (O'Connor, 2017; ONDCP, 2017). Early on, most of the purity-adjusted weight of fentanyl arrived from China, but numbers of seizures of direct-to-buyer orders from China have declined substantially since 2019 (DEA, 2021). Currently, the majority of synthesized fentanyl comes by land from Mexico. Law enforcement notes a large disparity in the purity of imported fentanyl; product coming from Mexico is of low purity, is often trafficked in larger quantities, and increasingly involves counterfeit tablets that contain small amounts of fentanyl. In comparison, smaller amounts of nearly pure fentanyl and a variety of analogs used to arrive directly to the United States from Asia (CBP, 2019).

By and large, distribution of fentanyl is not as well understood as illegal supply of heroin. Different actors are involved in importation and redistribution further downstream. Recent

FIGURE 7.5

Drug Seizures Involving Heroin and Synthetic Opioids in Selected States, 2012–2020

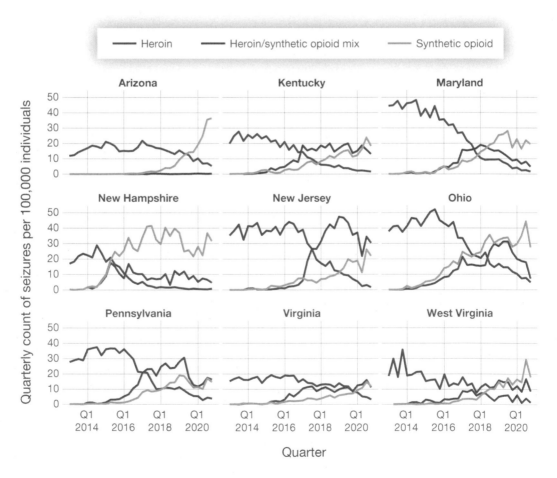

SOURCE: Commission on Combating Synthetic Opioid Trafficking, Technical Appendix B.

analysis of fentanyl seizures and federal law enforcement actions suggest that there appear to be variations in the supply of illicit fentanyl and that traditional drug trafficking organizations might be using other means, including the domestic postal system, to traffic fentanyl across the United States. New England may be supplied by traditional drug trafficking organizations, while markets in Ohio, until 2019, may have been supplied to a greater degree with product bought online and imported from China (Pardo, Davis, and Moore, 2019).

The typology of fentanyl dealers is not well understood, although it appears that some importers obtain substances from online vendors abroad, ordering large quantities that are shipped through the mail or private express consignment operators (e.g., FedEx, DHL) (Pardo, Davis, and Moore, 2019; U.S. Department of Justice, 2017). These individuals may then redistribute wholesale quantities (tens or hundreds of grams of fentanyl) via the dark net to local dealers who then cut it into heroin or press it into pills for supply further downstream (DEA, 2018b; Lamy et al., 2020). In other instances, product imported from Mexico arrives as powder or pressed into counterfeit tablets through traditional conveyances across the border.

Supply Control

Supply reduction and control, which refers to interventions to curtail the production, distribution, and retail sale of drugs, is a key pillar of drug policy. It often involves drug law enforcement and is therefore seen as the remit of law enforcement investigations and prosecutions. However, compared with law enforcement investigations and prosecutions, supply control has a broader reach that includes restrictions on precursor chemicals or other equipment to limit the production of drugs, diplomatic engagements to reduce source-country supply through institution-building or eradication, and alternative livelihood programs that convince rural farmers to cease cultivating poppy or coca.

As mentioned earlier, multiple entities are involved in attempting to control the supply of opioids. For drugs that are legally produced by pharmaceutical companies, the DEA and the FDA regulate production and wholesale distribution. Medical officials ultimately determine who can get a prescription for these drugs, and most prescribers and dispensers act in good faith. The U.S. Department of Justice, state and local criminal justice agencies, and medical boards are often involved in addressing those prescribers who break the law (e.g., knowingly overprescribing, engaging in payback schemes). Local law enforcement agencies typically take the lead in reducing the diversion of prescription pills that are being illegally distributed in street markets. The DEA also regulates the production, trade, and access to precursor chemicals needed to manufacture controlled drugs.

For illegally produced opioids like heroin and fentanyl, law enforcement agencies, the U.S. Postal Service, and some defense agencies are involved in trying to reduce supply and ultimately increase prices of these drugs at the retail level. But supply control efforts for synthetic opioids can also involve better monitoring and placing limits on the production of these drugs and their precursors.

To generalize, supply control and drug prohibition raise prices by imposing risks on suppliers (Reuter and Kleiman, 1986) and creating other inefficiencies in the distribution process—what Reuter, 1983, refers to as the "structural consequences of illegality." Drugs are sold in markets, and participants in those markets (e.g., dealers and consumers) respond to economic incentives, such as price. Therefore, considerable attention is paid to purity-adjusted price, or the price of a pure gram or kilogram of a drug, along the supply chain (Babor et al., 2010). We see price reductions in cannabis as more states move from prohibiting supply to allowing it (MPG Consulting and the University of Colorado Boulder Leeds School of Business, undated; Oregon Liquor and Cannabis Commission, undated; Smart et al., 2017). Prohibition and a base level of enforcement surely inflate the prices of illegally traded opioids, such as heroin. As discussed earlier, by the time a kilo of heroin leaves Mexico and ends up in New York City, the price jumps from under $20,000 to $50,000. (If one were to ship that same kilo via FedEx, it would cost less than $100 to transport.) But once a retail market is established, increasing enforcement (in terms of arrests or prison sentences) yields diminishing returns and is not expected to make much of a difference in the retail price (Pollack and Reuter, 2014). At best, there might be temporary disruption, but it does not take long for established markets to adapt (Caulkins and Reuter, 2010).

The evidence base for supply control and reduction interventions is limited. As discussed later, little existing drug research funding goes to studying supply control. However, those researchers who have examined instances of supply control interventions or other disruptions to illegal supply of drugs point to limited effectiveness. Pollack and Reuter, 2014, reviewed the thin literature base on supply control and price and found that there was limited evidence of elevated prices resulting from increasing the risk of arrest, incarceration, or seizure. Others have noted that increasing a drug's schedule (e.g., moving it from Schedule III to Schedule II) may reduce some use-related outcomes (Caulkins et al., 2021b). There is a considerable evidence base for controls on precursor chemicals. Elevating restrictions on chemical inputs needed to manufacture drugs, including cocaine and methamphetamine, have been shown to reduce the use and availability of illegally manufactured drugs (Cunningham, Callaghan, and Liu, 2015; Cunningham and Finlay, 2013; Dobkin, Nicosia, and Weinberg, 2014).

Leading drug researchers who conducted an extensive review of supply control and reduction interventions found limited evidence for various supply reduction interventions. There is almost no evidence showing the effectiveness of alternative development or livelihood programs on reducing drug use; crop eradication can sometimes create temporary market disruptions, although they are often overcome by farmers planting more crops (Babor et al., 2010). There is evidence of an association of interdiction and higher-level enforcement with distribution, which suggests that law enforcement interventions may result in temporary disruptions that may increase prices for end users, but there is limited ability to quantify the effect sizes of such interventions (Babor et al., 2010).

Although enforcement against higher stages of the supply chain will not eliminate the illegal supply of drugs or permanently raise prices by a large degree, supply control and drug law enforcement can be used to help reduce the harm surrounding drug markets (e.g., targeting the most-violent suppliers; trying to address open-air drug markets and the instability they cause by moving dealers indoors or toward delivery, which is less disorderly and less prone to violence). Focused deterrence is one such approach. The underlying premise of focused deterrence is to change the behavior of offenders, in this case drug dealers, "by implementing an appropriately focused blended strategy of law enforcement, community mobilization, and social service actions" (Braga, Weisburd, and Turchan, 2018, p. 206). Such strategies have had some success in reducing overt retail markets (Corsaro et al., 2012; Saunders, Robbins, and Ober, 2017), and some people have suggested using this approach to address harms caused by the most-violent drug trafficking organizations and even drug dealers handling or mixing synthetic opioids with non-opioids or manufacturers of counterfeit tablets containing fentanyl (Kleiman, 2012; Pardo and Reuter, 2020).

Surveillance of Drug Supply

There are several law enforcement data systems that are used to monitor illegal drug markets and the distribution of controlled drugs. For decades, the DEA has collected data on undercover buys and seizures that can be transformed into information about purity and prices through analysis in federal laboratories in an administrative data set known as STRIDE (which has been reinvented as STARLIMS). Although this is an administrative database that was not developed for research purposes, researchers have been able to develop algorithms to use this information to generate purity-adjusted price series for heroin, cocaine, and methamphetamine (e.g., Arkes et al., 2008; Midgette et al., 2019). This price information has been used to help estimate the size of drug markets (e.g., Kilmer et al., 2014; Rhodes et al., 2012) and conduct policy evaluations (e.g., Dobkin and Nicosia, 2009).

In addition to STARLIMS, the DEA manages other important data systems. The NFLIS collects results of forensic tests of seized drugs for many state and local law enforcement agencies; however, only aggregate-level reports—such as the share of all cocaine samples that also contained synthetic opioids—are made public. Now that there is a broad suite of opioids, not just heroin, and these opioids are showing up in packages of cocaine, it is important to start reporting counts of the various mixtures and combinations, not just total counts by chemical, or to let properly vetted researchers obtain access to underlying incident-level data. Additional information is available at the incident level, including purity, weight, and formulation of drugs.

The DEA also maintains ARCOS to track and record the movement of controlled substances from manufacturers to distributors to retail pharmacies or hospitals, where they are distributed to patients. The ARCOS system is useful to track and control the distribution of controlled drugs. It does not track controlled substances that are illegally produced, such as heroin or illegally manufactured and imported fentanyl. ARCOS data have been useful to show how access to prescription opioid analgesics, as measured by the distribution of prescriptions, is correlated with overdose outcomes (Alpert et al., 2019; Alpert, Powell, and Pacula, 2018).

Key Interactions with Other Components of the Ecosystem

The illegal supply of opioids, whether they are diverted prescription pain relievers, heroin, or fentanyl, affects and is affected by several other elements of the opioid ecosystem.

Criminal Legal System

The illegal supply of opioids is closely linked with the criminal legal system. Unlawful possession or supply of opioids is a criminal offense, often triggering law enforcement actions that result in an offender entering the criminal legal system. Individuals with OUD may go to extensive lengths, including selling drugs, to pay for their habit.

The criminal legal system is tasked with protecting public safety and addressing crimes related to drugs. The United States, more than most other Western countries, has generally taken a law enforcement–oriented approach to the illegal supply and possession of drugs (Babor et al., 2010), although that law enforcement focus was conspicuously absent until the mid to late 2010s with respect to the diversion of prescription opioids, in part because organized and violent criminal groups were not significantly involved in supply. Often, the criminal legal system dominates policy responses aimed at reducing the supply of illegal opioids. In this regard, law enforcement agencies aim to reduce the availability and raise prices of drugs sold in illegal markets.

There is a large body of literature on the effects of criminal justice interventions on the supply of illegal drugs and their prices. The effectiveness of enforcement might depend on the stage of the drug crisis. As Caulkins and Reuter argue,

> Enforcement is likely to be more effective in preventing the formation of a mass market than in suppressing such a market once it has formed. Once a mass market is established, there may be little return to intense enforcement. A modest level of enforcement may generate most of the benefits from prohibition. (Caulkins and Reuter, 2010, p. 213)

There is very little evidence to suggest that increasing prison sentences for street-level dealers in mature markets (especially drug homicide laws, as discussed in Chapter Six) will have any lasting effect on supply or purity-adjusted prices. These efforts should be considered alongside the impacts they have on these individuals and their communities.

What about efforts to increase enforcement against the higher levels of illegal drug markets (i.e.., above the street level)? It is hard to imagine these efforts influencing retail heroin prices given how well entrenched these markets are. For synthetically produced drugs, such as fentanyl, there is sometimes a focus on going after the precursor chemicals. Dobkin and Nicosia, 2009, evaluated an effort that shut down two suppliers that may have been providing more than half of the precursors used to produce methamphetamine in the mid-1990s. Although the intervention had a massive impact on retail markets and harms (as measured by purity, hospital admissions, drug treatment admissions, and arrests), the authors found that these outcomes returned to preintervention levels within 18 months of the end of the intervention. This does not mean that the intervention was not beneficial; rather, it speaks to the resiliency of these markets.

The dimensions of illegal supply have become increasingly complex with the introduction of fentanyl. The nature of fentanyl, and its ability to be shipped directly by mail to buyers, complicates criminal justice efforts aimed at regulating this substance, reducing its availability, and investigating and prosecuting individuals who supply it, in part because novel synthetic opioids are designed to circumvent drug control laws and efforts. For example, law enforcement officers that come across fentanyl might not have the ability to determine its presence because field drug kits are not designed to detect new chemicals. Fentanyl is often much cheaper and more potent (and thus easier to conceal) than diverted prescription pain relievers or heroin, making it an attractive alternative for drug distributors.

Medical Care

As discussed earlier, diverted prescription opioids can make their way into illicit markets, meaning that the health care system is an important source of potentially harmful substances. This is why federal regulatory authorities, such as the DEA and the FDA, limit the amount or type of scheduled drugs that can be produced and have systems in place to track their distribution. Because the medical system is a source of psychoactive drugs, individuals with OUD may try to obtain prescription medications at certain points in the medical system, including at emergency departments, via doctor or pharmacy shopping, or by accessing medications from unscrupulous pain management facilities.

As it pertains to the illegal supply of regulated pharmaceutical analgesics, the diversion of prescription opioids from the medical system is the principal concern. This is different from illegally manufactured heroin and fentanyl, the supply of which is wholly illegal. To reduce opportunities for diversion and overpromotion and to protect patient health, the medical system has long used the prescription system, which separates the prescriber from the dispenser. Yet many jurisdictions in the United States have adopted additional policy responses to enhance how the prescription system guards against diversion or oversupply.

PDMPs were started by states as a means to track prescribing and dispensing of controlled substances. Not all PDMPs are the same in their design or implementation (Pardo, 2017). Yet at their core, they are state-run administrative programs that collect and distribute information on patients, prescribers, and dispensers. In some states, PDMPs are administered by law enforcement agencies who analyze these data to identify suspicious prescribing habits or suspected diversion. Some states mandate that health care professionals query the database before writing or filling an opioid prescription.

Another set of laws and policies aimed at reducing diversion consists of pain clinic regulations. Pain clinics, the worst of which are referred to pejoratively as "pill mills," were common points of diversion of prescription opioids, especially during the 2000s. Although there are many legitimate pain management clinics, some operations were known to be sources of easily accessible prescription opioids. These facilities are often aimed at treating chronic pain and in some cases faced little regulatory scrutiny, allowing unscrupulous doctors and pharmacists to distribute large quantities of pain medications. Stories of doctors servicing large volumes of patients, especially those from out of state, suggest that these facilities did little to comprehensively treat patients but rather served as points of diversion. Over time, states adopted laws to regulate these facilities so as to reduce inappropriate prescribing and diversion (Dowell et al., 2016; Lyapustina et al., 2016; Rutkow et al., 2015).

Other efforts have been made to reduce oversupply of abusable medications. In 2010, OxyContin was reformulated into abuse-deterrent tablets intended to prevent crushing and injection. More recently, federal guidelines have focused on reducing excess supply of prescription medications for acute or chronic pain in an attempt to reduce diversion (Bohnert, Guy, and Losby, 2018; Dowell, Haegerich, and Chou, 2016). Although these well-intended policies reduced the misuse and diversion of prescription opioids, some experts have noted that they coincided with a marked increase in heroin use and overdose, suggesting that a segment of individuals with OUD switched to heroin after finding it difficult to obtain prescription opioids (Alpert et al., 2018; Cicero, Ellis, and Surratt, 2012; Mars et al., 2014).[7] In addition, the background rate at which people were already trading down to illegally produced opioids could have increased because the illegally produced opioids are generally less expensive on a morphine-equivalent basis.[8]

Substance Use Disorder Treatment

Drug treatment policies and services are linked with the supply of illegal opioids inasmuch as reducing use (either in treatment or during recovery) will shrink the broader market of drugs and its associated harms. For example, effective treatment for individuals with OUD can reduce the demand for opioids, potentially affecting supplier behavior at the retail level (e.g., user-sellers might no longer need to sell; Babor et al., 2010). Therefore, supply disruptions might have a more lasting impact when coupled with robust OUD treatment efforts.

First Responders

The evolution in the illegal supply of opioids affects first responders. As the risk of overdose increases, first responders have to use more naloxone to reverse opioid overdoses or attend to more repeat or more frequent overdose cases (Cash et al., 2018; Faul et al., 2017). Elevated risks and more frequent overdose calls may increase burnout and elevate stress levels of frontline workers (Jozaghi et al., 2018). First responder services are finite. Overdoses might not stress emergency response resources nationally, yet calls to attend to overdoses in hard-hit

---

[7] See also Martin et al., 2018, on the effect of restricting the legal supply of prescription opioids on buying through online illicit marketplaces.

[8] Oxycodone sold on the street generally trades for a $1 per milligram (Lebin et al., 2019), whereas the equivalent amount of heroin sells for about $0.90 (Midgette et al., 2019). After we factor in heroin's greater MED, heroin comes to about one-third the cost of oxycodone per morphine milligram equivalent.

regions might mean that the ability of emergency responders to attend to other calls for service is negatively affected (Pike et al., 2019), but we do not have systematic data on how often this happens.

Harm Reduction and Community-Initiated Interventions

Monitoring and early-warning systems are challenged by the emergence of synthetic opioids because many people are unknowingly using them, and there are often lags in the release of overdose and drug seizure reports that allow analysts to assess drug market trends. Individuals who use drugs might not accurately report their drug use given the introduction of fentanyl, and drug testing field kits might not be able to detect the presence of novel synthetic opioids, confounding measurement and appropriate responses. Public health and safety authorities will need to improve how they estimate and observe changes to the illegal supply of drugs. Efforts in other parts of the world have shown that innovative approaches, such as wastewater testing, might be useful to improve monitoring and surveillance (Castiglioni et al., 2014). Allowing people who use drugs to test their drugs (beyond fentanyl test strips, which provide only binary responses), as is done in parts of Canada and elsewhere, provides useful information to these individuals and to people who monitor these markets (e.g., see Toronto's Drug Checking Service, undated); however, this type of testing is generally prohibited in the United States.

Changes in the illegal supply of opioids can also have downstream public health effects. Although fentanyl is more potent than heroin, its effects typically do not last as long. Because of its shorter duration of effect, individuals with OUD might be injecting it more often (Buresh et al., 2019; Geddes et al., 2018; Lambdin et al., 2019; Peng and Sandler, 1999). This could increase the number of times each day they put themselves at risk of overdose or other harms. Ethnographic research suggests that individuals in some markets report injecting fentanyl twice as frequently as they inject heroin (Ciccarone, Ondocsin, and Mars, 2017). Increased injection frequency elevates the burden on public health measures and systems because individuals might overdose more often or are more likely to transmit blood-borne viruses. Harm reduction services might see increased need for needles and other injection equipment to prevent needlesharing or to reduce soft-tissue damage and infection caused by the dulling of needles from reuse. That said, there is some recent work documenting that some people are transitioning to smoking fentanyl instead of injecting it (e.g., Kral et al., 2021).

Similarly, the shift in the illegal supply or use of opioids will require new messaging and detection interventions. There is a growing effort to expand access to fentanyl test strips for individuals who use drugs to encourage them to test their drugs before use, thus allowing them to modulate their doses and perhaps lower their risk of overdose with fentanyl (Krieger et al., 2018; Peiper et al., 2019; Weicker et al., 2020; Zibbell et al., 2021). These low-threshold and low-cost tools were first distributed by harm reduction groups and were later distributed by public authorities, such as county and state departments of health. In 2021, the federal government, through the CDC and SAMHSA, expanded the use of fentanyl test strips and funded further research into this intervention (CDC, 2021a; The White House, 2021b).

Apart from increasing awareness of the presence of fentanyl in the drug supply, harm reduction campaigns might need to adapt to changes in routes of administration by people who use drugs. The risks and harms from ingesting prescription analgesics by mouth are different from the risks of injection drug use; the latter presents concerns over transmission of HIV or the hepatitis C virus. Public health campaigns to prevent drug use might need to be increasingly aimed at reducing harm, in addition to deterring initiation, as illegal supply changes.

Policy Opportunities and Considerations

Focusing Supply Reduction Efforts at Higher Levels of the Supply Chain

The potency of synthetic opioids and the small quantities needed to meet U.S. demand (Kilmer et al., 2022a) represent a serious challenge for interdiction and domestic law enforcement interventions aimed at disrupting the supply to and within the United States. Therefore, efforts to address the challenge at higher levels of the supply chain might merit particular attention. Source-country supply control has its limits (Babor et al., 2010), but improving oversight over large chemical and pharmaceutical sectors is not like forcing farmers to eradicate illicit crops that economically support their households.

Because most illegally manufactured synthetic opioids currently consumed in the United States are produced using input chemicals from China, efforts will be needed to strengthen the existing oversight and regulatory enforcement framework in China, increasing investigations over those who violate rules or are found to supply precursor chemicals to trafficking organizations. The recent shift in China from production of fentanyl and fentanyl analogs to production of precursor chemicals is linked to Beijing's decision to adopt a blanket ban over all fentanyl-related structures in 2019. Additional steps that China could take include extending regulatory control over chemicals with little or no use other than for the manufacture of synthetic opioids and improving its oversight and inspections of its pharmaceutical and chemical sectors. The Chinese government could also tighten its chemical export regulations by adopting "know-your-customer" laws, introducing restrictions on exports to countries with controls on the chemicals in question, enacting export controls on tableting equipment, and improving information-sharing with partner countries regarding chemical exports. However, there are limits to these efforts given that India's pharmaceutical and chemical sectors could easily pick up any slack left by greater enforcement by Chinese authorities.

Attempts to disrupt the flow of precursor chemicals to Mexico before they are used to produce synthetic opioids might be less problematic and easier to undertake than interdicting finished fentanyl at the border. U.S. authorities could work with their partners in Mexico to help strengthen the capacity of Mexican authorities to target suspicious incoming shipments, to detect chemicals and drugs coming through ports of entry, and to identify and share information on detected chemicals.

It is important to recognize that steps taken against higher levels of the supply chain will not eliminate the supply of synthetic opioids. However, these steps represent interventions that would be aimed at links in the chain where volumes are largest, and perhaps most pure, and would be directed at targets that minimize collateral damage. Supply reduction efforts have not been shown to be entirely successful in changing drug prices but have had limited disruptive effects in markets (Caulkins et al., 2021a; Pollack and Reuter, 2014). Furthermore, supply reduction in the form of domestic drug law enforcement aimed at users and street-level dealers has been found to generate harms and excesses of its own (Caulkins and Kleiman, 2018).

Getting More Innovative About Supply Disruption

Much of this section was previously published in Pardo et al., 2019.

The transition to fentanyl is driven by suppliers, so it makes sense to consider supply reduction as one piece of a comprehensive effort. Even if supply cannot be eliminated altogether, delaying the entrenchment of fentanyl in a market by even a few years could save lives. Yet there is a deserved rejection of some excesses of the recent past (e.g., aggressive policing of minority communities, aerial spraying of coca fields, mandatory minimum prison sentences). There is little reason to believe that tougher sentences, including sentences for violating drug-induced homicide laws for low-level retailers and easily replaced functionaries (e.g., couriers), will make a positive difference (see, e.g., Kleiman, 2009). There is also little reason to believe that synthetic opioid trafficking, which stems from easy access to precursors and finished product in Asia, could be curtailed in the short term (Pardo, Kilmer, and Huang, 2019). However, just as there are many types of harm reduction, there are many types of supply reduction—each with its own costs and benefits. Targeting importers and wholesalers of nearly pure fentanyl from China is very different from throwing the book at street-level retailers, who might not know the exact chemicals in or purity of the drugs they sell.

Efforts are already underway to improve technologies for detecting small shipments of drugs, particularly fentanyl, through the mail and parcel services (such as UPS and FedEx). The U.S. Postal Service might improve its knowledge of the patterns of dispatch by Chinese suppliers and use its monitoring capacities more efficiently. Although inventing technologies and reporting protocols that help detect fentanyl in parcels is innovative and could be of great value, the longer history of drug interdiction involves an arms race of constant technological adaptation by both sides. Improved detection leads smugglers to find new routes or importation methods, or both, to blunt the effectiveness of the new interdiction methods (Caulkins, Crawford, and Reuter, 1993). Guerrero Castro, 2016, refers to the "co-evolution of technology" by smugglers and interdictors (p. 9).

Synthetic opioids' extreme potency and resulting small volumes help smugglers and challenge interdictors. There could be other approaches to interdiction besides accelerating that arms race of detection and evasion technologies. As discussed at the beginning of this chapter, efforts could be made to target importers and distributors in the supply chain, who sometimes use the internet to obtain and distribute fentanyl. For example, although the legal dimensions could become complicated, the DEA or another federal agency could, in principle, set up phony drug-selling websites the way the Dutch police did with the Hansa network, to which many users migrated after the Alpha Bay cryptomarket website was shut down (Europol, 2018). Some sites could make controlled deliveries to buyers who import and are likely to be dealers themselves, so that these buyers could be arrested in "reverse stings." Other DEA-operated counterfeit sites could promise—but not deliver—synthetic opioids, sending either nothing or inert powders. Even if purchasers do not face arrest, the failure of some sites to fulfill orders might stimulate general wariness of online procurement, reducing the demand for actual fentanyl sellers. It is hard to determine how dealers would adapt to these supply-side efforts, but the fact that some of these individuals use the internet to transact sales offers law enforcement unique insights and opportunities.

The government could attempt to hack or disable websites that sell drugs, or at least swamp their comment boards with phony complaints. There is no doubt that there are legal issues that we are missing, so we offer this suggestion tentatively. However, conventional interdiction has involved active disruption, not just reactive investigation. As the adage holds, sometimes the best defense is a good offense, so it might be worth exploring the legality and feasibility of nontraditional options of this ilk (Freeborn, 2009). But the existence of online trade raises an interesting question: Would it be better to have all these transactions happen online if it meant reducing revenues to Mexican drug trafficking organizations, who appear to be capturing an increasing share of the U.S. fentanyl market? Of course, there will always be a large share of people who use opioids who do not have the means to obtain drugs online, and the drug trafficking organizations could always get involved in internet transactions, although criminal organizations in Mexico are increasingly expanding into fentanyl synthesis and trafficking. There is also the perennial question of how the drug trafficking organizations will react to online competition from suppliers in Asia. But thinking about who is supplying and the harms they cause will be important for helping law enforcement agencies prioritize efforts.

Finally, social network analysis is another opportunity to learn more about the suppliers and opportunities for disrupting them (Bichler, Malm, and Cooper, 2017; Morselli and Petit, 2007). This will require access to investigation reports and could be augmented with interviews with suppliers who are and are not incarcerated.

Rethinking Supply Reduction in the Fentanyl Era

This section summarizes Pardo and Reuter, 2020.

The move to fentanyl and other potent synthetic opioids is largely a decision by dealers to substitute new, cheaper opioids for expensive heroin. Although fentanyl has had a measurable impact on national overdose rates, it is now found most commonly in the eastern half of the United States, as reflected in the overdose rates involving synthetic opioids of more than 23 per 100,000 in New Hampshire, Ohio, and West Virginia and rates at or under ten per 100,000 in California, Oregon, and Washington (these data are for 2020 [CDC, 2021b]). Therefore, local law enforcement responses should vary depending on whether the illegal drug supply has transitioned to fentanyl.

The traditional goals of reducing the supply or raising the price of drugs through conventional enforcement tactics, such as buy and bust or restriction of access to precursor chemicals, will be limited in the fentanyl era. The marketplace for fentanyl is more dispersed than that for heroin given the ability of individuals (mostly low-level distributors) to source product online. Fentanyl is too easy to make, too cheap to obtain, increasingly accessible, and easier than heroin to conceal. All of these characteristics make it an attractive alternative for suppliers. As a consequence, drug enforcement agencies should consider alternative priorities that shape the behavior of retailers to (1) reduce the toxicity and increase the transparency of drugs sold in illegal markets and (2) reduce the crime, violence, and corruption produced by the supply network (at all levels). This might require greater coordination and cooperation between law enforcement and public health authorities.

Because the illegal supply of drugs is unregulated, dealers feel no obligation to adhere to truth in advertising, and they conceal risks of elevated potency of drugs. Counterfeit tablets containing fentanyl are often sold as the legitimate items; bags of powder containing fentanyl are sometimes sold as cocaine or heroin. Adapting from a focused deterrence approach, law enforcement could work to focus efforts on dealers that conceal fentanyl in counterfeit tablets or sell them as non-opioids (Pardo and Reuter, 2020; Saunders, Robbins, and Ober, 2017).

To this last point, lower-level enforcement against diverted opioid medications might be more harmful should counterfeits containing fentanyl replace them. This could be true even for MOUD. Emerging evidence suggesting that diverted MOUD, such as methadone and buprenorphine, are largely used for withdrawal management and self-treatment raises questions about the appropriate sanctions for unauthorized possession and distribution. As discussed earlier, some decisionmakers argue that prosecuting people for unauthorized possession and distribution of MOUD is too harsh, especially in places where availability of high-quality treatment is limited. For example, in 2019, prosecutors in Chittenden County, Vermont, announced that they would no longer charge individuals for illegally possessing the drug. Philadelphia adopted a similar approach in 2020. These efforts have yet to be evaluated, but they offer examples of a new policy approach at the intersection of illegal supply, criminal justice, and OUD treatment.

Finally, while reducing the illegal supply of opioids, particularly prescription opioids, is an important goal for many public safety and public health agencies, one must consider what successful supply reduction might mean for other segments of the illegal market and components of the ecosystem (e.g., medical care, substance use disorder treatment, harm reduction).

This is especially important in the context of local efforts to disrupt or limit the supply of opioid analgesics, which could lead some individuals who are dependent or addicted to start obtaining opioids from the illegal market or to move to injection.

Improving Data Collection in the Era of Fentanyl and Other Synthetic Opioids

Much of this section was previously published in Pardo et al., 2019.

An improved understanding of which synthesis route is used could offer additional insights into the supply of fentanyl. Being able to determine the chemical profiles of synthetic opioids could help law enforcement investigate supply sources and ascertain the impacts of precursor controls. The DEA's long-standing assertion that Colombian heroin continued to make its way to retail markets in the eastern half of the United States as late as 2012, when in fact Mexican drug traffickers had figured out the Colombian powder recipe, is just one example of the limits of signature profiling. Federal law enforcement should consider these limitations and the possibility that manufacturers are using a variety of synthesis methods beyond traditional approaches.

Understanding dealer decisionmaking is also critical for understanding the market and formulating innovative and effective policy interventions. Thus, an important task is to gain insights into how dealers who acquire synthetic opioids from the internet determine which chemicals they choose to purchase and how much they put into the heroin they sell or the counterfeit tablets they press; cocaine needs to be considered separately. A simple economic model of the heroin market suggests that profit-maximizing dealers would substitute cheap fentanyl for expensive heroin roughly up to the point at which the user notices a decline in the quality of the experience, assuming that quality differences can be perceived. One reason that a simple model of dealer behavior might have failed so far is that fentanyl is probably not readily available to all heroin wholesalers, and there might be long-standing factors that have limited the emergence of fentanyl in some markets (e.g., black and brown tar heroin found in the western United States may have prevented contamination of heroin with fentanyl; Commission on Synthetic Opioid Trafficking, 2022). Some dealers might be intimidated by the difficulty of dosing accurately with fentanyl. There also could be differential legal risks. The calculus underlying dealer decisions about how much to substitute fentanyl (or some other potent synthetic opioid) for heroin remains unknown; however, this calculus will determine the future pattern of such overdoses. Studies of street dealers have a long history of producing insights about the operation of markets (Johnson et al., 1985; Reuter et al., 1990). In that vein, interviews with dealers at various levels of supply (e.g., bulk importers, dark net distributors, and street dealers) would provide much-needed insight into the decisionmaking and operational processes of suppliers in markets affected by fentanyl.

As noted in Chapter Two, efforts should be made to learn from user experiences. This is particularly true for individuals who are at risk of overdose and are most likely to come into regular contact with synthetic opioids (Mars, Ondocsin, and Ciccarone, 2018). Many of these individuals engage with dealers, providing additional insights into prices and retail supply trends. Understanding how individuals who use drugs adapt to elevated overdose risk might allow more-targeted policy innovation, as well as help identify and overcome barriers to services and tools that can save lives (Park et al., 2019; Rouhani et al., 2019).

The possible mixing of fentanyl into the supply of cocaine raises different problems and potential research opportunities. In 2017, synthetic opioids were found in about as many fatal overdoses when combined with cocaine as when they were combined with heroin. Deliberate mixing is one possible explanation. As discussed in Daly, 2019, these mixtures might also be the consequence of cocaine users who separately buy fentanyl-contaminated heroin or of cocaine dealers who carelessly handle fentanyl-contaminated heroin before they package cocaine. It is plausible that all three explanations play a role; analysis of seizures and undercover purchases is one path forward to understanding how fentanyl gets into the supply of cocaine.

Finally, investment in the analysis of crowdsourced data sets and online marketplaces (on the dark and surface webs) could also provide useful information about the supply of these substances. A growing number of drugs are traded using online forums, and greater analysis of websites or forums might be needed to anticipate emerging drug trends. Crowdsourced websites that report transaction data (e.g., streetrx.com), such as price and quantity, as well as dark net marketplaces, can help measure supply trends in near real time. Researchers have started to analyze these sources, and some have reported logically consistent findings regarding drug prices and density of outlets or other traditional supply-side measures, such as seizures (Dasgupta et al., 2013; Giommoni and Gundur, 2018; Hswen, Zhang, and Brownstein, 2020; Lebin et al., 2019; Munksgaard and Tzanetakis, 2022). Other online forums might offer other insights into emerging drugs and drug sources.

In summary, supply control interventions get a substantial amount of the public resources allocated to reducing problems associated with drugs.[9] In 2005, the total supply control budget across all levels of government was estimated at $40 billion (Boyum and Reuter, 2005). However, relatively little is spent on evaluating these interventions or ways to improve drug law enforcement, compared with billions of dollars spent on research related to reducing demand for drugs. The National Institute on Drug Abuse has an annual budget of more than $1 billion dedicated to understanding drug demand and harm reduction interventions (Pardo and Reuter, 2018). In comparison, the National Institute of Justice receives one-quarter of that amount for all criminal justice research, of which drug-related issues make up only a fraction (Pardo and Reuter, 2018). This represents a misalignment of research and policy priorities, in that few research funding dollars are allocated to understanding or improving most operationally expensive and socially costly interventions that are aimed at reducing drug-related harms and other issues.

---

[9] The federal drug control budget has moved more toward spending on demand reduction programs in recent years, but about half of federal spending is dedicated to supply control; see Office of National Drug Control Policy, 2021. However, these figures do not include state budgets, which often focus on law enforcement efforts aimed at local retail markets.

Abbreviations

ARCOS	Automation of Reports and Consolidated Orders System
CBP	U.S. Customs and Border Protection
CDC	Centers for Disease Control and Prevention
CSA	Controlled Substances Act
DEA	Drug Enforcement Administration
FDA	Food and Drug Administration
MED	morphine-equivalent dose
MOUD	medications for opioid use disorder
NFLIS	National Forensic Laboratory Information System
NSDUH	National Household Survey on Drug Use and Health
ONDCP	Office of National Drug Control Policy
OUD	opioid use disorder
PDMP	prescription drug monitoring program
SAMHSA	Substance Abuse and Mental Health Services Administration
STRIDE	System to Retrieve Information About Drug Evidence

References

Abelson, Jenn, Andrew Ba Tran, Beth Reinhard, and Aaron C. Davis, "As Overdoses Soared, Nearly 35 Billion Opioids—Half of Distributed Pills—Handled by 15 Percent of Pharmacies," *Washington Post*, August 12, 2019.

Alpert, Abby E., William N. Evans, Ethan M. J. Lieber, and David Powell, *Origins of the Opioid Crisis and Its Enduring Impacts*, Cambridge, Mass.: National Bureau of Economic Research, Working Paper 26500, November 2019.

Alpert, Abby, David Powell, and Rosalie Liccardo Pacula, *Supply-Side Drug Policy in the Presence of Substitutes: Evidence from the Introduction of Abuse-Deterrent Opioids*, Cambridge, Mass.: National Bureau of Economic Research, Working Paper No. 23021, 2017.

Alpert, Abby, David Powell, and Rosalie Liccardo Pacula, "Supply-Side Drug Policy in the Presence of Substitutes: Evidence from the Introduction of Abuse-Deterrent Opioids," *American Economic Journal*, Vol. 10, No. 4, November 2018, pp. 1–35.

American Medical Association, "Opioid Prescriptions Decrease for 10th Consecutive Year," opioid prescription trends chart, September 2021. As of July 7, 2022: https://end-overdose-epidemic.org/wp-content/uploads/2021/09/IQVIA-opioid-prescription-trends-chart-Sept-2021-FINAL.pdf

Arkes, Jeremy, Rosalie Liccardo Pacula, Susan M. Paddock, Jonathan P. Caulkins, and Peter Reuter, *Why the DEA STRIDE Data Are Still Useful for Understanding Drug Markets*, Cambridge, Mass.: National Bureau of Economic Research, Working Paper No. 14224, August 2008.

Babor, Thomas F., Jonathan P. Caulkins, Griffith Edwards, Benedikt Fischer, David R. Foxcroft, Keith Humphreys, Isidore Obot, Jürgen Rehm, Peter Reuter, Robin Room, et al., *Drug Policy and the Public Good*, 1st ed., New York: Oxford University Press, 2010.

Barasch, Alex, "Is 20.8 Million Pain Pills Over a Decade a Lot for One Town? It Depends," *Slate*, January 30, 2018.

Betses, Mitch, and Troyen Brennan, "Abusive Prescribing of Controlled Substances—A Pharmacy View," *New England Journal of Medicine*, Vol. 369, 2013, pp. 989–991.

Bianchi, R., K. Ballard, C. Harte, and G. Vorsanger, "Fentanyl Extraction/Recovery Experiments: Simulation of Fentanyl Diversion," *Journal of Pain*, Vol. 6, No. 3, 2005.

Bichler, Gisela, Aili Malm, and Tristen Cooper, "Drug Supply Networks: A Systematic Review of the Organizational Structure of Illicit Drug Trade," *Crime Science*, Vol. 6, No. 2, 2017.

Bohnert, Amy S. B., Gery P. Guy, Jr., and Jan L. Losby, "Opioid Prescribing in the United States Before and After the Centers for Disease Control and Prevention's 2016 Opioid Guideline," *Annals of Internal Medicine*, Vol. 169, No. 6, 2018, pp. 367–375.

Boyum, David, and Peter Reuter, *An Analytic Assessment of U.S. Drug Policy*, Washington, D.C.: The AEI Press, 2005.

Braga, Anthony A., David Weisburd, and Brandon Turchan, "Focused Deterrence Strategies and Crime Control: An Updated Systematic Review and Meta-Analysis of the Empirical Evidence," *Criminology & Public Policy*, Vol. 17, No. 1, February 2018, pp. 205–250.

Braun, Richard L., "Uniform Controlled Substances Act of 1990," *Campbell Law Review*, Vol. 13, No. 3, Summer 1991, pp. 365–374.

Buresh, Megan, Becky L. Genberg, Jacquie Astemborski, Gregory D. Kirk, and Shruti H. Mehta, "Recent Fentanyl Use Among People Who Inject Drugs: Results from a Rapid Assessment in Baltimore, Maryland," *International Journal of Drug Policy*, Vol. 74, December 2019, pp. 41–46.

Butler, Stephen F., Natasha K. Oyedele, Taryn Dailey Govoni, and Jody L. Green, "How Motivations for Using Buprenorphine Products Differ from Using Opioid Analgesics: Evidence from an Observational Study of Internet Discussions Among Recreational Users," *JMIR Public Health and Surveillance*, Vol. 6, No. 1, 2020.

Cash, Rebecca E., Jeremiah Kinsman, Remle P. Crowe, Madison K. Rivard, Mark Faul, and Ashish R. Panchal, "Naloxone Administration Frequency During Emergency Medical Service Events—United States, 2012–2016," *Morbidity and Mortality Weekly Report*, Vol. 67, No. 31, 2018, pp. 850–853.

Castiglioni, Sara, Kevin V. Thomas, Barbara Kasprzyk-Hordern, Liesbeth Vandam, and Paul Griffiths, "Testing Wastewater to Detect Illicit Drugs: State of the Art, Potential and Research Needs," *Science of the Total Environment*, Vol. 487, 2014, pp. 613–620.

Caulkins, Jonathan P., Gordon Crawford, and Peter Reuter, *Simulation of Adaptive Response: A Model of Drug Interdiction*, Santa Monica, Calif.: RAND Corporation, RP-193, 1993. As of August 1, 2022:
https://www.rand.org/pubs/reprints/RP193.html

Caulkins, Jonathan P., Anne Gould, Bryce Pardo, Peter Reuter, and Bradley D. Stein, "Opioids and the Criminal Justice System: New Challenges Posed by the Modern Opioid Epidemic," *Annual Review of Criminology*, Vol. 4, January 2021a, pp. 353–375.

Caulkins, Jonathan P., Laura A. Goyeneche, Lingrong Guo, Kathryn Lenart, and Michael Rath, "Outcomes Associated with Scheduling or Up-Scheduling Controlled Substances," *International Journal of Drug Policy*, Vol. 91, May 2021b, pp. 1–12.

Caulkins, Jonathan P., and Mark Kleiman, "Lessons to be Drawn from U.S. Drug Control Policies," *European Journal on Criminal Policy and Research*, Vol. 24, No. 5, June 2018, pp. 125–144.

Caulkins, Jonathan P., and Peter Reuter, "How Drug Enforcement Affects Drug Prices," *Crime and Justice*, Vol. 39, No. 1, 2010, pp. 213–271.

CBP—*See* U.S. Customs and Border Protection.

CDC—*See* Centers for Disease Control and Prevention.

Centers for Disease Control and Prevention, "Federal Grantees May Now Use Funds to Purchase Fentanyl Test Strips," press release, April 7, 2021a.

Centers for Disease Control and Prevention, "National Center for Health Statistics: Provisional Drug Overdose Death Counts," webpage, 2021b. As of August 2, 2021: https://www.cdc.gov/nchs/nvss/vsrr/drug-overdose-data.htm

Centers for Disease Control and Prevention, Office for State, Tribal, Local and Territorial Support, *Menu of Pain Management Clinic Regulation*, Atlanta, Ga., 2012.

Ciccarone, Daniel, Jeff Ondocsin, and Sarah G. Mars, "Heroin Uncertainties: Exploring Users' Perceptions of Fentanyl-Adulterated and -Substituted 'Heroin,'" *International Journal of Drug Policy*, Vol. 46, 2017, pp. 146–155.

Cicero, Theodore J., Matthew S. Ellis, and Hilary L. Surratt, "Effect of Abuse-Deterrent Formulation of OxyContin," *New England Journal of Medicine*, Vol. 367, 2012, pp. 187–189.

Coleman, John J., *Fentanyl Analogs in Street Drugs*, Fairfax, Va.: Prescription Drug Research Center, 2007.

Commission on Combating Synthetic Opioid Trafficking, *Commission on Combating Synthetic Opioid Trafficking: Final Report*, Washington, D.C., February 2022.

Congressional Research Service, *Heroin Trafficking in the United States*, Washington, D.C., 2019.

Corsaro, Nicholas, Eleazer D. Hunt, Natalie Kroovand Hipple, and Edmund F. McGarrell, "Impact of Drug Market Pulling Levers Policing on Neighborhood Violence: An Evaluation of the High Point Drug Market Intervention," *Criminology & Public Policy*, Vol. 11, No. 2, May 2012, pp. 167–199.

Cunningham, James K., Russell C. Callaghan, and Lon-Mu Liu, "US Federal Cocaine Essential ('Precursor') Chemical Regulation Impacts on US Cocaine Availability: An Intervention Time-Series Analysis with Temporal Replication," *Addiction*, Vol. 110, No. 5, May 2015, pp. 805–820.

Cunningham, Scott, and Keith Finlay, "Parental Substance Use and Foster Care: Evidence from Two Methamphetamine Supply Shocks," *Economic Inquiry*, Vol. 51, No. 1, January 2013, pp. 764–782.

Daly, Max, "The Truth About Drug Dealers Lacing Cocaine with Fentanyl," *Vice*, April 5, 2019.

Daniulaityte, Raminta, Ramzi W. Nahhas, Sydney Silverstein, Silvia Martins, Angela Zaragoza, Avery Moeller, and Robert G. Carlson, "Patterns of Non-Prescribed Buprenorphine and Other Opioid Use Among Individuals with Opioid Use Disorder: A Latent Class Analysis," *Drug and Alcohol Dependence*, Vol. 204, 2019.

Dasgupta, Nabarun, Clark Freifeld, John S. Brownstein, Christopher Mark Menone, Hilary L. Surratt, H.L., Luke Poppish, Jody L. Green, Eric J. Lavonas, and Richard C. Dart, "Crowdsourcing Black Market Prices for Prescription Opioids," *Journal of Medical Internet Research*, Vol. 15, No. 8, 2013, pp. 1–11.

DEA—*See* Drug Enforcement Administration.

Devine, Ben, Kristin Gutierrez, and Roy Rogers, "Drug Diversion by Anesthesiologists: Identification Through Intensive Auditing," *American Journal of Health-System Pharmacy*, Vol. 69, No. 7, 2012, pp. 552–556.

Dhalla, Irfan A., Navindra Persaud, and David N. Juurlink, "Facing Up to the Prescription Opioid Crisis," *BMJ*, Vol. 343, 2011.

Dobkin, Carlos, and Nancy Nicosia, "The War on Drugs: Methamphetamine, Public Health, and Crime," *American Economic Review*, Vol. 99, No. 1, 2009, pp. 324–349.

Dobkin, Carlos, Nancy Nicosia, and Matthew Weinberg, "Are Supply-Side Drug Control Efforts Effective? Evaluating OTC Regulations Targeting Methamphetamine Precursors," *Journal of Public Economics*, Vol. 120, December 2014, pp. 48–61.

Dowell, Deborah, Tamara M. Haegerich, and Roger Chou, "CDC Guideline for Prescribing Opioids for Chronic Pain—United States, 2016," *JAMA*, Vol. 315, No. 15, 2016, pp. 1624–1645.

Dowell, Deborah, Kun Zhang, Rita K. Noonan, and Jason M. Hockenberry, "Mandatory Provider Review and Pain Clinic Laws Reduce the Amounts of Opioids Prescribed and Overdose Death Rates," *Health Affairs*, Vol. 35, 2016, pp. 1876–1883.

Drug Enforcement Administration, *National Heroin Threat Assessment Summary*, Springfield, Va., June 2016a.

Drug Enforcement Administration, *2016 National Drug Threat Assessment*, Springfield, Va., November 2016b.

Drug Enforcement Administration, *2017 National Drug Threat Assessment*, Springfield, Va., October 2017.

Drug Enforcement Administration, "Justice Department, DEA Propose Significant Opioid Manufacturing Reduction in 2019," press release, August 16, 2018a.

Drug Enforcement Administration, *2018 National Drug Threat Assessment*, Springfield, Va., October 2018b.

Drug Enforcement Administration, *2019 National Drug Threat Assessment*, Springfield, Va., December 2019.

Drug Enforcement Administration, *2020 National Drug Threat Assessment*, Springfield, Va., March 2021.

Europol, "Crime on the Dark Web: Law Enforcement Coordination Is the Only Cure," press release, May 29, 2018.

Faul, Mark, Peter Lurie, Jeremiah M. Kinsman, Michael W. Dailey, Charmaine Crabaugh, and Scott M. Sasser, "Multiple Naloxone Administrations Among Emergency Medical Service Providers Is Increasing," *Prehospital Emergency Care*, Vol. 21, No. 4, 2017, pp. 411–419.

Freeborn, Beth A., "Arrest Avoidance: Law Enforcement and the Price of Cocaine," *Journal of Law and Economics*, Vol. 52, No. 1, 2009, pp. 19–40.

Gallet, Craig A., "Can Price Get the Monkey off Our Back? A Meta-Analysis of Illicit Drug Demand," Health Economics, Vol. 23, No. 1, January 2014, pp. 55–68.

Geddes, Louise, Jenny Iversen, Sonja Memedovic, and Lisa Maher, "Intravenous Fentanyl Use Among People Who Inject Drugs in Australia," *Drug and Alcohol Review*, Vol. 37, No. S1, April 2018, pp. S314–S322.

Giommoni, Luca, and R. V. Gundur, "An Analysis of the United Kingdom's Cannabis Market Using Crowdsourced Data," *Global Crime*, Vol. 19, No. 2, 2018, pp. 85–106.

Gladden, R. Matthew, Pedro Martinez, and Puja Seth, "Fentanyl Law Enforcement Submissions and Increases in Synthetic Opioid–Involved Overdose Deaths—27 States, 2013–2014," *Morbidity and Mortality Weekly Report*, Vol. 65, No. 33, 2016, pp. 837–843.

Gluck, Abbe R., Ashley Hall, and Gregory Curfman, "Civil Litigation and the Opioid Epidemic: The Role of Courts in a National Health Crisis," *Journal of Law, Medicine, and Ethics*, Vol. 46, No. 2, June 2018, pp. 351–366.

Guerrero Castro, Javier Enrique, "Maritime Interdiction in the War on Drugs in Colombia: Practices, Technologies and Technological Innovation," thesis, University of Edinburgh, 2016.

Haffajee, Rebecca L., and Michelle M. Mello, "Drug Companies' Liability for the Opioid Epidemic," *New England Journal of Medicine*, Vol. 377, No. 24, 2017, pp. 2301–2305.

Han, Beth, Wilson M. Compton, Carlos Blanco, Elizabeth Crane, Jinhee Lee, and Christopher M. Jones, "Prescription Opioid Use, Misuse, and Use Disorders in U.S. Adults: 2015 National Survey on Drug Use and Health," *Annals of Internal Medicine*, Vol. 167, 2017, pp. 293–301.

Harris, Magdalena, and Tim Rhodes, "Injecting Practices in Sexual Partnerships: Hepatitis C Transmission Potentials in a "Risk Equivalence" Framework," *Drug and Alcohol Dependence*, Vol. 132, No. 3, 2013, pp. 617–623.

Hedegaard, Holly, Arialdi M. Miniño, and Margaret Warner, "Drug Overdose Deaths in the United States, 1999–2018," NCHS Data Brief, No. 394, December 2020.

Higham, Scott, Sari Horwitz, Steven Rich, and Meryl Kornfield, "The Opioid Files: Inside the Drug Industry's Plan to Defeat the DEA," *Washington Post*, September 13, 2019.

Hswen, Yulin, Amanda Zhang, and John S. Brownstein, "Leveraging Black-Market Street Buprenorphine Pricing to Increase Capacity to Treat Opioid Addiction, 2010–2018," *Preventive Medicine*, Vol. 137, 2020.

Inciardi, James A., Hilary L. Surratt, Steven P. Kurtz, and Theodore J. Cicero, "Mechanisms of Prescription Drug Diversion Among Drug-Involved Club- and Street-Based Populations," *Pain Medicine*, Vol. 8, No. 2, 2007, pp. 171–183.

Johnson, Bruce D., Paul J. Goldstein, Edward Preble, James Schmeidler, Douglas S. Lipton, Barry Spunt, and Thomas Miller, *Taking Care of Business: The Economics of Crime by Heroin Abusers*, Lexington, Mass.: Lexington Books, 1985.

Jozaghi, Ehsan, Russ Maynard, Zahra Dadakhah-Chimeh, Kevin Yake, and Sarah Blyth, "The Synthetic Opioid Epidemic and the Need for Mental Health Support for First Responders Who Intervene in Overdose Cases," *Canadian Journal of Public Health*, Vol. 109, No. 2, 2018, pp. 231–232.

Kennedy-Hendricks, Alene, Matthew Richey, Emma E. McGinty, Elizabeth A. Stuart, Colleen L. Barry, and Daniel W. Webster, "Opioid Overdose Deaths and Florida's Crackdown on Pill Mills," *American Journal of Public Health*, Vol. 106, 2016, pp. 291–297.

Khan, Nazleen F., Brian T. Bateman, Joan E. Landon, and Joshua J. Gagne, "Association of Opioid Overdose with Opioid Prescriptions to Family Members," *JAMA Internal Medicine*, Vol. 179, No. 9, 2019, pp. 1186–1192.

Kilmer, Beau, Jonathan P. Caulkins, Brittany M. Bond, and Peter H. Reuter, *Reducing Drug Trafficking Revenues and Violence in Mexico: Would Legalizing Marijuana in California Help?* Santa Monica, Calif.: RAND Corporation, OP-325-RC, 2010. As of August 1, 2022: https://www.rand.org/pubs/occasional_papers/OP325.html

Kilmer, Beau, Bryce Pardo, Jonathan P. Caulkins, and Peter Reuter, "How Much Illegally Manufactured Fentanyl Could the U.S. Be Consuming?" *American Journal of Drug and Alcohol Abuse*, July 22, 2022a, pp. 1–6.

Kilmer, Beau, Bryce Pardo, Toyya A. Pujol, and Jonathan P. Caulkins, "Rapid Changes in Illegally Manufactured Fentanyl Products and Prices in the United States," *Addiction*, May 11, 2022b, pp. 1–5.

Kilmer, Beau, Susan M. Sohler Everingham, Jonathan P. Caulkins, Gregory Midgette, Rosalie Liccardo Pacula, Peter Reuter, Rachel M. Burns, Bing Han, and Russell Lundberg, *What America's Users Spend on Illegal Drugs, 2000–2010*, Santa Monica, Calif.: RAND Corporation, RR-534-ONDCP, 2014. As of June 15, 2022: https://www.rand.org/pubs/research_reports/RR534.html

Kleiman, Mark A. R., *When Brute Force Fails: How to Have Less Crime and Less Punishment*, Princeton, N.J.: Princeton University Press, 2009.

Kleiman, Mark A. R., "Targeting Drug-Trafficking Violence in Mexico: An Orthogonal Approach," in Ernesto Zedillo and Haynie Wheeler, eds., *Rethinking the "War on Drugs" Through the US-Mexico Prism*, New Haven, Conn.: Yale Center for the Study of Globalization, 2012, pp. 125–136.

Kolodny, Andrew, David T. Courtwright, Catherine S. Hwang, Peter Kreiner, John L. Eadie, Thomas W. Clark, and G. Caleb Alexander, "The Prescription Opioid and Heroin Crisis: A Public Health Approach to an Epidemic of Addiction," *Annual Review of Public Health*, Vol. 36, 2015, pp. 559–574.

Kral, Alex H., Barrot H. Lambdin, Erica N. Browne, Lynn D. Wenger, Ricky N. Bluthenthal, Jon E. Zibbell, and Peter J. Davidson, "Transition from Injecting Opioids to Smoking Fentanyl in San Francisco, California," *Drug and Alcohol Dependence*, Vol. 227, October 2021, pp. 1–8.

Krieger, Maxwell S., William C. Goedel, Jane A. Buxton, Mark Lysyshyn, Edward Bernstein, Susan G. Sherman, Josiah D. Rich, Scott E. Hadland, Traci C. Green, and Brandon D. L. Marshall, "Use of Rapid Fentanyl Test Strips Among Young Adults Who Use Drugs," *International Journal of Drug Policy*, Vol. 61, 2018, pp. 52–58.

Lambdin, Barrot H., Ricky N. Bluthenthal, Jon E. Zibbell, Lynn Wenger, Kelsey Simpson, and Alex H. Kral, "Associations Between Perceived Illicit Fentanyl Use and Infectious Disease Risks Among People Who Inject Drugs," *International Journal of Drug Policy*, Vol. 74, December 2019, pp. 299–304.

Lamy, Francois R., Raminta Daniulaityte, Monica J. Barratt, Usha Lokala, Amit Sheth, and Robert G. Carlson, "Listed for Sale: Analyzing Data on Fentanyl, Fentanyl Analogs and Other Novel Synthetic Opioids on One Cryptomarket," *Drug and Alcohol Dependence*, Vol. 213, 2020.

Le Cour Grandmaison, Romain, Nathaniel Morris, and Benjamin T. Smith, *No More Opium for the Masses: From the U.S. Fentanyl Boom to the Mexican Opium Crisis: Opportunities Amidst Violence? Paris*: Noria Research, 2019.

Lebin, Jacob A., David L. Murphy, Stevan Geoffrey Severtson, Gabrielle E. Bau, Nabarun Dasgupta, and Richard C. Dart, "Scoring the Best Deal: Quantity Discounts and Street Price Variation of Diverted Oxycodone and Oxymorphone," *Pharmacoepidemiology and Drug Safety*, Vol. 28, No. 1, 2019, pp. 25–30.

Lofwall, Michelle R., and Sharon L. Walsh, "A Review of Buprenorphine Diversion and Misuse: The Current Evidence Base and Experiences from Around the World," *Journal of Addiction Medicine*, Vol. 8, No. 5, 2014, pp. 315–326.

Lyapustina, Tatyana, Lainie Rutkow, Hsien-Yen Chang, Matthew Daubresse, Alim F. Ramji, Mark Faul, Elizabeth A. Stuart, and G. Caleb Alexander, "Effect of a 'Pill Mill' Law on Opioid Prescribing and Utilization: the Case of Texas," *Drug and Alcohol Dependence*, Vol. 159, 2016, pp. 190–197.

Mars, Sarah G., Philippe Bourgois, George Karandinos, Fernando Montero, and Daniel Ciccarone, "'Every "Never" I Ever Said Came True': Transitions from Opioid Pills to Heroin Injecting," *International Journal of Drug Policy*, Vol. 25, No. 2, 2014, pp. 257–266.

Mars, Sarah G., Jeff Ondocsin, and Daniel Ciccarone, "Sold as Heroin: Perceptions and Use of an Evolving Drug in Baltimore, MD," *Journal of Psychoactive Drugs*, Vol. 50, No. 2, April–June 2018, pp. 167–176.

Martin, James, Jack Cunliffe, David Décary-Hétu, and Judith Aldridge, "Effect of Restricting the Legal Supply of Prescription Opioids on Buying Through Online Illicit Marketplaces: Interrupted Time Series Analysis," *British Medical Journal*, Vol. 361, 2018.

Midgette, Gregory, Steven Davenport, Jonathan P. Caulkins, and Beau Kilmer, *What America's Users Spend on Illegal Drugs, 2006–2016*, Santa Monica, Calif.: RAND Corporation, RR-3140-ONDCP, 2019. As of August 20, 2019:
https://www.rand.org/pubs/research_reports/RR3140.html

Monte, Andrew A., Todd Mandell, Bonnie B. Wilford, Joseph Tennyson, and Edward W. Boyer, "Diversion of Buprenorphine/Naloxone Coformulated Tablets in a Region with High Prescribing Prevalence," *Journal of Addictive Diseases*, Vol. 28, No. 3, 2009, pp. 226–231.

Morselli, Carlo, and Katia Petit, "Law-Enforcement Disruption of a Drug Importation Network," *Global Crime*, Vol. 8, No. 2, 2007, pp. 109–130.

MPG Consulting and the University of Colorado Boulder Leeds School of Business, 2020 Regulated Marijuana Market Update, Boulder, Colo., undated.

Munksgaard, Rasmus, and Meropi Tzanetakis, "Uncertainty and Risk: A Framework for Understanding Pricing in Online Drug Markets," *International Journal of Drug Policy*, Vol. 101, March 2022, pp. 1–13.

Musto, David F., *One Hundred Years of Heroin*, Westport, Conn.: Praeger, 2002.

O'Connor, Sean, *Meth Precursor Chemicals from China: Implications for the United States*, Washington, D.C.: U.S.-China Economic and Security Review Commission, 2016.

O'Connor, Sean, *Fentanyl: China's Deadly Export to the United States*, Washington, D.C.: U.S.-China Economic and Security Review Commission, 2017.

Office of National Drug Control Policy, *Response to Questions Concerning Fentanyl*, Washington, D.C.: Executive Office of the President, 2017.

Office of National Drug Control Policy, *New Annual Data Released by White House Office of National Drug Control Policy Shows Poppy Cultivation and Potential Heroin Production Remain at Record-High Levels in Mexico*, Washington, D.C.: Executive Office of the President, 2019.

Office of National Drug Control Policy, *National Drug Control Budget: FY 2022 Funding Highlights*, Washington, D.C., May 2021.

ONDCP—*See* Office of National Drug Control Policy.

Oregon Liquor and Cannabis Commission, "Marijuana and Hemp (Cannabis): Harvest, Price, and Sales Market Data," dataset, undated. As of November 10, 2022:
https://www.oregon.gov/olcc/marijuana/Pages/Marijuana-Market-Data.aspx

Pardo, Bryce, "Do More Robust Prescription Drug Monitoring Programs Reduce Prescription Opioid Overdose?" *Addiction*, Vol. 112, No. 10, 2017, pp. 1773–1783.

Pardo, Bryce, *Evolution of the U.S. Overdose Crisis: Understanding China's Role in the Production and Supply of Synthetic Opioids*, Santa Monica, Calif.: RAND Corporation, CT-497, 2018. As of April 11, 2019:
https://www.rand.org/pubs/testimonies/CT497.html

Pardo, Bryce, Lois M. Davis, and Melinda Moore, *Characterization of the Synthetic Opioid Threat Profile to Inform Inspection and Detection Solutions*, Homeland Security Operational Analysis Center operated by the RAND Corporation, RR-2969-DHS, 2019. As of May 25, 2022:
https://www.rand.org/pubs/research_reports/RR2969.html

Pardo, Bryce, Beau Kilmer, and Wenjing Huang, *Contemporary Asian Drug Policy: Insights and Opportunities for Change*, Santa Monica, Calif.: RAND Corporation, RR-2733-RC, 2019. As of May 25, 2022:
https://www.rand.org/pubs/research_reports/RR2733.html

Pardo, Bryce, and Peter Reuter, "Narcotics and Drug Abuse: Foreshadowing of 50 Years of Change," *Criminology & Public Policy*, Vol. 17, No. 2, May 2018, pp. 419–436.

Pardo, Bryce, and Peter Reuter, "China Can't Solve America's Fentanyl Problem: Why a Crackdown Won't Fix the Opioid Crisis," *Foreign Affairs*, 2019.

Pardo, Bryce, and Peter Reuter, *Enforcement Strategies for Fentanyl and Other Synthetic Opioids*, Washington, D.C.: Brookings Institution, June 22, 2020.

Pardo, Bryce, Jirka Taylor, Jonathan P. Caulkins, Beau Kilmer, Peter Reuter, and Bradley D. Stein, *The Future of Fentanyl and Other Synthetic Opioids*, Santa Monica, Calif.: RAND Corporation, RR-3117-RC, 2019. As of January 2, 2020:
https://www.rand.org/pubs/research_reports/RR3117.html

Park, Ju Nyeong, Emaan Rashidi, Kathryn Foti, Michael Zoorob, Susan Sherman, and G. Caleb Alexander, "Fentanyl and Fentanyl Analogs in the Illicit Stimulant Supply: Results from U.S. Drug Seizure Data, 2011–2016," *Drug and Alcohol Dependence*, Vol. 218, No. 8, 2021.

Park, Ju Nyeong, Susan G. Sherman, Saba Rouhani, Kenneth B. Morales, Michelle McKenzie, Sean T. Allen, Brandon D. L. Marshall, and Traci C. Green, "Willingness to Use Safe Consumption Spaces Among Opioid Users at High Risk of Fentanyl Overdose in Baltimore, Providence, and Boston," *Journal of Urban Health*, Vol. 96, No. 3, June 2019, pp. 353–366.

Peiper, Nicholas C., Sarah Duhart Clarke, Louise B. Vincent, Dan Ciccarone, Alex H. Kral, and Jon E. Zibbell, "Fentanyl Test Strips as an Opioid Overdose Prevention Strategy: Findings from a Syringe Services Program in the Southeastern United States," *International Journal of Drug Policy*, Vol. 63, 2019, pp. 122–128.

Peirce, Gretchen L., Michael J. Smith, Marie A. Abate, and Joel Halverson, "Doctor and Pharmacy Shopping for Controlled Substances," *Medical Care*, Vol. 50, No. 6, 2012, pp. 494–500.

Peng, Philip W. H., and Alan N. Sandler, "A Review of the Use of Fentanyl Analgesia in the Management of Acute Pain in Adults," *Journal of the American Society of Anesthesiologists*, Vol. 90, 1999, pp. 576–599.

Pike, Erika, Martha Tillson, J. Matthew Webster, and Michele Staton, "A Mixed-Methods Assessment of the Impact of the Opioid Epidemic on First Responder Burnout," *Drug and Alcohol Dependence*, Vol. 205, 2019, pp. 1–6.

Pollack, Harold A., and Peter Reuter, "Does Tougher Enforcement Make Drugs More Expensive?" *Addiction*, Vol. 109, No. 12, December 2014, pp. 1959–1966.

Reuter, Peter, *Disorganized Crime: The Economics of the Visible Hand*, Cambridge, Mass.: MIT Press, 1983.

Reuter, Peter, and Mark A. R. Kleiman, "Risks and Prices: An Economic Analysis of Drug Enforcement," *Crime and Justice*, Vol. 7, 1986, pp. 289–340.

Reuter, Peter, Robert J. MacCoun, Patrick Murphy, Allan Abrahamse, and Barbara Simon, *Money from Crime: A Study of the Economics of Drug Dealing in Washington, D.C.*, Santa Monica, Calif.: RAND Corporation, R-3894-RF, 1990. As of May 25, 2022: https://www.rand.org/pubs/reports/R3894.html

Rhodes, William, Christina Dyous, Dana Hunt, Jeremy Luallen, Myfanwy Callahan, and Rajen Subramanian, *What America's Users Spend on Illegal Drugs, 2000 Through 2006*, Washington, D.C.: Executive Office of the President, June 2012.

Rhodes, William, Mary Layne, Anne-Marie Bruen, Patrick Johnston, and Lisa Becchetti, *What America's Users Spend on Illegal Drugs 1988–2000*, Cambridge, Mass.: Abt Associates, December 2001.

Rouhani, Saba, Ju Nyeong Park, Kenneth B. Morales, Traci C. Green, and Susan G. Sherman, "Harm Reduction Measures Employed by People Using Opioids with Suspected Fentanyl Exposure in Boston, Baltimore, and Providence," *Harm Reduction Journal*, Vol. 16, No. 39, 2019.

Royal Canadian Mounted Police, "Massive Drug Lab Bust Highlights Coordinated Approach to Gangs and Organized Crime," press release, May 13, 2021.

Rutkow, Lainie, Hsien-Yen Chang, Matthew Daubresse, Daniel W. Webster, Elizabeth A. Stuart, and G. Caleb Alexander, "Effect of Florida's Prescription Drug Monitoring Program and Pill Mill Laws on Opioid Prescribing and Use," *JAMA Internal Medicine*, Vol. 175, No. 10, 2015, pp. 1642–1649.

Sacco, Lisa N., and Erin Bagalman, *The Opioid Epidemic and Federal Efforts to Address It: Frequently Asked Questions*, Washington, D.C.: Congressional Research Service, No. 44987, 2017.

Saunders, Jessica, Michael Robbins, and Allison J. Ober, "Moving from Efficacy to Effectiveness: Implementing the Drug Market Intervention Across Multiple Sites," *Criminology & Public Policy*, Vol. 16, No. 3, August 2017, pp. 787–814.

Scholl, Lawrence, Puja Seth, Mbabazi Kariisa, Nana Wilson, and Grant Baldwin, "Drug and Opioid-Involved Overdose Deaths—United States, 2013–2017," *Morbidity and Mortality Weekly Report*, Vol. 67, No. 5152, 2019, pp. 1419–1427.

Shover, Chelsea L., Titilola O. Falasinnu, Rohan B. Freedman, and Keith Humphreys, "Emerging Characteristics of Isotonitazene-Involved Overdose Deaths: A Case-Control Study," *Journal of Addiction Medicine*, Vol. 15, No. 5, 2021, pp. 429–431.

Silverstein, Sydney M., Raminta Daniulaityte, Shannon C. Miller, Silvia S. Martins, and Robert G. Carlson, "*On My Own Terms*: Motivations for Self-Treating Opioid-Use Disorder with Non-Prescribed Buprenorphine," *Drug and Alcohol Dependence*, Vol. 210, 2020.

Smart, Rosanna, Jonathan P. Caulkins, Beau Kilmer, Steven Davenport, and Greg Midgette, "Variation in Cannabis Potency and Prices in a Newly Legal Market: Evidence from 30 Million Cannabis Sales in Washington State," *Addiction*, Vol. 112, No. 12, December 2017, pp. 2167–2177.

Smith, Kirsten E., Martha D. Tillson, Michele Staton, and Erin M. Winston, "Characterization of Diverted Buprenorphine Use Among Adults Entering Corrections-Based Drug Treatment in Kentucky," *Drug and Alcohol Dependence*, Vol. 208, March 2020.

Spencer, Merianne Rose, Margaret Warner, Brigham A. Bastian, James P. Trinidad, and Holly Hedegaard, *Drug Overdose Deaths Involving Fentanyl, 2011–2016*, Washington, D.C.: U.S. Department of Health and Human Services, National Vital Statistics Reports, Vol. 68, No. 3, March 21, 2019.

Staman, Jennifer A., *The Opioid Epidemic and the Food and Drug Administration: Legal Authorities and Recent Agency Action*, Washington, D.C.: Congressional Research Service, No. R45218, December 27, 2018.

Substance Abuse and Mental Health Data Archive, "National Survey on Drug Use and Health, 2019: Crosstab Creator," web tool, Substance Abuse and Mental Health Services Administration, undated. As of July 7, 2022:
https://pdas.samhsa.gov/#/survey/NSDUH-2019-DS0001?column=UDPYPNR&results_received=true&row=SRCPNRNM2&run_chisq=false&weight=ANALWT_C

Substance Abuse and Mental Health Services Administration, *Key Substance Use and Mental Health Indicators in the United States: Results from the 2017 National Survey on Drug Use and Health*, Rockville, Md.: Center for Behavioral Health Statistics and Quality, 2018.

Toronto's Drug Checking Service, homepage, Centre on Drug Policy Evaluation, undated. As of July 7, 2022:
https://drugchecking.cdpe.org/

United Nations Office on Drugs and Crime, *México: Monitoreo de Cultivos de Amapola—2015–2016 y 2016–2017*, Mexico City, No. MEXK54, 2018.

United Nations Office on Drugs and Crime, *World Drug Report 2021: Global Overview—Drug Demand and Drug Supply*, Vienna, Austria, 2021.

UNODC—*See* United Nations Office on Drugs and Crime.

U.S. Customs and Border Protection, *CBP Strategy to Combat Opioids*, Washington, D.C.: U.S. Department of Homeland Security, 2019.

U.S. Department of Justice, "Justice Department Announces First Ever Indictments Against Designated Chinese Manufacturers of Deadly Fentanyl and Other Opiate Substances," press release, October 17, 2017.

U.S. Government Accountability Office, *Synthetic Opioids: Considerations for the Class-Wide Scheduling of Fentanyl-Related Substances*, Washington, D.C., GAO-21-499, April 2021.

U.S. Senate, Ensuring Patient Access and Effective Drug Enforcement Act of 2016, Bill S.483, April 19, 2016. As of May 25, 2022:
https://www.congress.gov/bill/114th-congress/senate-bill/483

Vardanyan, Ruben S., and Victor J. Hruby, "Fentanyl-Related Compounds and Derivatives: Current Status and Future Prospects for Pharmaceutical Applications," *Future Medicinal Chemistry*, Vol. 6, No. 4, 2014, pp. 385–412.

Weicker, Noelle P., Jill Owczarzak, Glenna Urquhart, Ju Nyeong Park, Saba Rouhani, Rui Ling, Miles Morris, and Susan G. Sherman, "Agency in the Fentanyl Era: Exploring the Utility of Fentanyl Test Strips in an Opaque Drug Market," *International Journal of Drug Policy*, Vol. 84, 2020.

The White House, "The Office of National Drug Control Policy Announces the Third Consecutive Year of Reduction in Poppy Cultivation and Potential Heroin Production in Mexico," press release, June 10, 2021a.

The White House, "ONDCP Funds Research to Support Evidence-Based State Drug Policies and Laws," press release, August 2, 2021b.

World Health Organization, *China Policies to Promote Local Production of Pharmaceutical Products and Protect Public Health*, Geneva, 2017.

Yeh, Brian T., *Legal Authorities Under the Controlled Substances Act to Combat the Opioid Crisis*, Washington, D.C.: Congressional Research Service, No. R45164, December 18, 2018.

Zibbell, Jon E., Arnie P. Aldridge, Dennis Cauchon, Jolene DeFiore-Hyrmer, and Kevin P. Conway, "Association of Law Enforcement Seizures of Heroin, Fentanyl, and Carfentanil with Opioid Overdose Deaths in Ohio, 2014–2017," *JAMA Network Open*, Vol. 2, No. 11, 2019.

Zibbell, Jon E., Nicholas C. Peiper, Sarah E. Duhart Clarke, Zach R. Salazar, Louise B. Vincent, Alex H. Kral, and Judith Feinberg, "Consumer Discernment of Fentanyl in Illicit Opioids Confirmed by Fentanyl Test Strips: Lessons from a Syringe Services Program in North Carolina," *International Journal of Drug Policy*, Vol. 93, 2021.

Harm Reduction and Community-Initiated Interventions

Martin Y. Iguchi, Jirka Taylor, Beau Kilmer

Overview

The U.S. approach to addressing problems with substance use has traditionally focused on two pillars: supply reduction and demand reduction. Compared with many other Western countries, the U.S. federal government has been slow to embrace *harm reduction* efforts, which focus on reducing the risk associated with drug consumption. For example, syringe service programs (SSPs)—which reduce infectious disease by providing clean syringes and other materials to people who use drugs (PWUD)—have been operating in hundreds of communities across the country, but it was not until 2016 that the federal government allowed, under certain circumstances, the use of federal funding to support these programs.

SSPs and other harm reduction programs often start as grassroots efforts, usually by nonprofit organizations and/or PWUD. This chapter focuses on harm reduction programs and community-initiated efforts to prevent and reduce drug consumption. Community engagement is necessary to avoid defaulting to institutional solutions that all too often come prepackaged, do not necessarily fit with community need, and fail to account for upstream social determinants of health. This is very much the case for the prevention, mitigation, and resolution of harms caused by opioid and other drug use.

Prevention Efforts Focused on Adverse Childhood Experiences and Substance Use

Children in socioeconomically disadvantaged communities, particularly children of color, are affected by a lack of resources, exposure to violence, challenging physical environments, regular exposure to microaggressions, and oppression associated with prejudice and stigma. These and other adverse events experienced by children are associated with higher rates of physical and mental health conditions, as well as other developmental issues. Public health–oriented prevention interventions for children and adolescents typically examine a variety of risk and protective factors and a wide variety of target problem areas, such as obesity, smoking, diabetes, heart disease, alcohol and drug use, depression, and exposure to violence.

But prevention efforts should not just be focused on youth, especially because most people do not start using heroin and other illegally produced opioids until they are adults. Multiple community-wide programs have been successfully implemented to engage and support communities in their efforts to select the best mix of evidence-based approaches for reducing or eliminating risk factors and building on strengths. Examples of science-guided, community-level interventions include the Communities That Care prevention program, Getting to Outcomes, and the Substance Abuse and Mental Health Services Administration (SAMHSA) community engagement approach.

Community-Based Efforts to Reduce Drug Use Harms

Treatment engagement and longer-term recovery are enhanced when PWUD engage with peers, non–drug using members of the community, and community resources, such as housing, education, and employment. One example of a program to promote community engagement by individuals who are in treatment for substance use disorders is the Community Reinforcement Approach. In addition to reinforcing engagement with treatment, this approach reinforces a variety of behaviors and activities that are intended to engage the individual with the larger community, including social or recreational counseling and job-hunting skills.

But efforts to reduce harms also need to include individuals who are neither seeking treatment nor in recovery. Coalitions to reduce drug use harms have their roots in self-organizing by people who use drugs in the Netherlands in the 1970s. The concept of early drug user unions involved peer support and activism to push back against the political scapegoating of drug users (Friedman, 1998), law enforcement harassment (Trautmann, 1995), and stigma and demonization (Johansson, Kjær, and Stothard, 2015). Over time, the work of community activists and a generation of research on harm reduction interventions have contributed to an ongoing, albeit limited, shift in the politics of harm reduction in the United States.

Harm Reduction Interventions to Reduce Risks and Stigma Associated with Drug Use

Examples of harm reduction interventions include opioid education and naloxone distribution programs (teaching PWUD and other community members about how to administer naloxone and/or providing it to them), street-outreach workers who engage with PWUD in a nonjudgmental manner, SSPs, drug content testing, and supervised drug consumption. Such interventions, and who is responsible for implementing them, often vary from community to community. In some places, these efforts are implemented by government agencies (e.g., state and local departments of public health); in others, they are government supported but implemented by other organizations. In many jurisdictions, they take place with little to no government support. Harm reduction is controversial in many parts of the United States, often leading to a very unstable funding environment.

Key Interactions with Other Components of the Ecosystem

To the extent that harm reduction interventions increase admissions to opioid use disorder (OUD) treatment (e.g., through direct referral, motivating behavior change, or increasing trust in the health system), these interventions directly affect the **medical care** and **specialty treatment systems**; however, the extent to which this happens is largely understudied. In addition to some medical care services being made available by harm reduction organizations, referrals to the medical care system might be made for infectious disease testing, access to medications that prevent disease spread (e.g., preexposure prophylaxis [PrEP]), and/or utilization of OUD treatment services. Within the specialty treatment system, harm reduction approaches have challenged orthodoxy (e.g., low-threshold methadone programs, heroin-assisted treatment outside the United States) while other measures have become more common (e.g., tolerance of ongoing substance use during treatment rather than mandated program discharge).

The relationships between **criminal legal agencies** and those operating and using harm reduction initiatives, such as SSPs and drug content testing, are complex. Possession of controlled substances without a prescription is illegal, and many jurisdictions prohibit drug paraphernalia, which can include harm reduction materials (such as fentanyl test strips). Thus, the successful operation of some of these programs requires at least tacit tolerance or nonintervention from law enforcement agencies, though there are non–government sanctioned harm reduction programs operating in the United States. Supervised consumption sites (SCSs) violate the "crack house statute" of the U.S. Controlled Substances Act (CSA), and various U.S. Department of Justice (DOJ) officials and a federal appellate court have made this argument. That said, New York City recently opened two SCSs, and the DOJ (as of January 2023) has not taken action against these facilities or against the individuals who operate and use them.

The **illegal drug supply** shapes the context in which community-initiated interventions operate because changes in drug supply can have serious implications for harm reduction efforts. The arrival of illegally manufactured synthetic opioids (such as fentanyl) has resulted in elevated risks to people who use opioids and to individuals using other drugs who may be unknowingly exposed to synthetic opioids, placing even greater importance on interventions that aim to minimize the harm stemming from drug use. Examples include using SSPs to help reduce the risks stemming from frequent injections, naloxone distribution programs to enable individuals to reverse an overdose, and drug checking programs to tell individuals whether their street-purchased drugs contain potent and/or unexpected substances.

Community-initiated interventions also interact significantly with other systems. Most obvious is the relationship between **community coalitions** that are focused on prevention and the **education systems**, because schools represent an important setting for prevention interventions. In addition, schools have increasingly been a venue for the storage and distribution of naloxone kits, as well as for providing training on how to administer naloxone.

Harm reduction interventions also interact with **first responders**, who may administer naloxone to reverse potentially fatal overdoses in the community. Despite an increase in the number of law enforcement officers equipped with naloxone, some agencies continue to refuse to take this step and continue to question the desirability of providing naloxone to PWUD. In some places, however, first responders—including law enforcement, fire departments, and emergency medical services (EMS) agencies—play an important role as naloxone distribution channels in the community.

Policy Opportunities and Considerations

Providing more funding for harm reduction programs—especially during an unprecedented overdose crisis—is critical. However, decisionmakers could use more information about how to best allocate available funds for harm reduction. For example, if a city has $5 million in new funds to support efforts to reduce overdose deaths, should it allocate those funds to create and staff an SCS, increase the availability of naloxone, implement drug checking services, expand treatment, provide more emergency services, implement some combination of these efforts, or should it spend the funds on something else? The most efficient allocation of these funds will depend on the resources and programs that already are available in that community. Additionally, the location of these programs—and whether they are colocated with other service components of the ecosystem—will have implications for the overall costs and benefits.

Although the federal government has announced that it will spend $30 million to advance harm reduction efforts (U.S. Department of Health and Human Services [HHS] Press Office, 2021), this is a very small investment compared with the more than $40 billion proposed in the 2022 federal budget for demand and supply reduction (Office of National Drug Control Policy, 2021).

Some laws and criminal legal efforts have been changed to make it easier for communities to implement harm reduction interventions, but more could be done. For example, law enforcement could make it clear that individuals will not be arrested for patronizing or working at SSPs or places where individuals can test the composition of their drug sample and find out whether it contains fentanyl (and, ideally, how much). With respect to SCSs, federal barriers could be reduced to make it easier for communities to pilot and evaluate these interventions.

More broadly, reforming drug possession laws could also be considered (further discussed in Chapter Six). Indeed, in some parts of the country, there appears to be a willingness to engage in discussions about reducing harms caused by criminal legal policies related to substance use; the added burdens of the unmet needs of those living with serious mental health problems; and the critical dimensions of poverty, lack of opportunity, and homelessness.

Introduction

The U.S. approach to addressing problems with substance use has traditionally focused on two pillars: supply reduction and demand reduction. Compared with many other Western countries, the U.S. government has been slow to embrace *harm reduction* efforts, which focus on reducing the risk associated with drug consumption.[1] For example, SSPs—which reduce infectious disease by providing clean syringes and other materials to PWUD—have been operating in hundreds of communities throughout the United States, but it was not until 2016 that federal money could be used in some circumstances to support these programs (Centers for Disease Control and Prevention [CDC], 2016). It was not until 2021 that the federal government indicated that these programs can use federal funding directly to purchase syringes for distribution (SAMHSA, 2021).

SSPs and other harm reduction programs often start as grassroots efforts, usually by nonprofit organizations and/or PWUD with extensive input from advocates, public health workers, and physicians (Szalavitz, 2021). Funding may eventually come from government agencies, but this is not always the case. Contemporary harm reduction efforts in the United States emerged as a response to the AIDS epidemic and have since been undergoing a transformation from a rather marginal phenomenon to a much more mainstream approach, although this transformation is still very much in progress.[2] The acceptability of different types of harm reduction approaches can vary widely from community to community, with many harm reduction approaches being quite controversial in many parts of the United States, making the funding environment unstable.

This chapter focuses on harm reduction programs and community-initiated efforts to prevent and reduce drug consumption. Community engagement is necessary to avoid defaulting to institutional solutions that come prepackaged; do not necessarily fit with community needs, priorities, or culture; and fail to take into account upstream social determinants of health (Wendel et al., 2018). There is also a need to engage communities in the overall effort to promote the widespread implementation of effective interventions, both to promote accountability and to assure sustainment of effort (Lancaster and Ritter, 2014; MacPhail et al., 2019; Palombi et al., 2019; SAMHSA, 2020; Story et al., 2018; Wells et al., 2018).

The chapter begins with an overview of these initiatives, followed by a discussion about how they interact with many other components of the opioid ecosystem (Figure 8.1). It concludes with a discussion about policy considerations and opportunities.

---

[1] In this chapter, we use the term *harm reduction* in line with its conceptualization by the National Harm Reduction Coalition, which encompasses both the practical strategies "aimed at reducing negative consequences associated with drug use" and the underlying social justice movement concerned with the rights of PWUD (National Harm Reduction Coalition, undated-a).

[2] Szalavitz, 2021, offers a comprehensive account of some key episodes in the history of harm reduction in the United States and elsewhere.

FIGURE 8.1

The Harm Reduction System and Its Interactions

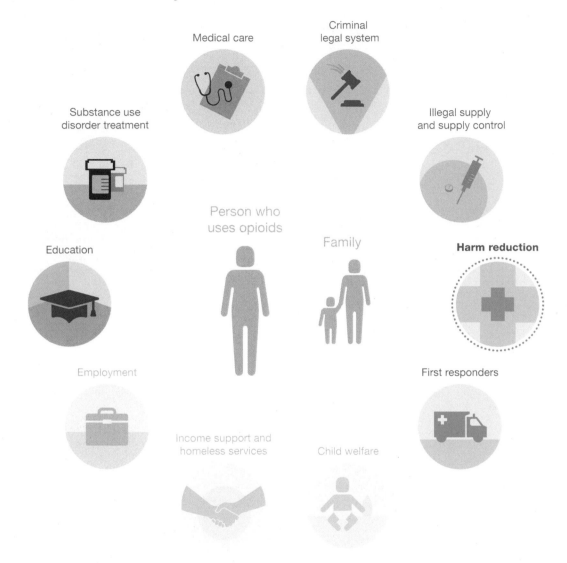

System Components and How They Interact with Opioids

Harm Reduction Interventions Intended to Reduce Risks and Stigma Associated with Opioid and Other Drug Use

This section largely focuses on the following harm reduction efforts that are intended to reduce the risks and stigma associated with opioid use: SSPs, naloxone, SCSs, drug checking services, prescription models, and nonprescription approaches to providing PWUD with drugs of known composition.

Street-Outreach Workers

There are several ways that the harms of injection drug use might be mitigated. In the early days of the HIV epidemic, one question that was frequently asked was, "Will intravenous drug users take steps to reduce their risk of getting AIDS?" (Des Jarlais and Friedman, 1987). Over time, it became abundantly clear that drug users were very interested in reducing their risk for infection and that they would be willing to adopt new behaviors to protect themselves. Early in the HIV/AIDS epidemic, peer-education and outreach efforts emphasized the following basic messages:

- Do not inject drugs.
- If drugs are to be injected, do not share your needles and injection works.
- Always clean your needles with bleach and clean water.

The use of condoms was encouraged to prevent the sexual spread of HIV/AIDS and other sexually transmitted infections from people who inject drugs (PWID) to their sexual partners. Other key message components were "Get Tested" and "Treatment Works" (Booth et al., 1998; Bux et al., 1993; Coyle, Needle, and Normand, 1998; Iguchi et al., 1990). Implementation of the early harm reduction messages to PWID required extensive street outreach, peer-reinforced messaging, and a large shift in PWID culture. Many communities resisted implementation of bleach and condom distribution, arguing that providing bleach to PWID "enabled" injection drug use and that condom distribution encouraged "promiscuous" sex (Rafferty and Radosh, 1997).

Syringe Service Programs

SSPs (also referred to as *needle exchange programs* [NEPs])[3] are community interventions that offer free access to sterile needles and syringes, as well as safe disposal of used needles (Des Jarlais et al., 2020). As SSPs began to spread, the message to clean needles and injection works changed to always use a clean and sterile needle and never share injection paraphernalia. As discussed earlier, needle exchange schemes were first implemented in Amsterdam in 1984 by a drug user union to combat the spread of hepatitis B. As the AIDS epidemic

---

[3] Currently, the terms SSP, NEP, and *syringe exchange program* are largely interchangeable, with SSP being the most commonly used term by U.S. policy authorities (see, e.g., CDC, 2019a) and in the literature. In the past, the term NEP was used more frequently, reflecting a historical requirement in some places that clients bring in used needles in exchange for sterile needles they obtain from the service (CDC, 2020). In this chapter, we use the term NEP when discussing the historical evolution of the service and SSP when discussing the current situation and state of the evidence. According to data from the North American Syringe Exchange Network (NASEN), the most common type ($n = 188$) of SSP is needs-based (i.e., without any requirement to bring in used syringes). NASEN data record 148 exchange-based SSPs (102 of them operating on a one-for-one basis and 42 running a "1+ exchange"). Another 99 sites are listed as "undisclosed," five as mobile, and five as secondary (NASEN, undated). Needs-based distribution policies have been found to be associated with higher syringe coverage among PWID (Bluthenthal et al., 2007) and with lower rates of syringe reuse (Kral et al., 2004).

spread rapidly around the globe, needle and syringe exchange programs were a central part of the harm reduction movement aimed at preventing infection and saving lives. Paraphernalia laws made NEPs illegal, so operating an exchange was an act of civil disobedience. Even as evidence mounted from studies conducted worldwide and in the United States that NEPs (1) significantly reduced the likelihood of HIV transmission in exchange users, (2) did not lead nonusers to begin drug use, (3) did not increase injection drug use, and (4) did not result in an increase in injection initiates (Bastos and Strathdee, 2000; Bravo et al., 2007; Drucker et al., 1998; Hagan et al., 2000; Wodak and Cooney, 2005), the response of federal leaders in the United States was one of skepticism and continued opposition. In 1998, section 300ee-5 of the Public Health and Welfare Act banned the use of federal funds to support NEPs. That law stood until 2009, when President Barack Obama lifted the ban on receipt of federal funds. His action was quickly reversed by the U.S. Congress in 2011. The use of federal funds to support NEPs (though not to purchase syringes) was finally allowed through the Consolidated Appropriations Act of 2016, and the use of federal funds for syringe purchases became possible with a December 2021 announcement of a $30 million harm reduction grant funding opportunity by SAMHSA (SAMHSA, 2021).[4] As an extension of NEPs, vending machines have been used in many countries to dispense needles and syringes (Islam, Wodak, and Conigrave, 2008; Moatti et al., 2001; Obadia et al., 1999).

Most SSPs also actively support "secondary" exchanges, whereby clients attending the service also exchange needles and syringes for peers who are not personally connected to the program (Des Jarlais et al., 2015). SSPs also typically provide education on safe injection practices and first aid and wound care and may provide a suite of other services. These additional services may include screening and counseling for HIV and hepatitis C, hepatitis A and B vaccination, distribution of naloxone kits, and overdose prevention education (Barocas et al., 2015; Goedel et al., 2020; Heinzerling et al., 2006; Teshale et al., 2019). In addition, for services that cannot be provided on-site, SSPs may be able to provide referrals for their clients, helping to connect them with various medical care, substance use treatment, and social and legal support interventions (Des Jarlais et al., 2015; Goedel et al., 2020). SSPs are generally low-threshold facilities designed to be as easy for PWUD to use as possible with minimum access requirements in an effort to maximize uptake (Allen et al., 2019; New York City Department of Health and Mental Hygiene, 2009). Therefore, they represent an important point of entry for PWUD, who may otherwise be reluctant to engage with services in more formalized settings (Goedel et al., 2020; United Nations Office on Drugs and Crime et al., 2017).

The coverage of SSPs across the United States remains limited. NASEN lists 445 programs currently operating in the United States (NASEN, undated).[5] However, the distribu-

---

[4] The reason why this funding mechanism can be used to purchase syringes is because it is funded via the American Rescue Plan Act. The American Rescue Plan Act does not include a prohibition on syringe purchases, unlike the regular appropriation act that funds HHS and some other departments (Davis, 2021).

[5] Note that this is very likely an undercount because NASEN relies on programs' voluntary self-registration with the network.

tion of SSPs remains uneven, with no NASEN-registered programs in eight states and with SSPs predominantly located in urban areas (Des Jarlais et al., 2015; Goedel et al., 2020). This severely limits the availability of harm reduction services to PWID who reside outside urban centers.[6] Despite the fact that SSPs have been operating in the United States for decades, their operations continue to be met with community and political opposition stemming from a variety of reasons, including concerns about negative neighborhood effects and stigmatizing attitudes toward services for PWUD, particularly those services that are seen as promoting further drug use (Goedel et al., 2020; Tempalski et al., 2007).[7] Yet evidence shows that many community concerns surrounding SSPs fail to materialize.[8] Multiple studies have found that SSPs have led to better safe needle disposal and have not resulted in an increase in discarded needles (Bluthenthal et al., 2007; Doherty et al., 2000; Tookes et al., 2012). In addition, studies from large cities did not find any effect of SSPs on crime following the introduction of SSPs (Galea et al., 2001; Marx et al., 2000).

Naloxone

A key part of responding to the overdose crisis is distributing naloxone to individuals who may be witnesses to an opioid overdose, such as friends or family of individuals who use opioids. The expansion of access to naloxone has taken numerous forms. All 50 states and the District of Columbia have adopted laws expanding access to naloxone via pharmacy-based dispensing (Guy et al., 2019). Depending on the legislative framework in each state, naloxone can be prescribed by physicians directly to the individual at risk, prescribed indirectly to those in a position to help others (so-called third-party prescription laws), or dispensed by pharmacists through standing order legislation, which enables anyone to obtain naloxone as if they had a prescription (Abouk, Pacula, and Powell, 2019; Guy et al., 2019; Smart, Pardo, and Davis, 2021). Relatedly, several states have started either requiring or recommending that certain patients who are considered at risk of an opioid overdose be prescribed naloxone along with their opioid prescription. As of September 2019, seven states required providers to prescribe naloxone in such situations, two states mandated prescribers to offer a naloxone prescription, and eight states made a recommendation to providers to prescribe naloxone in

---

[6] Specifically, with access to sterile syringes, pharmacies represent an alternative option with many more locations and often less limited hours of operation.

[7] For instance, Meyerson et al., 2017, and Goedel et al., 2020, describe the challenges associated with opening an SSP in response to an HIV outbreak in Indiana.

[8] While this report was being edited and formatted, an ecological study was published that found that "SEP openings decrease HIV rates by up to 18.2 percent . . . [and] increase rates of opioid-related mortality" (Doleac, 2019). We do not offer a specific review of this analysis (for additional discussion, see Doleac, 2019; Siegel, 2022; and Gelman, 2023) but note that ecological studies focused on drug overdose deaths in the age of fentanyl and other synthetic opioids should be interpreted with caution given the dynamics of these markets and the lack of reliable county-level information about the availability and prices of illegally produced synthetic opioids. For insights about improving supply-side data on synthetic opioids, see Pardo and Kilmer, 2022.

certain situations (Haffajee, Cherney, and Smart, 2020). Many who witness overdoses are themselves opioid users, so intervening or calling for assistance may be impeded by laws that criminalize their presence at the scene of active drug use or their own use of drugs at that scene. Most states also have Good Samaritan laws that protect bystanders who summon help from risk of arrest (Banta-Green et al., 2013; Davis and Carr, 2015; Davis, Webb, and Burris, 2013; Green et al., 2014; Prescription Drug Abuse Policy System, 2018), and many allow naloxone administration by nonmedical bystanders and exempt them from liability so long as compensation is not provided for the administration of the naloxone.[9]

Historically, many medical professionals have objected to lay administration of medications, citing concerns regarding potential side effects and secondary overdose (overdose victims can return to overdose status as naloxone wears off). Opponents voiced concerns that opioid overdose victims would not present for formal care—potentially avoiding referral to treatment (Coe and Walsh, 2015; Zuckerman, Weisberg, and Boyer, 2014). Some general practitioners also reported concern that serving as a training and dissemination agent for naloxone might also bring them into contact with PWUD, revealing an underlying issue of PWUD stigmatization (Beletsky et al., 2007; Matheson et al., 2014). A reported lack of training and discomfort with using and dispensing naloxone among medical and pharmacy professionals requires improved clinical guidelines and the development of educational programming (Agarin et al., 2015; Bachhuber et al., 2015; Green et al., 2014; Haegerich et al., 2014; Jones, Lurie, and Compton, 2016). Resistance to naloxone distribution is also raised by those who feel that it encourages opioid use, with some objectors citing anecdotes of individuals revived with naloxone requiring additional naloxone doses later in the same day (Maxwell et al., 2006; Seal et al., 2003; Wagner et al., 2010). Others raise the issue of needing formal deputation or authorization to dispense a prescription medication and related issues of liability. Progress continues on passing laws that allow health professionals, law enforcement officers, and the lay public to use naloxone (Davis et al., 2015; Davis et al., 2014; Davis, Webb, and Burris, 2013; Jones, Lurie, and Compton, 2016).

The expansion of naloxone access arrangements has resulted in a dramatic increase in the number of kits dispensed. Retail pharmacy–based dispensing rates of naloxone grew from 0.4 prescriptions per 100,000 pharmacies in 2012 to 170.2 per 100,000 in 2018, a more than 400-fold increase (Guy et al., 2019). Dispensing of naloxone alongside high-dose opioid prescriptions also increased substantially, more than doubling between 2017 and 2018. However, even in 2018, only 1.5 percent of high-opioid prescriptions were accompanied by naloxone (Guy et al., 2019), with low rates also found among individuals receiving long-term opioids

---

[9] See, for instance, Arizona's statutory language on the administration of opioid antagonists:

> A person who in good faith and without compensation administers an opioid antagonist to a person who is experiencing an opioid-related overdose is not liable for any civil or other damages as the result of any act or omission by the person rendering the care or as the result of any act or failure to act to arrange for further medical treatment or care for the person experiencing the overdose, unless the person while rendering the care acts with gross negligence, willful misconduct or intentional wrongdoing. (Arizona State Legislature, undated)

and among those receiving buprenorphine, indicating that more is needed for the practice to become much more common. In addition to pharmacy-based dispensing, an increasing volume of naloxone kits are distributed via other avenues, such as overdose education and naloxone distribution (OEND) programs, in which naloxone kits and concomitant education are provided at various venues, including primary care organizations, treatment programs, SSPs, and recovery support programs (Kerensky and Walley, 2017).[10] In a survey of SSPs in Lambdin et al., 2020, the vast majority of respondents (94 percent) indicated that they ran an OEND program, a substantial increase from 5 percent reported in 2013 (Des Jarlais et al., 2015). Evidence on OEND programs shows that they can contribute to reductions in opioid mortality and be cost-effective (Coffin and Sullivan, 2013; Walley et al., 2013).

More broadly, a systematic review in 2020 of the emerging literature on the effectiveness of naloxone access laws in the United States concludes that the

> existing literature on naloxone access laws in the United States supports beneficial effects for increased naloxone distribution, but provides inconclusive evidence for reduced fatal opioid overdose. Mixed findings may reflect variation in the laws' design and implementation, confounding effects of concurrent policy adoption, or differential effectiveness in light of changing opioid environments. (Smart, Pardo, and Davis, 2021, p. 6)[11]

In addition, the authors suggested that although naloxone access laws increase the number of kits distributed, these increases may not, in light of continuing barriers to access, be large enough to lead to population-level mortality reductions, at least for now (Smart, Pardo, and Davis, 2021). Recent movements in support of greatly expanded access to naloxone are apparent: e.g., the highlights from the 2019 American Medical Association (AMA) Annual Meeting (O'Reilly, 2019) and the AMA's Opioid Task Force 2020 progress report (AMA, 2020).

Supervised Consumption

Parts of this section are reproduced from Kilmer, 2020.

SCSs (also referred to as *overdose prevention centers, drug consumption rooms,* or *safe injection facilities*) are places where PWUD can consume drugs in the presence of trained staff who monitor for overdose or risky injection practices, intervening when necessary. More than 150 sites have been implemented in at least ten countries, and they are an important component of Canada's response to opioid-involved overdoses (Health Canada, 2018; Kilmer

---

[10] Statistics on pharmacy-based dispensing in this section do not include naloxone distributed by OEND programs.

[11] The authors reviewed ten peer-reviewed studies (Abouk, Pacula, and Powell, 2019; Atkins, Durrance, and Kim, 2019; Blanchard et al., 2018; Erfanian, Collins, and Grossman, 2019; Gertner, Domino, and Davis, 2018; Lambdin et al., 2018; McClellan et al., 2018; Rees et al., 2019; Sohn et al., 2019; and Xu et al., 2018) and one working paper (Doleac and Mukherjee, 2018). An updated version of this working paper was recently accepted for publication at the *Journal of Law and Economics*.

et al., 2018). SCSs provide a safe and sanitary environment for those who inject drugs and, at some sites, have ventilated spaces for people who choose to smoke drugs. They offer sterile injection and cleaning materials so PWUD can wash their injection sites, reducing the risk of infection. Some offer drug checking services (e.g., fentanyl test strips) and other services, such as treatment referrals for those who want them. They also typically serve as SSPs, where those who consume at the SCS, as well as those who do not, can obtain new injection supplies for use outside the facility.[12]

The available research on SCSs is overwhelmingly positive (see, for example, Potier et al., 2014; and Kennedy and Kerr, 2017), but most published studies do not have credible control groups or counterfactuals that allow strong causal inferences (Pardo, Caulkins, and Kilmer, 2018). Although the causal evidence on the population-level effects of these interventions is sparse and largely focused on just two locations, thousands of overdoses have been reversed at these sites around the world, and there appears to be little basis for concern about adverse effects in the communities where they operate, especially in terms of crime (Caulkins, Pardo, and Kilmer, 2019; Davidson et al., 2021).[13]

As noted in Chapter Six, there also are federal legal barriers to some harm reduction programs. For example, SCSs violate the "crack house statute" of the federal CSA (21 U.S.C. § 856(a) (2)). The U.S. Attorney for the Eastern District of Pennsylvania filed a preemptive injunction asking a federal judge to declare that Safehouse—the proposed SCS in Philadelphia—was in violation of the CSA. Although a federal judge ruled against the government, the case was subsequently overturned by the U.S. Court of Appeals, and the U.S. Supreme Court declined to hear the appeal. Despite the federal prohibition, two SCSs opened in New York City in November 2021; as of January 2023, the DOJ has not taken action against these facilities or against the individuals who operate and use them. In 2017, the AMA voted to support the creation of pilot SCS facilities in the United States. In an AMA press release, Patrice Harris, chair of the AMA Opioid Task Force and former president of the AMA, noted, "Pilot facilities will help inform U.S. policymakers on the feasibility, effectiveness and legal aspects of supervised

---

[12] The fact that SCSs provide these additional services can make it difficult to isolate the community-level benefits and costs of supervised consumption in a fixed location and compare it with other interventions. Such a comparison has been attempted, with Caulkins, Pardo, and Kilmer, 2019, p. 2111, noting,

> For example, Pinkerton estimates that Insite prevents 83.5 HIV infections per year, but 80.7 were due to Insite's syringe exchange program, with supervision within the facility preventing only an additional 2.8 infections. Pinkerton revised that upwards to 5.2, but that would still be only 6% of the total.

[13] With the proliferation of SCSs throughout many parts of Canada, we suspect that more research will be published on the community-level effects. Two new studies leverage the fact that multiple sites opened throughout British Columbia and Ontario (Panagiotoglou, 2022; Panagiotoglou and Lim, 2022). The study focused on British Columbia finds that SCSs "reduce opioid-related paramedic attendance and emergency department visit rates but no evidence that they reduce local hospitalization or mortality rates" (Panagiotoglou, 2022). The study of Ontario moves beyond counting sites and introduces a new concept of "booth hours" to account for the size and hours of operation for the sites (Panagiotoglou and Lim, 2022). The authors conclude that "Booth-hours had no population-level effect on opioid-related overdose [emergency department] visit, hospitalization, or death rates."

injection facilities in reducing harms and health care costs associated with injection drug use" (AMA, 2017). In late 2021, the National Institute on Drug Abuse, in collaboration with the CDC and HHS, published a review of the evidence, essentially echoing this sentiment:

> [T]here is a clear need for more rigorous research and evaluation of [overdose prevention centers (OPCs)]. Given the amount and quality of the existing data, it may be prudent to consider the American Medical Association's recommendation of developing and imple-menting OPC pilot programs in the United States designed, monitored, and evaluated to generate locality-relevant data to inform policymakers on the feasibility and effectiveness of OPCs in reducing harms and health care costs related to [injection drug use]. (National Institute on Drug Abuse, 2021, p. 11)

Within a few weeks of the release of that report, New York City became the first jurisdic-tion in the United States to authorize the opening of an SCS; two sites started serving clients on November 30, 2021.

Although New York is the first city to open a sanctioned SCS in the United States, it is in no way the first place where PWUD could go to consume while being supervised. Indeed, there is an unsanctioned SCS that has been operating in the United States since 2014 that has been extensively studied by Alex Kral and colleagues (Kral and Davidson, 2017). In a 2020 analysis published in the *New England Journal of Medicine*, Kral and colleagues observe that, from 2014 to 2019, there were 10,514 injections and 33 opioid-involved overdoses at the SCS, all of which were reversed by naloxone (Kral et al., 2020). It is also noteworthy that the number of supervised injections involving both opioids and stimulants (sometimes referred to as *speedballs* or *goofballs*) at that SCS increased from 5 percent in 2014 to 60 percent in 2019 (Figure 8.2). With the number of cocaine and methamphetamine overdose deaths involving opioids increasing (see Chapter Seven), researchers wondered how much of this increase was attributable to simultaneous use versus use of these drugs on different occasions (e.g., Pardo et al., 2019). Figure 8.2 does not answer that question because it is focused only on a subpopu-lation of PWUD at one location, but it highlights another potential benefit of SCSs: serving as an early-warning system for changes in drug use patterns.

As with the "not in my backyard" (or NIMBY) sentiments sometimes expressed during discussions of potential sites for drug treatment centers, some of the resistance to SCSs comes from the fact that some residents and businesses do not want to see a brick-and-mortar facil-ity in their neighborhood. Thus, it is imperative that thinking about supervising consump-tion not be linked to fixed sites. Some SCSs are mobile, and there has been a proliferation of less structured and less resource intensive *overdose prevention sites* in Canada. Additionally, "don't use alone" education campaigns and hotlines—which provide people with someone to listen on the phone while they inject and summon medical assistance if an overdose is suspected—can also reduce unsupervised consumption. There are also a growing number of phone apps intended to provide virtual supervision, including at least one that will notify selected contacts if the person using drugs is not moving and not responding to prompts from the application.

FIGURE 8.2

Type of Drugs Injected as a Percentage of All Drugs Injected at an Unsanctioned Supervised Consumption Site in the United States

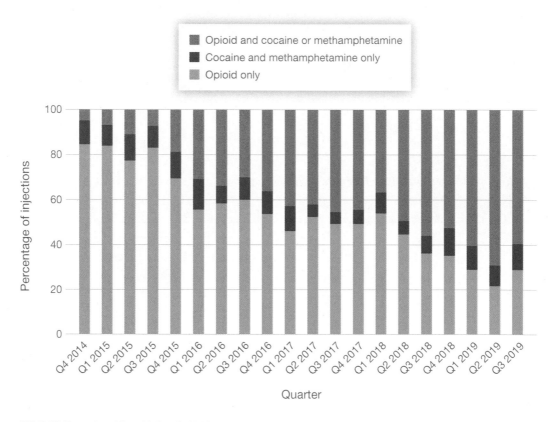

SOURCE: Reproduced from Kral et al., 2020.

A final point needs to be made about scalability. Kilmer et al., 2018, p. xii, offers a back-of-the-envelope calculation using the assumption that there are 1.5 million people in the United States injecting heroin and/or fentanyl on a daily or near daily basis:

> If these 1.5 million daily or near-daily heroin users injected an average of roughly twice a day (see Bayoumi and Zaric, 2008), that would be about 1.1 billion use sessions per year. Vancouver's Insite SCS supervised an average of 415 injections per day in 2017 (Vancouver Coastal Health, 2018), or roughly 150,000 per year. Even ignoring injection of methamphetamine and other drugs or the increased frequency of injecting associated with shorter-acting drugs such as fentanyl, this suggests that the United States would need more than 7,000 SCSs the size of Insite to supervise those use sessions, and, as of 2017, there were only about 100 SCSs operating worldwide. Of course, these figures tell us nothing about whether a local community should or should not adopt an SCS; they do, though, give a sense of scale and suggest that SCSs as implemented elsewhere would need to be part of a package of responses to the opioid crisis, not the only or primary piece.

Drug Checking Services

Another intervention that aims to reduce the risks associated with drug use is drug checking services, which offer PWUD the ability to have the content of their drugs analyzed before they consume. Available for decades in many international jurisdictions, primarily in the context of the dance scene originally (Brunt, 2017), they have become part of the response to the opioid crisis in certain North American jurisdictions (Karamouzian et al., 2018; Maghsoudi et al., 2020; Peiper et al., 2019). Because the arrival of illicitly manufactured synthetic opioids has introduced a new level of uncertainty to illicit opioid markets, drug checking services can help PWUD better understand what they bought and whether their sample is contaminated with fentanyl, its analogs (Peiper et al., 2019), or other contaminants. Typically, drug checking services in the context of illicit synthetic opioids take the form of distributing and administering fentanyl test strips, which can detect the presence of fentanyl in a sample. The evidence from studies on U.S.-based programs involving fentanyl test strips suggests that PWUD are very willing to use them (Krieger et al., 2018; Marshall, 2018; Sherman et al., 2018).[14] The effect of drug checking programs on PWUD is somewhat less well explored (Peiper et al., 2019). In a North Carolina–based program, however, 43 percent of respondents reported changes in drug-use behavior, with those who reported a positive test result being five times more likely to report a behavioral change (Peiper et al., 2019).

A simple binary indicator of the presence or absence of fentanyl in a given sample is less useful in markets where fentanyl has achieved a high degree of penetration: i.e., where opioid samples can be expected to contain fentanyl. However, such information is still very valuable to people who use other classes of drugs, such as stimulants, and who would thus not normally expect their samples to contain fentanyl. Some more-comprehensive drug checking services in Canada have been using more-sophisticated technologies, such as spectrometers, which provide more-comprehensive information on the composition of a given sample and the concentrations of its constituent parts. This information may be more valuable in markets where the presence of fentanyl is very likely but the purity of the sample could vary.[15] A 2021 pilot of a drug checking service in Chicago that incorporated both fentanyl test strips and spectrometer-based analysis demonstrated the feasibility of a similar intervention in the United States (Karch et al., 2021).[16]

Drug checking services can also be beneficial for the purpose of drug market surveillance. Findings from drug checking services can be communicated to the community, alert-

---

[14] For instance, in a North Carolina–based program, 81 percent of a surveyed sample of participants reported using strips before their consumption (Peiper et al., 2019). The survey was administered online and involved a sample of 125 PWID.

[15] More-complex technology has its downsides as well. Besides higher operational costs, some spectrometers (such as Fourier-transform infrared) may not detect concentrations under a certain threshold, which may exceed the concentration of fentanyl in common retail samples (Green et al., 2020).

[16] No cost information was reported as part of the study. These data will be important for comparing this intervention with others.

ing PWUD of shifts in drug supply and the emergence of new substances. Drug checking data can also feed into public health monitoring and early-warning systems (Bardwell and Kerr, 2018; Laing, Tupper, and Fairbairn, 2018).

Prescription and Nonprescription Approaches to Providing PWUD with Drugs of Known Composition

Much of this section is reproduced from Kilmer and Pardo, 2023.

There is a growing debate about providing PWUD with drugs of known composition in lieu of what is sold in illegal markets, sometimes referred to as *safe supply* or *safer supply* (Nolen, 2022; Select Special Committee to Examine Safe Supply, 2022; Csete and Elliott, 2021). However, these terms are used to describe a diverse set of interventions with different levels of evidence, target populations, outcomes, and regulatory involvement (Kilmer and Pardo, 2023). Thus, we urge caution when using the terms; policy discussions will likely be more productive if the focus is on the specific type of intervention.

One approach under the "safer supply" umbrella involves offering medications to PWUD: sometimes their drug of choice and sometimes an alternative. There is no consensus about which substances and what conditions of use constitute safer supply versus more-traditional treatments. Is liquid methadone consumed at a clinic a form of safer supply? What about diamorphine (heroin) or pharmaceutical-grade fentanyl?

Some countries allow doctors to prescribe pharmaceutical-grade heroin (diamorphine) for those with OUD; this is commonly referred to as *supervised-injectable heroin treatment* or *heroin-assisted treatment* (Bell, Belackova, and Lintzeris, 2018). In at least seven countries, heroin-assisted treatment is not a first-line treatment and is generally targeted at those with a long use history who have tried other treatments multiple times but are still using heroin (Strang et al., 2015). As with other types of medications for OUD, the main goals are to reduce patients' use of street-sourced heroin and help stabilize their lives (see, for example, Reuter, 2009). There is strong evidence that prescribing heroin as a form of medication treatment can lead to a variety of positive outcomes (see a review by Smart, 2018), although this evidence comes from trials conducted in countries with a much more robust set of nonpharmacological interventions and supports that routinely are provided—including stronger wraparound and other social service provision—than is available in the United States.

Health Canada distinguishes between the goals of opioid agonist treatment and safer supply, stating, "Usually, the goal of traditional [opioid agonist treatment] is for a patient to stop taking drugs. . . [whereas] safer supply refers to providing prescribed medications as a safer alternative to the toxic illegal drug supply to people who are at high risk of overdose" (Health Canada, 2022).

In response to the opioid crisis in Canada, additional options have been introduced for those who have not benefited from traditional medications, such as methadone and buprenorphine. These new options include slow-release oral morphine (Kadian) and, since 2019, injectable hydromorphone (Dilaudid). In Vancouver, there is also a very small pilot project prescribing fentanyl patches as an alternative opioid agonist therapy approach (Bardwell, Wood, and Brar, 2019). In 2021, a clinic combined with an overdose prevention site opened in Victoria, British Columbia, that also offered three fentanyl-based products: tablets, patches, and injections (Medrano, 2022).

There has also been innovation in how medications are supplied to PWUD. In Vancouver, a small number of patients diagnosed with OUD can visit a 24-hour, secure biometric vending machine, which will distribute hydromorphone pills that can be crushed, mixed with liquid, and then injected (Bonn, 2020). It is too early to know what the overall effect of the vending machine model will be, but it is an example of the type of outside-the-box thinking that should be piloted and evaluated if the United States is going to stem the tide of synthetic drug poisonings (Pardo et al., 2021).

Some are promoting other safer supply interventions outside the traditional prescription model. One approach that has been proposed is a cooperative purchase-based model of pharmaceutical-grade drugs (e.g., heroin) for members without a prescription to ensure quality and competitive pricing (British Columbia Centre on Substance Use, 2019). This model is based on the cannabis compassion clubs or buyers' clubs that emerged in the 1980s during the HIV/AIDS epidemic. It has been argued that this model "could have the immediate potential to reduce the number of fentanyl-related deaths and impacts of organized crime" (British Columbia Centre on Substance Use, 2019, p. 5). Although Vancouver's city council expressed unanimous support for the model's application for federal approval (Grochowski, 2021), this approach seems neither legally nor politically feasible in the United States at the moment. However, it highlights another example of a community-initiated intervention attempting to reduce harm for PWUD. But if this approach were to be seriously considered, it would be useful to assess the potential effects it might have on local prices and consumption patterns in addition to the effects on overdoses and other health consequences.

Another approach is for a group to purchase illegal drugs, test them, and then repackage and distribute them to PWUD. The Drug User Liberation Front in Vancouver has held at least five events where they have distributed the tested and repackaged drugs without inciting a crackdown by local law enforcement (Brogle, 2021; Canêdo et al., 2022). In August 2022, it was reported that a Cocaine, Heroin and Methamphetamine Compassion Club and Fulfilment Centre had been in operation in Vancouver for a month, although the club was not authorized by the government and the drugs were not sourced from a pharmaceutical company; they were purchased from the dark web, tested, and sold at cost (Gallant, 2022; Smart, 2022). Access to this club is limited to members of the Vancouver Area Network of Drug Users who are over 19 years old (Gallant, 2022). It is much too early to measure the effects of this approach, but the approach is worthy of a rigorous evaluation.

Other Harm Reduction Approaches

Additional harm reduction approaches include such technologies and interventions as low-dead-space syringes and needles, used needle drop boxes, and soft-tissue damage clinics. It has been suggested that syringes with high dead-space (fluid remaining in the space between the needle hub and the plunger, usually in syringes with detachable needles) versus low-dead-space syringes (typically used by those injecting insulin) are far more likely to transmit HIV and other blood-borne diseases, such as hepatitis B or C (Gyarmathy et al., 2010; Vickerman, Martin, and Hickman, 2013; Zule et al., 2013). Interventions to make communities safer from accumulating needles and syringes include needle drop boxes situated in areas with a higher density of PWID (de Montigny et al., 2010; Riley et al., 1998; Riley et al., 2010).

Community-Level Efforts to Prevent Drug Consumption

Children in socioeconomically disadvantaged communities (particularly, children of color) are affected by a lack of resources (Bird et al., 2010; Yousey-Hindes and Hadler, 2011), exposure to violence (Gelles, 1992; Guerra, Huesmann, and Spindler, 2003), challenging physical environments (Prescott, 2013), regular exposure to microaggressions (Matsuda, 1991; Torres-Harding and Turner, 2015), and oppression associated with prejudice and stigma (Pachter and Coll, 2009; Paradies, 2006; Priest et al., 2013). These intersecting factors create high levels of stress, referred to by some as *toxic stress* (Johnson et al., 2013; Shonkoff and Garner, 2012), that can influence the lifetime trajectory of children's development, negatively affecting their physical and mental health into adulthood (Campbell et al., 2014; Conti and Heckman, 2013; Delaney and Smith, 2012; Goodman, Joyce, and Smith, 2011; Smith, 2009; Smith and Smith, 2010). A strong association has been shown between the socioeconomic status of a community and allostatic load (a summary measure of biological risk across nine metabolic, inflammatory, and cardiovascular indices; Bird et al., 2010). Other studies examining children demonstrate the relationship between socioeconomic status and cortisol elevation (a hormonal marker of stress; see DeSantis et al., 2007; and Evans and Kim, 2007), as well as socioeconomic status and lower levels of activity in the prefrontal cortex (an area of the brain associated with executive function; Sheridan et al., 2012). There is also an increasing body of evidence in children that links exposure to stressful events (e.g., maternal depression, exposure to violence) with shortened telomere length (a marker for premature cellular aging; see Drury et al., 2014; Shalev et al., 2013; and Wojcicki et al., 2015). These and other adverse events experienced by children are associated with lower rates of school engagement and higher rates of chronic disease (Bethell et al., 2014), premature mortality (Brown et al., 2009), poor social development, poor mental health, and chronic medical conditions, with more chronic or cumulative exposures associated with worse outcomes (Kerker et al., 2015).

It is clear that a constellation of health risk behaviors, including substance use, delinquency and violence, and chronic health conditions, all may be linked to common risk and protective factors in individuals and their environments. Several community-wide programs have been successfully implemented to engage and support communities in their efforts to select the best mix of evidence-based approaches for reducing or eliminating risk factors and building on strengths.

Public health–oriented prevention interventions for children and adolescents typically examine a variety of risk and protective factors and a wide variety of target problem areas, such as obesity, smoking, diabetes, heart disease, alcohol and drug use, depression, and exposure to violence. At younger ages (before most problems emerge), risk factors across these and many other public health problems significantly overlap (Coie et al., 1993), with increasing recognition of common risk factors for multiple disorders (Meigs et al., 2008; Sheiham and Watt, 2000; Vitaro et al., 2001), risk factor clustering, and clustering of disorders in those with multiple risk factors (Danese et al., 2009; Pronk et al., 2004; Schuit et al., 2002). Examples of generic risk factors include extreme poverty, neighborhood disorganization, racial injustice, peer rejection, isolation, family conflict, child abuse, stressful life events, school failure, and poor work skills or habits, to name a few (Coie et al., 1993). Protective factors also appear to be common across many disorders (Coie et al., 1993; Greenberg, 2007). Examples of generic protective factors include high-quality schools, effective social policies (e.g., high taxes on tobacco or alcohol, extension of health coverage [as with the Affordable Care Act], clean air laws, or programs to alleviate food insecurity), safe neighborhoods, good parent relationships, social support (multiple levels and kinds), positive peer-modeling, self-efficacy, intelligence, and cognitive skills, to name a few (Durlak, 1998). Together, these observations indicate a need to increase the use of multiproblem and community-wide prevention approaches, rather than targeted prevention approaches, to address the factors underlying multiple health disorders (Durlak, 1998; Yoshikawa, 1995). Multiproblem approaches tend to build on strengths, with a focus on wellness rather than pathology, and have the advantage of improving conditions for all while helping the disadvantaged most and, perhaps, decreasing the stigma associated with being singled out for special attention.

One well-researched program is the Communities That Care (CTC) prevention program (Hawkins, Catalano, and Arthur, 2002). CTC engages public officials and community leaders in prevention planning and implementation, with an emphasis on prevention science, to develop a system that is grounded in theory and supported by scientific evidence. Briefly, CTC provides tools for using local data to identify elevated risk factors and lower protective factors that are specific to local communities. CTC then guides communities in the implementation of evidence-based interventions for decreasing risk factors and enhancing protective factors.

Another program for enhancing community-wide prevention is Getting to Outcomes (GTO; Chinman, Imm, and Wandersman, 2004). GTO, which emphasizes community participation in collaboration with the scientific community, is a toolkit meant to provide communities with a ten-step process to plan, select, implement, and evaluate the science-based prevention interventions that are best suited for the community. Extending the community-based participatory model, GTO draws from empowerment evaluation (Fetterman, Kaftarian, and Wandersman, 1996), emphasizing the need for prevention interventions to actively involve community members in the prevention intervention itself, calling such interventions *community based participatory interventions*. The GTO process also draws from results-based accountability (Osborne and Gaebler, 1992), as well as Continuous Quality Improvement (Deming, 1982), and involves the consideration of local goals and objectives, capacity, programmatic fit, outcome assessment, and sustainability.

SAMHSA promotes a community engagement approach that starts with a community readiness assessment that classifies communities into one of nine stages of community readiness, ranging from no awareness (Stage 1) or denial/resistance (Stage 2) to Confirmation/Expansion (Stage 8) or High Level of Community Ownership (Stage 9). The assessment provides a sense of where communities are starting and takes into account specific community strengths and weaknesses within the context of the communities' cultures, resources, needs, and circumstances. The assessment then guides the provision of technical assistance and identifies those in the community who should participate. Emphasis is placed on sustainability through collaboration and assessment (SAMHSA, 2020).

Collectively, community-tailored processes (such as those described in this section) emphasize the need to engage communities at all levels (individual, organizational, policy) to develop local support and ownership of selected science-based prevention interventions, enhance implementation integrity and evaluation, and increase the likelihood of sustainability. Community involvement also helps community members better understand (1) their collective roles and responsibilities with respect to the development and maintenance of a health-promoting ecosystem and (2) the need to develop individual strengths and community protective factors from the earliest years and beyond.

Development of Community Coalitions Aiming to Reduce Drug Use Harms and Stigma

Coalitions to reduce drug use harms have their roots in self-organizing by drug users in the Netherlands, who formed Junkiebunds (drug user unions) in the 1970s. The concept of early drug user unions involved peer support and activism to push back against the political scapegoating of drug users (Friedman, 1998), law enforcement harassment (Trautmann, 1995), and stigma and demonization (Johansson, Kjær, and Stothard, 2015). This concept also involved the introduction of harm reduction approaches, such as the first needle exchange in Amsterdam in 1984 to reduce the harms of hepatitis B and, later, HIV (Buning, 1989; O'Hare, 2013).

Building on the early drug user unions' demands for basic human rights, dignity, and social justice, harm reduction coalitions became far more common as the HIV epidemic spurred the development of coalitions around the world (Friedman et al., 2001) and, eventually, in the United States (Bluthenthal, 1998; Henman et al., 1998). Challenged by the immediate threat of HIV/AIDS, drug users and many public health professionals moved away from prohibitionist notions of abstinence and use reduction to the consideration of harm reduction and the avoidance of HIV spread as the social movement expanded from drug user unions to community coalitions (Bluthenthal, 1998; Boyd and MacPherson, 2018; Friedman, 1998; Wieloch, 2002). Today, there are drug user networks in numerous countries around the world.

Over time, harm reduction further expanded beyond interventions to reduce the harms associated with drug use as it related to HIV/AIDS to a broader notion of racial equity and harms to entire communities by drug policies that focused on use reduction and abstinence (see, e.g., National Harm Reduction Coalition, undated-a). As the opioid overdose crisis emerged in the United States, coalitions to prevent overdose appeared to be a natural extension of earlier efforts. One early example is Project Lazarus, a nonprofit established in 2007 in response to high overdose mortality rates in Wilkes County, North Carolina, by Fred Brason II. As a hospice chaplain, Brason became aware that prescription opioids were being regularly stolen from patients. He began to explore the issue and discovered that misuse of opioid prescriptions was rampant in the community, with overdose rates among the highest in the country. This led to the development of a community coalition that brought together diverse elements of the community to address the issue, including ministries, medical and public health professionals, the business community, law enforcement, educators, other civic organizations, and the community at large. The coalition's focus was on overdose prevention, treatment for OUD, prescribing practices and diversion control, community and provider education, and appropriate pain control for those requiring it. The effort resulted in a decrease in overdose deaths in Wilkes County from 46.6 deaths per 100,000 population in 2009 to 29.0 per 100,000 in 2010 (Albert et al., 2011; Brason, Roe, and Dasgupta, 2013). The international spread of harm reduction coalitions has been rapid and, in many cases, occurred well before community coalitions (such as Project Lazarus) made their appearance in the United States. Another early example is the Drug Overdose Prevention and Education (DOPE) project implemented in San Francisco. DOPE was a naloxone prescription program established by outreach workers and researchers in partnership with public health officials and treatment providers (Enteen et al., 2010) and has since grown to become the largest naloxone distribution program in the country (National Harm Reduction Coalition, undated-b).

Over time, the work of community activists and a generation of research on harm reduction interventions have contributed to an ongoing, albeit limited, shift in the politics of harm reduction in the United States (Des Jarlais, 2017; Moore and Clear, 2012). This shift is marked by greater support for syringe service access and (more recently, in connection with the opioid crisis) for programs to reduce overdose fatalities, such as naloxone distribution programs and drug checking services (Nadelmann and LaSalle, 2017). Along similar lines, the Biden administration has signaled greater acceptance of harm reduction principles (The White House, 2021); in a growing number of jurisdictions, law enforcement agencies are interested in nonpunitive and harm reduction approaches (Saloner et al., 2018; White et al., 2021). And yet, harm reduction interventions continue to face opposition, with policies and attitudes varying greatly across the United States and even among localities within states (Nadelmann and LaSalle, 2017; Owczarzak et al., 2020; Taylor et al., 2021). Alongside the continued lack of general acceptance, harm reduction approaches have historically suffered from inadequate levels of funding (Bluthenthal et al., 2008; Des Jarlais, McKnight, and Milliken, 2004; Showalter, 2018), although the variety of services that receive funding from federal, state, and local governments to offer financial support has increased over time.[17]

---

[17] In a recent example, federal funding can now be used to buy fentanyl test strips (CDC, 2021).

Key Interactions with Other Components of the Ecosystem

Harm reduction and community-initiated interventions interact with all aspects of the core systems, including the medical, opioid specialty care, criminal legal, and illegal supply systems. Furthermore, community engagement involves all core systems because interventions at all levels are more likely to be accepted if communities are engaged, are educated, and have input into processes. For example, community coalitions that promote prevention programming are very common. Treatment engagement and longer-term recovery are enhanced when drug users engage peers, non–drug using members of the community, and community resources (such as housing, education, and employment).

Criminal Legal System

Harm reduction programs frequently run afoul of criminal law because many interventions involve the distribution of drug use paraphernalia, such as syringes or fentanyl test strips. Because many established harm reduction initiatives essentially operate at the discretion of local law enforcement agencies (e.g., even if the programs are legally sanctioned, police could, in theory, arrest individuals seeking to test their drugs for possession or follow those leaving a syringe exchange program), they end up playing a critical role in terms of access to these public health services. As noted earlier, with respect to SCSs, the DOJ has actively blocked efforts for localities to pilot and study these interventions. It will be interesting to see whether any action is taken against the recently opened sites in New York City.

Traditionally, the simple fact that these drugs are illegal—coupled with a societal reliance on the criminal legal system and punishment—have driven opioid users underground, stigmatized them, and increased the harms of use. In response, some communities have implemented reforms that seek to divert drug users from adverse criminal outcomes, such as conviction and incarceration. Examples of policing innovations are rapidly increasing as many communities and their law enforcement authorities are coming to realize the harms associated with the criminalization of substance use and its disproportionate impact on communities of color, as well as the considerable costs to society of policing, the courts, and incarceration.

As the negative impacts of incarceration for drug offenses became increasingly clear, many criminal legal agencies began to organize alternative paths for PWUD. An early innovation was drug court, dating back to 1989 in Miami-Dade County. Since then, thousands of drug courts and specialty courts (such as treatment courts, family courts, and mental health courts) have been developed to increase treatment and/or drug monitoring and supervision as alternatives to incarceration (Longshore et al., 2001; Turner et al., 2002; further discussed in Chapter Six). Another early example of a diversion approach was California's Proposition 36, the Substance Abuse and Crime Prevention Act of 2000, which allowed adults convicted of nonviolent drug possession offenses to receive drug treatment in the community instead of being incarcerated (Anglin et al., 2013; Farabee et al., 2004; Gardiner, 2008; Kilmer and Iguchi, 2009; Worrall et al., 2009).

Other diversion schemes aiming to reduce the negative impacts of drug use criminalization include prosecutor-led initiatives and police-run deflection programs. These programs can take many forms, which are discussed in greater detail in Chapter Six. Overall, most of the research on these new diversion and deflection programs has been descriptive, and the impact of the programs has not been carefully studied. Survey research has found that clients, officers, treatment staff, and the public support these programs (Center for Technology and Behavioral Health, 2018; Ormsby, 2018; Reichert, 2017; Schiff et al., 2017).

Criminal legal agencies have also played an active role in community collaborations related to substance use prevention (e.g., Youth Empowerment Strategies), drug take-back programs, and focused-deterrence initiatives to address overt drug selling (e.g., Drug Market Initiatives; see Corsaro, Brunson, and McGarrell, 2010; Kennedy, 1997; and Saunders et al., 2016).

Medical Care

Interventions that touch on medical systems include overdose prevention in the form of naloxone distribution and related policies; interventions to decrease the spread of infectious diseases, such as HIV or hepatitis C testing, counseling, treatment, and PrEP for HIV; and soft-tissue wound clinics to prevent such problems as long-term bacterial infections and necrotizing fasciitis (an aggressive and deadly soft-tissue infection). Harm reduction interventions also touch on the medical system through drug take-backs and syringe distribution schemes involving pharmacies.

The arrival of antiretroviral medications at the turn of the century for the treatment of HIV has opened up opportunities for both PrEP and postexposure prophylaxis in PWID (Fauci et al., 2019).[18]

For those with ongoing HIV exposure risks, PrEP is recommended (CDC, 2018). However, studies focusing on PWID indicate relatively low levels of uptake (Leech et al., 2020; Walters et al., 2020). Reported possible contributing factors include such barriers as copays and concerns about the therapy, as well as low levels of awareness of PrEP among PWID and limited prevalence of PrEP prescribing among practitioners (Leech et al., 2020; Schneider et al., 2020; Walters et al., 2020). That said, among PWID aware of PrEP, studies report relatively high levels of interest (Schneider et al., 2020; Walters et al., 2020). Postexposure prophylaxis

---

[18] A randomized clinical trial in Thailand demonstrated that PWID provided with a daily oral dose of 300 mg tenofovir disoproxil fumarate (TDF) experienced a large reduction in HIV seroincidence. Following the release of the study, the CDC moved quickly to issue guidance for PrEP use by PWID. PrEP involves the prophylactic use of antiretroviral medication to reduce the likelihood that HIV will be transmitted from one individual to another through either sexual contact or injection drug use. In the United States, the Federal Drug Administration (FDA) has approved two oral medications for PrEP: Emtricitabine (F) 200 mg in combination with TDF 300 mg (F/TDF, commonly known by the brand name *Truvada*) and Emtricitabine (F) 200 mg in combination with tenofovir alafenamide (TAF) 25 mg (F/TAF, commonly known by the brand name *Descovy*). Currently, only F/TDF (Truvada) is recommended by the FDA for use by PWID (CDC, 2018).

involves taking antiretroviral medications no more than 72 hours after an event with a high potential for HIV exposure. The CDC recommends postexposure prophylaxis for those who have not tested positive for HIV when a condom breaks during sex, when needles or works used to prepare drugs are shared, or after a sexual assault. These guidelines assume an emergency situation; for PWID, this means an assumption of regular adherence to safe injection practices and regular use of a condom with sexual partners (CDC, 2019b).

Soft-tissue clinics also decrease harms associated with injection drug use in that they prevent soft-tissue wounds caused by injection drug use from becoming infected or necrotic, providing a timely medical intervention and relief for high-cost emergency rooms (Bassetti and Battegay, 2004; Binswanger et al., 2008; Takahashi, Maciejewski, and Bradley, 2010; Torres et al., 2017).

The primary objectives of SSPs are to promote safe injection practices and to reduce the risk of transmission of blood-borne infections (notably, hepatitis C and HIV). Evidence shows that SSPs are effective in helping prevent infection (Aspinall et al., 2014; Bluthenthal et al., 2007; Fernandes et al., 2017; Platt et al., 2017). Furthermore, some SSPs have a broader service portfolio and therefore can provide medical care and social services to their clients (Des Jarlais et al., 2015). Elsewhere, some SSPs are integrated or, at a minimum, colocated with primary care clinics and pharmacies where SSP clients can obtain medical services (Goedel et al., 2020; Hood et al., 2020). In other contexts, SSPs offer to link their clients with medical (and other) providers and thus represent an important access point for services (Des Jarlais et al., 2015; Goedel et al., 2020). Similarly, limited medical care and linkage to further medical providers are among the services provided at SCSs (Strang and Taylor, 2018).

Conversely, medical care providers also contribute to community-led harm reduction interventions. For instance, primary care clinics are one of many venues where people can obtain naloxone kits and be trained on their use (Kerensky and Walley, 2017).

Substance Use Disorder Treatment

Community-initiated interventions that interact with opioid treatment systems include efforts to engage people in treatment with the larger community, implement harm reduction interventions within treatment settings, and use community-based harm reduction efforts to interact with those who need or may eventually need treatment.

Community Engagement

One example of a program to promote community engagement by individuals in treatment for substance misuse is the Community Reinforcement Approach (Azrin, 1976; Hunt and Azrin, 1973). In addition to reinforcing treatment engagement, this approach reinforces a variety of behaviors and activities that are intended to engage the individual with the larger community (e.g., social recreational counseling, relationship counseling, job club). Another example is the use of clinic stores, where treatment recipients can draw rewards (in the case of contingency management) or aid from community-solicited goods. Researchers have found that the process of solicitation in the community and thank-you letters written by those in treatment or recovery help develop support from the community (Amass and Kamien, 2004; Kirby, Amass, and McLellan, 1999).

Efforts to reach out to non–substance-using friends and family members to involve them in the treatment process are also examples of engaging the community, as are efforts to involve community organizations (e.g., religious communities and nonprofits), because they serve to sensitize community members to the benefits of treatment and go a long way toward decreasing stigma for treatment participants.

Harm Reduction Innovations Within Treatment Settings

Early in the HIV epidemic, it was clear that those in methadone treatment were much less likely to be infected and die from HIV than those not in treatment (Grönbladh, Öhlund, and Gunne, 1990; Metzger et al., 1993; Zanis and Woody, 1998). One important harm reduction intervention implemented in methadone treatment programs was shifting from strict rules for drug use—which often led to methadone dose reductions and discharge from treatment—to (1) reinforcing approaches (Iguchi et al., 1988; Stitzer et al., 1993) and (2) allowing greater tolerance for ongoing substance use during treatment with greater attention to consumer preferences (Des Jarlais, 1990; Flynn et al., 2002; Rhoades et al., 1998). Low-threshold programs (medications for OUD and nonpharmacological interventions) were developed to engage and retain PWUD in treatment, often resulting in great discomfort among providers who were used to abstinence-only programming (de Leon, 1996; Klingemann, 1996). One residential drug treatment program in Sydney, Australia, placed clean needle kits in the bathrooms. When residents were asked whether the kits made them feel unsafe or triggered cravings, they replied that the kits triggered cravings but that they needed to learn to cope with those cravings. They also noted that the kits made them feel safer in the program because they showed that staff prioritized their safety and health above all else. These innovations continue today, as HIV, hepatitis C, and involvement with the criminal legal system are all significantly affected by time in treatment.

Using Harm Reduction Interventions to Engage Those Who Need or May Eventually Need Treatment

Providing information about available treatment options and linkage to treatment providers is one of the key services offered by SSPs (Des Jarlais et al., 2015; Goedel et al., 2020). There is evidence that SSPs can be effective in facilitating individuals' entry into treatment and helping them stay engaged with services (Hagan et al., 2000; Heimer, 1998; Strathdee et al., 1999). More recently, some SSPs have also become places where clients can obtain treatment medication prescriptions. For instance, a Philadelphia-based SSP implemented a buprenorphine treatment program integrated within the SSP and aimed at SSP clients who expressed an interest in ceasing illicit opioid use (Bachhuber et al., 2018). In Seattle, a low-threshold buprenorphine program was introduced that was colocated with an SSP, primary care clinic, and pharmacy. SSP clients are asked by the program staff about their interest in buprenorphine treatment; alternatively, individuals can self-refer into the program. Once treatment participants express readiness to do so, they are transferred to a community treatment provider for ongoing care (Hood et al., 2020). Along similar lines to SSPs, SCSs also represent possible sources of information about and linkage with treatment services for people with OUD. In some (though not all) instances, SCSs can also be colocated with treatment providers (Strang and Taylor, 2018).[19]

Illegal Supply

Illicit drug supply shapes the context in which community-initiated interventions operate. Different substances and different modalities of drug use (e.g., injecting heroin versus ingesting diverted pharmaceutical-grade analgesics) involve different harms and risks, which needs to be reflected in the design of interventions aiming to respond to these risks. By extension, changes in drug supply can have serious implications for community-led harm reduction efforts.

The arrival of such illicitly manufactured synthetic opioids as fentanyl over the past decade has resulted in elevated risks to people who use opioids stemming from the high potency of these new drugs, the higher frequency of use because of their shorter duration of effect, and their frequent marketing as heroin or their presence in counterfeit pills. This only increases the importance of interventions aiming to minimize the harm stemming from drug use. SSPs can help reduce the risks stemming from frequent injections. SCSs provide an ability to administer potent drugs under the supervision of trained staff, who can immediately reverse an overdose event. Naloxone distribution and education programs empower individuals and their family and friends to reverse an overdose. Lastly, drug checking programs can tell individuals whether their street-purchased drugs contain potent and/or unexpected substances and can thus inform their consumption. Conversely, information produced and collected by community-initiated interventions can yield important insights about the continuously changing drug supply.

First Responders

Community-initiated interventions interact in several ways with first responders—including law enforcement, nontransport fire departments, and EMS—who may administer naloxone (Narcan) to reverse potentially fatal opioid overdoses in the community. Although the number of first responders authorized to administer naloxone has been extended to all types of EMS staff (Bessen et al., 2019; Krohmer, 2017), law enforcement agencies in some communities continue to refuse to equip their officers with naloxone (Murphy and Russell, 2020). In some communities, the desirability of providing naloxone to drug users is some-

---

[19] By contrast, some localities operating SCSs make a conscious effort to keep them distinct from treatment facilities, although SCS clients are of course provided with information on and offered linkage with treatment services. This avoids a situation in which people in treatment use the same facility as people in active use and not in treatment.

times questioned by the police (Reichert, Lurigio, and Weisner, 2019). There are also reports that, in some places, some police officers confiscate naloxone kits (Marten, 2018; Winstanley et al., 2016). Furthermore, in the absence of Good Samaritan Laws offering broad protections, police may arrest those who report an overdose for drug or paraphernalia possession and other related crimes (Prescription Drug Abuse Policy System, 2018), but it is unclear how often this happens. Combined with other concerns, such as fear of loss of child custody or of facing serious charges in jurisdictions with drug-induced homicide laws in place, such practices contribute to PWUDs' reluctance to call for emergency assistance (Goulka et al., 2021; Koester et al., 2017; Wagner et al., 2019).

In addition, community-initiated interventions may have an impact on the first responders' work because the expansion of naloxone access means that there is an increased chance that overdose witnesses will have naloxone available to administer. In some instances, witnesses may subsequently feel it is no longer necessary to call 911, in which case the overdose may not become known to first responders and the broader public health system and will be missing in public surveillance data. In this context, the potency of fentanyl increases the odds that multiple doses of naloxone may be necessary, which may not be available to overdose witnesses. In addition, witnesses may not be able to address other challenges specific to fentanyl that may limit the effectiveness of naloxone, such as chest wall rigidity (Torralva and Janowsky, 2019).

Education

Schools interact with community-initiated interventions because they represent an important setting for prevention interventions. Relatedly, high-quality schools are a generic protective factor. Furthermore, schools have increasingly been a venue for the storage and distribution of naloxone kits and for providing training on how to administer naloxone. Training recipients include both school staff and students, who learn the skills to reverse an overdose among their friends or family (Levin, 2020). Higher-education institutions have also begun making naloxone available to students and campus-based EMS (Johnson et al., 2020).

The strength of community coalitions, however, is the ability to develop broad prevention solutions upstream from the education system, with the potential for attention to premature and underweight births, the first five years of development, child care, and other programs touching on social services and child welfare.

Policy Opportunities and Considerations

The SCS portion of this section is reproduced from Kilmer, 2020.

Providing more funding for harm reduction programs—especially during an unprecedented overdose crisis—is critical. However, questions remain about how to best allocate funds for harm reduction. For example, if a city is focused on reducing overdose deaths and has $5 million in new funds to support these efforts, should it allocate those efforts to creating and staffing an SCS, increasing the availability of naloxone in the community, implementing drug checking services, expanding treatment access, providing more emergency services, or some combination of these efforts, or should it spend the funds on something else? The most efficient allocation of these funds will depend on resources and programs already available in that community. Additionally, the location of these programs—and whether they are colocated with other service components of the ecosystem—will have implications for the overall costs and benefits.

Although the federal government announced in 2021 that it will spend $30 million to advance harm reduction efforts (HHS Press Office, 2021), this is a very small investment compared with the more than $40 billion proposed in the 2022 federal budget for demand and supply reduction (Office of National Drug Control Policy, 2021).

With respect to SCSs, federal barriers could be reduced to allow communities to pilot and evaluate these interventions. One federal option is to make a legislative change explicitly exempting SCSs from the CSA and to start funding demonstration programs. Of course, the new legislative language would have to be broad enough to ensure that those who worked there could not be sanctioned (e.g., lose the ability to prescribe drugs) and those who entered with drugs would not be arrested. (Although the federal government rarely makes arrests for possessing small amounts, such arrests are still a theoretical possibility even if not a practical issue.) Another option would be to pass a budget rider that prohibits federal funds from being used to enforce federal laws against those implementing, staffing, or using an SCS.[20] A recent precedent with respect to the CSA was the budget rider that prohibited federal funds from being used to enforce federal law against those participating in state-legal medical cannabis programs.

However, Congress does not have to pass legislation to reduce federal barriers to implementing SCSs. U.S. attorneys have discretion about the types of cases they pursue. U.S. attorneys could simply decide to not enforce federal laws against those implementing, staffing, or using SCSs, or they could issue guidance about the types of cases they will prioritize (Kilmer and Pardo, 2019).

The DOJ could also publish guidance indicating that it is not "legalizing" SCSs but will not make it an enforcement priority to target sites that are consistent with state and local laws. Additional guidelines could be added, for example, requiring that any new sites have a robust evaluation plan with a credible control condition and disinterested evaluator (e.g., the U.S. Government Accountability Office). Although this type of guidance could always be reversed, it would allow local governments to experiment with an intervention that may help reduce some of the harms associated with unsupervised consumption.

As noted earlier, there is much to learn about the community-level outcomes associated with implementing SCSs. Although only New York City has opened a sanctioned SCS in the United States, multiple jurisdictions seem poised for this, and now is the time to start collect-

---

[20] Leo Beletsky, personal communication with the authors, December 5, 2019.

ing pre-implementation data and thinking critically about possible control neighborhoods and cities for pilot studies.

Even when countries are successful in implementing SCSs, these sites address only a very small share of all opioid use. A much more fundamental change that affects many orders of magnitude more people would be to reform drug possession laws (further discussed in Chapter Six). Indeed, in some parts of the country, there appears to be a willingness to engage in discussions about reducing harms caused by criminal legal policies related to substance use; the added burdens of the unmet needs of those living with serious mental health problems; and the critical dimensions of poverty, lack of opportunity, and homelessness.

Abbreviations

AMA	American Medical Association
CDC	Centers for Disease Control and Prevention
CSA	U.S. Controlled Substances Act
CTC	Communities That Care
DOJ	U.S. Department of Justice
EMS	emergency medical services
GTO	Getting to Outcomes
HHS	U.S. Department of Health and Human Services
NASEN	North American Syringe Exchange Network
NEP	needle exchange program
OUD	opioid use disorder
PreP	preexposure prophylaxis
PWID	people who inject drugs
PWUD	people who use drugs
SAMHSA	Substance Abuse and Mental Health Services Administration
SCS	supervised consumption site
SSP	syringe service program

References

Abouk, Rahi, Rosalie Liccardo Pacula, and David Powell, "Association Between State Laws Facilitating Pharmacy Distribution of Naloxone and Risk of Fatal Overdose," *JAMA Internal Medicine*, Vol. 179, No. 6, 2019, pp. 805–811.

Agarin, Taghogho, Andrea M. Trescot, Aniefiok Agarin, Doreena Lesanics, and Claricio Decastro, "Reducing Opioid Analgesic Deaths in America: What Health Providers Can Do," *Pain Physician*, Vol. 18, No. 3, 2015, pp. E307–E322.

Albert, Su, Fred W. Brason II, Catherine K. Sanford, Nabarun Dasgupta, Jim Graham, and Beth Lovette, "Project Lazarus: Community-Based Overdose Prevention in Rural North Carolina," *Pain Medicine*, Vol. 12, Suppl. 2, 2011, pp. S77–S85.

Allen, Sean T., Suzanne M. Grieb, Allison O'Rourke, Ryan Yoder, Elise Planchet, Rebecca Hamilton White, and Susan G. Sherman, "Understanding the Public Health Consequences of Suspending a Rural Syringe Services Program: A Qualitative Study of the Experiences of People Who Inject Drugs," *Harm Reduction Journal*, Vol. 16, No. 1, December 2019.

AMA—*See* American Medical Association.

Amass, Leslie, and Jonathan Kamien, "A Tale of Two Cities: Financing Two Voucher Programs for Substance Abusers Through Community Donations," *Experimental and Clinical Psychopharmacology*, Vol. 12, No. 2, May 2004, pp. 147–155.

American Medical Association, "AMA Wants New Approaches to Combat Synthetic and Injectable Drugs," press release, Chicago, Ill., June 12, 2017.

American Medical Association, *Physicians' Progress Toward Ending the Nation's Drug Overdose and Death Epidemic: Opioid Task Force 2020 Progress Report*, Chicago, Ill., 2020.

Anglin, M. Douglas, Bohdan Nosyk, Adi Jaffe, Darren Urada, and Elizabeth Evans, "Offender Diversion into Substance Use Disorder Treatment: The Economic Impact of California's Proposition 36," *American Journal of Public Health*, Vol. 103, No. 6, June 2013, pp. 1096–1102.

Arizona State Legislature, Title 36, Public Health and Safety, Chapter 21.1, Emergency Medical Services, Article 4, Opioid Antagonists, Section 36-2267, Administration of Opioid Antagonist; Exemption from Civil Liability; Definition, undated.

Aspinall, Esther J., Dhanya Nambiar, David J. Goldberg, Matthew Hickman, Amanda Weir, Eva Van Velzen, Norah Palmateer, Joseph S. Doyle, Margaret E. Hellard, and Sharon J. Hutchinson, "Are Needle and Syringe Programmes Associated with a Reduction in HIV Transmission Among People Who Inject Drugs: A Systematic Review and Meta-Analysis," *International Journal of Epidemiology*, Vol. 43, No. 1, February 2014, pp. 235–248.

Atkins, Danielle N., Christine Piette Durrance, and Yuna Kim, "Good Samaritan Harm Reduction Policy and Drug Overdose Deaths," *Health Services Research*, Vol. 54, No. 2, April 2019, pp. 407–416.

Azrin, N. H., "Improvements in the Community-Reinforcement Approach to Alcoholism," *Behaviour Research and Therapy*, Vol. 14, No. 5, 1976, pp. 339–348.

Bachhuber, Marcus A., Emma E. McGinty, Alene Kennedy-Hendricks, Jeff Niederdeppe, and Colleen L. Barry, "Messaging to Increase Public Support for Naloxone Distribution Policies in the United States: Results from a Randomized Survey Experiment," *PLoS ONE*, Vol. 10, No. 7, 2015.

Bachhuber, Marcus A., Cole Thompson, Ann Prybylowski, José Benitez, Silvana Mazzella, and David Barclay, "Description and Outcomes of a Buprenorphine Maintenance Treatment Program Integrated Within Prevention Point Philadelphia, an Urban Syringe Exchange Program," *Substance Abuse*, Vol. 39, No. 2, 2018, pp. 167–172.

Banta-Green, Caleb J., Leo Beletsky, Jennifer A. Schoeppe, Phillip O. Coffin, and Patricia C. Kuszler, "Police Officers' and Paramedics' Experiences with Overdose and Their Knowledge and Opinions of Washington State's Drug Overdose-Naloxone-Good Samaritan Law," *Journal of Urban Health*, Vol. 90, No. 6, December 2013, pp. 1102–1111.

Bardwell, Geoff, and Thomas Kerr, "Drug Checking: A Potential Solution to the Opioid Overdose Epidemic?" *Substance Abuse Treatment, Prevention, and Policy*, Vol. 13, No. 1, 2018.

Bardwell, Geoff, Evan Wood, and Rupinder Brar, "Fentanyl Assisted Treatment: A Possible Role in the Opioid Overdose Epidemic?" *Substance Abuse Treatment, Prevention, and Policy*, Vol. 14, No. 50, 2019.

Barocas, Joshua A., Lisa Baker, Shawnika J. Hull, Scott Stokes, and Ryan P. Westergaard, "High Uptake of Naloxone-Based Overdose Prevention Training Among Previously Incarcerated Syringe-Exchange Program Participants," *Drug and Alcohol Dependence*, Vol. 154, September 1, 2015, pp. 283–286.

Bassetti, S., and M. Battegay, "Staphylococcus Aureus Infections in Injection Drug Users: Risk Factors and Prevention Strategies," *Infection*, Vol. 32, No. 3, 2004, pp. 163–169.

Bastos, F. I., and S. A. Strathdee, "Evaluating Effectiveness of Syringe Exchange Programmes: Current Issues and Future Prospects," *Social Science & Medicine*, Vol. 51, No. 12, 2000, pp. 1771–1782.

Beletsky, Leo, Robin Ruthazer, Grace E. Macalino, Josiah D. Rich, Litjen Tan, and Scott Burris, "Physicians' Knowledge of and Willingness to Prescribe Naloxone to Reverse Accidental Opiate Overdose: Challenges and Opportunities," *Journal of Urban Health*, Vol. 84, No. 1, 2007, pp. 126–136.

Bell, James, Vendula Belackova, and Nicholas Lintzeris, "Supervised Injectable Opioid Treatment for the Management of Opioid Dependence," *Drugs*, Vol. 78, No. 13, 2018, pp. 1339–1352.

Bessen, Sarah, Stephen A. Metcalf, Elizabeth C. Saunders, Sarah K. Moore, Andrea Meier, Bethany McLeman, Olivia Walsh, and Lisa A. Marsch, "Barriers to Naloxone Use and Acceptance Among Opioid Users, First Responders, and Emergency Department Providers in New Hampshire, USA," *International Journal of Drug Policy*, Vol. 74, 2019, pp. 144–151.

Bethell, Christina D., Paul Newacheck, Eva Hawes, and Neal Halfon, "Adverse Childhood Experiences: Assessing the Impact on Health and School Engagement and the Mitigating Role of Resilience," *Health Affairs*, Vol. 33, No. 12, 2014, pp. 2106–2115.

Binswanger, Ingrid A., Traci A. Takahashi, Katharine Bradley, Timothy H. Dellit, Kathryn L. Benton, and Joseph O. Merrill, "Drug Users Seeking Emergency Care for Soft Tissue Infection at High Risk for Subsequent Hospitalization and Death," *Journal of Studies on Alcohol and Drugs*, Vol. 69, No. 6, 2008, pp. 924–932.

Bird, Chloe E., Teresa Seeman, José J. Escarce, Ricardo Basurto-Dávila, Brian K. Finch, Tamara Dubowitz, Melonie Heron, Lauren Hale, Sharon Stein Merkin, Margaret Weden, Nicole Lurie, and Paul O'Neill Alcoa, "Neighbourhood Socioeconomic Status and Biological 'Wear and Tear' in a Nationally Representative Sample of US Adults," *Journal of Epidemiology and Community Health*, Vol. 64, No. 10, 2010, pp. 860–865.

Blanchard, Janice, Audrey J. Weiss, Marguerite L. Barrett, Kimberly W. McDermott, and Kevin C. Heslin, "State Variation in Opioid Treatment Policies and Opioid-Related Hospital Readmissions," *BMC Health Services Research*, Vol. 18, December 17, 2018.

Bluthenthal, Ricky N., "Syringe Exchange as a Social Movement: A Case Study of Harm Reduction in Oakland, California," *Substance Use & Misuse*, Vol. 33, No. 5, 1998, pp. 1147–1171.

Bluthenthal, Ricky N., Keith G. Heinzerling, Rachel Anderson, Neil M. Flynn, and Alex H. Kral, "Approval of Syringe Exchange Programs in California: Results from a Local Approach to HIV Prevention," *American Journal of Public Health*, Vol. 98, No. 2, February 2008, pp. 278–283.

Bluthenthal, Ricky N., Greg Ridgeway, Terry Schell, Rachel Anderson, Neil M. Flynn, and Alex H. Kral, "Examination of the Association Between Syringe Exchange Program (SEP) Dispensation Policy and SEP Client-Level Syringe Coverage Among Injection Drug Users," *Addiction*, Vol. 102, No. 4, 2007, pp. 638–646.

Bonn, Matthew, "Canada's Safe-Supply Vending Machines Project Is Even More Important Now," *Filter*, May 5, 2020.

Booth, Robert E., Carol Kwiatkowski, Martin Y. Iguchi, Francesca Pinto, and Debbie John, "Facilitating Treatment Entry Among Out-of-Treatment Injection Drug Users," *Public Health Reports*, Vol. 113, Suppl. 1, 1998, pp. 116–128.

Boyd, Susan, and Donald MacPherson, "Community Engagement—The Harms of Drug Prohibition: Ongoing Resistance in Vancouver's Downtown Eastside," *BC Studies*, Vol. 200, 2018, pp. 87–96.

Brason, Fred Wells, II, Candice Roe, and Nabarun Dasgupta, "Project Lazarus: An Innovative Community Response to Prescription Drug Overdose," *North Carolina Medical Journal*, Vol. 74, No. 3, 2013, pp. 259–261.

Bravo, Maria J., Luis Royuela, Gregorio Barrio, Luis de la Fuente, Mónica Suarez, and M. Teresa Brugal, "More Free Syringes, Fewer Drug Injectors in the Case of Spain," *Social Science & Medicine*, Vol. 65, No. 8, 2007, pp. 1773–1778.

British Columbia Centre on Substance Use, *Heroin Compassion Clubs: A Cooperative Model to Reduce Opioid Overdose Deaths and Disrupt Organized Crime's Role in Fentanyl, Money Laundering and Housing Unaffordability*, Victoria, British Columbia, February 2019.

Brogle, Courtney, "Free Heroin, Cocaine and Meth Distributed in Front of Police Department," *Newsweek*, July 16, 2021.

Brown, David W., Robert F. Anda, Henning Tiemeier, Vincent J. Felitti, Valerie J. Edwards, Janet B. Croft, and Wayne H. Giles, "Adverse Childhood Experiences and the Risk of Premature Mortality," *American Journal of Preventive Medicine*, Vol. 37, No. 5, 2009, pp. 389–396.

Brunt, Tibor, "Drug Checking as a Harm Reduction Tool for Recreational Drug Users: Opportunities and Challenges," European Monitoring Centre for Drugs and Drug Addiction, October 30, 2017.

Buning, E. C., *Effects of Amsterdam Needle and Syringe Exchange: Dutch-American Debate*, The Hague, Netherlands: Government Printing Office, 1989.

Bux, D. A., M. Y. Iguchi, V. Lidz, R. C. Baxter, and J. J. Platt, "Participation in an Outreach-Based Coupon Distribution Program for Free Methadone Detoxification," *Hospital & Community Psychiatry*, Vol. 44, No. 11, November 1993, pp. 1066–1072.

Campbell, Frances, Gabriella Conti, James J. Heckman, Seong Hyeok Moon, Rodrigo Pinto, Elizabeth Pungello, and Yi Pan, "Early Childhood Investments Substantially Boost Adult Health," *Science*, Vol. 343, No. 6178, 2014, pp. 1478–1485.

Canêdo, Joana, Kali-olt Sedgemore, Kelly Ebbert, Haleigh Anderson, Rainbow Dykeman, Katey Kincaid, Claudia Dias, Diana Silva, Youth Health Advisory Council, Reith Charlesworth, et al., "Harm Reduction Calls to Action from Young People Who Use Drugs on the Streets of Vancouver and Lisbon," *Harm Reduction Journal*, Vol. 19, No. 43, May 2022.

Caulkins, Jonathan P., Bryce Pardo, and Beau Kilmer, "Supervised Consumption Sites: A Nuanced Assessment of the Causal Evidence," *Addiction*, Vol. 114, No. 12, 2019, pp. 2109–2115.

CDC—*See* Centers for Disease Control and Prevention.

Center for Technology and Behavioral Health, "Safe Station: A Systematic Evaluation of a Novel Community-Based Model to Tackle the Opioid Crisis," September 2018.

Centers for Disease Control and Prevention, *Program Guidance for Implementing Certain Components of Syringe Services Programs*, Atlanta, Ga., 2016.

Centers for Disease Control and Prevention, *Preexposure Prophylaxis for the Prevention of HIV Infection in the United States—2017 Update: A Clinical Practice Guideline*, Atlanta, Ga., March 2018.

Centers for Disease Control and Prevention, "Federal Funding for Syringe Services Programs," webpage, May 23, 2019a. As of December 16, 2021:
https://www.cdc.gov/ssp/ssp-funding.html

Centers for Disease Control and Prevention, "PEP (Post-Exposure Prophylaxis)," webpage, July 2019b. As of December 16, 2021:
https://www.cdc.gov/hiv/basics/pep.html

Centers for Disease Control and Prevention, *Needs-Based Syringe Distribution and Disposal at Syringe Services Programs*, Atlanta, Ga., September 2020.

Centers for Disease Control and Prevention, "Federal Grantees May Now Use Funds to Purchase Fentanyl Test Strips," press release, April 7, 2021. As of June 7, 2022:
https://www.cdc.gov/media/releases/2021/p0407-Fentanyl-Test-Strips.html

Chinman, Matthew, Pamela Imm, and Abraham Wandersman, *Getting to Outcomes™ 2004: Promoting Accountability Through Methods and Tools for Planning, Implementation, and Evaluation*, Santa Monica, Calif.: RAND Corporation, TR-101-CDC, 2004. As of December 16, 2021:
https://www.rand.org/pubs/technical_reports/TR101.html

Coe, Marion A., and Sharon L. Walsh, "Distribution of Naloxone for Overdose Prevention to Chronic Pain Patients," *Preventive Medicine*, Vol. 80, 2015, pp. 41–43.

Coffin, Phillip O., and Sean D. Sullivan, "Cost-Effectiveness of Distributing Naloxone to Heroin Users for Lay Overdose Reversal," *Annals of Internal Medicine*, Vol. 16, No. 8, 2013, pp. 1051–1060.

Coie, John D., Norman F. Watt, Stephen G. West, J. David Hawkins, Joan R. Asarnow, Howard J. Markman, Sharon L. Ramey, Myrna B. Shure, and Beverly Long, "The Science of Prevention: A Conceptual Framework and Some Directions for a National Research Program," *American Psychologist*, Vol. 48, No. 10, 1993, pp. 1013–1022.

Conti, Gabriella, and James J. Heckman, "The Developmental Approach to Child and Adult Health," *Pediatrics*, Vol. 131, Suppl. 2, 2013, pp. S133–S141.

Corsaro, Nicholas, Rod K. Brunson, and Edmund F. McGarrell, "Evaluating a Policing Strategy Intended to Disrupt an Illicit Street-Level Drug Market," *Evaluation Review*, Vol. 34, No. 6, 2010, pp. 513–548.

Coyle, Susan L., Richard H. Needle, and Jacques Normand, "Outreach-Based HIV Prevention for Injecting Drug Users: A Review of Published Outcome Data," *Public Health Reports*, Vol. 113, Suppl. 1, 1998, pp. 19–30.

Csete, Joanne, and Richard Elliott, "Consumer Protection in Drug Policy: The Human Rights Case for Safe Supply as an Element of Harm Reduction," *International Journal of Drug Policy*, Vol. 91, May 2021.

Danese, Andrea, Terrie E. Moffitt, HonaLee Harrington, Barry J. Milne, Guilherme Polanczyk, Carmine M. Pariante, Richie Poulton, and Avshalom Caspi, "Adverse Childhood Experiences and Adult Risk Factors for Age-Related Disease: Depression, Inflammation, and Clustering of Metabolic Risk Markers," *Archives of Pediatrics and Adolescent Medicine*, Vol. 163, No. 12, 2009, pp. 1135–1143.

Davidson, Peter J., Barrot H. Lambdin, Erica N. Browne, Lynn D. Wenger, and Alex H. Kral, "Impact of an Unsanctioned Safe Consumption Site on Criminal Activity, 2010–2019," *Drug and Alcohol Dependence*, Vol. 220, 2021.

Davis, Corey, "American Rescue Plan Act Provides Opportunity for Syringe Access," Network for Public Health Law, March 30, 2021.

Davis, Corey S., and Derek Carr, "Legal Changes to Increase Access to Naloxone for Opioid Overdose Reversal in the United States," *Drug and Alcohol Dependence*, Vol. 157, 2015, pp. 112–120.

Davis, Corey S., Derek Carr, Jessica K. Southwell, and Leo Beletsky, "Engaging Law Enforcement in Overdose Reversal Initiatives: Authorization and Liability for Naloxone Administration," *American Journal of Public Health*, Vol. 105, No. 8, 2015, pp. 1530–1537.

Davis, Corey S., Sarah Ruiz, Patrick Glynn, Gerald Picariello, and Alexander Y. Walley, "Expanded Access to Naloxone Among Firefighters, Police Officers, and Emergency Medical Technicians in Massachusetts," *American Journal of Public Health*, Vol. 104, No. 8, 2014, pp. e7–e9.

Davis, Corey, Damika Webb, and Scott Burris, "Changing Law from Barrier to Facilitator of Opioid Overdose Prevention," *Journal of Law, Medicine, and Ethics*, Vol. 41, Suppl. 1, 2013, pp. 33–36.

de Leon, George, "Therapeutic Communities: AIDS/HIV Risk and Harm Reduction," *Journal of Substance Abuse Treatment*, Vol. 13, No. 5, 1996, pp. 411–420.

de Montigny, Luc, Anne Vernez Moudon, Barbara Leigh, and Sun Young Kim, "Assessing a Drop Box Programme: A Spatial Analysis of Discarded Needles," *International Journal of Drug Policy*, Vol. 21, No. 3, May 2010, pp. 208–214.

Delaney, Liam, and James P. Smith, "Childhood Health: Trends and Consequences over the Life Course," *Future Child*, Vol. 22, No. 1, 2012, pp. 43–63.

Deming, W. Edwards, *Out of the Crisis*, Cambridge, Mass.: MIT Press, 1982.

Des Jarlais, D. C., and S. R. Friedman, "HIV Infection Among Intravenous Drug Users: Epidemiology and Risk Reduction," *AIDS*, Vol. 1, No. 2, 1987, pp. 67–76.

Des Jarlais, Don C., "Stages in the Response of the Drug Abuse Treatment System to the AIDS Epidemic in New York City," *Journal of Drug Issues*, Vol. 20, No. 2, 1990, pp. 335–347.

Des Jarlais, Don C., "Harm Reduction in the USA: The Research Perspective and an Archive to David Purchase," *Harm Reduction Journal*, Vol. 14, No. 15, 2017.

Des Jarlais, Don C., Jonathan Feelemyer, Kamyar Arasteh, Paul LaKosky, and Kathryn Szymanowski, "Expansion of Syringe Service Programs in the United States, 2015–2018," *American Journal of Public Health*, Vol. 110, No. 4, 2020, pp. 517–519.

Des Jarlais, Don C., Courtney McKnight, and Judith Milliken, "Public Funding of US Syringe Exchange Programs," *Journal of Urban Health*, Vol. 81, No. 1, 2004, pp. 118–121.

Des Jarlais, Don C., Ann Nugent, Alisa Solberg, Jonathan Feelemyer, Jonathan Mermin, and Deborah Holtzman, "Syringe Service Programs for Persons Who Inject Drugs in Urban, Suburban, and Rural Areas—United States, 2013," *Morbidity and Mortality Weekly Report*, Vol. 64, No. 48, 2015, pp. 1337–1341.

DeSantis, Amy S., Emma K. Adam, Leah D. Doane, Susan Mineka, Richard E. Zinbarg, and Michelle G. Craske, "Racial/Ethnic Differences in Cortisol Diurnal Rhythms in a Community Sample of Adolescents," *Journal of Adolescent Health*, Vol. 41, No. 1, July 2007, pp. 3–13.

Doherty, Meg C., Benjamin Junge, Paul Rathouz, Richard S. Garfein, Elise Riley, and David Vlahov, "The Effect of a Needle Exchange Program on Numbers of Discarded Needles: A 2-Year Follow-Up," *American Journal of Public Health*, Vol. 90, No. 6, June 2000, pp. 936–939.

Doleac, Jennifer, "Analisa Packham on Syringe Exchange Programs," Probable Causation podcast, May 14, 2019.

Doleac, Jennifer L., and Anita Mukherjee, "The Moral Hazard of Lifesaving Innovations: Naloxone Access, Opioid Abuse, and Crime," IZA Institute of Labor Economics, April 2018.

Drucker, E., P. Lurie, A. Wodak, and P. Alcabes, "Measuring Harm Reduction: The Effects of Needle and Syringe Exchange Programs and Methadone Maintenance on the Ecology of HIV," *AIDS*, Vol. 12, Suppl. A, 1998, pp. S217–S230.

Drury, Stacy S., Emily Mabile, Zoë H. Brett, Kyle Esteves, Edward Jones, Elizabeth A. Shirtcliff, and Katherine P. Theall, "The Association of Telomere Length with Family Violence and Disruption," *Pediatrics*, Vol. 134, No. 1, 2014, pp. e128–e137.

Durlak, Joseph A., "Common Risk and Protective Factors in Successful Prevention Programs," *American Journal of Orthopsychiatry*, Vol. 68, No. 4, 1998, pp. 512–520.

Enteen, Lauren, Joanna Bauer, Rachel McLean, Eliza Wheeler, Emalie Huriaux, Alex H. Kral, and Joshua D. Bamberger, "Overdose Prevention and Naloxone Prescription for Opioid Users in San Francisco," *Journal of Urban Health*, Vol. 87, No. 6, 2010, pp. 931–941.

Erfanian, Elham, Alan R. Collins, and Daniel Grossman, "The Impact of Naloxone Access Laws on Opioid Overdose Deaths in the U.S.," *Review of Regional Studies*, Vol. 49, No. 1, 2019, pp. 45–72.

Evans, Gary W., and Pilyoung Kim, "Childhood Poverty and Health: Cumulative Risk Exposure and Stress Dysregulation," *Psychological Sciences*, Vol. 18, No. 11, 2007, pp. 953–957.

Farabee, David, Yih-ing Hser, M. Douglas Anglin, and David Huang, "Recidivism Among an Early Cohort of California's Proposition 36 Offenders," *Criminology & Public Policy*, Vol. 3, No. 4, 2004, pp. 563–584.

Fauci, Anthony S., Robert R. Redfield, George Sigounas, Michael D. Weahkee, and Brett P. Giroir, "Ending the HIV Epidemic: A Plan for the United States," *JAMA*, Vol. 321, No. 9, 2019, pp. 844–845.

Fernandes, Ricardo M., Maria Cary, Gonçalo Duarte, Gonçalo Jesus, Joana Alarcão, Carla Torre, Suzete Costa, João Costa, and António Vaz Carneiro, "Effectiveness of Needle and Syringe Programmes in People Who Inject Drugs—An Overview of Systematic Reviews," *BMC Public Health*, Vol. 17, 2017.

Fetterman, David M., Shakeh J. Kaftarian, and Abraham Wandersman, *Empowerment Evaluation: Knowledge and Tools for Self-Assessment and Accountability*, Washington, D.C.: Sage Publications, 1996.

Flynn, Patrick M., James V. Porto, Jennifer L. Rounds-Bryant, and Patricia L. Kristiansen, "Costs and Benefits of Methadone Treatment in DATOS-Part 1," *Journal of Maintenance in the Addictions*, Vol. 2, 2002, pp. 129–149.

Friedman, Samuel R., "The Political Economy of Drug-User Scapegoating—and the Philosophy and Politics of Resistance," *Drugs: Education, Prevention and Policy*, Vol. 5, No. 1, 1998, pp. 15–32.

Friedman, Samuel R., Matthew Southwell, Regina Bueno, Denise Paone, Jude Byrne, and Nick Crofts, "Harm Reduction—A Historical View from the Left," *International Journal of Drug Policy*, Vol. 12, No. 1, 2001, pp. 3–14.

Galea, Sandro, Jennifer Ahern, Crystal Fuller, Nicholas Freudenberg, and David Vlahov, "Needle Exchange Programs and Experience of Violence in an Inner City Neighborhood," *Journal of Acquired Immune Deficiency Syndromes*, Vol. 28, No. 3, November 1, 2001, pp. 282–288.

Gallant, Jacques, "Can Drug Users' Lives Be Saved by Giving Them Uncontaminated Heroin and Cocaine?" *Toronto Star*, October 23, 2022.

Gardiner, Christine Lynn, *From Inception to Implementation: How SACPA Has Affected the Case Processing and Sentencing of Drug Offenders in One California County*, University of California, Irvine, 2008.

Gelles, Richard J., "Poverty and Violence Toward Children," *American Behavioral Scientist*, Vol. 35, No. 3, 1992, pp. 258–274.

Gelman, Andrew, "Controversy Over an Article on Syringe Exchange Programs and Harm Reduction: As Usual, I'd Like to See More Graphs of the Data," *Statistical Modeling, Causal Inference, and Social Science* blog, February 10, 2023. As of February 17, 2023: https://statmodeling.stat.columbia.edu/2023/02/10/controversy-over-an-article-on-syringe-exchange-programs-and-harm-reduction-as-usual-id-like-to-see-more-graphs-of-the-data/

Gertner, Alex K., Marisa Elena Domino, and Corey S. Davis, "Do Naloxone Access Laws Increase Outpatient Naloxone Prescriptions? Evidence from Medicaid," *Drug and Alcohol Dependence*, Vol. 190, September 1, 2018, pp. 37–41.

Goedel, William C., Maximilian R. F. King, Mark N. Lurie, Sandro Galea, Jeffrey P. Townsend, Alison P. Galvani, Samuel R. Friedman, and Brandon D. L. Marshall, "Implementation of Syringe Services Programs to Prevent Rapid Human Immunodeficiency Virus Transmission in Rural Counties in the United States: A Modeling Study," *Clinical Infectious Diseases*, Vol. 70, No. 6, March 15, 2020, pp. 1096–1102.

Goodman, Alissa, Robert Joyce, and James P. Smith, "The Long Shadow Cast by Childhood Physical and Mental Problems on Adult Life," *Proceedings of the National Academy of Sciences of the United States of America*, Vol. 108, No. 15, 2011, pp. 6032–6037.

Goulka, Jeremiah, Valena Elizabeth Beety, Alex Kreit, Anne Boustead, Justine Newman, and Leo Beletsky, *Drug-Induced Homicide Defense Toolkit*, 2021 ed., Ohio State Public Law Working Paper No. 467, 2021.

Green, Traci C., Jef Bratberg, Emily F. Dauria, and Josiah D. Rich, "Responding to Opioid Overdose in Rhode Island: Where the Medical Community Has Gone and Where We Need to Go," *Rhode Island Medical Journal*, Vol. 97, No. 10, 2014, pp. 29–33.

Green, Traci C., Ju Nyeong Park, Michael Gilbert, Michelle McKenzie, Eric Struth, Rachel Lucas, William Clarke, and Susan G. Sherman, "An Assessment of the Limits of Detection, Sensitivity and Specificity of Three Devices for Public Health-Based Drug Checking of Fentanyl in Street-Acquired Samples," *International Journal of Drug Policy*, Vol. 77, 2020.

Greenberg, Mark T., "Promoting Resilience in Children and Youth: Preventive Interventions and Their Interface with Neuroscience," *Annals of the New York Academy of Sciences*, Vol. 1094, No. 1, 2007, pp. 139–150.

Grochowski, Sarah, "Cocaine, Heroin and Meth Buyers' Club Gets Vancouver's Approval to Secure a Safe Supply," *Vancouver Sun*, October 7, 2021.

Grönbladh, L., L. S. Öhlund, and L. M. Gunne, "Mortality in Heroin Addiction: Impact of Methadone Treatment," *Acta Psychiatrica Scandinavica*, Vol. 82, No. 3, 1990, pp. 223–227.

Guerra, Nancy G., L. Rowell Huesmann, and Anja Spindler, "Community Violence Exposure, Social Cognition, and Aggression Among Urban Elementary School Children," *Child Development*, Vol. 74, No. 5, 2003, pp. 1561–1576.

Guy, Gery P., Jr., Tamara M. Haegerich, Mary E. Evans, Jan L. Losby, Randall Young, and Christopher M. Jones, "Vital Signs: Pharmacy-Based Naloxone Dispensing—United States, 2012–2018," *Morbidity and Mortality Weekly Report*, Vol. 68, 2019, pp. 679–686.

Gyarmathy, V. Anna, Alan Neaigus, Nan Li, Eszter Ujhelyi, Irma Caplinskiene, Saulius Caplinskas, and Carl A. Latkin, "Liquid Drugs and High Dead Space Syringes May Keep HIV and HCV Prevalence High—A Comparison of Hungary and Lithuania," *European Addiction Research*, Vol. 16, No. 4, 2010, pp. 220–228.

Haegerich, Tamara M., Leonard J. Paulozzi, Brian J. Manns, and Christopher M. Jones, "What We Know, and Don't Know, About the Impact of State Policy and Systems-Level Interventions on Prescription Drug Overdose," *Drug and Alcohol Dependence*, Vol. 145, 2014, pp. 34–47.

Haffajee, Rebecca L., Samantha Cherney, and Rosanna Smart, "Legal Requirements and Recommendations to Prescribe Naloxone," *Drug and Alcohol Dependence*, Vol. 209, 2020.

Hagan, Holly, James P. McGough, Hanne Thiede, Sharon Hopkins, Jeffrey Duchin, and E. Russell Alexander, "Reduced Injection Frequency and Increased Entry and Retention in Drug Treatment Associated with Needle-Exchange Participation in Seattle Drug Injectors," *Journal of Substance Abuse Treatment*, Vol. 19, No. 3, 2000, pp. 247–252.

Hawkins, J. David, Richard F. Catalano, and Michael W. Arthur, "Promoting Science-Based Prevention in Communities," *Addictive Behaviors*, Vol. 27, No. 6, 2002, pp. 951–976.

Health Canada, "Supervised Consumption Sites and Services," webpage, 2018. As of September 11, 2020:
https://www.canada.ca/en/health-canada/services/substance-use/
supervised-consumption-sites.html

Health Canada, "Safer Supply," webpage, March 17, 2022. As of July 29, 2022:
https://www.canada.ca/en/health-canada/services/opioids/responding-canada-opioid-crisis/
safer-supply.html

Heimer, Robert, "Can Syringe Exchange Serve as a Conduit to Substance Abuse Treatment?" *Journal of Substance Abuse Treatment*, Vol. 15, No. 3, 1998, pp. 183–191.

Heinzerling, K. G., A. H. Kral, N. M. Flynn, R. L. Anderson, A. Scott, M. L. Gilbert, S. M. Asch, and R. N. Bluthenthal, "Unmet Need for Recommended Preventive Health Services Among Clients of California Syringe Exchange Programs: Implications for Quality Improvement," *Drug and Alcohol Dependence*, Vol. 81, No. 2, February 2006, pp. 167–178.

Henman, Anthony R., Denise Paone, Don C. Des Jarlais, Lee M. Kochems, and Samuel R. Friedman, "Injection Drug Users as Social Actors: A Stigmatized Community's Participation in the Syringe Exchange Programmes of New York City," *AIDS Care*, Vol. 10, 1998, pp. 397–408.

HHS—*See* U.S. Department of Health and Human Services.

Hood, Julia E., Caleb J. Banta-Green, Jeffrey S. Duchin, Joseph Breuner, Wendy Dell, Brad Finegood, Sara N. Glick, Malin Hamblin, Shayla Holcomb, Darla Mosse, Thea Oliphant-Wells, and Mi-Hyun Mia Shim, "Engaging an Unstably Housed Population with Low-Barrier Buprenorphine Treatment at a Syringe Services Program: Lessons Learned from Seattle, Washington," *Substance Abuse*, Vol. 41, No. 3, 2020, pp. 356–364.

Hunt, George M., and N. H. Azrin, "A Community-Reinforcement Approach to Alcoholism," *Behaviour Research and Therapy*, Vol. 11, No. 1, 1973, pp. 91–104.

Iguchi, M. Y., C. McCoy, W. Wiebel, J. Watters, D. Chitwood, L. Kotranski, P. Biernacki, M. Williams, J. Liebman, B. Brown, et al., "Early Indices of Efficacy in the NIDA AIDS Outreach Demonstration Projects," *Morbidity and Mortality Weekly Report*, 1990.

Iguchi, Martin Y., Maxine L. Stitzer, George E. Bigelow, and Ira A. Liebson, "Contingency Management in Methadone Maintenance: Effects of Reinforcing and Aversive Consequences on Illicit Polydrug Use," *Drug and Alcohol Dependence*, Vol. 22, No. 1–2, 1988.

Islam, Mofizul, Alex Wodak, and Katherine M. Conigrave, "The Effectiveness and Safety of Syringe Vending Machines as a Component of Needle Syringe Programmes in Community Settings," *International Journal of Drug Policy*, Vol. 19, 2008, pp. 436–441.

Johansson, Mikael, Jørgen Kjær, and Blaine Stothard, "Smørrebrød or Smörgåsbord: The Danish and Swedish Drug Users Unions: Contexts, Aims, Activities, Achievements," *Drugs and Alcohol Today*, Vol. 15, No. 1, 2015, pp. 38–48.

Johnson, Evan C., Ainsley E. Huffman, Hillary A. Yoder, Nicole M. Bordelon, Gretchen Sewczak-Claude, and Derek T. Smith, "Educational Intervention Changes College Students' Attitudes Toward Prescription Opioid Drug Use," *Substance Use & Misuse*, Vol. 55, No. 3, 2020, pp. 367–376.

Johnson, Sara B., Anne W. Riley, Douglas A. Granger, and Jenna Riis, "The Science of Early Life Toxic Stress for Pediatric Practice and Advocacy," *Pediatrics*, Vol. 131, 2013, pp. 319–327.

Jones, Christopher M., Peter G. Lurie, and Wilson M. Compton, "Increase in Naloxone Prescriptions Dispensed in US Retail Pharmacies Since 2013," *American Journal of Public Health*, Vol. 106, No. 4, 2016, pp. 689–690.

Karamouzian, Mohammad, Carolyn Dohoo, Sara Forsting, Ryan McNeil, Thomas Kerr, and Mark Lysyshyn, "Evaluation of a Fentanyl Drug Checking Service for Clients of a Supervised Injection Facility, Vancouver, Canada," *Harm Reduction Journal*, Vol. 15, No. 46, 2018.

Karch, Lydia, Samuel Tobias, Clare Schmidt, Maya Doe-Simkins, Nicole Carter, Elizabeth Salisbury-Afshar, and Suzanne Carlberg-Racich, "Results from a Mobile Drug Checking Pilot Program Using Three Technologies in Chicago, IL, USA," *Drug and Alcohol Dependence*, Vol. 228, 2021.

Kennedy, David M., "Pulling Levers: Chronic Offenders, High-Crime Settings, and a Theory of Prevention," *Valparaiso University Law Review*, Vol. 31, 1997, pp. 449–484.

Kennedy, Mary Clare, and Thomas Kerr, "Overdose Prevention in the United States: A Call for Supervised Injection Sites," *American Journal of Public Health*, Vol. 107, No. 1, 2017, pp. 42–43.

Kerensky, Todd, and Alexander Y. Walley, "Opioid Overdose Prevention and Naloxone Rescue Kits: What We Know and What We Don't Know," *Addiction Science & Clinical Practice*, Vol. 12, No. 4, 2017, pp. 1–7.

Kerker, Bonnie D., Jinjin Zhang, Erum Nadeem, Ruth E. K. Stein, Michael S. Hurlburt, Amy Heneghan, John Landsverk, and Sarah McCue Horwitz, "Adverse Childhood Experiences and Mental Health, Chronic Medical Conditions, and Development in Young Children," *Academic Pediatrics*, Vol. 15, No. 5, 2015, pp. 510–517.

Kilmer, Beau, *Reducing Barriers and Getting Creative: 10 Federal Options to Increase Treatment Access for Opioid Use Disorder and Reduce Fatal Overdoses*, Washington, D.C.: Brookings Institution, June 2020.

Kilmer, Beau, and Martin Y. Iguchi, *Drug Treatment for Drug-Abusing Criminal Offenders: Insights from California's Proposition 36 and Arizona's Proposition 200*, Princeton, N.J.: Robert Wood Johnson Foundation, Substance Abuse Policy Research Program, 2009.

Kilmer, Beau, and Bryce Pardo, "Addressing Federal Conflicts over Supervised Drug Consumption Sites," *The Hill*, March 14, 2019.

Kilmer, Beau, and Bryce Pardo, "Clarifying 'Safer Supply' to Enrich Policy Discussions," *Addiction*, 2023.

Kilmer, Beau, Jirka Taylor, Jonathan P. Caulkins, Pam A. Mueller, Allison J. Ober, Bryce Pardo, Rosanna Smart, Lucy Strang, and Peter H. Reuter, *Considering Heroin-Assisted Treatment and Supervised Drug Consumption Sites in the United States*, Santa Monica, Calif.: RAND Corporation, RR-2693-RC, 2018. As of May 25, 2022:
https://www.rand.org/pubs/research_reports/RR2693.html

Kirby, Kimberly C., Leslie Amass, and A. Thomas McLellan, "Disseminating Contingency Management Research to Drug Abuse Treatment Practitioners," in S. T. Higgins and K. Silverman, eds., *Motivating Behavior Change Among Illicit-Drug Abusers: Research on Contingency Management Interventions*, Washington, D.C.: American Psychological Association, 1999, pp. 327–344.

Klingemann, Harald K. H., "Drug Treatment in Switzerland: Harm Reduction, Decentralization and Community Response," *Addiction*, Vol. 91, No. 5, 1996, pp. 723–736.

Koester, Stephen, Shane R. Mueller, Lisa Raville, Sig Langegger, and Ingrid A. Binswanger, "Why Are Some People Who Have Received Overdose Education and Naloxone Reticent to Call Emergency Medical Services in the Event of Overdose?" *International Journal of Drug Policy*, Vol. 48, 2017, pp. 115–124.

Kral, Alex H., Rachel Anderson, Neil M. Flynn, and Ricky N. Bluthenthal, "Injection Risk Behaviors Among Clients of Syringe Exchange Programs with Different Syringe Dispensation Policies," *Journal of Acquired Immune Deficiency Syndromes*, Vol. 37, No. 2, 2004, pp. 1307–1312.

Kral, Alex H., and Peter J. Davidson, "Addressing the Nation's Opioid Epidemic: Lessons from an Unsanctioned Supervised Injection Site in the U.S.," *American Journal of Preventive Medicine*, Vol. 53, No. 6, 2017, pp. 919–922.

Kral, Alex H., Barrot H. Lambdin, Lynn D. Wenger, and Pete J. Davidson, "Evaluation of an Unsanctioned Safe Consumption Site in the United States," *New England Journal of Medicine*, Vol. 383, 2020, pp. 589–590.

Krieger, Maxwell S., William C. Goedel, Jane A. Buxton, Mark Lysyshyn, Edward Bernstein, Susan G. Sherman, Josiah D. Rich, Scott E. Hadland, Traci C. Green, and Brandon D. L. Marshall, "Use of Rapid Fentanyl Test Strips Among Young Adults Who Use Drugs," *International Journal of Drug Policy*, Vol. 61, 2018, pp. 52–58.

Krohmer, Jon R., "2007 National EMS Scope of Practice Model, Change Notice," memorandum to State EMS Directors, Washington, D.C.: U.S. Department of Transportation, National Highway Traffic Safety Administration, November 1, 2017.

Laing, Matthew K., Kenneth W. Tupper, and Nadia Fairbairn, "Drug Checking as a Potential Strategic Overdose Response in the Fentanyl Era," *International Journal of Drug Policy*, Vol. 62, 2018, pp. 59–66.

Lambdin, Barrot H., Ricky N. Bluthenthal, Lynn D. Wenger, Eliza Wheeler, Bryan Garner, Paul Lakosky, and Alex H. Kral, "Overdose Education and Naloxone Distribution Within Syringe Service Programs—United States, 2019," *Morbidity and Mortality Weekly Report*, Vol. 69, No. 33, August 21, 2020, pp. 1117–1121.

Lambdin, Barrot H., Corey S. Davis, Eliza Wheeler, Stephen Tueller, and Alex H. Kral, "Naloxone Laws Facilitate the Establishment of Overdose Education and Naloxone Distribution Programs in the United States," *Drug and Alcohol Dependence*, Vol. 188, July 1, 2018, pp. 370–376.

Lancaster, Kari, and Alison Ritter, "Making Change Happen: A Case Study of the Successful Establishment of a Peer-Administered Naloxone Program in One Australian Jurisdiction," *International Journal of Drug Policy*, Vol. 25, 2014, pp. 985–991.

Leech, Ashley A., Cindy L. Christiansen, Benjamin P. Linas, Donna M. Jacobsen, Isabel Morin, and Mari-Lynn Drainoni, "Healthcare Practitioner Experiences and Willingness to Prescribe Pre-Exposure Prophylaxis in the US," *PLoS ONE*, Vol. 15, No. 9, 2020.

Levin, Dan, "Teaching Children How to Reverse an Overdose," *New York Times*, February 23, 2020.

Longshore, Douglas, Susan Turner, Suzanne Wenzel, Andrew Morral, Adele Harrell, Duane McBride, Elizabeth Deschenes, and Martin Iguchi, "Drug Courts: A Conceptual Framework," *Journal of Drug Issues*, Vol. 31, No. 1, 2001, pp. 7–25.

MacPhail, Catherine, Nomhle Khoza, Sarah Treves-Kagan, Amanda Selin, Xavier Gómez-Olivé, Dean Peacock, Dumisani Rebombo, Rhiani Twine, Suzanne Maman, Kathleen Kahn, et al., "Process Elements Contributing to Community Mobilization for HIV Risk Reduction and Gender Equality in Rural South Africa," *PLoS One*, Vol. 14, 2019.

Maghsoudi, N., K. McDonald, C. Stefan, D. R. Beriault, K. Mason, L. Barnaby, J. Altenberg, R. D. MacDonald, J. Caldwell, R. Nisenbaum, et al., "Evaluating Networked Drug Checking Services in Toronto, Ontario: Study Protocol and Rationale," *Harm Reduction Journal*, Vol. 17, No. 9, 2020, pp. 1–10.

Marshall, Kristen, "Fentanyl Test Strip Pilot," National Harm Reduction Coalition, February 18, 2018. As of July 27, 2022:
https://harmreduction.org/issues/fentanyl/fentanyl-test-strip-pilot/

Marten, Lucas, "Investigation: Where Are Naloxone Confiscations Happening the Most?" *Filter*, March 6, 2018.

Marx, Melissa A., Byron Crape, Ronald S. Brookmeyer, Benjamin Junge, Carl Latkin, David Vlahov, and Steffanie A. Strathdee, "Trends in Crime and the Introduction of a Needle Exchange Program," *American Journal of Public Health*, Vol. 90, No. 12, December 2000, pp. 1933–1936.

Matheson, Catriona, Christiane Pflanz-Sinclair, Lorna Aucott, Philip Wilson, Richard Watson, Stephen Malloy, Elinor Dickie, and Andrew McAuley, "Reducing Drug Related Deaths: A Pre-Implementation Assessment of Knowledge, Barriers and Enablers for Naloxone Distribution Through General Practice," *BMC Family Practice*, Vol. 15, No. 12, 2014.

Matsuda, Mari J., "Voices of America: Accent, Antidiscrimination Law, and a Jurisprudence for the Last Reconstruction," *Yale Law Journal*, Vol. 100, No. 5, 1991, pp. 1329–1407.

Maxwell, Sarz, Dan Bigg, Karen Stanczykiewicz, and Suzanne Carlberg-Racich, "Prescribing Naloxone to Actively Injecting Heroin Users: A Program to Reduce Heroin Overdose Deaths," *Journal of Addictive Disorders*, Vol. 25, 2006, pp. 89–96.

McClellan, Chandler, Barrot H. Lambdin, Mir M. Ali, Ryan Mutter, Corey S. Davis, Eliza Wheeler, Michael Pemberton, and Alex H. Kral, "Opioid-Overdose Laws Association with Opioid Use and Overdose Mortality," *Addictive Behaviors*, Vol. 86, 2018, pp. 90–95.

Medrano, Kastalia, "A BC Safe Supply Program Pushes the Medical Model as Far as It Will Go," *Filter*, February 3, 2022.

Meigs, James B., Peter Shrader, Lisa M. Sullivan, Jarred B. McAteer, Caroline S. Fox, Josée Dupuis, Alisa K. Manning, Jose C. Florez, Peter W. F. Wilson, and Ralph B. D'Agostino, Sr., "Genotype Score in Addition to Common Risk Factors for Prediction of Type 2 Diabetes," *New England Journal of Medicine*, Vol. 359, 2008, pp. 2208–2219.

Metzger, David S., George E. Woody, A. Thomas McLellan, Charles P. O'Brien, Patrick Druley, Helen Navaline, Dominick DePhilippis, Paul Stolley, and Elias Abrutyn, "Human Immunodeficiency Virus Seroconversion Among Intravenous Drug Users in- and out-of-Treatment: An 18-Month Prospective Follow-Up," *Journal of Acquired Immune Deficiency Syndromes*, Vol. 6, No. 9, 1993, pp. 1049–1056.

Meyerson, Beth E., Carrie A. Lawrence, Laura Miller, Anthony Gillespie, Daniel Raymond, Kristen Kelley, and D. J. Shannon, "Against the Odds: Syringe Exchange Policy Implementation in Indiana," *AIDS and Behavior*, Vol. 21, 2017, pp. 973–981.

Moatti, J. P., D. Vlahov, I. Feroni, V. Perrin, and Y. Obadia, "Multiple Access to Sterile Syringes for Injection Drug Users: Vending Machines, Needle Exchange Programs and Legal Pharmacy Sales in Marseille, France," *European Addiction Research*, Vol. 7, No. 1, 2001, pp. 40–45.

Moore, Lisa, and Allan Clear, "History and Context of Harm Reduction in the United States," in Richard Pates and Diane Riley, eds., *Harm Reduction in Substance Use and High-Risk Behaviour*, Hoboken, N.J.: John Wiley and Sons, 2012, pp. 382–394.

Murphy, Jennifer, and Brenda Russell, "Police Officers' Views of Naloxone and Drug Treatment: Does Greater Overdose Response Lead to More Negativity?" *Journal of Drug Issues*, Vol. 50, No. 4, 2020, pp. 455–471.

Nadelmann, Ethan, and Lindsay LaSalle, "Two Steps Forward, One Step Back: Current Harm Reduction Policy and Politics in the United States," *Harm Reduction Journal*, Vol. 14, No. 37, 2017.

NASEN—*See* North American Syringe Exchange Network.

National Harm Reduction Coalition, "Principles of Harm Reduction," webpage, undated-a. As of September 23, 2021:
https://harmreduction.org/about-us/principles-of-harm-reduction/

National Harm Reduction Coalition, "Who We Are," webpage, undated-b. As of September 23, 2021:
https://harmreduction.org/about-us/

National Institute on Drug Abuse, *Overdose Prevention Centers*, Washington, D.C.: U.S. Department of Health and Human Services, 2021.

New York City Department of Health and Mental Hygiene, *Recommended Best Practices for Effective Syringe Exchange Programs in the United States: Results of a Consensus Meeting*, 2009.

Nolen, Stephanie, "Fentanyl from the Government? A Vancouver Experiment Aims to Stop Overdoses," *New York Times*, July 26, 2022.

North American Syringe Exchange Network, "SSP Locations," webpage, undated. As of December 16, 2021:
https://nasen.org/map/

Obadia, Yolande, Isabelle Feroni, Vincent Perrin, David Vlahov, and Jean-Paul Moatti, "Syringe Vending Machines for Injection Drug Users: An Experiment in Marseille, France," *American Journal of Public Health*, Vol. 89, No. 12, 1999, pp. 1852–1854.

Office of National Drug Control Policy, *National Drug Control Budget: FY 2022 Funding Highlights*, Washington, D.C., May 2021.

O'Hare, P. A., "Preface: A Note on the Concept of Harm Reduction," in E. C. Buning, E. Drucker, A. Matthews, R. Newcombe, and P. A. O'Hare, eds., *The Reduction of Drug-Related Harm*, New York: Routledge, 2013.

O'Reilly, Kevin B., "Highlights from the 2019 AMA Annual Meeting," webpage, June 13, 2019. As of November 16, 2020:
https://www.ama-assn.org/house-delegates/annual-meeting/
highlights-2019-ama-annual-meeting

Ormsby, David, "Poll: 69% Back Illinois Law Pushing Drug Treatment over Arrest," *Chicago Tribune*, November 28, 2018.

Osborne, David, and Ted Gaebler, *Reinventing Government: How the Entrepreneurial Spirit Is Transforming the Public Sector*, Reading, Mass.: Wiley Publishing Company, Inc., 1992.

Owczarzak, Jill, Noelle Weicker, Glenna Urquhart, Miles Morris, Ju Nyeong Park, and Susan G. Sherman, "'We Know the Streets:' Race, Place, and the Politics of Harm Reduction," *Health & Place*, Vol. 64, July 2020.

Pachter, Lee M., and Cynthia Garcia Coll, "Racism and Child Health: A Review of the Literature and Future Directions," *Journal of Developmental and Behavioral Pediatrics*, Vol. 30, No. 3, 2009, pp. 255–263.

Palombi, Laura, Michelle Olivarez, Laura Bennett, and Amanda N. Hawthorne, "Community Forums to Address the Opioid Crisis: An Effective Grassroots Approach to Rural Community Engagement," *Substance Abuse*, Vol. 13, 2019.

Panagiotoglou, Dimitra, "Evaluating the Population-Level Effects of Overdose Prevention Sites and Supervised Consumption Sites in British Columbia, Canada: Controlled Interrupted Time Series," *PLoS ONE*, Vol. 17, No. 3, March 2022.

Panagiotoglou, Dimitra, and Jihoon Lim, "Using Synthetic Controls to Estimate the Population-Level Effects of Ontario's Recently Implemented Overdose Prevention Sites and Consumption and Treatment Services," *International Journal of Drug Policy*, Vol. 110, December 2022.

Paradies, Yin, "A Systematic Review of Empirical Research on Self-Reported Racism and Health," *International Journal of Epidemiology*, Vol. 35, No. 4, August 2006, pp. 888–901.

Pardo, Bryce, Jonathan P. Caulkins, and Beau Kilmer, *Assessing the Evidence on Supervised Drug Consumption Sites*, Santa Monica, Calif.: RAND Corporation, WR-1261-RC, 2018. As of May 25, 2022:
https://www.rand.org/pubs/working_papers/WR1261.html

Pardo, Bryce, and Beau Kilmer, *Giving Drug Policy Decisionmakers the Data They Need*, Santa Monica, Calif.: RAND Corporation, CT-A2133-1, 2022. As of February 24, 2023:
https://www.rand.org/pubs/testimonies/CTA2133-1.html

Pardo, Bryce, Jirka Taylor, Jonathan P. Caulkins, Beau Kilmer, Peter Reuter, and Bradley D. Stein, *The Future of Fentanyl and Other Synthetic Opioids*, Santa Monica, Calif.: RAND Corporation, RR-3117-RC, 2019. As of May 25, 2022: https://www.rand.org/pubs/research_reports/RR3117.html

Pardo, Bryce, Jirka Taylor, Jon Caulkins, Peter Reuter, and Beau Kilmer, "The Dawn of a New Synthetic Opioid Era: The Need for Innovative Interventions," *Addiction*, Vol. 116, No. 6, June 2021, pp. 1304–1312.

Peiper, Nicholas C., Sarah Duhart Clarke, Louise B. Vincent, Dan Ciccarone, Alex H. Kral, and Jon E. Zibbell, "Fentanyl Test Strips as an Opioid Overdose Prevention Strategy: Findings from a Syringe Services Program in the Southeastern United States," *International Journal of Drug Policy*, Vol. 63, 2019, pp. 122–128.

Platt, Lucy, Silvia Minozzi, Jennifer Reed, Peter Vickerman, Holly Hagan, Clare French, Ashly Jordan, Louisa Degenhardt, Vivian Hope, Sharon Hutchinson, et al., "Needle Syringe Programmes and Opioid Substitution Therapy for Preventing Hepatitis C Transmission in People Who Inject Drugs," *Cochrane Database of Systematic Reviews*, Vol. 9, No. 9, 2017.

Potier, Chloé, Vincent Laprévote, Françoise Dubois-Arber, Olivier Cottencin, and Benjamin Rolland, "Supervised Injection Services: What Has Been Demonstrated? A Systematic Literature Review," *Drug and Alcohol Dependence*, Vol. 145, 2014, pp. 48–68.

Prescott, Susan L., "Early-Life Environmental Determinants of Allergic Diseases and the Wider Pandemic of Inflammatory Noncommunicable Diseases," *Journal of Allergy and Clinical Immunology*, Vol. 131, No. 1, 2013, pp. 23–30.

Prescription Drug Abuse Policy System, "Good Samaritan Overdose Prevention Laws," webpage, updated 2018. As of May 25, 2022: http://pdaps.org/datasets/good-samaritan-overdose-laws-1501695153

Priest, Naomi, Yin Paradies, Brigid Trenerry, Mandy Truong, Saffron Karlsen, and Yvonne Kelly, "A Systematic Review of Studies Examining the Relationship Between Reported Racism and Health and Wellbeing for Children and Young People," *Social Science and Medicine*, Vol. 95, 2013, pp. 115–127.

Pronk, Nicolaas P., Louise H. Anderson, A. Lauren Crain, Brian C. Martinson, Patrick J. O'Connor, Nancy E. Sherwood, and Robin R. Whitebird, "Meeting Recommendations for Multiple Healthy Lifestyle Factors: Prevalence, Clustering, and Predictors Among Adolescent, Adult, and Senior Health Plan Members," *American Journal of Preventive Medicine*, Vol. 27, Suppl. 2, 2004, pp. 25–33.

Rafferty, Y., and A. Radosh, "Attitudes About AIDS Education and Condom Availability Among Parents of High School Students in New York City: A Focus Group Approach," *AIDS Education and Prevention*, Vol. 9, No. 1, 1997, pp. 14–30.

Rees, Daniel I., Joseph J. Sabia, Laura M. Argys, Dhaval Dave, and Joshua Latshaw, "With a Little Help from My Friends: The Effects of Good Samaritan and Naloxone Access Laws on Opioid-Related Deaths," *Journal of Law and Economics*, Vol. 62, No. 1, February 2019.

Reichert, Jessica, "Fighting the Opioid Crisis Through Substance Use Disorder Treatment: A Study of a Police Program Model in Illinois," Illinois Criminal Justice Information Authority, September 7, 2017.

Reichert, Jessica, Arthur J. Lurigio, and Lauren Weisner, "The Administration of Naloxone by Law Enforcement Officers: A Statewide Survey of Police Chiefs in Illinois," *Law Enforcement Executive Forum*, Vol. 19, No. 4, 2019, pp. 1–14.

Reuter, Peter, *Can Heroin Maintenance Help Baltimore?* Baltimore: Abell Foundation, January 2009.

Rhoades, H. M., D. Creson, R. Elk, J. Schmitz, and J. Grabowski, "Retention, HIV Risk, and Illicit Drug Use During Treatment: Methadone Dose and Visit Frequency," *American Journal of Public Health*, Vol. 88, No. 1, 1998, pp. 34–39.

Riley, Elise, Peter Beilenson, David Vlahov, Laura Smith, Matthew Koenig, T. Stephen Jones, and Meg Doherty, "Operation Red Box: A Pilot Project of Needle and Syringe Drop Boxes for Injection Drug Users in East Baltimore," *Journal of Acquired Immune Deficiency Syndromes and Human Retrovirology*, Vol. 18, Suppl. 1, 1998, pp. S120–S125.

Riley, Elise D., Alex H. Kral, Thomas J. Stopka, Richard S. Garfein, Paul Reuckhaus, and Ricky N. Bluthenthal, "Access to Sterile Syringes Through San Francisco Pharmacies and the Association with HIV Risk Behavior Among Injection Drug Users," *Journal of Urban Health*, Vol. 87, 2010, pp. 534–542.

Saloner, Brendan, Emma E. McGinty, Leo Beletsky, Ricky Bluthenthal, Chris Beyrer, Michael Botticelli, and Susan G. Sherman, "A Public Health Strategy for the Opioid Crisis," *Public Health Reports*, Vol. 133, Suppl. 1, 2018, pp. 24S–34S.

SAMHSA—*See* Substance Abuse and Mental Health Services Administration.

Saunders, Jessica, Allison J. Ober, Beau Kilmer, and Sarah Michal Greathouse, *A Community-Based, Focused-Deterrence Approach to Closing Overt Drug Markets: A Process and Fidelity Evaluation of Seven Sites*, Santa Monica, Calif.: RAND Corporation, RR-1001-NIJ, 2016. As of May 25, 2022:
https://www.rand.org/pubs/research_reports/RR1001.html

Schiff, Davida M., Mari-Lynn Drainoni, Zoe M. Weinstein, Lisa Chan, Megan Bair-Merritt, and David Rosenbloom, "A Police-Led Addiction Treatment Referral Program in Gloucester, MA: Implementation and Participants' Experiences," *Journal of Substance Abuse Treatment*, Vol. 82, 2017, pp. 41–47.

Schneider, Kristin E., Rebecca Hamilton White, Rashelle J. Musci, Allison O'Rourke, Michael E. Kilkenny, Susan G. Sherman, and Srean T. Allen, "The Relationship Between Polysubstance Injection Drug Use, HIV Risk Behaviors, and Interest in Pre-Exposure Prophylaxis (PReP) Among People Who Inject Drugs in Rural West Virginia," *Journal of Studies on Alcohol and Drugs*, Vol. 81, No. 6, 2020, pp. 740–749.

Schuit, A. Jantine, A. Jeanne M. van Loon, Marja Tijhuis, and Marga C. Ocké, "Clustering of Lifestyle Risk Factors in a General Adult Population," *Preventive Medicine*, Vol. 35, No. 3, 2002, pp. 219–224.

Seal, Karen H., Moher Downing, Alex H. Kral, Shannon Singleton-Banks, Jon-Paul Hammond, Jennifer Lorvick, Dan Ciccarone, and Brian R. Edlin, "Attitudes About Prescribing Take-Home Naloxone to Injection Drug Users for the Management of Heroin Overdose: A Survey of Street-Recruited Injectors in the San Francisco Bay Area," *Journal of Urban Health*, Vol. 80, 2003, pp. 291–301.

Select Special Committee to Examine Safe Supply, *Final Report to Examine Safe Supply*, Committees of the Legislative Assembly of Alberta, June 2022.

Shalev, I., T. E. Moffitt, K. Sugden, B. Williams, R. M. Houts, A. Danese, J. Mill, L. Arseneault, and A. Caspi, "Exposure to Violence During Childhood Is Associated with Telomere Erosion from 5 to 10 Years of Age: A Longitudinal Study," *Molecular Psychiatry*, Vol. 18, 2013, pp. 576–581.

Sheiham, Aubrey, and Richard Geddie Watt, "The Common Risk Factor Approach: A Rational Basis for Promoting Oral Health," *Community Dentistry and Oral Epidemiology*, Vol. 28, No. 6, 2000, pp. 399–406.

Sheridan, Margaret A., Khaled Sarsour, Douglas Jutte, Mark D'Esposito, and W. Thomas Boyce, "The Impact of Social Disparity on Prefrontal Function in Childhood," *PLoS One*, Vol. 7, 2012.

Sherman, Susan G., Ju Nyeong Park, Jennifer Glick, Tricia Christensen, Kenneth Morales, Traci C. Green, and Michelle McKenzie, "Fentanyl Overdose Reduction Checking Analysis Study," Johns Hopkins Bloomberg School of Public Health, February 6, 2018.

Shonkoff, Jack P., and Andrew S. Garner, "The Lifelong Effects of Early Childhood Adversity and Toxic Stress," *Pediatrics*, Vol. 129, No. 1, 2012, pp. e232–e246.

Showalter, David, "Federal Funding for Syringe Exchange in the US: Explaining a Long-Term Policy Failure," *International Journal of Drug Policy*, Vol. 55, May 2018, pp. 95–104.

Siegel, Zachary, "Blame Overdoses on Syringe Programs? Classic." *Substance* Substack, November 4, 2022. As of February 17, 2023:
https://tanag.substack.com/p/blame-overdoses-on-syringe-programs

Smart, Amy, "Vancouver Club Will Continue to Distribute Hard Drugs in Bid to Save Lives, Despite Health Canada Rejection," CBC News, August 31, 2022.

Smart, Rosanna, *Evidence on the Effectiveness of Heroin-Assisted Treatment*, Santa Monica, Calif.: RAND Corporation, WR-1263-RC, 2018. As of May 25, 2022:
https://www.rand.org/pubs/working_papers/WR1263.html

Smart, Rosanna, Bryce Pardo, and Corey S. Davis, "Systematic Review of the Emerging Literature on the Effectiveness of Naloxone Access Laws in the United States," *Addiction*, Vol. 116, No. 1, 2021, pp. 6–17.

Smith, James P., "The Impact of Childhood Health on Adult Labor Market Outcomes," *Review of Economics and Statistics*, Vol. 91, No. 3, 2009, pp. 478–489.

Smith, James Patrick, and Gillian C. Smith, "Long-Term Economic Costs of Psychological Problems During Childhood," *Social Science Medicine*, Vol. 71, No. 1, 2010, pp. 110–115.

Sohn, Minji, Jeffery C. Talbert, Zhengyan Huang, Michelle R. Lofwall, and Patricia R. Freeman, "Association of Naloxone Coprescription Laws with Naloxone Prescription Dispensing in the United States," *JAMA Network Open*, Vol. 2, No. 6, 2019.

Stitzer, Maxine L., Martin Y. Iguchi, Michael Kidorf, and George E. Bigelow, "Contingency Management in Methadone Treatment: The Case for Positive Incentives," *National Institute on Drug Abuse Research Monographs*, Vol. 137, 1993.

Story, Chandra R., Wei-Kang Kao, Joe Currin, Colton Brown, and Vignetta Charles, "Evaluation of the Southern Harm Reduction Coalition for HIV Prevention: Advocacy Accomplishments," *Health Promotion Practices*, Vol. 19, No. 5, 2018, pp. 695–703.

Strang, John, Teodora Groshkova, Ambros Uchtenhagen, Wim van den Brink, Christian Haasen, Martin T. Schechter, Nick Lintzeris, James Bell, Alessandro Pirona, Eugenia Oviedo-Joekes, Roland Simon, and Nicola Metrebian, "Heroin on Trial: Systematic Review and Meta-Analysis of Randomised Trials of Diamorphine-Prescribing as Treatment for Refractory Heroin Addiction," *British Journal of Psychology*, Vol. 207, No. 1, July 2015, pp. 5–14.

Strang, Lucy, and Jirka Taylor, *Heroin-Assisted Treatment and Supervised Drug Consumption Sites: Experience from Four Countries*, Santa Monica, Calif.: RAND Corporation, WR-1262-RC, 2018. As of May 25, 2022:
https://www.rand.org/pubs/working_papers/WR1262.html

Strathdee, Steffanie A., David D. Celentano, Nina Shah, Cynthia Lyles, Veronica A. Stambolis, Grace Macalino, Kenrad Nelson, and David Vlahov, "Needle-Exchange Attendance and Health Care Utilization Promote Entry into Detoxification," *Journal of Urban Health*, Vol. 76, No. 4, December 1999, pp. 448–460.

Substance Abuse and Mental Health Services Administration, "Community Engagement Process," webpage, 2020. As of July 20, 2020:
https://www.samhsa.gov/tribal-ttac/training-technical-assistance/community-engagement-process

Substance Abuse and Mental Health Services Administration, "SAMHSA Announces Unprecedented $30 Million Harm Reduction Grant Funding Opportunity to Help Address the Nation's Substance Use and Overdose Epidemic," press release, December 8, 2021.

Szalavitz, Maia, *Undoing Drugs: The Untold Story of Harm Reduction and the Future of Addiction*, New York: Hachette Go, 2021.

Takahashi, Traci A., Matthew L. Maciejewski, and Katharine Bradley, "US Hospitalizations and Costs for Illicit Drug Users with Soft Tissue Infections," *Journal of Behavioral Health Services & Research*, Vol. 37, No. 4, 2010, pp. 508–518.

Taylor, Jirka, Allison J. Ober, Beau Kilmer, Jonathan P. Caulkins, and Martin Y. Iguchi, "Community Perspectives on Supervised Consumption Sites: Insights from Four US Counties Deeply Affected by Opioids," *Journal of Substance Abuse Treatment*, Vol. 131, 2021.

Tempalski, Barbara, Risa Friedman, Marie Keem, Hannah Cooper, and Samuel R. Friedman, "NIMBY Localism and National Inequitable Exclusion Alliances: The Case of Syringe Exchange Programs in the United States," *Geoforum*, Vol. 38, No. 6, 2007, pp. 1250–1263.

Teshale, Eyasu H., Alice Asher, Maria V. Aslam, Ryan Augustine, Eliana Duncan, Alyson Rose-Wood, John Ward, Jonathan Mermin, Kwame Owusu-Edusei, and Patricia M. Dietz, "Estimate Cost of Comprehensive Syringe Service Program in the United States," *PLoS One*, Vol. 14, No. 4, April 2019.

Tookes, Hansel E., Alex H. Kral, Lynn D. Wenger, Gabriel A. Cardenas, Alexis N. Martinez, Recinda L. Sherman, Margaret Pereyra, David W. Forrest, Marlene LaLota, and Lisa R. Metsch, "A Comparison of Syringe Disposal Practices Among Injection Drug Users in a City With Versus a City Without Needle and Syringe Programs," *Drug and Alcohol Dependence*, Vol. 123, No. 1–3, June 1, 2012, pp. 255–259.

Torralva, Randy, and Aaron Janowsky, "Noradrenergic Mechanisms in Fentanyl-Mediated Rapid Death Explain Failure of Naloxone in the Opioid Crisis," *Journal of Pharmacology and Experimental Therapeutics*, Vol. 371, No. 2, 2019, pp. 453–475.

Torres, Jesus, Nathaniel Avalos, Lamarr Echols, Jillian Mongelluzzo, and Robert M. Rodriguez, "Low Yield of Blood and Wound Cultures in Patients with Skin and Soft-Tissue Infections," *American Journal of Emergency Medicine*, Vol. 35, No. 8, 2017, pp. 1159–1161.

Torres-Harding, Susan, and Tasha Turner, "Assessing Racial Microaggression Distress in a Diverse Sample," *Evaluation & the Health Professions*, Vol. 38, No. 4, 2015, pp. 464–490.

Trautmann, Franz, "Peer Support as a Method of Risk Reduction in Injecting Drug-User Communities: Experiences in Dutch Projects and the 'European Peer Support Project,'" *Journal of Drug Issues*, Vol. 25, No. 3, 1995, pp. 617–628.

Turner, Susan, Douglas Longshore, Suzanne Wenzel, Elizabeth Deschenes, Peter Greenwood, Terry Fain, Adele Harrell, Andrew Morral, Faye Taxman, Martin Iguchi, Judith Greene, and Duane McBride, "A Decade of Drug Treatment Court Research," *Substance Use & Misuse*, Vol. 37, No. 12-13, 2002, pp. 1489–1527.

United Nations Office on Drugs and Crime, International Network of People Who Use Drugs, Joint United Nations Programme on HIV/AIDS, United Nations Development Programme, United Nations Population Fund, World Health Organization, and United States Agency for International Development, *Implementing Comprehensive HIV and HCV Programmes for People Who Inject Drugs: Practical Guidance for Collaborative Interventions*, Vienna, Austria, 2017.

U.S. Code, Title 21, Section 856, Maintaining Drug-Involved Premises, January 3, 2005.

U.S. Department of Health and Human Services Press Office, "SAMHSA Announces Unprecedented $30 Million Harm Reduction Grant Funding Opportunity to Help Address the Nation's Substance Use and Overdose Epidemic," press release, December 8, 2021.

Vickerman, P., N. K. Martin, and M. Hickman, "Could Low Dead-Space Syringes Really Reduce HIV Transmission to Low Levels?" *International Journal of Drug Policy*, Vol. 24, No. 1, 2013, pp. 8–14.

Vitaro, Frank, Mara Brendgen, Robert Ladouceur, and Richard E. Tremblay, "Gambling, Delinquency, and Drug Use During Adolescence: Mutual Influences and Common Risk Factors," *Journal of Gambling Studies*, Vol. 17, No. 3, 2001, pp. 171–190.

Wagner, Karla D., Robert W. Harding, Richard Kelley, Brian Labus, Silvia R. Verdugo, Elizabeth Copulsky, Jeanette M. Bowles, Maria Luisa Mittal, and Peter J. Davidson, "Post-Overdose Interventions Triggered by Calling 911: Centering the Perspectives of People Who Use Drugs (PWUDs)," *PLoS One*, Vol. 14, No. 10, 2019.

Wagner, Karla D., Thomas W. Valente, Mark Casanova, Susan M. Partovi, Brett M. Mendenhall, James H. Hundley, Mario Gonzalez, and Jennifer B. Unger, "Evaluation of an Overdose Prevention and Response Training Programme for Injection Drug Users in the Skid Row Area of Los Angeles, CA," *International Journal of Drug Policy*, Vol. 21, No. 3, 2010, pp. 186–193.

Walley, Alexander Y., Ziming Xuan, H. Holly Hackman, Emily Quinn, Maya Doe-Simkins, Amy Sorenson-Alawad, Sarah Ruiz, and Al Ozonoff, "Opioid Overdose Rates and Implementation of Overdose Education and Nasal Naloxone Distribution in Massachusetts: Interrupted Time Series Analysis," *BMJ*, 2013.

Walters, Suzan M., Alex H. Kral, Kelsey A. Simpson, Lynn Wenger, and Ricky N. Bluthenthal, "HIV Pre-Exposure Prophylaxis Prevention Awareness, Willingness, and Perceived Barriers Among People Who Inject Drugs in Los Angeles and San Francisco, CA, 2016–2018," *Substance Use & Misuse*, Vol. 55, No. 14, 2020, pp. 2409–2419.

Wells, Kenneth B., Katherine E. Watkins, Brian Hurley, Linggi Tang, Felicia Jones, and James Gilmore, "Commentary: Applying the Community Partners in Care Approach to the Opioid Crisis," *Ethnicity & Disease*, Vol. 28, 2018, pp. 381–388.

Wendel, Monica L., Whitney R. Garney, Billie F. Castle, and C. Monique Ingram, "Critical Reflexivity of Communities on Their Experience to Improve Population Health," *American Journal of Public Health*, Vol. 108, No. 7, 2018, pp. 896–901.

White, Michael D., Dina Perrone, Seth Watts, and Aili Malm, "Moving Beyond Narcan: A Police, Social Service, and Researcher Collaborative Response to the Opioid Crisis," *American Journal of Criminal Justice*, Vol. 46, No. 4, 2021, pp. 626–643.

The White House, *The Biden-Harris Administration's Statement of Drug Policy Priorities for Year One*, Washington, D.C.: Executive Office of the President, Office of National Drug Control Policy, 2021.

Wieloch, Neil, "Collective Mobilization and Identity from the Underground: The Deployment of 'Oppositional Capital' in the Harm Reduction Movement," *Sociological Quarterly*, Vol. 43, 2002, pp. 45–72.

Winstanley, Erin L., Angela Clark, Judith Feinberg, and Christine M. Wilder, "Barriers to Implementation of Opioid Overdose Prevention Programs in Ohio," *Substance Abuse*, Vol. 37, No. 1, 2016, pp. 42–46.

Wodak, Alex, and Annie Cooney, "Effectiveness of Sterile Needle and Syringe Programmes," *International Journal of Drug Policy*, Vol. 16, Suppl. 1, 2005, pp. 31–44.

Wojcicki, J. M., M. B. Heyman, D. Elwan, S. Shiboski, J. Lin, E. Blackburn, and E. Epel, "Telomere Length Is Associated with Oppositional Defiant Behavior and Maternal Clinical Depression in Latino Preschool Children," *Translational Psychiatry*, Vol. 5, No. 6, 2015.

Worrall, John L., Scott Hiromoto, Nancy Merritt, Dan Du, Jerry O. Jacobson, and Martin Y. Iguchi, "Crime Trends and the Effect of Mandated Drug Treatment: Evidence from California's Substance Abuse and Crime Prevention Act," *Journal of Criminal Justice*, Vol. 37, No. 2, 2009, pp. 109–113.

Xu, Jing, Corey S. Davis, Marisa Cruz, and Peter Lurie, "State Naloxone Access Laws Are Associated with an Increase in the Number of Naloxone Prescriptions Dispensed in Retail Pharmacies," *Drug and Alcohol Dependence*, Vol. 189, August 2018, pp. 37–41.

Yoshikawa, Hirokazu, "Long-Term Effects of Early Childhood Programs on Social Outcomes and Delinquency," *Future of Children*, Vol. 5, No. 3, 1995, pp. 51–75.

Yousey-Hindes, Kimberly M., and James L. Hadler, "Neighborhood Socioeconomic Status and Influenza Hospitalizations Among Children: New Haven County, Connecticut, 2003–2010," *American Journal of Public Health*, Vol. 101, No. 9, 2011, pp. 1785–1789.

Zanis, David A., and George E. Woody, "One-Year Mortality Rates Following Methadone Treatment Discharge," *Drug and Alcohol Dependence*, Vol. 52, No. 3, 1998, pp. 257–260.

Zuckerman, Matthew, Stacy N. Weisberg, and Edward W. Boyer, "Pitfalls of Intranasal Naloxone," *Prehospital Emergency Care*, Vol. 18, No. 4, 2014, pp. 550–554.

Zule, William A., Harry E. Cross, John Stover, and Carel Pretorius, "Are Major Reductions in New HIV Infections Possible with People Who Inject Drugs? The Case for Low Dead-Space Syringes in Highly Affected Countries," *International Journal of Drug Policy*, Vol. 24, No. 1, 2013, pp. 1–7.

CHAPTER NINE

First Responders

Jirka Taylor

Overview

First responders—including law enforcement, fire departments, and emergency medical services (EMS)—provide assistance in emergency situations, including drug overdoses. These are the three main groups of responding entities that make up the emergency response system in the United States. The organization of the emergency response system varies across jurisdictions: In many areas, ambulance services are part of the fire department (transporting fire departments), but other models exist, such as private ambulance agencies or those that are part of hospitals or public safety agencies. Similarly, the availability of each type of responding entity differs across locations, as does the way in which emergency calls are handled and first responders dispatched.

Helping victims of opioid overdose typically involves the administration of naloxone, which is an opioid antagonist that reverses the effect of opioids. Assistance may also involve rescue breathing and chest compressions. EMS or transporting fire departments usually transport the overdose victim to an emergency department (ED) for definitive care, unless the individual refuses medical transport.

First responders play a critical role in mitigating the impact of the opioid crisis by helping reduce opioid overdose deaths. Providing timely assistance reduces the number of overdoses that become fatal and other opioid-related harms. Available data indicate that there has been a substantial increase in naloxone administrations by first responders in recent years. To illustrate, the rate of naloxone administration by EMS for suspected opioid overdoses increased 119 percent between 2012 and 2016 (Cash et al., 2018).

With the arrival of more-potent synthetic opioids, such as fentanyl, one dose of naloxone may no longer be sufficient to prevent a lethal overdose, requiring first responders to administer multiple doses. To meet the increased need for emergency response for opioid overdoses, states have expanded the number and type of personnel allowed to carry and administer naloxone. All states and the District of Columbia now provide naloxone authorization to EMS personnel of all licensure levels; in 2013, only 13 states did so.

The opioid crisis has not only increased the number of individuals served by first responders but also increased the complexity of the environment in which naloxone is administered. In some instances, the first dose of naloxone may be administered before the arrival of first responders (e.g., by friends or family of the victim). Coupled with the prevailing uncertainty within illicit markets, in which even victims of overdoses frequently are not sure what they consumed, these factors make it increasingly challenging for first responders to provide adequate overdose management.

The increased demand for emergency response in the context of opioid overdoses has placed a substantial burden on first responder agencies. No systematic data exist on this topic. However, the overdose crisis has imposed notable opportunity costs, and first responders report negative effects on their ability to respond to other calls for service and on the quality of their services. The overdose crisis has affected first responder well-being, with reports of increased emotional strain and higher rates of burnout. Related negative impacts reported in the literature include feelings of helplessness and compassion fatigue on the part of responding entities, who frequently respond to repeated calls for service for the same individuals. These negative outcomes can result in longer-term impacts, such as higher rates of substance use disorder or posttraumatic stress disorder among first responders. In addition, the opioid crisis has given rise to concerns regarding the safety of responding staff, who may be exposed to potent toxic substances.

Key Interactions with Other Components of the Ecosystem

EMS agencies are closely linked with the **medical care system** because they often transport victims of overdose to EDs for care. Proper handoffs between EMS and ED providers are very important to avoid gaps in care. First responders also sometimes interact with the **opioid use disorder (OUD) treatment system** because they are in a position to influence an individual's decision to seek and stay engaged with treatment services. Nonfatal overdoses represent a moment of personal crisis, which may increase an individual's readiness for change. Interactions with first responders may help convince individuals to seek treatment, particularly if the first responders can offer information on available services and how to access them. Conversely, negative experiences with first responders (such as being a target of stigmatizing behavior stemming from first responder fatigue) can deter future change.

Some jurisdictions have launched post-overdose outreach programs, whereby recent victims of an overdose are contacted by teams that include first responders, who offer assistance with accessing services. Elsewhere, first responders have set up designated locations, such as fire stations, where self-referring individuals can seek help without repercussions.

First responders also closely interact with the **criminal legal system**, not least because police are a type of emergency responder. Other first responders interact with the criminal legal system via emergency dispatch protocols, which give rise to issues related to whether first responders (such as law enforcement) are summoned to an overdose in the first place.

Fear of police has been consistently reported as a major reason why people who use drugs (PWUD) or those close to them do not call 911 in the event of an emergency. In some instances, this is directly related to fear of arrest for drug-related charges. In other cases, the concern may be the consequences of a parole or probation violation, fear of losing custody of children, or fear of homicide-related charges, if the overdose ends up being fatal. Numerous jurisdictions have adopted Good Samaritan laws, which offer some immunity to those calling for help. However, in some jurisdictions, the protection of these laws does not extend to all the issues noted in this section, and evidence of their effectiveness on willingness to call 911 appears to be mixed.

First responders interface with the **harm reduction and community-initiated intervention system** in two principal ways. First, first responders have become a channel through which naloxone can be distributed to PWUD and their friends and families. Recently, some EMS agencies have implemented naloxone leave-behind programs, whereby emergency responders leave naloxone with the overdose victim or their family and friends for future use. Second, EMS data represent a surveillance tool that can be used to monitor trends in opioid overdoses, such as changes in their rates, seasonality, geographic distribution, demographic distribution, and other indicators of interest.

Policy Opportunities and Considerations

Interactions between first responders and other systems reveal some policy opportunities. Efforts to use first responders as a naloxone distribution channel could be intensified. Naloxone leave-behind programs could be expanded. In addition, first responder agencies could serve as naloxone distribution centers even outside the context of responding to overdoses, akin to other places (such as pharmacies) where the general public can access naloxone. Relatedly, steps can be taken to further increase the number of law enforcement officers and non-EMS firefighters carrying naloxone.

The interaction between first responders and the criminal legal system suggests opportunities related to 911 calls. To alleviate fears of calling 911 on the part of PWUD or their families or friends, the scope of Good Samaritan laws could be expanded to cover areas not directly related to drug-related offenses, such as breaches of parole or probation. Awareness of existing laws and their provisions among both the general public and law enforcement personnel could be increased. Another solution could be introducing an emergency reporting system for reporting drug overdoses: e.g., via a dedicated non-911 emergency number or through modifications to dispatch protocols, such that callers would be guaranteed that the police would not be among the dispatched responding personnel. Of course, such an option is viable only in areas where first responders other than the police are able to provide a timely response.

Lastly, another set of opportunities and considerations revolves around support for first responders irrespective of their interactions with other systems. The impact of the opioid crisis may be mitigated by training to improve the resiliency of emergency personnel, mitigating the risk of burnout and compassion fatigue. Other areas suitable for first responder training include education on addiction and recovery and on how to make referrals to services. This can also help reduce the risk of stigmatizing behavior on the part of first responders and improve the chances that overdose victims will be effectively handed off to appropriate services.

Introduction

Within the emergency response system, first responders are professionals who might arrive at the scene of an overdose to provide emergency assistance. There are three broad types of agencies that fall under the umbrella term of first responders: EMS, fire departments, and law enforcement agencies. The organization of the emergency response system varies substantially across U.S. jurisdictions and depends on a variety of factors, such as local and state requirements, urbanicity, communities served, and types of services required and provided (Mulcahy et al., 2019; National Association of State Emergency Management Services Officials [NASEMSO], 2020; Taymour et al., 2018). Correspondingly, the universe of entities involved in responding to drug overdoses in the United States is extremely large. There are nearly 18,000 law enforcement agencies in the country, and the number of EMS agencies is even higher, estimated at more than 23,000 (NASEMSO, 2020).[1]

The most pertinent type of EMS operator with respect to drug overdoses is an ambulance agency responding to a 911 call and (possibly) transporting the patient to a hospital. Such agencies represent approximately half (49 percent) of all EMS agencies. The next largest group of EMS agencies (29 percent) also responds to 911 calls but without the subsequent transport (NASEMSO, 2020). An example is fire trucks arriving at a scene from the nearest fire station before the local ambulance service (i.e., a nontransporting fire department).[2]

Many EMS agencies are funded and run by local governments, either as stand-alone organizations or in combination with fire departments. Transporting fire departments (with either cross-trained or separate EMS personnel) account for slightly less than half of all ambulance services in the United States, while stand-alone EMS agencies, which operate concurrently with fire departments in their areas, account for about half as big a share (National Highway Traffic Safety Administration [NHTSA], 2012; Taymour et al., 2018). Elsewhere, local governments contract with private for-profit or nonprofit agencies for the provision of EMS. Importantly, not all ambulance agencies necessarily provide emergency services; some (predominantly, for-profit operators) focus on nonemergency services, such as transports between medical facilities (Mulcahy et al., 2019).[3]

The level of resources available and the type of community served also affect how emergency services are provided. In rural areas, local governments are more likely to retain control over the provision of ambulance services. These organizations are comparatively smaller and transport patients over greater distances, resulting in higher response times. Rural-based

---

[1] The 2020 National EMS Assessment reported a total of 23,272 EMS agencies in the United States. However, this number does not include any organizations from Louisiana, American Samoa, or Puerto Rico. Furthermore, differing licensing practices and definitional differences across states complicate the count (NASEMSO, 2020).

[2] The other type of typical 911 responder agency is air medical services, which account for approximately 3 percent of EMS agencies (NASEMSO, 2020).

[3] Other, less frequent, business models exist as well. These include a public-private partnership and the organization of ambulance services as a public utility (Taymour et al., 2018).

ambulance agencies are also more likely to use volunteer labor than their counterparts in other areas (Mulcahy et al., 2019).

Individual EMS agencies can be licensed to provide different levels of care. Although licensing regimes vary across states (and some states do not license by level of care), two broad categories of EMS staff can be distinguished (NASEMSO, 2020). Basic life support (BLS) services, typically staffed by emergency medical responders or emergency medical technicians, are generally authorized, skilled, and trained to provide more-limited medical support, whereas advanced life support (ALS) services, typically staffed by advanced emergency medical technicians or paramedics, receive more training and, correspondingly, have the skills and authorization to respond to emergency situations of greater complexity and acuity (NHTSA, 2019). The advantages of BLS units are that they are less costly and, because they are more numerous, their response times are usually shorter. Therefore, they are particularly well placed for situations in which the priority is quick transport for definitive care (Brennan, 2020). By contrast, ALS units are able to provide an advanced level of care on the scene and during longer transports. However, the number of calls for service in which the difference in the level of care makes a big difference may be limited (Staats, 2017). The geographical distribution of levels of care also remains uneven, with rural areas more likely to be served by BLS units (NASEMSO, 2020).

Lastly, a critical role in the emergency response system is played by the 911 call processing system and associated dispatching protocols. Emergency 911 calls are received by public service answering points (PSAPs). There are more than 6,000 independently operating PSAPs in the United States, with varying management arrangements and operational protocols (Neusteter et al., 2019). Their staff take 911 calls and interact with the callers to identify the nature and location of the emergency. Using this information, the staff decide what resources should be deployed in response (Sanko, Lane, and Eckstein, 2020). In addition to these initial interrogatory duties, 911 call-takers in some areas double as dispatchers: That is, they directly interact with first responder agencies (Neusteter et al., 2019). Elsewhere, 911 calls, or information provided by the caller, are transferred to a specialized dispatch center, which then manages the dispatch of responding personnel (Neusteter et al., 2019). In instances in which information is transferred to a specialized dispatch center, the original call-taker may still remain on the line to provide emergency assistance over the phone (e.g., providing cardiopulmonary resuscitation [CPR] instruction) before first responders reach the scene of the emergency (NASEMSO, 2020; Wise, Freeman, and Edemekong, 2019).

The specialized agencies for dispatching EMS units are emergency medical dispatch (EMD) centers. There are more than 1,400 EMD centers in the country (NASEMSO, 2020), some of which are colocated with a PSAP, whereas others are separate (Fales, 2019). The organization and oversight of EMDs vary across jurisdictions: In some states, they are regulated by the state EMS office, while elsewhere they fall under the remit of agencies dealing with such areas as communications and public utilities. In 20 states, EMDs remain unregulated at the state level (NASEMSO, 2020). The variability in the organization of 911 processing and dispatch across jurisdictions and available resources means that similar calls for service may be attended to differently in various parts of the country. For instance, given the geographical distribution and concentration of first responders, law enforcement in some areas may arrive at the scene of an overdose before EMS (Townsend et al., 2019), particularly in rural areas, where law enforcement personnel greatly outnumber EMS personnel (Lurigio, Andrus, and Scott, 2018).[4]

System Components and How They Interact with Opioids

How First Responders Are Able to Affect the Opioid Crisis

First responders play an important role in mitigating harms stemming from the opioid crisis by providing timely assistance to victims of opioid overdose and thus reducing the number of fatal overdoses and other severe opioid use–related harms (Figure 9.1). Assisting victims of opioid overdose typically involves the administration of naloxone and may involve rescue breathing and chest compressions, followed by transportation to a hospital, unless the victim refuses to go to the hospital (Bagley et al., 2019).[5]

Increase in the Number of Calls for Service and Naloxone Administrations

As the opioid crisis in the United States worsened and was accentuated by the arrival of potent synthetic opioids, such as fentanyl and its analogs, the number and rate of naloxone administrations by first responders increased dramatically. According to analysis by Cash et al., 2018, the rate of naloxone administration by EMS rose 75 percent between 2012 and 2016, from 574 administrations per 100,000 EMS events in 2012 to 1,004 per 100,000 EMS events in 2016.[6] This growth rate is broadly similar to the increase in the rate of deaths involving opioids over the same period. Looking only at a subset of events involving suspected opioid overdoses (defined as cases with documented evidence of drug consumption or poisoning), the rate of naloxone administration by EMS increased 119 percent between 2012 and 2016 (Cash et al., 2018). Similar findings of a substantial increase in naloxone administrations by EMS were also reported by Geiger, Smart, and Stein, 2019. Examining the period 2013–2016, the authors

---

[4] For instance, in a statewide survey of naloxone use among Pennsylvania law enforcement, Jacoby et al., 2020, found that police were the first to arrive at an overdose scene in 73 percent of calls.

[5] Naloxone is an opioid antagonist that acts to reverse overdoses by binding to opioid receptors and thus blocking the effect of opioids (Moss and Carlo, 2019). The rates of refusal of transport to the hospital reported in the literature vary. For instance, Faul et al., 2017, reports that less than 3 percent of patients were released after naloxone administration, some of whom refused transport. By contrast, Glenn et al., 2021, drawing on data from the Tucson, Arizona, EMS system, reports refusal rates after naloxone administration of 14.6 percent before the coronavirus disease 2019 (COVID-19) pandemic and 35.9 percent during the pandemic.

[6] The denominator for this analysis included all 911 responses, special event coverage, and care provided during ambulance intercepts or mutual aid to another ambulance response. It excluded transfers and transports, events with disposition codes "canceled" and "no patient found," and events in Guam and the U.S. Virgin Islands.

FIGURE 9.1

First Responder System and Its Interactions

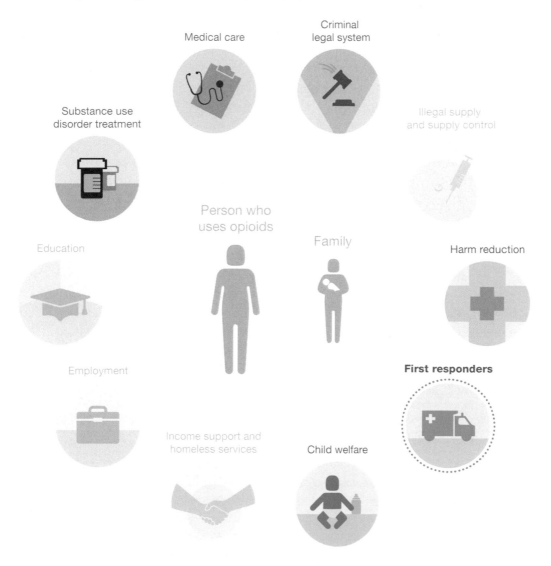

noted variations across locations and regions. Nationally, suburban locations had the highest rate of naloxone administration, although urban locations saw the highest increase over the reference period. The study also found a significant trend toward naloxone administration events in streets and other public places (such as bars) and, consistent with the findings by Cash et al., 2018, a shift toward young adults as recipients of naloxone (Geiger, Smart, and Stein, 2019). Broken down by census regions, the Northeast saw the fastest growth in naloxone administration, while comparatively little growth was reported in the West. More-recent raw data collected by the National Emergency Medical Services Information System

(NEMSIS) show that growth in the number and rate of naloxone administrations by EMS also occurred between 2018 and 2021 (NEMSIS, undated).[7]

Expansion in the Number of People Able to Administer Naloxone

The increases in naloxone administration rates in recent years were accompanied by an expansion in the types of emergency responders authorized to carry and administer naloxone. Historically, only certain types of personnel were equipped with naloxone. The *National EMS Scope of Practice Model*, published in 2007 by the NHTSA, identified naloxone administration as a skill requirement for ALS but not for BLS personnel (NHTSA, 2007). This arrangement limited the ability of EMS to provide effective assistance to victims of opioid overdose because non-ALS units are vastly outnumbered by BLS teams and law enforcement patrol, particularly in rural areas, which have less access to ALS (Faul et al., 2017; Gulec et al., 2018; Kinsman and Robinson, 2018; Lurigio, Andrus, and Scott, 2018). Therefore, limiting authorization for naloxone administration to more-skilled emergency responders could substantially lengthen the time between overdose and naloxone administration beyond the window when it can reverse a potentially fatal overdose (Weiner et al., 2017).

In recognition of this limitation, states have taken steps to ensure that a broader array of first responders are equipped with naloxone (Davis et al., 2014; Watson et al., 2018). To illustrate, 13 states allowed BLS personnel to administer naloxone in 2013; one year later, the number had increased to 37 and continued increasing thereafter (Geiger, Smart, and Stein, 2019; Gulec et al., 2018). A review of state laws by Kinsman and Robinson, 2018, found that 49 states and Washington, D.C., had authorized staff of all EMS licensure levels to administer naloxone; since the publication of the review, the remaining exception (Wyoming) has also extended naloxone authorization to all EMS certification levels (Bessen et al., 2019). The *National EMS Scope of Practice Model* was updated in 2017 in line with these changes at the state level, and the administration of naloxone was added to the scope of practice for BLS staff (Krohmer, 2017). At the time of the update, the NHTSA was unable to draw on any published studies to compare naloxone administration by BLS and ALS personnel, although some studies appear to offer evidence that BLS staff are as effective in naloxone administration as advanced EMS providers (Gulec et al., 2018; Weiner et al., 2017).

Moving beyond EMS, law enforcement officers can also effectively administer naloxone (Kitch and Portela, 2016). Indeed, naloxone administration by law enforcement has become

---

[7] The absolute number of EMS activations in which naloxone administrations were recorded in the public NEMSIS dashboard grew from 161,687 activations in 2018 to 357,487 in 2020, and the share of naloxone administrations for all EMS activations grew from 0.6 percent in January 2018 to 0.9 percent in November 2021 (NEMSIS, undated). Note that these rates are somewhat lower than those reported by Cash et al., 2018, and the two analyses are not perfectly comparable. Unlike Cash et al., 2018, the NEMSIS public dashboard has no exclusion criteria related to the type of service requested or to incident or patient disposition, resulting in a larger denominator. Another difference between the two analyses is that the population of agencies reporting to NEMSIS changes over time. Still, irrespective of the data analysis used, naloxone administrations represent a growing, albeit still relatively small (approximately 1 percent), share of all EMS events.

an increasingly common phenomenon as a growing number of agencies have equipped their officers with naloxone. The precise number of law enforcement agencies equipping their officers with naloxone is not known. The North Carolina Harm Reduction Coalition maintains a tally of 2,482 agencies (as of November 2018). However, according to the organization's disclaimer, this is certainly an undercount because some agencies that carry naloxone have not registered with the website (North Carolina Harm Reduction Coalition, undated). However, despite the proliferation of officers carrying naloxone, many agencies continue to resist the move. Reasons for some law enforcement agencies expressing opposition to equipping their officers with naloxone include a reluctance to administer prescription drugs, which has been seen as a role for medical professionals (Slade, 2017); the costs of officer training that would be required; the costs of naloxone itself (Associated Press, 2016; Gilmore, 2019);[8] and concerns over exposure to legal liability (Reichert, Lurigio, and Weisner, 2019). The acceptance of naloxone by law enforcement agencies is also impeded by stigmatizing attitudes among some officers toward PWUD, which have been reported in multiple studies (Murphy and Russell, 2020; Wagner et al., 2016). Furthermore, some officers harbor reservations about the usefulness of naloxone, particularly when they believe it could promote further drug use (Green et al., 2013; Reichert, Lurigio, and Weisner, 2019). There is evidence suggesting that reservations about naloxone may be more common among officers who are more frequently involved in drug-related emergency calls. Murphy and Russell, 2020, noted in a survey of Pennsylvania law enforcement officers that officers who have responded to higher numbers of overdoses are more likely to believe naloxone use should be limited. Similarly, Carroll et al., 2020, in a survey of officers in 20 eastern states, found that officers with a more frequent history of responding to overdose calls were significantly less likely to express support for responding to overdoses.

Lastly, nontransporting fire departments have also increasingly equipped their staff with naloxone, with the support (in some cases) of targeted state-level efforts to distribute naloxone kits and train non-EMS first responders in their use (see, e.g., Rudisill et al., 2021; and Wood et al., 2021). However, as with law enforcement, reports of non-EMS fire departments failing to carry or administer naloxone persist (Paris, 2021; Police Executive Research Forum, 2021).

More-Complex Requirements for Naloxone Administrations

The opioid crisis has not only increased the number of individuals served by first responders but also increased the complexity of the environment in which naloxone is administered. With the arrival of potent synthetic opioids, higher doses of naloxone may be necessary to

---

[8]   Note that naloxone is available over the counter in some states, and most states have adopted naloxone standing orders, which means the state bears the costs rather than the agencies that are equipping themselves with naloxone (Reichert and Charlier, 2017).

counter their effects (Moss and Carlo, 2019).[9] Furthermore, naloxone itself has a relatively short duration of activity (Moss and Carlo, 2019; Pergolizzi et al., 2019), and it may need to be administered multiple times because one dose may not be enough to reverse the effects of a synthetic opioid (Faul et al., 2017). Alternatively, in cases in which the first dose of naloxone has been administered before the arrival of first responders (for example, by friends of the victim or a bystander), first responders may need to administer additional doses. To illustrate, according to 2016 data (i.e., in the early stages of synthetic opioids' expansion), EMS administered more than one dose in more than 20 percent of cases in which naloxone was administered (Geiger, Smart, and Stein, 2019; Morgan and Jones, 2018). Furthermore, the possibility of rebound toxicity, also accentuated by the emergence of potent synthetic opioids, has led to the suggestion that first responders stay with the victim for some time to be in a position to offer further assistance if necessary (Pergolizzi et al., 2019; World Health Organization, 2014). At the same time, the risk of rebound toxicity may not be as big of a concern as feared: A systematic review of studies on mortality after EMS naloxone administration and release ($n = 7$ studies) found that the mortality rate was less than 0.1 percent (Greene et al., 2019). Generally, dosing naloxone is difficult because the effective dose is dependent on numerous contextual factors that first responders may not know about, such as the volume and purity of the drugs consumed (Pergolizzi et al., 2019). The proliferation of novel synthetic opioids with varying levels of potency and concomitant uncertainty in the illicit markets, whereby even victims of overdoses are frequently not sure what they consumed, only accentuates the response complexity.[10] In this context, educating and training first responders about proper naloxone administration remains paramount to help ensure effective overdose management. However, there is some evidence of persistent gaps in EMS knowledge about naloxone administration (Kilwein et al., 2019).

How First Responders Are Affected by the Opioid Crisis

EMS personnel and other first responders have been affected by the opioid crisis in a variety of ways. In this section, we discuss three principal mechanisms: (1) an increase in demands on first responding agencies, (2) responder safety, and (3) the impact on the responder workforce.

Opportunity Costs and Competing Demands

As discussed earlier, the opioid crisis has resulted in an increase in demand for emergency services because of opioid-related overdoses (Cash et al., 2018). This has led to increased strain on responding agencies, without a corresponding increase in available resources (Knaak et al., 2019). First responders have reported that this increased demand for their services has

---

[9] In addition to fentanyl's higher potency, a contributing factor is its rapid onset of action, which needs to be countered by correspondingly high doses of naloxone.

[10] Relatedly, differences in overdose management requirements are not confined to synthetic opioids. For instance, Banta-Green et al., 2017, described differences between responses to cases involving heroin and those involving prescription opioids.

imposed opportunity costs, affected their ability to address other issues, and made it more difficult to perform their jobs (Pike et al., 2019). In addition, first responders have reported that (1) this increased workload has affected the quality of provided services because agencies are required to do more for less or the same amount and (2) services have become less efficient as a result (Pike et al., 2019). Relatedly, a lack of resources and understaffing have also been noted as major challenges in qualitative research involving first responders (Knaak et al., 2019; Saunders et al., 2019), and rural agencies with fewer resources can be expected to be particularly affected by these developments (Hancock et al., 2017). In addition to increased demand on the responder workforce, the cost of naloxone has been noted as an increased burden on agencies' resources (Kodjak, 2017).

Responder Safety

The opioid crisis has given rise to a series of considerations about the safety of first responders. First, Wermeling, 2015, noted the existence of concerns about an accidental needlestick injury and HIV or hepatitis infection transmission when responding to an overdose scene. Second, first responders face risks to their safety if revived individuals undergo acute opioid withdrawal and become agitated (Pike et al., 2019; Wermeling, 2015). First responders' safety concerns may affect how they respond to calls for their services. In a survey of and focus groups with EMS personnel in Wyoming, Kilwein et al., 2019, found that agencies operating in areas with longer transport times and less access to backup by law enforcement were more likely to report titrating naloxone. One participant said that this was a way to lessen the odds of a withdrawal and thus make the patient less combative, because patients who use opioids often become combative after the reversal agent is administered. Furthermore, to address the possibility of violent encounters when responding to overdoses, several cities have started implementing violence mitigation training programs (Keseg et al., 2019).

Lastly, the proliferation of unknown and more-potent synthetic opioids has also led to concerns over first responders' exposure to illicit drugs (in particular, fentanyl and related substances), notably via inhalation, dermal exposure, or mucous membrane exposure (Chiu et al., 2019; Keseg et al., 2019). Correspondingly, some police departments have reported that they stopped performing field drug tests because of concerns about the chemical exposure of their personnel (Howard and Hornsby-Myers, 2018). In response, numerous authorities, such as the National Institute for Occupational Safety and Health and the Office of National Drug Control Policy, have developed guidance on how emergency responders should protect themselves from fentanyl and fentanyl analogs (National Institute for Occupational Safety and Health, undated; Office of National Drug Control Policy, undated). In assessing the overall risk, the American College of Medical Toxicology and the American Academy of Clinical Toxicology stated in 2017 that the risks of clinically significant exposure among emergency responders were "extremely low" and added, "To date, we have not seen reports of emergency responders developing signs or symptoms consistent with opioid toxicity from incidental contact with opioids. Incidental dermal absorption is unlikely to cause opioid toxicity" (American College of Medical Toxicology, undated). Relatedly, others have pointed out that responders' risk perceptions may not correspond to the true extent of the risk, which could be addressed by efforts to improve responders' understanding of the risk and to modulate their expectations (Chiu et al., 2019). Since then, there have been many more media reports of first responders being exposed to fentanyl, and some of these stories have gone viral (Siegel, 2022). These stories rarely, if ever, provide evidence that fentanyl intoxication led to the reported symptoms. The Centers for Disease Control and Prevention removed a video from its website after experts expressed concerns that the video, which was about the risks of fentanyl exposure to law enforcement officers, mischaracterized these risks (D'Ambrosio, 2022).

More recently, the COVID-19 pandemic has led to concerns among law enforcement professionals about their inability to maintain social distancing when responding to drug overdoses and administering naloxone. In response, some law enforcement agencies reportedly refused to administer naloxone during the pandemic (Blanchard, 2020; Newberry, 2020).

Responder Well-Being

The last type of impact is on personnel and their well-being, which can affect the way first responders go about their jobs. Numerous sources have reported that care for victims of overdose has led to emotional strain on first responders and feelings of burnout (Elliott, Bennett, and Wolfson-Stofko, 2019; Knaak et al., 2019; Saunders et al., 2019).[11] To illustrate, in a survey and interviews with various types of first responders in a county in Kentucky (undertaken by Pike et al., 2019), nearly all participants indicated that opioid use was a significant problem for their community, and the majority of them felt that this had resulted in burnout among their colleagues. Although this was not a random sample, the study showed that EMS and fire personnel were significantly more likely to agree that the opioid crisis had resulted in burnout compared with their law enforcement counterparts. Related negative impacts on first responder personnel well-being reported in the literature include vicarious trauma (Saunders et al., 2019), feelings of helplessness (Pike et al., 2019), and compassion fatigue (Knaak et al., 2019).

A variety of factors have been reported as contributing to these outcomes. These factors include first responders' experiences with responding to repeated calls for the same individu-

---

[11] As a thought exercise regarding the degree of firsthand experience with overdose responses among first responders, consider the following data points. According to the 2020 National EMS Assessment, there are slightly more than 1 million licensed EMS professionals in the United States (including all license levels but excluding dispatchers; NASEMSO, 2020). According to 2021 NEMSIS data, there were approximately 350,000 naloxone administrations performed by EMS in 2020 (NEMSIS, undated). On average, this corresponds to approximately one naloxone administration per EMS professional every three years. However, because calls for service typically are staffed by more than one person, the average frequency with which EMS professionals attend suspected opioid overdoses is likely much higher. Of course, this is only a very rough illustration because the burden of responding to overdoses is not spread equally across EMS agencies. To illustrate, the National EMS Assessment counted 19,520 EMS agencies in the country. Naloxone administrations recorded in NEMSIS since 2018 come from 11,589 EMS agencies, suggesting that fewer than 60 percent of EMS agencies are responsible for all or nearly all naloxone administrations in the past four years. This further underscores the relatively high degree of firsthand experience with overdose response in some parts of the country.

als (particularly, over short periods or even as part of the same shift) and the refusal of revived patients to be transported to the hospital and to seek further assistance (Pike et al., 2019). Relatedly, some EMS personnel highlighted feeling disappointed that their well-intentioned and medically appropriate advice was not being followed by their patients and that no behavioral change was likely to result from the overdose episode (Bessen et al., 2019; Elliott, Bennett, and Wolfson-Stofko, 2019).

Burnout and compassion fatigue among first responders can translate into a variety of other negative outcomes. Secondary outcomes that affect emergency responders include substance use disorders and posttraumatic stress disorder (Jozaghi et al., 2018; Katzman et al., 2019). In addition, burnout and compassion fatigue may be a source of stigmatizing attitudes on the part of first responders, negatively affecting victims of overdose (Bessen et al., 2019; Elliott, Bennett, and Wolfson-Stofko, 2019; Farrugia, 2019; Knaak et al., 2019).[12]

In an effort to address the challenges discussed in this section, some agencies have introduced policies and practices to help deal with the impact and stress of responding to the opioid crisis, although, in some instances, the opioid crisis may not have been the sole impetus behind these initiatives (Goodison et al., 2019). This is not surprising because secondary trauma that affects first responders has always been a concern, albeit exacerbated by the crisis (Austin, Pathak, and Thompson, 2018; Papazoglou and Tuttle, 2018; Rudofossi, 2017). Initiatives reported by law enforcement agencies include training on addiction and trauma, mandatory mental wellness check-ins, and embedding trauma or mental health specialists with agencies (Gerdes, 2020; Goodison et al., 2019).

Key Interactions with Other Components of the Ecosystem

Medical Care

Direct Link to Emergency Departments and Health Care System

In cases in which an overdose victim does not refuse further care, they typically are transported by EMS to the ED, where they are handed over to the hospital's medical professionals. This handoff between EMS and ED personnel may give rise to various challenges because they each have different clinical responsibilities and do not generally share working locations, creating the potential for communication gaps that can be detrimental to the care of the patient (Meisel et al., 2015). A smooth handoff is also important for subsequent interventions in the medical care system, during which professionals may help connect individuals with treatment and other services in the community or may start treatment in the ED and subsequently refer individuals to a community-based provider (Fox and Nelson, 2019; Lowenstein et al., 2019).

---

[12] For a concrete illustration of stigmatizing attitudes, see, e.g., Limmer, 2016.

Substance Use Disorder Treatment

Linkage to Treatment

First responders interact with the OUD treatment system to the extent that they can help overdose survivors access treatment services. This is of utmost importance because prior overdoses have been found to be associated with a significantly higher risk of a (repeat) overdose (Bagley et al., 2019; Kelty and Hulse, 2017; Olfson et al., 2018). First responders are the first to engage with opioid overdose victims in a moment of personal crisis, which can act as a potential facilitator for change in the lives of people with OUD (Saunders et al., 2019). Individuals can demonstrate an increased willingness or readiness to change at certain moments of their lives, including after a life-threatening event (DiClemente, 2018). Thus, there is a possibility that the interaction with first responders in the aftermath of an overdose may help convince individuals to seek treatment and recovery, especially if responders are in a position to provide information and concrete options to overdose victims (Langabeer et al., 2020).

However, there is ample evidence that a notable share of people who survive an overdose do not receive support and are not connected to services after hospital discharge, even if not every overdose survivor is interested in such linkage (Formica et al., 2018; Naeger et al., 2016). For instance, an analysis of Medicaid claims data from West Virginia covering opioid overdose survivors who enrolled under the Affordable Care Act expansion found that the use of buprenorphine increased significantly post-overdose but remained extremely low,[13] at less than 10 percent at both six months and 12 months after the overdose (Koyawala et al., 2019). Further exacerbating the situation is the fact that there do not appear to be established and accepted standards of care in post-overdose situations (targeting either the overdose victim or their families and other close ones; Bagley et al., 2019).

In response, some jurisdictions have started introducing post-overdose outreach programs that aim to engage overdose survivors in the community, typically involving response teams that draw on personnel from public health and public safety agencies (Formica et al., 2018; Formica et al., 2021; Streisel et al., 2019; Wagner et al., 2019). First responders from a variety of agencies are frequently included in these efforts (Bagley et al., 2019). The target population for these efforts includes overdose survivors who left the ED unconnected to any services (because of either not accepting or not being offered any services or information),[14] those who were attended to by first responders but refused further care or transport,[15] and

[13] Methadone is not covered by Medicaid in West Virginia. The use of naltrexone in the study sample was very low.

[14] For instance, in interviews with people who inject drugs in Baltimore, a group of researchers found that only 17 percent of respondents were given information on treatment options from emergency medical technicians (Pollini, McCall, Mehta, Vlahov, and Strathdee, 2006). The shares for receiving information from ED staff and hospital staff were 26 percent and 43 percent, respectively.

[15] The proportion of overdose victims who are not subsequently transported to a hospital is relatively small. Using an analysis of NEMSIS data from 2012 to 2015, Faul et al., 2017, noted that the vast majority of naloxone recipients (91 percent) were transported to the ED.

those who have never become known to the medical system in the first place (Formica et al., 2018; Formica et al., 2021).

Post-overdose outreach programs can take many forms. In a scoping review by Bagley et al., 2019, the authors identified 27 programs, which they categorized in five distinct groups depending on where they were implemented. Apart from programs that were implemented wholly or partly in the ED or correctional institutions, the review found ten community-based programs that took place either in individuals' homes or at the place of the overdose. Furthermore, four identified programs were not site-specific or were "mobile" (Bagley et al., 2019). Formica et al., 2018, surveyed fire and police departments in Massachusetts and found that approximately one-fifth (21 percent) of respondents were actively implementing a post-overdose outreach program. The authors identified four types of programs, three of which involved trying to reach overdose survivors in the community via (1) a multidisciplinary intervention team, (2) police officers followed by a referral to a treatment service, or (3) a clinician. The fourth type of program was location-based outreach, whereby survivors were encouraged to visit a specific location where they could seek assistance.[16] In a more recent study, Formica et al., 2021, surveyed municipalities in Massachusetts, in which nearly half (44 percent, $n = 156$) reported running a post-overdose outreach program, with 75 percent of these programs introduced since 2016. In line with earlier studies, the survey revealed differences in the implementation of these programs, though they commonly relied on police data to identify overdose survivors; involved police officers, recovery coaches, and harm reduction specialists in their outreach teams; and focused on linkage with overdose prevention, treatment, and recovery support services.

First responders in several other states have set up pathways to treatment and diversion services with designated intake locations. For instance, several fire stations in New Hampshire, Maryland, and Rhode Island run programs (referred to as *safe stations*) where individuals with OUD can ask for help with accessing services without any fear of criminal liability or other negative repercussions (Sacco, Unick, and Gray, 2018). These initiatives operate on a similar basis as police-led self-referral programs, a type of deflection program in which individuals with OUD can seek help at participating police stations (Hoke, Baker, and Wenrich, 2020; Reichert, 2017). Of course, the advantage of fire department or EMS-led safe stations is that clients do not have to be willing to come into contact with law enforcement to engage with support services, even though going through police-led programs officially does not expose individuals to any risks either.

---

[16] The number of post-overdose outreach programs in the country is not known, although some state-level implementation data are available. For instance, as of December 2019, there were 18 counties with active post-overdose outreach programs in North Carolina, with another 13 counties planning to introduce such programs (North Carolina Harm Reduction Coalition, 2020). In Ohio, at least 41 agencies in 31 counties received grants to set up response teams (Ohio Attorney General, 2019). Formica et al., 2018, identified 20 post-overdose programs operating in Massachusetts.

Challenges to Post-Overdose Outreach Programs

The implementation of post-overdose programs gives rise to several challenges and concerns. First, there is a concern about loss of privacy because individuals selected for outreach need to be identified by agencies participating in the program. The sharing of personal information on vulnerable individuals and communities among public health and public safety agencies can lead to a variety of negative outcomes, such as stigma or eviction (Formica et al., 2018). Conversely, the sharing of information and associated loss of privacy may also result in over-dose survivors' loss of trust in service providers, particularly if law enforcement officers are involved in the outreach effort (Bagley et al., 2019). Second, there may be concerns stemming from the fact that, compared with their public health counterparts, law enforcement officers and other public safety agency staff are likely to be less well trained on working with over-dose survivors and their families and close contacts (Formica et al., 2018). Another potential challenge is the sustainability of outreach programs and their dependence on potentially pre-carious funding streams. To illustrate, a survey of programs in Massachusetts by Formica et al., 2021, found that 76 percent of programs relied on external grants, with many pro-grams reporting that they draw on multiple sources of funding. The loss of grant funding may not necessarily mean the termination of outreach programs, but the question of how to provide long-term funding for outreach programs without external support requires further attention.

Further Challenges to Effective Linkage

Multiple other factors also influence the ability of first responders to link individuals with treatment services. As discussed earlier, an overly antagonistic reaction to the administration of naloxone can lead to opioid withdrawal (Bessen et al., 2019), as well as to a refusal of fur-ther care by the overdose victim (Neale and Strang, 2015). Severe post-naloxone withdrawal can contribute to individuals' perceived negative experience with first responders, as can situations in which overdose victims feel they are being judged or subjected to stigmatizing behavior by emergency personnel (Biancarelli et al., 2019; Motavalli et al., 2021). Such expe-riences can act as an obstacle to reductions in risky behaviors on the part of PWUD or to their readiness to attempt to stop their substance use (Elliott, Bennett, and Wolfson-Stofko, 2019; Farrugia, 2019). Along similar lines, a previous negative experience has been identified as a major reason why PWUDs may be reluctant to place an emergency call in the first place (Koester et al., 2017; Sherman et al., 2008). This is a challenge that, as discussed earlier, may be exacerbated by the negative impacts of the opioid crisis on first responders. For instance, in a survey of Pennsylvania law enforcement officers, Murphy and Russell, 2020, found that officers who responded more frequently to overdoses were less likely to believe police should help make referrals to treatment and more likely to express skepticism about the effectiveness of treatment.

Furthermore, the ability of first responders to assist with effective linkage depends on the availability of treatment services in the local area. Several studies examining first responder attitudes suggested that first responders frequently perceive local service provision to be inadequate or not easily accessible, which may contribute to their job-related frustrations. In interviews conducted by Saunders et al., 2019, p. 7, first responders "overwhelmingly" reported feeling frustrated by what they perceived to be policy, economic, and physical barriers to their ability to refer individuals to treatment services. Similarly, first responders reported in focus groups that PWUD lacked access to treatment and care services (Knaak et al., 2019).

Criminal Legal System

First responders also closely interact with the criminal legal system, not least because police are a type of emergency responder, and all three types of first responders work closely together to respond to all sorts of emergencies that are unrelated to opioids. They are partners and complementary components of first-line response to everything from traffic accidents to hurricanes. EMS and nontransport fire departments interact with the criminal legal system via dispatch protocols, which relate to issues regarding whether first responders are called to an overdose in the first place.

Issues Surrounding Calling EMS

The interaction between EMS and law enforcement in dispatch protocols has direct implications for whether emergency services are called to attend to an overdose. Numerous studies have reported fear of police as a reason not to call 911 (Koester et al., 2017; Townsend et al., 2019). Furthermore, evidence suggests that this fear may be more prevalent among nonmajority groups, such as undocumented migrants, low-income populations, and PWUD (Wagner et al., 2019). The extent of this phenomenon inevitably varies across contexts, and reported rates of calling emergency services for overdose cases vary in the literature. For instance, in a study of PWUD in Baltimore, Tobin, Davey, and Latkin, 2005, reported that 911 was called in 23 percent of cases. In another study from Baltimore (Pollini, McCall, Mehta, Celentano, et al., 2006), the reported rate was much higher (at 63.4 percent), although more than half of participants who called 911 reported delaying the call by at least five minutes, with fear of police indicated as one of the reasons for doing so. Wagner et al., 2010, evaluating an overdose prevention program for PWUD in Skid Row in Los Angeles, reported that the rate of calling 911 in response to opioid overdoses was 60 percent. These latter results are similar to those reported in a study from British Columbia (Ambrose, Amlani, and Buxton, 2016), in which 911 was called in 54 percent of cases, with overdoses taking place on the street (as opposed to in private residences) having significantly higher odds of 911 being called.[17]

In many cases, the reason for wanting to avoid the involvement of law enforcement is fear of arrest, either for drug-related charges connected with the overdose event or for other out-

---

[17] Of course, there are other reasons for not calling 911 that are not related to fears of law enforcement involvement. One such reason frequently reported in the literature is that PWUD did not think it was necessary to call for medical assistance (Bohnert et al., 2011; Koester et al., 2017). Not having immediate access to a phone may also be an obstacle (Seal et al., 2005).

standing warrants. However, the variety of reasons for not wanting to place an emergency call can be much broader. Other reasons reported in the literature include fear of consequences of a parole or probation violation, fear of losing custody of children, and fear of homicide-related charges, if the overdose ends up being fatal (Follett et al., 2014; Koester et al., 2017; Wagner et al., 2019).

In response to individuals' concerns about law enforcement when considering whether to call 911, numerous states have adopted so-called Good Samaritan laws, which offer immunity or other legal protections to overdose victims and other people involved on the scene in the event of calling for help in response to a drug overdose. As of July 2018, 45 states and the District of Columbia had some form of a drug overdose Good Samaritan law (Prescription Drug Abuse Policy System, 2018), with state laws differing in the breadth of the protections they offer.[18] For both controlled substance possession laws and drug paraphernalia laws, some states offer protection from arrest, charge, and prosecution, whereas other states cover only the latter. In a few other states, laws only consider calling 911 in response to an overdose to be an affirmative defense. Furthermore, states with Good Samaritan laws were equally split (as of 2018) on whether they provided protection from parole or probation violations (Prescription Drug Abuse Policy System, 2018).

The evidence on the effectiveness of Good Samaritan laws in terms of the likelihood to call 911 appears to be mixed.[19] Some studies suggest that such laws may play a role in some individuals' decisionmaking. For instance, in an evaluation of the law's implementation in the state of Washington (Banta-Green et al., 2011), most opiate users (88 percent) reported being more likely to place a 911 call during an overdose after becoming aware of the law, although the evaluation did not find any evidence of the law's direct impact on the actual number of calls, largely because of other contemporaneous developments (Banta-Green, 2013). Elsewhere, however, evidence suggests that 911 continues to not be called in some overdose cases despite the existence of Good Samaritan laws, even in instances when people are aware of the law's protections (Townsend et al., 2019; Watson et al., 2018). For instance, in interviews with PWUDs in Colorado (Koester et al., 2017), participants said they were not necessarily the most worried about possession and paraphernalia laws: It was standard procedure to get rid of any problematic items before the arrival of first responders. The most pressing concern was that responding law enforcement would run background checks on the victim or witnesses, which may result in arrests because of outstanding warrants or incarceration if individuals are found to be in violation of their parole or probation. Along similar lines, in a study of syringe service program (SSP) clients in New York, Zadoretzky et al., 2017, concluded that some of the reasons for not calling 911 that were provided by participants would not have

---

[18] The remaining five states without such a law were Kansas, Maine, Oklahoma, Texas, and Wyoming.

[19] There also is mixed, and still emerging, evidence with respect to the potential wider impacts of Good Samaritan laws, such as changes in drug-related mortality or ED visits. See, e.g., McClellan et al., 2018; Nguyen and Parker, 2018; and Rees et al., 2019.

been addressed even by greater awareness of the state's Good Samaritan law, because the concerns of PWUD extended to other legal issues not covered by the law's protections.

Harm Reduction and Community-Initiated Interventions

Naloxone Leave-Behind Programs

First responders have become a channel through which naloxone can be distributed to PWUD and their friends and families. In recent years, some emergency responder agencies have implemented naloxone leave-behind programs, whereby emergency responders leave naloxone with the overdose victim or their family and friends for future use (Ray et al., 2018). In some contexts, the primary beneficiaries are intended to be those who refuse transportation to the hospital and may need another dose soon (Mechem et al., 2020), although naloxone kits distributed as part of a response to a call for service can be used over a longer time frame.

The number of jurisdictions nationwide that have introduced naloxone leave-behind programs is not known, though information from some states suggests that these programs have become a relatively common occurrence. For instance, there were 26 naloxone leave-behind programs in North Carolina as of December 2019 (North Carolina Harm Reduction Coalition, 2020).

Because of their relative novelty, there is little evidence on the effectiveness and impact of naloxone leave-behind programs. The literature so far is generally limited to demonstrating the existence of these programs and to describing how individual programs have been implemented. One of the emerging insights from studies focusing on naloxone leave-behind programs is that they may also help family members and friends promote their close one's engagement in treatment and other services. In a study on the implementation of an naloxone leave-behind program in Howard County, Maryland, Scharf et al., 2021, found that overdose victims whose family members or friends received a naloxone kit and information about services were subsequently significantly more likely to be connected with peer-support services. The authors also identified a series of implementation lessons and challenges, including difficulties in overcoming record-sharing issues between health and fire departments and the importance of stakeholder buy-in, including from EMS providers.

Emergency Medical Services Data as a Useful Surveillance Tool

Data collected by EMS agencies represent a valuable source of information and a tool for a variety of monitoring and surveillance efforts (see Chapter Seven). First and foremost, these data are a surveillance tool that can be used to monitor trends in opioid overdoses, such as changes in their rates, seasonality, geographic distribution, demographic distribution, and other indicators of interest (Faul et al., 2017; Garza and Dyer, 2016; Knowlton et al., 2013; Moore et al., 2017). Furthermore, EMS data can be used as a mechanism for developing and targeting various outreach interventions, including post-overdose outreach programs (Garza and Dyer, 2016; Wagner et al., 2019). EMS data possess several qualities that make them a valuable source of information. They are timely, without any substantial time lag between the event of interest and the logging of information. They are tied to geographic indicators, enabling an analysis pertaining to a defined geographic area. The population captured in EMS data is relatively sizeable, producing a large number of observations for various statistical analyses. In addition, given the fact that some overdose victims refuse further care, EMS data include individuals who would otherwise not appear in any other health records (Garza and Dyer, 2016; Knowlton et al., 2013).

EMS data are also subject to limitations. First, not every overdose event will be captured in EMS data because a substantial proportion of overdoses does not involve calling 911. This limitation is further accentuated by ongoing naloxone distribution programs, which result in greater numbers of naloxone administrations being performed by members of the public because someone on the scene already has naloxone and is ready to use it (Garza and Dyer, 2016). This may increase the number of overdoses not attended by EMS. Furthermore, EMS data may not capture naloxone administered by first responders prior to EMS arrival. There also is the possibility of an overcount in EMS data because naloxone, given its safety and the risks inherent in delaying a response to a suspected opioid overdose, may be administered in different types of health events that do not actually constitute an overdose (Knowlton et al., 2013).

Child Welfare

EMS professionals have an obligation to report suspected cases of child maltreatment (Lynne et al., 2015). On the one hand, first responders can thus help improve child welfare in the event of maltreatment. Furthermore, because many calls for services involve the presence of children, first responders need to respond in a sensitive manner that supports the children's well-being. On the other hand, as discussed earlier, the role of first responders as mandatory reporters may affect the decision of whether to call for emergency help in the event of an overdose. This presents a standing conflict between the need to safeguard children's safety and the need to remove any barriers to effective emergency help.

Policy Opportunities and Considerations

Interactions between first responders and other components of the opioid ecosystem suggest some policy opportunities. Regarding the interaction between first responders and harm reduction and community-initiated interventions, more can be done to increase the use of first responders as a naloxone distribution channel to people who use opioids and their families and friends. Recently introduced naloxone leave-behind programs are an example of such a mechanism, and their number could be expanded. In addition, first responder agencies could be systematically used as naloxone distribution places, complementing other locations where members of the general public can access naloxone kits, such as pharmacies and SSPs. Relatedly, there continue to be gaps in the degree to which first responders are equipped with naloxone and thus able to administer it in the event of an opioid overdose. This is an observation pertaining primarily to law enforcement agencies and non-EMS fire departments, some of which continue to operate without carrying naloxone. Closing this gap would further increase the likelihood that naloxone is available as a response in the event of an opioid overdose.

Interaction with the criminal legal system (and further potential interactions with other systems, such as child welfare) suggests opportunities and considerations related to calls for service in emergency situations. To alleviate fears of calling 911, the scope of existing Good Samaritan laws could be expanded to cover areas not directly related to drug-related offenses, such as breaches of parole or probation. Relatedly, efforts to educate the general public, as well as law enforcement personnel, about these laws could be increased (Watson et al., 2018).[20] This step could have the effect of improving people's understanding of the protections afforded by the law in the event of calling 911 in response to a drug overdose and could reduce the potential for differences between what the laws state and how the police choose to interpret such laws.[21] Therefore, these efforts could help address people's fear of police involvement, one of the major barriers to calling 911. Although there is some evidence that, even in some instances in which people know about the law and its provisions, they decide not to call 911, the adoption of Good Samaritan laws elsewhere appears to have helped increase the odds of 911 being called.

Another solution to address negative interactions with the criminal legal system could be introducing a system for the purpose of reporting drug overdoses, in which callers would be guaranteed that the police would not be among the responding personnel. For instance, some participants in a qualitative study by Koester et al., 2017, noted they were more likely to call 911 because of their prior experiences with overdose emergency calls, which were attended to only by EMS and the fire department. They also reported that, when calling 911, they would use language that would avoid positively identifying the case as an overdose, for fear that this would increase the odds of law enforcement being dispatched. This approach is also in line with guidance provided by the National Harm Reduction Coalition (Wheeler et al., 2012). Options to exclude law enforcement from overdose responses include (1) introducing a non-911 emergency number dedicated to drug overdoses that would connect callers with local responders or (2) making modifications to existing dispatch protocols. In line with the

---

[20] To illustrate, in a survey of law enforcement officers in Washington state, Banta-Green et al., 2013, found that only a small share of officers (16 percent) knew about the state's Good Samaritan law one year after its adoption despite the majority of respondents having been at the scene of an overdose within the past 12 months. An even smaller share of respondents correctly identified the scope of the law: specifically, what types of immunities it confers and to whom. In a more recent survey of police officers in 20 eastern states, Carroll et al., 2020, found that the vast majority of respondents (91 percent) correctly reported the existence of a Good Samaritan law in their jurisdiction. However, only about one-quarter (26 percent) correctly described the protections it afforded.

[21] See, e.g., Beletsky et al., 2015, on the differences between the law on the books and the law as applied on the street by police officers when it comes to drug paraphernalia and SSP clients.

latter suggestion, the city of Eugene, Oregon, introduced a program called Cahoots, in which some mental health–related 911 calls are attended to by medics and crisis workers alone: i.e., without a police officer (Elinson, 2018). The model has since been replicated in Denver in a program called STAR, in which some mental health and substance use–related 911 calls are attended to by a medic and a social worker (Enos, 2020). A similar program is underway in Olympia, Washington, and other cities have announced plans to develop programs that involve civilian first responders in the aftermath of protests following the death of George Floyd in 2020 (Thompson, 2020). Notably, however, in the existing programs mentioned in this section, the decision regarding whether a police officer is sent to the scene rests with the dispatch staff, so 911 callers who may fear law enforcement involvement are not guaranteed that there will be none. Admittedly, some non–law enforcement responders may be hesitant to forgo police protection while on the scene. That said, the various models of 911 response that result in law enforcement not being present for some calls do not appear to have had notable adverse impacts on first responder safety.[22] Furthermore, it is important to recognize that excluding law enforcement from responding to overdose calls may not be an option for every community. For instance, law enforcement in rural communities is often the nearest available responding agency, and its exclusion could mean unacceptable delays in response times. For these reasons, communities could decide which approach works best for their local circumstances.

Lastly, there are opportunities that pertain primarily to first responders themselves. To counter the effect of the opioid crisis on first responders, training and further support to improve resiliency could be stepped up (Keseg et al., 2019; Knaak et al., 2019; Murphy and Russell, 2020). This could have a positive effect on job-related stress, burnout, and responder fatigue, and this effect could result in improved services for PWUD and reductions in their perceived negative experiences with first responders. In addition, the provision of education on addiction, treatment, and recovery for first responders (particularly, law enforcement officers) can be expanded (Elliott et al., 2019; Keseg et al., 2019; Knaak et al., 2019). This step would have the benefit of improving first responders' understanding of the situation in which PWUD find themselves and help modulate first responders' expectations from their encounters with PWUD. By extension, these changes could result in reductions in stigmatizing attitudes and behaviors on the part of first responders, as well as more-effective provision of services (Murphy and Russell, 2020). Relatedly, first responders should be provided with continuous education on how to make referrals (Keseg et al., 2019). This step could improve the process of linking overdose victims with treatment and other services and make first responders more effective in the process.

---

[22] For example, in the Cahoots program in Eugene, the rate at which medics and crisis workers request police backup is approximately 2 percent for calls coded as "Check Welfare," "Assist Public," or "Transport," though it is notably higher for more-policing-style calls, such as "Criminal Trespass" (Eugene Police Crime Analysis Unit, 2020).

Abbreviations

ALS	advanced life support
BLS	basic life support
COVID-19	coronavirus disease 2019
ED	emergency department
EMD	emergency medical dispatch
EMS	emergency medical services
NASEMSO	National Association of State Emergency Management Services Officials
NEMSIS	National Emergency Medical Services Information System
NHTSA	National Highway Traffic Safety Administration
OUD	opioid use disorder
PSAP	public service answering point
PWUD	people who use drugs
SSP	syringe service program

References

Ambrose, Graham, Ashraf Amlani, and Jane A. Buxton, "Predictors of Seeking Emergency Medical Help During Overdose Events in a Provincial Naloxone Distribution Programme: A Retrospective Analysis," *BMJ Open*, Vol. 6, 2016.

American College of Medical Toxicology, *ACMT and AACT Position Statement: Preventing Occupational Fentanyl and Fentanyl Analog Exposure to Emergency Responders*, Phoenix, Ariz., undated.

Associated Press, "Just Say No to Narcan? Heroin Rescue Efforts Draw Backlash," *CBS News*, September 26, 2016.

Austin, Cindy L., Manoj Pathak, and Simon Thompson, "Secondary Traumatic Stress and Resilience Among EMS," *Journal of Paramedic Practice*, Vol. 10, No. 6, 2018, pp. 240–247.

Bagley, Sarah M., Samantha F. Schoenberger, Katherine M. Waye, and Alexander Y. Walley, "A Scoping Review of Post Opioid-Overdose Interventions," *Preventive Medicine*, Vol. 128, 2019.

Banta-Green, C. J., P. C. Kuszler, P. O. Coffin, and J. A. Schoeppe, *Washington's 911 Good Samaritan Drug Overdose Law: Initial Evaluation Results*, Seattle, Wash.: University of Washington, Alcohol and Drug Abuse Institute, November 2011.

Banta-Green, Caleb, "Good Samaritan Overdose Response Laws: Lessons Learned from Washington State," Obama White House blog, March 29, 2013. As of May 25, 2022: https://obamawhitehouse.archives.gov/blog/2013/03/29/good-samaritan-overdose-response-laws-lessons-learned-washington-state

Banta-Green, Caleb J., Leo Beletsky, Jennifer A. Schoeppe, Phillip O. Coffin, and Patricia C. Kuszler, "Police Officers' and Paramedics' Experiences with Overdose and Their Knowledge and Opinions of Washington State's Drug Overdose-Naloxone-Good Samaritan Law," *Journal of Urban Health*, Vol. 90, No. 6, December 2013, pp. 1102–1111.

Banta-Green, Caleb J., Phillip O. Coffin, Jennie A. Schoeppe, Joseph O. Merrill, Lauren K. Whiteside, and Abigail K. Ebersol, "Heroin and Pharmaceutical Opioid Overdose Events: Emergency Medical Response Characteristics," *Drug and Alcohol Dependence*, Vol. 178, 2017.

Beletsky, Leo, Jess Cochrane, Anne L. Sawyer, Chris Serio-Chapman, Marina Smelyanskaya, Jennifer Han, Natanya Robinowitz, and Susan G. Sherman, "Police Encounters Among Needle Exchange Clients in Baltimore: Drug Law Enforcement as a Structural Determinant of Health," *American Journal of Public Health*, Vol. 105, No. 9, September 2015, pp. 1872–1879.

Bessen, Sarah, Stephen A. Metcalf, Elizabeth C. Saunders, Sarah K. Moore, Andrea Meier, Bethany McLeman, Olivia Walsh, and Lisa A. Marsch, "Barriers to Naloxone Use and Acceptance Among Opioid Users, First Responders, and Emergency Department Providers in New Hampshire, USA," *International Journal of Drug Policy*, Vol. 74, 2019, pp. 144–151.

Biancarelli, Dea L., Katie B. Biello, Ellen Childs, M. Drainoni, Peter Salhaney, Alberto Edeza, Matthew J. Mimiaga, Richard Saitz, and Angela R. Bazzi, "Strategies Used by People Who Inject Drugs to Avoid Stigma in Healthcare Settings," *Drug and Alcohol Dependence*, Vol. 198, 2019, pp. 80–86.

Blanchard, Sessi Kuwabara, "An Indiana Police Dept. No Longer Reversing Overdoses During Pandemic," *Filter*, April 9, 2020.

Bohnert, Amy S. B., Arijit Nandi, Melissa Tracy, Magdalena Cerdá, Kenneth J. Tardiff, David Vlahov, and Sandro Galea, "Policing and Risk of Overdose Mortality in Urban Neighborhoods," *Drug and Alcohol Dependence*, Vol. 113, No. 1, 2011, pp. 62–68.

Brennan, Erin, *BLS Is More Than Basic, It's Fundamental to Good Care*, National Association of EMS Physicians, 2020.

Carroll, Jennifer J., Sasha Mital, Jessica Wolff, Rita K. Noonan, Pedro Martinez, Melissa C. Podolsky, John C. Killorin, and Traci C. Green, "Knowledge, Preparedness, and Compassion Fatigue Among Law Enforcement Officers Who Respond to Opioid Overdose, *Drug and Alcohol Dependence*, Vol. 217, 2020.

Cash, Rebecca E., Jeremiah Kinsman, Remle P. Crowe, Madison K. Rivard, Mark Faul, and Ashish R. Panchal, "Naloxone Administration Frequency During Emergency Medical Service Events—United States, 2012–2016," *Morbidity and Mortality Weekly Report*, Vol. 67, No. 31, 2018, pp. 850–853.

Chiu, S. K., J. L. Hornsby-Myers, M. A. de Perio, J. E. Snawder, D. M. Wiegand, D. Trout, and J. Howard, "Health Effects from Unintentional Occupational Exposure to Opioids Among Law Enforcement Officers: Two Case Investigations," *American Journal of Industrial Medicine*, Vol. 62, No. 5, 2019, pp. 439–447.

D'Ambrosio, Amanda, "CDC Nixes Misleading Video About Cops' Risk of Fentanyl Overdose," MedPage Today, July 14, 2022.

Davis, Corey S., Jessica K. Southwell, Virginia Radford Niehaus, Alexander Y. Walley, and Michael W. Dailey, "Emergency Medical Services Naloxone Access: A National Systematic Legal Review," *Academic Emergency Medicine*, Vol. 21, No. 10, 2014, pp. 1173–1177.

DiClemente, Carlo C., *Addiction and Change: How Addictions Develop and Addicted People Recover*, 2nd ed., New York: Guilford Publications, 2018.

Elinson, Zusha, "When Mental-Health Experts, Not Police, Are the First Responders," *Wall Street Journal*, November 24, 2018.

Elliott, Luther, Alex S. Bennett, and Brett Wolfson-Stofko, "Life After Opioid-Involved Overdose: Survivor Narratives and Their Implications for ER/ED Interventions," *Addiction*, Vol. 114, No. 8, August 2019, pp. 1379–1386.

Enos, Gary, "Denver Initiative Should Reduce Need for Police on Some Emergency Calls," *Mental Health Weekly*, Vol. 30, No. 25, 2020.

Eugene Police Crime Analysis Unit, *CAHOOTS Program Analysis*, Eugene, Ore., August 21, 2020.

Fales, William, *EMS Dispatch—Function: Call Taking, Pre-Arrivals, and System Integration*, paper presented at the NAEMSP 2019 Annual Meeting, Austin, Tex., January 7–12, 2019.

Farrugia, Adrian, "Commentary on Elliot et al. (2019): How Stigma Shapes Overdose Revival and Possible Avenues to Disrupt It," *Addiction*, Vol. 114, No. 8, August 2019, pp. 1387–1388.

Faul, Mark, Peter Lurie, Jeremiah M. Kinsman, Michael W. Dailey, Charmaine Crabaugh, and Scott M. Sasser, "Multiple Naloxone Administrations Among Emergency Medical Service Providers Is Increasing," *Prehospital Emergency Care*, Vol. 21, No. 4, 2017, pp. 411–419.

Follett, Kayla M., Anthony Piscitelli, Michael Parkinson, and Felix Munger, "Barriers to Calling 9-1-1 During Overdose Emergencies in a Canadian Context," *Critical Social Work*, Vol. 15, No. 1, 2014.

Formica, Scott W., Robert Apsler, Lindsay Wilkins, Sarah Ruiz, Brittni Reilly, and Alexander Y. Walley, "Post Opioid Overdose Outreach by Public Health and Public Safety Agencies: Exploration of Emerging Programs in Massachusetts," *International Journal of Drug Policy*, Vol. 54, 2018, pp. 43–50.

Formica, Scott W., Katherine M. Waye, Allyn O. Benintendi, Shapei Yan, Sarah M. Bagley, Leo Beletsky, Jennifer J. Carroll, Ziming Xuan, David Rosenbloom, Robert Apsler, Traci C. Green, Allie Hunter, and Alexander Y. Walley, "Characteristics of Post-Overdose Public Health-Public Safety Outreach in Massachusetts," *Drug and Alcohol Dependence*, Vol. 219, February 1, 2021.

Fox, Lindsay, and Lewis S. Nelson, "Emergency Department Initiation of Buprenorphine for Opioid Use Disorder: Current Status, and Future Potential," *CNS Drugs*, Vol. 33, No. 12, 2019, pp. 1147–1154.

Garza, Alex, and Sophia Dyer, "EMS Data Can Help Stop the Opioid Epidemic," *Journal of Emergency Medical Services*, 2016.

Geiger, Caroline, Rosanna Smart, and Bradley D. Stein, "Who Receives Naloxone from Emergency Medical Services? Characteristics of Calls and Recent Trends," *Substance Abuse*, Vol. 41, No. 3, 2019, pp. 400–407.

Gerdes, Scott, "The Case for Mandatory Annual Mental Health Checkups," *Police Chief*, November 2020, pp. 20–22.

Gilmore, Ginger, *Equipping Law Enforcement Officers with the Opioid Antagonist Naloxone*, Wichita Falls, Tex.: Wichita Falls Police Department, June 2019.

Glenn, Melody J., Amber D. Rice, Keith Primeau, Adrienne Hollen, Isrealia Jado, Philipp Hannan, Sharon McDonough, Brittany Arcaris, Daniel W. Spaite, and Joshua B. Gaither, "Refusals After Prehospital Administration of Naloxone During the COVID-19 Pandemic," *Prehospital Emergency Care*, Vol. 25, No. 1, 2021, pp. 46–54.

Goodison, Sean E., Michael J. D. Vermeer, Jeremy D. Barnum, Dulani Woods, and Brian A. Jackson, *Law Enforcement Efforts to Fight the Opioid Crisis: Convening Police Leaders, Multidisciplinary Partners, and Researchers to Identify Promising Practices and to Inform a Research Agenda*, Santa Monica, Calif.: RAND Corporation, RR-3064-NIJ, 2019. As of July 22, 2022:
https://www.rand.org/pubs/research_reports/RR3064.html

Green, Traci C., Nickolas Zaller, Wilson R. Palacios, Sarah E. Bowman, Madeline Ray, Robert Heimer, and Patricia Case, "Law Enforcement Attitudes Toward Overdose Prevention and Response," *Drug and Alcohol Dependence*, Vol. 133, No. 2, 2013, pp. 677–684.

Greene, Jennifer Anne, Brent J. Deveau, Justine S. Dol, and Michael B. Butler, "Incidence of Mortality Due to Rebound Toxicity After 'Treat and Release' Practices in Prehospital Opioid Overdose Care: A Systematic Review," *Emergency Medicine Journal*, Vol. 36, No. 4, 2019, pp. 219–224.

Gulec, Nazey, Joseph Lahey, James C. Suozzi, Matthew Sholl, Charles D. MacLean, and Daniel L. Wolfson, "Basic and Advanced EMS Providers Are Equally Effective in Naloxone Administration for Opioid Overdose in Northern New England," *Prehospital Emergency Care*, Vol. 22, No. 2, 2018, pp. 163–169.

Hancock, Christine, Heidi Mennenga, Nikki King, Holly Andrilla, Eric Larson, and Pat Schou, *Treating the Rural Opioid Epidemic*, Washington, D.C.: National Rural Health Association, 2017.

Hoke, Scott, Kerrie Baker, and Kristen Wenrich, "An Assessment of Officer Attitudes Toward the Training and Use of a Pre-Booking Diversionary Program," *Journal of Substance Abuse Treatment*, Vol. 115, 2020.

Howard, John, and Jennifer Hornsby-Myers, "Fentanyls and the Safety of First Responders: Science and Recommendations," *American Journal of Industrial Medicine*, Vol. 61, No. 8, 2018, pp. 633–639.

Jacoby, Jeanne L., Lauren M. Crowley, Robert D. Cannon, Kira D. Weaver, Tara K. Henry-Morrow, Kathryn A. Henry, Allison N. Kayne, Colleen E. Urban, Robert A. Gyory, and John F. McCarthy, "Pennsylvania Law Enforcement Use of Narcan," *American Journal of Emergency Medicine*, Vol. 38, No. 9, 2020, pp. 1944–1946.

Jozaghi, Ehsan, Russ Maynard, Zahra Dadakhah-Chimeh, Kevin Yake, and Sarah Blyth, "The Synthetic Opioid Epidemic and the Need for Mental Health Support for First Responders Who Intervene in Overdose Cases," *Canadian Journal of Public Health*, Vol. 109, No. 2, 2018, pp. 231–232.

Katzman, Neil, Jessica Medrano, Robin Swift, and Paige Menking, "First Responder ECHO: Developing an Innovative Telementoring Program," *Creative Education*, Vol. 10, No. 9, 2019, pp. 1982–1987.

Kelty, Erin, and Gary Hulse, "Fatal and Non-Fatal Opioid Overdose in Opioid Dependent Patients Treated with Methadone, Buprenorphine or Implant Naltrexone," *International Journal of Drug Policy*, Vol. 46, 2017, pp. 54–60.

Keseg, David P., James J. Augustine, Raymond L. Fowler, Kenneth A. Scheppke, David A. Farcy, and Paul E. Pepe, "Annotated Guidance and Recommendations for the Role and Actions of Emergency Medical Services Systems in the Current Opioid and Drug-Related Epidemics," *Journal of Emergency Medicine*, Vol. 57, No. 2, 2019, pp. 187–194.

Kilwein, Tess M., Laurel A. Wimbish, Lauren Gilbert, and Rodney A. Wambeam, "Practices and Concerns Related to Naloxone Use Among Emergency Medical Service Providers in a Rural State: A Mixed-Method Examination," *Preventive Medicine Reports*, Vol. 14, 2019.

Kinsman, Jeremiah M., and Kathy Robinson, "National Systematic Legal Review of State Policies on Emergency Medical Services Licensure Levels' Authority to Administer Opioid Antagonists," *Prehospital Emergency Care*, Vol. 22, No. 5, 2018, pp. 650–654.

Kitch, Bryan B., and Roberto C. Portela, "Effective Use of Naloxone by Law Enforcement in Response to Multiple Opioid Overdoses," *Prehospital Emergency Care*, Vol. 20, No. 2, 2016, pp. 226–229.

Knaak, Stephanie, Sue Mercer, Romie Christie, and Heather Stuart, *Stigma and the Opioid Crisis: Final Report*, Ottawa, Ontario: Mental Health Commission of Canada, 2019.

Knowlton, Amy, Brian W. Weir, Frank Hazzard, Yngvild Olsen, Junette McWilliams, Julie Fields, and Wade Gaasch, "EMS Runs for Suspected Opioid Overdose: Implications for Surveillance and Prevention," *Prehospital Emergency Care*, Vol. 17, No. 3, 2013, pp. 317–329.

Kodjak, Alison, "First Responders Spending More on Overdose Reversal Drug," NPR, August 8, 2017.

Koester, Stephen, Shane R. Mueller, Lisa Raville, Sig Langegger, and Ingrid A. Binswanger, "Why Are Some People Who Have Received Overdose Education and Naloxone Reticent to Call Emergency Medical Services in the Event of Overdose?" *International Journal of Drug Policy*, Vol. 48, 2017, pp. 115–124.

Koyawala, Neel, Rachel Landis, Colleen L. Barry, Bradley D. Stein, and Brendan Saloner, "Changes in Outpatient Services and Medication Use Following a Non-Fatal Opioid Overdose in the West Virginia Medicaid Program," *Journal of General Internal Medicine*, Vol. 34, No. 6, 2019, pp. 789–791.

Krohmer, Jon R., "2007 National EMS Scope of Practice Model, Change Notice," memorandum to state EMS directors, Washington, D.C.: U.S. Department of Transportation, National Highway Traffic Safety Administration, November 1, 2017.

Langabeer, James, Tiffany Champagne-Langabeer, Samuel D. Luber, Samuel J. Prater, Angela Stotts, Katherine Kirages, Andrea Yatsco, and Kimberly A. Chambers, "Outreach to People Who Survive Opioid Overdose: Linkage and Retention in Treatment," *Journal of Substance Abuse Treatment*, Vol. 111, 2020, pp. 11–15.

Limmer, Dan, "Naloxone Reversal: Turning Helpers into Haters," EMS1.com, February 3, 2016. As of May 25, 2022:
https://www.ems1.com/ems-social-media/articles/
naloxone-reversal-turning-helpers-into-haters-Pq5WSuWLOq0DQbES/

Lowenstein, Margaret, Austin Kilaru, Jeanmarie Perrone, Jessica Hemmons, Dina Abdel-Rahman, Zachary F. Meisel, and M. Kit Delgado, "Barriers and Facilitators for Emergency Department Initiation of Buprenorphine: A Physician Survey," *American Journal of Emergency Medicine*, Vol. 37, No. 9, 2019, pp. 1787–1790.

Lurigio, Arthur J., Justine Andrus, and Christy K. Scott, "The Opioid Epidemic and the Role of Law Enforcement Officers in Saving Lives," *Victims and Offenders*, Vol. 13, No. 8, 2018, pp. 1055–1076.

Lynne, Ellen Grace, Elizabeth J. Gifford, Kelly E. Evans, and Joel B. Rosch, "Barriers to Reporting Child Maltreatment: Do Emergency Medical Services Professionals Fully Understand Their Role as Mandatory Reporters?" *North Carolina Medical Journal*, Vol. 76, No. 1, 2015, pp. 13–18.

McClellan, Chandler, Barrot H. Lambdin, Mir M. Ali, Ryan Mutter, Corey S. Davis, Eliza Wheeler, Michael Pemberton, and Alex H. Kral, "Opioid-Overdose Laws Association with Opioid Use and Overdose Mortality," *Addictive Behaviors*, Vol. 86, 2018, pp. 90–95.

Mechem, C. Crawford, Crystal A. Yates, Maureen S. Rush, Arturo Alleyne, H. Jay Singleton, and Tabitha L. Boyle, "Deployment of Alternative Response Units in a High-Volume, Urban EMS System," *Prehospital Emergency Care*, Vol. 24, No. 3, 2020, pp. 378–384.

Meisel, Zachary F., Judy A. Shea, Nicholas J. Peacock, Edward T. Dickinson, Breah Paciotti, Roma Bhatia, Egor Buharin, and Carolyn C. Cannuscio, "Optimizing the Patient Handoff Between Emergency Medical Services and the Emergency Department," *Annals of Emergency Medicine*, Vol. 65, No. 3, 2015, pp. 310–317.

Moore, P. Quincy, Joseph Weber, Steven Cina, and Steven Aks, "Syndrome Surveillance of Fentanyl-Laced Heroin Outbreaks: Utilization of EMS, Medical Examiner and Poison Center Databases," *American Journal of Emergency Medicine*, Vol. 35, No. 11, 2017, pp. 1706–1708.

Morgan, Jody, and Alison L. Jones, "The Role of Naloxone in the Opioid Crisis," *Toxicology Communications*, Vol. 2, No. 1, 2018, pp. 15–18.

Moss, Ronald B., and Dennis J. Carlo, "Higher Doses of Naloxone Are Needed in the Synthetic Opioid Era," *Substance Abuse Treatment, Prevention, and Policy*, Vol. 14, No. 6, 2019.

Motavalli, Delia, Jessica L. Taylor, Ellen Childs, Pablo K. Valente, Peter Salhaney, Jennifer Olson, Dea L. Biancarelli, Alberto Edeza, Joel J. Earlywine, Brandon D. L. Marshall, et al., "'Health Is on the Back Burner': Multilevel Barriers and Facilitators to Primary Care Among People Who Inject Drugs," *Journal of General Internal Medicine*, Vol. 36, 2021, pp. 129–137.

Mulcahy, Andrew, Kirsten Becker, Jonathan Cantor, Scott Ashwood, Jeanne Ringel, Lisa Sontag-Padilla, Christine Buttorff, Michael Robbins, Susan Lovejoy, Thomas Goughnour, et al., *Medicare's Ground Ambulance Data Collection System: Sampling and Instrument Considerations and Recommendations*, Washington, D.C.: MITRE Corporation, 2019.

Murphy, Jennifer, and Brenda Russell, "Police Officers' Views of Naloxone and Drug Treatment: Does Greater Overdose Response Lead to More Negativity?" *Journal of Drug Issues*, Vol. 50, No. 4, 2020, pp. 455–471.

Naeger, Sarah, Ryan Mutter, Mir M. Ali, Tami Mark, and Lauren Hughey, "Post-Discharge Treatment Engagement Among Patients with an Opioid-Use Disorder," *Journal of Substance Abuse Treatment*, Vol. 69, 2016, pp. 64–71.

NASEMSO—*See* National Association of State Emergency Management Services Officials.

National Association of State Emergency Management Services Officials, *2020 National Emergency Medical Services Assessment*, Washington, D.C.: U.S. Department of Transportation, May 2020.

National Emergency Medical Services Information System, "Public Naloxone Administration Dashboard," webpage, undated. As of December 7, 2021: https://nemsis.org/view-reports/public-reports/version-3-public-dashboards/public-naloxone-administration-dashboard/

National Highway Traffic Safety Administration, *National EMS Scope of Practice Model*, Washington, D.C.: U.S. Department of Transportation, 2007.

National Highway Traffic Safety Administration, *2011 National EMS Assessment*, Washington, D.C.: U.S. Department of Transportation, 2012.

National Highway Traffic Safety Administration, *National EMS Scope of Practice Model 2019*, Washington, D.C.: U.S. Department of Transportation, 2019.

National Institute for Occupational Safety and Health, "Fentanyl: Emergency Responders at Risk—Preventing Emergency Responders' Exposures to Illicit Drugs," webpage, undated. As of May 25, 2022:
https://www.cdc.gov/niosh/topics/fentanyl/risk.html

Neale, Joanne, and John Strang, "Naloxone—Does Over-Antagonism Matter? Evidence of Iatrogenic Harm After Emergency Treatment of Heroin/Opioid Overdose," *Addiction*, Vol. 110, No. 10, 2015, pp. 1644–1652.

NEMSIS—*See* National Emergency Medical Services Information System.

Neusteter, S. Rebecca, Maris Mapolski, Mawia Khogali, and Megan O'Toole, *The 911 Call Processing System: A Review of the Literature as It Relates to Policing*, New York: Vera Institute of Justice, July 2019.

Newberry, Bryce, "Austin Police Department Refuses Narcan Donation as Community Leaders Question Why, Overdoses Spike," KVUE, April 21, 2020.

Nguyen, Holly, and Brandy R. Parker, "Assessing the Effectiveness of New York's 911 Good Samaritan Law—Evidence from a Natural Experiment," *International Journal of Drug Policy*, Vol. 58, 2018, pp. 149–156.

NHTSA—*See* National Highway Traffic Safety Administration.

North Carolina Harm Reduction Coalition, "U.S. Law Enforcement Who Carry Naloxone," webpage, undated. As of May 25, 2022:
http://www.nchrc.org/law-enforcement/us-law-enforcement-who-carry-naloxone/

North Carolina Harm Reduction Coalition, "Monthly Update: December 2019," slides, 2020.

Office of National Drug Control Policy, *Advisory: Fentanyl Safety Recommendations for First Responders*, Washington, D.C., undated.

Ohio Attorney General, "AG Yost Sends $1.3 Million to Local Drug Abuse Response Teams," press release, October 28, 2019.

Olfson, Mark, Melanie Wall, Shuai Wang, Stephen Crystal, and Carlos Blanco, "Risks of Fatal Opioid Overdose During the First Year Following Nonfatal Overdose," *Drug and Alcohol Dependence*, Vol. 190, 2018, pp. 112–119.

Papazoglou, Konstantinos, and Brooke McQuerrey Tuttle, "Fighting Police Trauma: Practical Approaches to Addressing Psychological Needs of Officers," *Sage Open*, Vol. 8, No. 3, 2018.

Paris, F., "Many, But Not All, Berkshire Police Officers Carry Narcan. This Bill Could Make It Universal," *Berkshire Eagle*, October 23, 2021.

Pergolizzi, J. V., J. A. LeQuang, R. Taylor, and R. B. Raffa, "The Place of Community Rescue Naloxone in a Public Health Crisis of Opioid Overdose," *Pharmacology & Pharmacy*, Vol. 10, No. 2, 2019, pp. 61–81.

Pike, Erika, Martha Tillson, J. Matthew Webster, and Michele Staton, "A Mixed-Methods Assessment of the Impact of the Opioid Epidemic on First Responder Burnout," *Drug and Alcohol Dependence*, Vol. 205, 2019.

Police Executive Research Forum, *Policing on the Front Lines of the Opioid Crisis*, Washington, D.C.: Office of Community Oriented Policing Services, 2021.

Pollini, Robin A., Lisa McCall, Shruti H. Mehta, David D. Celentano, David Vlahov, and Steffanie A. Strathdee, "Response to Overdose Among Injection Drug Users," *American Journal of Preventive Medicine*, Vol. 31, No. 3, 2006, pp. 261–264.

Pollini, Robin A., Lisa McCall, Shruti H. Mehta, David Vlahov, and Steffanie A. Strathdee, "Non-Fatal Overdose and Subsequent Drug Treatment Among Injection Drug Users," *Drug and Alcohol Dependence*, Vol. 83, No. 2, 2006, pp. 104–110.

Prescription Drug Abuse Policy System, "Good Samaritan Overdose Prevention Laws," webpage, updated 2018. As of May 25, 2022: http://pdaps.org/datasets/good-samaritan-overdose-laws-1501695153

Ray, Bradley R., Evan M. Lowder, Aaron J. Kivisto, Peter Phalen, and Harold Gil, "EMS Naloxone Administration as Non-Fatal Opioid Overdose Surveillance: 6-Year Outcomes in Marion County, Indiana," *Addiction*, Vol. 113, No. 12, 2018, pp. 2271–2279.

Rees, Daniel I., Joseph J. Sabia, Laura M. Argys, Dhaval Dave, and Joshua Latshaw, "With a Little Help from My Friends: The Effects of Good Samaritan and Naloxone Access Laws on Opioid-Related Deaths," *Journal of Law and Economics*, Vol. 62, No. 1, 2019.

Reichert, J., *Fighting the Opioid Crisis Through Substance Use Disorder Treatment: A Study of a Police Program Model in Illinois*, Chicago, Ill., September 2017.

Reichert, Jessica, and Jac Charlier, *Exploring Effective Post-Opioid Overdose Reversal Responses for Law Enforcement and Other First Responders*, Chicago, Ill., November 29, 2017.

Reichert, Jessica, Arthur J. Lurigio, and Lauren Weisner, "The Administration of Naloxone by Law Enforcement Officers: A Statewide Survey of Police Chiefs in Illinois," *Law Enforcement Executive Forum*, Vol. 19, No. 4, 2019, pp. 1–14.

Rudisill, Toni Marie, Alexandria J. Ashraf, Herbert I. Linn, Sheena Sayres, James E. Jeffries, and Kelly K. Gurka, "Facilitators, Barriers and Lessons Learnt from the First State-Wide Naloxone Distribution Conducted in West Virginia," *Injury Prevention*, Vol. 27, No. 4, 2021, pp. 369–374.

Rudofossi, Daniel, *A Cop Doc's Guide to Public Safety Complex Trauma Syndrome: Using Five Police Personality Styles*, New York: Taylor and Francis, 2017.

Sacco, Paul, G. Jay Unick, and Christina Gray, "Enhancing Treatment Access Through 'Safe Stations,'" *Journal of Social Work Practice in the Addictions*, Vol. 18, No. 4, 2018, pp. 458–464.

Sanko, Stephen, Christianne Lane, and Marc Eckstein, "Effect of New 9-1-1 System on Efficiency of Initial Resource Assignment," *Prehospital Emergency Care*, Vol. 24, No. 5, 2020, pp. 634–643.

Saunders, Elizabeth, Stephen A. Metcalf, Olivia Walsh, Sarah K. Moore, Andrea Meier, Bethany McLeman, Samantha Auty, Sarah Bessen, and Lisa A. Marsch, "'You Can See Those Concentric Rings Going Out': Emergency Personnel's Experiences Treating Overdose and Perspectives on Policy-Level Responses to the Opioid Crisis in New Hampshire," *Drug and Alcohol Dependence*, Vol. 204, 2019.

Scharf, Becca M., David J. Sabat, James M. Brothers, Asa M. Margolis, and Matthew J. Levy, "Best Practices for a Novel EMS-Based Naloxone Leave Behind Program," *Prehospital Emergency Care*, Vol. 25, No. 3, 2021, pp. 418–426.

Seal, Karen H., Robert Thawley, Lauren Gee, Joshua Bamberger, Alex H. Kral, Dan Ciccarone, Moher Downing, and Brian R. Edlin, "Naloxone Distribution and Cardiopulmonary Resuscitation Training for Injection Drug Users to Prevent Heroin Overdose Death: A Pilot Intervention Study," *Journal of Urban Health*, Vol. 82, No. 2, 2005, pp. 303–311.

Sherman, Susan G., Donald S. Gann, Gregory Scott, Suzanne Carlberg, Dan Bigg, and Robert Heimer, "A Qualitative Study of Overdose Responses Among Chicago IDUs," *Harm Reduction Journal*, Vol. 5, No. 2, 2008.

Siegel, Zachary, "What's Really Going On in Those Police Fentanyl Exposure Videos?" *New York Times Magazine*, July 13, 2022.

Slade, H. K., "An Argument Against Narcan," Calibre Press, March 9, 2017. As of May 25, 2022: https://www.calibrepress.com/2017/03/an-argument-against-narcan/

Staats, Kathy, "Who Do You Want on Your 911 Call? The ALS Versus BLS Debate," presentation at the EMSAAC Conference, San Diego, Calif., May 9, 2017.

Streisel, Shannon, Christy Visher, Daniel O'Connell, and Steven S. Martin, "Using Law Enforcement to Improve Treatment Initiation and Recovery," *Federal Probation Journal*, Vol. 83, No. 2, 2019.

Taymour, Rekar K., Mahshid Abir, Margaret Chamberlin, Robert B. Dunne, Mark Lowell, Kathy Wahl, and Jacqueline Scott, "Policy, Practice, and Research Agenda for Emergency Medical Services Oversight: A Systematic Review and Environmental Scan," *Prehospital and Disaster Medicine*, Vol. 33, No. 1, 2018, pp. 89–97.

Thompson, Christie, "This City Stopped Sending Police to Every 911 Call," The Marshall Project, July 24, 2020.

Tobin, Karin E., Melissa A. Davey, and Carl A. Latkin, "Calling Emergency Medical Services During Drug Overdose: An Examination of Individual, Social and Setting Correlates," *Addiction*, Vol. 100, No. 3, 2005, pp. 397–404.

Townsend, Tarlise, Freida Blostein, Tran Doan, Samantha Madson-Olson, Paige Galecki, and David W. Hutton, "Cost-Effectiveness Analysis of Alternative Naloxone Distribution Strategies: First Responder and Lay Distribution in the United States," *International Journal of Drug Policy*, Vol. 75, 2019.

Wagner, Karla D., L. James Bovet, Bruce Haynes, Alfred Joshua, and Peter J. Davidson, "Training Law Enforcement to Respond to Opioid Overdose with Naloxone: Impact on Knowledge, Attitudes, and Interactions with Community Members," *Drug and Alcohol Dependence*, Vol. 165, 2016, pp. 22–28.

Wagner, Karla D., Robert W. Harding, Richard Kelley, Brian Labus, Silvia R. Verdugo, Elizabeth Copulsky, Jeanette M. Bowles, Maria Luisa Mittal, and Peter J. Davidson, "Post-Overdose Interventions Triggered by Calling 911: Centering the Perspectives of People Who Use Drugs (PWUDs)," *PLoS One*, Vol. 14, No. 10, 2019.

Wagner, Karla D., Thomas W. Valente, Mark Casanova, Susan M. Partovi, Brett M. Mendenhall, James H. Hundley, Mario Gonzalez, and Jennifer B. Unger, "Evaluation of an Overdose Prevention and Response Training Programme for Injection Drug Users in the Skid Row Area of Los Angeles, CA," *International Journal of Drug Policy*, Vol. 21, No. 3, 2010, pp. 186–193.

Watson, Dennis P., Bradley Ray, Lisa Robison, Philip Huynh, Emily Sightes, La Shea Walker, Krista Brucker, and Joan Duwve, "Lay Responder Naloxone Access and Good Samaritan Law Compliance: Postcard Survey Results from 20 Indiana Counties," *Harm Reduction Journal*, Vol. 15, No. 1, 2018.

Weiner, Scott G., Patricia M. Mitchell, Elizabeth S. Temin, Breanne K. Langlois, and K. Sophia Dyer, "Use of Intranasal Naloxone by Basic Life Support Providers," *Prehospital Emergency Care*, Vol. 21, No. 3, 2017, pp. 322–326.

Wermeling, Daniel P., "Review of Naloxone Safety for Opioid Overdose: Practical Considerations for New Technology and Expanded Public Access," *Therapeutic Advances in Drug Safety*, Vol. 6, No. 1, 2015, pp. 20–31.

Wheeler, Eliza, Katie Burk, Hilary McQuie, and Sharon Stancliff, *Guide to Developing and Managing Overdose Prevention and Take-Home Naloxone Projects*, New York: National Harm Reduction Coalition, Fall 2012.

Wise, Stefanie L., Clifford L. Freeman, and Peter F. Edemekong, "EMS Pre-Arrival Instructions," *StatPearls*, Treasure Island, Fla.: StatPearls Publishing, 2019.

Wood, Claire A., Alex Duello, Phil Horn, Rachel Winograd, Lillie Jackson, Sandra Mayen, and Karen Wallace, "Overdose Response Training and Naloxone Distribution Among Rural First Responders," *Journal of Rural Mental Health*, Vol. 45, No. 3, 2021, pp. 207–218.

World Health Organization, *Community Management of Opioid Overdose*, Geneva, 2014.

Zadoretzky, Cathy, Courtney McKnight, Heidi Bramson, Don Des Jarlais, Maxine Phillips, Mark Hammer, and Mary Ellen Cala, "The New York 911 Good Samaritan Law and Opioid Overdose Prevention Among People Who Inject Drugs," *World Medical & Health Policy*, Vol. 9, No. 3, 2017, pp. 318–340.

CHAPTER TEN

Child Welfare

Dionne Barnes-Proby

Overview

Children of parents who struggle with substance use, including opioid use, suffer a wide variety of adverse consequences and are at high risk of becoming involved with the child welfare system. The child welfare system comprises a group of public and private services designed to achieve three primary goals: (1) ensure that children are safe, (2) ensure that children live in stable and permanent environments, and (3) support child well-being.

Most children initially become involved in the child welfare system after a report to local authorities of suspected child maltreatment (i.e., neglect or physical, emotional, or sexual abuse). Child Protective Services (CPS), a component of the child welfare system, investigates these allegations. Substantiated cases are assessed further to determine the level of risk of continued or future maltreatment. Depending on the level of risk, children are permitted to remain in their home while the family receives supportive services (e.g., parent education, planning to ensure child safety, counseling), or they are cared for in an out-of-home placement (e.g., foster care, kinship care, congregate care).

Research indicates that it is preferable for children to remain in the home with their parents, which is most often the outcome for children who are involved with the child welfare system (National Conference of State Legislatures, 2019). Parents of children who are placed outside the home may be offered services to reduce the risk of future maltreatment in hopes of reunification. Concurrently, alternatives for permanency are explored, including adoption or transferring custody to a relative. Permanency plans must be approved by a dependency court within 12 months of the child entering foster care.

After a significant decline in child welfare caseloads from 2006 to 2012 (Child Trends, 2019), the opioid crisis appears to have sparked an increase in foster care placements. Between 2012 and 2016, there was a 10-percent increase in the national foster care caseload, with some states experiencing an increase greater than 50 percent (i.e., Alabama, Georgia, Minnesota, Indiana, Montana, and New Hampshire; Radel et al., 2018a). As caseloads surged, a greater proportion of children in the foster care system were placed in kinship foster care (an increase from 24 percent in 2008 to 32 percent in 2016; Generations United, 2018). Even more children are living with relatives outside the child welfare system. The timing of this rise in foster and kinship care appears to correlate with the national rise in drug overdose death rates, which increased by three times from 1999 to 2016 (Ghertner, Waters, et al., 2018).

Once placed in out-of-home care, children with opioid-dependent parents typically stay in care longer and are less likely to reunify with their families (Falletta et al., 2018; Hall et al., 2016). In addition, child welfare agencies in some communities observe intergenerational substance use problems, which makes it challenging to find qualified relative caregivers and results in a greater need for nonrelative foster families.

Most parents who have opioid use disorder (OUD) or who use opioid medications for non-prescribed purposes want to be good parents and experience great moral injury when their substance use disorder (SUD) hinders their ability to properly fulfill parental roles (Snoek and Horstkötter, 2021). Parental opioid use can generate adverse outcomes for children, in both the short term and the long term. Children exposed to opioids prenatally may be born with neonatal opioid withdrawal syndrome (NOWS), which is associated with many conditions at birth, including low birth weight, respiratory problems, and other developmental limitations (Krans and Patrick, 2016), as well as behavioral, cognitive, and psychomotor issues in early childhood (Normile, Hanlon, and Eichner, 2018). Parental substance use is also associated with increased risk of trauma, adverse childhood experiences, and high rates of behavior problems for older children and adolescents, including truancy, school suspension, involvement with the police, and substance use (Mirick and Steenrod, 2016; Normile, Hanlon, and Eichner, 2018).

Opioid misuse can also affect the parent-child dyad, as well as caretakers of dependent children (i.e., children under the custody of a child welfare agency). Separating children from their families detrimentally affects both parents and children, reducing opportunities for parent-child bonding and, possibly, negatively affecting the child's ability to form new attachments (Mirick and Steenrod, 2016). Removing children may also have detrimental effects on treatment outcomes for parents: For example, removing a child is associated with an increased risk of overdose (Thumath et al., 2021), and women tend to stay in treatment longer if they can continue to care for their children while in treatment (Health Resources and Services Administration [HRSA], 2018). Given the negative effects of separation on both the parent and the child, child welfare agencies attempt to preserve the family unit while providing supportive services to ensure parental health and child well-being and safety.

Key Interactions with Other Components of the Ecosystem

Families involved with child welfare often face a plethora of interrelated issues, including financial instability, housing and food insecurity, domestic violence, mental illness, long histories of traumatic experiences, involvement with the criminal legal system, and health issues. To address these challenges, child welfare agencies may partner with key systems that are focused on **harm reduction** and **community engagement, behavioral health care and substance use treatment, the criminal legal system,** and **education**.

In part, state policies drive the link between the publicly funded health care and child welfare systems. Almost half of the states consider substance use during pregnancy to be reportable child abuse and/or require health care professionals to report suspected prenatal drug use to child welfare authorities. This can discourage mothers from seeking prenatal care because of fears that they may lose custody of their children.

There is also an intersection between child welfare and behavioral **health care and substance use treatment systems**. This collaboration is crucial: Children spend less time in foster care when parents (1) engage in treatment quickly, (2) spend more time in treatment, or (3) successfully complete it. Recognizing the benefits of treatment, some child welfare agencies have staff who specialize in SUD treatment colocated in their offices. One often-cited, evidence-based example of a child welfare–based program is the Sobriety Treatment and Recovery Team, which relies on collaboration between child welfare workers and community providers to provide direct services to children, referrals for supportive services, and rapid access to SUD treatment, including medications for OUD (MOUD). Families who participate in this program enter state custody at almost half the rate of similar families, and more than 40 percent were reunified when their cases were closed (Hall et al., 2016), although other variables may have contributed to these outcomes.

Strong linkages also exist between the child welfare and **criminal legal agencies,** including family and criminal courts. Examples of partnerships between the two systems include family drug courts and safe baby courts, which provide judicial monitoring, wraparound services, and substance use treatment with the goal of family reunification. In addition, Arizona and Tennessee are pilot testing pre-petition court programs that identify and support families who are at risk for involvement in the child welfare system because of an SUD (National Judicial Opioid Task Force, 2019).

Because schools are a primary place where children spend their time outside the home, prevention and intervention strategies are often implemented in the **school setting**. Child welfare systems may partner with schools to ensure that administrators, educators, and counselors are trained to (1) identify challenges and intervene to support children with opioid-dependent parents and (2) promote access to academic supports for children who need individualized education plans as a result of parents' prior exposure to opioids.

Child welfare also interacts with the **employment system**, given the direct relationship with economic status, and is closely linked to labor force participation and family and child well-being. Furthermore, parents with OUD who are involved with the child welfare system often rely on a wide variety of **social service programs**. Child welfare agencies have sought to collaborate with social service agencies to help families meet their concrete needs in an effort to keep families together and prevent future risk of child maltreatment.

Lastly, the child welfare system interacts with **first responders**, who are mandatory reporters of child maltreatment. The relationship navigates a difficult balance regarding the need to ensure the safety and well-being of children while minimizing fears of calling 911 in the event of an opioid-related emergency.

Policy Opportunities and Considerations

One legislative effort that specifically aims to address the opioid crisis through collaboration between the child welfare and substance use treatment systems is the Families First Prevention Services Act of 2018 (FFPSA). Effective October 1, 2019, FFPSA aims to preserve families by allowing states, for the first time, to use funds for evidence-based and trauma-informed (i.e., with awareness of and sensitivity to the needs of trauma-exposed children and families) **prevention services** (e.g., mental health, substance use, and parenting skills) for parents at risk of child welfare involvement. States have struggled to implement FFPSA because of limited capacity and financial resources, as well as misinterpretation of the law (Jordan and McKlindon, 2020; Patrick et al., 2019). In December 2019, Congress passed the Family First Transition Act to help states overcome these implementation challenges. As of May 2020, 25 states had enacted some portion of FFPSA.

Additional reforms to child welfare system policies should be informed by the substance use treatment system to address barriers to best practices for **treating parents** with SUDs. For example, the Adoption and Safe Families Act requires termination of parental rights if a parent is not ready for reunification after the child has been in foster care for 15 of the past 22 months (Tabashneck, 2018). As a result, when parents struggle with OUD, they generally are not afforded the time to engage in treatment while retaining custody of their children; because of federal guidelines on permanency planning, they sometimes are unable to complete their treatment plans in time to reunite with their children. In addition, despite evidence that MOUD are more effective than other OUD treatments and that parents who receive MOUD may be more likely to have better permanency outcomes (Hall et al., 2016), child welfare professionals may be reticent to allow children to remain in their homes or be reunited with their families if the parent is receiving MOUD.

Although parent and child outcomes improve when parents and children engage in comprehensive family-centered treatment that meets the needs of the whole family, there is a dearth of family-oriented treatment programs in most child welfare agencies. And family drug courts—which, in most cases, focus on the whole family—are underutilized because of a lack of awareness and lack of buy-in from child welfare agencies (Children and Family Futures, 2017).

One risk of attempting more-holistic approaches and greater coordination across contexts is an expansion in duties and expectations for individual agencies without a concomitant increase in resources. As a result, one or more systems may become overburdened. The opioid crisis has significantly overburdened the underresourced child welfare system. The system cannot sustain the current rate of growth in the national child welfare caseload without additional resources and extensive collaboration with other key systems. Partnerships are critical to prevent the involvement of child welfare, preserve families when possible, support parent engagement in evidence-based treatment, and, ultimately, improve child outcomes.

Introduction

Children of parents who struggle with substance use, including opioid use, are at high risk of becoming involved with the child welfare system because of concerns of child maltreatment, which includes abuse or neglect. Research shows that there is a greater likelihood that children with parents who use substances will experience abuse or neglect when compared with children in other environments (Child Welfare Information Gateway, 2014; Spehr et al., 2017) and have unstable and unstructured home settings (Ghertner, Waters, et al., 2018). Despite parents' desire to provide a safe and healthy environment for their children, parental use of opioids can compromise the safety of children. In response to concerns about child safety, all states; Washington, D.C.; Guam; and the U.S. Virgin Islands have child protection laws that address parental substance use (Child Welfare Information Gateway, 2019a). In addition, some states have expanded their definitions of child abuse and neglect to include parental use of substances that diminish the parent's ability to care for a child.

Children who are victims of maltreatment may be referred to the child welfare system for protection and support. The child welfare system comprises federal, state, tribal, and public child welfare agencies working in collaboration with other public and private child-serving agencies and communities to achieve three primary goals:

1. **safety** to ensure children are safe and protected from abuse and neglect
2. **permanency** to ensure children live in stable and permanent environments
3. **well-being** to meet the physical, emotional, and social needs of children and youth who have experienced and/or been exposed to trauma (DePanfilis, 2018).

Although the federal government has a major supportive role in administering funds and developing legislation for child welfare system programs, states and local governments are primarily responsible for service delivery (Child Welfare Information Gateway, 2020b). The Children's Bureau, an agency of the U.S. Department of Health and Human Services' Administration for Children and Families, implements federal family and child legislation, and each state establishes its own child welfare system, which often is administered at the county level. To receive funding for child welfare programs, states and local governments are required to comply with federal requirements and guidelines. The key federal legislation that significantly enhanced the child welfare system is the Child Abuse Prevention and Treatment Act (CAPTA), which was enacted in 1974 and most recently reauthorized in 2019 (Child Welfare Information Gateway, 2019b). CAPTA provides federal funding to states to support prevention, assessment, investigation, prosecution, and treatment services for child maltreatment (Child Welfare Information Gateway, 2019b). The child welfare system is also supported by Titles IV-B and IV-E of the Social Security Act.

Most children initially become involved in the child welfare system after a report to local authorities of suspected *child maltreatment*, defined by CAPTA as serious harm—neglect, physical abuse, sexual abuse, or emotional abuse—to children by parents or primary caregivers. CPS, a component of the child welfare system, receives and investigates these allegations and provides a broad variety of services to promote child safety and well-being. Substantiated cases are assessed further to determine the level of risk of continued or future maltreatment. In 2018, CPS received an estimated 4.3 million referrals for alleged neglect or abuse, of which more than 50 percent were screened for either investigation or alternative response (i.e., a response other than an investigation to determine child and family needs; U.S. Department of Health and Human Services, Administration for Children and Families, Administration on Children, Youth and Families, Children's Bureau, 2020). The vast majority of cases are unsubstantiated. Victimization rates are highest for children younger than age one, girls, and Native American and Black children. For substantiated reports, depending on the level of risk, children are permitted to remain in their home while the family receives supportive services (e.g., parent education, planning to ensure child safety, counseling), or the children are cared for in an out-of-home placement (e.g., foster care, kinship or relative care, congregate or group care). Most children remain in their home; for those who are placed outside the home, their parents may be offered services to reduce the risk of future maltreatment in the hope that the parents will be reunited with their children. There are as many as 15 reasons for removing a child from their home identified in the Adoption and Foster Care Analysis and Reporting System, "a federally mandated data collection system that receives case-level information on all children in foster care in the United States": physical abuse, sexual abuse, neglect, child disability, child behavior problem, child alcohol use, child drug use, parental alcohol use, **parental drug use**, parental death, parental incarceration, caretaker inability to cope, abandonment, relinquishment, and inadequate housing (Meinhofer et al., 2020, p. 2). According to a 2021 Children's Bureau report, child removal was the result of parental drug use—an official child welfare agency designation that is applied when the primary caretaker has a "compulsive use of drugs that is not of a temporary nature" (Meinhofer et al., 2020, p. 2)—in more than one-third (35.3 percent) of cases (Child Welfare Information Gateway, 2021b).

Foster care with nonrelative caregivers and foster care with relative caregivers are the most common types of out-of-home placement (46 percent and 32 percent, respectively; National Conference of State Legislatures, 2019). Children of parents with substance use issues are more likely to be placed in and remain in out-of-home care for a longer period than other children (Child Welfare Information Gateway, 2014). Native American, Black, and multiracial children are disproportionately represented in foster care (Meinhofer et al., 2020). While children are in foster care, the child welfare system develops a plan for reunification with the parent and explores alternatives for permanency, which may include adoption or transferring custody to a relative. One of the primary goals of *concurrent planning* is to reduce the timeline for the child to achieve a permanent placement either with a safe return to their parents or through another custody option (Child Welfare Information Gateway, 2021a). Permanency plans must be approved by a dependency court within 12 months of the child entering foster care.

Family or juvenile dependency courts also have a critical role in the child welfare process. Once a child welfare agency determines that a child should be placed in foster care, there is a series of hearings with a judge to assess the veracity of the allegations and determine where the child will live. If the judge agrees with the child welfare agency's determination that the child should be placed in out-of-home care, the judge grants legal custody of the child to the child welfare agency, and the family is assigned a caseworker. The caseworker develops a case plan, with family reunification as the primary goal. Case plans outline specific tasks and activities that parents are required to complete to improve their ability to provide a protective environment for their children (e.g., attend anger management classes, complete a substance use treatment program, participate in supervised or unsupervised visits with the child). Throughout the process, the judge and child welfare agency are responsible for deciding what types of services, actions, and orders serve the best interest of the child. Figure 10.1 illustrates the child welfare case flow process, from allegation to final disposition.

Families involved with the child welfare system often face a wide variety of interrelated issues, such as health issues, mental illness, involvement with the criminal legal system, and financial instability, which necessitate collaboration with other key systems to address these challenges. Figure 10.2 illustrates the various systems with which the child welfare system interacts to support children and families affected by SUD, including opioid use. In the remainder of this chapter, we review specific examples of these interactions and offer policy considerations that may contribute to improving the outcomes of children, parents, and families affected by SUD.

System Components and How They Interact with Opioids

Drug overdose deaths involving opioids have increased annually since the beginning of the 21st century. In the span of 20 years, the United States has seen a nearly sevenfold increase in the per capita death rate involving opioid overdoses, from nearly three per 100,000 in 2000 to more than 20 per 100,000 in 2020. Since 2016, opioid overdose death rates have surpassed fatalities for every other form of accidental death, including those involving firearms or motor vehicles (Centers for Disease Control and Prevention, 2016; Centers for Disease Control and Prevention, 2021; National Highway Traffic Safety Administration, 2020). A co-occurring outcome of drug dependency epidemics is the removal of vulnerable children from their homes. During the crack epidemic, the number of children in foster care climbed from 400,000 in 1990 to an apex of 567,000 in 1999, and it was not until 2012 that the number of children in foster care declined to less than 400,000 (Kohomban, Rodriguez, and Haskins, 2018). One critical lesson learned from prior epidemics is that a singular focus on criminalizing parental substance use has detrimental effects on children and families. A public health response is preferable because it promotes holistic efforts to support both parents and children affected by substance use.

FIGURE 10.1

Child Welfare Case Flow

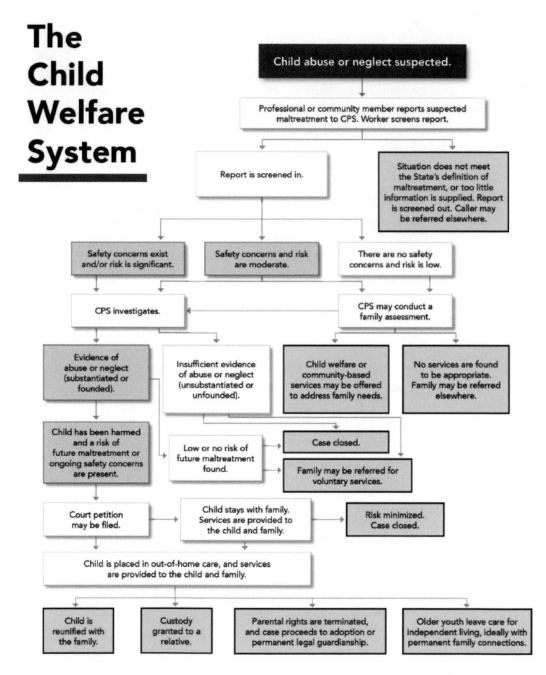

The Child Welfare System

Child abuse or neglect suspected.

Professional or community member reports suspected maltreatment to CPS. Worker screens report.

Report is screened in.

Situation does not meet the State's definition of maltreatment, or too little information is supplied. Report is screened out. Caller may be referred elsewhere.

Safety concerns exist and/or risk is significant.

Safety concerns and risk are moderate.

There are no safety concerns and risk is low.

CPS investigates.

CPS may conduct a family assessment.

Evidence of abuse or neglect (substantiated or founded).

Insufficient evidence of abuse or neglect (unsubstantiated or unfounded).

Child welfare or community-based services may be offered to address family needs.

No services are found to be appropriate. Family may be referred elsewhere.

Child has been harmed and a risk of future maltreatment or ongoing safety concerns are present.

Low or no risk of future maltreatment found.

Case closed.

Family may be referred for voluntary services.

Court petition may be filed.

Child stays with family. Services are provided to the child and family.

Risk minimized. Case closed.

Child is placed in out-of-home care, and services are provided to the child and family.

Child is reunified with the family.

Custody granted to a relative.

Parental rights are terminated, and case proceeds to adoption or permanent legal guardianship.

Older youth leave care for independent living, ideally with permanent family connections.

SOURCE: Child Welfare Information Gateway, 2020b, p. 8.

FIGURE 10.2

The Child Welfare System and Its Interactions

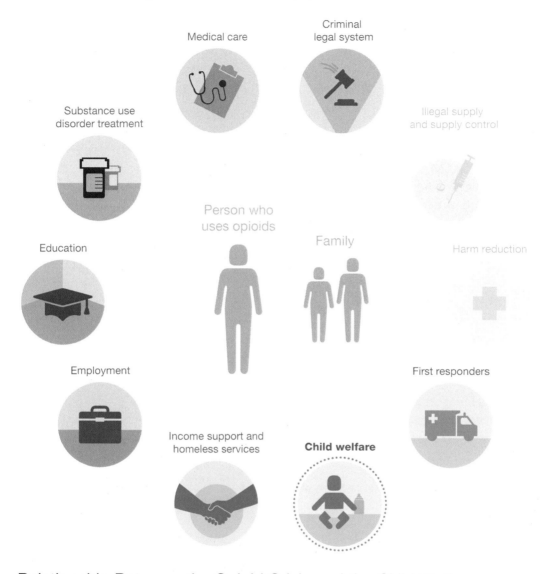

Relationship Between the Opioid Crisis and the Child Welfare System

After a significant decline in child welfare caseloads in the first decade of the 21st century, the opioid crisis appears to have resulted in an increase in child welfare caseloads and foster care placements. Between 2012 and 2016, there was a 10-percent increase in the national foster care caseload, with some states (i.e., Alabama, Georgia, Indiana, Minnesota, Montana, and New Hampshire) experiencing an increase greater than 50 percent (Radel et al., 2018a). Although the research to determine a causal link between child welfare caseloads and opioid use is nascent, Figure 10.3 illustrates a corresponding increase in opioid overdose deaths and foster care entries starting in 2013, although the increase in foster care entries is more gradual.

Other research demonstrates a positive relationship between opioid use and child maltreatment, as measured by hospital discharges involving prescription opioid overdose and hospital discharges related to child maltreatment (Wolf et al., 2016), reports to the child welfare system of infants with likely NOWS (Lynch et al., 2018), and drug overdose death and drug-hospitalization rates and measures of child welfare caseloads (Ghertner, Baldwin, et al., 2018). However, there is substantial variation in state-level associations between child removals and opioid prescription rates (a measure of potential opioid use). One study found a positive association in 23 states, a negative association in 15 states, and 12 states that did not have a statistically significant association (Quast, 2018).

Among children in the foster care system, the proportion of children in kinship foster care increased from 24 percent to 32 percent from 2008 to 2016, and even more children are living with relatives outside the child welfare system (Generations United, 2018). According to 2009 and 2014 data from the National Survey on Drug Use and Health, 8.7 million children under the age of 18 (12 percent of children in the United States) lived in households with at least one parent who had an SUD, and 2.1 million children (3 percent) lived in households in which at least one parent had an SUD associated with an illicit substance in the past year (Lipari and Van Horn, 2017). Although these children are at greater risk of child welfare system involvement, many have not yet experienced the type of crisis that often precipitates child removal. This rise in foster and kinship care appears to correlate with the national rise

FIGURE 10.3

Overdose Deaths and Foster Care Caseloads, 2002–2016

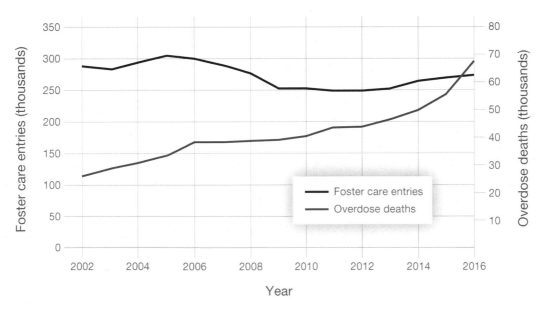

SOURCE: Adapted from Radel et al., 2018a, p. 3.

in drug overdose death rates, which increased by three times from 1999 to 2016 (Ghertner, Waters, et al., 2018).

Despite the increase in kinship care provision, child welfare agencies in some communities observe intergenerational substance use, which makes it challenging to find qualified relative caregivers and results in a greater need for nonrelative foster families (Mathur and Torres, 2018; Winstanley and Stover, 2019). Some child welfare agencies have ramped up recruitment to increase the already short supply of foster families to address the surge in caseloads (Haskins, Kohomban, and Rodriguez, 2019).

Cases involving parents with SUD are the most complex, most challenging, and most prevalent, with 50 percent to 80 percent of families within the child welfare system affected in some way by an SUD (Bosk et al., 2019). Between 2008 and 2017, Native American children represented the highest level and fastest growth in parental substance use entries into foster care when compared with children of other races and ethnicities, as well as the highest level of disproportionality in foster care (Meinhofer et al., 2020). For the most part, child welfare agencies do not systematically track the type of drug used by parents; rather, they document general substance use as a possible contributing factor during their investigations. However, according to data from treatment providers in one study, approximately one-third of mothers in treatment for OUD ($n = 211$) have had a child removed from their homes (Taplin and Mattick, 2015). In addition, research shows that children with substance-dependent parents experience the worst permanency outcomes at every point in the child welfare process, including lower reunification rates, longer stays in care, and reentry into foster care (Bosk et al., 2019; Falletta et al., 2018; Hall et al., 2016; Sanmartin et al., 2020). Altogether, the opioid crisis has resulted in substantial costs for the child welfare system. Some estimates have put these costs at nearly $3 billion between 2011 and 2016 (Crowley et al., 2019).

Effects of Parental Substance Use on Children

In addition to the effects of interaction with the child welfare system, children experience short- and long-term adverse outcomes from before birth to adolescence as a result of parental opioid use. Children prenatally exposed to opioids are sometimes born with NOWS, which refers to withdrawal symptoms resulting from exposure to a variety of substances, including opioids (Patrick, 2020). The number of children reported to have NOWS has increased substantially since 2004, rising from seven to 27 cases per 1,000 admissions to neonatal intensive care units for NOWS between 2004 and 2013 (Morton and Wells, 2017). Children born with NOWS experience many conditions, including low birth weight, sleep disturbances, gastrointestinal issues, and respiratory problems (HRSA, 2018). Overall, however, NOWS is highly treatable and need not lead to long-term harms. Children born with NOWS also have a higher rate of cognitive impairments and executive function deficits, as well as other developmental limitations (Krans and Patrick, 2016; Mathur and Torres, 2018).

In early childhood, children who were drug-exposed in utero exhibit behavioral, cognitive, and psychomotor issues (Normile, Hanlon, and Eichner, 2018). Parental substance use is also associated with increased risk of trauma and adverse childhood experiences. Children are at risk of depression, anxiety, and other trauma or mental health issues, as well as difficulty learning and concentrating, controlling their responses to stress, and forming trusting relationships (Child Welfare Information Gateway, 2014; Stulac et al., 2019). School absenteeism is also a problem, because parents are unable to take their children to school because of drug use. In addition, there has been a significant increase in pediatric hospitalizations resulting from opioid ingestion and poisoning for all ages, but especially for children ages five and younger (Normile, Hanlon, and Eichner, 2018).

Although there has been extensive research on prenatal drug exposure and the effect of parental opioid use on infants and young children, as well as on child welfare policies that address these issues, less is known about older children who are reared in homes with a parent who misuses opioids. Older children and adolescents are at risk of higher rates of mental health and behavior problems, including aggression, truancy, school suspension, impaired social functioning, and involvement with the juvenile justice system (Morton and Wells, 2017). These youth may feel responsible for their parents' choices to use substances, and they may become "parentified" as they take on the added burden of caring for their parents and siblings in the absence of adequate parental supervision and support (Stulac et al., 2019). Adolescents with prolonged exposure to parents' substance use may also turn to substance use, including opioids, as a way of coping with stress or because drug use has been normalized in their households (Mirick and Steenrod, 2016; Normile, Hanlon, and Eichner, 2018; Stulac et al., 2019). A literature review revealed the rate of substance use for youth living with a parent with OUD ranged from 47 percent to 59 percent (Morton and Wells, 2017).

Opioid use can also directly affect the parent and child unit and negatively affect a parent's ability to function effectively in their role. Parents with an SUD often

- have concurrent mental health problems, histories of trauma, posttraumatic stress disorder, interpersonal violence, and social isolation, which can contribute to the development of maladaptive parenting skills, including a reduced capacity to meet their children's basic needs and respond to child cues
- have difficulty regulating emotions
- prioritize time using or trying to acquire drugs
- are sometimes incarcerated (Child Welfare Information Gateway, 2014; Mirick and Steenrod, 2016; Substance Abuse and Mental Health Services Administration, 2016; Stulac et al., 2019).

In these instances, as children learn that they cannot count on their parents to meet their emotional and physical needs, they begin to view relationships as disengaged, unpredictable, and unsafe, which can affect their ability to form relationships in adulthood (Bosk et al., 2019).

However, separating children from their families can have detrimental effects on both parents and children as well, including reducing opportunities for parent-child attachment and, possibly, negatively affecting the child's ability to form new attachment relationships (Mirick and Steenrod, 2016). Parent treatment outcomes also suffer from child removal: Women tend to stay in treatment longer if they are able to continue to care for their children while in treatment (HRSA, 2018), and child removal is associated with higher risks of maternal overdose (Thumath et al., 2021). By contrast, parents who retain custody of their children have higher recovery rates compared with those whose children were removed from their homes (Casey Family Programs, 2019; Winstanley and Stover, 2019).

Key Interactions with Other Components of the Ecosystem

Medical Care

In part, state policies drive the link between the publicly funded health care and child welfare systems. Almost half of all states consider substance use during pregnancy to be reportable child abuse and/or require health care professionals to report suspected prenatal drug use to child welfare authorities (Stulac et al., 2019). This can discourage mothers from seeking prenatal care because of fears that they may lose custody of their children (Sanmartin et al., 2020). In addition, pediatricians and primary care providers are mandated reporters of suspected child maltreatment (Substance Abuse and Mental Health Services Administration, 2016), although maltreatment should not be a prerequisite for these professionals to intervene and offer support to parents who experience an SUD.

Primary Care Providers

Federal and state law, policies, and procedures address prenatal drug exposure and the experiences of children living with a parent with a drug dependency. Specifically, there are civil child welfare statutes in 24 states and in Washington, D.C., in which substance use during pregnancy is considered child abuse, which could result in the termination of parental rights (Stulac et al., 2019). Health care personnel are required to notify CPS of children who are born exposed to substances and to create a safe plan for infants. For example, New Hampshire recently passed legislation requiring health care providers to develop safe care plans for any new infant born with substance exposure. It should be noted that the planning for safe care has been an explicit requirement of child welfare agencies since 2003, but recent legislation (e.g., the SUPPORT for Patients and Communities Act of 2018) in response to the opioid crisis has intensified efforts to support multisystem safe care planning (National Center on Substance Abuse and Child Welfare, undated-a). This plan should include a treatment plan that addresses the health and safety needs of the infant, as well as parents' SUD treatment needs. This law also clarifies that prenatal substance exposure does not by itself warrant mandatory reporting and aims to improve the identification of parental OUD and to connect children and parents to services. However, given wide variation across the states in terms of the requirements for reporting suspected prenatal and postnatal substance use, primary care providers sometimes struggle to interpret these policies and to understand how the child welfare system will respond.

Pediatric providers' responsibilities extend beyond reporting parental substance use. These providers are also expected to respond to the opioid crisis by identifying intrauterine exposure, screening for parental opioid use, being knowledgeable about child welfare involvement, and understanding current health policy related to caring for children and families with SUDs. However, they experience multiple challenges in these areas, including lack of reliable indications of prenatal drug exposure, lack of a universal screening protocol to assess for parental substance use, and limited screening tools for parental opioid use in a pediatric setting (Spehr et al., 2017). And although both pediatricians and child welfare agencies seek to promote child safety and well-being, there is a conflict in their approach to care. Pediatric care providers are sometimes reluctant to screen for parental substance use because they are concerned about the detrimental effect that screening may have on the relationship with their patients, and they are hesitant to report substance use because they fear that parents who misuse substances will not engage in health care because of the risk of child welfare involvement (Spehr et al., 2017). It is important for pediatric primary care providers and child welfare organizations to seek to understand and reconcile their approaches and work collaboratively to achieve their shared goal of child well-being. Child welfare agencies should proactively engage primary care providers to facilitate an understanding of the roles of their agencies and relevant internal and external policies and procedures, and providers should seek to leverage child welfare agencies as a resource to ensure comprehensive care for children and families. In addition, there should be increased efforts to understand how best to honor a patient's privacy and confidentiality rights and build trusting relationships with parents while still protecting children.

Mental Health

National data indicate that just more than one-third of adults with SUDs have a co-occurring mental illness, including posttraumatic stress disorder, often the result of childhood trauma (Child Welfare Information Gateway, 2014). Research estimates that up to 75 percent of individuals who have accessed drug dependency treatment services have experienced child maltreatment or trauma (Bosk et al., 2019). Adults who were victims of child abuse or neglect are at greater likelihood of opioid dependence and of their children becoming involved in the child welfare system (Morton and Wells, 2017). Substance use and mental health issues are not uncommon for child welfare–involved families. Approximately 60 percent of child welfare–involved caregivers struggle with issues related to substance use, and 30 percent to 35 percent experience mental health difficulties (treated or untreated), which can be a key barrier to family reunification (Mowbray et al., 2017). Because child welfare agencies provide a variety of services to families in an effort to promote child safety and permanency, they typically screen parents to identify a need for substance use and mental health services. It is common for child welfare staff to make referrals for treatment to address these needs.

Medicaid

Medicaid provides resources for medical care, including substance use treatment, for both parents and children. Nearly one-third of people receiving treatment for OUD are insured by Medicaid (Leslie et al., 2019). Children born exposed to opioids also benefit from Medicaid, which funds 80 percent of their medical treatment (Ko et al., 2016). However, proposed changes to Medicaid that would roll back program expansions that provided funding that some states used to increase addiction treatment for low-income individuals, including those with OUD (Young and Zur, 2017), do not account for the current crisis and could have negative implications for families (Feder, Letourneau, and Brook, 2019; Mathur and Torres, 2018). For example, parents with OUD may have a difficult time meeting imposed work requirements to receive benefits (Sommers et al., 2019). Another challenge that affects parents is limited access to evidence-based treatment, such as MOUD, because physicians who prescribe MOUD (e.g., buprenorphine) often do not accept Medicaid (Radel et al., 2018b). In addition, there are Medicaid utilization restrictions (e.g., prior authorization and annual limits) that limit the availability of buprenorphine (Andrews et al., 2019). And funding cuts through caps or block grants could significantly affect access to mental health and physical health services for children in foster care (Mathur and Torres, 2018). The child welfare system should ensure coordination with Medicaid to support coverage for substance use treatment for pregnant women, parents, and adolescents.

Criminal Legal System

Strong linkages exist between the child welfare and criminal legal agencies, including correctional facilities, community supervision, and family and criminal courts. Some parents who have an open child welfare case because of substance use also have an active criminal case. Among children who enter the child welfare system, 15 percent to 20 percent have an incarcerated parent (Johnson-Peterkin, 2003). Parent involvement in the lives of children placed in out-of-home care because of parental incarceration is often undervalued and unsupported (LaLiberte, Barry, and Walthour, 2018). However, to support child well-being, it is important for the child welfare and criminal legal systems to collaborate to maintain the parent-child relationship (LaLiberte, Barry, and Walthour, 2018). One strategy that child welfare practitioners can use to cultivate this relationship is to include activities in their case plans to encourage parent-child contact (e.g., letters, phone calls, in-person visits) and work with prison-based program staff to assist parents with meeting their child welfare requirements, including treatment services for substance use issues (LaLiberte, Barry, and Walthour, 2018). In addition, because many parents are incarcerated as a result of opioid-related offenses, it is important for child welfare professionals to understand the collateral consequences of incarceration (e.g., unemployment, lack of affordable housing, limited access to drug treatment services, conditions of parole or probation) and work with parents before and after their releases and with prison and community supervision agencies to support successful family reunification.

Another example of a partnership between the child welfare and criminal legal systems is family drug treatment courts (FDTCs), which are distinct from traditional adult drug treatment courts in that the latter do not focus on child or family outcomes. Although there is evidence that drug treatment courts are effective at reducing criminal behavior and drug use, one study revealed a high referral rate to CPS one to three years following parent participation in a drug treatment court (LaLiberte, Barry, and Walthour, 2018, p. 18). Conversely, FDTCs—which provide judicial monitoring, wraparound services, and substance use treatment, with the goal of family reunification—have demonstrated improvements in treatment enrollment completion and family reunification (Marlowe and Carey, 2012). For example, parents who participated in the King County Family Treatment Court in Washington state—which uses early intervention and comprehensive, individualized, holistic services for the entire family—entered treatment sooner and successfully completed the program, and their children spent less time in out-of-home care than children in the comparison group (Bruns et al., 2012). In addition, in a meta-analysis of 17 studies from 2004 to 2018, participants in FDTCs were substantially more likely to achieve reunification without increasing the risk of foster care reentry or maltreatment report (Zhang et al., 2019). However, with only 300 FDTCs across the country, the benefits of this collaborative treatment approach are limited. Additional court collaborations with child welfare include pilot programs in Arizona and Tennessee, which are testing pre-petition court programs that identify and support families who are at risk for involvement in the child welfare system because of an SUD (National Judicial Opioid Task Force, 2019).

Substance Use Disorder Treatment

Child welfare and SUD treatment systems often intersect to improve child and family well-being. This collaboration is crucial: Children spend less time in foster care when parents (1) engage in treatment quickly, (2) spend more time in treatment, or (3) successfully complete treatment (HRSA, 2018; Winstanley and Stover, 2019). Public awareness and funding for programming have increased dramatically in the past few years, in part because of the U.S. government declaring the opioid crisis a national emergency. There are several examples of federal efforts to address the opioid crisis (e.g., the SUPPORT for Patients and Community Act of 2018 and the Stop Opioid Abuse and Reduce Drug Supply and Demand Initiative). However, one legislative effort that specifically aims to address the impact of this crisis through collaboration between the child welfare and substance use treatment systems is the FFPSA.

Effective October 1, 2019, the FFPSA aims to preserve families by allowing states, for the first time, to use Title IV-E funds—the primary source of funding for foster care—for evidence-based and trauma-informed prevention services (e.g., mental health, substance use, and parenting skills) for parents at risk of child welfare involvement (Lindell, Sorenson, and Mangold, 2020). The FFPSA provides funds to states and counties for all children to safely remain in their homes while their parents receive necessary treatment and services (Waite, Greiner, and Laris, 2018), which may incentivize the use of this option instead of placing these kids in foster care. This legislation epitomizes a family-centered philosophy related to opioids that emphasizes the importance of keeping families together and decreasing foster care placement.

Recognizing the benefits of treatment, some child welfare agencies colocate staff who specialize in SUD in their offices, engage in cross-training between child welfare and substance use treatment professionals, or develop protocols to share information across systems (e.g., screening and assessment results, case plans, treatment plans, goal progress). One example of this colocation strategy is Project First Step in New Hampshire, which embeds licensed alcohol and drug counselors in select child welfare offices to train staff to facilitate access to SUD treatment and community services. Another approach to facilitate coordination between child welfare and treatment providers is the use of recovery coaches. Recovery coaches provide intensive outreach and engagement with parents, child welfare case workers, and treatment agencies to address barriers to treatment and provide support for reunification. Outcomes across multiple programs have shown increases in access and engagement in treatment, reductions in out-of-home care, and quicker reunification for program participants than for nonprogram participants (National Center on Substance Abuse and Child Welfare, undated-b). One experimental study found that, compared with families who received the usual care, parents who worked with recovery coaches were more likely to rapidly engage in substance use treatment, reunify with their children, and reduce the length of time children spent in out-of-home care (Ryan and Huang, 2012).

One often-cited, evidence-based example of a child welfare–based program that focuses on families with co-occurring substance use and child maltreatment issues is the Sobriety Treatment and Recovery Team (START) program. This is an evidence-based, integrative intervention that aims to facilitate early and rapid access to care for families and children affected by opioid use, with the goal of keeping children at home if this is a safe option. The START program relies on collaboration between child welfare workers and community organizations to provide direct services to children, referrals for supportive services, and rapid access to SUD treatment, including MOUD. Families who participate in this program enter state custody at almost half the rate of similar families, and more than 40 percent were reunified when their cases were closed (Hall et al., 2016).

Although a large proportion of parents who are involved with the child welfare system require substance use treatment, there are numerous barriers to accessing these services. Treatment availability is often scarce in certain geographic areas and for certain populations. Research indicates that treatment options are less available and less accessible in rural communities than they are in urban areas (Winstanley and Stover, 2019). One study found that patients in rural areas often have to travel more than an hour per treatment visit and that many patients rely on public transportation to travel to and from appointments (Ghertner, Waters, et al., 2018). Service availability is also limited for some high-need populations. For example, less than 20 percent of rehabilitation facilities have sufficient programs for pregnant or postpartum women with SUD, and only seven states give priority for pregnant women to access treatment services (LaLiberte, Barry, and Walthour, 2018). Another critical barrier to treatment is that parents may choose not to engage in opioid treatment because of a fear of child welfare involvement (Grella, Hser, and Huang, 2006).

Some child welfare agencies have also invested in family-based residential treatment programs to address parental SUDs and mitigate outcomes that could provoke child welfare involvement. These residential programs are an example of collaboration between child welfare and substance use treatment systems that are often separate, and they offer parents access to treatment and parenting education while allowing them to preserve their relationships with their children by permitting children to live with or frequently visit their parents while they are in treatment (Casey Family Programs, 2019). In addition to focusing on recovery, these programs aim to prevent child maltreatment, promote family preservation and reunification, and support family self-sufficiency (Hammond and McGlone, 2013). Program results include longer treatment stays, greater likelihood of treatment completion, and less likelihood of parents having their children removed or remaining in out-of-home care (Casey Family Programs, 2019).

Despite some examples of collaboration or partnership between child welfare agencies and SUD treatment providers, this collaborative approach is still used infrequently. One major barrier to coordination is a difference in perspectives. Child welfare agencies traditionally focus primarily (if not exclusively) on child well-being and are less attentive to parents' needs for recovery or the development of parenting capacity, whereas treatment programs tend to prioritize parents' recovery in lieu of the child's interests. There is also disagreement between child welfare personnel and treatment staff about the utility of evidence-based programs. Despite positive outcomes associated with MOUD (e.g., significantly higher chances of retaining custody of children, higher reunification rates), child welfare agencies often require complete sobriety, including abstinence from MOUD. Another critical challenge relates to the typical time frames to achieve parent and child goals. Parent substance use treatment plans, accounting for high rates of relapse, often exceed the time allotted to parents to reunify with their children (Winstanley and Stover, 2019). Delays in treatment may be attributable to the limited availability of programs in low-resource communities or to parental incarceration (Winstanley and Stover, 2019). Parents' rights may be terminated while they are still engaged in or attempting to access treatment (Rippey, 2020).

Education

It is estimated that at least 25 percent of kindergarten through 12th-grade students live in homes that are affected by an alcohol or other substance use issue (National Association for Children of Addiction, 2018). Teachers, school counselors, school social workers, and administrators are often the first to identify possible evidence of child maltreatment. The highest percentage of reports of child abuse and neglect (20.5 percent) are from education personnel (U.S. Department of Health and Human Services, Administration for Children and Families, Administration on Children, Youth and Families, Children's Bureau, 2020). However, the educators' role extends beyond that of a mandated reporter. Education staff increasingly

- provide assistance to support child welfare staff with their investigations (i.e., sharing relevant information about families and children)
- provide services to children, parents, and families (e.g., developing individual education plans for students; offering counseling services to children and parents; providing job skills training, substance use counseling, or other education programs to parents)
- participate in multidisciplinary teams (i.e., school or community-based professionals who represent various areas of expertise and roles to respond to child abuse reports and other school crises; Crosson-Tower, 2003).

Children living with parents who struggle with SUD often experience difficulties in school (e.g., higher rates of school absenteeism, truancy, and suspension) and are more likely to not complete high school (National Association for Children of Addiction, 2018). Because students spend a large proportion of their waking hours during school days in school, this could be a prime setting for offering prevention and intervention strategies to address social, emotional, and behavioral concerns, which affect academic performance. Educators are uniquely positioned to work with child welfare agencies to provide valuable support to children affected by the opioid crisis. One example of this type of collaboration is the Child Protection Team program (or crisis teams). These teams comprise school-based professionals and a representative from the local child welfare agency. Child Protection Teams are designed to provide guidance to educators about when and how they should report suspected child maltreatment and how they can support students and families after a report is made (Crosson-Tower and Rizzuto, undated).

Employment

There is a direct relationship between economic status and family and child well-being. Low-income families are at greater risk of both substance use and child maltreatment. Families who struggle with substance use, including opioid dependence, experience declines in labor force participation, which significantly affect family finances (Mathur and Torres, 2018). Areas with higher rates of opioid prescriptions per capita have seen faster declines in labor force participation, and men who are out of the labor force are more than twice as likely to take a prescription pain medication every day compared with those who are employed or unemployed (Krueger, 2017). Because OUD may be a more severe addiction that results in lower functioning than other SUDs, mothers with this disorder struggle to secure and maintain employment (Winstanley and Stover, 2019). Employment outcomes for formerly incarcerated parents are even more dire, because there are numerous barriers to employment for individuals with a criminal record (e.g., social stigma, institutional barriers). In addition, as family members assume responsibility for children living with parents who use opioids, the financial situation of the family members may worsen. Many of these individuals are already living below the poverty line (Mathur and Torres, 2018). As parents' job participation declines or discontinues, their ability to retain their children or reunify with them if the children are placed in foster care also diminishes. As caseworkers develop a plan to support parents dealing with opioid use, especially those with a criminal record, they should explore resources to assist parents with securing employment or training to develop job skills and address other institutional barriers.

Income Support and Homeless Services

Because individuals who live below the poverty line are more likely to be dependent on opioids (Germain, 2018), it is unsurprising that parents with OUD who are involved with the child welfare system rely on a wide variety of social service programs (e.g., Temporary Assistance for Needy Families, housing, child care, transportation). Almost half (47 percent) of the children placed in out-of-home care because of substantiated allegations of child abuse or neglect were removed from homes that struggled to meet basic necessities (Martin and Citrin, 2014). Often, eligibility for social service programs is tied to the children in the home. When children are removed from their homes, parents are at risk of losing their benefits, which exacerbates preexisting income, housing, food, and health care insecurity. Typically, income and housing stability are important considerations for family reunification and for accessing treatment for substance use (if this was a reason for child removal), so disqualification from social services could jeopardize parents' ability to reunite with their children or could result in permanent termination of parental rights (Child Welfare Information Gateway, 2016; Dworsky, 2014).

Child welfare agencies have sought to collaborate with social service agencies to help families meet their concrete needs in an effort to keep families together and prevent future risk of child maltreatment. One example of this approach is a Kentucky-based program called the Targeted Assessment Program (TAP). TAP colocates experienced staff at child welfare and Temporary Assistance for Needy Families offices to evaluate and assess participants for barriers to self-sufficiency and fulfillment of parental responsibilities (e.g., SUD, mental health issues, intimate partner violence, and unmet needs for housing, transportation, and child care). TAP specialists develop a treatment plan to address identified barriers. In addition, specialists provide training to agency staff and offer case consultation. A 2012 study demonstrated a reduction in the percentage of participants assessed to have a substance use issue from 48 percent to 38 percent, and researchers observed improvements in self-sufficiency measures (e.g., needs for transportation and child care; Ramlow and Leukefeld, 2020).

First Responders

Child welfare agencies have fairly frequent interactions with one major group of first responders: law enforcement. Law enforcement officials are one of the primary reporters of allegations of child maltreatment (LaLiberte, Barry, and Walthour, 2018). In addition, they often are the first responders to incidents involving a drug overdose. Given that a large proportion of adults with opioid dependency have at least one child living with them (about 41 percent; Feder et al., 2018), it is critical that law enforcement personnel understand how to manage these situations with sensitivity and compassion and that they make decisions that support the safety and well-being of affected children.

Child welfare agencies also establish formal partnerships with law enforcement to assist with CPS investigations. According to a national study of children involved in CPS investigations in 2008 and 2009 across 82 agencies and 30 states, law enforcement participated in investigations for 28 percent of the cases, which varied substantially by the type of maltreatment (i.e., sexual abuse, physical abuse, neglect, and other maltreatment; LaLiberte, Barry, and Walthour, 2018).

Because of their role in reporting child maltreatment, this interaction with first responders gives rise to a conflict between the need to ensure children's safety and well-being and the need to respond to medical emergencies. This is because the fears of CPS involvement and of loss of custody of children are among the reasons reported by people who use drugs for not calling 911 to respond to a drug overdose (14 percent of respondents; Follett et al., 2014). Other top reasons for not calling include fear of arrest or probation violation (28 percent and 16 percent, respectively), lack of access to a phone (15 percent), not wanting friends or family to find out, and the fear of getting drugs confiscated (14 percent for both responses; Follett et al., 2014). Some jurisdictions have taken steps to limit the involvement of law enforcement officers in responding to SUD-related calls for service (see, e.g., Elinson, 2018), which may play a role in some individuals' considerations regarding whether to call 911, but such efforts do not ultimately address the conflict described in this section.

Policy Opportunities and Considerations

This chapter has documented the huge role that SUD and OUD have had in increasing the prevalence of child maltreatment and the many ripple effects of this increase as the child welfare system interacts with other systems. Research evidence reveals some opportunities to improve child welfare outcomes. We briefly summarize a few examples here. When considering the following opportunities, keep in mind that most parents with OUD or who make nonmedical use of opioid medications want to be good parents and experience great moral injury when their SUDs hinder their ability to properly fulfill parental roles (Snoek and Horstkötter, 2021).

Criminal legal system–focused policies that aim to reduce prenatal substance use can have negative, unintended consequences in health care behavior. Research shows that, in states with punitive prenatal substance use policies, some pregnant women are reluctant to seek prenatal care because of a fear of criminal charges or of losing their children to the child welfare system (Sanmartin et al., 2020). In addition, once an infant is removed from their home because of parental substance use in states that implement criminal legal system–focused policies, they have a lower chance of reunification with their parent when compared with states that have not adopted such policies (Sanmartin et al., 2020). To reduce the number of potentially unnecessary separations between parent and child, Congress passed the Comprehensive Addiction and Recovery Act of 2016, which directs states to develop safe care plans to address the health and substance use treatment needs of infants who are affected by prenatal substance exposure, as well as the affected family and caregiver, following the child's release from the care of a health care provider. Safe care plans, or Plans of Safe Care, are required to be developed by child welfare agencies in 33 states, but states have flexibility in who initiates Plans of Safe Care (e.g., CPS, health care professionals, substance use treatment providers) and how they are implemented (Child Welfare Information Gateway, 2020a). Plans should include the direct services and supports needed for the infant and their family to ensure the infant's safety and well-being (e.g., physical and mental health support, substance use treatment, parenting education, infant developmental screening; National Quality Improvement Center for Collaborative Community Court Teams, undated). Further exploration into the effectiveness of safe care planning and other nonpunitive strategies to support children and families can balance health care professionals' and child welfare agencies' roles and approaches and better promote their shared interests in child safety, permanency, and well-being.

Relatedly, family outcomes may be improved by addressing the intersection between the criminalization of drug use and child welfare. For instance, the reunification of family members can be rendered more difficult because of an inability to access housing caused by past criminal records. Automatically sealing drug possession records could represent one way to address this challenge. Furthermore, some lawmakers have started to attend to the punitive impacts of the child welfare system (Scott, 2020), although the impact of such efforts is yet to be demonstrated because of their recency. For instance, in 2019, New York state passed two laws to (1) allow some children who were adopted from foster care to keep in contact with their parents and (2) raise the evidence standard for being listed on the state's abuse and neglect registry (McCarthy, 2019). The latter law was vetoed by the governor, although it passed with veto-proof majorities (Williams, 2019).

Because the expanded Medicaid program has been a powerful, sustainable funding source to increase access to care, including clinical SUD treatment services and recovery supports (Bailey et al., 2021), it is vital to efforts to prevent child abuse and reduce foster care placements caused by SUD. Research indicates that individuals with Medicaid coverage are more likely to engage in treatment than those without Medicaid coverage. Child welfare agencies should leverage this program to support pregnant mothers and parents who need substance use treatment and should advocate for expansion in those states that have not yet accepted this option.

To improve permanency outcomes, efforts should be made to increase funding for prevention and treatment services (e.g., the FFPSA) and support the implementation of similar programs, especially in communities that are hardest hit by the crisis (e.g., rural communities). In addition, the FFPSA should be expanded to include all MOUD treatment options. Currently, the Department of Health and Human Services, which is responsible for approving programs funded by the FFPSA, has only approved methadone maintenance therapy, despite evidence that newer MOUD options (such as buprenorphine treatment) have also proven to be effective. Although states can defer the implementation of the FFPSA for up to two years, it is crucial that they begin planning to leverage these new funds to better support families struggling with SUDs who are involved with the child welfare system. States have struggled to implement the FFPSA because of limited capacity and financial resources, as well as misinterpretation of the law (Jordan and McKlindon, 2020; Patrick et al., 2019). In December 2019, Congress passed the Family First Transition Act to help states overcome these implementation challenges. As of May 2020, 25 states had enacted some portion of the FFPSA (National Conference of State Legislatures, 2021).

Although the FFPSA supports both prevention and treatment programs, programs appear to be more treatment focused. Greater attention to upstream, primary prevention is also needed to address the underlying factors that drive opioid and substance misuse and addiction (Prevention Institute, 2017). Efforts should be made to improve societal issues that contribute to the opioid crisis, such as social and economic instability and decline, loss of living-wage jobs, underfunded schools, criminalization of substance use, limited access to health care providers and behavioral health services, structural racism, intergenerational poverty, social isolation, and underfunded social services (Prevention Institute, 2017). Child welfare planning might include linkages to services and supports to directly address these issues (e.g., collaboration with job training programs to improve employment outcomes).

It is also important to continue funding to support collaboration between child welfare and substance use treatment and other important stakeholders, such as the In-Depth Technical Assistance program, which is an 18- to 24-month program provided by the National Center on Substance Abuse and Child Welfare to build the capacity of states, tribes, and community partner agencies to improve outcomes for families affected by SUDs (Patrick, 2020).

Increasing support for adolescent victims of OUD who are involved with the child welfare system is also critical. Adolescents involved with the child welfare system are at high risk of OUD. Sixty percent of drug overdose deaths among adolescents in 2016 were caused by opioids (Winstanley and Stover, 2019). Child welfare agencies should collect indicators related to behavioral and substance use outcomes for youth and employ evidence-informed interventions to support the well-being of this vulnerable population. They should also conduct screenings using evidence-based tools, such as the CRAFFT, because early intervention is critical to preventing addiction (Winstanley and Stover, 2019).

Although parent and child outcomes improve when parents and children engage in comprehensive family-centered treatment that meets the needs of the whole family, there is a dearth of family-oriented treatment programs in most child welfare agencies. There is a need to increase support for this approach to treatment, because these programs recognize the ubiquitous effects of substance use on the entire family, focus treatment on the opioid-dependent parent, and attend to the needs of the children, the parent-child relationship, and the rest of the family. One study found that women who participated in family-centered substance use treatment programs demonstrated reduced mental health symptoms, reduction in risky behavior, and longer program retention and were twice as likely to reunify with their children as those in the comparison group, who received the usual care (Grella, Hser, and

Huang, 2006; Zweben et al., 2015). In addition, despite evidence that (1) MOUD are more effective than other OUD treatments and (2) parents who receive MOUD may be more likely to have better permanency outcomes than those who do not receive MOUD (Hall et al., 2016), child welfare professionals and judges are reticent to allow children to remain in their homes or be reunited with their families if the parent is receiving MOUD (Hall et al., 2016; Radel et al., 2018b). And family drug courts—which, in most cases, focus on the whole family—are underutilized because of a lack of awareness and lack of buy-in from child welfare agencies (Children and Family Futures, 2017).

Typically, once children are placed in out-of-home care, parents' rights are terminated if the placement exceeds 15 of the previous 22 months, unless the state can identify a good reason not to do so. Washington state recognized the disproportionate impact this requirement would have on incarcerated parents and implemented a statutory exception to the 15-month deadline for parents whose rights were to be terminated for no other reason than their incarceration (Rippey, 2020). New York implemented a similar exception that also allows child welfare agencies to delay termination proceedings if the child's foster care placement was primarily attributable to their parent's incarceration or participation in a substance use treatment program (Rippey, 2020). Child welfare agencies should explore widespread implementation of exceptions for parents engaged in opioid use treatment.

The Fostering Connections to Success and Increasing Adoptions Act of 2008 requires local education and child welfare agencies in each state to work together to improve educational success for children; however, barriers to full collaboration are persistent in many localities (Rubin et al., 2013). Barriers to partnership include federal and state laws that restrict sharing information (e.g., the Family Education Rights and Privacy Act), cultural differences between systems, confusion over roles, inconsistent knowledge of relevant policies and practices, and lack of trust (National Center for Mental Health Promotion and Youth Violence Prevention, 2010; Rubin et al., 2013). To improve child well-being, especially for high-risk children (such as those involved with the child welfare system because of parental opioid dependence), it is important that these systems better align policies and practices and improve communication and interaction. Additional suggestions include having school personnel develop good relationships with senior supervisory child welfare agency staff, developing clear guidelines to facilitate information-sharing across systems, defining each agency's role, convening regular case management meetings with representatives from both systems, and providing cross-training for staff across agencies (National Center for Mental Health Promotion and Youth Violence Prevention, 2010).

The Supporting Grandparents Raising Grandchildren Act of 2018 seeks to understand and support the needs of the more than 2.6 million grandparents who are raising the children of parents who are unable to care for them because of substance use (Generations United, 2018). Given the large number of children living with relatives (either formally or informally) as the result of parental substance use, relative caregivers require adequate financial, emotional, and social support to meet the needs of these children (Dolbin-MacNab and O'Connell, 2021). Evidence shows that children in relative foster care fare better than those with nonrelative foster families (Generations United, 2018). Currently, collaborative efforts between child welfare agencies and several core and other systems are limited to parents who are misusing substances, foster parents, and children. These linkages should be expanded to improve the level of support provided to kinship caregivers.

As a final consideration, it is important to add that one risk of attempting more-holistic approaches and greater coordination across contexts is an expansion in duties and expectations for individual agencies without a concomitant increase in the resources available. As a result, one or more systems may become overburdened. The system cannot sustain the current rate of growth in the national child welfare caseload without additional resources and extensive collaboration with other key systems. Partnerships are critical to prevent the involvement of child welfare, preserve families when possible, support parent engagement in evidence-based treatment, and, ultimately, improve child, parent, and family outcomes.

Abbreviations

CAPTA	Child Abuse Prevention and Treatment Act
CPS	Child Protective Services
FDTC	family drug treatment court
FFPSA	Families First Prevention Services Act of 2018
HRSA	Health Resources and Services Administration
MOUD	medications for opioid use disorder
NOWS	neonatal opioid withdrawal syndrome
OUD	opioid use disorder
SUD	substance use disorder
TAP	Targeted Assessment Program

References

Andrews, Christina M., Amanda J. Abraham, Colleen M. Grogan, Melissa A. Westlake, Harold A. Pollack, and Peter D. Friedmann, "Impact of Medicaid Restrictions on Availability of Buprenorphine in Addiction Treatment Programs," *American Journal of Public Health*, Vol. 109, No. 3, 2019, pp. 434–436.

Bailey, Anna, Kyle Hayes, Hannah Katch, and Judith Solomon, *Medicaid Is Key to Building a System of Comprehensive Substance Use Care for Low-Income People*, Washington, D.C.: Center on Budget and Policy Priorities, March 18, 2021.

Bosk, Emily A., Ruth Paris, Karen E. Hanson, Debra Ruisard, and Nancy E. Suchman, "Innovations in Child Welfare Interventions for Caregivers with Substance Use Disorders and Their Children," *Children and Youth Services Review*, Vol. 101, 2019, pp. 99–112.

Bruns, Eric J., Michael D. Pullmann, Ericka S. Weathers, Mark L. Wirschem, and Jill K. Murphy, "Effects of a Multidisciplinary Family Treatment Drug Court on Child and Family Outcomes: Results of a Quasi-Experimental Study," *Child Maltreatment*, Vol. 17, No. 3, 2012, pp. 218–230.

Casey Family Programs, *How Can Family-Based Residential Treatment Programs Help Reduce Substance Use and Improve Child Welfare Outcomes?* Seattle, Wash., August 2019.

Centers for Disease Control and Prevention, "Motor Vehicle Crash Deaths: How Is the US Doing?" webpage, updated July 6, 2016. As of August 2, 2021:
https://www.cdc.gov/vitalsigns/motor-vehicle-safety/index.html

Centers for Disease Control and Prevention, "Fast Facts: Firearm Violence Prevention," webpage, 2021. As of August 2, 2021:
https://www.cdc.gov/violenceprevention/firearms/fastfact.html

Child Trends, *Child Maltreatment Databank Indicator*, Bethesda, Md., May 7, 2019.

Child Welfare Information Gateway, *Parental Substance Use and the Child Welfare System*, Washington, D.C.: U.S. Department of Health and Human Services, Administration for Children and Families, Children's Bureau, October 2014.

Child Welfare Information Gateway, *Reunification: Bringing Your Children Home from Foster Care*, Washington, D.C.: U.S. Department of Health and Human Services, Administration for Children and Families, Children's Bureau, May 2016.

Child Welfare Information Gateway, *Parental Substance Use as Child Abuse*, Washington, D.C.: U.S. Department of Health and Human Services, Administration for Children and Families, Children's Bureau, 2019a.

Child Welfare Information Gateway, *About CAPTA: A Legislative History*, Washington, D.C.: U.S. Department of Health and Human Services, Administration for Children and Families, Children's Bureau, February 2019b.

Child Welfare Information Gateway, *Plans of Safe Care for Infants with Prenatal Substance Exposure and Their Families*, Washington, D.C.: U.S. Department of Health and Human Services, Administration for Children and Families, Children's Bureau, 2020a.

Child Welfare Information Gateway, *How the Child Welfare System Works*, Washington, D.C.: U.S. Department of Health and Human Services, Administration for Children and Families, Children's Bureau, October 2020b.

Child Welfare Information Gateway, *Concurrent Planning for Timely Permanency for Children*, Washington, D.C.: U.S. Department of Health and Human Services, Administration for Children and Families, Children's Bureau, 2021a.

Child Welfare Information Gateway, *Parental Substance Use: A Primer for Child Welfare Professionals*, Washington, D.C.: U.S. Department of Health and Human Services, Administration for Children and Families, Children's Bureau, January 2021b.

Children and Family Futures, *National Strategic Plan for Family Drug Courts*, Lake Forest, Calif., March 2017.

Crosson-Tower, Cynthia, *The Role of Educators in Preventing and Responding to Child Abuse and Neglect*, Washington, D.C.: U.S. Department of Health and Human Services, 2003.

Crosson-Tower, Cynthia, and Anthony P. Rizzuto, *Designing and Implementing a School Reporting Protocol: A How-To Manual for Massachusetts Educators*, 2nd ed., Boston, Mass.: Children's Trust Fund, undated.

Crowley, Daniel Max, Christian M. Connell, Damon Jones, and Michael W. Donovan, "Considering the Child Welfare System Burden from Opioid Misuse: Research Priorities for Estimating Public Costs," *American Journal of Managed Care*, Vol. 25, Suppl. 13, 2019, pp. S256–S263.

DePanfilis, Diane, *Child Protective Services: A Guide for Caseworkers*, Washington, D.C.: U.S. Department of Health and Human Services, Administration for Children and Families, Administration on Children, Youth and Families, Children's Bureau, 2018.

Dolbin-MacNab, Megan L., and Lyn M. O'Connell, "Grandfamilies and the Opioid Epidemic: A Systemic Perspective and Future Priorities," *Clinical Child and Family Psychology Review*, Vol. 24, No. 2, 2021, pp. 207–223.

Dworsky, Amy, *Families at the Nexus of Housing and Child Welfare*, State Policy Advocacy and Reform Center, November 2014.

Elinson, Zusha, "When Mental-Health Experts, Not Police, Are the First Responders," *Wall Street Journal*, November 24, 2018.

Falletta, Lynn, Kelsey Hamilton, Rebecca Fischbein, Julie Aultman, Beth Kinney, and Deric Kenne, "Perceptions of Child Protective Services Among Pregnant or Recently Pregnant, Opioid-Using Women in Substance Abuse Treatment," *Child Abuse & Neglect*, Vol. 79, 2018, pp. 125–135.

Feder, Kenneth A., Elizabeth J. Letourneau, and Jody Brook, "Children in the Opioid Epidemic: Addressing the Next Generation's Public Health Crisis," *Pediatrics*, Vol. 143, No. 1, 2019.

Feder, Kenneth A., Ramin Mojtabai, Rashelle J. Musci, and Elizabeth J. Letourneau, "U.S. Adults with Opioid Use Disorder Living with Children: Treatment Use and Barriers to Care," *Journal of Substance Abuse Treatment*, Vol. 93, 2018, pp. 31–37.

Follett, Kayla M., Anthony Piscitelli, Michael Parkinson, and Felix Munger, "Barriers to Calling 9-1-1 During Overdose Emergencies in a Canadian Context," *Critical Social Work*, Vol. 15, No. 1, 2014.

Generations United, *Raising the Children of the Opioid Epidemic: Solutions and Supports for Grandfamilies*, Washington, D.C., 2018.

Germain, Justin, *Opioid Use Disorder, Treatment, and Barriers to Employment Among TANF Recipients*, Washington, D.C.: Office of Family Assistance, Administration for Children and Families, U.S. Department of Health and Human Services, February 2018.

Ghertner, Robin, Melinda Baldwin, Gilbert Crouse, Laura Radel, and Annette Waters, "The Relationship Between Substance Use Indicators and Child Welfare Caseloads," *Foster Care*, Vol. 300, 2018.

Ghertner, Robin, Annette Waters, Laura Radel, and Gilbert Crouse, "The Role of Substance Use in Child Welfare Caseloads," *Children and Youth Services Review*, Vol. 90, 2018, pp. 83–93.

Grella, Christine E., Yih-Ing Hser, and Yu-Chuang Huang, "Mothers in Substance Abuse Treatment: Differences in Characteristics Based on Involvement with Child Welfare Services," *Child Abuse and Neglect*, Vol. 30, No. 1, 2006, pp. 55–73.

Hall, Martin T., Jordan Wilfong, Ruth A. Huebner, Lynn Posze, and Tina Willauer, "Medication-Assisted Treatment Improves Child Permanency Outcomes for Opioid-Using Families in the Child Welfare System," *Journal of Substance Abuse Treatment*, Vol. 71, 2016, pp. 63–67.

Hammond, Gretchen Clark, and Amanda McGlone, "Residential Family Treatment for Parents with Substance Use Disorders Who Are Involved with Child Welfare: Two Perspectives on Program Design, Collaboration, and Sustainability," *Child Welfare*, Vol. 92, No. 6, 2013, pp. 131–150.

Haskins, Ron, Jeremy Kohomban, and Jennifer Rodriguez, *Keeping Up with the Caseload: How to Recruit and Retain Foster Parents*, Washington, D.C.: Brookings Institution, 2019.

Health Resources and Services Administration, *HRSA's Home Visiting Program: Supporting Families Impacted by Opioid Use and Neonatal Abstinence Syndrome*, Rockville, Md.: U.S. Department of Health and Human Services, 2018.

HRSA—*See* Health Resources and Services Administration.

Johnson-Peterkin, Yolanda, *Information Packet: Children of Incarcerated Parents*, New York: National Resource Center for Foster Care and Permanency Planning, May 2003.

Jordan, Elizabeth, and Amy McKlindon, *The Family First Transition Act Provides New Implementation Supports for States and Tribes*, Bethesda, Md.: Child Trends, March 10, 2020.

Ko, Jean Y., Stephen W. Patrick, Van T. Tong, Roshni Patel, Jennifer N. Lind, and Wanda D. Barfield, "Incidence of Neonatal Abstinence Syndrome—28 States, 1999–2013," *Morbidity and Mortality Weekly Report*, Vol. 65, No. 31, 2016, pp. 799–802.

Kohomban, Jeremy, Jennifer Rodriguez, and Ron Haskins, *The Foster Care System Was Unprepared for the Last Drug Epidemic—Let's Not Repeat History*, Washington, D.C.: Brookings Institution, 2018.

Krans, Elizabeth E., and Stephen W. Patrick, "Opioid Use Disorder in Pregnancy: Health Policy and Practice in the Midst of an Epidemic," *Obstetrics and Gynecology*, Vol. 128, No. 1, 2016, pp. 4–10.

Krueger, Alan B., "Where Have All the Workers Gone? An Inquiry into the Decline of the U.S. Labor Force Participation Rate," *Brookings Papers on Economic Activity*, Fall 2017.

LaLiberte, Traci, Korina Barry, and Kate Walthour, eds., *Criminal Justice Involvement of Families in Child Welfare*, St. Paul, Minn.: Center for Advanced Studies in Child Welfare, Spring 2018.

Leslie, Douglas L., Djibril M. Ba, Edeanya Agbese, Xueyi Xing, and Guodong Liu, "The Economic Burden of the Opioid Epidemic on States: The Case of Medicaid," *American Journal of Managed Care*, Vol. 25, Suppl. 13, 2019, pp. S243–S249.

Lindell, Karen U., Christina K. Sorenson, and Susan V. Mangold, "The Family First Prevention Services Act: A New Era of Child Welfare Reform," *Public Health Reports*, Vol. 135, No. 2, 2020, pp. 282–286.

Lipari, Rachel N., and Struther L. Van Horn, *Children Living with Parents Who Have a Substance Use Disorder*, Washington, D.C.: Substance Abuse and Mental Health Services Administration, August 24, 2017.

Lynch, Sean, Laura Sherman, Susan M. Snyder, and Margaret Mattson, "Trends in Infants Reported to Child Welfare with Neonatal Abstinence Syndrome (NAS)," *Children and Youth Services Review*, Vol. 86, 2018, pp. 135–141.

Marlowe, Douglas B., and Shannon M. Carey, *Research Update on Family Drug Courts*, Alexandria, Va.: National Association of Drug Court Professionals, May 2012.

Martin, Megan, and Alexandra Citrin, *Prevent, Protect and Provide: How Child Welfare Can Better Support Low-Income Families*, Washington, D.C.: Center for the Study of Social Policy, 2014.

Mathur, Rricha, and Kristen Torres, "Opioids, Poverty, and the Child Welfare System," *Our Kids, Our Future*, Washington, D.C.: First Focus, 2018.

McCarthy, Nora, "New York's Child Welfare Laws Will Advance Justice," The Appeal, November 13, 2019. As of October 7, 2020:
https://theappeal.org/new-yorks-child-welfare-laws-will-advance-justice/

Meinhofer, Angelica, Erica Onuoha, Yohanis Angleró-Díaz, and Katherine M. Keyes, "Parental Drug Use and Racial and Ethnic Disproportionality in the US Foster Care System," *Children and Youth Services Review*, Vol. 118, 2020.

Mirick, Rebecca G., and Shelley A. Steenrod, "Opioid Use Disorder, Attachment, and Parenting: Key Concerns for Practitioners," *Child and Adolescent Social Work Journal*, Vol. 33, No. 6, 2016, pp. 547–557.

Morton, Cory, and Melissa Wells, "Behavioral and Substance Use Outcomes for Older Youth Living with a Parental Opioid Misuse: A Literature Review to Inform Child Welfare Practice and Policy," *Journal of Public Child Welfare*, Vol. 11, No. 4–5, 2017, pp. 546–567.

Mowbray, Orion, Joseph P. Ryan, Bryan G. Victor, Gregory Bushman, Clayton Yochum, and Brian E. Perron, "Longitudinal Trends in Substance Use and Mental Health Service Needs in Child Welfare," *Children and Youth Services Review*, Vol. 73, 2017.

National Association for Children of Addiction, *Children Impacted by Addiction: A Toolkit for Educators*, Kensington, Md., 2018.

National Center for Mental Health Promotion and Youth Violence Prevention, *The Role of Schools in Supporting Children in Foster Care*, March 2010.

National Center on Substance Abuse and Child Welfare, "Plans of Safe Care," webpage, undated-a. As of December 17, 2021:
https://ncsacw.samhsa.gov/topics/plans-of-safe-care.aspx

National Center on Substance Abuse and Child Welfare, *The Use of Peers and Recovery Specialists in Child Welfare Settings*, undated-b.

National Conference of State Legislatures, "The Child Welfare Placement Continuum: What's Best for Children?" webpage, November 3, 2019. As of November 6, 2020:
https://www.ncsl.org/research/human-services/
the-child-welfare-placement-continuum-what-s-best-for-children.aspx

National Conference of State Legislatures, "Family First Legislation," webpage, January 15, 2021. As of December 17, 2021:
https://www.ncsl.org/research/human-services/family-first-updates-and-new-legislation.aspx

National Highway Traffic Safety Administration, "Early Estimates of 2019 Motor Vehicle Traffic Data Show Reduced Fatalities for Third Consecutive Year," press release, May 5, 2020.

National Judicial Opioid Task Force, *Convening, Collaborating, Connecting: Courts as Leaders in the Crisis of Addiction*, Washington, D.C., 2019.

National Quality Improvement Center for Collaborative Community Court Teams, *Plans of Safe Care: An Issue Brief for Judicial Officers*, undated.

Normile, Becky, Carrie Hanlon, and Hannah Eichner, *State Strategies to Meet the Needs of Young Children and Families Affected by the Opioid Crisis*, Washington, D.C.: National Academy for State Health Policy, 2018.

Patrick, Stephen W., "Understanding the Needs of Families During the Opioid Crisis," *IRP Focus*, Vol. 36, No. 1, 2020, pp. 7–15.

Patrick, Stephen W., Richard G. Frank, Elizabeth McNeer, and Bradley D. Stein, "Improving the Child Welfare System to Respond to the Needs of Substance-Exposed Infants," *Hospital Pediatrics*, Vol. 9, No. 8, 2019, pp. 651–654.

Prevention Institute, "To Address Opioids, We Need to Think Upstream," press release, October 27, 2017.

Quast, Troy, "State-Level Variation in the Relationship Between Child Removals and Opioid Prescriptions," *Child Abuse and Neglect*, Vol. 86, 2018, pp. 306–313.

Radel, Laura, Melinda Baldwin, Gilbert Crouse, Robin Ghertner, and Annette Waters, *Substance Use, the Opioid Epidemic, and the Child Welfare System: Key Findings from a Mixed Methods Study*, Washington, D.C.: U.S. Department of Health and Human Services, Office of the Assistant Secretary for Planning and Evaluation, March 7, 2018a.

Radel, Laura, Melinda Baldwin, Gilbert Crouse, Robin Ghertner, and Annette Waters, *Medication-Assisted Treatment for Opioid Use Disorder in the Child Welfare Context: Challenges and Opportunities*, Washington, D.C.: U.S. Department of Health and Human Services, Office of the Assistant Secretary for Planning and Evaluation, November 2018b.

Ramlow, Barbara, and Carl G. Leukefeld, "Supporting Treatment and Recovery in Human Services Programs," *IRP Focus*, Vol. 36, No. 2, 2020, pp. 21–23.

Rippey, Sayer, "Incarcerated Parents and Child Welfare in Washington," *Washington Law Review*, Vol. 95, No. 1, 2020, pp. 531–554.

Rubin, David, Amanda O'Reilly, Sarah Zlotnik, Taylor Hendricks, Catherine Zorc, Meredith Matone, and Kathleen Noonan, *Improving Education Outcomes for Children in Child Welfare*, The Children's Hospital of Philadelphia: PolicyLab, 2013.

Ryan, Joseph P., and Hui Huang, *Illinois AODA IV-E Waiver Demonstration: Final Evaluation Report*, Urbana, Ill.: University of Illinois, Children and Family Research Center, July 2012.

Sanmartin, Maria X., Mir M. Ali, Sean Lynch, and Arda Aktas, "Association Between State-Level Criminal Justice–Focused Prenatal Substance Use Policies in the US and Substance Use–Related Foster Care Admissions and Family Reunification," *JAMA Pediatrics*, Vol. 174, No. 8, 2020, pp. 782–788.

Scott, Katie, "Stretched Thin: Parents Lacking Resources Who Are Accused of Negligent Child Abuse Need Solutions, Not Prisons," *Minnesota Journal of Law and Inequality*, 2020.

Snoek, Anke, and Dorothee Horstkötter, "Parental Substance and Alcohol Abuse: Two Ethical Frameworks to Assess Whether and How Intervention Is Appropriate," *Bioethics*, Vol. 35, No. 9, November 2021, pp. 916–924.

Sommers, Benjamin D., Anna L. Goldman, Robert J. Blendon, E. John Orav, and Arnold M. Epstein, "Medicaid Work Requirements—Results from the First Year in Arkansas," *New England Journal of Medicine*, Vol. 381, No. 11, 2019, pp. 1073–1082.

Spehr, Michelle K., Jennifer Coddington, Azza H. Ahmed, and Elizabeth Jones, "Parental Opioid Abuse: Barriers to Care, Policy, and Implications for Primary Care Pediatric Providers," *Journal of Pediatric Health Care*, Vol. 31, No. 6, 2017, pp. 695–702.

Stulac, Sara, Megan Bair-Merritt, Elisha M. Wachman, Marilyn Augustyn, Carey Howard, Namrata Madoor, and Eileen Costello, "Children and Families of the Opioid Epidemic: Under the Radar," *Current Problems in Pediatric and Adolescent Health Care*, Vol. 49, No. 8, 2019.

Substance Abuse and Mental Health Services Administration, *A Collaborative Approach to the Treatment of Pregnant Women with Opioid Use Disorders: Practice and Policy Considerations for Child Welfare, Collaborating Medical, and Service Providers*, Rockville, Md., 2016.

Tabashneck, Stephanie, "Family Drug Courts: Combatting the Opioid Epidemic," *Family Law Quarterly*, Vol. 52, No. 1, 2018, pp. 183–202.

Taplin, Stephanie, and Richard P. Mattick, "The Nature and Extent of Child Protection Involvement Among Heroin-Using Mothers in Treatment: High Rates of Reports, Removals at Birth and Children in Care," *Drug and Alcohol Review*, Vol. 34, No. 1, 2015, pp. 31–37.

Thumath, Meaghan, David Humphreys, Jane Barlow, Putu Duff, Melissa Braschel, Brittany Bingham, Sophie Pierre, and Kate Shannon, "Overdose Among Mothers: The Association Between Child Removal and Unintentional Drug Overdose in a Longitudinal Cohort of Marginalised Women in Canada," *International Journal of Drug Policy*, Vol. 91, May 2021.

U.S. Department of Health and Human Services, Administration for Children and Families, Administration on Children, Youth and Families, Children's Bureau, *Child Maltreatment 2018*, Washington, D.C., 2020.

Waite, Douglas, Mary V. Greiner, and Zach Laris, "Putting Families First: How the Opioid Epidemic Is Affecting Children and Families, and the Child Welfare Policy Options to Address It," *Journal of Applied Research on Children*, Vol. 9, No. 1, 2018.

Williams, Zach, "Cuomo Vetoes Bill Aimed to Help People of Color Keep Custody of Their Kids," City and State New York, December 16, 2019.

Winstanley, Erin L., and Amanda N. Stover, "The Impact of the Opioid Epidemic on Children and Adolescents," *Clinical Therapeutics*, Vol. 41, No. 9, 2019, pp. 1655–1662.

Wolf, Jennifer Price, William R. Ponicki, Nancy J. Kepple, and Andrew Gaidus, "Are Community Level Prescription Opioid Overdoses Associated with Child Harm? A Spatial Analysis of California Zip Codes, 2001–2011," *Drug and Alcohol Dependence*, Vol. 166, 2016, pp. 202–208.

Young, Katherine, and Julia Zur, *Medicaid and the Opioid Epidemic: Enrollment, Spending, and the Implications of Proposed Policy Changes*, San Francisco, Calif.: Kaiser Family Foundation, issue brief, July 2017.

Zhang, Saijun, Hui Huang, Qi Wu, Yong Li, and Meirong Liu, "The Impacts of Family Treatment Drug Court on Child Welfare Core Outcomes: A Meta-Analysis," *Child Abuse and Neglect*, Vol. 88, 2019.

Zweben, Joan E., Yael Moses, Judith B. Cohen, Genny Price, William Chapman, and Joanna Lamb, "Enhancing Family Protective Factors in Residential Treatment for Substance Use Disorders," *Child Welfare*, Vol. 94, No. 5, 2015, pp. 145–166.

CHAPTER ELEVEN

Income Support and Homeless Services

Lois M. Davis

Overview

Individuals experiencing homelessness suffer from substance use disorders (SUDs), poor health, and mortality from opioid overdose at rates higher than the national average (Warfield and DiPietro, 2016). Similarly, among individuals in poverty, the rates of illegal opioid use and opioid use disorders (OUDs) exceed those among populations with incomes more than 200 percent of the federal poverty line (Ghertner and Groves, 2018). Hence, policies that aim to address (1) the needs of low-income individuals with an OUD and (2) homelessness and housing requirements can play a role in promoting better OUD outcomes.

Among the wide variety of social services provided by the government, income-security programs (or *income-security means-tested entitlements*) address the needs of individuals in poverty by providing direct monetary or noncash assistance. Because a notable share of people with an OUD are living at or below the poverty level, these programs are a crucial component of this population's social protection net. In addition, housing and homeless services that provide aid in kind are critical supports for this population.

In this chapter, we focus on three federal income-security programs that provide income support to individuals and families: (1) the Temporary Assistance for Needy Families (TANF) program, which provides cash assistance to families and includes the noncash Supplemental Nutrition Assistance Program (SNAP), which provides food assistance; (2) Supplemental Security Income (SSI), a means-tested program with a strict set of financial requirements, intended to meet the basic needs of elderly, blind, and disabled individuals with limited resources; and (3) Social Security Disability Insurance (SSDI), a federal insurance program providing income support funded via a payroll tax for disabled workers and their dependents. In addition, we address housing and services for those experiencing homelessness that provide aid in kind.

System Components

Supplemental Security Income and Social Security Disability Insurance

Both programs are administered by the Social Security Administration (SSA). SSI is a *means-tested program*, while SSDI is an *entitlement program*. SSDI recipients have high rates of prescription opioid use, some develop an OUD during their time on SSDI, and rates of opioid prescriptions and disability insurance (DI) claims are correlated (U.S. Government Accountability Office [GAO], 2020). Government guidance is that individuals with an OUD for whom the disorder is a major contributor to their disability should be denied SSDI. However, an SUD (including illegal use of opioids) is seldom the reason why the SSA may deny benefits (GAO, 2020).

Temporary Assistance for Needy Families

TANF assists families with children when parents or other responsible relatives cannot provide for the family's basic needs.[1] TANF is carried out by states and territories based on grants from the federal government; the states have substantial flexibility in determining what their TANF programs will cover. SNAP provides food assistance, whereas TANF provides cash assistance. Most TANF recipients also receive SNAP benefits, and most TANF programs automatically enroll participants in SNAP (Zedlewski, 2012). Because there is little research on how common OUDs are among individuals receiving TANF or who are eligible for the program, researchers have drawn inferences about the TANF population from what is known about opioid use by low-income individuals. Estimates of the prevalence of substance use among TANF recipients have ranged widely between 4 percent and 37 percent (Radel, Joyce, and Wulff, 2011).

Homeless and Housing Programs

Individuals' housing situation is among the key social determinants of health. Two-thirds of people experiencing homelessness have had SUDs during their lifetimes, and overdose deaths are a notable driver of mortality among this population experiencing homelessness (Warfield and DiPietro, 2016; Substance Abuse and Mental Health Services Administration [SAMHSA], 2018). A study of adults experiencing homelessness in Boston found that drug overdose was the cause in 17 percent of deaths among people experiencing homelessness; 81 percent of these deaths involved opioids (Baggett et al., 2013). Specifically among men and women aged 25 to 44 experiencing homelessness, the opioid overdose death rates were nine times higher than among their housed counterparts (Baggett et al., 2013). Therefore, OUD is not rare among people experiencing homelessness, even if individuals experiencing homelessness represent only a fraction of those with OUD.

---

[1] According to the Benefits.gov website,

> To be eligible for this benefit program, applicants must be a resident of the state in which they apply, and a U.S. citizen, legal alien or qualified alien. You must be unemployed or underemployed and have low or very low income. ("Temporary Assistance for Needy Families," undated)

Government, nonprofit, and private agencies provide housing services (including government-subsidized housing) to people experiencing homelessness in need of transitional or permanent housing. At the federal level, the U.S. Department of Housing and Urban Development (HUD) manages the Housing Choice Voucher Program Section 8, which provides federal funds to local public housing agencies (PHAs) to issue housing vouchers to very low-income families, the elderly, and the disabled. HUD also manages the Continuum of Care (CoC) Homeless Assistance Program to help individuals and families experiencing homelessness with finding and moving into transitional and permanent housing (HUD, undated).

Of the different housing models within the CoC program, Housing First has been cited as a promising approach for those illegally using opioids or who have an OUD. Housing First takes a harm reduction approach to housing, offering access to permanent housing options with few to no treatment preconditions (Kerman et al., 2021). Existing evidence suggests that, compared with other types of programs, Housing First approaches lead to between 75-percent and 95-percent higher improvements in housing stability rates (Padgett, Henwood, and Tsemberis, 2015). In addition, programs that consistently implement Housing First principles generally have seen better outcomes related to housing and substance use among individuals with SUD who experience chronic homelessness (Davidson et al., 2014). However, more research is needed on how Housing First approaches affect overdose risk and other harms related to drug use, especially in the age of illegally manufactured synthetic opioids (Kerman et al., 2021).

Key Interactions with Other Components of the Ecosystem
Medical Care
Nearly all TANF recipients are eligible for Medicaid—in 2009, approximately 98 percent of TANF cases were enrolled in Medicaid (Germain, 2018). Given the high degree of program overlap, research on the Medicaid population offers some insights about the TANF population. Medicaid recipients' SUD rates are estimated to be ten times higher than those of the general population (Germain, 2018). In fiscal year (FY) 2013, about 636,000 Medicaid enrollees were reported to have an OUD (Young and Zur, 2017). In general, some researchers have estimated that approximately three in ten nonelderly people with OUDs are covered by Medicaid (Kaiser Family Foundation, 2017), although there are serious questions about existing estimates of OUD (see Chapter Two). In addition, Medicaid programs in numerous states have introduced measures to curb the prescribing of opioids (Kaiser Family Foundation, 2019).

Substance Use Treatment
Medicaid expansion has provided states with additional resources to cover many adults with SUDs. It is estimated that, between 2005 and 2015, Medicaid expansion doubled the number of nonelderly adults with OUD covered by the Medicaid program (Kaiser Family Foundation, 2017). Treatment providers have noted several challenges that TANF participants with SUD

have faced in meeting work requirements if the treatment (e.g., using medications for OUD [MOUD]) they are engaged with does not meet the criteria for an allowable activity under the TANF rules in their states (Germain, 2018; Benoit et al., 2004).

Criminal Legal System

Having an SUD and a criminal record can affect an individual's ability to get a job. In addition, some states still bar people convicted of a drug felony from even accessing TANF or SNAP benefits, even though Congress granted states the ability not to enforce this requirement. The vast majority of states have used this prerogative or have at least modified the ban to impose less severe restrictions (Polkey, 2019). Illicit drug use also affects an individual's eligibility for public housing. PHAs have the ability, granted by federal policies, to ban people with histories of drug use or those considered at risk of illegal drug use from obtaining housing assistance (HUD, Office of Public and Indian Housing [PIH], 2019).

Employment

Intersection with employment is relevant for TANF participants with OUD. A key component of TANF is providing job services and support to help a participant become ready for work and find employment. In Germain, 2018, a literature review of OUD among TANF recipients identified numerous barriers to employment associated with an OUD, such as limited work experience, domestic violence, low levels of education, and mental health disorders. Furthermore, information is limited regarding opioid treatment strategies focusing on people receiving TANF and their employment and work-readiness (Germain, 2018).

Child Welfare

Parents dealing with substance use problems sometimes have trouble caring for their children, finding and maintaining employment, and addressing health concerns. Analyses in Radel et al., 2018, found a positive correlation between (1) rates of overdose deaths and drug hospitalizations and (2) child welfare caseload rates. There are major challenges that affect the interaction between (1) child welfare agencies and families and (2) options for substance use treatment, including MOUD. Three of these challenges are the timeliness of assessments and the inconsistent assessment of parents' substance use, misunderstanding of how treatment works and mistrust of MOUD for parents, and treatment shortages of publicly available funded programs (Radel et al., 2018).

Policy Opportunities and Considerations

Improving Access to Social Security Disability Insurance and Supplemental Security Income

Although opioid use (illegal or prescribed) is seldom a key factor in denying DI benefits, many individuals find it challenging to complete the benefits application, which requires extensive documentation of disabilities and sometimes involves multiple hearings (Bloom, Loprest, and Zedlewski, 2011). To help applicants, some states are connecting recipients to legal services and other providers who can assist with this process (Bloom, Loprest, and Zedlewski, 2011). One promising approach is SAMHSA's SSI/SSDI Outreach, Access, and Recovery (SOAR) program, which "aims to improve access to SSI and SSDI for people who are homeless or at risk of becoming homeless, with a particular focus on people with mental illness" (Kauff et al., 2016). Case managers trained by SOAR assist eligible individuals with their SSI and SSDI applications. Analyses of SSA administrative data found that initial SSDI or SSI applications submitted through the SOAR process were approved at almost double the rate of those among all applicants experiencing homelessness (50 percent versus 28 percent) (Kauff et al., 2016).

Mitigating the Consequences of a Drug-Related Criminal Record

The existence of a criminal record can constrain an individual's ability to receive support from the social services system, specifically by limiting eligibility for public benefits or access to public housing. One way to mitigate these negative consequences would be to change the eligibility rules pertaining to an applicant's criminal history; an alternative would be to seal or expunge relevant criminal records. These changes could be done by systematically helping individuals petition the court or by establishing rules for an automatic sealing or expungement after a certain period has elapsed since the offense.

Improving Information and Research on Welfare and TANF Populations and Their Use of Opioids

A major limitation facing policymakers is the lack of contemporary research on opioid use by people who are receiving or eligible for TANF; many research studies predate the current opioid crisis (Germain, 2018). As a result, studies available on TANF clients and SUDs have tended to focus on general SUDs rather than OUDs (Germain, 2018). There remains an important need for better information about the prevalence of substance use and SUDs among TANF recipients, how it might affect the employability of low-income individuals, and the degree to which services are available for those with OUDs receiving TANF (Germain, 2018; Morgenstern and Blanchard, 2006).

Developing Opioid Use Disorder Treatment and Prevention Strategies Specifically Targeted to TANF and TANF-Eligible Populations

As noted earlier, welfare offices typically rely on recipients' self-disclosure of use of opioids and other substances. However, many welfare recipients might be reluctant to disclose substance use because of the stigma associated with it and out of concern about losing their welfare benefits. As a result, TANF agencies are screening and referring to treatment a substantially lower number of people than would be expected based on prevalence rates (Germain, 2018; Radel, Joyce, and Wulff, 2011). Walker and Franklin, 2018, in their assessment of drug-testing programs for welfare recipients, concluded that—in addition to being expensive—drug-testing programs are often viewed as punitive and, in general, are not an effective means for facilitating treatment entry. Instead, programs that combine treatment methods—such as

Intensive Case Management (ICM)[2] or the Individual Placement and Support (IPS) model of supported employment—are considered promising approaches for TANF recipients with an OUD (Germain, 2018; Lones et al., 2017).

Implementing a Housing First Approach to Address the Intersection of the Opioid Crisis and Homelessness

The Housing First approach is an alternative to traditional housing models in which individuals experiencing homelessness first have to take part in and successfully complete short-term residential and treatment programs before receiving permanent housing (HUD, 2014). Key features of a Housing First approach that offers people experiencing homelessness access to permanent housing options include (1) few to no treatment preconditions; (2) low-barrier admission policies; (3) rapid and streamlined entry into housing; (4) voluntary supportive services; and (5) the incorporation of practices and policies that prevent lease violations and evictions among tenants (HUD, 2014). In addition, a Housing First approach is intended to provide tenants with legal protections and to be applicable in a variety of housing models (HUD, 2014).

The Housing First model has been cited by SAMHSA and HUD as a best practice for reducing chronic homelessness (Pfefferle, Karon, and Wyant, 2019). The U.S. Interagency Council on Homelessness (USICH) also supports a Housing First approach (Pfefferle, Karon, and Wyant, 2019). In September 2021, the Biden administration launched *House America*, a partnership between HUD and USICH, which adopts a Housing First approach to address the crisis of homelessness (HUD, 2021).

A body of research has found that Housing First appears to be an effective strategy for providing stable housing for people experiencing chronic homelessness (Kerman et al., 2021; Padgett, Henwood, and Tsemberis, 2015). However, Kerman et al., 2021, cautions that evidence regarding Housing First approaches and harm reduction outcomes remains limited, with most studies focusing only on general indicators of substance use problems. According to a systematic review of the literature on harm reduction outcomes and practices in Housing First models in Kerman et al., 2021, authors concluded that additional research is needed on how Housing First affects unsupervised drug use, polysubstance use, and access to and use of naloxone and equipment for safer drug use.

---

[2] A 2006 random-assignment study showed that ICM, which involves individual-level monitoring and social service support over an extended period, improved outcomes of TANF recipients, including employment, treatment attendance, and substance use patterns (Germain, 2018).

Introduction

People experiencing homelessness are estimated to be more likely to suffer from SUDs, poorer health, and mortality by opioid overdose in comparison with national averages (Warfield and DiPietro, 2016). In addition, individuals in poverty have higher rates of OUD than those who have incomes exceeding 200 percent of the federal poverty line (Ghertner and Groves, 2018).

Social services in the United States encompass a wide variety of programs and supports provided by government, for-profit organizations, and nonprofit organizations that are intended to improve the well-being of individuals, families, and communities. Among the wide variety of social services provided by the government, income-security programs (or *income-security means tested entitlements*) address the needs of individuals in poverty by providing direct monetary or noncash assistance (U.S. House of Representatives Committee on the Budget, 2017). Because a notable share of people with an OUD are living at the poverty level, these programs are an important part of the social safety net for them. The share of individuals with an OUD living in poverty is substantially higher than that of the general population. According to the 2020 National Survey on Drug Use and Health (which misses a large share of people who use illegally produced opioids; see Chapter Two), 36 percent of individuals with an OUD were living in poverty,[3] compared with a national poverty rate of 11.4 percent (Substance Abuse and Mental Health Data Archive, undated; Shrider et al., 2021).

It is beyond the scope of this chapter to address the full variety of programs and supports that fall within income support and homeless services.[4] Instead, we focus on three federal income-security programs that provide income support to individuals and families: (1) TANF, which provides cash assistance to families and includes the noncash program (SNAP) that provides food assistance (U.S. Department of Health and Human Services [HHS], Administration for Children and Families, Office of Family Assistance, 2020); (2) SSI, a means-tested program with a strict set of financial requirements, intended to satisfy the basic needs of elderly, blind, and disabled individuals with limited resources (SSA, undated-f); and (3) SSDI, a payroll tax–funded federal insurance program that provides income supplements to disabled workers and their dependents (SSA, undated-c). In addition, we focus on housing and homeless services that provide aid in kind. These programs and in-kind services are critical supports to individuals with OUDs and interact in important ways with other components of the opioid ecosystem, as discussed later in this chapter. Next, we discuss each system component in turn.

---

[3] The share of individuals living in poverty is even higher when looking only at individuals with heroin use disorder (51.22 percent) and at those with heroin and prescription OUD (71.21 percent) (see Substance Abuse and Mental Health Data Archive, undated).

[4] For an overview of the different types of programs that fall within this category, see U.S. House of Representatives Committee on the Budget, 2017.

System Components and How They Interact with Opioids

Social Security Disability Insurance and Supplemental Security Income

Given the prevalence of opioid use nationwide and the proportion of new SSDI awardees who have conditions (e.g., musculoskeletal conditions) related to opioid use, Wu, Hoffman, and O'Leary, 2019, found that opioid use appears to have increased among SSDI applicants. The authors estimated that opioid use from 2007 to 2017 was self-reported by between one-quarter and one-third of those applying for SSDI (Wu, Hoffman, and O'Leary, 2019). This section discusses the role of SSDI and SSI in providing insurance and cash payments to individuals with opioid use.

SSDI and SSI are two federal programs disbursing cash payments to those who meet the federal definition of *disabled*[5]—specifically,

- SSDI pays benefits to individuals and certain members of their families if an individual is *insured*, meaning that the individual has a long enough history of employment and Social Security tax payments.
- SSI pays benefits to disabled adults and children with limited income and resources ("Temporary Assistance for Needy Families," undated).

Both programs are administered by the SSA. Eligibility for benefits under either program is limited to individuals with a disability who meet medical criteria (SSA, undated-a; SSA, undated-c).

Federal law requires the denial of DI benefits to claimants if an alcohol use disorder or another SUD is a contributing factor to be considered for the purposes of disability determination; however, SUDs (including illegal use of opioids) are seldom the reason why the SSA may deny benefits (42 U.S.C. § 423(d)(2)(C), 2012; GAO, 2020). The decision process about DI eligibility of claimants with an SUD, including nonmedical use of prescription opioids, is complex, and there is a lot of uncertainty in how these decisions are actually made.[6] The reasons for this uncertainty are severalfold: (1) It is not clear under what circumstances to carry out a drug addiction and alcoholism evaluation; (2) the policies guiding the determination of

---

[5] The SSA offers a description of how it determines whether an individual is disabled for the purposes of its programs (see SSA, undated-b).

[6] For example, in GAO, 2020, welfare program staff interviewed in three states commented on the subjectivity involved in conducting drug addiction and alcoholism evaluations:

> Staff told us that making DI eligibility decisions for claims involving substance use disorders, including prescription opioids not taken as prescribed, can be complex. For example, staff in our three selected states noted challenges with subjectivity in conducting [drug addiction or alcoholism] evaluations, particularly when the claim involves mental health conditions. They said that certain conditions, such as depression or psychosis, can be exacerbated by substance use disorders.

In addition, program staff reported challenges in understanding and following SSA policies.

Social Security Disability Insurance and Supplemental Security Income Programs

SSI is a means-tested program intended to meet the basic needs of elderly, blind, and disabled individuals with limited resources and, thus, has a strict set of financial requirements (SSA, undated-e). The monthly benefit amount for SSI is set each year by Congress, and many states provide additional financial support.

SSDI, a payroll tax–funded federal insurance program, provides income supplements to individuals who are physically restricted in their ability to work because of a disability. SSDI is available to any person who has paid into the Social Security system for at least ten years, regardless of current income and assets (GAO, 2020).

SSI and SSDI benefits vary considerably in the amount of money that is provided. For 2020, the SSI monthly maximum federal amounts were $783 for an eligible individual, $1,175 for an eligible individual with an eligible spouse, and $392 for an essential person (i.e., a person who lives with an SSI beneficiary and provides essential care) (SSA, undated-d). The average SSDI payment in 2020 was estimated to be $1,258 per month (Laurence, 2021).

what is a medically determinable impairment for people with SUDs are not always clear; and (3) there is missing or incomplete documentation (GAO, 2020).

Trends Show That Social Security Disability Insurance Recipients Have High Prescription Opioid Use

Wu, Hoffman, and O'Leary, 2019, looked at trends in opioid use among SSDI applicants. They estimated the proportion of SSDI applicants reporting opioid use from 2007 through 2017 to be more than 30 percent, with increasing rates until 2012, followed by declines through 2017.

GAO, 2020, examined the relationship at the county level between opioid prescriptions and DI claims for the 2006–2017 period. The GAO found a positive correlation between prescribing rates and DI claims, even after adjusting for economic, demographic, and other factors. The GAO noted that this correlation was expected given that musculoskeletal conditions, such as back and joint impairments—which might involve prescription opioids for the treatment of associated pain—accounted for nearly one-third of all impairments among disabled workers in 2018 (GAO, 2020). The GAO analysis also found a correlation between opioid prescription *rates* on one side and poverty rates, population size, and access to health insurance on the other. In addition, the GAO analysis found a positive correlation between rates of DI claims and poverty rates and between rates of DI claims and unemployment, age, and race.

Expanded Availability of Opioid Prescription Medication Affects Social Security Disability Insurance and Supplemental Security Income Enrollment

Cutler, Meara, and Stewart, 2017, examined the effects of increased availability of prescription opioids on enrollment in SSDI and SSI. They found that between 2006 and 2012, the proportion of disabled beneficiaries receiving a high dose of opioid drugs was 5.8 percent nationally; the range of this rate across all states was 1.6 percent to 11.5 percent. Their analysis also found a relationship between the rates of change in opioid availability and DI enrollment. In other words, localities where the availability of opioids grew faster also saw more-pronounced growth in DI enrollment. Specifically, the results showed that a 30-percent increase in opioid shipments in a given area corresponded to an increase of 5 percent in DI applications.

TANF, Income Support, and SNAP

This section discusses the role of TANF in providing income support and the role of SNAP in providing in-kind assistance in the form of food assistance to low-income individuals who misuse opioids or who have an OUD. The TANF program provides cash assistance to low-income families. The federal government provides grants to states and territories to run the TANF program. State-administered TANF programs provide families with financial assistance and related support services, which may include work and child care assistance, and

---

Temporary Assistance for Needy Families Program

The TANF program assists families with children when the parents or other responsible relatives cannot provide for the family's basic needs. The federal government provides grants to states and territories to run the TANF program. State-administered TANF programs provide families with financial assistance and related support services that may include child care assistance, job preparation, and work assistance.

To qualify for TANF, an applicant must be either pregnant or responsible for a child younger than 19 years of age; be a U.S. national, citizen, legal alien, or permanent resident; have low or very low income; and be underemployed (working for very low wages), unemployed, or about to become unemployed.

Although the federal government provides grants to the states, the states have broad flexibility in carrying out their TANF programs. States determine the designs of their TANF programs, the types and amounts of assistance payments, the variety of other services to be provided, and the rules for determining who is eligible for benefits. Each state and territory also establishes the eligibility criteria for receiving financial assistance payments or other types of benefits and services.

SOURCES: "Temporary Assistance for Needy Families," undated; HHS, 2012; HHS, Administration for Children and Families, Office of Family Assistance, 2018.

The Supplemental Nutrition Assistance Program

SNAP is broadly available to households with low incomes (Center on Budget and Policy Priorities, 2019). SNAP eligibility rules and benefit levels, for the most part, are set at the federal level and are uniform across the nation, though states have flexibility to tailor certain aspects of the program. Under federal rules, to qualify for SNAP benefits, a household must meet three criteria:

- Its gross monthly income generally must be at or below 130 percent of the poverty line.
- Its net monthly income, or income after deductions are applied for items, such as high housing costs and child care, must be less than or equal to the poverty line.
- Its assets must fall below certain limits: In FY 2019, the limits were $2,250 for households without an elderly or disabled member and $3,500 for those with an elderly or disabled member.

SOURCE: This description of SNAP is largely drawn from Center on Budget and Policy Priorities, 2019.

job preparation. Importantly, states and territories enjoy great flexibility in determining what their TANF programs will cover.

SNAP (formerly known as food stamps) is the largest federal nutrition assistance program. It uses an electronic transfer card to provide benefits to eligible low-income individuals and families. SNAP provides food assistance, whereas TANF provides cash assistance. Most TANF recipients also receive SNAP benefits; most TANF programs automatically enroll participants in SNAP (Zedlewski, 2012). For example, in FY 2014, the vast majority (84 percent) of families receiving TANF were also SNAP recipients (HHS, Administration for Children and Families, Office of Family Assistance, 2018).

Research on TANF and Opioid Use Disorder

The role of TANF in providing income support to low-income individuals who use opioids for nonprescribed purposes or who have an OUD has not been extensively researched (Germain, 2018). Thus, there is limited data on the prevalence of OUD within the TANF and TANF-eligible populations. Instead, researchers have drawn inferences about the TANF population from what is known about opioid use by low-income individuals. Individuals in poverty have higher rates of opioid use and OUD than those with incomes more than 200 percent of the federal poverty line (Ghertner and Groves, 2018).

Germain, 2018, conducted a literature review of OUD among TANF recipients. The author found that much of the contemporary research on the opioid use surge focuses instead on the general population. The challenges of collecting data on the prevalence of OUD among the TANF population include (1) underreporting of substance use by individuals across all income levels; (2) reliance on TANF recipients' self-reports of SUD; (3) concern among lower-income individuals that they may lose welfare benefits if they reveal an addiction; and (4) TANF agencies undertaking substantially fewer screenings and referrals than would be expected given existing prevalence rates (Germain, 2018; Radel, Joyce, and Wulff, 2011). As a result, there is little accurate data on the prevalence of OUD among the TANF population and on the frequency of use rates. Furthermore, studies of the prevalence of substance use among TANF recipients have varied widely, with rates ranging between 4 percent and 37 percent (Radel, Joyce, and Wulff, 2011). As noted in Radel, Joyce, and Wulff, 2011, the reasons for this are severalfold:

> . . . studies that define welfare to include General Assistance (GA) beneficiaries often find higher rates. Typically, lower end estimates of around 5 percent or less focus on indications of diagnosable abuse of or dependence on illicit drugs among TANF or (for early estimates) Aid to Families with Dependent Children (AFDC) Program clients. Higher rates, in the 10 percent range, tend to include any past month use of illicit drugs. Rates in the highest ranges (15 percent or more) usually define substance abuse to include alcohol abuse and include any past year (rather than past month) use of illicit drugs.

States also vary in how they provide treatment services for TANF recipients. To illustrate, some states (Illinois and Washington) give priority to TANF recipients and their families for treatment services; in other states (e.g., New Jersey), TANF funding covers recipients' SUD assessment and treatment needs (Germain, 2018).

Germain argues that research on the Medicaid population instead can offer insights on the TANF population because of program overlap. Studies examining SUDs overall have found that Medicaid recipients have rates of SUD that are ten times higher than those of the general population (Germain, 2018), although there is a lot of uncertainty surrounding estimates of those with OUDs.[7] In general, approximately three in ten nonelderly people with OUDs are estimated to be covered by Medicaid (Kaiser Family Foundation, 2017).

Drug screening of welfare recipients is controversial. Walker and Franklin, 2018, used a proportionality approach to assess drug-testing programs of welfare recipients. They concluded that drug screening of welfare recipients is expensive, but the practice is also often seen as punitive and not effective in facilitating treatment entry. They also concluded that drug testing of welfare recipients does not meet the criteria for being ethically acceptable.[8] Instead, programs that combine treatment methods, such as ICM or the IPS model,[9] of sup-

---

[7] In 2013, one study estimated that 636,000 Medicaid enrollees suffered from an OUD (Young and Zur, 2017).

[8] Walker and Franklin, 2018, noted that "[f]or ethical acceptability a practice must be reasonably likely to meet its aims, sufficiently important in purpose as to outweigh harms incurred, and lower in costs than feasible alternatives."

[9] As noted in Germain, 2018, p. 9, "Successful IPS programs have assisted individuals with financial management, mental health, substance use disorder, and vocational services, and encourage employment that

ported employment are considered promising approaches for TANF recipients with OUDs (Germain, 2018; Lones et al., 2017).

Homeless and Housing Programs

People experiencing homelessness are estimated to have higher rates of SUDs, poorer health, and higher opioid-involved mortality rates than national averages (Warfield and DiPietro, 2016). According to Poe and Boyer, 2017, p. 2, "Housing is a major social determinant of health, and lack of housing has been shown to negatively impact physical and behavioral health among individuals experiencing homelessness." Hence, policies related to homelessness and housing can play a role in promoting better OUD outcomes.

Nationally, two-thirds of people experiencing homelessness are estimated to have had an SUD during their lifetimes (SAMHSA, 2018). Furthermore, overdose is a major cause of death among those experiencing homelessness. A study of adults experiencing homelessness in Boston found that drug overdose was the cause in 17 percent of deaths among homeless people; 81 percent of these deaths involved opioids (Baggett et al., 2013). Specifically among men and women aged 25 to 44 experiencing homelessness, opioid overdose death rates were nine times higher than among their housed counterparts. OUD is common among people experiencing homelessness, even if individuals experiencing homelessness represent only a fraction of those with OUD.[10]

At the federal level, USICH is tasked with coordinating the federal response to homelessness (USICH, undated). In 2017, USICH outlined five strategies that communities can use to (1) assess the scope of the problem and build partnerships and (2) adopt best practices and evidence-based programs to address the opioid crisis among people locally experiencing homelessness (USICH, 2017). These five strategies are discussed later in this chapter.

Continuum-of-Care Homeless Assistance Program

HUD manages the CoC Homeless Assistance Program. CoC programs were established in 1995 to (1) streamline funding and grant-making processes for assistance programs targeting people experiencing homelessness and (2) support the coordination at the local level of planning and the provision of housing and services for people experiencing homelessness (Burt et al., 2002). CoC programs are the primary coordinating bodies for homeless services in the United States (Fowler et al., 2019). To achieve its objectives, the CoC program provides funding for the quick rehousing of individuals and families experiencing homelessness. Recipients of this funding include state and local governments and nonprofit providers (HUD Exchange, undated). There are four parts to a CoC model: outreach, intake, and assessment; emergency shelter; transitional housing with supportive services; and permanent supportive

---

promotes recovery."

[10] This is based on the 2020 estimate of 580,000 people experiencing homelessness in the United States (see USICH, 2021). Also, see Chapter Two for estimates of the total population of individuals with OUDs.

housing (PSH) with services, if needed. In addition, the CoCs conduct biannual counts of the homeless population (National Alliance to End Homelessness, 2010).

There have been only a few evaluations of the CoC model. In 2002, the Urban Institute examined how the development of 25 CoC programs across the United States was influenced by federal funding being available for homeless assistance programs and by a requirement introduced by HUD that communities organize themselves to provide coherent systems of care (Burt et al., 2002). According to the study, "Respondents reported increased capacity, increased diversity, and increased coordination of their homeless-specific programs and services" (Burt et al., 2002). Most of the 25 communities in the study also reported that the CoC funding structure improved coordination and planning and led to a greater number of stakeholder participants in the planning process (Burt et al., 2002).

Fowler et al., 2019, undertook an evaluation that aimed to capture perceptions of service delivery gaps in a Midwestern CoC. The review of the literature in Fowler et al., 2019, found few research studies on various aspects of CoC functioning, including coordination governance and planning methods, with the available research instead focusing on the relationship between policies governing homeless services, coordination, and service integration. The authors also found little research on considerations regarding the distribution of CoC funding across different service types. Examples of recipients of CoC funding include emergency shelter, permanent housing, supportive services, and prevention services.

Housing Models

Government and nonprofit public or private agencies provide housing services (including government-subsidized housing) to homeless people in need of transitional or permanent housing. To improve the understanding of housing models suitable for supporting individuals with OUDs, Pfefferle, Karon, and Wyant, 2019, undertook an environmental scan of the literature and conducted interviews with experts in OUD or SUD and homelessness and with housing providers and collaborative partners in four communities. Regardless of what housing model was being used to provide housing for individuals experiencing homelessness and SUD, the environmental scan and expert interviews identified three important elements of a housing model: (1) that it fosters social support; (2) that it takes a trauma-informed approach; and (3) that it involves personal choice, allowing individuals to choose their own recovery environments (Pfefferle, Karon, and Wyant, 2019). The environmental scan in Pfefferle, Karon, and Wyant, 2019, identified only a few programs specifically focused on individuals with OUD and experiencing housing instability. That said, the authors highlighted a list of four housing models for homeless individuals with OUD. We also included in the list a fifth housing model (rapid rehousing) identified in National Alliance to End Homelessness, 2016. The housing models are shown in the box titled "Possible Housing Models for Homeless Individuals with Opioid Use Disorder." Except for recovery housing, all of the housing models incorporate elements of the Housing First model.

Existing evidence suggests that, compared with other types of programs, Housing First approaches led to between 75-percent and 95-percent higher improvements in housing sta-

Possible Housing Models for People Experiencing Homelessness with Opioid Use Disorder

Housing First: A Housing First approach is an alternative to the traditional approach of having people experiencing homelessness first participate in and graduate from short-term residential and treatment programs before obtaining permanent housing (HUD, 2014). Instead, using a Housing First approach, homeless people are offered access to permanent housing options with the following features: (1) few to no treatment preconditions or other barriers to entry, such as sobriety, treatment, or service participation requirements; (2) low-barrier admission policies; (3) rapid and streamlined entry into housing; (4) voluntary supportive services; (5) tenants having full rights, responsibilities, and legal protections; (6) the incorporation of practices and policies that prevent lease violations and evictions among tenants; and (7) applicability in a variety of housing models (HUD, 2014). A central tenet of Housing First is harm reduction.

Rapid rehousing: This housing model follows the Housing First approach but differs in implementation. This model provides short-term rental assistance and services and is employed for a wide variety of individuals and families. The goals are to help people obtain housing quickly, increase self-sufficiency, and remain housed. The core components of rapid rehousing—housing identification, rent and move-in assistance, and case management and services—operationalize Housing First principles.

PSH: This model is targeted to households that have at least one member with a chronic disabling condition who requires ongoing support for the household to live independently. PSH projects provide permanent housing (either in a permanent housing property or through tenant-based rental subsidies) and services to support residents' needs. PSH is targeted to individuals and families with chronic illnesses, disabilities, mental health issues, or SUDs who have experienced long-term or repeated homelessness. It provides long-term rental assistance and supportive services. Some PSH programs use the Housing First philosophy, while some PSH models require SUD treatment and abstinence.

Housing Choice:[a] This is a combined approach that incorporates elements of both recovery housing and Housing First to allow individuals to select housing based on their personal needs. Individuals can choose from a variety of housing options, including transitional housing, PSH, family housing, Housing First, and recovery housing.

Recovery housing: These programs are intended to support individuals with an SUD in their recovery, often as a step down from inpatient or residential SUD treatment. The recovery housing approach considers that individuals with a history of SUD are better off in a home environment that emphasizes abstinence.

SOURCES: The description of the Housing First model is largely drawn from HUD, 2014. The descriptions of the other housing models are largely drawn from Pfefferle, Karon, and Wyant, 2019.

[a] Housing Choice was developed by Central City Concern in Portland, Oregon.

bility rates (Padgett, Henwood, and Tsemberis, 2015). For example, a systematic literature review and meta-analysis of randomized controlled trials in Baxter et al., 2019, identified four studies that reported housing stability measures. In all four studies, Housing First recipients saw notable increases in their housing stability compared with treatment as usual: The approximate effect estimate was that Housing First participants had housing stability rates that were 2.5 times higher after 18 to 24 months than their control counterparts.

Davidson et al., 2014, examined how the implementation of Housing First affected housing and substance use outcomes. The study included 358 individuals with histories of chronic homelessness and problematic substance use who were housed in nine Housing First programs in New York City. Client interviews were conducted at baseline and 12 months to assess substance use. The authors also incorporated a measure of program fidelity based on eight core program components deemed essential to high fidelity to Housing First principles. Davidson et al., 2014, found that retention in housing was significantly better in Housing First programs judged to have consistently implemented consumer participation components. Furthermore, participants in these programs also had significantly lower rates of self-reported stimulant or opioid use at follow-up.[11]

Harm reduction is a central tenet of the Housing First program model. Kerman et al., 2021, examined the connection between Housing First and harm reduction outcomes and practices in the following four domains: substance-related harms, viral health, sexual health, and harm reduction services. In a systematic review of the published literature, Kerman et al., 2021, identified 35 original research studies.[12] Of the 13 studies that examined substance use, most employed indicators of general substance use problems, frequency of drinking to intoxication, and/or binge drinking. Housing First was found to have only minimal effects on these outcomes. For example, one randomized controlled trial examining a high-fidelity intervention in five Canadian cities failed to find a difference in substance-related outcomes over time between Housing First and the control intervention (treatment as usual, up to six years postrandomization) (Kerman et al., 2021). Similar results were reported by three quasi-experimental studies examining different types of Housing First interventions. The authors concluded that the research evidence suggests that Housing First does not enable substance use harm reduction, adding that more research was needed on the effects of Housing First on other outcomes, including unaccompanied drug use, polysubstance use, and access to and use of naloxone and equipment for safer drug use. In addition, in light of differential overdose

---

[11] The odds ratio was 0.17, the confidence interval was 0.07–0.57, and the p-value was 0.002 (Davidson et al., 2014).

[12] As Kerman et al., 2021, pp. 3 and 8, noted,

> Studies were variable in quality; seven were assessed as being high quality, 18 were moderate quality, and 10 were low quality. . . . High quality studies comprised . . . primary analyses from well-controlled studies with or without randomization, as well as two detailed qualitative studies involving robust designs. Moderate quality articles included a range of quasi-experiments and qualitative studies, as well as secondary analyses from larger research projects. . . . Low quality articles included mostly small retrospective cohort studies and program evaluations.

risks by substance, Kerman et al., 2021, asserted that it would be important to examine harms specific to various drug types.

Austin et al., 2021, examined the association between housing stress and later substance use. To do so, they conducted a systematic review of the literature on housing stress, substance use, and epidemiologic research.[13] Their review of 38 articles published between 1991 and 2020 "demonstrated an association of homelessness with an increased likelihood of substance use, substance use disorders (SUD), and overdose death."

Interactions with Other Components of the Ecosystem

Figure 11.1 highlights the ecosystem components that interact with the income support and homeless services component in regard to opioids: medical care, SUD treatment, the criminal legal system, child welfare, and employment. In this section, we discuss the interactions between these components and the social services programs and services discussed in this chapter.

Medical Care

The medical care component covers physical and mental health care beyond specialty SUD treatment. It includes health care providers, health care delivery organizations, insurers, pharmaceutical companies, medical training organizations, and various regulatory bodies. We highlight here the interaction of the social services programs discussed in this chapter with the insurance component of medical care. That is, the same clients are eligible for both sets of programs, as discussed next.

The interaction with the medical care system primarily lies in the fact that beneficiaries of social services usually receive access to medical care via publicly funded health care programs. In addition, the medical care system can serve as an access point and source of referral for individuals to various social services (Andermann, 2018).

As noted earlier in this chapter, SSI beneficiaries typically receive Medicaid,[14] whereas SSDI provides access to Medicare (Academy of Special Needs Planners, 2022). In most cases, a person who receives SSI is immediately eligible for Medicaid. In addition to monthly financial benefits, SSDI beneficiaries become eligible for Medicare two years after they can receive

---

[13] According to Austin et al., 2021, p. 2, eligibility criteria

included articles that examined the association of housing stress (i.e., housing instability, insecurity, or insufficiency, homelessness, eviction, overcrowding, poor physical housing conditions, frequent moves, high housing cost relative to income) with substance use outcomes (i.e., substance use, misuse, or use disorders, motivation or intention to change use, fatal and nonfatal overdose, treatment initiation, retention, and completion).

[14] Medicaid is a joint state and federal health insurance program for qualifying low-income adults.

FIGURE 11.1

Income Support and Homeless Services' Interactions with Key Components of the Opioid Ecosystem

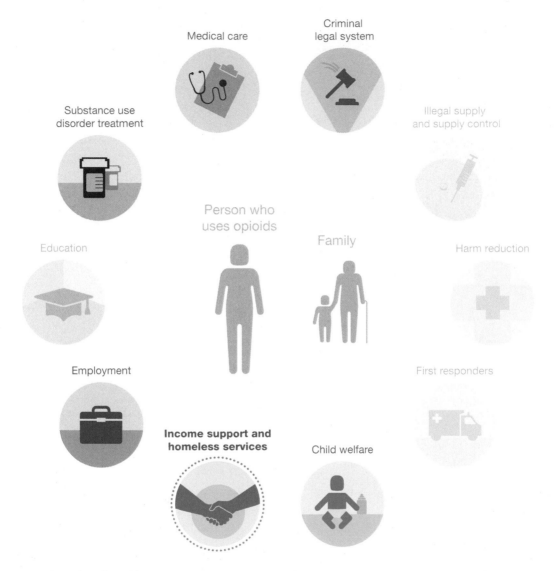

SSDI benefits.[15] Furthermore, SSDI and SSI beneficiaries are dually eligible for Medicare and Medicaid health insurance. About three-quarters of SSDI recipients are also enrolled in Medicaid and in SSI (Finkelstein, Gentzkow, and Williams, 2018). However, important segments

---

[15] People who receive SSDI are eligible for Medicare and, in most cases, are automatically enrolled in Medicare after a two-year waiting period. The waiting period does not apply if an individual is 65 years old or older (Centers for Medicare and Medicaid Services [CMS], 2021).

of the SSDI population do not receive Medicaid and, thus, face additional service barriers (Armour and O'Hanlon, 2019).

Similarly, nearly all TANF cases also receive Medicaid, with TANF programs usually automatically enrolling beneficiaries in Medicaid (Zedlewski, 2012). Given the high degree of program overlap between TANF and Medicaid, the Medicaid population offers some insights about the TANF population. For example, in FY 2013, about 635,000 people enrolled in Medicaid had an OUD—a prevalence of 889 per 100,000 (Young and Zur, 2017). In 2017, Medicaid provided coverage for four in ten nonelderly individuals with an OUD (Kaiser Family Foundation, 2019).

Substance Use Disorder Treatment

One area where the income support and homeless services component interacts with the OUD treatment system is where social service beneficiaries participate in treatment programs. As discussed earlier, Medicaid expansion has provided states with additional resources to cover many adults with an SUD. Three MOUD—methadone, buprenorphine, and extended-release naltrexone—have been shown to be effective in reducing opioid use and adverse health outcomes (Haffajee et al., 2019). All state Medicaid programs cover at least two MOUD, and most cover all three (Kaiser Family Foundation, 2019).[16] In 2018, many state Medicaid programs that covered OUD treatment services had implemented measures to curb opioid prescribing (Kaiser Family Foundation, 2019).[17]

Low-income individuals with an SUD, including TANF recipients, typically can access a variety of medical, behavioral, case management, and community-based treatment options, including MOUD (Germain, 2018). Treatment providers have noted several challenges that TANF participants with SUDs have faced in meeting work requirements if their treatments are not an allowable activity under their state TANF programs (Germain, 2018; Benoit et al., 2004).

The second area where the income support and homeless services component and OUD treatment intersect is housing. In 2017, USICH outlined five strategies addressing the intersection of homelessness and the opioid crisis that illustrate the interactions with a variety of other systems, such as OUD treatment. USICH asserts that these strategies illustrate the types of interactions homeless service agencies need to have with a variety of other systems to effectively address this issue. They include

---

[16] The three MOUD are methadone (covered by 40 states and the District of Columbia), buprenorphine (covered by 50 states and the District of Columbia), and naltrexone (covered by 50 states and the District of Columbia).

[17] Forty-three states covered inpatient detoxification, 33 states covered residential rehabilitation, 31 states covered outpatient detoxification, and 38 states covered intensive outpatient treatment (see Kaiser Family Foundation, 2019).

- assessing the prevalence of OUD and opioid misuse among individuals experiencing homelessness
- developing and implementing overdose prevention and response strategies (e.g., improving access to naloxone)
- strengthening partnerships between housing and health care providers
- improving access to MOUD, such as through connections between homelessness and health care service providers, landlords, and housing providers at the local level
- removing barriers to housing (this strategy includes using a Housing First approach to offer access to permanent housing).

Criminal Legal System

Here, we address the intersection between the income support and homeless services component and the criminal legal system. For individuals with a criminal record, their ability to access these programs can be affected in several ways, as discussed next.

Suspension or Termination of Medicaid Benefits

Individuals who are incarcerated in jail or prison will have their Medicaid benefits either suspended or, in some instances, terminated. Section 1905(a)(A) of the Social Security Act excludes federal Medicaid funding for medical care provided to "inmates of a public institution" (National Association of Counties, 2017).[18] Although states are directed to only suspend (i.e., not terminate) Medicaid benefits for those who are incarcerated, some states still discontinue Medicaid enrollment at the time of jail booking or entry into prison. In such cases, the reapproval for Medicaid upon reentry can be a very lengthy process. This factor, in turn, may lead to interruptions in access to medical, mental health, and addiction treatment services and, for those released from jail or prison, affect an individual's ability to continue receiving treatment out in the community that began while incarcerated.

This issue is also relevant to those individuals who have been released to halfway houses. People involved with the criminal legal system who are not incarcerated but under community supervision (e.g., probation, parole) may receive Medicaid benefits if they meet the state's eligibility criteria required of all residents (Pew Charitable Trusts, 2016). In guidance from CMS, HHS reversed previous policy that prohibited the coverage of services for Medicaid-eligible persons residing in state or local community residential facilities under correctional supervision (e.g., halfway houses).

Lifetime Ban on TANF or SNAP for Individuals Convicted of a Drug Felony

As part of the welfare reform legislation entitled the Personal Responsibility and Work Opportunity Reconciliation Act of 1996, states could impose a lifetime ban on TANF or SNAP to

---

[18] This *inmate exception* has been a feature of the Social Security Act since its inception in 1965.

anyone convicted of a drug felony.[19] Congress allowed states not to enforce this requirement. The vast majority of states have used this prerogative or have at least modified the ban to impose less severe restrictions (Polkey, 2019).[20] As of March 2019, ten states have a full drug ban on TANF benefits; 21 states and the District of Columbia have a modified ban; and 17 states have no ban on TANF benefits. Fewer states have a drug ban for SNAP (Thompson and Burnside, 2019).[21]

Impact on Access to Public Housing

Illicit drug use also affects an individual's eligibility for public housing. PHAs have the ability, granted by federal policies, to ban people with histories of drug use or those considered at risk of illegal drug use from obtaining housing assistance (HUD and PIH, 2019). Specifically, as noted in HUD and PIH, 2019, PHAs must deny admission if

> [t]he PHA determines that a household member is currently illegally using a controlled substance or such household member's illegal use (or pattern of illegal use) of a controlled substance, or abuse (or pattern of abuse) of alcohol, is determined by the PHA to interfere with the health, safety, or right to peaceful enjoyment of the premises by other residents. The PHA may consider whether such household member has taken steps to rehabilitate or has been rehabilitated and is no longer engaging in the illegal use of a controlled substance or abuse of alcohol.[22]

Prior research has found that some PHAs have created more-extensive bans than required in interpreting these policies. For example, Lundgren, Curtis, and Oettinger, 2010, analyzed postincarceration policies in relation to housing assistance and other federal programs. They found that the length of housing assistance bans imposed on those convicted of a drug felony frequently exceeded the three-year ban required in the federal mandates. Curtis, Garlington, and Schottenfeld, 2013, analyzed data from 40 PHAs to examine alcohol, drug, and criminal

---

[19] As Polkey, 2019, notes, "Among the new requirements was one that disqualified individuals from accessing public benefits if they have been convicted of a federal or state offense for the possession, use or distribution of a controlled substance."

[20] As noted in Polkey, 2019,

> The vast majority of states have opted out of the restriction or imposed less severe restrictions through a modified ban. Examples of modified approaches include:
>
> - Limiting the circumstances in which the permanent disqualification applies (in the cases when convictions involve the sale of drugs).
> - Requiring the convicted person to submit to drug testing.
> - Requiring participation in a drug treatment program.
> - Imposing a two-year temporary disqualification period for those who violate parole.

[21] Only three states have a full drug ban for SNAP benefits; 24 states have a modified ban; and 24 states plus the District of Columbia have no ban (Thompson and Burnside, 2019).

[22] In addition, PHAs are directed to deny admission to public housing if a member of the household was convicted of producing methamphetamine on the premises of federally assisted housing.

history provisions related to access to or eviction from public housing.[23] They found wide variations among PHAs in the ban lengths and definitions of problematic alcohol or drug behavior, noting that, in part, these variations may be due to the fact that PHAs are given broad discretion in enforcing and interpreting the rules. As a result, the authors noted that similar households may encounter different rules across and within PHAs in their efforts to gain or keep access to housing assistance.

Employment

Intersection with employment is relevant for TANF participants with an OUD. A key component of TANF is providing job services and support to help a participant become ready for work and find employment. A literature review of OUDs among TANF recipients identified numerous barriers to employment associated with an OUD, such as limited work experience, domestic violence, low levels of education, and mental health disorders (Germain, 2018).

As detailed in Chapter Twelve, negative labor market outcomes to which the opioid crisis has contributed likely lead to an increase in social services spending. Furthermore, reductions in employment can also have a negative impact on the ability to provide social services via lower tax revenue. Although there is an important connection among experiencing a workplace injury, using opioids, departing from the labor force, and receiving SSDI, the sizes of any causal relationships among these phenomena are challenging to measure.

Child Welfare

As noted in Chapter Ten, the opioid crisis has had devastating effects on children and families. Parents dealing with substance use, including opioid use, often have trouble finding and maintaining employment, caring for their children, and/or addressing health concerns, and some families experience homelessness as a result (Martin et al., 2016). In addition, these families often touch many social services systems, including the child welfare system and TANF. Analyses in Radel et al., 2018, found a positive correlation between rates of overdose deaths and drug hospitalizations and child welfare caseload rates.

Departments of social services that run a state's TANF program will often contract with private child welfare agencies and community-based organizations to provide services to families, including SUD treatment (Child Welfare Information Gateway, 2020). In addition, states may use TANF to fund various child welfare activities, including family reunification services and crisis intervention (Child Welfare Information Gateway, 2020). For example, as part of its TANF program, California's Department of Social Services funded the Family Stabilization Program to support families in crisis, providing them with intensive case management and other services to help them overcome an identified situation or crisis (Davis et al., 2020). Destabilizing conditions include homelessness, domestic violence, and untreated or

---

[23] Specifically, they collected and analyzed Admissions and Continued Occupancy Policy documents for 40 PHAs.

undertreated mental health or substance use problems. In addition, the Family Stabilization Program enables counties to provide direct services to the children of these families.

Major challenges affecting the interactions between child welfare agencies and families and SUD treatment options, including MOUD, are (1) timeliness of assessments and the inconsistent assessment of parents' substance use, (2) misunderstanding and mistrust of MOUD for parents, and (3) treatment shortages of publicly available funded programs and limited family-friendly treatment options (Radel et al., 2018).

Policy Opportunities and Considerations

Next, we discuss policy implications of these findings. We acknowledge that the coronavirus disease 2019 (COVID-19) pandemic has had a large effect on demand for income support and homeless services programs and on the funding available. We did not address these issues in our analysis, but they will have to be taken into consideration by programs moving forward.

Improving Access to Social Security Disability Insurance and Supplemental Security Income

As noted earlier, opioid use (illegal or prescribed) is seldom a key factor in denying DI benefits (GAO, 2020). However, one of the challenges is that the SSI application requires extensive documentation of disabilities and, sometimes, involves multiple hearings (Bloom, Loprest, and Zedlewski, 2011). To assist applicants in completing the form, some states have connected recipients to legal services and other providers to help them with the process (Loprest et al., 2007).

Another approach has been SAMHSA's SOAR program, which "aims to improve access to SSI and SSDI for people who are homeless or at risk of becoming homeless, with a particular focus on people with mental illness" (Kauff et al., 2016). Case managers trained by SOAR assist eligible individuals with their SSI and SSDI applications. Analyses of SSA administrative data found that initial SSDI or SSI applications submitted through the SOAR process were approved almost twice as often as applications submitted by all homeless applicants (50 percent versus 28 percent) (Kauff et al., 2016).

Consider Mitigating the Consequences of a Drug-Related Criminal Record

As discussed earlier, the existence of a criminal record constrains an individual's ability to receive support from the social services system, specifically by limiting the individual's eligibility for public benefits or access to public housing. One way to mitigate some of these negative consequences is to change the rules on eligibility, such as for housing assistance, TANF, or SNAP, pertaining to an applicant's criminal history. However, there could be some political resistance to such a move—but, as noted in Chapter Six, several states have removed some of these restrictions.

A related alternative would be to seal or expunge relevant criminal records for some drug offenses. Pursuant to state laws, these efforts could be done by systematically helping individuals petition the court or by establishing rules for an automatic sealing or expungement after a certain amount of time has elapsed since the offense (see the discussion in Chapter Six). However, as noted in Chapter Two, many of those with criminal records for drug offenses also have records for other offenses. This factor may limit any benefits associated with only expunging drug offenses.

Improving Information and Research on Populations on Welfare or TANF Populations and Their Use of Opioids

A major limitation facing policymakers is the lack of contemporary research on opioid use by TANF and TANF-eligible populations; much of the research predates the current opioid crisis (Germain, 2018). As a result, available studies have tended to focus on TANF clients and on general SUDs rather than OUDs (Germain, 2018). There remains an important need for information about the scope of the opioid crisis and its effects on the employability of low-income individuals, the prevalence of substance use and OUD among TANF recipients, and the availability of services for TANF recipients with OUD (Germain, 2018; Morgenstern and Blanchard, 2006).

Developing Opioid Use Disorder Treatment and Prevention Strategies Specifically Targeted to the TANF and TANF-Eligible Populations

As noted earlier, welfare offices typically rely on recipients' self-disclosure about use of opioids and other substances. However, many welfare recipients may be reluctant to disclose substance use because of the stigma associated with it and out of concern about losing their welfare benefits. As a result, TANF agencies are screening and referring to treatment a substantially lower number of people than would be expected based on prevalence rates (Germain, 2018; Radel, Joyce, and Wulff, 2011). In an assessment of drug-testing programs for welfare recipients, Walker and Franklin, 2018, concluded that, in addition to being expensive, drug-testing programs are often viewed as punitive and, in general, are not an effective means for facilitating treatment entry. Instead, programs that combine such treatment methods as ICM[24] or the IPS model of supported employment are considered promising approaches for TANF recipients with OUDs (Germain, 2018; Lones et al., 2017).

---

[24] ICM, which involves long-term, personal monitoring and social service assistance, was shown in a 2006 random-assignment study to improve TANF recipients' employment, substance abstinence, and treatment attendance outcomes (Germain, 2018).

Implementing a Housing First Approach to Address the Intersection of the Opioid Crisis and Homelessness

The Housing First model has been cited by SAMHSA and HUD as a best practice for reducing chronic homelessness (Pfefferle, Karon, and Wyant, 2019). In addition, the model and a systemwide Housing First orientation enjoy the support of the USICH (Pfefferle, Karon, and Wyant, 2019). In September 2021, the Biden administration launched House America (a partnership between HUD and USICH), which adopts a Housing First approach to address the crisis of homelessness by immediately rehousing and creating more housing for people experiencing homelessness (HUD, 2021).[25]

Research has shown that Housing First appears to be effective in providing stable housing for people experiencing chronic homelessness (Kerman et al., 2021; Padgett, Henwood, and Tsemberis, 2015). Although the evidence base supports the idea that Housing First does not reduce substance use harms, Kerman et al., 2021, cautions that evidence regarding Housing First approaches and harm reduction outcomes remains limited, largely because most studies have focused instead on broader indicators of substance use. Additional research is needed to assess the Housing First model's effectiveness (specifically for people with OUD), including research on the effects of Housing First on other outcomes, such as unaccompanied drug use, polysubstance use, and access to and use of naloxone and equipment for safer drug use (Kerman et al., 2021).

---

[25] As stated in HUD, undated,

> House America calls on state, tribal, and local leaders to partner with HUD and USICH to use American Rescue Plan resources, alongside other federal, tribal, state, and local resources to set and achieve ambitious goals to rehouse households experiencing homelessness through a Housing First approach, and to add new units of affordable housing into the development pipeline by December 31, 2022.

Abbreviations

CMS	Centers for Medicare and Medicaid Services
CoC	Continuum of Care
DI	disability insurance
FY	fiscal year
GAO	U.S. Government Accountability Office
HUD	U.S. Department of Housing and Urban Development
ICM	Intensive Case Management
IPS	Individual Placement and Support
MOUD	medications for opioid use disorder
OUD	opioid use disorder
PHA	public housing agency
PIH	Office of Public and Indian Housing
PSH	permanent supportive housing
SAMHSA	Substance Abuse and Mental Health Services Administration
SNAP	Supplemental Nutrition Assistance Program
SOAR	SSI/SSDI Outreach, Access, and Recovery
SSA	Social Security Administration
SSDI	Social Security Disability Insurance
SSI	Supplemental Security Income
SUD	substance use disorder
TANF	Temporary Assistance for Needy Families
USICH	U.S. Interagency Council on Homelessness

References

Academy of Special Needs Planners, "Three Big Differences Between SSI and SSDI," webpage, March 18, 2022. As of November 6, 2020:
https://specialneedsanswers.com/three-big-differences-between-ssi-and-ssdi-14866

Andermann, Anne, "Screening for Social Determinants of Health in Clinical Care: Moving from the Margins to the Mainstream," *Public Health Reviews*, Vol. 39, No. 19, 2018.

Armour, Philip, and Claire O'Hanlon, *How Does Supplemental Medicare Coverage Affect the Disabled Under-65 Population? An Exploratory Analysis of the Health Effects of States' Medigap Policies for SSDI Beneficiaries*, Cambridge, Mass.: National Bureau of Economic Research, Working Paper No. 25564, February 2019.

Austin, Anna E., Kristin Y. Shiue, Rebecca B. Naumann, Mary C. Figgatt, Caitlin Gest, and Meghan E. Shanahan, "Associations of Housing Stress with Later Substance Use Outcomes: A Systematic Review," *Addictive Behaviors*, Vol. 123, December 2021.

Baggett, Travis P., Stephen W. Hwang, James J. O'Connell, Bianca C. Porneala, Erin J. Stringfellow, E. John Orav, Daniel E. Singer, and Nancy A. Rigotti, "Mortality Among Homeless Adults in Boston: Shifts in Causes of Death over a 15-Year Period," *JAMA Internal Medicine*, Vol. 173, No. 3, 2013, pp. 189–195.

Baxter, Andrew, S. Vittal Katikireddi, Hilary Thomson, and Emily Tweed, "The Effects of Housing First and Other Permanent, Non-Contingent Housing Provision Interventions on the Health and Wellbeing of Homeless Adults: Protocol for a Systematic Review of Randomised Controlled Trials," *Journal of Epidemiology and Community Health*, Vol. 73, No. 5, May 2019, pp. 379–387.

Benoit, Ellen, Rebecca Young, Stephen Magura, and Graham L. Staines, "The Impact of Welfare Reform on Methadone Treatment: Policy Lessons from Service Providers in New York City," *Substance Use & Misuse*, Vol. 39, No. 13–14, 2004, pp. 2355–2390.

Bloom, Dan, Pamela J. Loprest, and Sheila R. Zedlewski, *TANF Recipients with Barriers to Employment*, Washington, D.C.: Urban Institute, August 2011.

Burt, Martha R., Dave Pollack, Abby Sosland, Kelly S. Mikelson, Elizabeth Drapa, Kristy Greenwalt, Patrick Sharkey, Aaron Graham, Martin Abravanel, and Robin Smith, *Evaluation of Continuums of Care for Homeless People: Final Report*, Washington, D.C.: Urban Institute, May 2002.

Center on Budget and Policy Priorities, *Policy Basics: The Supplemental Nutrition Assistance Program (SNAP)*, Washington, D.C., June 25, 2019.

Centers for Medicare and Medicaid Services, "Top 5 Things You Need to Know About Medicare Enrollment," webpage, last updated December 1, 2021. As of June 16, 2022: https://www.cms.gov/Outreach-and-Education/Find-Your-Provider-Type/Employers-and-Unions/Top-5-things-you-need-to-know-about-Medicare-Enrollment

Child Welfare Information Gateway, *How the Child Welfare System Works*, Washington, D.C.: U.S. Department of Health and Human Services, October 2020.

Curtis, Marah A., Sarah Garlington, and Lisa S. Schottenfeld, "Alcohol, Drug, and Criminal History Restrictions in Public Housing," *Cityscape*, Vol. 15, No. 3, 2013, pp. 37–52.

Cutler, David, Ellen Meara, and Susan Stewart, *Has Wider Availability of Prescription Drugs for Pain Relief Affected SSDI and SSI Enrollment?* Cambridge, Mass: National Bureau of Economic Research Disability Research Center, September 2017.

Davidson, Clare, Charles J. Neighbors, Gerod Hall, Aaron Hogue, Richard Cho, Bryan Kutner, and Jon Morgenstern, "Association of Housing First Implementation and Key Outcomes Among Homeless Persons with Problematic Substance Use," *Psychiatric Services*, Vol. 65, No. 11, 2014, pp. 1318–1324.

Davis, Lois M., Lynn A. Karoly, Dionne Barnes-Proby, Beverly A. Weidmer, Praise O. Iyiewuare, Robert Bozick, Gabriele Fain, Sami Kitmitto, Cheryl Graczewski, Eric Larsen, Johannes M. Bos, Melissa Arellanes, Andrew Horinouchi, Jennifer Anthony, Marina Castro, Kaitlin Fronberg, Connie Chandra, and Anlan Zhang, *Evaluation of the SB 1041 Reforms to California's CalWORKs Welfare-to-Work Program: Updated Findings Regarding Policy Implementation and Outcomes*, Santa Monica, Calif.: RAND Corporation, RR-1894-CDSS, 2020. As of May 25, 2022: https://www.rand.org/pubs/research_reports/RR1894.html

Finkelstein, Amy, Matthew Gentzkow, and Heidi Williams, *What Drives Prescription Opioid Abuse? Evidence from Migration*, Stanford, Calif.: Stanford Institute for Economic Policy Research, August 2018.

Fowler, Patrick J., Kenneth Wright, Katherine E. Marcal, Ellis Ballard, and Peter S. Hovmand, "Capability Traps Impeding Homeless Services: A Community-Based System Dynamics Evaluation," *Journal of Social Service Research*, Vol. 45, No. 3, 2019, pp. 348–359.

GAO—*See* U.S. Government Accountability Office.

Germain, Justin, *Opioid Use Disorder, Treatment, and Barriers to Employment Among TANF Recipients*, Washington, D.C.: Office of Family Assistance, Administration for Children and Families, U.S. Department of Health and Human Services, February 2018.

Ghertner, Robin, and Lincoln Groves, *The Opioid Epidemic and Economic Opportunity*, Washington, D.C.: Office of the Assistant Secretary for Planning and Evaluation, working paper, last updated September 2018.

Haffajee, Rebecca L., Lewei Allison Lin, Amy S. B. Bohnert, and Jason E. Goldstick, "Characteristics of US Counties with High Opioid Overdose Mortality and Low Capacity to Deliver Medications for Opioid Use Disorder," *JAMA Network Open*, Vol. 2, No. 6, 2019.

HHS—*See* U.S. Department of Health and Human Services.

HUD—*See* U.S. Department of Housing and Urban Development.

HUD and PIH—*See* U.S. Department of Housing and Urban Development, Office of Public and Indian Housing.

HUD Exchange, "Continuum of Care (CoC) Program," webpage, undated. As of June 16, 2022: https://www.hudexchange.info/programs/coc/

Kaiser Family Foundation, *The Opioid Epidemic and Medicaid's Role in Treatment: A Look at Changes over Time*, San Francisco, Calif., June 29, 2017.

Kaiser Family Foundation, *Medicaid's Role in Addressing the Opioid Epidemic*, San Francisco, Calif., June 3, 2019.

Kauff, Jacqueline F., Elizabeth Clary, Kristin Sue Lupfer, and Pamela J. Fischer, "An Evaluation of SOAR: Implementation and Outcomes of an Effort to Improve Access to SSI and SSDI," *Psychiatric Services*, May 2, 2016.

Kerman, Nick, Alexia Polillo, Geoff Bardwell, Sophia Gran-Ruaz, Cathi Savage, Charlie Felteau, and Sam Tsemberis, "Harm Reduction Outcomes and Practices in Housing First: A Mixed-Methods Systematic Review," *Drug and Alcohol Dependence*, Vol. 228, 2021.

Laurence, Bethany K., "How Much in Social Security Disability Benefits Can You Get?" webpage, November 8, 2021. As of June 15, 2022: https://www.disabilitysecrets.com/how-much-in-ssd.html

Lones, Carrie E., Gary R. Bond, Mark P. McGovern, Kathryn Carr, Teresa Leckron-Myers, Tim Hartnett, and Deborah R. Becker, "Individual Placement and Support (IPS) for Methadone Maintenance Therapy Patients: A Pilot Randomized Controlled Trial," *Administration and Policy in Mental Health and Mental Health Services Research*, Vol. 44, No. 3, 2017, pp. 359–364.

Loprest, Pamela, Pamela A. Holcomb, Karin Martinson, and Sheila R. Zedlewski, *TANF Policies for the Hard to Employ: Understanding State Approaches and Future Directions*, Washington, D.C.: Urban Institute, July 2007.

Lundgren, Lena M., Marah A. Curtis, and Catherine Oettinger, "Postincarceration Policies for Those with Criminal Drug Convictions: A National Policy Review," *Families in Society: The Journal of Contemporary Human Services*, Vol. 91, No. 1, 2010, pp. 31–38.

Martin, Megan, Rosalynd Erney, Alex Citrin, and Rhiannon Reeves, *20 Years of TANF: Opportunities to Better Support Families Facing Multiple Barriers*, Washington, D.C.: Center for the Study of Social Policy, August 2016.

Morgenstern, Jon, and Kimberly A. Blanchard, "Welfare Reform and Substance Abuse Treatment for Welfare Recipients," *Alcohol Research and Health*, Vol. 29, No. 1, 2006.

National Alliance to End Homelessness, "What Is a Continuum of Care?" webpage, January 14, 2010. As of May 25, 2022:
https://endhomelessness.org/resource/what-is-a-continuum-of-care/

National Alliance to End Homelessness, "Housing First," webpage, April 20, 2016. As of May 25, 2022:
https://endhomelessness.org/resource/housing-first/

National Association of Counties, *Medicaid Coverage and County Jails: Understanding Challenges and Opportunities for Improving Health Outcomes for Justice-Involved Individuals*, Washington, D.C., February 2017.

Padgett, Deborah K., Benjamin F. Henwood, and Sam J. Tsemberis, *Housing First: Ending Homelessness, Transforming Systems, and Changing Lives*, New York: Oxford University Press, 2015.

Pew Charitable Trusts, *How and When Medicaid Covers People Under Correctional Supervision*, Philadelphia, Pa., Issue Brief, 2016.

Pfefferle, Susan G., Samantha S. Karon, and Brandy Wyant, *Choice Matters: Housing Models That May Promote Recovery for Individuals and Families Facing Opioid Use Disorder*, Washington, D.C.: U.S. Department of Health and Human Services, Office of the Assistant Secretary for Planning and Evaluation, June 2019.

Poe, Brett, and Alaina Boyer, *Addressing the Opioid Epidemic: How the Opioid Crisis Affects Homeless Populations*, Nashville, Tenn.: National Health Care for the Homeless Council, August 2017.

Polkey, Chesterfield, "Most States Have Ended SNAP Ban for Convicted Drug Felons," *The NCSL Blog*, July 30, 2019. As of June 16, 2022:
https://www.ncsl.org/blog/2019/07/30/most-states-have-ended-snap-ban-for-convicted-drug-felons.aspx

Radel, Laura, Melinda Baldwin, Gilbert Crouse, Robin Ghertner, and Annette Waters, *Substance Use, the Opioid Epidemic, and the Child Welfare System: Key Findings from a Mixed Methods Study*, Washington, D.C.: U.S. Department of Health and Human Services, Office of the Assistant Secretary for Planning and Evaluation, March 7, 2018.

Radel, Laura, Kristen Joyce, and Carli Wulff, *Drug Testing Welfare Recipients: Recent Proposals and Continuing Controversies*, Washington, D.C.: U.S. Department of Health and Human Services, Office of the Assistant Secretary for Planning and Evaluation, October 2011.

SAMHSA—*See* Substance Abuse and Mental Health Services Administration.

Shrider, Emily A., Melissa Kolar, Frances Chen, and Jessica Semega, *Income and Poverty in the United States: 2020*, Washington, D.C.: U.S. Census Bureau and U.S. Department of Commerce, September 2021. As of June 16, 2022:
https://www.census.gov/library/publications/2021/demo/p60-273.html

Social Security Administration, "Benefits for People with Disabilities," webpage, undated-a. As of June 15, 2022:
https://www.ssa.gov/disability/

Social Security Administration, "Code of Federal Regulations: 416.222. Who Is an Essential Person," webpage, undated-b. As of June 15, 2022:
https://www.ssa.gov/OP_Home/cfr20/416/416-0222.htm

Social Security Administration, "Disability Insurance," webpage, undated-c. As of June 15, 2022:
https://www.ssa.gov/benefits/disability/

Social Security Administration, "SSI Federal Payment Amounts for 2022," webpage, undated-d. As of June 15, 2022:
https://www.ssa.gov/oact/cola/SSI.html

Social Security Administration, "Supplemental Security Income," webpage, undated-e. As of June 15, 2022:
https://www.ssa.gov/benefits/ssi/

Social Security Administration, "What Is Supplemental Security Income?" webpage, undated-f. As of June 15, 2022:
https://www.ssa.gov/ssi/

SSA—*See* Social Security Administration.

Substance Abuse and Mental Health Data Archive, "National Survey on Drug Use and Health, 2020: Crosstab Creator," undated. As of June 16, 2022:
https://pdas.samhsa.gov/#/survey/NSDUH-2020-DS0001?column=UDPYOPI&results_received=true&row=POVERTY3&run_chisq=false&weight=ANALWTQ1Q4_C

Substance Abuse and Mental Health Services Administration, "SSI/SSDI Outreach, Access, and Recovery (SOAR): Understanding and Documenting Opioid and Other Substance Use Disorders for SSI/SSDI Claims," webinar, December 12, 2018.

"Temporary Assistance for Needy Families," Benefits.gov, webpage, undated. As of June 16, 2022:
https://www.benefits.gov/benefit/613

Thompson, Darrel, and Ashley Burnside, *No More Double Punishments: Lifting the Ban on SNAP and TANF for People with Prior Felony Drug Convictions*, Washington, D.C.: Center for Law and Social Policy, updated March 2019.

U.S. Code, Title 42, Section 423, Disability Insurance Benefit Payments, January 3, 2012.

U.S. Department of Health and Human Services, "What Is TANF?" webpage, 2012. As of May 16, 2022:
https://www.hhs.gov/answers/programs-for-families-and-children/what-is-tanf/index.html

U.S. Department of Health and Human Services, Administration for Children and Families, Office of Family Assistance, *Temporary Assistance for Needy Families: TANF 12th Report to Congress—Fiscal Years 2014 and 2015*, Washington, D.C., January 25, 2018.

U.S. Department of Health and Human Services, Administration for Children and Families, Office of Family Assistance, "Temporary Assistance for Needy Families (TANF)," webpage, last updated November 2020. As of June 15, 2022:
https://www.acf.hhs.gov/ofa/programs/temporary-assistance-needy-families-tanf

U.S. Department of Housing and Urban Development, "House America: Frequently Asked Questions," webpage, undated. As of June 16, 2022:
https://www.hud.gov/house_america/faq

U.S. Department of Housing and Urban Development, *Housing First in Permanent Supportive Housing*, Washington, D.C., July 2014.

U.S. Department of Housing and Urban Development, "Biden-Harris Administration Launches *House America* Initiative to Address Homelessness Crisis," press release, HUD No. 21-152, September 20, 2021.

U.S. Department of Housing and Urban Development, Office of Public and Indian Housing, "Eligibility Determination and Denial of Assistance," *Housing Choice Voucher Program Guidebook*, Washington, D.C., November 2019.

U.S. Government Accountability Office, *Social Security Disability: Action Needed to Help Agency Staff Understand and Follow Policies Related to Prescription Opioid Misuse*, Washington, D.C., GAO-20-120, January 2020.

U.S. House of Representatives Committee on the Budget, *What You Need to Know About Means-Tested Entitlements*, Washington, D.C., May 1, 2017.

U.S. Interagency Council on Homelessness, "About USICH," webpage, undated. As of June 16, 2022:
https://www.usich.gov/about-usich/

U.S. Interagency Council on Homelessness, *Strategies to Address the Intersection of the Opioid Crisis and Homelessness*, Washington, D.C., February 2017.

U.S. Interagency Council on Homelessness, "Key Findings of 2020 Point-in-Time Count," webpage, last updated July 28, 2021. As of June 16, 2022:
https://www.usich.gov/tools-for-action/2020-point-in-time-count

USICH—*See* U.S. Interagency Council on Homelessness.

Walker, Mary J., and James Franklin, "An Argument Against Drug Testing Welfare Recipients," *Kennedy Institute of Ethics Journal*, Vol. 28, No. 3, 2018, pp. 309–340.

Warfield, Matt, and Barbara DiPietro, *Medication-Assisted Treatment: Buprenorphine in the HCH Community*, Nashville, Tenn.: National Health Care for the Homeless Council, May 2016.

Wu, April Yanyuan, Denise Hoffman, and Paul O'Leary, *Trends in Opioid Use Among Social Security Disability Insurance Applicants*, paper presented at the 21st Annual SSA Research Consortium Meeting, Washington, D.C., April 1–2, 2019.

Young, Katherine, and Julia Zur, *Medicaid and the Opioid Epidemic: Enrollment, Spending, and the Implications of Proposed Policy Changes*, San Francisco, Calif.: Kaiser Family Foundation, Issue Brief, July 2017.

Zedlewski, Sheila, *TANF and the Broader Safety Net*, Washington, D.C.: Urban Institute, January 2012.

CHAPTER TWELVE

Employment

Michael Dworsky

Overview

The relationships between opioid use and various employment outcomes are complex. Although opioid use may help some people who are experiencing pain stay in their jobs, others with opioid addiction may become less productive and, ultimately, be fired (or laid off and not rehired). These facts have implications not only for these individuals and their families but also for their employers, coworkers, and possibly taxpayers. Having a job may also influence one's decisions to use opioids, but such decisions depend on several factors, ranging from the type of job to the availability of employer-sponsored health insurance. Related to these components, there is also growing debate about the "deaths of despair" hypothesis, which argues that the disappearance of high-paying jobs from particular communities is strongly associated with rising midlife mortality, not only from opioid-related overdoses but also from alcohol-related liver disease and suicide.

Given the interactions between employment and many other components of the ecosystem (e.g., criminal legal system, income support and homeless services, medical care), it is critical to understand the evidence on these relationships—not only whether it is positive, negative, or both but also the magnitude of the association. This chapter slightly differs from the others in that it spends more time critically reviewing the evidence on these complex relationships, with a special focus on studies that use methods to assess a causal relationship versus a simple correlation.

In our discussion, we attempt neither to estimate the costs and benefits of opioids relevant to employment outcomes nor to assess the precise share of these consequences that can be attributed to different pathways. Numerous studies have attempted to estimate the economic burden of opioids, but many suffer from important methodological limitations. Furthermore, there are other costs—such as the secondary effects that addiction and mortality have on the employment outcomes of family members, or opioid-involved embezzlement from employers—that have not been the subject of much empirical research. Similarly, few studies have rigorously considered the extent to which opioid use may improve some employment outcomes (e.g., helping those with chronic pain stay in the workforce).

Direct evidence on how opioid use affects productivity losses on the job (known as *presenteeism*) or absenteeism remains sparse; most published estimates of productivity losses because of opioids are extrapolated from studies that measure the average effect of all illicit substances.

However, a smaller number of studies specifically on opioids confirm that misuse and untreated addiction are associated with reduced productivity on the job and reduced work hours (Goplerud, Hodge, and Benham, 2017; Henke et al., 2020; Rice et al., 2014; Van Hasselt et al., 2015). Long-term opioid prescribing has also been shown to increase the duration of temporary disability among workers receiving workers' compensation temporary disability benefits (Savych, Neumark, and Lea, 2019).

The evidence on how opioids affect labor supply and employment rates is stronger, and several well-designed studies have found that higher prescription opioid dispensing leads to reduced labor force participation and employment in a local labor market (Aliprantis, Fee, and Schweitzer, 2018; Beheshti, 2019; Harris et al., 2020). These negative effects of opioid prescribing on labor market outcomes are observed among both men and women, but effects for men are estimated to be several times larger (Aliprantis, Fee, and Schweitzer, 2018; Krueger, 2017). In contrast to alcohol and some other drugs, the adverse effects of opioids on employment and labor force participation are complicated by the role of opioids in pain treatment: Pain is highly prevalent among working-age adults and is concentrated among those who are out of the labor force (Krueger, 2017).

Work and the labor market have also shaped the opioid crisis and society's response to it. The burden of the opioid crisis is not distributed evenly across the workforce: Prescription opioid use varies widely across occupations (Asfaw, Alterman, and Quay, 2020), and overdose mortality rates per worker are extremely high in some industries (Hawkins et al., 2019). One factor that seems to explain this variation is the level of physical demand and risk of workplace injury. For individuals who are currently employed, workplace injuries can result in chronic pain and are frequently treated with prescription opioids. Studies of patients who received workers' compensation for nonfatal injuries have shown frequent high-duration prescribing leading to overdose deaths (Franklin et al., 2005); a long-term study also found substantial increases in drug overdose mortality and suicide for workers with nonfatal injuries that led to lost workdays (Applebaum et al., 2019). In principle, employment should have some countervailing protective effects against opioid misuse by providing workers with incentives for sobriety and resources to avoid or manage opioid dependence.

Unemployment and declining labor demand have also been identified as factors that contributed to the rise of the opioid crisis. Local economic conditions, specifically widespread job losses resulting from the disappearance of high-paying manufacturing jobs, are strongly associated with opioid overdose mortality (Pierce and Schott, 2020; Venkataramani et al., 2020). Similar patterns have been documented for suicide and deaths from alcohol-related liver disease, which, along with deaths from opioids, have been termed *deaths of despair* in Case and Deaton, 2015. The same authors attributed rising mid-life mortality from deaths of despair to *cumulative disadvantage*, which they defined as the cumulative effect of long-term hardship relative to one's own expectations for life (Case and Deaton, 2017; Case and Deaton, 2020). This factor is a bigger story than just declining labor demand, but the disappearance of high-quality jobs for less-educated non-Hispanic White men and women is identified by Case and Deaton as the prime mover.

However, it is important not to conflate the *deaths of despair* mechanism with the opioid crisis as a whole, and studies of industries other than manufacturing suggest that working conditions and the consequences of workplace injuries also contribute to opioid overdose mortality. In short, employment affects the opioid crisis through multiple channels, and the effort to understand these different pathways is an active area of research.

There is strong evidence that opioid use disorder (OUD) is associated with reduced productivity and labor supply among currently employed workers. However, the impact of opioids on those who are currently employed does not appear to be anywhere near large enough to explain the overall loss of economic output that is typically assumed in total burden estimates.

Key Interactions with Other Components of the Ecosystem

The availability and generosity of employer-sponsored health insurance, which is the dominant source of health care financing for nonelderly adults, are strongly influenced by labor market conditions. Prior to the enaction of the Mental Health Parity and Addiction Equity Act (MHPAEA) in 2008 and the Affordable Care Act in 2010, coverage of **mental health and substance use treatment** in private insurance (or employer-sponsored health insurance) was often limited compared with public insurance. Even among those with private insurance that covers substance use disorder (SUD) treatment, stigma—including fear of labor market consequences—remains a widely reported reason that privately insured individuals with SUDs do not seek treatment (Ali et al., 2017). Job changes or job loss can also lead to transitions in coverage or coverage loss (Schaller and Stevens, 2015). This has the potential to impede access to treatment at a time when workers would benefit from care.

A more subtle interaction between the **medical care system** and the labor market's influence on the opioid crisis stems from the financing of employer-sponsored insurance through employer contributions. Rapid growth in health care spending demands higher employer contributions and drives up the total employer cost of compensation, with a larger impact relative to total compensation for lower-wage and less-skilled workers. Case and Deaton, 2020, argued that rising health care spending has accelerated the disappearance of good jobs for lower-skilled workers, fueling the opioid crisis and the other deaths of despair. We note that some of these issues may be consequences of the U.S. system of employer-sponsored health insurance.

The opioid crisis also affects the labor market by disrupting other systems addressed in this report. Interrupted schooling (**the education system**) undermines accumulation of human capital (i.e., the availability of workers with a given skill level) in the workforce, reducing labor supply. The demands of caregiving for family members with SUDs also reduce labor supply (and have other consequences; see Chapter Three), as does the higher prevalence of incarceration and criminal history related to the opioid crisis.

The labor market effects discussed earlier in this chapter may adversely affect **health care**, **education**, and **criminal legal** systems because of the impact on workers employed in these systems. Although one study from Massachusetts showed that health care support workers have higher overdose mortality rates than average, available evidence on opioid mortality does not suggest that other occupational groups important to these systems (educators, health care providers, or first responders) are more susceptible than other workers to OUD and its adverse labor market effects (Hawkins et al., 2019). Yet it would also be inaccurate to assume that any group of workers in the United States is entirely unaffected.

In addition to contributing to opioid overdoses and the deaths of despair, declining labor demand increases participation in **federal disability insurance programs** (Black, Daniel, and Sanders, 2002; Pierce and Schott, 2020). One study suggests that reduced opioid prescribing volumes lead to lower Social Security Disability Insurance (SSDI) participation rates independent of their association with declining labor demand (Beheshti, 2019), but more work is needed to disentangle how labor market conditions and opioid supply affect participation in disability programs. Finally, reduced employment attributable to the opioid crisis is estimated to have reduced state and federal tax revenue (by a total amount of $26 billion in 2000 and $11.8 billion in 2016) (Segel et al., 2019), depriving governments of resources needed to address this and other crises.

Policy Opportunities and Considerations

Effective pain management without the catastrophic side effects of widespread opioid prescribing is needed to enable adults suffering from chronic pain to participate in the labor force. Eliminating prescription opioids without providing alternative pain management can reduce labor supply among workers who live with chronic pain (Kilby, 2015); for example, earlier research shows that withdrawing COX-2 inhibitors from the market substantially reduced labor supply for older adults with arthritis (Garthwaite, 2012). More broadly, the mechanisms that drive differences across demographic groups, occupations, and industries in the relationship between labor market conditions and opioid overdose remain underexamined. In particular, it remains unclear whether the factors that make some industries and occupations particularly prone to opioid misuse can be modified through public policy or changes in the organization of work. We also note that research on illegal opioids and the labor market is very sparse compared with the literature on prescription opioids; the generalizability of estimates from earlier stages of the opioid crisis to the current stage of the crisis is an open question (see Chapter Two for an evolution of the stages of the opioid crisis).

Changing working conditions to reduce occupational health risks that could spark opioid use could be a helpful direction for employers and labor regulators seeking to manage the opioid crisis, but evidence on the effectiveness of such interventions as a response to the opioid crisis is limited. In the meantime, numerous interventions have attempted to leverage various aspects of the workplace to detect opioid misuse earlier and facilitate employment among individuals in recovery. Few of these have operated on a large scale or been targeted beyond very specific populations already involved in the criminal legal system (Vine et al., 2020). Identifying and expanding successful interventions that address the opioid crisis through the workplace remains an important area for research.

Introduction

Opioid misuse, addiction, and overdose mortality affect the labor market by reducing productivity (the amount of output produced in an hour of labor) and by reducing labor supply (the quantity of labor that workers are willing and able to provide at a given wage). (See Chapter Two for definitions of opioid *use* versus *misuse*.) Premature death also reduces labor supply by reducing the number of available workers in the population. In addition to reduced labor supply from individuals with OUD, the opioid crisis imposes burdens on others—specifically, family members of individuals with OUD—that make it more difficult to work (further reducing labor supply). Incarceration related to opioids also removes working-age adults from the labor force, and it can be argued that labor provided to the illegal markets also reduces the supply of workers available to the formal economy.

Work and the labor market have also shaped both the opioid crisis and society's response to it: Opioid use and overdose mortality vary widely across occupations and industries, and workplace injury has been shown to predict overdose mortality. In addition to the direct effects of working conditions and occupational health on opioid misuse, unemployment and labor force exits because of declining labor demand have been identified as factors that contributed to the rise of the opioid crisis. Local economic conditions, specifically widespread job losses because of the disappearance of high-paying production jobs for less-educated workers, are strongly associated with opioid overdose mortality, suicide, and mortality from alcohol-related liver disease.

As the above discussion makes clear, the linkages between the opioid crisis, work, and the labor market are numerous and complex: The opioid crisis affects work and the labor market through various channels; simultaneously, working conditions and changes in the U.S. labor market over past decades have contributed to the opioid crisis. Causal arrows between the opioid crisis and the labor market run in both directions, posing a substantial challenge for researchers seeking to understand the opioid crisis or address it through policies focused on the labor market: Any policy-relevant attempt to understand how opioids affect the labor market—or vice versa—must address the problem of reverse causation.

However, the relationship between work and the opioid crisis is an extremely active area of research, and credible findings are beginning to emerge about both the effects of opioids on work and the role that labor markets have played in the opioid crisis.

This chapter is laid out as follows. As background, we define some concepts and measures used in the analysis of labor markets (see the box on the next page). We then review research findings about the relationship between opioids, work, and the labor market, structuring our discussion around the two directions of causation linking employment and the opioid crisis. First, we examine impacts of the opioid crisis on work and the labor market; then, we turn to the question of how changes in the labor market have contributed to the opioid crisis. Throughout this review, we seek to distinguish between studies that document associations (or correlations) between opioids and the labor market and those that credibly address the causal relationships between opioids and the labor market.

Labor Market Terminology

Before discussing evidence on the relationship between opioids, work, and the labor market, it is important to define some concepts and terminology that are central to economic analysis of labor markets. Different studies discussed here focus on different measures of labor market activity or distress—specifically, the *unemployment rate*, the *labor force participation rate*, and the *employment-to-population ratio*. These quantities measure different concepts, and some familiarity with the differences between these measures is important for interpreting empirical findings.

Economists define the *labor force* at a given point in time to encompass all individuals who are currently either (1) working for pay or (2) jobless, looking for work, and available for work. That is, the labor force is the sum of the *employed* and the *unemployed*. Individuals who are neither working nor looking for work are counted as *not in the labor force*. Individuals may be not in the labor force for a wide variety of reasons, including retirement, disability, school attendance, and caregiving. Some may also be working in the illegal economy. The group of workers who are not in the labor force also includes those who want a job and are available to work but who have stopped looking for work, either because jobs are scarce or for other reasons.[a]

Studies discussed in this chapter use various measures of labor market conditions. There are some subtle differences in the concepts captured by these different measures, and it will be useful to review these differences before turning to our review of the literature. The *unemployment rate* is the proportion of individuals in the labor force who are unemployed but looking for work. The *labor force participation rate* is the proportion of all individuals who are participating in the labor force (including both the employed and the unemployed) relative to the total population. The *employment-to-population ratio* is the number of currently employed workers as a percentage of the total population.[b] Data on wages, hours worked, worker demographics and health status, occupational safety, and other aspects of working conditions are also used widely in the studies examined in this chapter. Readers should refer to the studies cited for further details.

The quantity of labor supplied depends not just on the number of workers (or *payroll employment*) but also on the number of hours worked by each worker. Economists define *labor productivity* as the quantity of output (either goods or services) produced per unit of labor input. Equipment and other nonlabor inputs supplied by businesses to workers are referred to as *capital*, and worker productivity depends on the availability of capital inputs and other factors, such as the organization of work and, in team production processes involving coordination between multiple workers, the labor input and productivity of other workers.

Research on the relationship between health and labor productivity often distinguishes between *absenteeism* and *presenteeism* as two mechanisms through which health problems, including opioid misuse, affect the production process. *Absenteeism* refers to unscheduled absence from work. *Presenteeism* refers to reduced labor productivity while on the job. Absenteeism reduces a business's output by reducing the quantity (i.e., number of hours) of labor supplied, while presenteeism (by definition) reduces output through lower productivity.

It is important to note that economists use very different terminology from the public health and medical communities in describing the economic burden of opioid misuse and other diseases. In these fields, the term *lost productivity* is widely used to refer to any reduction in economic output attributable to a disease, including reductions in output because of reduced hours worked; reduced employment; labor force exits because of disability, incarceration, or other reasons; and mortality. In economics, and in this chapter, these are all considered reductions in the quantity of labor supplied rather than the productivity of labor.

---

[a] This paragraph draws on definitions provided by the U.S. Bureau of Labor Statistics (BLS) (see BLS, 2015).

[b] The labor force participation rates and employment-to-population ratios reported by BLS are calculated relative to the civilian, noninstitutionalized population aged 16 and older. Populations excluded from the labor force participation rate include those in prison, the active-duty armed forces, and those in nursing homes or other long-term care facilities.

Interactions with other systems described in this report are then discussed. For example, employment interacts with the health care system through employer-sponsored health insurance, which affects access to and cost of prescriptions and treatment. A portion of the negative labor supply impact of the opioid crisis is driven by incarceration and barriers to hiring for formerly incarcerated individuals, suggesting that interactions with the criminal legal system are also important (see Figure 12.1).

We conclude by considering what might be done to improve things, either by mitigating the opioid crisis's impacts on workers, their families, and the labor market or by leveraging employers and the workforce system to address the opioid crisis. Barriers to change and opportunities for progress are discussed, and we highlight some key questions that should be addressed to guide better policy responses in the future.

System Components and How They Interact with Opioids

We organize our discussion of these many pathways into three broad categories. First, we assess the effect of opioids on currently employed workers. Second, we discuss the potential for opioids to affect whether individuals are employed. Third, we consider the effect of work and labor market conditions on the use of opioids. This last section addresses the ongoing debate about deaths of despair.

Figure 12.2 illustrates the complexity of actual or potential (hypothesized but perhaps not well-substantiated) causal linkages between employment and opioids, many of which we discuss in this chapter. As we discuss briefly next, we take the perspective of labor economics, in which labor market outcomes (the number of workers with different skill levels and the wages they are paid) are the result of labor demand (i.e., employers buying labor) interacting with labor supply (i.e., workers selling labor). Similarly, quantitative outcomes of the opioid crisis (such as the volume of opioids prescribed, the prevalence of opioid misuse, or the overdose mortality rate) are affected by both the demand for and the supply of opioids. As Figure 12.2 makes clear, efforts to learn about the effect of employment on opioids must deal with the fact that causation runs in both directions between the employment system and opioids through a large number of mechanisms.

FIGURE 12.1

The Employment System and Its Interactions

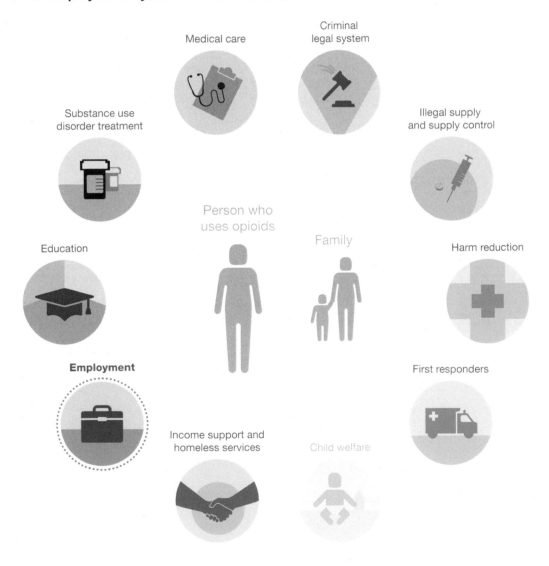

FIGURE 12.2

Overview of Potential Causal Relationships Between Employment, Opioids, and Other Factors

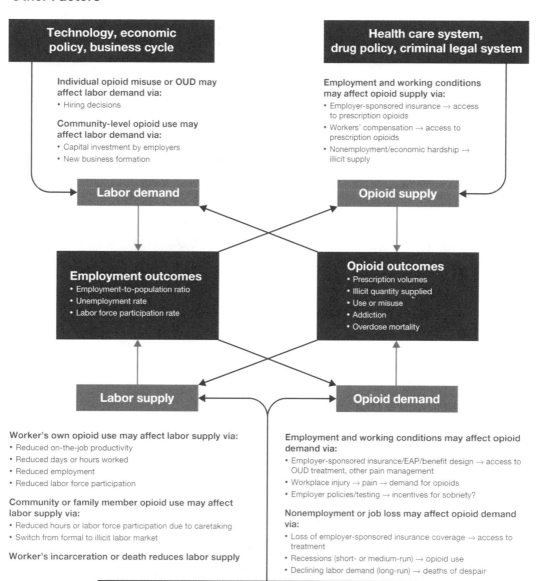

NOTE: Arrows indicate substantiated or hypothesized causal linkages between entities. Employment outcomes and opioid outcomes are, by definition, influenced by both supply and demand. Text adjacent to arrows lists mechanisms contributing to causal connections from opioid outcomes to labor supply and demand and from employment outcomes to opioid supply and demand. EAP = employee assistance program.

Similarly, other factors (such as the prevalence of chronic pain or other aspects of population health) can drive variation in both opioid and employment outcomes. If unmeasured or unmodeled, these external factors can also pose serious challenges for understanding the relationship between opioids and employment. Under some circumstances, however, changes in external factors that clearly affect only one piece of the system depicted in Figure 12.2 offer opportunities for researchers to learn about the causal arrows between employment and opioids in isolation from the vast number of confounding factors that can make it challenging to draw policy conclusions from observational studies. Throughout this chapter, we seek to highlight studies that have provided credible evidence on the direction and strength of causation between opioids and employment.

Effects of Opioids on Work and Labor Markets

In this section, we identify different mechanisms through which the opioid crisis has affected the labor market and review the strength of the evidence on the importance of these different channels. In general, SUDs reduce worker productivity, and intoxication on the job can undermine workplace safety. In comparison with the effects of alcohol and some other drugs, the effect of opioids on the workforce is complicated by the fact that there can be therapeutic benefits to appropriate opioid use. In this section, we first discuss evidence on the effects of opioid misuse on the productivity of the current workforce and the frequency of lost workdays because of workplace injury and illness, sick leave utilization, or short-term disability. We briefly discuss the limited evidence on opioids and workplace safety before turning to impacts on employment rates and labor force participation.

We note some limitations in the scope of this chapter. We briefly discuss estimates of lost economic output because of opioid-related mortality, but we do not focus on this channel at length, in contrast to the other channels through which opioid misuse affects labor supply. Although the effect of opioid-related mortality on employment outcomes when compared with other pathways has been considered in the economic burden studies described later, we caution against drawing strong conclusions from some of these studies.

Our review also does not include estimates of labor supply impacts on family members of OUD patients or overdose victims, or on the individual- or community-level impacts of incarceration related to the opioid crisis. We know, in general, that caretaking responsibilities can reduce labor supply, that incarceration prevents prisoners from working in the noncarceral labor market, and that formerly incarcerated individuals face numerous barriers to employment. Given the scale of the opioid crisis, these effects are likely to be quantitatively quite important and likely contribute to community-level estimates (discussed next) of the impact of opioid supply on local labor market outcomes. However, it is not clear that we would expect the labor market impacts of caretaking responsibilities or incarceration related to opioids to differ systematically from effects driven by other difficult family situations or crimes, and we did not find research specifically on those questions.

We also do not address the effect that employee opioid use may have on embezzlement and theft from employers. This is not because we do not believe this happens, but the extent to which it does is not well documented.

From the perspective of labor economics, these effects of opioid misuse, addiction, and overdose mortality are conceptualized as most directly affecting labor supply and worker productivity. Employer responses to the opioid crisis, such as changing decisions about where to locate production facilities, are understood to be reactions to changes in the supply of workers (or, potentially, the productivity of available workers) in a local labor market brought about by opioids. Our discussion, and the bulk of the evidence, is accordingly structured around effects of opioids on workers via negative impacts on productivity, workplace safety, or labor supply.

Productivity, Absenteeism, and Lost Workdays Among Currently Employed Workers

In this section, we review studies on the effects of opioid misuse on labor productivity on the job, as well as absence from work among those who are currently employed. As discussed above, the literature in medicine and public health—including studies that have calculated the social cost or *total burden* of the opioid crisis—generally uses *productivity* as a catch-all term for the sum of all effects on output, including reduced productivity on the job, work absence, and reduced employment, including reduced employment because of incarceration and premature death. That is, what these studies call *productivity* is what economists would call *production* or *economic output*.

Viewed through the lens of the labor market, overdose mortality can dramatically reduce aggregate labor supply—especially because overdose mortality often kills young workers who would otherwise spend decades in the labor force. Another important cause of lost production is incarceration, which mechanically removes workers from the labor force while they are imprisoned. (It is not clear that total burden estimates account for economic output produced by prison labor or for reductions in employment caused by reduced labor demand for the formerly incarcerated.)

Studies on the total burden of the opioid crisis indicate that most of the reduction in economic output caused by the opioid crisis is attributable to overdose mortality. Florence et al., 2016, estimated that, in 2013, the opioid crisis reduced economic output by $42 billion in 2013 dollars ($46.7 billion in 2020 dollars), accounting for just more than half of the estimated $78.5 billion total burden of opioid abuse[1] and dependence in 2013. Half ($21.4 billion) of this lost economic output was attributable to overdose mortality, $4 billion was attributable to reduced labor supply of incarcerated individuals, and the rest ($16 billion) was attributable to reduced labor supply and productivity associated with use by nonincarcerated individuals.

---

[1] We do not condone the use of the word *abuse*, but, as noted earlier in this report, this was a clinical term for a diagnosis that was included in many prior studies. We use it in this section when referring to findings or inferences in those prior studies.

Total burden estimates with similar methods in Council of Economic Advisers, 2017, and Davenport, Weaver, and Caverly, 2019, have used or updated (with minimal changes) the economic output figures reported in Florence et al., 2016.[2] An independently produced grey literature estimate by the Altarum Institute attributes a similar proportion of the total burden of the opioid crisis as of 2016 to lost economic output (Rhyan, 2017). However, the Altarum study estimates that 77 percent of the lost output is attributable to overdose mortality, 3 percent is attributable to incarceration, and 20 percent is attributable to misuse and dependence. The Altarum estimate did not appear in a peer-reviewed journal, and the methods are only briefly described; thus, we do not give it as much weight as other studies. One possible reason for its higher estimate of lost production as a result of fatal overdose is the sharp rise in opioid overdose mortality between 2013 and 2016 following the rapid diffusion of fentanyl into the U.S. illegal drug supply. This chapter is not intended to catalog or correct the limitations of these total burden estimates, and we mention them here mostly to provide context for our narrower discussion of labor market effects that result from opioid use.

In this section, we largely focus on the impact of opioid misuse on productivity as defined by labor economists (i.e., quantity of output produced per hour of labor input) and the number of hours or days worked by currently employed workers. Studies on the effect of opioids on employment and labor force participation are discussed later in this chapter. Together, these channels correspond to what the total burden estimates refer to as the *productivity costs of OUD*, and this is where most of the research and debate have focused.

Impacts of Opioid Use Disorder on Labor Productivity (Presenteeism)

Reduced labor productivity because of health problems, including OUD, is widely referred to in the medical literature as *presenteeism*. Reductions in the number of hours or days worked by currently employed workers, whether because of sick leave, short-term disability leave or workers' compensation temporary total disability, or unplanned work absence, are widely referred to in the medical literature as *absenteeism*.

Evidence on the effect of OUD on labor productivity was limited to one published report—Henke et al., 2020. The authors used a large database of medical claims linked to health risk assessment data containing employee self-reports on the annual number of days when the worker's health interfered with work. Adjusting for worker and job characteristics, they compared days with lost productivity across three groups: workers without a diagnosed OUD, workers with a diagnosed OUD who are receiving medications for OUD (MOUD), and work-

---

[2] The Council of Economic Advisers simply scaled up the Florence et al., 2016, estimate of productivity loss and other costs of nonfatal opioid misuse (including the costs of substance use treatment and incarceration) to account for growth over time in the number of people with OUD. The Society of Actuaries produced its own estimates but essentially followed the same approach as Florence et al., 2016, combining more-recent data on the population with OUD with an estimate of potential productivity per person and then multiplying the total potential productivity by the estimated percentage productivity loss from the National Drug Intelligence Center (NDIC) study discussed in the text box titled "Using Caution When Quoting Social Cost of Opioid Use Disorder Estimates."

Using Caution When Quoting Social Cost of Opioid Use Disorder Estimates

Currently available estimates of the cost of OUD are largely based on cross-sectional comparisons of lost workdays between workers with and workers without SUDs, and published estimates differ in terms of the form of opioid misuse (or misuse of other substances) that they measure, the outcome variables, and the care that is exercised in adjusting for observed or unobserved factors that are likely to be confounded with opioid misuse.

In terms of its impact on policy analysis, the most important estimate comes from a study produced for the NDIC in 2011. Among four studies on the total burden of the opioid crisis that calculated the contribution of reduced productivity and absenteeism, all relied on an estimate produced in NDIC, 2011; these four studies are Council of Economic Advisers, 2017; Davenport, Weaver, and Caverly, 2019; Florence et al., 2016; and Rhyan, 2017. The authors of the NDIC report analyzed the 2007 National Survey on Drug Use and Health (NSDUH) and found that prior-year abuse or dependence on illicit drugs (including controlled pharmaceuticals) was associated with 17 percent fewer hours of work for men and 18 percent fewer hours of work for women after controlling for age, marital status, education, and alcohol abuse or dependence. (See Chapter Two for a discussion of known issues with the NSDUH.) The sample used in these estimates appears to include all NSDUH respondents aged 15 and older and thus includes currently employed workers, the unemployed, and those who are not in the labor force. The NDIC estimates would thus appear to capture reductions in hours worked because of absenteeism among the workforce, reductions in employment because of job loss or higher unemployment duration among those in the labor force, and exit from the labor force. Capturing all these channels in a single number makes the NDIC estimate convenient for total burden estimation.

Unfortunately, there are serious methodological problems with the NDIC study, and there are further reasons to question its direct applicability to the opioid crisis. A handful of subsequent, better-executed studies have done much to address these limitations (discussed below), but these results do not yet appear to have been incorporated into estimates of the productivity costs of the opioid crisis. Given the widespread use of the NDIC estimate in total burden estimation, its limitations warrant some discussion.

One problem is that there is clear potential for reverse causation from an individual's employment status and economic situation to substance use: This is more or less the central premise of the deaths of despair argument that we discuss later in this chapter. However, there can also be reverse causation in the other direction (higher incomes increase consumption of many goods, potentially including consumption of drugs). Under the assumption that the first mechanism (job loss and economic hardship increase substance use) is quantitatively larger, this reverse causation will tend to introduce bias toward overestimating the reduction in employment that is actually caused by substance use. Reverse causation is an issue with any cross-sectional comparison between individuals with and individuals without opioid misuse, so the use of regression-adjustment with all relevant control variables or other research strategies becomes critically important for such comparisons to yield internally valid results.

Unfortunately, because opioids are widely used to treat chronic pain, it seems likely that unobserved differences in the prevalence of chronic pain between workers with and workers without OUD could also contribute to the incremental absenteeism associated with OUD. The NDIC estimates do not control for chronic pain, mental distress, or any other measure of health status or health-related work limitations apart from alcohol abuse or dependence.

These limitations should raise questions about the validity of total burden estimates based on the NDIC study, given that more-recent studies using NSDUH data suggest that patterns of absenteeism associated with SUD are systematically different across different substances, and that the estimated increase in absenteeism associated with OUD is highly sensitive to the inclusion of other control variables. The evolution of the opioid crisis since 2007 should also raise concerns about the current relevance of estimates based on the NDIC study.

ers with OUD who are not receiving MOUD. Workers with untreated OUD experienced 14 additional days per year in which their health interfered with work, while the productivity of workers with OUD who received MOUD was not statistically significantly different from the productivity of similar workers without OUD. This research suggests that the productivity impact of OUD is large, but it is not possible to infer from the data available what this precisely means in terms of lost economic output.[3]

Impacts of Opioid Misuse on Hours or Days Worked (Absenteeism)

Compared with presenteeism, which is notoriously difficult to measure and monetize, reduced work hours and lost workdays are conceptually clear and can be quantified in survey data or, frequently, captured in administrative databases. There is, accordingly, much more research on the relationship between opioid misuse, OUD, and the number of hours or days worked.

There are relatively few studies that convincingly measure differences in work absence between currently employed workers with and without opioid misuse, and even the methodologically sound studies (Henke et al., 2020; Rice et al., 2014; Van Hasselt et al., 2015) use a variety of different data sets and methods to reach a wide variety of estimates. Henke et al., 2020, who analyzed OUD-diagnosed workers with and without MOUD separately, have the smallest estimates. Although these estimates might reflect recall bias in those workers' self-reported absence measures, a more hopeful possibility is that, by using more-recent data

---

[3] That said, it might be possible to generate some insightful back-of-the-envelope calculations using some of the figures about OUD and treatment utilization described in Chapter Two. One would also have to make some strong assumptions about the extent to which the existing employment-related research applies to the current situation with illegally produced synthetic opioids in many parts of the United States.

in which a slight majority (58 percent) of OUD-diagnosed workers in the sample received MOUD, Henke and colleagues captured a new reality in which relatively effective MOUD are increasingly available to workers with high-quality insurance (Henke et al., 2020). It is understandable, given the unsettled state of the currently available evidence, that the simpler NDIC estimates are still used in cost-effectiveness analyses and total burden estimates (see the box titled "Using Caution When Quoting Social Cost of Opioid Use Disorder Estimates"). Yet it would also be fair to conclude that, beyond multiple studies finding more work absences among individuals misusing opioids or with diagnosed OUD, we still do not have a clear picture of the actual effect of opioid misuse on hours or days worked among the currently employed. We also do not know much about the effect that a long absence from the workforce (or educational system) as a result of OUD has on human capital formation and future employment outcomes.

Impact of Opioids on Disability Costs and Disability Duration

Opioids are often prescribed after surgery or an injury or to treat pain resulting from an ongoing health condition, so researchers have also used administrative data to estimate the association between opioid prescribing and the duration of episodes of disability covered by either workers' compensation (which covers work-related injuries) or short-term disability insurance (which covers episodes of disability regardless of whether they are work-related). These estimates reflect the timing of return to work after an initial spell of work disability rather than the average amount of lost work time and so cannot be compared directly with the absenteeism and presenteeism estimates reported above without incorporating data or assumptions on the incidence of injuries or work disability episodes. That said, workers experiencing a spell of work disability are likely much more vulnerable than the average worker to serious consequences from opioid misuse.

Johnston et al., 2016, using the same data set analyzed by Henke et al., 2020, examined the association between diagnosed OUD and the duration of short-term disability spells and workers' compensation temporary total disability spells. The distinction between these two types of events is that workers' compensation covers disability caused by work-related injury and illness, while short-term disability covers injury and illness because of all other causes. Johnston et al., 2016, found that diagnosed OUD is not associated with disability duration for workers' compensation claimants, but they found a strong association between diagnosed OUD and higher short-term disability duration after adjusting for individual characteristics.

With its narrower set of precipitating causes, workers' compensation is a particularly interesting context for studying the effects of opioid prescribing and OUD. The mix of health conditions treated in workers' compensation today is dominated by sprains, strains, and other musculoskeletal disorders, especially low-back injuries.[4] These injuries can develop into disabling chronic pain, which can lead to opioid prescribing, and musculoskeletal dis-

---

[4] The extent to which these claims are fraudulent and used to obtain opioids that can be sold in illegal markets is unknown, but it is plausible that this has happened.

orders account for a large share of the caseload enrolled in SSDI. Not surprisingly, workplace injury places workers at substantially elevated risk of permanent disability, which often results in labor force exits. One study found that a lost-time workplace injury roughly doubles the risk that a worker will enter SSDI over the next decade (O'Leary et al., 2012). Medical care provided through workers' compensation has also been identified as a setting where inappropriate opioid prescribing was common early in the opioid crisis (Franklin et al., 2005).

Franklin et al., 2008, studied opioid prescribing and disability duration among workers' compensation claims from Washington state for back injuries. Adjusting for covariates, the authors compared workers who received seven days' supply or more of opioids in the first six months after an injury with those with lower doses or no opioids. They showed that opioid prescribing is strongly associated with long-term disability, increasing the odds that a worker remained on total disability after one year by a factor of 2.2. Despite having rich data available (including both administrative records and survey data) to adjust for confounding factors, Franklin et al., 2008, could not rule out the possibility of reverse causation: Patients who receive more opioids may be those with more-severe injuries, even after controlling for all observable factors.

Savych, Neumark, and Lea, 2019, used workers' compensation claims from multiple states to revisit the relationship between opioid prescribing and workers' compensation disability duration using a more credible research design. They used a large multistate database of workers' compensation claims to estimate the effects of various opioid prescribing patterns on temporary disability duration for workers with low-back injuries and more than seven days of lost work time. Whereas the studies discussed so far in this section estimate a potentially noncausal association between opioid prescribing or OUD and measures of productivity or labor supply, Savych, Neumark, and Lea, 2019, used an instrumental variables strategy that leverages variation across health care markets in the rate at which health care providers prescribe opioids.[5] Their main findings focus on long-term opioid prescribing, which they define as receipt of one or more opioid prescriptions in the first three months after injury and three or more opioid prescriptions in the sixth through 12th months after injury.

There are two important findings in Savych, Neumark, and Lea, 2019. First, the researchers found that long-term opioid prescribing results in more than a tripling (251-percent increase) of temporary disability duration relative to injured patients who received no prescription opioids. This result represents the first estimate of the causal effect of opioid prescribing on disability duration among injured workers. A second and more subtle finding is

---

[5] Instrumental variables are an estimation method widely used in economics to estimate causal relationships in observational data when reverse causation, omitted variables bias, or other issues would make the association between two variables (say, X and Y) a misleading estimate of the true causal impact of one variable on the other (holding all other observed and unobserved factors constant). The basic idea is to estimate how Y changes with X when the variation in X is caused by a third variable (Z) that is known to have no effect on Y. In this case, Savych, Neumark, and Lea, 2019, studied how changes in opioid prescribing (X) driven by geographic variation in prescribing rates (Z) affect temporary disability duration (Y). See Angrist and Krueger, 2001, for a nontechnical overview.

that the researchers' instrumental variable estimates for most other opioid prescribing patterns are dramatically different from regression estimates that do not attempt to isolate exogenous variation in opioid prescribing. Regression-adjusted ordinary least squares estimates show that any opioid prescribing, including short-term prescribing without longer-term prescribing, is associated with large increases (60-percent to 80-percent increases) in disability duration. Instrumental variable estimates for these shorter-term forms of opioid prescribing are much smaller (20-percent to 50-percent increases) and are not statistically significant.

Impacts of Opioids on Workplace Safety

Occupational health researchers have highlighted multiple channels through which opioid misuse among the workforce seems likely to reduce workplace safety. Examples identified in a literature review include slowed response times, cognitive effects of long-term opioid use, increased risk of car crashes, and increased risk of falling (Kowalski-McGraw et al., 2017). Some of these mechanisms were substantiated with experimental or other high-quality study designs, but we could not find estimates quantifying overall safety effects of individual-level opioid use or community-level opioid supply measures, making it difficult to quantify how many additional workplace accidents are actually attributable to opioids.

Summary of Evidence on Opioids' Impacts on Productivity, Absenteeism, and Workplace Safety

The studies reviewed above indicate that untreated OUD is associated with lower productivity on the job. Evidence on the association between OUD and absenteeism is less clear, with estimates from well-designed studies varying widely. Studies on temporary disability duration following a workplace injury indicate that prescription opioid receipt is associated with much longer disability duration, but this association also reflects, in part, reverse causality: Unmeasured differences in health status or injury severity across individuals drive both opioid prescribing and higher disability duration. Evidence on workplace safety effects of prescription opioid use is also very limited. Although it seems likely (and is perhaps tautologically true) that opioid misuse adversely affects all these dimensions of productivity, labor supply, and workplace safety, many workers use opioids to manage pain that might also interfere with work. The results from Henke et al., 2020, also emphasize the importance of OUD treatment in modifying the impact of OUD on workers' productivity and absenteeism.

This is not to say that opioid use is benign; the studies discussed earlier indicate that it is not. Rather, individual-level evidence on associations between opioid use and productivity may overstate the short-term economic harms of opioid use unless researchers are able to either control for health status or use research designs (as in Savych, Neumark, and Lea, 2019) that identify causal effects. As we discuss next, the most-harmful effects of the opioid crisis on the labor market and the economy are likely to operate not through reduced worker productivity or other effects on workers who are currently employed, but rather through reductions in employment and labor force participation.

Impacts of Opioids on Labor Force Participation and Employment Rates

We have seen that opioid misuse and diagnosed OUD are strongly associated with reduced productivity on the job and reduced days worked among current employees and higher disability duration among workers using short-term disability benefits or who filed a workers' compensation claim. Unfortunately, even the high-quality studies yielded a wide variety of estimates (between 0.32 and 13.3 days per year) for the reduction in days worked associated with OUD (Henke et al., 2020; Rice et al., 2014). Although the best of these studies are careful to control for relevant worker and job characteristics, we saw only one study that clearly isolates the causal effect of opioid prescribing on the currently employed workforce: the study of low-back injuries in workers' compensation by Savych, Neumark, and Lea, 2019, which found that long-term opioid prescribing more than tripled the duration of temporary disability.

We also noted that widely cited estimates of lost economic output as a result of the opioid crisis generally used an assumption about the productivity and labor supply impacts of opioids that is not based on the higher-quality studies, but rather is drawn from an older estimate that had serious methodological limitations and uncertain external validity for the opioid crisis (NDIC, 2011). The key parameter drawn from the NDIC study is that opioid abuse or dependence predicts a reduction in annual hours worked of 17 percent for men and 18 percent for women.

As a very rough way to illustrate the range of estimates among the above studies in terms comparable with those of the NDIC estimate, we calculated the percentage reduction in workdays associated with opioid misuse for a full-time, full-year worker with two weeks' vacation, who would be assumed to work 250 days per year. The NDIC study estimate would imply reductions from this base of 42.5 days for men and 45 days for women, several times larger than the 13.3-day reduction estimated by Rice et al., 2014, and two orders of magnitude larger than the 0.32- to 0.67-day reduction reported in Henke et al., 2020. Although there is strong evidence that OUD is associated with reduced productivity and labor supply among currently employed workers, the impact of opioids on those who are currently employed does not appear to be anywhere near large enough to explain the overall loss of economic output that is typically assumed in total burden estimates.

To reconcile the various estimates in the studies mentioned earlier, we need to consider the effects of opioids on the probability of employment. It has long been established in the health economics literature that income losses because of health problems are primarily driven by nonemployment and labor force exits; the impacts of reductions in hours worked and slower wage growth, while also measurable, are of secondary importance in explaining why poor health is associated with lower income (Currie and Madrian, 1999). This suggests that we should expect to see larger impacts of opioid misuse on employment than we saw on productivity or hours worked.

Fortunately, several studies have used strong research designs to isolate the causal effect of opioid supply on employment or labor force participation rates. These studies generally focused on aggregate data at the level of the local labor market (e.g., counties, commuting zones, or other substate regions) rather than the individual level. Researchers have had much greater success in finding valid quasi-experiments in which opioid prescribing rates or shipment volumes varied across regions for reasons plausibly unrelated to the labor market than they have in studies that seek to explain individual-level outcomes (such as those discussed earlier).

Before turning to these studies on the causal effect of opioids on local labor markets, we consider a study that used individual-level data to document strong associations between chronic pain, prescription pain medication use, and labor force nonparticipation. Krueger (2017) analyzed American Time Use Survey data from 2010 through 2013 and documented several suggestive facts about the conditions of individuals who are out of the labor force and the role of chronic pain and prescription pain medication, including opioids. He found that men who are not in the labor force report being in pain much more of the time (53 percent of the time) than those who are in the labor force (30 percent for employed men and 29 percent for unemployed men). He also found that men who are not in the labor force are twice as likely as men who are in the labor force to have taken pain medication on any given day (43.5 percent of men who are not in the labor force versus 20 percent of working men and 19 percent of unemployed men).

The high prevalence of pain and high rates of pain medication use among those who are not in the labor force are consistent with a causal relationship between labor force participation, chronic pain, and the use of opioids and other pain medication. However, this evidence is not sufficient to distinguish between several possible explanations:

1. Use of opioids leads to reduced labor force participation.
2. Chronic pain both reduces labor force participation and leads to use of pain medication, including opioids.
3. Labor force nonparticipation in response to declining labor demand leads to substance use, including use of opioids.

Several high-quality studies using different research strategies have gone beyond correlational evidence and have successfully isolated the causal effects of opioid prescribing on local labor market outcomes. Three of these showed that increased opioid prescribing in a region reduces labor force participation or employment (Aliprantis, Fee, and Schweitzer, 2018; Beheshti, 2019; Harris et al., 2020). And a fourth study examining substitution of OxyContin with illicit opioids also showed large negative impacts on employment (Park and Powell, 2021). These findings are contradicted by a working paper that found no relationship between opioid prescriptions and labor force participation for men and a positive relationship for women (Currie, Jin, and Schnell, 2018). Still, a separate report addressing the methodological limitations of previous studies found an even larger negative relationship (Maestas and Sherry, 2020). Taken together, these studies appear to confirm that there is a causal link from higher opioid prescribing to *reduced labor supply* (defined in these studies as a lower employment-to-population ratio or labor force participation rate).

The studies vary in their measures of opioid supply, in substate geographic definitions, and, perhaps most importantly, in the source of variation in opioid supply that they use to estimate causal effects. However, three of these studies rely, in one form or another, on differences in the probability of physicians to prescribe opioids. The report on workers' compensation disability duration by Savych, Neumark, and Lea, 2019, that was discussed earlier in this chapter used a similar approach. Such variation in physician practice styles is widely used in health economics, and Finkelstein, Gentzkow, and Williams, 2018, showed convincingly that such geographic variation in physician practice styles has a large effect on the risk that a patient will be exposed to high-risk opioid prescribing patterns, including high dosages, high-duration prescription episodes, and overlapping prescriptions from multiple providers. As long as we are willing to assume that physician practice styles are not somehow correlated with future labor market conditions, then these studies offer a way to learn the true causal effect of opioid prescribing on local labor market outcomes.

Aliprantis, Fee, and Schweitzer combined 2007–2016 data from the American Community Survey with Centers for Disease Control and Prevention (CDC) data on the county-level rate of opioid prescriptions per capita to explore both directions of causality between opioids and local labor market outcomes (Aliprantis, Fee, and Schweitzer, 2018).[6] Their research strategy was to focus on changes within local areas (metropolitan counties or larger substate rural areas), controlling for nationwide changes over time and permanent differences across geographic areas. They found evidence of a strong negative relationship between changes in local opioid prescribing volumes and changes in employment and labor force participation. Notably, the employment and labor force participation responses were nearly identical, suggesting that employment reductions associated with increased opioid prescription are coming from workers leaving the labor force rather than becoming unemployed. Their estimates suggest that a 10-percent increase in the number of opioid prescriptions per capita causes a 0.61-percentage-point reduction in the employment-to-population ratio. Effects for men were about three times as large as effects for women.

Harris et al., 2020, used 2010–2015 data from ten state prescription drug monitoring programs (PDMPs) to identify individual providers at the top of the nationwide opioid prescribing distribution. They used the locations of these heavy prescribers within each state to predict local opioid prescribing volumes, using a statistical specification that effectively isolates within-county changes in opioid prescribing because of changes in the locations of these heavy prescribers. This is similar in spirit to the Savych, Neumark, and Lea, 2019, study on workers' compensation discussed earlier, in that differences in the supply of opioids that are driven by different physician practice styles are assumed to be uncorrelated with unob-

---

[6]   They used a geographic unit of analysis that combines boundaries of counties with Public Use Microdata Areas (PUMAs) used in American Community Survey data. This hybrid geography, which is also used in Case and Deaton, 2017; Maestas and Sherry, 2020; and others, is called the *couma* (for county/PUMA) in this literature. We refer to this as *the county* for simplicity, but we note that rural counties with fewer than about 100,000 people will typically be aggregated to match PUMA boundaries.

servable factors that affect labor market outcomes. Consistent with Aliprantis, Fee, and Schweitzer, 2018, Harris and colleagues estimated large negative effects of prescription opioid supply on labor force participation: A 10-percent increase in prescriptions per capita reduced county-level labor force participation by 0.56 percentage points (Harris et al., 2020).

Beheshti, 2019, used a third approach to isolate variation in the prescription opioid supply across three-digit ZIP codes, measuring per capita opioid supply using recently published U.S. Drug Enforcement Administration Automated Reports and Consolidated Ordering System (ARCOS) data on drug shipments. In 2010, hydrocodone was rescheduled from Schedule III to Schedule II, adding oversight and administrative hassle to physicians wishing to prescribe hydrocodone. Prior to the rescheduling, there was wide variation across local areas in the volume of hydrocodone prescribed, so the rescheduling differentially reduced prescription volumes in areas with high hydrocodone prescribing. Substitution from hydrocodone to other opioids was modest, so this change represented a sharp reduction in the total prescription opioid supply. Beheshti, 2019, estimates larger effects than do Harris et al., 2020, and Aliprantis, Fee, and Schweitzer, 2018, finding that a 10-percent reduction in *hydrocodone* prescribing (not total opioid prescribing) increased labor force participation by 0.7 percentage points.

Park and Powell, 2021, examined the effect of illicit opioid supply on labor markets. The authors used an innovative research design that compares geographic areas with differing rates of OxyContin prescribing at the time, in 2010, when the reformulation of OxyContin (which replaced pills that could be crushed and snorted with an abuse-deterrent version) spurred opioid users to substitute to heroin and other illicit opioids. They found that employment-to-population ratios fell by more in areas that, because of their greater baseline use of OxyContin, saw a larger shift toward illicit opioids.

However, a working paper by Currie, Jin, and Schnell that also used geographic differences in opioid prescribing patterns failed to find a negative relationship between opioid prescribing rates and local labor market outcomes (Currie, Jin, and Schnell, 2018). Opioid prescribing rates were measured at the county level using data on retail pharmacy transactions from IQVIA, a market intelligence firm. The researchers measured physician practice styles using data on prescriptions billed to Medicare Part D, under the assumption that prescriptions for elderly and disabled Medicare enrollees are not driven by labor market conditions. Although some Medicare enrollees remain in the labor force, this assumption seems reasonable. When the researchers estimated the effect of opioid prescriptions per capita on the employment-to-population ratio, they found no relationship for men and a *positive* effect for women, especially for women aged 45 to 64: A 10-percent increase in opioid prescriptions per capita increased the female employment-to-population ratio by 3.5 percent for women in counties with higher rates of educational attainment and 4.3 percent for women in counties with lower rates of educational attainment.

Taken together, these papers seem to indicate that the opioid crisis has had a substantial negative effect on labor supply, resulting in lower employment and labor force participation. Taken at face value, the magnitude of the effects estimated in Aliprantis, Fee, and Schweitzer,

2018; Beheshti, 2020; and Harris et al., 2020, is large enough to suggest that the opioid crisis is an important explanation (though probably not the most important one) for the declining employment and labor force participation rates observed in the United States since 2000. Yet the contrary findings of Currie, Jin, and Schnell, 2018, raise some questions about the interpretation of these findings.

One concern is that these reports differ in their geographic coverage and their treatment of nonmetropolitan counties: Harris et al., 2020, used county-level data, but only from ten states, while Aliprantis, Fee, and Schweitzer, 2018, collapsed nonmetropolitan areas in many states because of data limitations. A related point is that the research designs used in Harris et al., 2020, Beheshti, 2020, and Currie, Jin, and Schnell, 2018, employ different measures of opioid prescribing and leverage different sources of variation in prescribing rates. The *instrumental variables* estimation method used in Harris et al., 2020, and Currie, Jin, and Schnell, 2018, and used implicitly in Beheshti, 2020, to express his results as an effect of opioid prescribing on employment, captures causal effects that may be specific to the source of variation used in the model (Angrist and Pischke, 2009). Furthermore, differing geographic coverage of different studies may contribute to differences in the findings if the effects of opioids on employment vary in important ways across populations or settings. It is conceivable that areas with heavy opioid prescribers (as in Harris et al., 2020) and where high rates of hydrocodone prescribing responded sharply to additional oversight (as in Beheshti, 2019) or where the OxyContin reformulation sharply changed prescribing behavior (as in Park and Powell, 2021) are not representative of the nationwide effects more likely to be captured in the study design of Currie, Jin, and Schnell, 2018.

A related challenge in the papers that use geographic variation in prescribing rates is that the data sources used to measure opioid prescribing rarely contain sufficiently detailed information about patients receiving opioids. This makes it hard to rule out the possibility that what is being labeled variation in practice styles is really unmeasured variation in the prevalence of chronic pain or other conditions that might directly affect labor supply, employment, and labor force participation.

An innovative working paper by Maestas and Sherry, 2020, does much to address both of these limitations in the earlier geographic variation reports discussed earlier in this chapter. The researchers used individual-level microdata from a large, nationwide commercial claims database to measure the probability that providers in a local geographic area prescribe opioids to opioid-naïve[7] patients, while adjusting for the presence of pain-related diagnoses and other individual-level patient characteristics. These county-level prescribing propensities were then used as instrumental variables for county-level opioid prescribing volumes between 2012 and 2018, which were measured using nationwide CDC data similar to the data used in Aliprantis, Fee, and Schweitzer, 2018, and Currie, Jin, and Schnell, 2018. Maestas and Sherry, 2020, found that higher rates of opioid prescribing reduce employment by a substan-

---

[7] *Opioid naïve* is a term used to define individuals with "no opioid prescriptions or evidence of OUD in the 6 months prior to the index prescription" (Burke et al., 2020, p. 495).

tial amount: Ten additional opioid prescriptions per 100 adults in a county (about one-third of a standard deviation) reduced the county's employment-to-population ratio by 1.1 percentage points, an even larger effect than that estimated in Beheshti, 2019.

We note that the employment and labor force participation effects estimated in these reports all represent aggregate- or community-level relationships (typically county-level) between opioid supply and local labor market outcomes, such as the employment-to-population ratio or the labor force participation rate. This aspect makes it somewhat challenging to compare the magnitude of these effects with the effects discussed earlier in this chapter on productivity, absenteeism, and disability duration, which are estimates of the effect of individual-level opioid use (or prescription opioid receipt) on individual-level outcomes, because spillover effects of an individual's opioid misuse on the labor supply of other individuals in the same labor market will be captured in estimates of the community-level relationship but not the individual-level relationship. The direction of these spillover effects (i.e., positive or negative) is *a priori* unclear; we can imagine spillovers that would reduce labor supply (e.g., one spouse reduces labor supply in response to caretaking needs or other disruptions because of the other spouse's opioid misuse), but we can also imagine spillovers that might work in the opposite direction (e.g., one spouse increases work hours or reenters the labor force to offset income losses because of the other spouse's opioid misuse). On a longer time scale, labor demand (employer-side) responses—such as those reported in Ouimet, Simintzi, and Ye, 2019, and Rietveld and Patel, 2021—would also feed into the aggregate-level estimates, but not individual-level estimates using other individuals in the same labor market as a control group.

Summary of Evidence on Opioids' Impacts on Employment and Labor Force Participation

There are several studies that show, using several highly credible research designs, that increased opioid supply has large negative impacts on employment and other labor market outcomes in local labor markets. We caution that not all well-designed studies reach this conclusion, and Currie, Jin, and Schnell, 2018, highlight potentially important gender differences in the labor market impacts of opioids. However, Maestas and Sherry, 2020, addressed many of the limitations in earlier studies, and Park and Powell, 2021, and Beheshti, 2019, which used somewhat different research designs, reached qualitatively similar conclusions.

Labor Demand and Business Formation Impacts of Opioids

We have framed the impact of the opioid crisis on the labor market as operating primarily through reductions in labor supply. This is not to say that employers have not also responded. Ouimet, Simintzi, and Ye, 2019, explored whether employers have responded to opioid-related reductions in labor supply by investing in automation and other labor-saving information technology (IT) (i.e., substituting for labor with capital). To reduce the threat of reverse-causality from technology-driven disemployment to opioid prescription rates, the researchers estimated the relationship between growth in county-level opioid prescription rates between 2006 and 2010 and establishment-level IT investment growth from 2011 to 2015. They found that a 10-percent increase in opioid prescriptions per capita over a four-year period leads to a 3.9-percent increase in IT investment, compared with IT investment in areas with lower growth in opioid prescriptions per capita. This finding from Ouimet, Simintzi, and Ye, 2019, is potentially quite important because it suggests that the declining labor supply caused by the opioid crisis is leading firms to change production processes in ways that will reduce future labor demand. Similarly, Rietveld and Patel, 2021, showed that higher opioid prescribing rates at the county and state levels are associated with lower levels of entrepreneurship on several measures, including lower rates of new business formation.

Effects of Work and Labor Markets on Opioids

Work and labor markets are likely to affect the opioid crisis through several channels. For the population of currently employed workers, workplace injuries and chronic pain related to workplace injuries can contribute to demand for prescription opioids. Workplace injuries may be especially problematic for opioids because medical care provided through workers' compensation (as opposed to health insurance) has been shown to involve high rates of inappropriate prescribing, with deadly consequences for workers who entered the workers' compensation system with nonfatal injuries, such as a sprained back (Franklin et al., 2008). In principle, drug testing and other drug-free workplace policies provide incentives for sobriety that may discourage use, although anecdotal evidence suggests that these policies can also penalize workers in recovery who are receiving MOUD.

The loss of employment opportunities has also been identified as an important contributing factor to the opioid crisis. Labor markets are inherently local, and the disappearance of high-paying jobs from particular communities is strongly associated with rising midlife mortality, not only from opioid-related overdoses but also from alcohol-related liver disease and suicide—the deaths of despair.

Before turning to studies that examine the specific mechanisms through which work and the labor market have shaped the opioid crisis, we review descriptive evidence on the distribution of opioid use and opioid-related mortality across different types of workers.

Patterns of Opioid Use and Mortality Across Industries and Occupations

The opioid crisis has played out differently for different groups of workers, and recent research has documented dramatic differences across occupations and industries in rates of prescription opioid use and opioid-related mortality. As we will discuss later in this chapter, some promising new research has also started to link geographic variation in the opioid crisis to working conditions and economic fluctuations in specific industries.

A recent article by National Institute for Occupational Safety and Health (NIOSH) researchers used the Medical Expenditure Panel Survey-Household Component (MEPS-HC) to characterize the prevalence of opioid prescribing among workers (Asfaw, Alterman, and Quay, 2020). After adjusting for demographic characteristics and source of health insurance, they found that workers in farming, fishing, and forestry; construction and extraction; production and transportation; and service occupations were more likely to receive prescription opioids than white-collar workers in finance and management occupations were. Other occupational groups did not have statistically significantly higher rates of prescription opioid receipt.

Similarly, Hawkins et al., 2019, used vital records and employment data from Massachusetts to examine opioid-related overdose mortality rates by occupation and industry. Patterns of opioid mortality across industries appear consistent with the occupational patterns in opioid prescribing documented by Asfaw, Alterman, and Quay, 2020. Compared with the statewide average, industry-specific opioid-related overdose rates were dramatically higher in construction; agriculture, forestry, fishing, and hunting; transportation and warehousing; administrative and support and waste management services; accommodations and food services; and other service industries. Similarly, occupation-specific overdose rates were higher in construction and extraction; farming, fishing, and forestry; material moving; installation, maintenance, and repair; transportation; production; food preparation and serving; and health care support. The variation in mortality rates was quite stark across occupations: Opioid-related mortality rates for men in construction and extraction and farming, fishing, and forestry occupations were more than five times the average across all occupations. These occupational and industrial patterns in opioid-related overdose mortality aligned closely with differences in physical job demands and injury rates across industries, as well as job insecurity and lower availability of paid sick leave (Hawkins et al., 2019).

Differences in overdose death rates by workplace injury rates are particularly striking: Industries with 200 or more injuries per 10,000 full-time workers had nearly 70 opioid-related overdose deaths per 100,000 workers, compared with roughly 20 overdose deaths per 100,000 workers for industries with 100 to 199 injuries per 10,000 full-time workers, and below ten overdose deaths per 100,000 workers for industries with the lowest injury rates (0 to 49 injuries per 100,000 workers). Injury rates and other dimensions of working conditions are correlated with the other risk factors identified in Hawkins et al., 2019, including job insecurity and physical job demands, and these associations do not prove a causal connection between any single job characteristic and opioid overdose mortality. Even so, these sharp differences warrant closer examination.

Workplace Injuries, Workers' Compensation, and Overdose Mortality

Workplace injuries and workers' compensation came up earlier when we discussed evidence on the effect of opioid prescribing on disability duration. There is also evidence that workplace injury can expose workers to risky opioid prescribing, often from medical care provided through the workers' compensation system. Franklin and colleagues from the Washington state workers' compensation system have documented widespread opioid prescribing among patients with back injuries, doing so at an early stage of the opioid crisis (Franklin et al., 2005). In particular, they showed that patients who received workers' compensation for non-fatal injuries frequently received high-duration prescribing in workers' compensation, leading to overdose deaths (Franklin et al., 2005).

Several recent studies have shown that nonfatal workplace injuries with lost workdays lead to substantial increases in long-term drug overdose mortality and suicide (Applebaum et al., 2019). Using data on workplace injuries between 1994 and 2000, researchers found that a lost-time injury increased the hazard (i.e., the instantaneous probability) of mortality from drug overdose or suicide by 42 percent for men and 163 percent for women. Martin et al., 2020, reported similar findings for West Virginia workers who suffered low-back injuries in 1999 and 2000. They found that, compared with the general population of West Virginia, a lost-time low-back injury increased the hazard of opioid-related drug overdose by 89 percent. Similarly, the hazard of suicide increased by 85 percent. These grim findings clearly indicate that the risk of workplace injury and resulting exposure to opioids are important mechanisms underlying the patterns of industry-specific overdose mortality highlighted in Hawkins et al., 2019.

Incentives for Sobriety and Access to Treatment Outside Health Insurance

Notwithstanding the clear risks posed by workplace injuries, employment should also offer some protective effects against substance use, including opioid misuse. Work provides many people with a sense of meaning and is an important venue for social interaction, both elements of a good life that can mitigate feelings of mental distress that lead to substance use. Conversely (as we discuss at length later in this chapter), lack of work and financial hardship are likely triggers for substance use. Cross-sectional patterns consistent with the protective effect of work are reported by Perlmutter et al., 2017, who analyzed the 2011–2013 NSDUH to compare rates of past-year prescription opioid misuse among full-time workers, part-time workers, the unemployed, and individuals not in the labor force. After adjusting for demographics and psychological distress, they found that the unemployed had higher rates of prescription opioid misuse than currently employed workers, but that those who were not in the workforce had *lower* rates of prescription opioid misuse than currently employed workers. Note, however, that this appears to go against the findings of Krueger, 2017—who used a different nationally representative data set from the same years—that daily prescription pain medication use was more than twice as high for men who are not in the labor force as it was for either currently employed workers or the unemployed.

Presumably, work and employer policies have an important role to play in deterring or treating opioid misuse. Drug-free workplace policies and drug testing (whether pre-employment, random, or postaccident) should serve as powerful deterrents for employees to use illicit substances. Work should also provide workers with resources that can help them avoid or manage opioid dependence, either through health insurance that provides access to substance use treatment or through EAPs. Some studies show associations between drug testing (and related employer policies) and reduced substance use by workers. Carpenter, 2007, analyzed 2000–2001 NSDUH data to study the association between workplace drug testing and past-month marijuana use. He showed that workplace testing is associated with reduced past-month marijuana use, with lower rates of use in workplaces with more-frequent testing, random testing after hiring, and more-severe penalties. He also found that some of the bivariate association between testing and past-month use was attributable to other correlated employer policies (such as drug education, official written policies regarding substance use, and EAPs).

We did not find evidence on this question specifically for opioids, although Van Hasselt et al., 2015, in the analysis of the 2008–2012 NSDUH discussed earlier in this chapter, reported unadjusted comparisons of workplace policies between workers with and without past-month prescription drug misuse. Without controlling for other worker characteristics, the researchers reported that workers reporting past-month prescription drug misuse are less likely to have a written drug and alcohol policy (69 percent versus 77 percent of nonusers) and less likely to have workplace drug and alcohol testing (43 percent versus 49 percent of nonusers). Workplace policies are likely to be correlated with other unobserved job characteristics affecting substance use, however, in which case cross-sectional comparisons like these have little, if any, policy implications.

Underscoring the lack of strong evidence on employer policies to deter opioid misuse and other drug problems, a new and far-reaching systematic review in Akanbi et al., 2020, failed to find consistently strong evidence for the effectiveness of any of the most widespread and widely recommended workplace interventions to prevent or manage employee drug use. The researchers searched the worldwide literature (with no language restrictions) through 2019 for studies focused on six types of interventions recommended by the Substance Abuse and Mental Health Services Administration:

- employee education
- drug testing
- EAPs
- supervisor training
- written workplace drug-free policies
- restructuring of employee health benefit plans.

Although they found studies on all of these interventions, only four were randomized controlled trials, and the quality of all of the studies was rated as "fair" or "poor." Each intervention was effective in at least one study, but none was effective in a majority of included studies.

Declining Labor Demand and Deaths of Despair

The opioid crisis arose in the context of several major changes that have reshaped the U.S. labor market over the past several decades. The most striking of these changes has been declining employment and labor force participation among working-age adults. The employment-to-population ratio has fallen from 64.3 percent in 1999 to 60.4 percent in 2018, a pattern that is mirrored in declining labor force participation. This trend represents a reversal in the decades-long expansion in overall employment that was observed as women entered the workforce in the mid- and late 20th century. Declining employment rates have also been accompanied by changes in the structure of wages for workers with different levels of education, as the gap in wages between workers with and without a college degree has also widened in recent decades.

These long-term changes reflect many factors. Abraham and Kearney, 2018, identified import competition from China and adoption of industrial robots as the most-important factors underlying this decline, accounting for 24 percent and 11 percent, respectively, of the total 3.8-percentage-point decline in employment rates over the past two decades. These factors have reduced labor demand, especially for workers with less educational attainment. Other contributing factors that Abraham and Kearney considered well-substantiated include higher minimum wages at the state level[8] (reducing labor demand), increased receipt of federal disability benefits (reducing labor supply), and higher rates of incarceration (reducing labor supply).

In addition to rising inequality between less-educated and more-educated workers, recent decades have seen changes in the nature of inequality across places within the United States. Before 1980, the 20th century saw a pattern of regional convergence between lower-income and higher-income states within the United States, with faster economic growth in initially lower-income states. However, regional convergence has slowed dramatically since 1980, meaning places that started out lower income have remained low income. Slowing regional convergence has been accompanied by a decline in migration rates of less-educated workers from lower-wage to higher-wage labor markets (Ganong and Shoag, 2017).

These changes in the labor market and patterns of regional economic growth add up to reduced economic opportunities for lower-skilled workers, particularly those in less prosperous places. In 2015, Case and Deaton reported that death rates involving substance use and suicide were rising dramatically for non-Hispanic White men and women at midlife. Case and Deaton, 2015, labeled three self-inflicted causes of death—drug poisoning, suicide, and alcohol-related liver disease—as deaths of despair. They documented the importance of geographic variation in these deaths, showing a strong correlation across U.S. states in suicide and drug poisoning mortality. They also suggested that slow earnings growth and financial insecurity might be underlying causes worth investigating. Finally, the 2015 study also identified the deaths of despair as a uniquely U.S. phenomenon, showing that mortality trends in European countries that also experienced slow earnings growth for less-educated workers did not in any way mirror the pattern seen for White non-Hispanic people in the United States.

The findings of Case and Deaton seeded a rapidly growing literature seeking to identify the mechanisms driving the deaths of despair and tease apart the causal arrows that run in both directions between opioid use (and mortality) and lack of economic opportunity. We discuss this literature in detail in the rest of this section, before moving on to a discussion of connections between employment and other systems, as well as policy implications.

Since the seminal Case and Deaton, 2015, study, some of the literature on opioid overdoses and other deaths of despair has noted worrisome trends in opioid mortality and other deaths of despair in populations other than non-Hispanic White men and women in the United

---

[8] The federal minimum wage has not been raised since 2009. It remains at $7.25 per hour.

States. In particular, it is important to note that opioid overdose mortality has increased rapidly among Black non-Hispanic men and women over the past two decades, as documented in Hoopsick, Homish, and Leonard, 2021, with growth in the overdose rate for Black men and women (of any ethnicity) accelerating in 2012 and later years (Furr-Holden et al., 2021). Looking abroad, there are also worrisome midlife mortality trends in the United Kingdom, especially in Scotland (Allik et al., 2020). We wish to be clear that the long-run trends in midlife mortality among non-Hispanic White workers that were highlighted by Case and Deaton's original 2015 report should not be conflated with the opioid crisis as a whole—a point that Case and Deaton, 2018, made in subsequent writing. That said, the important role of the labor market (and declining labor demand) in Case and Deaton's theory makes it an important argument to examine in this chapter.

When we look across different geographic areas at a given point in time (i.e., in a cross-section), drug overdose mortality is strongly associated with local economic conditions. Monnat, 2018, confirmed that *economic distress*—defined as an index reflecting labor market conditions, poverty rates, disability program participation, and other indicators of hardship—predicted higher drug-related mortality during the period from 2006 to 2015: A 1–standard deviation increase in the economic distress index predicted a 6.4-percent increase in the age-adjusted drug overdose mortality rate. Controlling for the economic distress index, industry mix also mattered: Overdose mortality was higher in local economies that were more dependent on mining or less dependent on the public sector. In addition to these economic factors, family distress (proxied by the proportion of separated or divorced adults and single-parent families) and low social capital (proxied by religious establishments and other community institutions) independently predicted higher drug-related mortality over and above the economic distress index.[9]

This cross-sectional relationship leaves open the question of whether opioid misuse and its downstream consequences are responsive to short-run economic fluctuations (i.e., recessions and recoveries) or only to long-run or permanent changes (e.g., manufacturing plant closures). Several studies have shown that differences across geographic areas in the severity of the 2008–2009 Great Recession were associated with short-run changes in opioid misuse and mortality. Carpenter, McClellan, and Rees, 2017, using NSDUH data from 2002 to 2015, showed that increases in the state-level unemployment rate predicted increases in oxycodone use, heroin use, and the prevalence of diagnosable pain medication use disorders. Hollingsworth, Ruhm, and Simon, 2017, which applied a similar research design to emergency department discharge and mortality data from 2004 to 2014, found that a 1-percentage-point increase in the county unemployment rate increases emergency department visits for opioid overdose by 7 percent and increases opioid overdose mortality by 3.6 percent. Consistent with

---

[9] We note that the opioid crisis continues to evolve, most recently with the greatly expanded supply of fentanyl, which has led to rising overdose mortality rates in areas that had been less affected by earlier phases of the crisis. The geographic correlates of opioid overdose mortality have likely changed in the past few years, so extrapolation to conditions in 2023 should be approached with caution.

Case and Deaton, 2015, the adverse effects found in both of these reports were driven by overdoses and deaths among White men and women.

These studies clearly show that short-run economic fluctuations affect opioid misuse and adverse outcomes. However, Case and Deaton argued that the long-run nature of the opioid crisis suggests that short-run business-cycle fluctuations are not an adequate explanation for the observed relationship between poor labor market conditions and the opioid crisis (Case and Deaton, 2017; Case and Deaton, 2020). They also argued that a theory of the relationship between the labor market and the opioid crisis needs to explain why opioid-related mortality and the other deaths of despair did not follow a similar trajectory for Hispanic or Black men and women, given that these groups have long experienced greater economic hardship and were more severely affected by the Great Recession than were non-Hispanic White men and women.

To explain the racial and ethnic differences in the deaths of despair, Case and Deaton, 2017, proposed a theory of *cumulative disadvantage*, which they defined as the cumulative effect of long-term hardship relative to one's own expectations for life. They argued that the conditions of life for White working-class men and women have deteriorated on other important dimensions (such as family structure, civic engagement, and religious involvement) that go far beyond the labor market (Case and Deaton, 2020). The disappearance of high-quality jobs for less-educated White workers, however, is identified by Case and Deaton as the prime mover in all aspects of racial and ethnic differences in the deaths of despair. The literature we reviewed in this chapter does not explore the role of culture, life expectations, or social capital, but these observations are consistent with the cross-sectional patterns reported in Monnat, 2018.

Several recent studies have shown a causal connection between reduced manufacturing employment and deaths of despair. Pierce and Schott, 2020, studied changes in unemployment between 1990 and 2013 that resulted from the accession of China to the World Trade Organization in 2000, measuring import exposure at the local labor market level by comparing the mix of products in an area's manufacturing output with changes in tariffs. They found that exposure to Chinese import competition is strongly related to higher rates of suicide and accidental poisoning deaths; these effects are driven by White workers (Hispanic ethnicity is not available in all years of the authors' data), with larger effects for men than for women. The magnitude of the researchers' estimated effects is striking: A 1-percentage-point increase in the county unemployment rate causes an additional 1.5 accidental poisoning deaths per 100,000 population, an increase of 32 percent. Venkataramani et al., 2020, used a different research strategy, comparing counties with auto plant closures between 1999 and 2016 with other counties with auto plants that did not close. They found very large mortality effects associated with large declines in labor demand, with opioid-related mortality increasing by 85 percent as of five years after the plant closure. Taken together, these reports strongly corroborate the hypothesis that the disappearance of manufacturing jobs was an important driver of the opioid crisis.

Although the work of Pierce and Schott, 2020, and Venkataramani et al., 2020, provides convincing evidence of a causal connection from manufacturing job losses to opioid-related mortality, others have emphasized that the deaths of despair mechanism should not be taken as a monocausal explanation for the opioid crisis. Ruhm, 2019, modeled the change between 1999 and 2015 in state-level drug overdose mortality rates and various measures of economic conditions, including unemployment, poverty, household income, and exposure to import competition; other deaths of despair (including suicide and alcohol-related liver disease) were also examined. Although he found a relationship between long-run declines in local economic conditions and long-run increases in drug-related mortality, the proportion of the long-run variation in mortality rates that is explained by the economic measures taken together is arguably quite small—less than 10 percent of the total increase in opioid-related overdose rates. Ruhm argued that this analysis shows that factors other than declining labor demand—most notably the supply of opioids through the health care system and the illicit market—should be considered more-important explanations of the opioid crisis and that policy interventions focused on the labor market may have limited success in addressing the opioid crisis. Case and Deaton, 2018, responded that Ruhm's perspective is somewhat of a straw man argument that defines the relevant mechanisms too narrowly.

Well-designed studies that look at different industries beyond the manufacturing sector also paint a more nuanced picture of the relationship between labor market conditions and the opioid crisis. Metcalf and Wang, 2019, examined the effects of coal mine employment on opioid mortality and more or less reached the opposite conclusion from Pierce and Schott, 2020, and Venkataramani et al., 2020, about the relationship between labor demand and opioid overdose mortality. Specifically, they found that coal mine employment *increases* opioid overdose mortality: A 1-percentage-point increase in the share of coal miners in the county workforce caused an increase of 1.1 opioid-related overdose deaths per 100,000 people over the following three years. Other researchers who looked at employment across all industries (not just manufacturing) also found that the effect of employment rates on opioid prescribing differed meaningfully by educational attainment and gender (Currie, Jin, and Schnell, 2018) and by the industry-level workplace injury rate (Musse, 2020). Similarly, Betz and Jones, 2018, explored heterogeneity across industries and demographic groups in the effect of changes in labor demand on opioid overdose deaths and found that, although greater labor demand in low-wage and medium-wage industries reduced the opioid overdose death rate, greater labor demand in high-wage industries increased the opioid overdose death rate. They also found—contrary to the popular view that deaths of despair are uniquely a phenomenon of White men in rural areas—that labor demand in low- and medium-wage industries reduced the opioid overdose death rate for Black people, women, and those in metropolitan areas.

One plausible explanation for this apparent heterogeneity across industries is that there are multiple pathways leading from employment to opioid use, with the importance of these different mechanisms depending on worker demographics and workplace safety. On the one hand is the deaths of despair mechanism: Loss of employment because of declining labor demand leads to despair, then death. On the other hand is the mechanism suggested by

Musse, 2020—specifically, that higher-injury industries increase opioid utilization by injuring workers or wearing them down and, therefore, increasing the prevalence of pain and the demand for pain relief. This mechanism suggests that higher labor demand increases opioid utilization and, with it, the risks of accidental overdose and addiction. This suggestion would square with Franklin et al., 2005, who documented large numbers of accidental opioid overdose deaths for Washington state workers' compensation patients in the late 1990s, as well as the studies discussed earlier in this chapter that showed how nonfatal workplace injury places workers at elevated risk for opioid overdose and suicide in the long term. Other explanations are possible, however, and the complex relationship between labor demand and the opioid crisis remains an active area of research.

We conclude this section by noting that the spread of illegally produced synthetic opioids like fentanyl and the availability of naloxone, the overdose reversal drug, may complicate some of these studies and raise questions about their utility going forward. Given the data limitations described in Chapter Two, it is hard to incorporate information on the availability and use of illegally produced synthetic opioids—which are much more likely to lead to overdose—into research on the effect of employment on overdose mortality or other opioid-related outcomes. These changes in the opioid ecosystem raise questions about how research done earlier in the course of the opioid crisis can be extrapolated to policy decisions in the present day. In addition, the fact that the drug-involved overdose rate is now higher for Black Americans than it is for White Americans (Friedman and Hansen, 2021) suggests that the standard deaths of despair argument may need to be amended or augmented.

Key Interactions with Other Components of the Ecosystem

Labor markets and employment interact with the systems at the core of the opioid ecosystem in several ways. The most-important interactions are with the medical care system, and there are notable interactions with the treatment system and criminal legal system. There is less evidence on interactions with illegal supply, and the research discussed above is not able to distinguish illegal supply or diversion from prescription opioids provided by physicians and pharmacies.

One common interaction across nearly all these systems is that their functioning is reliant upon the health and productivity of their workers. The negative impacts of the opioid crisis on workers and the labor market also affect these systems. This is especially true of medical care and first responders, who are deterred from disclosing SUDs and seeking treatment by the threat of professional consequences. Nonphysician health care workers, police, and firefighters also have high physical job demands and high injury rates, which would tend to place them at risk for exposure to prescription opioids and, potentially, misuse. Workers in some of these occupations may also face more-stringent drug-testing requirements that can create further barriers to receiving MOUD. Although impacts on the physician, nursing, police, and firefighter workforces have been most thoroughly studied, no occupational group or industry is untouched by the opioid crisis, so this form of interaction should be viewed as affecting all systems considered in this report.

Medical Care

Employer-sponsored health insurance is the primary source of health insurance coverage for nonelderly Americans, so employment rates, labor productivity, and employer decisions about benefit design play enormous roles in determining who has access to medical care, which treatments and providers are covered, and what it costs to patients.

Due in part to America's reliance on employer-sponsored health insurance, the medical care system also has impacts on labor markets that have been identified by some observers as worrisome. A large portion of the exceptionally high level of health spending in the United States is financed by employer contributions to employer-sponsored insurance. In 2019, employer costs of providing health insurance were 8.3 percent of total employee compensation for civilian workers. Economists generally believe that the employer costs of health insurance are ultimately paid by workers in the form of lower wages (Gruber, 1994). In their recent book on deaths of despair, Case and Deaton, 2020, point out that this approach to financing health insurance functions like a head tax that has helped to depress wages for lower-skilled workers and that deters businesses from hiring them. America's failure to control health spending growth since the 1980s has ratcheted up the size of this head tax, further undermining labor demand for less productive (lower-skilled) workers.

Substance Use Disorder Treatment

Employer decisions about health insurance benefit design, EAPs, and other optional benefits also play an important role in shaping access to drug treatment for workers and their dependents. Even in the presence of stronger mental health parity laws (including MHPAEA and the Affordable Care Act), parity on all dimensions of insurance benefit design (such as network adequacy) may be difficult to monitor and enforce. If employers are biased against hiring workers with OUD, they may be less likely to choose benefit designs, networks, or optional benefits (such as EAPs) that may be especially important to workers with OUD. Henke et al., 2020, found that workers with diagnosed OUD who are receiving MOUD did not exhibit decreased productivity compared with workers without OUD; however, participation in MOUD does not guarantee that the individual will remain in recovery (see Chapter Four).

The OUD treatment system plays a critical role in enabling workers with OUD to remain in or reenter employment. As we discuss below, public workforce system interventions to promote employment among workers with OUD are frequently administered by (or integrated with) SUD treatment facilities. In some, productive employment is used as an element of recovery by providing structure, meaning, and (perhaps implicitly) financial incentives for continued sobriety to individuals undergoing treatment.

Criminal Legal System

In the context of the opioid crisis, probably the most-notable interactions between the labor market and the criminal legal system revolve around the barriers to hiring that many workers with a history of OUD or participation in the illicit market might face because of their criminal records (see Chapter Six for more on this factor). We also note, as we discussed earlier in the context of total burden estimates, that reductions in the labor force because of incarceration for opioid-related crimes are estimated to make up around 10 percent of the total amount of lost economic output because of the impact of the opioid crisis on labor supply, around $4 billion in 2013 (in 2013 dollars) (Florence et al., 2016).

We noted earlier that state workforce agencies seeking to promote employment among workers with OUD have started with programs focused on the OUD treatment system. Some of these efforts have also explicitly focused on formerly incarcerated individuals. One relatively unexplored interaction is whether occupational licensing requirements create undue barriers for formerly incarcerated individuals to apply credentials or work experience acquired in prison. For example, inmate firefighters in California had historically been barred from receiving emergency medical technician licenses necessary to become firefighters after release; in 2020, California enacted Assembly Bill 2147 to address this issue by allowing inmate firefighters to expunge their convictions under certain circumstances. Broader efforts to remove barriers to employment among formerly incarcerated individuals seem likely to benefit those whose criminal records are somehow related to opioids.

Illegal Supply

Employment can be said to contribute to illegal supply via diversion of prescription opioids obtained through employer-sponsored insurance or workers' compensation. Similarly, employment opportunities in the legal labor market may reduce labor supply to the criminal labor market, including opioid supply.

Being a source of opioids, illegal supply surely affects labor markets, workers, and employers through many of the channels identified in this chapter. As we note here, evidence specifically linking illegal supply to labor market outcomes appears to be nonexistent (or, at least, far rarer than the literature on prescription opioids). Some employers do report that the workplace is a venue for illegal sales of prescription drugs, but employers reported nearly all other concerns and incidents related to the opioid crisis much more frequently (Abd-Elsayed et al., 2020).

First Responders

One widely publicized concern for first responders is the risk of opioid poisoning in the line of duty, a concern that has become quite urgent given the rise of fentanyl. NIOSH has developed recommendations for first responders and hospital-based health care workers to minimize workplace exposure to fentanyl and other illicit drugs. The scale and severity of this problem remains largely unsubstantiated; however, the professional organizations for toxicologists state that "for routine handling of drug[s], nitrile gloves provide sufficient dermal protection. In exceptional circumstances where there are drug particles or droplets suspended in the air, an N95 respirator provides sufficient protection" (Moss et al., 2017, p. 347). Some observers have argued that the focus on accidental fentanyl poisoning in the line of duty primarily reflects—and propagates—stereotypes that can undermine other efforts to control the opioid crisis (Del Pozo, Rich, and Carroll, 2022). (See also Chapters Six and Nine.)

In addition to concerns over exposure to toxic substances, the opioid crisis has exacerbated workplace stressors affecting first responders. The increased volume of calls for service has led to increased workload with negative implications for agencies' ability to respond to other situations (Knaak et al., 2019; Pike et al., 2019). Furthermore, the opioid crisis has adversely affected first responders' well-being, with reports of emotional strain, burnout, vicarious trauma, and compassion fatigue (Elliott, Bennett, and Wolfson-Stofko, 2019; Saunders et al., 2019).

Income Support and Homeless Services

From the perspective of public budgets, negative labor market impacts of the opioid crisis are likely to result in increased social services spending at the local, state, and federal levels because loss of employment or family income ultimately resulting from the opioid crisis may result in increased eligibility for means-tested programs, such as Temporary Assistance for Needy Families and the Supplemental Nutrition Assistance Program. In hard-hit labor markets, reductions in employment can harm state and local revenues because of reduced income tax revenues; the resulting loss of labor income is also likely to reduce sales tax revenue, which is a particularly important revenue source for local government. Nationwide, lost tax revenue between 2000 and 2016 because of reduced labor supply (including both overdose mortality and nonfatal use) was calculated to average $694 million per year to state governments (primarily because of reduced income taxes) and $1.5 billion per year to the federal government (Segel et al., 2019). Consistent with this channel, Ouimet, Simintzi, and Ye, 2019, found reduced business revenues in areas with higher growth in opioid prescriptions per capita. By eroding government revenues while increasing expenditure needs, opioid-related declines in local labor markets would appear to be an important mechanism through which the opioid crisis may strain social services systems.[10]

There is a major nexus between workplace injury, opioid use, labor force exits, and participation in SSDI, but the magnitude of the causal effects between each of these phenomena has been challenging to measure. Musculoskeletal disorders, pain, and prescription opioid use are highly prevalent among SSDI beneficiaries (Morden et al., 2014). The causal relationship

---

[10] There have been studies examining whether the excise taxes paid and/or contributions to Social Security and other government programs by those who use tobacco or alcohol offset the public expenditures related to the costs of these substances (see, e.g., Manning et al., 1989). Most people who die from opioid overdoses do not collect Social Security, and none impose costs on other systems after they die, but we are not aware of any studies that have attempted to compare the full effects on public budgets.

between opioid prescribing and SSDI participation is likely to be quite complex. Cutler, Meara, and Stewart found some evidence of an association between state-level opioid prescribing patterns and SSDI application volumes (Cutler, Meara, and Stewart, 2016; Cutler, Meara, and Stewart, 2017), but the causal direction of this aggregate relationship remains unclear given that, like opioid prescription volumes, applications to SSDI rise when labor demand falls in a local labor market (Black, Daniel, and Sanders, 2002). It is important to remember that the Personal Responsibility and Work Opportunity Reconciliation Act of 1996 changed the eligibility criteria for SSDI and Supplemental Security Income—the primary federal disability insurance programs—so that individuals for whom SUD was a "contributing factor" to their disability would not be eligible for an award of benefits. These individuals seem likely to be more reliant on state and local social services, such as general assistance programs, or to fall into homelessness.

As noted below, public workforce system interventions to promote employment among workers with OUD are sometimes administered by (or integrated with) SUD treatment facilities.

Education

Because education helps determine the supply of workers at different skill levels, disruptions to education or job training by opioid misusers undermine the human capital of the labor force. Similarly, criminal justice involvement can also disrupt education, which reduces human capital. If shortages of less-educated workers as a result of the opioid crisis were large enough, they would eventually drive up wages or lead to more widespread job vacancies in jobs with lower skill requirements. In theory, higher wages for less-skilled workers could draw youth away from high school or college by making work more attractive than continued schooling. In practice, it seems unlikely that shortages of less-skilled workers caused by the opioid crisis would outweigh the relative scarcity of college graduates that has driven up the college wage profile in recent decades.

Education in the United States is overwhelmingly financed by state and local government, so the public finance impacts of disruptions to the labor market are a potential channel through which the impacts of the opioid crisis on the labor market may affect the education system. The estimated nationwide-average impact of the opioid crisis on government revenues appears modest in comparison with the overall size of public budgets (Segel et al., 2019), but there are likely states and counties where tax revenue losses have had larger impacts on public school funding.

Harm Reduction and Community-Initiated Interventions

To the extent that harm reduction services keep people who use drugs healthier and alive, this factor could have implications for various labor market outcomes; however, we are not aware of any studies that have specially addressed this relationship. Some employers may seek out naloxone kits and trainings provided by public health agencies, but the extent to which these options happen is unknown.

There is also the role that local businesses may play in blocking or helping facilitate the opening of harm reduction services in their neighborhoods. They are, of course, not the only local stakeholders involved in these decisions. However, those seeking to provide these services should have an understanding about how the surrounding businesses feel, providing education about the services when appropriate.

Finally, there is the role that harm reduction programs play in providing employment opportunities to people with lived or living experience of drug use (see, e.g., Olding et al., 2021). We are unaware of any estimates of the size of the workforce distributing naloxone and working at syringe service programs in the United States, let alone what share have lived or living experience of drug use. But the CDC recommends that syringe service programs involve people who inject drugs in all aspects of program design, implementation, and service delivery (CDC, 2020).

Policy Opportunities and Considerations

The rise of widespread opioid prescribing in the 1990s was a response to increased focus on chronic pain, including among those in the workforce. Lost economic output because of chronic pain is estimated to be about ten times larger than lost economic output because of the opioid crisis (Gaskin and Richard, 2012; Florence et al., 2016; Rhyan, 2017). The withdrawal of Vioxx and other COX-2 inhibitors (a type of nonsteroidal anti-inflammatory drug) from the U.S. market in 2004 offers a cautionary example of the economic costs that might result from changes that reduce access to pain treatment. After the removal of COX-2 inhibitors, labor supply among older adults with chronic pain declined sharply, with the estimated loss of wages comparable in magnitude with estimates of lost economic output because of nonfatal opioid use (Garthwaite, 2012). Similarly, Kilby (2015) found that introducing a PDMP without providing alternative pain management can reduce labor supply among workers who live with chronic pain. The fact that there is some evidence that reducing access to pain medication reduces labor supply among those with chronic pain does not imply that widespread opioid prescribing is the best way to keep workers with chronic pain in the labor force, especially given the lack of evidence that the clinical benefits of long-term opioid therapy for chronic pain management outweigh the harms (see Chapter Two). However, this consideration does suggest that when policymakers take actions to reduce access to prescription opioids, they need to be thoughtful about how individuals with chronic pain will respond to reduced access. Will these individuals have ready access to non-opioid alternatives to pain management? How many of them will just turn to illegal markets and possibly use illegally produced opioids that increase the risk of overdose? Ultimately, we have to acknowledge (1) that using opioids to address chronic pain has had disastrous consequences and (2) that treating and managing chronic pain in a way that facilitates employment will remain an important challenge.

Coverage of non-opioid pain management therapy, including complementary and alternative medicine, through employee benefits appears to be rare. A survey by the National Safety Council asked surveyed employers about their interest in covering a wide variety of non-opioid pain treatment through health insurance, including physical therapy, cognitive behavioral therapy for pain, massage, mindfulness meditation, acupuncture, yoga, and tai chi (Abd-Elsayed et al., 2020). Other than tai chi, two-thirds or more of surveyed employers expressed some interest in covering each modality. Yet the proportion actually covering these benefits was very low. Thirty-one percent covered physical therapy, but the percentages of employers covering the other modalities were in the single digits or low teens.

It is also plausible that the basic structure of the U.S. health insurance system, with its reliance on employer-sponsored insurance and fees for service, has undermined access to non-opioid pain management and OUD treatment. Authority for regulating the design of employer-sponsored insurance is split between states (who have oversight of health insurance products sold by commercial insurers) and the federal government (which regulates self-funded health insurance plans). Earlier state-level parity laws may have had limited effectiveness in changing benefits available to the majority of workers who are covered by self-funded employer plans. And even in the presence of stronger federal parity laws, ensuring access to mental health and SUD treatment may require further steps to close all the loopholes. For instance, California enacted a law (California Senate Bill 855, 2020) regulating the definition of *medical necessity* to prevent insurers from making medical necessity decisions that undermine the spirit of existing state and federal parity laws. Job loss or job changes often lead to changes or gaps in insurance coverage, which can reduce the continuity of care. However, the importance of insurance churning for workers with OUD in particular has not been established empirically.

Existing drug-testing policies also create challenges for employers who are in recovery from OUD, especially those receiving MOUD. In particular, the U.S. Government Accountability Office's (GAO's) review of workforce system interventions highlights some unfortunate interactions between employer drug-testing policies and the Americans with Disabilities Act (ADA), which established employment protections for workers with disabilities. Workforce agency officials reported to GAO investigators that some employers try to work around the ADA by discriminating against workers in OUD recovery at the hiring stage to avoid a situation where they are forced to provide accommodation to a worker. Other employers might rely on zero-tolerance policies (automatically firing workers upon a positive drug test) to provide them legal cover against ADA lawsuits. Employers who want to help may need to revisit their drug-testing or zero-tolerance policies, but mitigating these unintended consequences of antidiscrimination laws may need legislative changes.

An open question about the deaths of despair mechanism is whether the driving force is the loss of work and the inability to fill expected social roles or the financial insecurity and material hardship that result from declining labor demand. It is hard to identify small-scale changes that would reverse the secular trend toward declining labor demand for less-educated workers, but financial insecurity may be relatively easy to fix in the short term through tax credits, wage subsidies (including basic income), or minimum wages. Dow et al., 2019, examined whether increases between 1999 and 2015 in the minimum wage or the Earned Income Tax Credit—two policies designed to raise wages and incomes for low-wage workers—reduce mortality from deaths of despair. To the extent that the effects of declining labor demand on the opioid crisis operate through financial hardship alone, these measures might be expected to reduce opioid mortality by raising family incomes even if they do not increase employment. Dow et al., 2019, found that the minimum wage and Earned Income Tax Credit reduced nondrug suicides, but both factors had no significant effect on drug-related mortality. The Dow et al., 2019, findings suggested that these existing policies are not likely to reduce mortality because of drug overdoses. As in Pierce and Schott, 2020, nondrug suicides appear more responsive than drug-related mortality to economic hardship.

The federal-state workforce development system seems like a promising platform for policy responses to mitigate the effects of the opioid crisis on the labor market. The U.S. Department of Labor has made multiple grants to state workforce agencies to develop and implement programs focused specifically on promoting employment among workers in OUD recovery. Initial efforts were conducted under the Workforce Innovation and Opportunity Act, with additional opioid-focused funding provided through the 2018 SUPPORT Act. A May 2020 report by the GAO notes that these efforts are too new to have been evaluated for effectiveness or scalability. Vine et al., 2020, in a literature review covering employment interventions for workers with OUD, highlighted several intervention models, some of which were highlighted in the chapter of this report on the treatment system. Evidence on effectiveness was limited, and these models were largely implemented within the context of existing behavioral health programs, but some showed promise.

Vine et al., 2020, pointed out that employers might give workers who test positive for opioids the opportunity to provide a letter from their physician or other documentation that their test result reflects prescribed use rather than misuse. Other roles have been proposed for employers. New Hampshire has established a "recovery friendly workplace" designation, which employers can receive by implementing several of the strategies identified above. New Hampshire workforce agency staff told GAO investigators that some employers did not want to be designated as recovery-friendly workplaces because of concerns that customers would avoid businesses known to employ workers with a history of OUD (GAO, 2020). More broadly, workforce agencies reported stereotyping and discrimination of workers with OUD by employers as a barrier to employment efforts for their clients.

Both Ruhm, 2018, and Currie and Schwandt, 2020, argued that the importance of changes in the labor market to the opioid crisis has been overstated, and that the more promising strategies for reducing overdose mortality are those that focus on reducing inappropriate prescribing (e.g., PDMPs and prescribing guidelines) and rescuing overdose victims (i.e., expanding access to naloxone). This is fair enough as a public health strategy for addressing the urgent needs presented by the opioid crisis and saving lives. However, changing the opioid environment without changing the labor market may be insufficient to eliminate the other deaths of despair (Case and Deaton, 2020).

Limitations and Research Needs

Data limitations have constrained our ability to answer many policy-relevant hypotheses about the effect of opioids on workers' labor market outcomes or about the effects of employment, working conditions, and economic hardship on opioid use and mortality. To address some of the most-pressing questions that we examine in this chapter, it would be ideal to use individual-level data capturing demographics and labor market outcomes alongside information about opioid use—both legal and illicit—and health status for representative samples of individuals across many different geographic areas. Although some data sets fit this description, they may not have sufficiently large sample sizes or sufficient detail about employment and labor market conditions to yield very informative answers.

We note that this is not true of all the questions we examine: Hypotheses linking opioid misuse to declining regional economies (or linking local economic conditions to a high prevalence of opioid misuse) are framed in terms of community-level phenomena and can be most directly addressed using aggregate data. Unfortunately, even questions that fundamentally rely on mechanisms that operate at the level of individual biology or labor supply decisions are frequently addressed using aggregate data. In addition to all the challenges that generally affect observational studies (such as omitted variables bias and reverse causation), studies that use aggregate data to draw inferences about mechanisms of individual behavior require extra care to avoid the ecological fallacy.

One important way in which data limitations have shaped the evidence base is that all current studies on the causal effect of opioid supply on labor market outcomes have had to rely on measures of legal opioid supply. This leaves us with an inadequate evidence base to quantify increases in labor supply or productivity that would result from enforcement or other strategies to curb illegal opioid supply. The study on the OxyContin reformulation in Park and Powell, 2021, is a good step in this direction; similar evidence from more-recent phases of the opioid crisis would be valuable. It is also not clear to what extent labor market opportunities in the illegal opioid markets affect labor supply or career development by diverting school-age youth or young workers away from the formal labor market. Casual empiricism on this question abounds (Vance, 2016), but data and rigorous analysis are scarce.

Not surprisingly, given the broad scope of questions in this chapter, more research is needed on many of the topics discussed here. Policies to reconnect individuals with a history of opioid use to the labor market could help mitigate the negative impacts of opioids on the labor market, but the discussion above indicates that many of these efforts have not been very successful or well-substantiated yet. As noted earlier in this chapter, rigorous evidence on employer-based interventions to prevent or treat prescription drug misuse is too limited to be very useful for guiding policy formation—for example, by facilitating cost-effectiveness analysis or other evaluations of the employer and society-wide cost-effectiveness of specific interventions (Akanbi et al., 2020).

We also note that we did not discuss research on labor market discrimination against formerly incarcerated people in this chapter, but it is likely that these challenges fall disproportionately on Black workers. There is likely scope for research on interventions to promote employment among workers with a history of justice involvement related to opioids, and potentially for interventions that might be tailored to the different structural forces that affect different racial and ethnic groups.[11]

As discussed earlier, there are still some unresolved questions about the relationship between employment, loss of employment, and opioid misuse, especially related to heterogeneity in effects across industries, demographic groups, and adults at different points in the life course. Another area that could benefit from more sustained attention is the ways in which the U.S. system of employer-sponsored health insurance might have unintended consequences that exacerbate (or make it harder to address) the opioid crisis. It is reasonable to believe that the incentives for benefit design inherent in the employer-sponsored insurance system have contributed to the lack of true parity of treatment for SUD and OUD in health insurance (which we discuss at greater length in Chapter Five), but it has been difficult to test this hypothesis or to develop policy solutions that are likely to be widely adopted by employers. As discussed earlier in this chapter, employers have not voluntarily provided widespread access to nonpharmaceutical pain treatment. Although stronger parity laws or other regulation of benefit design might seem to offer a simple solution to these challenges, the logic highlighted by Case and Deaton, 2020, in which the high cost of employer-sponsored insurance helps drive the decline in labor demand for less-educated workers (and thus fuels opioid misuse and other deaths of despair), points toward a potential downside from policies that would seek to expand access to MOUD or nonpharmaceutical pain treatment by imposing mandates on employer-sponsored insurance design. This is not to say that parity laws or benefit mandates are necessarily a misguided solution, but rather to highlight the need for more empirical evidence on how labor demand might respond to any such benefit mandates.

Similarly, although Case and Deaton's work on the deaths of despair has been invaluable in drawing attention to connections between the labor market and the opioid crisis, the emphasis in their original study on midlife mortality among non-Hispanic White workers should not obscure the difficulties facing other demographic groups—especially because the racial dynamics of opioid-involved overdose deaths have changed dramatically since 2010.

---

[11] There should also be a focus on evaluating workplace efforts to address the stigma associated with SUD (e.g., see McGinty and Barry, 2020).

Abbreviations

ADA	Americans with Disabilities Act
BLS	U.S. Bureau of Labor Statistics
CDC	Centers for Disease Control and Prevention
EAP	employee assistance program
GAO	U.S. Government Accountability Office
IT	information technology
MHPAEA	Mental Health Parity and Addiction Equity Act
MOUD	medications for opioid use disorder
NDIC	National Drug Intelligence Center
NIOSH	National Institute for Occupational Safety and Health
NSDUH	National Survey on Drug Use and Health
OUD	opioid use disorder
PDMP	prescription drug monitoring program
PUMA	Public Use Microdata Area
SSDI	Social Security Disability Insurance
SUD	substance use disorder

References

Abd-Elsayed, Alaa, Mathew Fischer, Jonathan Dimbert, and Kenneth James Fiala, "Prescription Drugs and the US Workforce: Results from a National Safety Council Survey," *Pain Physician*, Vol. 23, No. 1, 2020.

Abraham, Katharine G., and Melissa S. Kearney, *Explaining the Decline in the U.S. Employment-to-Population Ratio: A Review of the Evidence*, Cambridge, Mass.: National Bureau of Economic Research, Working Paper No. 24333, February 2018.

Akanbi, Maxwell O., Cassandra B. Iroz, Linda C. O'Dwyer, Adovich S. Rivera, and Megan C. McHugh, "A Systematic Review of the Effectiveness of Employer-Led Interventions for Drug Misuse," *Journal of Occupational Health*, Vol. 62, No. 1, January 2020.

Ali, Shahid, Barira Tahir, Shagufta Jabeen, and Madeeha Malik, "Methadone Treatment of Opiate Addiction: A Systematic Review of Comparative Studies," *Innovations in Clinical Neuroscience*, Vol. 14, No. 7–8, 2017, pp. 7–19.

Aliprantis, Dionissi, Kyle Fee, and Mark Schweitzer, *Opioids and the Labor Market*, Cleveland, Ohio: Federal Reserve Bank of Cleveland, Working Paper No. 18 07R2, 2018.

Allik, Mirjam, Denise Brown, Ruth Dundas, and Alastair H. Leyland, "Deaths of Despair: Cause-Specific Mortality and Socioeconomic Inequalities in Cause-Specific Mortality Among Young Men in Scotland," *International Journal for Equity in Health*, Vol. 19, No. 215, 2020.

Angrist, Joshua D., and Alan B. Krueger, "Instrumental Variables and the Search for Identification: From Supply and Demand to Natural Experiments," *Journal of Economic Perspectives*, Vol. 15, No. 4, 2001, pp. 69–85.

Angrist, Joshua D., and Jörn-Steffen Pischke, Mostly Harmless Econometrics: An Empiricist's Companion, Princeton, N.J.: Princeton University Press, 2009.

Applebaum, Katie M., Abay Asfaw, Paul K. O'Leary, Andrew Busey, Yorghos Tripodis, and Leslie I. Boden, "Suicide and Drug-Related Mortality Following Occupational Injury," *American Journal of Industrial Medicine*, Vol. 62, No. 9, September 2019, pp. 733–741.

Asfaw, Abay, Toni Alterman, and Brian Quay, "Prevalence and Expenses of Outpatient Opioid Prescriptions, with Associated Sociodemographic, Economic, and Work Characteristics," *International Journal of Health Services*, Vol. 50, No. 1, 2020, pp. 82–94.

Beheshti, David, "The Impact of Opioids on the Labor Market: Evidence from Drug Rescheduling," *Journal of Human Resources*, 2019.

Betz, Michael R., and Lauren E. Jones, "Wage and Employment Growth in America's Drug Epidemic: Is All Growth Created Equal?" *American Journal of Agricultural Economics*, Vol. 100, No. 5, October 2018, pp. 1357–1374.

Black, Dan, Kermit Daniel, and Seth Sanders, "The Impact of Economic Conditions on Participation in Disability Programs: Evidence from the Coal Boom and Bust," *American Economic Review*, Vol. 92, No. 1, March 2002, pp. 27–50.

BLS—*See* U.S. Bureau of Labor Statistics.

Burke, Laura G., Xiner Zhou, Katherine L. Boyle, E. John Orav, Dana Bernson, Maria-Elena Hood, Thomas Land, Monica Bharel, and Austin B. Frakt, "Trends in Opioid Use Disorder and Overdose Among Opioid-Naive Individuals Receiving an Opioid Prescription in Massachusetts from 2011 to 2014," *Addiction*, Vol. 115, No. 3, 2020, pp. 493–504.

California Senate Bill 855, Health Coverage: Mental Health or Substance Use Disorders, September 25, 2020.

Carpenter, Christopher S., "Workplace Drug Testing and Worker Drug Use," *Health Services Research*, Vol. 42, No. 2, April 2007, pp. 795–810.

Carpenter, Christopher S., Chandler B. McClellan, and Daniel I. Rees, "Economic Conditions, Illicit Drug Use, and Substance Use Disorders in the United States," *Journal of Health Economics*, Vol. 52, March 2017, pp. 63–73.

Case, Anne, and Angus Deaton, "Rising Morbidity and Mortality in Midlife Among White Non-Hispanic Americans in the 21st Century," *Proceedings of the National Academy of Sciences*, Vol. 112, No. 49, 2015, pp. 15078–15083.

Case, Anne, and Angus Deaton, "Mortality and Morbidity in the 21st Century," *Brookings Papers on Economic Activity*, Spring 2017, pp. 397–476.

Case, Anne, and Angus Deaton, "Deaths of Despair Redux: A Response to Christopher Ruhm," 2018.

Case, Anne, and Angus Deaton, *Deaths of Despair and the Future of Capitalism*, Princeton, N.J.: Princeton University Press, 2020.

CDC—*See* Centers for Disease Control and Prevention.

Centers for Disease Control and Prevention, *Needs-Based Syringe Distribution and Disposal at Syringe Services Programs*, Atlanta, Ga., September 2020.

Council of Economic Advisers, *The Underestimated Cost of the Opioid Crisis*, Washington, D.C., November 2017.

Currie, Janet, Jonas Y. Jin, and Molly Schnell, *U.S. Employment and Opioids: Is There a Connection?* Cambridge, Mass.: National Bureau of Economic Research, Working Paper No. 24440, 2018.

Currie, Janet, and Brigitte Madrian, "Chapter 50: Health, Health Insurance and the Labor Market," *Handbook of Labor Economics*, Vol. 3, Part C, 1999, pp. 3309–3416.

Currie, Janet, and Hannes Schwandt, *The Opioid Epidemic Was Not Caused by Economic Distress but by Factors That Could Be More Rapidly Addressed*, Cambridge, Mass.: National Bureau of Economic Research, Working Paper No. 27544, July 2020.

Cutler, David M., Ellen Meara, and Susan Stewart, *The Rise of Prescription Opioids and Enrollment in Disability Insurance*, Cambridge, Mass.: National Bureau of Economic Research, Working Paper No. DRC NB16-03, September 2016.

Cutler, David, Ellen Meara, and Susan Stewart, *Has Wider Availability of Prescription Drugs for Pain Relief Affected SSDI and SSI Enrollment?* Cambridge, Mass: National Bureau of Economic Research Disability Research Center, September 2017.

Davenport, Stoddard, Alexandra Weaver, and Matt Caverly, *Economic Impact of Non-Medical Opioid Use in the United States: Annual Estimates and Projections for 2015 through 2019*, Schaumburg, Ill.: Society of Actuaries, 2019.

Del Pozo, Brandon, Josiah D. Rich, and Jennifer J. Carroll, "Reports of Accidental Fentanyl Overdose Among Police in the Field: Toward Correcting a Harmful Culture-Bound Syndrome," *International Journal on Drug Policy*, Vol. 100, 2022.

Dow, William H., Anna Godøy, Christopher A. Lowenstein, and Michael Reich, *Can Economic Policies Reduce Deaths of Despair?* Cambridge, Mass.: National Bureau of Economic Research, Working Paper No. 25787, April 2019.

Elliott, Luther, Alex S. Bennett, and Brett Wolfson-Stofko, "Life After Opioid-Involved Overdose: Survivor Narratives and Their Implications for ER/ED Interventions," *Addiction*, Vol. 114, No. 8, August 2019, pp. 1379–1386.

Finkelstein, Amy, Matthew Gentzkow, and Heidi Williams, *What Drives Prescription Opioid Abuse? Evidence from Migration*, Stanford, Calif.: Stanford Institute for Economic Policy Research, August 2018.

Florence, Curtis, Feijun Luo, Likang Xu, and Chao Zhou, "The Economic Burden of Prescription Opioid Overdose, Abuse, and Dependence in the United States, 2013," *Medical Care*, Vol. 54, No. 10, October 2016, pp. 901–906.

Franklin, Gary M., Jaymie Mai, Thomas Wickizer, Judith A. Turner, Deborah Fulton-Kehoe, and Linda Grant, "Opioid Dosing Trends and Mortality in Washington State Workers' Compensation, 1996–2002," *American Journal of Industrial Medicine*, Vol. 48, No. 2, August 2005, pp. 91–99.

Franklin, Gary M., Bert D. Stover, Judith A. Turner, Deborah Fulton-Kehoe, and Thomas M. Wickizer, "Early Opioid Prescription and Subsequent Disability Among Workers with Back Injuries: The Disability Risk Identification Study Cohort," *Spine*, Vol. 33, No. 2, 2008, pp. 199–204.

Friedman, Joseph, and Helena Hansen, "Black and Native Overdose Mortality Overtook That of White Individuals During the COVID-19 Pandemic," *medRxiv*, November 3, 2021.

Furr-Holden, Debra, Adam J. Milam, Ling Wang, and Richard Sadler, "African Americans Now Outpace Whites in Opioid-Involved Overdose Deaths: A Comparison of Temporal Trends from 1999 to 2018," *Addiction*, Vol. 116, No. 3, 2021, pp. 677–683.

Ganong, Peter, and Daniel Shoag, "Why Has Regional Income Convergence in the U.S. Declined?" *Journal of Urban Economics*, Vol. 102, 2017, pp. 76–90.

GAO—*See* U.S. Government Accountability Office.

Garthwaite, Craig L., "The Economic Benefits of Pharmaceutical Innovations: The Case of Cox-2 Inhibitors," *American Economic Journal: Applied Economics*, Vol. 4, No. 3, July 2012, pp. 116–137.

Gaskin, Darrell J., and Patrick Richard, "The Economic Costs of Pain in the United States," *Journal of Pain*, Vol. 13, No. 8, August 2012, pp. 715–724.

Goplerud, Eric, Sarah Hodge, and Tess Benham, "A Substance Use Cost Calculator for US Employers With an Emphasis on Prescription Pain Medication Misuse," *Journal of Occupational and Environmental Medicine*, Vol. 59, No. 11, 2017, pp. 1063–1071.

Gruber, Jonathan, "State-Mandated Benefits and Employer-Provided Health Insurance," *Journal of Public Economics*, Vol. 55, No. 3, November 1994, pp. 433–464.

Harris, Matthew C., Lawrence M. Kessler, Matthew N. Murray, and Beth Glenn, "Prescription Opioids and Labor Market Pains: The Effect of Schedule II Opioids on Labor Force Participation and Unemployment," *Journal of Human Resources*, Vol. 55, No. 4, Fall 2020, pp. 1319–1364.

Hawkins, Devan, Cora Roelofs, James Laing, and Letitia Davis, "Opioid-Related Overdose Deaths by Industry and Occupation—Massachusetts, 2011–2015," *American Journal of Industrial Medicine*, Vol. 62, No. 10, October 2019, pp. 815–825.

Henke, Rachel Mosher, David Ellsworth, Lauren Wier, and Jane Snowdon, "Opioid Use Disorder and Employee Work Presenteeism, Absences, and Health Care Costs," *Journal of Occupational and Environmental Medicine*, Vol. 62, No. 5, May 2020, pp. 344–349.

Hollingsworth, Alex, Christopher J. Ruhm, and Kosali Simon, "Macroeconomic Conditions and Opioid Abuse," *Journal of Health Economics*, Vol. 56, 2017, pp. 222–233.

Hoopsick, Rachel A., Gregory G. Homish, and Kenneth E. Leonard, "Differences in Opioid Overdose Mortality Rates Among Middle-Aged Adults by Race/Ethnicity and Sex, 1999–2018," *Public Health Reports*, Vol. 136, No. 2, March 2021, pp. 192–200.

Johnston, Stephen S., Andrea H. Alexander, Elizabeth T. Masters, Jack Mardekian, David Semel, Elisabetta Malangone-Monaco, Ellen Riehle, Kathleen Wilson, and Alesia Sadosky, "Costs and Work Loss Burden of Diagnosed Opioid Abuse Among Employees on Workers Compensation or Short-Term Disability," *Journal of Occupational and Environmental Medicine*, Vol. 58, No. 11, November 2016, pp. 1087–1097.

Kilby, Angela E., "Opioids for the Masses: Welfare Tradeoffs in the Regulation of Narcotic Pain Medications," working paper, 2015.

Knaak, Stephanie, Sue Mercer, Romie Christie, and Heather Stuart, *Stigma and the Opioid Crisis: Final Report*, Ottawa, Ontario: Mental Health Commission of Canada, 2019.

Kowalski-McGraw, Michele, Judith Green-McKenzie, Sudha P. Pandalai, and Paul A. Schulte, "Characterizing the Interrelationships of Prescription Opioid and Benzodiazepine Drugs with Worker Health and Workplace Hazards," *Journal of Occupational and Environmental Medicine*, Vol. 59, No. 11, November 2017, pp. 1114–1126.

Krueger, Alan B., "Where Have All the Workers Gone? An Inquiry into the Decline of the U.S. Labor Force Participation Rate," *Brookings Papers on Economic Activity*, Fall 2017.

Maestas, Nicole, and Tisamarie Sherry, *Opioid Treatment for Pain and Work and Disability Outcomes: Evidence from Health Care Providers' Prescribing Patterns*, Cambridge, Mass.: National Bureau of Economic Research, Center Paper NB19-28-2, October 2020.

Manning, Willard G., Emmett B. Keeler, Joseph P. Newhouse, Elizabeth M. Sloss, and Jeffrey Wasserman, *The Taxes of Sin: Do Smokers and Drinkers Pay Their Way?* Santa Monica, Calif.: RAND Corporation, March 1989. As of May 25, 2022:
https://www.rand.org/pubs/notes/N2941.html

Martin, Christopher J., ChuanFang Jin, Stephen J. Bertke, James H. Yiin, and Lynne E. Pinkerton, "Increased Overall and Cause-Specific Mortality Associated with Disability Among Workers' Compensation Claimants with Low Back Injuries," *American Journal of Industrial Medicine*, Vol. 63, No. 3, March 2020, pp. 209–217.

McGinty, Emma E., and Colleen L. Barry, "Stigma Reduction to Combat the Addiction Crisis— Developing an Evidence Base," *New England Journal of Medicine*, Vol. 382, No. 14, 2020, pp. 1291–1292.

Metcalf, Gilbert E., and Qitong Wang, *Abandoned by Coal, Swallowed by Opioids?* Cambridge, Mass.: National Bureau of Economic Research, Working Paper No. 26551, December 2019.

Monnat, Shannon M., "Factors Associated with County-Level Differences in U.S. Drug-Related Mortality Rates," *American Journal of Preventive Medicine*, Vol. 54, No. 5, May 2018, pp. 611–619.

Morden, Nancy E., Jeffrey C. Munson, Carrie H. Colla, Jonathan S. Skinner, Julie P. W. Bynum, Weiping Zhou, and Ellen Meara, "Prescription Opioid Use Among Disabled Medicare Beneficiaries: Intensity, Trends, and Regional Variation," *Medical Care*, Vol. 52, No. 9, September 2014, pp. 852–859.

Moss, Michael J., Brandon J. Warrick, Lewis S. Nelson, Charles A. McKay, Pierre-André Dubé, Sophie Gosselin, Robert B. Palmer, and Andrew I. Stolbach, "ACMT and AACT Position Statement: Preventing Occupational Fentanyl and Fentanyl Analog Exposure to Emergency Responders," *Clinical Toxicology*, Vol. 56, No. 4, 2017, pp. 297–300.

Musse, Isabel, "Employment Shocks and Demand for Pain Medication," Social Science Research Network, March 10, 2020.

National Drug Intelligence Center, *The Economic Impact of Illicit Drug Use on American Society*, Washington, D.C.: U.S. Department of Justice, April 2011.

NDIC—*See* National Drug Intelligence Center.

Olding, Michelle, Allison Barker, Ryan McNeil, and Jade Boyd, "Essential Work, Precarious Labour: The Need for Safer and Equitable Harm Reduction Work in the Era of COVID-19," *International Journal of Drug Policy*, Vol. 90, No. 103076, April 2021.

O'Leary, Paul, Leslie I. Boden, Seth A. Seabury, Al Ozonoff, and Ethan Scherer, "Workplace Injuries and the Take-Up of Social Security Disability Benefits," *Social Security Bulletin*, Vol. 72, No. 3, November 2012.

Ouimet, Paige, Elena Simintzi, and Kailei Ye, "The Impact of the Opioid Crisis on Firm Value and Investment," Social Science Research Network, 2019.

Park, Sujeong, and David Powell, "Is the Rise in Illicit Opioids Affecting Labor Supply and Disability Claiming Rates?" *Journal of Health Economics*, Vol. 76, No. 102430, March 2021.

Perlmutter, Alexander S., Sarah C. Conner, Mirko Savone, June H. Kim, Luis E. Segura, and Silvia S. Martins, "Is Employment Status in Adults over 25 Years Old Associated with Nonmedical Prescription Opioid and Stimulant Use?" *Social Psychiatry and Psychiatric Epidemiology*, Vol. 52, No. 3, 2017, pp. 291–298.

Pierce, Justin R., and Peter K. Schott, "Trade Liberalization and Mortality: Evidence from U.S. Counties," *American Economic Review: Insights*, Vol. 2, No. 1, March 2020, pp. 47–64.

Pike, Erika, Martha Tillson, J. Matthew Webster, and Michele Staton, "A Mixed-Methods Assessment of the Impact of the Opioid Epidemic on First Responder Burnout," *Drug and Alcohol Dependence*, Vol. 205, 2019.

Rhyan, Corwin N., *The Potential Societal Benefit of Eliminating Opioid Overdoses, Deaths, and Substance Use Disorders Exceeds $95 Billion per Year*, Ann Arbor, Mich.: Altarum Institute, November 16, 2017.

Rice, J. Bradford, Noam Y. Kirson, Amie Shei, Alice Kate G. Cummings, Katharine Bodnar, Howard G. Birnbaum, and Rami Ben-Joseph, "Estimating the Costs of Opioid Abuse and Dependence from an Employer Perspective: A Retrospective Analysis Using Administrative Claims Data," *Applied Health Economics and Health Policy*, Vol. 12, No. 4, 2014, pp. 435–446.

Rietveld, Cornelius A., and Pankaj C. Patel, "Prescription Opioids and New Business Establishments," *Small Business Economics*, Vol. 57, No. 3, 2021, pp. 1175–1199.

Ruhm, Christopher J., "Drug Mortality and Lost Life Years Among U.S. Midlife Adults, 1999–2015," *American Journal of Preventive Medicine*, Vol. 55, No. 1, 2018, pp. 11–18.

Ruhm, Christopher J., "Drivers of the Fatal Drug Epidemic," *Journal of Health Economics*, Vol. 64, 2019, pp. 25–42.

Saunders, Elizabeth, Stephen A. Metcalf, Olivia Walsh, Sarah K. Moore, Andrea Meier, Bethany McLeman, Samantha Auty, Sarah Bessen, and Lisa A. Marsch, "'You Can See Those Concentric Rings Going Out': Emergency Personnel's Experiences Treating Overdose and Perspectives on Policy-Level Responses to the Opioid Crisis in New Hampshire," *Drug and Alcohol Dependence*, Vol. 204, 2019.

Savych, Bogdan, David Neumark, and Randall Lea, "Do Opioids Help Injured Workers Recover and Get Back to Work? The Impact of Opioid Prescriptions on Duration of Temporary Disability," *Industrial Relations: A Journal of Economy and Society*, Vol. 58, No. 4, 2019, pp. 549–590.

Schaller, Jessamyn, and Ann Huff Stevens, "Short-Run Effects of Job Loss on Health Conditions, Health Insurance, and Health Care Utilization," *Journal of Health Economics*, Vol. 43, September 2015, pp. 190–203.

Segel, Joel E., Yunfeng Shi, John R. Moran, and Dennis P. Scanlon, "Revenue Losses to State and Federal Government from Opioid-Related Employment Reductions," *Medical Care*, Vol. 57, No. 7, 2019, pp. 494–497.

U.S. Bureau of Labor Statistics, "How the Government Measures Unemployment," webpage, last updated October 8, 2015. As of February 19, 2020: https://www.bls.gov/cps/cps_htgm.htm

U.S. Government Accountability Office, *Workforce Innovation and Opportunity Act: Additional DOL Actions Needed to Help States and Employers Address Substance Use Disorder*, Washington, D.C., GAO-20-337, May 2020.

Van Hasselt, Martijn, Vincent Keyes, Jeremy Bray, and Ted Miller, "Prescription Drug Abuse and Workplace Absenteeism: Evidence from the 2008–2012 National Survey on Drug Use and Health," *Journal of Workplace Behavioral Health*, Vol. 30, No. 4, 2015, pp. 379–392.

Vance, J. D., *Hillbilly Elegy: A Memoir of a Family and Culture in Crisis*, New York: Harper, 2016.

Venkataramani, Atheendar S., Elizabeth F. Bair, Rourke L. O'Brien, and Alexander C. Tsai, "Association Between Automotive Assembly Plant Closures and Opioid Overdose Mortality in the United States: A Difference-in-Differences Analysis," *JAMA Internal Medicine*, Vol. 180, No. 2, 2020, pp. 254–262.

Vine, Michaela, Colleen Staatz, Crystal Blyler, and Jillian Berk, *The Role of the Workforce System in Addressing the Opioid Crisis: A Review of the Literature*, Washington, D.C.: Mathematica, February 2020.

CHAPTER THIRTEEN

Education

Susan M. Gates

Overview

The opioid ecosystem influences schools most directly through its effect on students and their social and emotional well-being. Opioid use by students could affect learning and school safety. Data suggest that opioids are present in U.S. middle and high schools. In 2022, 1.7 percent of 12th-graders surveyed reported that they had used "narcotics other than heroin" (i.e., prescription opioids) for nonmedical purposes in the past 12 months, down from a peak of 9.5 percent in 2004 (Johnston et al., 2023). With respect to heroin, 0.5 percent of high school seniors reported ever having used the drug, and 0.3 percent reported heroin use in the preceding 12 months (Johnston et al., 2023).

Opioids also influence the education system indirectly based on the fact that more than 20 percent of people with opioid use disorder (OUD) live in a household with children (Substance Abuse and Mental Health Services Administration [SAMHSA], 2020). Living with someone who has a substance use problem is an adverse childhood experience (ACE) and can increase the risk of exposure to other ACEs, such as neglect, abuse, parental incarceration, death of a parent, or economic hardship (Lima et al., 2010; Spehr et al., 2017; Yoshikawa, Aber, and Beardslee, 2012). Research has demonstrated that exposure to ACEs is related to problems in school and a variety of social and behavior problems over a lifetime, including self-harm and violence toward others.

The opioid crisis can also influence schools through the well-being and engagement of parents and other community members. These influences may overlap with challenges stemming from other drug problems (including alcohol use disorder), poverty, parental incarceration, and mental illness. To the extent that effects of parental and community engagement and well-being on the education system are measured, the opioid crisis cannot be easily isolated from other factors in either statistics or policy. A study attempting to do so found some correlation between county-level indicators of third-grade test scores and county-level drug overdose mortality rates (Darolia and Tyler, 2020).

The impact of the opioid crisis on higher education has received very little attention in the policy realm, although that is beginning to change (Anderson, 2019). A 2017 Maryland law (Start Talking Maryland Act; see Maryland Senate Bill 1060, 2017) requires kindergarten through 12th-grade (K–12) school districts and colleges and universities that receive state funds to provide a drug prevention curriculum. Some schools and postsecondary institutions are developing approaches to support students who may be in recovery or struggling with addiction—for example, by providing support services or sober dormitories—although in most cases such supports are not focused on opioid addiction.

The opioid crisis may also influence the education system as an employer. In communities with high rates of opioid addiction, local school districts may face a shortage of people with no criminal records (especially crimes related to child abuse or neglect) to fill school positions. Educators may have lower productivity if they or a family member are struggling with opioid addiction. Educators may suffer from trauma and burnout as they strive to address the needs of students, family members, and community members. There are anecdotal descriptions of such challenges at the K–12 level, but there is little research documenting prevalence.

At the federal level, the Safe and Drug-Free Schools and Communities Act calls on the education system to play a role in drug prevention efforts, including opioids. The act provides states with resources to support local drug prevention and early intervention programs in school districts and community organizations. Although these efforts, if effective, have the potential to reduce opioid consumption, addiction, and related harms at comparatively low cost, more research is needed to understand the implications of evidence-based programs for opioid use specifically and to evaluate the effectiveness of opioid-centered programs.

Nevertheless, some states require school districts to provide opioid prevention instruction. In addition, according to a 2016 survey, approximately 37 percent of school districts had adopted a student drug-testing policy. In theory, drug tests could deter or reduce student drug use by identifying people who use drugs and referring them to treatment; however, the evidence on this is mixed (e.g., Sznitman et al., 2012).

Key Interactions with Other Components of the Ecosystem

The education system interacts with the **child welfare**, **harm reduction and community-initiated interventions**, **first responders**, and **criminal legal system** components on an as-needed basis, based on circumstances or events. Those interactions are not specific to opioids, but the need for such interactions might arise from opioid use and misuse. For example, educators are required to report child abuse and neglect to the child welfare system and may report parents who are abusive or neglectful because of opioid addiction.

Similarly, schools interact with other local systems and entities, such as the **health care system**, **mental health system**, **law enforcement**, **income support and homeless services**, religious organizations, and nonprofits. There are some examples of communities severely affected by the opioid crisis that have worked to promote cross-system communication for the benefit of children—for example, emergency medical technicians (EMTs) notifying schools when they are called to a home about an overdose or law enforcement alerting schools when a parent is arrested. These are anecdotal examples, and there is no information on their prevalence.

Policy Opportunities and Considerations

A key takeaway of this review is a call for more data-gathering and research about students who are affected directly or indirectly by OUD and the programs that are developed to support these students. There is a particular need to understand the applicability of evidence-based drug prevention programs to the opioid setting.

In response to research documenting lower graduation rates, educational attainment, and other adverse outcomes for students in the foster care system, several states have made policy changes in the past decade designed to enhance support for foster youth (Evans and McCann, 2020). Such policy changes include enrollment flexibilities to promote continuity of education regardless of residence, additional funding for districts that serve foster youth, and subsidies for higher education.

Some students with parents experiencing an OUD enter the foster care system. But many other children continue to be cared for by one or both parents (possibly including a parent with an OUD) or extended family members, such as grandparents, aunts, and uncles, in an arrangement called *kinship care*. These children are not formally part of the foster system, but they may face many of the same challenges that contribute to poor educational outcomes for foster youth, including residential mobility and exposure to trauma. States should consider how they might modify and extend policies designed to support better education outcomes for foster youth to include children who are at risk of being in the foster care system (e.g., because of parental OUD).

The past two decades have seen the emergence of the community schools approach, in which schools partner with other organizations in the community to address academic, health, developmental, and mental health needs not only of the student but of the entire family and to promote community engagement. This approach has been implemented in multiple high-needs communities across the country. It is not a highly prescriptive program with rigid features but rather a flexible approach that is "grounded in the principle that all students, families, and communities benefit from strong connections between educators, local resources, supports, and people" (Maier et al., 2017, p. 12). Although community schools programs in urban areas, such as New York, Oakland, and Hartford, Connecticut, have garnered much attention, Kentucky has been supporting these approaches through family resource and youth service centers across the state for 30 years (Kentucky Cabinet for Health and Family Services, 2020; McDaniels, 2018). Research suggests that students who participate in community schools programs have higher test scores and grades, better attendance, and a higher degree of school engagement than those who do not and that the return on investment from wraparound services and other features of community schools is in the range of $3 to $15 for each dollar spent (Maier et al., 2017).

Communities hard hit by the opioid crisis may need to consider cross-system approaches that promote collaboration and allocate resources intentionally across community needs. There are examples of cross-system collaboration to point to—for example, the Jackson County Anti-Drug Coalition in Jackson County, West Virginia, where the health department has partnered with schools, hospitals, law enforcement, mental health organizations, and faith organizations with support from the Drug Free Communities program; or a state effort in Massachusetts that supports drug treatment counselors in schools across the state; or the Handle With Care program in West Virginia, which provides for law enforcement to communicate with school administrators about traumatic events that occur in the home and the example of community schools that try to integrate parental support, education, nutrition, and mental health care (Gaines et al., 2017).

Introduction

The opioid crisis affects the education system in indirect ways through its effect on students, their families, education system employees, and communities in which they reside. Because the effects of the opioid crisis on the education system are primarily indirect in nature, they are often overlooked in the broader policy discussions. But that does not mean that the effects are less important. Additionally, the education system can potentially be an avenue for mitigating effects of the opioid crisis through drug prevention efforts and by giving individuals the education and skills they need to succeed in the workforce.

The education system in the United States is not a single monolithic entity. Public primary education and secondary education are governed by local school systems. There are more than 13,000 such public school systems in the country operating nearly 100,000 schools and serving roughly 50 million students. Although these systems are governed locally, they are also subject to both federal and state laws and regulations. An additional 35,000 private schools serve about 5.8 million students. These independent schools are subject to fewer laws and regulations. The higher education system consists of a combination of local, state, and independent entities—about 6,600 in total—that offer a wide variety of degree and nondegree enrollment options. Together, they serve nearly 20 million students. These, too, are subject to some federal and state laws and regulations (National Center for Education Statistics [NCES], Institute of Education Sciences, 2019; U.S. Department of Education, 2005).

This chapter summarizes what is known about the interactions between the education system and other aspects of the opioid ecosystem (see Figure 13.1). It is based on a review of research specifically linking opioids or OUD to the education system; a review of research linking drug use and misuse to the education system; and a discussion of some research linking the opioid crisis to specific changes in student, family, and community characteristics that are related to educational outcomes. The summary is, admittedly, limited because there is very little research that focuses *explicitly* on the implications of the opioid crisis for the education system. That is not to say that decisionmakers in the education system are unaware of and unresponsive to the opioid crisis. Rather, with the variety of challenges that the education system faces in meeting the needs of students, it is uncommon for the opioid crisis to be called out as a focal issue or for opioids to be the focus of education policy research or drug prevention efforts. That is beginning to change, especially in states and locales with a high prevalence of OUD. For the purposes of this review, we tapped relevant research related to other substance use disorders (SUDs) and research linking likely implications of OUD, such as exposure to trauma, to the education system. The chapter concludes with some policy considerations.

System Components and How They Interact with Opioids

Other chapters in this report have documented the wide-ranging effects of the opioid crisis, including death, overdose, lost work, increase in neonatal exposure, increase in trauma,

FIGURE 13.1

The Education System and Its Interactions

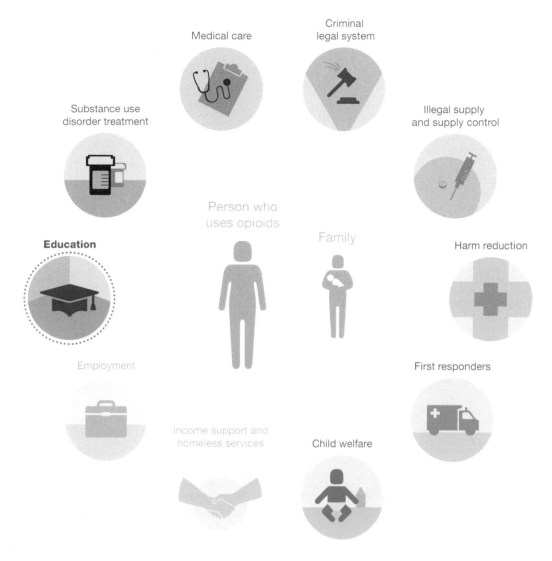

increased housing insecurity, and lack of parental supervision. As a result of the opioid crisis, a nontrivial number of students are showing up at the doors of U.S. schools, colleges, and universities having experienced the adverse effects of having a parent or other household member who suffered or is suffering from an OUD. The crisis also means that schools at the primary and secondary levels and institutions at the postsecondary level are serving students and employing people who are addicted to or recovering from an addiction to opioids—or are at risk of such an addiction.[1] Opioid use by students at all levels of the system could affect learning, the safety of others, and the learning environment more generally. For this reason, schools and postsecondary institutions may have an interest in identifying and addressing instances of drug misuse and being prepared to respond to overdoses.

By ensuring student success, the education system can potentially limit future opioid misuse and fatal overdoses stemming from such misuse. Higher educational attainment and employment (versus unemployment) have been related to lower risk of fatal opioid overdose (Altekruse et al., 2020), and educational attainment has been associated with lower rates of opioid misuse (Ford et al., 2020; Schepis, Teter, and McCabe, 2018). Educational attainment is also associated with better labor market outcomes, which, in turn, are related to lower risk of OUD and other types of "deaths of despair" (for more information on this issue, see Chapter Twelve) (Case and Deaton, 2020).

The effects of the opioid crisis are concentrated in particular states and locales, and this location factor has implications for the education system. A high prevalence of opioid misuse in a community is associated with a greater risk that an individual student is exposed to and potentially influenced by opioid misuse in their own home and higher levels of community-wide crime and violence. It can also mean that there are fewer adults who are willing and eligible to work or volunteer in schools (e.g., playground monitors, tutors) or community organizations, such as the Boys and Girls Club. In a community with a high prevalence of opioid misuse, the education system—whose funding comes primarily from state and local resources—will be competing with other sectors, including health care, criminal justice, child and family services, and income support and homeless service systems, for scarce resources.

Because students at the primary and secondary levels are required to attend school each day, schools are on the front lines when it comes to not only prevention efforts but also detection, response, and support when those prevention efforts fail. Local, state, and federal policymakers recognize that the education system can be a focal point for prevention and referrals to treatment for a wide variety of drugs, including opioids. However, there is wide variation in how schools approach their responsibilities and how they interface with other community supports.

The Concentrated Nature of the Opioid Crisis Has Implications for the Primary and Secondary Education System

Prior research has established that the effects of the opioid crisis are concentrated in particular states and locales. The crisis has placed a financial burden on state and local governments through increased costs to the health care and criminal legal systems and lost labor productivity (Brundage, Fifield, and Partridge, 2019; Florence et al., 2016; Scavette, 2019).

---

[1] Throughout this chapter, we use the term *schools* to refer to the places where the education system delivers primary or secondary education and *institutions* to refer to the places where the education system delivers postsecondary education.

One study estimates the average per capita cost of the crisis at $1,672 nationally. State-specific estimates—ranging from a high of $4,000 per capita in West Virginia to a low of $394 per capita in Nebraska—highlight the concentration of the financial burden in particular states (Brill and Ganz, 2018). Cornaggia et al., 2021, suggest that higher levels of opioid misuse in a community have a negative effect on municipal finance through lower property tax revenue, lower credit ratings, and higher borrowing costs. This means that municipalities most affected by the opioid crisis may have fewer options available to them for financing efforts to address the crisis.

Like other crucial social services affected by the opioid crisis, the K–12 public school system gets most of its funding from nonfederal sources, with state and local funding accounting for more than 90 percent (Maciag, 2019; U.S. Census Bureau, 2020). This dependence on nonfederal financing means that schools facing the greatest need as a result of the opioid crisis must compete with other strained local entities for increasingly scarce resources (Hefling, 2018). In the communities with the most need, the effects of the opioid crisis may increase demand on the dwindling available resources to support these services. Although this dynamic is not unique to the opioid crisis or to the education system, it is worth emphasizing here as we consider the implications of the opioid crisis for primary and secondary education.

Darolia, Owens, and Tyler, 2020, posit that neighborhood factors (i.e., how intense the opioid crisis is in a community) along with individual exposure to adverse effects of the crisis and individual vulnerability to those adverse effects work together to influence educational outcomes. Vulnerability can be influenced by supports provided by family, schools, and the community. However, the ability of schools and the community to provide those supports can be strained in these communities.

Drug Prevention and Education Efforts and the Education System

At the federal level, the Safe and Drug-Free Schools and Communities Act calls on the education system to play a role in drug prevention efforts. The act provides states with resources to support local drug prevention and early intervention programs in school districts and community organizations. These efforts, which have been shown to be effective in reducing consumption, addiction, and related harms at comparatively low cost (Caulkins et al., 1999; Miller and Hendrie, 2008), could potentially be leveraged to prevent opioid addiction specifically. However, most evidence-based programs described in this chapter focus on alcohol or substances other than opioids, and program effectiveness with regard to opioid use has not been demonstrated. There is also evidence that high schools that effectively implement school-wide positive behavioral interventions and supports have lower reported prevalence of illegal drug and alcohol use generally (Bastable et al., 2015).

The federal government has a variety of resources to support schools, districts, and universities in identifying effective programs and other supports. For example, the National Institute on Drug Abuse (NIDA) for Teens (NIDA, undated) promotes the use of evidence-based prevention curricula through a searchable repository of lesson plans and classroom resources on teens and drugs based on work funded by the agency. The federal Office of National Drug Policy hosts a substance use prevention school resource guide (Office of National Drug Control Policy, 2020). The site includes information about a national helpline that can provide immediate assistance with an SUD, a Behavioral Health Treatment Services Locator (SAMHSA, undated) hosted by the U.S. Department of Health and Human Services, a link to evidence-based Positive Behavioral Interventions and Supports (PBIS, undated-a) hosted by the U.S. Department of Education, with a section titled "Opioid Crisis and Substance Misuse" (PBIS, undated-b), and a tool developed by the Centers for Disease Control and Prevention (CDC) for assessing prevention curricula as part of a health education curriculum (CDC, 2012). The site also links to the Operation Prevention website with a variety of standards-based resources for schools focused specifically on opioid use prevention (Operation Prevention, undated). The resources include lessons and videos that can be used by individuals or in a classroom setting, educator guides, exercises, virtual field trips, and an educator training video. Ramos et al., 2018, identified four promising evidence-based school-based prevention programs. Three are classroom-based programs (LifeSkills Training, Project Toward NO Drug Abuse, Good Behavior Game), and a fourth leverages school-community-university partnerships (PROSPER).

States have historically been active in encouraging or even requiring drug education as part of the health curriculum in primary and secondary schools. In recent years, some state legislatures have passed legislation to expand the scope of these requirements to explicitly include education on opioids (Rafa, 2019). For example, Michigan Public Act 255, 2018, required the state's department of education to develop a curriculum for instruction on opioids. The Michigan Model for Health curriculum, including content on opioids, was launched in fall 2019. Ohio provides another example of an explicitly stated policy related to opioids. The state requires its schools to adopt a health curriculum that teaches students about the risks of prescription opioid misuse. Ohio has developed the Health and Opioid Prevention Education Curriculum (State of Ohio, undated) designed for K–12 educators with lesson plans organized by grade level, assessments, and instructional materials along with a teacher guide and school administrator guide (Rural Health Information Hub, 2019). Preliminary anecdotal feedback about the program has been positive. As noted earlier, further research is needed to understand the implications of most prevention programs for opioid use by looking explicitly at opioid-related outcomes for more-general or non-opioid prevention programs or by rigorously evaluating newer opioid-centric programs.

Although the school setting may be an expedient way to reach youth for the purposes of drug prevention and treatment, there is anecdotal evidence to suggest that some school districts resist prevention education as a result of parental opposition, questions about the appropriateness of such training, and concerns that it may cut into instructional time and push out the core curriculum. (Of note, there has been similar pushback about active shooter drills and other types of trainings provided by third-party organizations.) State requirements may relieve districts of the political burden associated with implementing such curricula.

State policy efforts to encourage or require prevention efforts targeting postsecondary institutions have been more limited, although that is beginning to change. A 2017 Maryland law (Start Talking Maryland Act; see Maryland Senate Bill 1060, 2017) requires K–12 school districts, colleges, and universities that receive state funds to provide a drug prevention curriculum. Individual institutions of higher education or higher education systems are recognizing a need to support students who may be in recovery or struggling with addiction—for example, by providing support services or sober dormitories—although, in most cases, such support efforts or programs are not focused on opioid addiction.

Opioid Use Among Students and Education System Staff and Its Implications

Despite federal and state crime reporting requirements, information about the prevalence of opioid possession and use in schools and in postsecondary education institutions is sparse.

Adolescent (ages 12 to 17) drug use has been a concern for decades. National survey data suggest that opioids are present in U.S. middle and high schools but not prevalent—at least relative to other drugs. In 2022, 1.7 percent of 12th-graders surveyed reported that they had used "narcotics other than heroin" (i.e., prescription opioids) for nonmedical purposes in the past 12 months, down from a peak of 9.5 percent in 2004 (Johnston et al., 2023). With respect to heroin, 0.5 percent of high school seniors reported ever having used the drug, and 0.3 percent reported heroin use in the preceding 12 months (Johnston et al., 2023). In contrast, 31 percent of 12th-graders reported using cannabis in the past year (Johnston et al., 2023). But recent research has also pointed to hot spots of adolescent opioid use in the United States where rates of opioid use are substantially higher (Jones et al., 2019). That study reported rates of heroin use as high as 7.6 percent in Baltimore, Maryland, and 6.4 percent in Shelby County, Tennessee. Rates of nonmedical prescription opioid use were as high as 18.1 percent in Duval County, Florida. The American Academy of Pediatrics does not advocate for drug testing in schools because of concerns about the implications of such screening programs, such as referral to the criminal legal system (Council on School Health and Committee on Substance Abuse, 2007; Sznitman et al., 2012).

We are not aware of data on drug use among education system staff, but there have been media reports of overdoses or drug arrests of school staff. It stands to reason that school staff would not be immune to the risks of drug addiction plaguing the local community.

The education system as an employer faces competing pressures at the federal, state, and local levels when crafting drug-testing policies (Bleasdale, 2014; Camera, 2019; Los Angeles Unified School District, 2018). On the one hand, employers that receive federal funds (as most schools and postsecondary institutions do) must abide by the federal Drug Free Workplace Act. However, federal law leaves employers with a fair amount of flexibility with regard to drug testing, including opportunities to justify random testing on the basis of safety or a compelling government interest. On the other hand, employers must respect employees' constitutional right to privacy, and broad drug-testing policies by school districts have been struck down in courts. State law may require districts to engage in drug testing of individuals in certain safety-sensitive positions, such as school bus drivers. Employee drug testing falls within the strictures of state law so long as parameters of the drug testing respect an employee's constitutional right to privacy. At the K–12 level, when a scandal strikes a local community involving drug use or possession by a teacher, there can be calls from the community for the district to adopt drug testing. Despite these calls, it appears to be uncommon for districts to impose random drug testing of teachers. Districts do have the authority to require drug testing in response to suspicion or evidence of drug use.

With regard to drug testing of students, schools and districts are allowed to perform random drug tests for middle and high school students who participate in competitive extracurricular activities. According to a 2016 survey, approximately 37 percent of school districts (CDC, 2016) had adopted a drug-testing policy for students. Although such policies aim to deter student drug use or refer students into treatment, there is only limited evidence that such policies actually reduce or deter drug use (James-Burdumy et al., 2012; Levy, Schizer, and Committee on Substance Abuse, 2015). Public health officials have raised concerns about the potential stigma of such testing and urged districts to have comprehensive plans in place, carefully consider approaches to drug screening, and emphasize referrals to treatment over legal consequences (Council on School Health and Committee on Substance Abuse, 2007). Research suggests that student athletes may be more likely than other students to use opioids. A recent meta-analysis found evidence of "concerningly high rates of [opioid] use among high school athletes" (Ekhtiari et al., 2020, p. 537) during their lifetimes of between 28 percent and 46 percent. Male athletes and those involved in contact sports, such as football, hockey, and wrestling, appear to be at greater risk (Ekhtiari et al., 2020; Ford et al., 2018), as are people who experience an undiagnosed concussion and experience unemployment. These findings are based largely on data from earlier periods during which opioids were being prescribed more aggressively for pain management, and they may not reflect current risk patterns for high school athletes. Nevertheless, our review highlights a need for attention to the population of high school and college athletes.

Although staff or counselors at schools and postsecondary institutions may be in a position to identify youth who might be suffering from OUDs and address their needs, privacy laws can limit responses that involve the sharing of private information about a student. The Family Education Rights Privacy Act prevents any school (including institutions of higher education) that receives funding from the U.S. Department of Education from releasing educational records to third parties without permission, with exceptions for health or safety emergencies. However, parents have a right to access the educational records of their minor children. When a child turns 18 or attends an institution of higher education, those privacy rights transfer to the student for the most part and the institution needs the student's permission to release information—even to the parents. However, institutions of higher education can disclose information to a parent if the student is considered a dependent for tax purposes; in the case of a health or safety emergency involving their child; or if the student is younger than age 21 and has committed a violation related to alcohol or a controlled substance.

How the Education System Is Affected by Opioids

The opioid crisis affects the education system in a variety of direct and indirect ways that increase or complicate the responsibilities and challenges faced by schools and districts. The opioid ecosystem influences the education system most directly through its effect on the education readiness and social and emotional well-being of students (Darolia and Tyler, 2020). The ecosystem also influences the education system through its effect on teachers, family members, and the community as a whole (Superville, 2017). The opioid crisis may also influence the education system as an employer. In communities with high rates of opioid addiction, local school districts and institutions of higher education may face a shortage of people with no criminal records (especially crimes related to child abuse or neglect) to fill school positions. Educators may have lower productivity if they or their family members are struggling with opioid addiction. Educators may suffer from trauma and burnout as they strive to address the needs of students, family members, and community members. There are anecdotal descriptions of such challenges, but there is little research documenting prevalence.

The Opioid Crisis Can Increase the Needs of Students and Affect Key Student Outcomes

It is widely recognized that key outcomes of the education system—especially academic achievement and educational attainment of students served—are influenced by student, family, and community characteristics, along with the services that schools provide (Hanushek, 2008). When student, family, and community characteristics shift in a way that is associated with poorer educational outcomes for students, schools and postsecondary institutions need to do more to maintain similar outcomes.

The Opioid Crisis Contributes to Adverse Childhood Experiences

Research has demonstrated that exposure to ACEs is related to problems in school and a variety of social and behavior problems over a lifetime, including self-harm and violence toward others. Living with someone who has a substance use problem is an ACE and can increase the risk of exposure to other ACEs, such as parental incarceration, death of a parent, or economic hardship (Lima et al., 2010; Yoshikawa, Aber, and Beardslee, 2012). It stands to reason that in communities with higher rates of opioid addiction, children will have higher rates of exposure to ACEs. However, ACEs are not unique to the opioid crisis. The influence of the opioid crisis on child outcomes may overlap or combine with challenges stemming from other substances (including alcohol), poverty, parental incarceration, and mental illness—each of which has the potential to limit parental effectiveness (Lander, Howsare, and Byrne, 2013). A meta-analysis of research on the effects of parental opioid addiction on child outcomes suggests that parental opioid addiction is associated with "suboptimal child development and behavioral outcomes" (Romanowicz et al., 2019, p. 1).

Overall, 12 percent of children in the United States were living with a parent with an SUD of some kind in the past year (i.e., in the 12 months before the survey question is asked). Ten percent were living with a parent with an alcohol use disorder, and 3 percent were living with a parent with an illegal drug use disorder (Lipari and Van Horn, 2017).[2]

At the level of the individual child, research has demonstrated that ACEs are associated with negative childhood outcomes of importance to the education system, including behavioral problems, diagnosis of attention deficit hyperactivity disorder, literacy and math skills, behavioral problems, and aggression (Hunt, Slack, and Berger, 2017; Jimenez et al., 2016; McKelvey et al., 2016). Stempel et al., 2017, found a positive relationship between exposure to one or more ACE and *chronic absenteeism* (defined as being absent 15 or more days per year) among school-aged children. Porche et al., 2011, found that those who experienced childhood trauma were more likely to drop out of school than those who did not experience trauma. At the community level, statistics show that children in some states have greater exposure to ACEs and to ACEs related to drug use than children in other states (Sacks and Murphey, 2018). A study found some correlation between county-level indicators of third-grade test scores and county-level drug overdose mortality rates (Darolia and Tyler, 2020). In response to this growing body of research on the implications of exposure to trauma for schools, districts and states have begun to emphasize trauma-informed school approaches that emphasize safety, trust, peer support, collaboration, empowerment, and cultural sensitivity (Overstreet and Chafouleas, 2016).

The Opioid Crisis May Increase the Need for Special Education Services

Neonatal exposure to drugs has been on the rise. As summarized by Morgan and Wang, 2019, neonatal opioid withdrawal syndrome (NOWS) increased dramatically in the United States between 2000 and 2013. In West Virginia, the incidence of NOWS per 1,000 live births increased from 0.5 to 33.4 in this time frame. The geography and timing of the increases suggest strongly that they are driven in large part by the opioid crisis. NOWS has been associated with a variety of developmental and behavioral delays and impairments that could decrease academic achievement and increase the need for special education services. Finally, studies have shown that children experiencing NOWS were more likely to be diagnosed with an education disability.

Morgan and Wang, 2019, estimated that the costs associated with providing services for one birth cohort of children in Pennsylvania born with diagnoses of NOWS amount to more than $16 million, of which about half is attributable to the costs of providing special education services. This estimate is based on data suggesting that the cost of providing special edu-

---

[2] To offer some indication of the magnitude of this phenomenon specifically for opioids, consider the following. Per the 2020 National Survey on Drug Use and Health (NSDUH), 22 percent of people with OUD lived in a household with children (8.8 percent with one child, 5.7 percent with two children, and 8 percent with three or more children) (SAMHSA, 2020). If we assume there are 4 million people with OUD and count only three children for the largest households, that yields 1.8 million children living in households with a person with OUD. Counting only three children in the largest household group likely undercounts the true number, but this is offset (though to an unknown extent) by the fact that there may be more than one adult person with OUD living in the household. Importantly, NSDUH survey data are subject to notable limitations, as discussed in Chapter Two.

cation is about twice the cost of providing general education. The Individuals with Disabilities Education Act requires school districts to provide appropriate special education services to students with special educational needs (U.S. Department of Education, undated). When passing the law in 1975, the U.S. Congress indicated that the federal government would cover 40 percent of the additional costs associated with this requirement, but it has never met that target. Therefore, states and districts have been on the hook for covering most of these costs (Balonon-Rosen, 2018). Indeed, Morgan and Wang's 2019 estimate assumed that the federal government would cover 15 percent of the costs of providing special education.

The Opioid Crisis Can Limit Family and Community Involvement

There is long-standing recognition and strong research evidence suggesting that families and communities have an important influence on education outcomes (Henderson, 1987; Henderson and Mapp, 2002). Parental involvement and the quality of social relationships are positively related to academic achievement—especially when defined in terms of high expectations for students by parents (Bryk and Schneider, 2020; Eskelsen Garcia and Thornton, 2014; Konstantopoulos and Borman, 2011; Wilder, 2014). This research base drives school and district leaders, states, and the U.S. Department of Education to promote community and family involvement as a strategy for improving student outcomes. There is ample anecdotal evidence of diminished family and community involvement in schools within communities hit hard by the opioid crisis. Some states, such as Pennsylvania, have a requirement for school volunteers to undergo a background check covering child abuse and criminal history (Pennsylvania Department of Education, undated). In states without such a policy, many districts have their own policies on this issue. Such policies can further limit involvement in communities with a high prevalence of opioid misuse.

Opioid Crisis and Higher Education

Research suggests that OUD is associated with lower educational attainment—both high school graduation rates and the completion of postsecondary degrees. Ellis, Kasper, and Cicero, 2020, analyzed survey data about educational attainment of adult patients entering opioid treatment between 2010 and 2018 and compared survey responses with national data. They found that individuals entering opioid treatment were much less likely to have earned a bachelor's degree. They also learned that the majority of those entering treatment reported that they started using opioids while they were in high school or college. Additionally, about two-thirds of those entering treatment reported that opioids had a negative effect on their ability to complete their education. This study illustrates that the opioid crisis likely affects higher education completion rates and has created a need for supports for students struggling with OUD.

There is limited research about what colleges and universities are doing about these challenges, although there is anecdotal evidence that higher education leaders are keenly aware of the challenges and developing strategies for addressing them on their campuses and in their systems (Anderson, 2019; Ashford, 2017; Hedegaard, Warner, and Miniño, 2017; Kadvany, 2020). Although the overdose rate among traditional college-aged individuals is lower than for other age groups, colleges have grown concerned about the possibility of inadvertent fentanyl overdose among students using other illegal drugs that are cross-contaminated with fentanyl (Kadvany, 2020; Pardo et al., 2019) and about how to address the needs of students who are in recovery (Field, 2018).

The Opioid Crisis Can Make Education System Employees Less Productive or Ineligible for Their Jobs

Primary and secondary schools often hire school staff from the local community. In communities hit hard by the opioid crisis, teachers and administrators may experience trauma because of the challenges they see in the classroom, in their own homes, or in community organizations of which they are a part. This could potentially affect physical and mental health, have implications for health insurance costs and absenteeism, and place a burden on the local health and mental health systems.

In communities with high rates of opioid addiction, local school districts may face a shortage of people with no criminal records to fill school positions. Kelly, 2016, described the variable nature of state and local policies related to teacher background checks. Local school boards set hiring policies, and states set requirements for certification of staff working in public K–12 schools. In setting such policies, officials must balance concerns about safety with privacy and fairness aims. All states have licensure requirements for public school educators. Felony offenses in general—specifically, offenses that involve child endangerment—typically prevent individuals from obtaining the licensure needed to be hired by districts. But states vary in terms of how thorough the background check is, whether it taps a national crime database in addition to the state database, and whether it is conducted by the state licensing agency or the local district.

There is also variation in terms of state requirements for reporting misconduct by school personnel once they are employed to national and state databases. Some states require districts to report cases of firing and resignation because of misconduct. Some states also require teachers to report personnel misconduct when they observe it. When it comes to nonfelony offenses, including drug-related offenses, school boards have discretion over employment policies so long as they fall within state and federal guidelines. Anecdotal evidence suggests that, in setting such policies, local boards must balance objectives that are sometimes at odds—promoting a safe school environment conducive to learning, offering second-chance opportunities for community members, and treating current employees with fairness and respect (Attorneys at the Legal Action Center, 2009; Chen, 2020; Klazema, 2016; Neal, 2017; Peacock Dunn, 2018; Texas Association of School Boards, 2019).

In addition, working with traumatized children can itself lead to secondary traumatic stress among teachers and other school staff (Walker, 2019). These stressors can lead to burnout and potentially affect physical and mental health with implications for productivity, health insurance costs, and absenteeism (Griffith, 2019). A survey of more than 2,000 teachers in West Virginia, one of the states hardest hit by the opioid crisis, revealed that student trauma because of the opioid crisis is creating challenges for teachers for which they are not prepared (Anderson et al., 2020). More than 70 percent of respondents described an increase in students affected by substance use in the home. Only 10 percent of the teachers surveyed felt confident in their ability to support children affected by substance misuse. The teachers' responses also pointed to "burnout—emotional exhaustion and cynicism and a lack of personal accomplishment." Seventy percent of teachers reported burnout on at least a monthly basis, and more than one-third reported frequent burnout. Only 7 percent of teachers reported that they felt "very confident" in their ability to support children with a parent suffering from addiction (West Virginia University, undated).

We did not identify any research regarding opioid-related employment challenges facing postsecondary education institutions.

Key Interactions with Other Components of the Ecosystem

The education system interacts directly with the child welfare system, income support and homeless services, harm reduction and community-initiated interventions, first responders, and the criminal legal systems on an as-needed basis depending on the circumstances or events. Those interactions, circumstances, or events are not specific to opioids, but opioid use and misuse may create a need for such interactions. For example, educators are mandatory reporters to the child welfare system about child abuse and neglect. They may report parents who are abusive or neglectful because of opioid addiction—but the reporting is driven by the abuse or neglect, not the addiction.

It is not uncommon for schools and postsecondary institutions to interact with other local systems and entities, such as the health care system, harm reduction and community-initiated interventions, criminal legal system, social services, religious organizations, and nonprofits—either to provide services and supports to students or to comply with requirements. There are some examples of communities severely affected by the opioid crisis that have worked to promote cross-system communication for the benefit of children—for example, EMTs notifying schools when they are called to a home about an overdose or law enforcement alerting schools when a parent is arrested. These are anecdotal examples, and there is no comprehensive information on their prevalence. Next, we describe what is known about the interactions between the education system and other systems.

Substance Use Disorder Treatment

Approximately one in 20 adolescents and one in six young adults are estimated to need substance use treatment, but only about 11 percent receive treatment at a specialized facility (Lipari and Van Horn, 2017; Passetti, Godley, and Kaminer, 2016). Regardless of whether individuals receive treatment at a specialized facility, schools and postsecondary institutions across the country encounter people with unmet treatment needs or in recovery on a daily basis. Traditional primary and secondary schools offer few options and limited support for kids struggling with addiction, and the return to school may simply return the student to an environment that was driving the drug use (Morello, 2017). Research shows that adolescents in recovery benefit from continuing care but are unlikely to access it (Morello, 2017; Passetti, Godley, and Kaminer, 2016). A lack of mental health counselors in public schools might contribute to a lack of access to recovery care. Although almost 90 percent of school districts have at least one school counselor (who might fill numerous roles in addition to identifying and supporting students in need of SUD treatment), research indicates that the median ratio of students to school counselors is 411:1 (Gagnon and Mattingly, 2016).

Recovery high schools are secondary schools for students recovering from an SUD (Moberg, Finch, and Lindsley, 2014). They are designed to meet both academic and therapeutic needs of these students. The Association of Recovery Schools provides resources and support and offers accreditation. The association currently lists 43 such schools across the country, operated as public, private, or charter schools.

At the postsecondary level, especially in institutions with residential dormitories, there is recognition of the need to provide recovery resources and living arrangements that can support recovery. Some colleges have established recovery programs that provide supports beyond a substance-free living environment (e.g., social events, 12-step programs, and counseling) (Bohanon, 2017). According to Field, 2018, there are about 200 such programs in colleges in the United States. Three states (New Jersey, West Virginia, and North Carolina) provide grants to colleges to support the recovery programs. New Jersey requires colleges with more than 25 percent of students living on campus to provide a recovery housing option and provides resources to support these efforts (Hoover, 2018). The nonprofit Transforming Youth Recovery also provides grants for such programs.

A systematic review of student recovery programs concluded that there is insufficient evidence as to whether recovery high schools or collegiate recovery communities improve outcomes; the available evidence consisted of a "single study with a serious risk of bias" (Hennessy et al., 2018).

Medical Care

According to the most-recent data from NCES, in school year 2015–2016, 82 percent of U.S. public schools had at least one full- or part-time nurse on staff, with 52 percent having at least one full-time nurse (NCES, Institute of Education Sciences, 2020). Traditional public schools are substantially more likely to have a nurse than public charter schools. School nurses are employees of the school or school district. They can play a key role in identifying and addressing both physical and mental health needs among students and school staff and build bridges between education and health care systems. Interactions between the education system and the mental health system are typically grounded in local relationships and operate on a referral model. As noted earlier, the median number of students per counselor in U.S. public schools would not support robust in-school mental health treatment. In communities ravaged by the opioid crisis, there are examples of schools partnering with addiction counselors who come into schools to provide mental health support to students (Gotbaum, 2018).

Criminal Legal System

In meeting their education mission, schools at all levels are focused on creating a school environment that is safe. Illegal activities are illegal in schools as they are anywhere else. Public school districts and institutions of higher education have authority to regulate and impose consequences for student behavior—including illegal drug-related behavior—that is detrimental to the education process or threatens the safety of other students, staff, or school property. This is widely understood to include behavior that occurs on school property and can extend outside those boundaries when a student is participating in a school activity, such as a field trip. K–12 school districts must balance the right to an education with these other considerations when imposing consequences, such as suspension or expulsion, for such offenses.

Many states have Safe Schools Acts that outline requirements for districts regarding how they respond to certain types of offenses. These laws are intended to balance the safety of students with access to education. For example, in Texas, the Safe Schools Act (Texas American Federation of Teachers, undated) requires mandatory removal and placement in a disciplinary alternative education program of any student who uses, possesses, or sells alcohol or illegal drugs within 300 feet of school property or at a school event.

Many states have laws that require schools to involve state or local law enforcement when certain crimes are committed on campuses and impose minimum consequences for certain types of offenses, and illegal drug–related offenses are often on those lists (Porter and Clemons, 2013). Federal law provides for enhanced penalties for federal drug-related crimes that take place in or near a school zone. Additionally, all states have their own drug-free zone laws that apply more-stringent enforcement and penalties for drug-related crimes that take place in or near a school zone.

Drug-free school and safe schools laws could drive schools and districts to respond to drug-related infractions by suspending students or referring students to the legal system rather than the mental health or drug treatment systems. Research suggests that punitive approaches, such as suspensions, can lead to further criminal offenses (Cuellar and Markowitz, 2015). Schools with school resource officers may be more likely to involve the criminal legal system. Research provides some evidence that schools with school resource officers have higher levels of exclusionary discipline for a variety of offenses, including drug possession or use (Fisher and Hennessy, 2016). A different study suggests that school resource officers do not affect school safety (Anderson, 2018).

The Clery Act of 1990 (Public Law 101-542) established a requirement for all institutions of higher education that receive federal funding to publicly report crime incidents, including arrests and referrals for disciplinary action stemming from drug use and liquor law violations. Although aggregate statistics are reported to the federal government, there is no parallel requirement for K–12 schools. States are responsible for establishing requirements for communication between law enforcement and local education agencies about students or school employees. For example, the state of Michigan requires annual reporting by school districts on a variety of crimes and violations, including illegal drug use, overdose possession or sale, and possession of alcohol or tobacco products by a minor.

Illegal Supply

Information about the prevalence of illegal opioid sales on school campuses is sparse, making it difficult to understand the relationships between the education system and illegal supply.

Harm Reduction and Community-Initiated Interventions

In recent years, several states have passed legislation to promote the use of overdose reversal agents in schools by requiring the development of policies on overdose reversal agent use, encouraging or requiring schools to identify and train school personnel to administer overdose reversal agents, and providing legal protections related to their use (Rafa, 2019). In other states, the decision is left up to the local community. Although school nurses may be on the front line as schools roll out policies that allow school staff to administer overdose reversal agents, most legislation allows for other school personnel to be trained to administer overdose reversal agents as well. Some colleges have started stocking kits in dormitories (Alltucker, 2018; Baker, 2019; Brean, 2019; Guydish, 2019). Some public health agencies are partnering with schools to get them to stock naloxone, train staff to administer it, and even train students on administration so that they could save a family member. In one Tennessee community, the county's drug prevention coalition offered training and kits to 600 children in three years. More than 100 of those children have returned to get more of the antidote, suggesting that they had to make use of the training (Levin, 2020).

First Responders

The education system typically interacts with first responders in the case of an emergency facing a member of the school or the school facility and to offer crime or drug prevention programs for youth. Some school districts and more colleges and universities have their own law enforcement officers. Although there is no research on the extent to which education system interactions relate to opioid use and misuse, there are examples of explicit partnerships or programs that have been driven by opioid-related concerns. The Handle With Care program, which originated in West Virginia and has since been adopted in other states, requires law enforcement to notify schools when they are called to an incident when children are present but not directly involved as perpetrators or victims, such as an overdose in a household with children. Schools are simply told that they should handle the child with care. The program also supports training for educators to support kids who experience trauma and to hire therapists in schools (Hefling, 2018; Johnson, 2019). In Virginia, school leaders are alerted when law enforcement officers are called to a student's home. This provides schools with awareness about recent trauma a student may be experiencing.

Child Welfare

Under federal law, all states must have provisions for reporting child abuse and neglect. Although states craft their own legislation to meet this requirement, most states consider educators to be mandatory reporters to the child welfare system (Child Welfare Information Gateway, 2019). Many states require school districts to provide training to staff about the mandatory reporting obligations.

Among children entering foster care in fiscal year 2017, more than one-third had parental drug use listed as a reason for entering the system (Sepulveda and Williams, 2019). The opioid crisis is likely to increase child neglect and abuse and, in turn, child interactions with the child welfare system (Litvinov, 2019). Under federal law, states are required to ensure continuity of education for children in foster care. The Every Student Succeeds Act emphasizes that educating children in foster care is a joint responsibility of the child welfare system and state and local education agencies (U.S. Department of Education and U.S. Department of Health and Human Services, 2016). Collaboration is needed to promote stability so that children can remain in the same school despite movements into, out of, or between foster care placements. Other foci are support for transportation and support for transitions to higher education. States have laws designed to support such interagency collaboration and information-sharing in the interests of stability, access, and continuity of education (National Conference of State Legislatures, 2016). States also provide additional resources to districts to support these efforts. However, a review conducted by the U.S. Government Accountability Office (GAO) suggests that effective collaboration to ensure continuity of education for foster youth is limited by agency capacity and staff turnover issues (GAO, 2019; National Conference of State Legislatures, 2016).

Protections focused on foster youth may not extend to all children suffering parental neglect (e.g., those who are directed to kinship care or who do not enter the child welfare system at all). The opioid crisis is likely to increase the number of children experiencing parental neglect (see Chapter Ten for a more-detailed discussion on this topic). There is anecdotal evidence of grandparents and other family members stepping in to care for the children of those suffering from opioid addictions (García Mathewson, 2016; Litvinov, 2019), suggesting that only a fraction of such children will formally enter the foster care system. Although children in kinship care may experience similar disruptions as those who are officially in the foster care system, they may not be afforded the resources and flexibilities available to foster youth when it comes to the education system. For example, although foster youth would be allowed to remain enrolled in their districts of origin even if they move because of foster placement, they may not be allowed to do so in the event that they move in with a grandparent.

Policy Opportunities and Considerations

This review illustrates the extent of gaps in researcher, policymaker, and practitioner knowledge about the interactions between the opioid ecosystem and the education system. Although it seems obvious that the education system would both influence and be influenced by the opioid crisis, these relationships have not been the focus of much research. Recent research has documented relationships between the prevalence of opioid use and misuse in particular locales and regions and education system outcomes and explored the theoretical foundations of this relationship. These research observations have prompted further interest in issues that have not been well studied, such as the effectiveness of opioid-focused drug prevention programs or targeted support programs for students affected indirectly (e.g., through family or community use) or directly by OUD. Much of what we know today is derived from more-general drug prevention or student support programs, but even there, the knowledge base is limited. A key takeaway of this review is a call for more data-gathering and research about students who are affected directly or indirectly by OUD and the programs that are developed to support them. There is a particular need to understand the applicability of evidence-based drug prevention programs to the opioid crisis.

Community-Wide Approaches That Cut Across Systems Hold Promise

Interactions between the education system and the medical, mental health, and public health systems are typically grounded in the initiative of individual districts or communities. Recognition is growing about the advantages of tighter linkages among these systems as reflected in the community school model. The advantages of a systems approach may be amplified in communities where resources are scarce and demands from the social welfare systems are high. Rather than competing over resources, community-wide approaches can promote collaboration to allocate resources intentionally across the full range of community needs. The community school model advances a comprehensive, neighborhood-based approach to education in which schools (1) partner with other organizations in the community to address academic, health, developmental, and mental health needs not only of the student but of the entire family and (2) promote community engagement (Diamond and Freudenberg, 2016). This approach has been implemented in several high-needs communities across the country. It is not a highly prescribed program with rigid features but rather a flexible approach that is "grounded in the principle that all students, families, and communities benefit from strong connections between educators, local resources, supports, and people" (Maier et al., 2017). Although community school programs in urban areas, such as New York, Oakland, and Hartford, have garnered much attention, Kentucky has been supporting these approaches through school-based family resource and youth service centers across the state for 30 years (Kentucky Cabinet for Health and Family Services, 2020; McDaniels, 2018). A comprehensive review of research studies evaluating the community schools approach in a variety of settings concluded that students who participate in the programs have higher test scores and grades, better attendance, and a higher degree of school engagement. Much of the research does not support causal conclusions, although the consistency of findings across studies and settings is promising (Maier et al., 2017). A quasi-experimental study examining outcomes for the community school approach in New York City found a positive effect of the program on a variety of outcomes, including attendance, on-time grade progression, graduation, discipline, and student achievement (Johnston et al., 2017; Johnston et al., 2020). Four community school studies included a cost-benefit component. Those studies suggest that the return on investment from wraparound services and other community school features is in the range of $3 to $15 for each dollar spent (Maier et al., 2017, pp. 99–104).

When applying the flexible and adaptable community school model in communities that are hard hit by the opioid crisis, policymakers would be advised to consider or even build on community-based approaches targeting the opioid crisis that originate outside but include the education system. As an example of such cross-system collaboration, in Jackson County, West Virginia, the Anti-Drug Coalition has partnered with schools, hospitals, law enforcement, mental health organizations, and faith organizations with support from the Drug Free Communities program. In Massachusetts, the state government supports drug treatment counselors in schools across the state. The Handle With Care program (in use in several states) promotes collaboration among schools, law enforcement agencies, and mental health providers and encourages involvement with other community organizations as well (Gaines et al., 2017).

Trauma-Sensitive Schools

The prevalence of ACE exposure implies that teachers across the country—especially teachers in communities hardest hit by the opioid crisis—are educating children suffering from the effects of trauma. As noted earlier, schools, districts, and states have begun to emphasize trauma-informed school approaches (Overstreet and Chafouleas, 2016). Some models of trauma-informed schools involve multitiered systems of support and cross-sector collaboration with community and university partners (Kataoka et al., 2018). Child advocates urge schools to respond to ACE exposure by fostering positive relationships, emphasizing the development of social-emotional skills, attending to physical and mental health needs of students, and putting in place a school culture that emphasizes safety and support rather than punitive practices that have the potential to retraumatize students (Jones, Berg, and Osher, 2018; Murphey and Sacks, 2019). In the case of students who have a family member experiencing an OUD, alternative solutions that keep students in school may be particularly important because traditional punishments like suspension could have the unintended effect of exposing these students to even more trauma in the home environment.

The U.S. Department of Education has created a menu of options to help schools and districts identify a suitable trauma-informed approach (Institute of Education Sciences, 2020). Many of these approaches emphasize social-emotional learning (Hamilton, Doss, and Steiner, 2019). Although such a resource is useful, state or other support may be needed to ensure that schools have the partners and resources available to implement such programs—especially the more-comprehensive ones (RAND Corporation, undated).

Although the trauma-sensitive school approaches seem well suited to populations affected by the opioid crisis, there is no research we are aware of that tailors the models and examines the effectiveness of these approaches for such communities. Such targeted studies would be useful.

Targeted Support for Students Whose Caretakers Are Experiencing Opioid Use Disorder and the Schools That Serve Them

In response to research documenting lower graduation rates, educational attainment, and other adverse outcomes for students in the foster care system, several states have made policy changes in the past decade designed to enhance support for foster youth (Evans and McCann, 2020). Such policy changes include enrollment flexibilities to promote continuity of education regardless of residence, additional funding for districts that serve foster youth, and subsidies for higher education. Some students with parents experiencing an OUD enter the foster care system. But many other children continue to be cared for by one or both parents (possibly including a parent with an OUD) or extended family members, such as grandparents, aunts, and uncles, in a kinship care arrangement and are not formally part of the foster system. These youth may face many of the same challenges that contribute to poor educational outcomes for foster youth, including residential mobility and exposure to trauma. States should consider how they might include children with a parent suffering from OUD in policies to support better education outcomes for foster youth.

Abbreviations

ACE	adverse childhood experience
CDC	Centers for Disease Control and Prevention
EMT	emergency medical technician
GAO	U.S. Government Accountability Office
K–12	kindergarten through 12th grade
NCES	National Center for Education Statistics
NIDA	National Institute on Drug Abuse
NOWS	neonatal opioid withdrawal syndrome
NSDUH	National Survey on Drug Use and Health
OUD	opioid use disorder
PBIS	Center on Positive Behavioral Interventions and Supports
SAMHSA	Substance Abuse and Mental Health Services Administration
SUD	substance use disorder

References

Alltucker, Ken, "Naloxone Can Reverse Opioid Overdoses, but Does the Drug Belong in Elementary Schools?" *USA TODAY*, September 11, 2018.

Altekruse, Sean F., Candace M. Cosgrove, William C. Altekruse, Richard A. Jenkins, and Carlos Blanco, "Socioeconomic Risk Factors for Fatal Opioid Overdoses in the United States: Findings from the Mortality Disparities in American Communities Study (MDAC)," *PLoS ONE*, Vol. 15, No. 1, 2020.

Anderson, Greta, "Wake-Up Call," Inside Higher Ed, November 15, 2019. As of May 24, 2022: https://www.insidehighered.com/news/2019/11/15/ colleges-determine-how-protect-students-opioid-epidemic

Anderson, Kenneth Alonzo, "Policing and Middle School: An Evaluation of a Statewide School Resource Officer Policy," *Middle Grades Review*, Vol. 4, No. 2, September 2018.

Anderson, Sara, Jessica Troilo, Frankie Tack, Lauren Prinzo, Megan Mikesell, and Sloane Strauss, "A Crisis in the Classroom: West Virginia Teachers and the Opioid Epidemic," presented at the National Association of Community Development Extension Professionals virtual conference, May 29–June 3, 2020.

Ashford, Ellie, "Campuses Tackle the Opioid Epidemic," *Community College Daily*, August 25, 2017. As of May 24, 2022: https://www.ccdaily.com/2017/08/campuses-tackle-opioid-epidemic/

Attorneys at the Legal Action Center, *Know Your Rights: Rights for Individuals on Medication-Assisted Treatment*, Rockville, Md.: Center for Substance Abuse Treatment, Substance Abuse and Mental Health Services Administration, 2009.

Baker, Vicky, "Opioid Crisis: US Schools Prepare for Student Overdoses," BBC News, March 11, 2019.

Balonon-Rosen, Peter, "Economics of Disability: Special Education Costs Add Up for Parents, Schools as Federal Law Remains Underfunded," *Marketplace*, June 22, 2018.

Bastable, Eoin, Angus Kittelman, Kent McIntosh, and Rob Hoselton, *Do High Schools Implementing SWPBIS Have Lower Rates of Illegal Drug and Alcohol Use?* Washington, D.C.: U.S. Department of Education, Office of Special Education Programs and Office of Elementary and Secondary Education, Center on Positive Behavioral Interventions & Supports (PBIS), March 2015.

Bleasdale, Timothy, *Drug Testing in the Workplace and in Public Schools*, Hartford, Conn.: Connecticut General Assembly, Office of Legislative Research, 2014.

Bohanon, Mariah, "The Opioid Crisis Comes to College," *Insight into Diversity*, October 17, 2017.

Brean, Berkeley, "Teacher Who Overdosed in School and Then Charged Allegedly Had 13 Baggies of Fentanyl in Lunch Bag," WHEC-TV, December 17, 2019.

Brill, Alex, and Scott Ganz, *The Geographic Variation in the Cost of the Opioid Crisis*, Washington, D.C.: American Enterprise Institute, Working Paper 2018-03, March 2018.

Brundage, Suzanne C., Adam Fifield, and Lee Partridge, *The Ripple Effect: National and State Estimates of the U.S. Opioid Epidemic's Impact on Children*, New York: United Hospital Fund, November 2019.

Bryk, Anthony S., and Barbara Schneider, *Trust in Schools: A Core Resource for Improvement*, New York: Russell Sage Foundation, 2020.

Camera, Lauren, "Teaching to the Drug Test," *U.S. News & World Report*, February 8, 2019.

Case, Anne, and Angus Deaton, *Deaths of Despair and the Future of Capitalism*, Princeton, N.J.: Princeton University Press, 2020.

Caulkins, Jonathan P., C. Peter Rydell, Susan S. Everingham, James Chiesa, and Shawn Bushway, *An Ounce of Prevention, a Pound of Uncertainty: The Cost-Effectiveness of School-Based Drug Prevention Programs*, Santa Monica, Calif.: RAND Corporation, MR-923-RWJ, 1999. As of July 26, 2020:
https://www.rand.org/pubs/monograph_reports/MR923.html

CDC—*See* Centers for Disease Control and Prevention.

Center on Positive Behavioral Intervention and Supports, homepage, undated-a. As of May 25, 2022:
https://www.pbis.org/

Center on Positive Behavioral Intervention and Supports, "Opioid Crisis and Substance Misuse," webpage, undated-b. As of May 25, 2022:
https://www.pbis.org/topics/opioid-crisis-and-substance-misuse

Centers for Disease Control and Prevention, *HECAT Module AOD: Alcohol- and Other Drug-Use Prevention Curriculum*, Atlanta, Ga., 2012.

Centers for Disease Control and Prevention, *Results from the School Health Policies and Practices Study*, Atlanta, Ga.: National Center for HIV/AIDS, Viral Hepatitis, STD, and TB Prevention, Division of Adolescent and School Health, 2016.

Chen, Grace, "Should Schools Conduct Background Checks on Teachers?" *Public School Review* blog, 2020. As of May 24, 2022:
https://www.publicschoolreview.com/blog/
should-schools-conduct-background-checks-on-teachers

Child Welfare Information Gateway, *Mandatory Reporters of Child Abuse and Neglect*, Washington, D.C.: U.S. Department of Health and Human Services, Children's Bureau, April 2019.

Cornaggia, Kimberly R., John Hund, Giang Nguyen, and Zihan Ye, "Opioid Crisis Effects on Municipal Finance," Social Science Research Network, working paper, April 14, 2021.

Council on School Health and Committee on Substance Abuse, "The Role of Schools in Combating Illicit Substance Abuse," *Pediatrics*, Vol. 120, No. 6, 2007, pp. 1379–1384.

Cuellar, Alison Evans, and Sara Markowitz, "School Suspension and the School-to-Prison Pipeline," *International Review of Law and Economics*, Vol. 43, 2015, pp. 98–106.

Darolia, Rajeev, Sam Owens, and John Tyler, *The Opioid Crisis and Educational Performance*, Providence, R.I.: Annenberg Institute at Brown University, EdWorkingPaper No. 20-322, 2020.

Darolia, Rajeev, and John Tyler, *The Opioid Crisis and Community-Level Spillovers onto Children's Education*, Washington, D.C.: Brookings Institution, 2020.

Diamond, Catherine, and Nicholas Freudenberg, "Community Schools: A Public Health Opportunity to Reverse Urban Cycles of Disadvantage," *Journal of Urban Health*, Vol. 93, 2016, pp. 923–939.

Ekhtiari, Seper, Ibrahim Yusuf, Yosra AlMakadma, Austin MacDonald, Timothy Leroux, and Moin Khan, "Opioid Use in Athletes: A Systematic Review," *Sports Health*, Vol. 12, No. 6, November–December 2020.

Ellis, Matthew S., Zachary A. Kasper, and Theodore J. Cicero, "The Impact of Opioid Use Disorder on Levels of Educational Attainment: Perceived Benefits and Consequences," *Drug and Alcohol Dependence*, Vol. 206, January 2020.

Eskelsen Garcia, Lily, and Otha Thornton, *The Enduring Importance of Parental Involvement*, Washington, D.C.: National Education Association, 2014.

Evans, Alyssa, and Meghan McCann, *Support for Students in Foster Care*, Denver, Colo.: Education Commission of the States, September 2020.

Field, Kelly, "A New Challenge for Colleges: Opioid-Addicted Students," The Hechinger Report, September 13, 2018. As of May 24, 2022: https://hechingerreport.org/a-new-challenge-for-colleges-opioid-addicted-students/

Fisher, Benjamin W., and Emily A. Hennessy, "School Resource Officers and Exclusionary Discipline in U.S. High Schools: A Systematic Review and Meta-Analysis," *Adolescent Research Review*, Vol. 1, 2016, pp. 217–233.

Florence, Curtis, Feijun Luo, Likang Xu, and Chao Zhou, "The Economic Burden of Prescription Opioid Overdose, Abuse, and Dependence in the United States, 2013," *Medical Care*, Vol. 54, No. 10, October 2016, pp. 901–906.

Ford, J. A., C. Pomykacz, P. Veliz, S. E. McCabe, and C. J. Boyd, "Sports Involvement, Injury History, and Non-Medical Use of Prescription Opioids Among College Students: An Analysis with a National Sample," *American Journal on Addictions*, Vol. 27, No. 1, 2018, pp. 15–22.

Ford, Jason A., Corey R. Pomykacz, Kasim Ortiz, Sean Esteban McCabe, and Ty S. Schepis, "Educational Attainment and Prescription Drug Misuse: The Importance of Push and Pull Factors for Dropping Out," *Journal of Criminal Justice*, Vol. 66, January–February 2020.

Gagnon, Douglas J., and Marybeth J. Mattingly, *Most U.S. School Districts Have Low Access to School Counselors*, Durham, N.H.: University of New Hampshire, Carsey School of Public Policy, National Issue Brief No. 108, Fall 2016.

Gaines, Elizabeth, Olivia Allen, Neeja Patel, and Natalie Logan, *2017 State Policy Survey: Child and Youth Policy Coordinating Bodies in the U.S.—Summary of Findings*, Washington, D.C.: Forum for Youth Investment, 2017.

GAO—*See* U.S. Government Accountability Office.

García Mathewson, Tara, "More Grandparents Are Raising Grandchildren. Here's How to Help Them," The Hechinger Report, September 2, 2016. As of May 24, 2022:
https://hechingerreport.org/
parent-substance-abuse-incarceration-drives-increase-in-grandparents-raising-grandchildren/

Gotbaum, Rachel, "Addiction Counselors Embed in Schools Dealing with the Opioid Crisis," The Hechinger Report, September 23, 2018. As of May 24, 2022:
https://hechingerreport.org/
addiction-counselors-embed-in-schools-dealing-with-the-opioid-crisis/

Griffith, Conor, "Opioid Crisis Hurting Student and Teacher Success," *WVNews*, June 24, 2019.

Guydish, Mark, "WVW Teacher Grievance Sheds Light on Fentanyl Fears in Grade School," *Times Leader*, December 11, 2019.

Hamilton, Laura S., Christopher Joseph Doss, and Elizabeth D. Steiner, *Teacher and Principal Perspectives on Social and Emotional Learning in America's Schools: Findings from the American Educator Panels*, Santa Monica, Calif.: RAND Corporation, RR-2991-BMGF, 2019. As of May 25, 2022:
https://www.rand.org/pubs/research_reports/RR2991.html

Hanushek, Eric A., "Education Production Functions," in Steven N. Durlauf and Lawrence E. Blume, eds., *The New Palgrave Dictionary of Economics*, 2008.

Hedegaard, Holly, Margaret Warner, and Arialdi M. Miniño, "Drug Overdose Deaths in the United States, 1999–2016," NCHS Data Brief, No. 294, December 2017.

Hefling, Kimberly, "Cash-Strapped Schools Struggle to Help Children of Opioid Epidemic," *Politico*, June 18, 2018.

Henderson, Anne T., *The Evidence Continues to Grow: Parent Involvement Improves Student Achievement—An Annotated Bibliography*, Columbia, Md.: National Committee for Citizens in Education, 1987.

Henderson, Anne T., and Karen L. Mapp, *A New Wave of Evidence: The Impact of School, Family, and Community Connections on Student Achievement—Annual Synthesis*, Austin, Tex.: Southwest Educational Development Lab, 2002.

Hennessy, Emily A., Emily E. Tanner-Smith, Andrew J. Finch, Nila Sathe, and Shannon Kugley, "Recovery Schools for Improving Behavioral and Academic Outcomes Among Students in Recovery from Substance Use Disorders: A Systematic Review," *Campbell Systematic Reviews*, Vol. 14, No. 1, 2018.

Hoover, Amanda, "As N.J. Colleges Expand Recovery Housing, Here's What Others Can Learn," NJ.com, May 20, 2018. As of May 25, 2022:
https://www.nj.com/news/2018/05/can_nj_lead_the_way_on_recovery_housing.html

Hunt, Tenah K. A., Kristen S. Slack, and Lawrence M. Berger, "Adverse Childhood Experiences and Behavioral Problems in Middle Childhood," *Child Abuse & Neglect*, Vol. 67, May 2017, pp. 391–402.

Institute of Education Sciences, "Menu of Trauma-Informed Programs for Schools," REL Appalachia Cross-State Collaborative to Support Schools in the Opioid Crisis (CCSSOC), April 8, 2020.

James-Burdumy, Susanne, Brian Goesling, John Deke, and Eric Einspruch, "The Effectiveness of Mandatory-Random Student Drug Testing: A Cluster Randomized Trial," *Journal of Adolescent Health*, Vol. 50, No. 2, February 2012, pp. 172–178.

Jimenez, Manuel E., Roy Wade, Jr., Yong Lin, Lesley M. Morrow, and Nancy E. Reichman, "Adverse Experiences in Early Childhood and Kindergarten Outcomes," *Pediatrics*, Vol. 137, No. 2, February 2016.

Johnson, Shauna, "What's Working, What's Not Is Focus of Handle With Care Outside Evaluation," *MetroNews*, March 31, 2019.

Johnston, Lloyd D., Richard A. Miech, Megan E. Patrick, Patrick M. O'Malley, John E. Schulenberg, and Jerald G. Bachman, *Monitoring the Future National Survey Results on Drug Use, 1975–2022: 2022 Overview—Findings on Adolescent Drug Use*, Ann Arbor, Mich.: Institute for Social Research, University of Michigan, January 2023.

Johnston, William R., John Engberg, Isaac M. Opper, Lisa Sontag-Padilla, and Lea Xenakis, *Illustrating the Promise of Community Schools: An Assessment of the Impact of the New York City Community Schools Initiative*, Santa Monica, Calif.: RAND Corporation, RR-3245-NYCCEO, 2020. As of May 25, 2022:
https://www.rand.org/pubs/research_reports/RR3245.html

Johnston, William R., Celia J. Gomez, Lisa Sontag-Padilla, Lea Xenakis, and Brent Anderson, *Developing Community Schools at Scale: Implementation of the New York City Community Schools Initiative*, Santa Monica, Calif.: RAND Corporation, RR-2100-NYCCEO, 2017. As of May 25, 2022:
https://www.rand.org/pubs/research_reports/RR2100.html

Jones, Abenaa A., Kristin E. Schneider, Sherri-Chanelle Brighthaupt, Julie K. Johnson, Sabriya L. Linton, and Renee M. Johnson, "Heroin and Nonmedical Prescription Opioid Use Among High School Students in Urban School Districts," *Drug and Alcohol Dependence*, Vol. 205, 2019.

Jones, Wehmah, Juliette Berg, and David Osher, *Trauma and Learning Policy Initiative (TLPI): Trauma-Sensitive Schools Descriptive Study: Final Report*, Washington, D.C.: American Institutes for Research, October 2018.

Kadvany, Elena, "Stanford Student Died from Accidental Fentanyl Overdose, Coroner Confirms," *Palo Alto Weekly*, February 27, 2020.

Kataoka, Sheryl H., Pamela Vona, Alejandra Acuna, Lisa Jaycox, Pia Escudero, Claudia Rojas, Erica Ramirez, Audra Langley, and Bradley D. Stein, "Applying a Trauma Informed School Systems Approach: Examples from School Community-Academic Partnerships," *Ethnicity & Disease*, Vol. 28, Suppl. 2, 2018, pp. 417–426.

Kelly, John, "How USA TODAY Graded the States on Teacher Background Checks," *USA Today*, February 14, 2016.

Kentucky Cabinet for Health and Family Services, *2020 Status Report: Kentucky Family Resource and Youth Services Centers*, Frankfort, Ky.: Kentucky Family Resource and Youth Services Centers, 2020.

Klazema, Michael, "Indiana General Assembly Considering Stricter School Background Checks," Backgroundchecks.com, August 18, 2016. As of May 25, 2022:
https://www.backgroundchecks.com/community/Post/4667/Indiana-General-Assembly-Considering-Stricter-School-Background-Checks

Konstantopoulos, Spyros, and Geoffrey D. Borman, "Family Background and School Effects on Student Achievement: A Multilevel Analysis of the Coleman Data," *Teachers College Record*, Vol. 113, No. 1, January 2011, pp. 97–132.

Lander, Laura, Janie Howsare, and Marilyn Byrne, "The Impact of Substance Use Disorders on Families and Children: From Theory to Practice," *Social Work in Public Health*, Vol. 28, No. 3-4, 2013, pp. 194–205.

Levin, Dan, "Teaching Children How to Reverse an Overdose," *New York Times*, February 23, 2020.

Levy, Sharon, Miriam Schizer, and Committee on Substance Abuse, "Adolescent Drug Testing Policies in Schools," *Pediatrics*, Vol. 135, No. 4, April 2015.

Lima, Julie, Margaret Caughy, Saundra M. Nettles, and Patricia J. O'Campo, "Effects of Cumulative Risk on Behavioral and Psychological Well-Being in First Grade: Moderation by Neighborhood Context," *Social Science & Medicine*, Vol. 71, No. 8, 2010, pp. 1447–1454.

Lipari, Rachel N., and Struther L. Van Horn, *Children Living with Parents Who Have a Substance Use Disorder*, Washington, D.C.: Substance Abuse and Mental Health Services Administration, August 24, 2017.

Litvinov, Amanda, *Teaching the Children of the Opioid Crisis*, Washington, D.C.: National Education Association, January 14, 2019.

Los Angeles Unified School District, *Covered Employees Drug and Alcohol Testing Program: Policy Guide*, Los Angeles, Calif., October 20, 2018.

Maciag, Michael, "States That Spend the Most (and the Least) on Education," Governing: The Future of States and Localities, June 3, 2019. As of May 25, 2022: https://www.governing.com/topics/education/gov-state-education-spending-revenue-data.html

Maier, Anna, Julia Daniel, Jeannie Oakes, and Livia Lam, *Community Schools as an Effective School Improvement Strategy: A Review of the Evidence*, Palo Alto, Calif.: Learning Policy Institute, National Education Policy Center, December 2017.

Maryland Senate Bill 1060, Heroin and Opioid Education and Community Action Act of 2017 (Start Talking Maryland Act), 2017.

McDaniels, Abel, *Building Community Schools Systems: Removing Barriers to Success in U.S. Public Schools*, Washington, D.C.: Center for American Progress, August 22, 2018.

McKelvey, Lorraine M., Leanne Whiteside-Mansell, Nicola A. Conners-Burrow, Taren Swindle, and Shalese Fitzgerald, "Assessing Adverse Experiences from Infancy Through Early Childhood in Home Visiting Programs," *Child Abuse and Neglect*, Vol. 51, January 2016, pp. 295–302.

Michigan Public Act 255, Require Opioid Abuse Training in Schools, 2018.

Miller, T., and D. Hendrie, *Substance Abuse Prevention Dollars and Cents: A Cost-Benefit Analysis*, Rockville, Md.: Center for Substance Abuse Prevention, Substance Abuse and Mental Health Services Administration, 2008.

Moberg, D. Paul, Andrew J. Finch, and Stephanie M. Lindsley, "Recovery High Schools: Students and Responsive Academic and Therapeutic Services," *Peabody Journal of Education*, Vol. 89, No. 2, 2014, pp. 165–182.

Morello, Rachel, "Kids Struggling with Addiction Need School, Too, but There Are Few Options," NPR, July 8, 2017.

Morgan, Paul L., and Yangyang Wang, "The Opioid Epidemic, Neonatal Abstinence Syndrome, and Estimated Costs for Special Education Services," *American Journal of Managed Care*, Vol. 25, Suppl. 13, July 2019, pp. S264–S269.

Murphey, David, and Vanessa Sacks, "Supporting Students with Adverse Childhood Experiences: How Educators and Schools Can Help," American Federation of Teachers, 2019.

National Center for Education Statistics, Institute of Education Sciences, "List of 2019 Data Tables," webpage, 2019. As of May 25, 2022:
https://nces.ed.gov/programs/digest/2019menu_tables.asp

National Center for Education Statistics, Institute of Education Sciences, *School Nurses in U.S. Public Schools*, Washington, D.C., NCES 2020-086, April 2020.

National Conference of State Legislatures, *Educating Children in Foster Care State Legislation 2008–2015*, Washington, D.C., September 27, 2016.

National Institute on Drug Abuse, "Lesson Plan and Activity Finder," webpage, undated. As of May 25, 2022:
https://teens.drugabuse.gov/teachers/lessonplans

National Institute on Drug Abuse, "Teens Using Vaping Devices in Record Numbers," news release, December 17, 2018.

NCES—*See* National Center for Education Statistics.

Neal, James, "State Rules Wouldn't Prevent Hiring a Teacher with Drug Charges," *Enid News & Eagle*, March 9, 2017.

NIDA—*See* National Institute on Drug Abuse.

Office of National Drug Control Policy, "Substance Use Prevention: A Resource Guide for School Staff," webpage, 2020. As of May 25, 2022:
https://trumpwhitehouse.archives.gov/ondcp/additional-links-resources/resource-guide-for-school-staff/

Operation Prevention, "School Resources: Opioid and Prescription Drugs," webpage, undated. As of June 8, 2022:
https://operationprevention.com/opioid-and-prescription-drugs

Overstreet, Stacy, and Sandra M. Chafouleas, "Trauma-Informed Schools: Introduction to the Special Issue," *School Mental Health: A Multidisciplinary Research and Practice Journal*, Vol. 8, No. 1, 2016.

Pardo, Bryce, Jirka Taylor, Jonathan P. Caulkins, Beau Kilmer, Peter Reuter, and Bradley D. Stein, *The Future of Fentanyl and Other Synthetic Opioids*, Santa Monica, Calif.: RAND Corporation, RR-3117-RC, 2019. As of May 25, 2022:
https://www.rand.org/pubs/research_reports/RR3117.html

Passetti, Lora L., Mark D. Godley, and Yifrah Kaminer, "Continuing Care for Adolescents in Treatment for Substance Use Disorders," *Child and Adolescent Psychiatric Clinics of North America*, Vol. 25, No. 4, October 2016, pp. 669–684.

PBIS—*See* Center on Positive Behavioral Intervention and Supports.

Peacock Dunn, Kelli, "Criminal Offenses That Will Stop Teacher Certification," *Chron*, March 30, 2018.

Pennsylvania Department of Education, "Clearances/Background Checks," webpage, undated. As of May 25, 2022:
https://www.education.pa.gov/Educators/Clearances/Pages/default.aspx

Porche, Michelle V., Lisa R. Fortuna, Julia Lin, and Margarita Alegria, "Childhood Trauma and Psychiatric Disorders as Correlates of School Dropout in a National Sample of Young Adults," *Child Development*, Vol. 82, No. 3, May–June 2011, pp. 982–998.

Porter, Nicole D., and Tyler Clemons, *Drug-Free Zone Laws: An Overview of State Policies*, Washington, D.C.: The Sentencing Project, December 20, 2013.

Public Law 101-542, Student Right-to-Know and Campus Security, November 8, 1990.

Rafa, Alyssa, *Education Policy Responses to the Opioid Crisis*, Denver, Colo.: Education Commission of the States, September 2019.

Ramos, Christal, Lisa Clemans-Cope, Haley Samuel-Jakubos, and Luis Basurto, *Evidence-Based Interventions for Adolescent Opioid Use Disorder: What Might Work for High-Risk Ohio Counties?* Washington, D.C.: Urban Institute, September 2018.

RAND Corporation, "Research on the Partnerships for Social and Emotional Learning Initiative," webpage, undated. As of May 25, 2022: https://www.rand.org/education-and-labor/projects/pseli.html

Romanowicz, Magdalena, Jennifer L. Vande Voort, Julia Shekunov, Tyler S. Oesterle, Nuria J. Thusius, Teresa A. Rummans, Paul E. Croarkin, Victor M. Karpyak, Brian A. Lynch, and Kathryn M. Schak, "The Effects of Parental Opioid Use on the Parent-Child Relationship and Children's Developmental and Behavioral Outcomes: A Systematic Review of Published Reports," *Child and Adolescent Psychiatry and Mental Health*, Vol. 13, 2019.

Rural Health Information Hub, "School-Based Drug Misuse Prevention Program," webpage, 2019. As of May 25, 2022: https://www.ruralhealthinfo.org/project-examples/1050

Sacks, Vanessa, and David Murphey, *The Prevalence of Adverse Childhood Experiences, Nationally, by State, and by Race or Ethnicity*, Bethesda, Md.: Child Trends, 2018.

SAMHSA—*See* Substance Abuse and Mental Health Services Administration.

Scavette, Adam, "Exploring the Economic Effects of the Opioid Epidemic," *Federal Reserve Bank of Philadelphia*, 2019.

Schepis, Ty S., Christian J. Teter, and Sean Esteban McCabe, "Prescription Drug Use, Misuse and Related Substance Use Disorder Symptoms Vary by Educational Status and Attainment in U.S. Adolescents and Young Adults," *Drug and Alcohol Dependence*, Vol. 189, 2018, pp. 172–177.

Sepulveda, Kristin, and Sarah Catherine Williams, *One in Three Children Entered Foster Care in 2017 Because of Parental Drug Abuse*, Bethesda, Md.: Child Trends, 2019.

Spehr, Michelle K., Jennifer Coddington, Azza H. Ahmed, and Elizabeth Jones, "Parental Opioid Abuse: Barriers to Care, Policy, and Implications for Primary Care Pediatric Providers," *Journal of Pediatric Health Care*, Vol. 31, No. 6, 2017, pp. 695–702.

State of Ohio, "The Health and Opioid-Abuse Prevention Education Curriculum," Start Talking Ohio, undated. As of May 25, 2022: https://starttalking.ohio.gov/Schools/The-HOPE-Curriculum

Stempel, Hilary, Matthew Cox-Martin, Michael Bronsert, L. Miriam Dickinson, and Mandy A. Allison, "Chronic School Absenteeism and the Role of Adverse Childhood Experiences," *Academic Pediatrics*, Vol. 17, No. 8, 2017, pp. 837–843.

Substance Abuse and Mental Health Services Administration, "Behavioral Health Treatment Services Locator," webpage, undated. As of May 25, 2022: https://findtreatment.samhsa.gov/

Substance Abuse and Mental Health Services Administration, *Key Substance Use and Mental Health Indicators in the United States: Results from the 2019 National Survey on Drug Use and Health*, Rockville, Md.: Center for Behavioral Health Statistics and Quality, 2020.

Superville, Denisa R., "Absences, Trauma, and Orphaned Children: How the Opioid Crisis Is Ravaging Schools," *Education Week*, November 20, 2017.

Sznitman, Sharon R., Sally M. Dunlop, Priya Nalkur, Atika Khurana, and Daniel Romer, "Student Drug Testing in the Context of Positive and Negative School Climates: Results from a National Survey," *Journal of Youth Adolescence*, Vol. 41, No. 2, February 2012, pp. 146–155.

Texas American Federation of Teachers, "Safe Schools Act," webpage, undated. As of May 25, 2022:
https://www.texasaft.org/resources/safe-schools-act/

Texas Association of School Boards, *Criminal History Reviews of District Employees and Volunteers*, Austin, Tex., 2019.

U.S. Census Bureau, "Annual Survey of School System Finances," webpage, 2020. As of May 25, 2022:
https://www.census.gov/programs-surveys/school-finances.html

U.S. Department of Education, "About IDEA," webpage, undated. As of May 25, 2022:
https://sites.ed.gov/idea/about-idea/

U.S. Department of Education, *Education in the United States: A Brief Overview*, Washington, D.C., September 2005.

U.S. Department of Education and U.S. Department of Health and Human Services, *Non-Regulatory Guidance: Ensuring Educational Stability for Children in Foster Care*, Washington, D.C., 2016.

U.S. Government Accountability Office, *Foster Care: Education Could Help States Improve Educational Stability for Youth in Foster Care*, Washington, D.C., GAO-19-616, 2019.

Walker, Tim, *"I Didn't Know It Had a Name": Secondary Traumatic Stress and Educators*, Washington, D.C.: National Education Association, October 18, 2019.

West Virginia University, "West Virginia Teachers and the Opioid Epidemic," webpage, undated. As of January 1, 2023:
https://appliedhumansciences.wvu.edu/academics/school-of-counseling-and-well-being/project-train/project-background

Wilder, S., "Effects of Parental Involvement on Academic Achievement: A Meta-Synthesis," *Educational Review*, Vol. 66, No. 3, 2014, pp. 377–397.

Yoshikawa, Hirokazu, J. Lawrence Aber, and William R. Beardslee, "The Effects of Poverty on the Mental, Emotional, and Behavioral Health of Children and Youth: Implications for Prevention," *American Psychologist*, Vol. 67, No. 4, May–June 2012, pp. 272–284.

CHAPTER FOURTEEN

Synthesis: A Strategy That Reflects the Ecosystem Perspective

The preceding chapters review the components of the opioid ecosystem in detail and describe how they interact. Each chapter highlights policy opportunities for improving the lives of people who use opioids, along with their families and communities. However, the sum of these opportunities is greater than their parts. Indeed, it is only after reviewing the ecosystem in its entirety that we can identify barriers requiring multisectoral collaboration and offer cross-cutting portfolios of action that emerge from many of the components.

Our motivation for taking an ecosystem approach is to identify

- **new perspectives:** The scope and persistence of the problem demand innovative new approaches, which require looking at the problem in a novel (or at least unconventional) way.
- **contradictions:** Policies designed to help in one arena can cause harm in others, counteracting each other and often wasting resources.
- **synergies:** Policies interact with each other in ways that can multiply their impacts.
- **unintended consequences:** System components interconnect, sometimes in unexpected ways. As a result, policies targeting one part of the system can have unintended consequences, affecting systems that they were not intended to target.
- **transitions:** Policies need to be designed so that the individuals who are the intended targets of interventions do not get lost between components as their situations evolve.
- **the importance of families:** Families sometimes suffer because of a relative's substance use but also are key players in many components of the ecosystem.

We begin this synthesis chapter by describing barriers to progress that are salient across multiple components of the opioid ecosystem. We then focus on nine portfolios of action: three of which directly address these barriers and six of which are germane to multiple system components.

It is beyond our study's scope to conduct a benefit-cost analysis of the options within these portfolios; however, after discussing the portfolios, we offer thoughts about prioritizing options.

Our focus on people who use opioids does not mean that we should ignore our country's problems with other drugs. The United States confronts multiple challenges, from long-standing problems related to alcohol to a dramatic rise in harms related to methamphetamine use. Correspondingly, some of the observations and suggestions made in this chapter will be applicable to contexts other than opioids. However, opioids play a vital role in medicine and an outsized role in America's drug problems. They deserve special attention.

Cross-Sector Barriers to Change

Previous chapters identified barriers to change that are common across multiple components of the ecosystem. Understanding these barriers could provide a roadmap for policymakers seeking to address them.

Who Is Responsible as Individuals Move Across Components of the Ecosystem?

It is common for individuals to move across components of the ecosystem. Insufficient information and a lack of a well-defined handoff between system components often create disconnects at juncture points, challenging the ability of individuals to successfully navigate across system components. There are benefits to ensuring that individuals can do so successfully; however, it is not clear who is responsible for ensuring that an individual is appropriately and successfully connected with multiple components of the ecosystem. Examples include individuals with opioid use disorder (OUD) being released from incarceration but unable to successfully engage in treatment; those involved with social services being unable to obtain OUD treatment; individuals receiving services from first responders or in emergency rooms but not transitioning to OUD treatment; and children who are informally moved to a relative's home because of parental substance use not being referred to services they may need.

Such failings can stem from insufficient capacity in one part of the ecosystem—for example, not enough treatment availability. They can also result from insufficient information to facilitate a successful transition and from ambiguity about who is responsible for supporting a transition. Put another way, is it the system component from which an individual is coming that is responsible for managing the transition, or is it the system component to which the individual is going? Who takes ownership of assisting people in their journey or transition through the systems?

This challenge is further exacerbated by the fragmented geography of government in the United States, with multiple potentially relevant layers of governance (federal, state, county, municipal) and silos within relevant layers that complicate the organization, oversight, and funding of the relevant programs and initiatives, some of which are delivered by private for-profit and not-for-profit organizations. One manifestation of this phenomenon is that multiple governmental programs and initiatives commonly target the same populations and issues that abut or overlap with—but are implemented and managed by—different entities.

Policies Reflect the Mission of Each System Component

Each of the components of the opioid ecosystem has its own mission and priorities. Although addressing treatment of individuals with OUD is central to the substance use disorder (SUD) specialty system, the opioid crisis is not central to most components' missions and priorities. For example, the mission of the child welfare system is the safety, health, and well-being of child welfare–involved children and their safe reunification with their biological families when possible.[1] The education system seeks to promote student achievement and foster educational excellence. Social services, which are provided by both the government and non-profit public or private organizations, are intended to aid disadvantaged, distressed, or vulnerable persons or groups. First responders are trained professionals who provide medical assistance in emergency situations, only one of which is drug overdose.

As a result, we often observe that policies furthering the mission of one part of the ecosystem may create barriers to progress for people with OUD in other parts of the ecosystem. For example, child welfare policies regarding parental drug use that are designed to ensure a safe environment for children may prevent a parent who uses drugs from having contact with their child. The policy may inadvertently create a disincentive for some parents with OUD who believe that, by revealing their drug use as part of seeking treatment, they would have less contact with their child. By contrast, policies that enhance monitoring while supporting the parent in getting treatment could enhance treatment engagement while also providing a safe environment for the child. As another example, housing assistance programs that are intended to support individuals in need of shelter sometimes turn away those with SUD to protect other residents and the staff. Because housing can help improve quality of life and treatment outcomes, this can create a vicious cycle: Excluding those who use drugs may worsen their addiction, thus making it even harder to obtain housing and other services in the future. At the same time, it may improve outcomes for other equally deserving clients of public housing.

All of these examples highlight the uncertainty inherent in trying to balance the interests of different stakeholders.

Stigma Regarding Drugs and People Who Use Drugs Creates Barriers to Change

Nora Volkow, the director of the U.S. National Institute on Drug Abuse, argued that, while progress has been made toward reducing stigma associated with mental health disorders in the United States, less has been made with regard to SUDs:

---

[1] According to a 2021 Children's Bureau report, child removal was the result of parental drug use—an official child welfare agency designation when the primary caretaker has a "compulsive use of drugs that is not of a temporary nature" (Meinhofer et al., 2020, p. 2)—in more than one-third (35.3 percent) of cases (Child Welfare Information Gateway, 2021, p. 3).

Stigma associated with many mental health conditions is a well-recognized problem. But whereas considerable progress has been made in recent decades in reducing the stigma associated with some psychiatric disorders such as depression, such change has been much slower in relation to substance use disorders. One obstacle is that this stigma has causes beyond those that apply to most other conditions. People who are addicted to drugs sometimes lie or steal and can behave aggressively, especially when experiencing withdrawal or intoxication-triggered paranoia. These behaviors are transgressions of social norms that make it hard even for their loved ones to show them compassion, so it is easy to see why strangers or health care workers may be rejecting or unsympathetic. (Volkow, 2020, p. 1289)

In many cases, stigma can be exacerbated by the dominant culture in parts of the overall system, hampering effective cross-system responses.

Drug laws and some criminal justice interventions seek to reify social disapproval of drug use; the stigmatization of people who use and/or sell drugs is a feature of—not a bug in—the current system, as it is for other forms of criminal activity. However, illegality is only one cause of stigmatization. For example, there is also considerable stigma associated with alcohol use disorder (Killian et al., 2021).

Using social and legal pressure to discourage drug use can generate both benefits and harms. On one hand, the legal repercussions of illegal drug activity may make it easier to persuade some people to avoid drugs, get those with OUD who come into contact with law enforcement into treatment (e.g., via deflection programs or drug courts), and provide police with an important tool for controlling retail drug selling. Illegality also prevents for-profit firms from actively promoting drug use, and it greatly increases price and reduces the availability of drugs.

On the other hand, stigma may reduce the probability that those with OUD ask for help or seek services. This is especially a concern for people of color, who disproportionately bear the brunt of drug law enforcement and many of whom distrust the health care and social service systems because of historical discrimination and exploitation (Armstrong et al., 2013; Corbie-Smith, Thomas, and St. George, 2002; Whetten et al., 2006). Populations of color and individuals who live in communities with a higher percentage of racial/ethnic minorities are also less likely to receive the most-effective treatment for OUD (Lagisetty et al., 2019; Schuler, Dick, and Stein, 2021; Stein et al., 2018). And for those with a criminal record, the impact of the conviction can linger long after they have paid their debt to society.

Indeed, having a criminal record—including for a drug offense involving possession—has implications for many other parts of the opioid ecosystem. Arrests and convictions can make it harder to get a job, access public housing, and obtain social services. A drug offense can alert child protective services to investigate a parent and possibly remove the children if there is a perceived or observed threat to the children. Whether this ultimately benefits the children or the parents is often unclear. The fear and stigma associated with criminalization can drive people who use drugs away from such harm reduction programs as syringe service programs and drug content testing.

Stigma and discrimination are also reflected in many components of the ecosystem beyond the criminal legal system—for example, despite the passage of the 2008 Mental Health Parity Addiction Equity Act, lack of parity in insurance coverage for treatment of alcohol and other SUDs through nonquantitative limits still creates barriers. Complicating matters further, there is also stigma associated with medications for OUD (MOUD), which reduces the availability of evidence-based treatment options. Some of this stigma comes from the belief that MOUD, like methadone or buprenorphine, are simply *substitutes* for heroin and fentanyl. Technically, this is true; the initial goal is for people who use drugs to replace one opioid with another. But this does not mean that the goal of MOUD is to "substitute" or "trade" one addiction or SUD for another. Addiction is best characterized as continued use despite harmful consequences—which is different from being physically dependent on a drug (e.g., those with diabetes are dependent on—but not addicted to—insulin). When someone transitions to MOUD, they will remain dependent on opioids, but the goal is to make sure that they are no longer *addicted* to opioids. Some individuals receiving MOUD—but not all—will eventually abstain from opioid use, and achieving abstinence often requires multiple treatment episodes.

One must also account for the fact that these substances have very different harm profiles from those of street-sourced opioids. Methadone can lead to overdose if too much is consumed, but the current OUD treatment regulatory system, with its focus on in-clinic administration and limits on take-home doses, reduces the risk of methadone overdose and diversion.[2] Overdoses involving Suboxone, which includes buprenorphine and naloxone and is the most common formulation of buprenorphine used in MOUD, are very rare and are often linked to the co-use of it and other substances (Lofwall and Walsh, 2014). In fact, the use of diverted Suboxone is most commonly consistent with therapeutic use and has been associated with lower risk of drug overdose (Carlson et al., 2020; Cicero, Ellis, and Chilcoat, 2018).

It is also the case that many primary care physicians are not interested in providing MOUD (Kennedy-Hendricks et al., 2020) and that higher levels of stigmatized attitudes about people with OUD are strongly associated with lower rates of providing MOUD (Stone et al., 2021). The very limited training that most physicians receive for treating SUDs (Howley, Whelan, and Rasouli, 2018; Isaacson et al., 2000; Morreale et al., 2020) likely contributes to and exacerbates this stigma.

Many communities are reluctant to accept public housing, drug treatment facilities, syringe service programs, and safe consumption sites (Davidson and Howe, 2014; Strang and Taylor, 2018). Opposition typically stems from concerns that these facilities would reduce property values and attract "undesirable individuals" to the neighborhood, who would

---

[2] In response to the coronavirus disease 2019 (COVID-19) pandemic, some of the restrictions about take-home doses and in-person visits were relaxed. It is unclear whether these measures will be made permanent, but there is some evidence to suggest that they did not lead to increases in methadone overdoses (Brothers, Viera, and Heimer, 2021). Related to expanding access to methadone, although not directly related to the pandemic, is that, in June 2021, the U.S. Drug Enforcement Administration (DEA) streamlined rules for obtaining a mobile methadone van license (The White House, 2021).

increase crime, disorder, and antisocial behavior and litter the community with discarded drug paraphernalia (Bernstein and Bennett, 2013; Takahashi, 1997). Communities may also be opposed to spending public money on individuals whom they perceive as undeserving, perhaps even seeing them as responsible for their difficult situations (Taylor et al., 2021; Tempalski et al., 2007).

As a result, those who have entered treatment for SUDs may find opportunities for social interactions and employment sharply curtailed relative to what would have been the case had they never started using drugs; if they start using again after treatment, those opportunities are further reduced. These attitudes, in turn, create a barrier or disincentive for individuals with OUD to identify themselves.

Nine Portfolios of Action

Each of the preceding chapters offers ideas for addressing opioid-related problems, and all of these ideas are listed in Appendix A. Some of the policy opportunities we describe, such as increasing funding of and access to effective treatment for OUD, safer opioid prescribing, and other efforts to reduce the nonprescribed use of opioids, are also discussed in many other publications (e.g., Christie et al., 2017; Frank, Humphreys, and Pollack, 2021; Humphreys et al., 2022; Saloner et al., 2018).

However, the main contribution of this study is to identify opportunities at the intersections of the ecosystem's components and highlight other cross-sector initiatives that could mitigate the harmful effects of opioids. To this end, the remainder of our discussion focuses on two areas of policy opportunities: (1) changes *across* components of the ecosystem and (2) changes *within* components of the ecosystem. To keep the latter area manageable, we limit our discussion to those components within which a change could have the largest ripple effects: SUD treatment, medical care, the criminal legal system, illegal supply and supply control, and harm reduction and community-initiated interventions. Our goal is not to be exhaustive, but rather to highlight opportunities within each sector that have the potential to make the largest overall contributions to confronting the crisis.

We offer nine portfolios of action that could help decisionmakers prioritize and organize their efforts to address the opioid crisis:

1. supporting individuals as they move across ecosystem components
2. coordinating across components and addressing different priorities
3. addressing legal consequences and stigma associated with drug use or possession
4. preventing nonprescribed opioid use and escalation to OUD
5. identifying individuals who need treatment, increasing access to effective treatment, and enhancing support to make treatment more effective
6. reducing the probability that an overdose is fatal
7. addressing nontreatment needs of individuals using opioids for nonprescribed purposes

8. mitigating the burdens that opioids impose on family members
9. improving the data infrastructure for understanding people who use drugs, drug consumption, and drug markets.

The first three portfolios directly address the cross-sector barriers we have just described. The other six not only reflect common themes emerging from this report but also suggest where an ecosystem approach offers insights for moving forward. The evidence for the ideas making up the portfolios varies dramatically. In some cases, an idea is supported by peer-reviewed research. Other ideas may have worked as a pilot, may be a logical extension from research in a similar area, or may be a theoretically grounded suggestion with little or no empirical support. For each idea, we characterize the nature of the evidence, identify which level of government would be most relevant for its implementation, and note whether the idea originates at the intersection of multiple system components or originates within a component but has important consequences for the rest of the ecosystem.

In some cases, it would seem to make sense to proceed—for example, by enhancing access to an intervention with demonstrated effectiveness. However, we might note that there is no research showing that a particular action (e.g., a suggested way of enhancing access) will generate benefits. The absence of evidence is not necessarily evidence of absence, particularly for things that have not been studied at all.

We caution that including an idea in one of these portfolios should not be considered a full-throated endorsement; we recognize the complexities, challenges, and potential downsides and opportunity costs of implementing these ideas. More importantly, the scope of the problem, the service infrastructure, and the policy environment vary dramatically across the country; thus, a universal recommendation for all states and localities would be presumptuous, inappropriate, and, in many places, politically unfeasible.

However, the opioid crisis is not lessening; it is intensifying. Hence, all these suggestions merit serious consideration and analysis.

Supporting Individuals as They Move Across Ecosystem Components

Several steps can be taken to address the challenges that occur as individuals move across components of the ecosystem. At the juncture between components, it is unclear who is responsible for a successful transition. In many cases, this means that no part of the system has primary responsibility.

Someone should take ownership of assisting people in their journey through the ecosystem. Although many components use case managers, some of whom work across components (e.g., treatment providers helping patients get access to social services), individuals with OUD often fall through the cracks. Some of the disconnects hampering treatment and support could be diminished if each community had some entity that was clearly responsible at these junctures and could provide the resources necessary to cover the additional responsibility.

One model that could address this disconnect is providing some individuals with OUD with comprehensive case management services that go beyond traditional case management approaches in continuity of service and in the extent to which the services stay engaged with the individuals. Existing evidence supports the benefits of various case management models, including those with more-intensive engagement with clients (Penzenstadler et al., 2017). However, the effect of case management intensity remains underexplored (Vanderplasschen et al., 2019), and existing models likely stop short of the long-term continuous engagement we call for here.

A second and related challenge is the paucity of information regarding what happens to individuals when they leave a system component. For example, SUD clinicians may learn what happens to a patient who leaves treatment if the patient relapses and returns to specialty care, but they are much less likely to know whether a patient is able to stay employed or has a fatal overdose. Yet information about what happens outside one's own system is critical to knowing how one's actions affect individuals across the ecosystem and understanding one's role in the system.

Data limitations have constrained our ability to provide continuous support for individuals across system components and to answer many policy-relevant questions, some of which are as basic as knowing how many people use opioids and what share of those people have OUD. There are important data limitations because of privacy concerns; however, there are examples of merging individual-level information in a way that protects privacy but still provides substantial information about what happens across components.

Massachusetts and Maryland are examples of successful approaches to merging data, and studies show how these data can be used. For instance, Smart et al.'s 2018 report, *Data Sources and Data-Linking Strategies to Support Research to Address the Opioid Crisis*, highlights that

> **Massachusetts** is a noted example of state success in linking [Prescription Drug Monitoring Program (PDMP)] data to a broad range of other public health and criminal justice data sources. Chapter 55 of the Acts of 2015 permitted the linkage and analysis of several government data sources to inform programmatic decisions, guide the development of policies, and advance understanding of the opioid crisis.[3] Under Chapter 55, Massachusetts' Department of Public Health has connected (in most cases, at the individual level) ten data sources managed by five state agencies to develop a data warehouse structure. The system also collects community-level data on naloxone (e.g., enrollments, refills, and rescues through the Massachusetts Department of Public Health Naloxone program), drug seizures, and socioeconomic and demographic characteristics. . . .
>
> **Maryland** is another example of a state that has overcome interpretational challenges of 42 CFR Part II (establishing special privacy protections for health care records related to the treatment of substance use disorders) and is currently advancing efforts to link person-level data from the PDMP, drug use and alcohol treatment admissions, hospi-

---

[3] Data assembled under Chapter 55 are now referred to as the Public Health Data system.

tal admissions, fatalities investigated by the medical examiner, and criminal justice data.... (Smart et al., 2018, p. 48)

However, we are unaware of studies demonstrating the effects of merging data in this way.

We offer some thoughts for using case management to support individuals in their transit across ecosystem components and suggest ways in which data can be merged to understand these interactions while also responding to data privacy concerns. (Additional ideas about improving data collection and analyses to support these efforts are provided in the box.)

Coordinating Across Components and Addressing Different Priorities

Leaders within each part of the ecosystem will continue to make policies and decisions that they believe are best aligned with their missions. Taking an ecosystem approach can provide more clarity about the contradictions and conflicts across these components and force policymakers (especially those tasked with coordinating these efforts and/or allocating funds) to be more explicit about the trade-offs they confront and compromises they have to make. Ultimately, decisions will be based on the values of those in positions of power, and this is certainly not unique to drug policy.

Ideas to Support Individuals Moving Across Ecosystem Components

Support individuals with comprehensive case management, an approach that is based on proactively addressing the needs of individuals in multiple ways. This model should go beyond regular case management by helping people with OUD navigate the landscape of existing providers; developing a plan for appropriate services; and establishing linkages and relationships with corresponding agencies, among other actions. Such comprehensive case managers could remain involved with individuals throughout periods when more-traditional case managers are not involved, such as during an individual's incarceration. This involvement would enable managers to address needs proactively during high-risk periods, such as release from incarceration. Such a model would likely require new sources of funding, probably from state and local governments or foundations; therefore, case managers would be involved with individuals when they are uninsured and not supported by social services. (Policy level: state and/or local; Evidence: emerging; Relevant chapter: Fourteen.)

Merge individual-level data across multiple components to better understand how components interact and how individuals flow across them. This information could also be used to conduct more-rigorous evaluations of policy interventions intended to reduce nonprescribed use of opioids and related harms. (Policy level: state and/or local; Evidence: studies have shown how data can be used, but we are unaware of studies demonstrating the effects of such use; Relevant chapter: Fourteen.)

At the federal level, the Office of National Drug Control Policy (ONDCP) was created to help coordinate the various federal systems addressing substance use and drug problems. Unfortunately, ONDCP played a diminished role in the Trump administration, partially because of staffing and funding issues (Bellware and O'Harrow, 2020), but also because of other federal efforts seeking to serve a similar role (Ehley and Karlin-Smith, 2018; Mann, 2020). ONDCP is playing a more active role in the Biden administration and should continue to work closely with the U.S. Department of Health and Human Services, the U.S. Department of Justice, and other federal entities to help prioritize how federal funds are spent to address drug problems. The bipartisan, bicameral, and multiagency Commission on Combating Synthetic Opioid Trafficking also recommends that the head of ONDCP rejoin the President's cabinet (Commission on Combating Synthetic Opioid Trafficking, 2022).

At the state and local levels, similar coordination issues and mission conflicts persist. That said, some states have been successful at creating interagency task forces stood up by governors to mitigate opioid-related harms, involving people from the health, criminal justice, and social service systems (see, e.g., Pennsylvania Opioid Command Center, undated). In the areas of health and well-being, the idea of cultivating and supporting "system stewards" is increasingly discussed as an approach to addressing cross-sectoral challenges and exploiting opportunities at the intersections of these systems. Broadly speaking, these stewards are described as "leaders (people and organizations) who take responsibility for forming working relationships with others to drive transformative change" (ReThink Health, undated). The idea of stewardship in the realm of public service is not new (see, e.g., Armstrong, 1997); however, we are unaware of any efforts to cultivate stewards focused specifically on issues surrounding the opioid ecosystem.

Another opportunity would be to engage leaders in opioid gaming exercises that prompt them to consider new approaches and work through how those decisions may affect the various system components and their interactions. This approach became popular in the 1940s as a way to think about nuclear deterrence, but it has been adapted to multiple social policy areas, including drug policy (Kahan et al., 1992). Gaming is also consistent with calls to use additional methods to understand the "bigger opioid picture" and its complexities and interrelationships (Jalali et al., 2020). The exercises bring coordination issues and mission conflicts to the forefront, making it easier to identify both cross-sector barriers and opportunities. (Ideas about promoting coordination across system components are provided in the box on the next page.)

Ideas to Promote Coordination Across System Components

Improve systems-level coordination on opioid policy at the federal level by streamlining the multiple federal opioid efforts that exist and reviving ONDCP's role as the primary coordinating body on issues surrounding substance use and drug policy. (Policy level: federal; Evidence: no empirical studies of effectiveness.)

Cultivate, identify, and support stewards who are tasked with addressing cross-sectoral challenges and exploiting opportunities at the intersections of these sectors. This is a position that could be funded by government or foundations, but the desire to create such a role must be endorsed by local decisionmakers. (Policy level: state and/or local; Evidence: no empirical studies of effectiveness.)

Create opioid policy gaming exercises with state and local system leaders to consider new approaches and work through how these decisions may affect the various systems and their interactions. The games could be coordinated by government officials, nonprofit organizations, and/or philanthropic foundations. (Policy level: state and/or local; Evidence: no empirical studies of effectiveness for opioids.)

Addressing Legal Consequences and Stigma Associated with Drug Use or Possession

State and federal laws allow—and sometimes require—that individuals with criminal records be prevented from certain government services or opportunities, and some of these laws are specific to those with criminal records for drug violations. (Additional ideas about addressing legal consequences and stigma are provided in the box on the next page.)

Changing these laws could reduce some of these barriers, but so could changing drug laws and making it easier to expunge or seal minor drug-specific criminal offenses. Of course, many individuals with records for drug offenses have other offenses on their records, potentially limiting the impact of any legal reforms (see Chapter Two).

Decriminalizing the possession of drugs might influence how people think about drug use and people who use drugs, but there has not been much empirical investigation of this claim. It is clearly not an automatic connection: Some U.S. states decriminalized cannabis in the 1970s, but then attitudes toward cannabis hardened considerably during the 1980s. Thus, the correlation between (1) decriminalization—and even legalization of cannabis more recently—and (2) growing societal acceptance is not automatic. In addition, the direction of the causal arrow(s) is not entirely clear, even if they are present. There are other consequences of decriminalization to be considered. (We discuss these consequences further in Chapter Six).

It should be noted that decriminalization need not be a permanent change. Cautious jurisdictions could implement decriminalization (or other reforms related to possession) with a sunset provision that could give them an escape clause if the changes do not work as expected.

Ideas to Address Legal Consequences and Stigma Associated with Drug Use or Possession

Across system components

- **Increase education for the media and decisionmakers in the use of nonstigmatizing language** related to SUDs. Ashford, Brown, and Curtis, 2019, and the Northeastern University School of Law's Health in Justice Action Lab, 2019, offer useful suggestions for discussing substance use, addiction, and people who use drugs in a nonstigmatizing manner. (Policy level: federal, state, local, and nongovernmental; Evidence: no empirical studies of effectiveness.)

Within system components

- **Increase preclinical and clinical training for treating SUDs.** Many medical students, physician residents, and other clinical trainees receive minimal instruction for treating SUDs. Enhancing such training will increase awareness that individuals with OUD and other SUDs can be successfully treated. The training would also normalize the treatment of such disorders. (Policy level: nongovernmental; Evidence: emerging evidence of effectiveness discussed in Chapter Five.)
- **Make it easier for individuals with minor drug convictions to expunge or seal these offenses from their criminal records.** This change can reduce barriers to social services and possibly increase employment opportunities. The adjustment will require legal changes. In some states, the process could be made automatic instead of putting the onus on the individual to petition the court. (Policy level: federal, state, and local; Evidence: no empirical studies of effectiveness for drug offenses; Relevant chapters: Chapters Six, Ten, and Eleven.)
- **Consider reforming drug possession laws and/or how they are enforced.** Reforms to heroin- and other drug–possession laws have been implemented in other countries, and decriminalizing possession—which was approved by Oregon voters in November 2020—is supported by international organizations including the World Health Organization and the Organization of American States. Reducing the expected sanction for possessing drugs can take many forms, from changing policing practices, to reducing penalties, to legalizing possession (not sales). The potential pros and cons of each approach deserve more attention. It should be noted that Portugal's oft-cited reforms, as well as Oregon's, included much more than decriminalizing drug possession. (Policy level: primarily state and local, but could happen at the federal level; Evidence: no empirical studies of decriminalization in the United States beyond cannabis, and we are not aware of any that measure effects on stigma; Relevant chapters: Chapter Six.)

But the stigma associated with opioid use and some evidence-based treatments extends beyond the sphere of the criminal legal system, and even countries that take a much less punitive approach to drug policy—such as Canada—report that stigma continues to be a barrier (Public Health Agency of Canada, 2020).

Preventing Nonprescribed Opioid Use and Escalation to Opioid Use Disorder

A common theme appearing in multiple chapters is the importance of preventing opioid misuse, particularly for individuals at higher risk of developing OUD. Multiple evidence-based interventions focus on general risk factors for youth and barriers to development that are not opioid-specific; however, they have been demonstrated to produce a modest but statistically significant reduction in drug use initiation by youth by delaying or preventing experimentation and misuse of other drugs. Some may target youth in schools (e.g., Life Skills; see Botvin and Griffin, 2004), while others can involve a larger community effort (e.g., Getting to Outcomes; see Wandersman et al., 2000). It is possible that these efforts might improve outcomes related to opioids, but they could also help build skills that could ultimately affect other systems, such as education, social services, and employment. (Ideas about preventing nonprescribed opioid use are provided in the box on the next page.)

Of course, the risk of prescribed or nonmedical opioid use escalating to OUD is not salient only among youth. For example, the employment chapter (Chapter Twelve) highlighted a touch point where work-related or work-caused pain can lead to prescriptions for opioid analgesics, which, in turn, may lead to dependence for a small percentage of individuals and, for some, may lead to addiction. Likewise, the opportunity to make money (sometimes a lot of money) by obtaining prescription opioids and selling them in illegal markets can generate supply that supports misuse and addiction. Efforts to decrease clinically unnecessary prescribing of opioids can decrease the numbers of individuals exposed to opioids, either directly or via people obtaining prescription opioids to divert. Such efforts often decrease the amount of opioids individuals receive. Receipt of clinically unnecessary opioids may be decreased, but in other cases, these policies might have the unintended consequence of decreasing access for individuals who benefit from opioid analgesics (see Chapter One for more information).

Efforts to decrease clinically unnecessary use of opioids can be supported in several ways. Making it easier for these individuals to access non-opioid–related pain therapies can, in some cases, decrease or even eliminate the need for opioid therapy. Similarly, employers who can help employees suffering from chronic pain transition to less physically demanding jobs may reduce the probability that opioid use escalates to a disorder.

There is also a broader variety of more-general efforts to decrease the clinically unnecessary prescribing of and general availability of opioid analgesics that could be misused or diverted for misuse by others. These efforts include clinical prescribing guidelines, prescription limits, changes to defaults in electronic prescribing systems, feedback to clinicians regarding opioid prescribing or outcomes, and the provision of safe ways to dispose of unused

Ideas to Prevent Nonprescribed Opioid Use and Escalation to OUD

Across system components

- **Increase referrals and access to quality mental health care.** Increasing the likelihood that individuals with mental health disorders receive quality care can reduce the odds that they will be prescribed opioids and that they will misuse opioids and develop an OUD. Steps to achieve this goal touch on many components of the opioid ecosystem and include increasing treatment capacity, incentivizing use of effective mental health interventions, promoting integration of SUD and mental health treatment, and enhancing reimbursement of mental health treatment. (Policy level: federal, state, local, and nongovernmental; Evidence: no empirical studies; Relevant chapters: Chapter Five.)

Within system components

- **Reduce barriers to nonmedication treatments for chronic pain.** The more than 19 million Americans with severe chronic pain need better access to effective nonaddictive pain management. Improved access could include increased insurance coverage of nonpharmacological interventions, increased access to nonpharmacological approaches to pain management (in person or virtually when appropriate), and efforts to develop effective nonaddictive analgesic medications. (Policy level: federal, state, local, and nongovernmental; Evidence: no clinical trials of effectiveness; Relevant chapters: Chapters Five and Twelve.)
- **Take steps to reduce unnecessary prescribing of opioid analgesics.**[a] In addition to offering alternatives to opioid analgesics, efforts can be made to decrease the availability of prescribed opioid analgesics that could be misused. Prescribers should, however, be mindful of potential unintended consequences of reducing access to beneficial medications. Such steps to decrease availability include clinical prescribing guidelines, prescription limits, changes to defaults in electronic prescribing systems, feedback to clinicians regarding opioid prescribing or outcomes, and safe ways to dispose of unused or expired opioid analgesics. (Policy level: federal, state, local, and nongovernmental; Evidence: no clinical trials of effectiveness in preventing misuse or escalation; Relevant chapters: Chapters Four, Five, and Twelve.)
- **Enhance efforts to offer evidence-based skills training and drug prevention,** especially when school-based programs coordinate with community-based initiatives. (Policy level: state, local, and nongovernmental; Evidence: empirical studies provide some evidence that such programs can decrease use of other substances, no empirical studies of reducing opioid misuse that we are aware of; Relevant chapters: Chapters Ten and Thirteen.)

---

[a] After this report went to press, legislation introduced requirements for education of opioid prescribers.

or expired opioid analgesics. It is important to note, however, that some of these approaches have also raised concerns about unintended consequences of decreasing clinically beneficial opioid prescribing, and not all will work with those who are trying to profit from diverted prescription opioids. For example, offering the chance to dispose of unused opioids will have no effect on people who obtained prescriptions for the express purpose of reselling the pills to make money.

Better treatment of mental health disorders could also help prevent OUD, given that mental health disorders increase the likelihood of being prescribed opioids and the risk of opioid misuse and OUD. Efforts in this area could include increasing mental health treatment capacity, incentivizing the use of mental health interventions that have been demonstrated to be effective, enhancing reimbursement for the treatment of mental health disorders, and better integrating treatment for individuals with comorbid mental health disorders and SUDs to facilitate concurrent treatment of both disorders.

Identifying Individuals Who Need Treatment, Increasing Access to Effective Treatment, and Enhancing Support to Make Treatment More Effective

The United States needs to do a better job of identifying individuals who need treatment and making it easier for them to access and engage in it—whether that population includes those involved with the criminal legal system, parents grappling with the child welfare system, individuals receiving social services, individuals identified by their primary care doctors as having OUD, or those resuscitated by first responders with naloxone. Across all of these populations, a reoccurring theme is the urgent need to identify individuals who need treatment, remove barriers and disincentives to obtaining specialty care, and implement systemic changes to support successful engagement and retention in treatment.

Estimating the cost of providing high-quality OUD treatment to everyone who wants it is challenging because we do not know the underlying demand for treatment (see Chapter Two). But to help put the issue in perspective, we provide a back-of-the-envelope calculation that yields an order-of-magnitude estimate.[4] One study estimated that, in 2019, there were approximately 1 million people receiving MOUD (Krawczyk et al., 2022). If one sought to double this figure, total costs for the increase would likely be in the single-digit billions per year.[5] That sounds like a lot of money, but it is not when compared with the societal costs of OUD.

---

[4] This paragraph and the subsequent footnote are largely reproduced from Kilmer, 2020, p. 20.

[5] The Washington State Institute for Public Policy puts the per-participant costs of providing 12 months of methadone and buprenorphine treatment at $3,962 (+/– 20 percent) and $4,859 (+/– 60 percent), respectively (Washington State Institute for Public Policy, 2019b and 2019a, respectively). Some of the estimates appear to include some fixed costs and differ depending on services provided (see Kilmer et al., 2018, p. 37, footnote 37). For rough calculations, at $4,000 per year, getting 1 million more people into medication treatment with additional services for a year would cost in the ballpark of $4 billion annually. Doubling the

OUD is a chronic illness in which relapse is common; many individuals require ongoing treatment. To address their needs, the SUD workforce should be increased (Hoge et al., 2007), with an emphasis on providing training in effective interventions. Clinical training programs also need to enhance the training of the more general clinical workforce regarding the treatment of SUDs; such training has historically been neglected in many treatment programs.

Efforts to ensure that individuals receive the appropriate level and intensity of specialty SUD treatment may also have a role in increasing access to effective treatment (see, e.g., Mee-Lee et al., 2013). Recent research suggests that some individuals may be receiving intensive care in restricted settings without first being assessed to determine whether care in a less intensive setting would be appropriate (Beetham et al., 2021), while others are unable to access the level of care needed to address the severity of their illness.

But many other parts of the ecosystem contain barriers and disincentives to receiving or staying in treatment. Only by addressing these barriers and implementing systemic changes in systems that support engagement and ongoing treatment can stakeholders offer individuals the services likely to address their OUD.

None of the systems we have described has "hindering treatment for OUD" as one of its goals. But many of the systems, in pursuing their individual missions, can make it more difficult to connect individuals with needed treatment and help them remain engaged. These systems can also create barriers to supporting families of those with OUD.

We offer examples of these kinds of interactions in the box on the next page, suggesting how changes in multiple systems could facilitate making the needed connections and indicating how the changes could be initiated—e.g., by changing existing laws or practices or by creating new programs. Some of the ideas are quite focused; others are systemic.

Reducing the Probability That an Overdose Is Fatal

Preventing overdoses and the probability that they are fatal must be a top priority. Overdose death rates involving opioids were high when the problem was mostly with prescription opioids. As some people traded down to heroin, death rates became worse. Now, the proliferation of potent synthetic opioids has made them catastrophic. Synthetic opioids, which are sometimes sold as other substances and disguised in counterfeit pills, have increased uncertainty in illicit drug markets and elevated risks for people who use drugs, putting a premium on interventions that aim to reduce the likelihood that an overdose is fatal.

Because one of the factors contributing to elevated risks is uncertainty and lack of information about what a substance purchased in an illegal drug market actually contains, existing surveillance efforts across all components of the ecosystem should be intensified and new

---

methadone clients would likely require creating new clinics that should also be factored into these calculations. In addition, one should factor in the funds devoted to increasing outreach to those with OUD and increasing incentives to physicians to treat these patients. Costs could also be higher depending on the types of services provided beyond medication.

Ideas to Identify Individuals Who Need Treatment, Increase Treatment Access, and Make Treatment More Effective

Across system components

- **Promote interagency collaboration and care integration** by developing networks linking buprenorphine-prescribing primary care providers and substance use treatment experts, but also by fostering links between SUD treatment and almost all other systems. Efforts should be made to develop integrated health and social service models that screen for vulnerabilities in social determinants of health at any point of entry (the medical care system, SUD treatment system, child welfare system, criminal legal system, etc.), tailor services to individual needs, and provide integrated services in the setting most convenient for the patient. (Policy level: state, local, and nongovernmental; Evidence: growing evidence that such approaches are effective; Relevant chapters: Chapters Four, Five, Six, Eight, Nine, Ten, Eleven, and Thirteen.)
- **Develop local networks of service providers to identify individuals who could benefit from engaging in multiple services, and develop an outreach and engagement plan.** An emerging model of such an arrangement is the Hub model of service engagement (Nilson, 2016; Public Safety Canada, 2014), which originated in Canada and is being implemented in a small number of localities in Massachusetts. The model brings together representatives of relevant service providers and partner organizations (education, mental health, SUD treatment, social workers, law enforcement, etc.) on a regular basis to confidentially discuss individuals who present frequently at the services of one or more participants and are at elevated risk of adverse outcomes (not limited to SUD-related risks). If there is consensus that the person is at risk, the group develops an individual intervention plan to engage with the individual and offer access to services; these are typically led by representatives of the agency with which the person has already been in touch. (Policy level: local and nongovernmental; Evidence: no evidence of effectiveness in the United States but some from Canada.)

Within system components

- **Increase capacity for quality SUD treatment in specialty settings** to enhance access for individuals requiring specialty treatment for OUD and to ensure that the treatment is effective and likely to result in positive outcomes. Achieving this will require multiple efforts, including an expansion of the SUD workforce, an emphasis on training clinicians in effective treatment approaches, and an infusion of funds to support an expanded system providing higher-quality care.[a] (Policy level: federal, state, local, and nongovernmental; Evidence: clear evidence of MOUD effectiveness in general, no clinical trials of capacity expansion; Relevant chapters: Chapters Four and Five.)
- **Increase access to quality MOUD in primary care settings** by supporting the training of primary care clinicians in the use of buprenorphine and providing the incentives and infrastructure to support buprenorphine-trained clinicians in the ongo-

ing treatment of individuals with OUD. Access to MOUD may also be improved by reducing or eliminating federal regulations that govern the use of opioid agonists in treatment of OUD, such as the requirement to obtain a waiver from the DEA to prescribe buprenorphine and limits on the number of patients that can be treated concurrently.[b] (Policy level: federal, state, local, and nongovernmental; Evidence: clear evidence of MOUD effectiveness in general, no clinical trials of increased access in primary care settings; Relevant chapters: Chapters Four and Five.)

- **Reduce barriers to effective OUD treatment for individuals involved in the criminal legal system.** State and local criminal justice agencies could intensify existing efforts to implement various forms of diversion and deflection programs intended to (1) connect individuals with OUD with treatment services before or during their involvement with the criminal legal system and (2) reduce barriers to community corrections–based OUD treatment. Expansion of Medicaid can also help people involved in the criminal legal system access treatment for OUD. (Policy level: federal, state, and local; Evidence: existing evidence of effectiveness; Relevant chapters: Chapters Four, Six, and Nine.)

- **Implement and enforce laws and regulations requiring true parity in coverage of SUD and OUD services.** The Mental Health Parity and Addiction Equity Act of 2008 and the Affordable Care Act of 2010 sought to create parity of coverage between medical surgical care and mental health and SUD treatment. However, there are aspects of treatment, such as prior authorizations, concurrent review, and reimbursement rates, where disparities likely remain (Carlo, Barnett, and Frank, 2020). Ongoing efforts could improve OUD services and decrease the frequency with which individuals seek care outside network and pay more out of pocket—which is an expense many cannot afford. (Policy level: state and federal; Evidence: some evidence to suggest that parity matters; Relevant chapters: Chapters Four and Twelve.)

- **Change laws so that Medicaid benefits are not terminated as a result of incarceration,** which would help retain and increase access to treatment and other health services. (Policy level: federal, state; Evidence: no empirical studies of effectiveness, but there is evidence that access to Medicaid can improve outcomes for this population; Relevant chapter: Chapter Six.)

---

[a] Given the volume of current treatment needs, it appears more urgent to expand the provision of existing good-quality treatment services as opposed to investing in increasing access to the highest-tier treatment options. This step should be complemented by the deimplementation of low-quality treatment programs with little supporting evidence.

[b] After this volume went to press, the waiver requirement for prescribing buprenorphine for OUD was eliminated.

forms of market monitoring should be introduced. The capacity to undertake forensic examinations and analyses of law enforcement seizures should be strengthened to quickly capture information about the emergence of novel substances in the market.

In addition, such programs as wastewater monitoring and drug checking services could be introduced to provide near–real-time information on what is being consumed or purchased in a given jurisdiction. That information should be made available to health care and criminal justice professionals and to people who use drugs. This is especially important with respect to novel synthetic opioids and the heightened risks they produce. Drug checking services and wastewater monitoring have been introduced as regular market surveillance techniques in jurisdictions outside the United States (Castiglioni et al., 2021; Karamouzian et al., 2018; Tupper et al., 2018), but there are no formal evaluations of how these programs affect fatal overdoses.

Places that are not saturated with fentanyl can benefit greatly from improved surveillance, and places with an entrenched fentanyl problem may also benefit. Although individuals who use street-sourced powders in these communities may already suspect that fentanyl is in the drugs they are buying, those using pills may not. There is also concern about people purchasing other drugs, such as cocaine, that may be contaminated with fentanyl (perhaps inadvertently) (Nolan et al., 2019). There are dozens of synthetic opioids, and communities with a fentanyl problem will want to know whether more-potent synthetic opioids, such as carfentanil (which is roughly 100 times more potent than fentanyl) have entered the local market (Jalal and Burke, 2021).

Within individual system components, additional steps could be taken to further increase distribution of naloxone to maximize its availability in the community. First responder agencies, while increasingly equipped with naloxone themselves, could serve as an important distribution outlet for community members. Expanding access to naloxone through community overdose education and naloxone distribution (OEND) programs would also increase the availability of naloxone for individuals who may be in a position to administer it during an overdose. Similarly, increasing pharmacy distribution of naloxone can increase its availability to be administered during an overdose (Smart, Pardo, and Davis, 2021).[6]

To complement naloxone distribution, communities could invest in implementing drug checking services, where members of the public can test the content of their already purchased street drugs—for instance, by distributing fentanyl test strips or by implementing more-elaborate programs that offer on-demand chemical analysis of submitted samples. This is an important service not only for people who use opioids but also for those who use other substances and may be at risk of consuming a sample containing potent synthetic opioids without their knowledge. Drug checking can also provide public health and public safety

---

[6] There have also been calls for making naloxone an over-the-counter drug (see, e.g., Davis and Carr, 2020). As noted by Kilmer, 2020:

> Davis and Carr (2020) acknowledge that this move will likely reduce insurance coverage for the medication and increase costs for some people, but they cite a modelling study (Murphy et al., 2019) suggesting this would likely lead to a total increase in pharmacy sales. Murphy et al. note that the public health impact of such a move 'will depend on how likely the new population of [over-the-counter] naloxone consumers are to encounter an overdose and use the product relative to the population of existing naloxone consumers.' The overall impact will also depend on whether this change influences the consumption behaviors of people who use opioids. (Kilmer, 2020, p. 17)

departments with information about the emergence of new substances (or combinations of substances) in the local market. The emerging evidence on fentanyl strips suggests that some people who use drugs are interested in using the service (Krieger et al., 2018; Peiper et al., 2019), but, to date, there is no empirical evidence that the programs reduce overdoses.[7]

Relatedly, criminal justice agencies can reduce barriers faced by people who use drugs in accessing harm reduction services. For example, federal and state lawmakers can make it easier to implement and evaluate supervised consumption sites (SCSs). Local law enforcement agencies can clearly communicate that they will not interfere with SCSs and other harm reduction programs and that people who use drugs will not face any consequences for engaging with these services. There are no formal evaluations of such police declarations; however, lessons from the implementation of harm reduction programs and SCSs abroad suggest that police noninterference or cooperative attitudes are essential for program functioning (Strang and Taylor, 2018).[8]

In addition, addressing people's concerns about involving law enforcement when calling 911 may increase the likelihood that first responders are called to an opioid overdose. One way to address such concerns would be to introduce an emergency response system guaranteeing that the police would not be among the responding personnel. Some communities may decide to introduce a non-911 emergency number that is dedicated to reporting overdoses and that connects to local responders; the 911 option remains available to those who wish to use it. Other communities may instruct dispatchers not to summon the police for calls involving drug overdoses. Some communities have applied the latter principle in introducing nonpolice responders and co-responder models for mental health emergency calls because of concerns about police responding to a mental health crisis (particularly without accompanying co-responders) (Enos, 2020).

Excluding law enforcement from responding to overdose calls may not be an option for every community. For instance, in rural communities, law enforcement is often the nearest available responding agency, and excluding them could mean unacceptable delays in response times. For this reason, communities could decide which approach works best for their local circumstances.

Lastly, to reduce illegal supply, public health and safety agencies need to get innovative, especially when it comes to potent fentanyl and other synthetic opioids. With respect to law enforcement, efforts could be made to target importers and wholesalers higher in the supply chain who often use the internet to obtain and distribute fentanyl. The government could

---

[7] This is an area that is ripe for cost-benefit analysis, especially because the results may differ by type of testing and by the saturation of illegally produced synthetic opioids in the community.

[8] One noted limitation of SCSs is their scalability; it would be practically infeasible for SCSs to cover every use session, given the number of facilities needed. Pardo et al., 2019, showed that the United States would likely need more than 7,000 SCSs the size of Insite (which is in Vancouver and is probably the largest SCS in the world) to cover every use session in the country. That said, neither researchers nor practitioners nor policymakers consider perfect coverage a realistic goal, and existing evidence regarding the potential benefits of SCSs is already based on the fact that only a small share of use sessions takes place in SCSs.

attempt to disable websites that sell drugs, or at least swamp their comment boards with phony complaints. The DEA or another federal agency could set up phony drug-selling websites the way the Dutch police did with the Hansa network, to which many users migrated after the Alpha Bay cryptomarket website was shut down (Europol, 2018). Other DEA-operated counterfeit sites could promise—but not deliver—synthetic opioids, sending either nothing or inert powders. Even if purchasers do not face arrest, the failure of some sites to fulfill orders might stimulate general wariness of online procurement, reducing the demand for actual fentanyl sellers. (Additional ideas about reducing the probability that an overdose is fatal are provided in the box.)

It is hard to determine how dealers would adapt to these supply-side efforts. However, the fact that some of these individuals use the internet to transact sales offers law enforcement unique insights and opportunities.[9]

Ideas to Reduce the Probability That an Overdose Is Fatal

Across system components

- **Increase market surveillance so that people who use drugs, along with public health and public safety practitioners, know what is being consumed or purchased, especially in areas that are at risk of synthetic opioid exposure.** Surveillance should include not only traditional efforts, such as forensic examinations and law enforcement seizure analyses, but also novel programs, such as wastewater monitoring or drug checking services, to offer real-time information on substances available in a given jurisdiction. (Policy level: federal, state, and local; Evidence: no empirical evidence of effectiveness; Relevant chapters: discussed in Chapters Seven and Eight and in the box titled "Ideas to Improve the Data Infrastructure for Understanding People Who Use Drugs, Drug Consumption, and Drug Markets" later in this chapter.)

Within system components

- **Increase funding for community provision of naloxone.** Greater investment should be made to increase the availability of this overdose reversal agent in the community. Such funding could support training and distribution of OEND programs, first responder use of naloxone, and naloxone dispensed through pharmacies when it is not covered by insurance. Funding could also be used to support first responder naloxone leave-behind programs and enable first responder agencies to serve as naloxone distribution centers even outside the context of responding to overdoses. (Policy level: federal, state, local, and nongovernmental; Evidence: emerging evidence that increased access and training is associated with fewer fatal overdoses; Relevant chapters: Chapters Eight and Nine.)

---

[9] The last two paragraphs are largely reproduced from Pardo et al., 2019.

- **Increase community provision of drug content testing services** (e.g., fentanyl test strip distribution schemes), where members of the public can confirm the chemical composition of the drugs they purchased before consuming them. Where the testing is done by service providers rather than by people who use drugs themselves, results may also be provided to public health and public safety authorities for market surveillance purposes. (Policy level: federal, state, and local; Evidence: no empirical studies of effectiveness on reducing overdoses; Relevant chapter: Chapter Eight.)

- **Reduce state and federal barriers to local experimentation with and implementation of SCSs.** For example, the U.S. Department of Justice could make it easier for local jurisdictions to pilot and evaluate SCSs by releasing a memorandum indicating that it will not prioritize targeting sites that conform with state and local laws. (Policy level: federal, state, and local; Evidence: most international studies on SCSs are positive, but there are relatively few high-quality studies with strong comparison groups; Relevant chapters: Chapters Six and Eight.)

- **Law enforcement could clearly communicate that individuals will not be arrested for patronizing or working at syringe service programs or places where individuals can test the content of their drugs** to guard against inadvertent inclusion of contaminants, such as fentanyl. This could also send a signal that individuals who use drugs and those who help them are valuable members of the community and should not be stigmatized. (Policy level: state and local; Evidence: no empirical studies of effectiveness; Relevant chapters: Chapters Six and Eight.)

- **Introduce an emergency response system for reporting suspected drug overdoses** (e.g., via a dedicated non-911 number or through dispatch arrangements), so that callers would be guaranteed that law enforcement officials would not be among the dispatched responding personnel. (Policy level: state and local; Evidence: no empirical studies of effectiveness; Relevant chapter: Chapter Nine.)

- **Get creative about disrupting the supply of illegally produced synthetic opioids.** We do not think it is possible to eliminate the supply of illegally produced fentanyl and other synthetic opioids. However, delaying the entrenchment of fentanyl in a community's drug supply could save many lives. To the extent that some wholesalers are accessing these substances via the internet, disrupting these transactions by hacking into or creating fake websites is a low-cost approach worth considering. (Policy levels: federal, state, and local; Evidence: no evidence of effectiveness about the effect of disrupting web transactions; Relevant chapter: Chapter Seven.)

Addressing Nontreatment Needs of Individuals Using Opioids for Nonprescribed Purposes

Stability in an individual's life often promotes reduced drug use and better treatment outcomes. Many chapters identified policies designed to enhance other services that are likely to improve the outcomes of individuals with OUD. Housing is consistently identified as one of the main facilitators of recovery from OUD.

Housing First has emerged as an approach that addresses the needs and concerns of individuals who are homeless (Pfefferle, Karon, and Wyant, 2019). In contrast with recovery housing options, Housing First has few or no entry requirements related to treatment participation or other conditions. Existing literature demonstrates that the approach is effective in providing stable housing and availability of services (Kerman et al., 2021), but evidence with respect to clients with OUD needs strengthening.

In the box, we offer examples of how changing existing policies and practices—and, in some cases, implementing new programs—could help address nontreatment needs.

Ideas to Address Nontreatment Needs of Individuals Using Opioids for Nonprescribed Purposes

Across system components

- **Build on efforts to revise laws and other policies that make it harder for those with drug convictions to access services, such as nutritional assistance and public housing.** (Policy level: federal, state, and local; Evidence: there are studies documenting barriers and some negative effects of these restrictions, but we are not aware of studies evaluating the effects of removing these barriers; Relevant chapters: Chapters Six, Ten, Eleven, and Thirteen.)
- **Support research and data-collection efforts to learn more about size and characteristics of this population and how it is changing.** Better understanding drug markets in the era of fentanyl and other synthetic opioids (e.g., via qualitative research methods) and resurrecting some version of the Arrestee Drug Abuse Monitoring (ADAM) program would help with these efforts. (Policy level: federal, state, local, and nongovernmental; Evidence: surveillance is critical for understanding the problem and evaluating interventions; Relevant chapters: discussed in Chapters Two, Six, Seven, Ten, and Eleven and in the box titled "Ideas to Improve the Data Infrastructure for Understanding People Who Use Drugs, Drug Consumption, and Drug Markets" later in this chapter.)

Within system components

- **Expand integration of the Housing First model with OUD treatment.** Some shelters prohibit those who use drugs from entering, and individuals with a drug conviction can have problems obtaining public housing. However, being housed greatly

---

increases an individual's ability to find work and stay in treatment. (Policy level: state and local; Evidence: good evidence about homelessness in general, emerging evidence with respect to SUDs; Relevant chapters: discussed in Chapters Four and Eleven.)

- **Consider expanding SOAR.** Social Security Insurance/Social Security Disability Insurance (SSI/SSDI) Outreach, Access, and Recovery (SOAR), which is funded by the Substance Abuse and Mental Health Services Administration, "is a national program designed to increase access to the disability income benefit programs administered by the Social Security Administration (SSA) for eligible adults and children who are experiencing or are at risk of homelessness and have a serious mental illness, medical impairment, and/or a co-occurring substance use disorder" (National Alliance to End Homelessness, 2016). The program was begun to help address the low benefit-approval rates for people experiencing homelessness. SOAR facilitates communication among SSI/SSDI benefit applicants, case managers, SSA, Disability Determination Services, and community providers, helping ensure that an application for disability moves forward smoothly and does not fall between system cracks. (Policy level: federal; Evidence: no empirical studies of effectiveness; Relevant chapter: Chapter Eleven.)

Mitigating the Burdens That Opioids Impose on Family Members

The fallout from OUD reaches far beyond individuals who have OUD. The burdens it can impose on family members include financial stress, emotional hardship, impacts on physical health, and involvement with the criminal legal system (e.g., if the family member has drugs in their household). It is hard to precisely calculate the harms OUD imposes on family members, but the toll is large and meaningful. A back-of-the-envelope calculation offered in Chapter Three (and inspired by Mark Kleiman) helps make this point: What is the average person's willingness to pay to avoid having a family member struggle with OUD for a year? We are unaware of anyone who has yet tried to estimate the number, but suppose, for the sake of argument, that it is $10,000. If there were approximately 4 million Americans struggling with OUD and, on average, they had two family members willing to pay that amount, then families' collective willingness to pay to avoid that OUD is 4 million × 2 × $10,000 = $80 billion per year.

Reducing the probability of OUD and shortening the time until someone with OUD is in treatment and/or recovery are paramount. However, there are additional opportunities to improve the lives of those with OUD and their families. Continuing to make it easier for families to access and use naloxone could reduce the probability that an overdose becomes fatal and thus help alleviate at least some of family members' concerns.

However, much more could be done. For example, social service and medical care agencies could help family members deal with the stress and other psychological consequences of having a family member with OUD—perhaps as part of a follow-up after an overdose. This is already part of some post-overdose outreach programs, which, in addition to engaging with the affected individual, offer information on and linkages to support services for family members (Formica et al., 2021). Providing additional support for informal caretakers for the children of individuals with OUD may relieve stress on the caretakers and reduce the probability that these children suffer a variety of adverse outcomes, including ending up in the child welfare system.[10] In the box, we discuss ideas for mitigating burdens imposed on family members of those with OUD.

Ideas to Mitigate Burdens Imposed on Family Members of Those with Opioid Use Disorder

Across system components

- **Help family members cope with the stress and other psychological consequences of having a family member with OUD.** This could require efforts to enhance the linkages between (1) systems serving individuals with OUD and their families and (2) local mental health providers, efforts to increase the services provided to family members by clinical systems serving individuals with OUD, and efforts to educate families and address the stigma of having a family member with OUD. (Policy level: state, local, and nongovernmental; Evidence: no empirical studies of effectiveness; Relevant chapters: Chapters Three, Four, Ten, and Thirteen.)
- **Provide additional support for those who serve as informal caretakers** for the children of people with OUD to relieve stress on the caretakers and reduce the probability that the children end up in the child welfare system. (Policy level: state, local, and nongovernmental; Evidence: no empirical studies of effectiveness; Relevant chapters: Chapters Three, Four, and Ten.)
- **Amend punitive state laws regarding drug use in pregnancy** because such laws may deter women from seeking treatment, increasing the risk that a child will be born with neonatal opioid withdrawal syndrome. (Policy level: state; Evidence: some empirical evidence regarding the effects of such laws; Relevant chapter: Chapter Ten.)

Within system components

- **Increase access to naloxone and trainings on how to administer it** to family members and friends of those who use opioids. This could be a coordinated effort with first responders and community organizations focused on harm reduction. These efforts can also be used to educate families about Good Samaritan laws. (Policy level: federal, state, local, and nongovernmental; Evidence: emerging evidence that increased access and training is associated with fewer fatal overdoses, but this evidence is not specific to families; Relevant chapters: Chapters Three, Eight, and Nine.)

---

[10] Another idea would be to provide vouchers (and/or tax relief) for those living in households affected by OUD. Policymakers do not do this for other chronic conditions, and it raises important questions about unintended consequences and equity. We discuss this question in greater detail in Chapter Three.

> • **Consider amending the Adoption and Safe Families Act**, which requires terminating a parent's rights if the parent is not ready for reunification after a child has been in foster care for 15 of the past 22 months. As a result, when parents struggle with OUD, they are sometimes unable to complete treatment in time to reunite with their children. (Policy level: federal; Evidence: no empirical studies of effectiveness; Relevant chapter: Chapter Ten.)

Improving the Data Infrastructure for Understanding People Who Use Drugs, Drug Consumption, and Drug Markets

The United States lacks critical information about the number of people with OUD and/or those using illegally produced opioids. This creates challenges for efficiently allocating resources, monitoring changes in these markets, and conducting rigorous program and policy evaluations.

The HIV/AIDS crisis prompted large-scale investments in new data and monitoring systems, such as the National HIV Behavioral Surveillance system. Overdose deaths involving opioids, which now kill more people than HIV/AIDS did at its peak, have not elicited any comparable investment in data infrastructure.

It is necessary to step up efforts to learn more about the size and characteristics of the population of people who use opioids and how it is changing. Better understanding drug markets in the era of fentanyl and other synthetic opioids (e.g., via qualitative research methods) and resurrecting some version of the ADAM program would help with these efforts. Indeed, one could imagine a version of ADAM, supported by the various federal agencies that address this population (e.g., the U.S. Department of Justice, U.S. Department of Health and Human Services, ONDCP, U.S. Department of Housing and Urban Development, U.S. Department of Labor), that could sharpen understanding of these individuals and their needs, service utilization, and cross-sector barriers to reducing drug-related harms. (We discuss ideas to improve the data infrastructure in the box on the next page.)

Ideas to Improve the Data Infrastructure for Understanding People Who Use Drugs, Drug Consumption, and Drug Markets

Across system components

- **Introduce a community behavioral surveillance program.** One option to generate knowledge about local drug markets and collect insights from people who use opioids is to introduce a community-based behavioral surveillance program. Such a program could engage with individuals who are neither in treatment nor subject to criminal justice supervision, thus addressing a major information gap. One such model that could be adapted for work with individuals who use opioids is the National HIV Behavioral Surveillance program. A similar principle, perhaps involving low-threshold facilities, such as syringe service programs, could be applied in the context of people who use opioids. (Policy level: federal, state, and local; Relevant chapter: Chapter Two.)

- **Use wastewater testing to track and possibly measure drug consumption, including synthetic opioids.** Novel approaches to measuring drug consumption might be needed, especially because many fentanyl analogs and other synthetic opioids enter and exit markets quickly. Users themselves might not know that they consumed a synthetic opioid, let alone be able to point to which compound was supplied. Wastewater testing is another way to monitor the spread of new psychoactive substances and to measure consumption (Castiglioni, 2016). This technique—which is used in Europe and to a much lesser extent in the United States—can supplement traditional epidemiological drug indicators (such as prevalence rates or overdoses). For example, wastewater analysis in Washington state found sharp increases in cannabis consumption after legalization (Burgard et al., 2019). In Oregon, it showed that higher concentrations of drug metabolites were found in municipalities that reported higher rates of drug use (Banta-Green et al., 2009). (Policy level: federal, state, and local; Relevant chapter: Chapter Two.)

- **Resurrect some version of the ADAM program.** The ADAM program collected rich drug market data (including urinalysis results) from thousands of individuals arrested and jailed for any offense. As with wastewater testing, ADAM's biological testing could serve as an early-warning and monitoring system. One could also imagine modules (funded by the National Institutes of Health, National Institute of Justice, and other federal agencies or departments) that ask people who use and/or sell heroin about their experiences and decisions around fentanyl and other synthetic opioids. (Policy level: federal, state, and local; Relevant chapter: Chapter Two.)

Within system components

- **Improve analyses of data collected by the DEA.** For decades, the DEA has collected data on the price and purity of drugs purchased in undercover buys and the purity of seizures analyzed in federal laboratories in an administrative data set known as the System to Retrieve Information About Drug Evidence (STRIDE, which has now been reinvented as STARLIMS). These price and purity data have been a mainstay of empirical research in drug markets, but it has become increasingly difficult for researchers to access these data. The National Forensic Laboratory Information System collects results of forensic tests of seized drugs for many state and local law enforcement agencies; however, only aggregate-level reports—such as the share of all cocaine samples that also contained a synthetic opioid—are made public. Much could be learned by making the incident-level data available for research purposes, with appropriate privacy protections, such as removing exact dates and locations. (Policy level: federal; Relevant chapter: Chapter Seven.)

- **Validate the National Survey on Drug Use and Health (NSDUH) and add questions specific to synthetic opioid use and the consequences of opioid use on families.** Because it seems likely that NSDUH will continue to play a major role in policy discussions and evaluations on drug-related matters, researchers need to know whether it is accurate. Validation need not happen annually, but incorporating a regular validity test into a survey that costs approximately $50 million per year seems like a wise investment—especially as researchers seek more information about illegally produced fentanyl that respondents may not know they are consuming. It would also be astute to add a market module that focuses on the amount of opioids obtained during the most recent or typical transaction; whether the respondent paid for them and, if so, how much; and whether they resold or gave any opioids away. NSDUH could add questions to learn more about how families are affected by a relative's opioid use and/or OUD. Indeed, getting a better sense of how many people have been negatively affected and how they have been affected would be immensely helpful for understanding the full social costs of OUD. (Policy level: federal; Relevant chapter: Chapter Two.)

Prioritizing Policy Considerations

We remind readers that just because an idea appears in the previous boxes does not mean it is a priority option—or even a good option—for every community. We recognize the complexities, challenges, and potential downsides of implementing these ideas. For some, there is a strong evidence base; others are ideas that have potential and deserve consideration. That said, some of the ideas, if implemented, might not be as effective as envisioned or could have detrimental unintended consequences.

But now is not the time to be timid.

So, how should decisionmakers choose among these options? The ideas are not mutually exclusive, but the costs of implementing them—the fiscal costs, as well as the political capital and coordination costs—indicate that trade-offs will have to be made. However, the trade-offs involved will differ depending on the existing service infrastructure and programs available within a particular jurisdiction and on the values of the people who live there.

Furthermore, the nature of the opioid crisis and its manifestation in various communities, along with community characteristics, are important determinants of which policies and interventions may be particularly welcome in which communities. Here are some examples highlighting both the nature of the required trade-offs and the difficulty of making them:

- Jurisdictions with markets that have been severely affected by synthetic opioids may want to prioritize ideas to reduce the probability that an overdose is fatal.
- Communities that have seen a substantial increase in the utilization of foster care and in the incidence of neonatal opioid withdrawal syndrome may want to pay attention to suggestions focused on addressing families' needs and improving access to treatment.
- In jurisdictions where there may be ongoing concerns about overprescribing opioid analgesics, ideas focused on preventing misuse and escalation to OUD would be highly relevant.
- Communities where work remains to be done on establishing an effective partnership between public health and public safety agencies may give special consideration to suggestions addressing stigma and discrimination.
- Rural communities may be keen to explore ways to better connect people with services dispersed across larger areas: for instance, by launching mobile methadone vans.

Key Takeaways

This report is arguably the most comprehensive analysis of opioids in 21st century America. The following four core messages can be derived from the detailed assessment:

- **U.S. issues surrounding opioids are most appropriately viewed in the context of an ecosystem.** Ecosystem components often focus on individuals, but their families also lie at the heart of the ecosystem. Each ecosystem component has its own mission, priorities, and funding, but policies furthering those priorities may hamper the efforts of other system components.
- **Current responses to U.S. opioid problems are insufficient—we need to innovate.** The federal government should make it easier—not harder—for states or localities to pilot and implement interventions. Because criminalization of drug possession and use creates barriers in many components of the ecosystem, jurisdictions could consider alternatives on a spectrum from changing enforcement practices to changing laws.
- **Individuals with OUD often touch multiple components of the ecosystem, but it is not always clear who is responsible for coordinating among components or managing the transition from one component to another.** Comprehensive case management that continues when traditional case management stops (e.g., incarceration) may be particularly helpful.
- **The United States is often flying blind, which makes it difficult to evaluate existing interventions, invent new ones, or improve understanding of ecosystem interactions.** The data infrastructure for understanding people who use drugs, drug consumption, and markets urgently needs improving.

Viewing the opioid crisis as an ecosystem requires adopting a comprehensive perspective. We have offered a detailed explanation of why that shift in perspective is so challenging, while also arguing that it is essential. Different actors in the ecosystem focus primarily on one population, each component of the system has its own priorities and policies, and initiatives target different components. No one has taken ownership of assisting people in their journey through the systems. Poor information hampers researchers' ability to understand how different parts of the ecosystem interact and how that interaction affects people passing through parts of the ecosystem.

Understanding the nature of the opioid ecosystem is a necessary step for decisionmakers seeking to move forward. They need to pay attention to multiple parts of the ecosystem at the same time. And they need reliable information to understand how policies interact and what the effects of the interactions are likely to be.

Moving away from siloed thinking and adopting an ecosystem approach will not only help stem the tide of the opioid crisis. It should also help mitigate the harmful consequences of other drug problems.

Abbreviations

ADAM	Arrestee Drug Abuse Monitoring
DEA	Drug Enforcement Administration
MOUD	medications for opioid use disorder
NSDUH	National Survey on Drug Use and Health
OEND	overdose education and naloxone distribution
ONDCP	Office of National Drug Control Policy
OUD	opioid use disorder
SCS	supervised consumption site
SUD	substance use disorder

References

Armstrong, Jim, *Stewardship and Public Service: A Discussion Paper*, Ottawa, Canada: James L. Armstrong and Associates, March 31, 1997.

Armstrong, Katrina, Mary Putt, Chanita Hughes Halbert, David Grande, J. Sanford Schwartz, Kaijun Liao, Noora Marcus, Mirar Bristol Demeter, and Judy A. Shea, "Prior Experiences of Racial Discrimination and Racial Differences in Health Care System Distrust," *Medical Care*, Vol. 51, No. 2, 2013, pp. 144–150.

Ashford, Robert David, Austin Brown, and Brenda Curtis, "Expanding Language Choices to Reduce Stigma: A Delphi Study of Positive and Negative Terms in Substance Use and Recovery," *Health Education*, Vol. 119, No. 1, 2019, pp. 51–62.

Banta-Green, Caleb J., Jennifer A. Field, Aurea C. Chiaia, Daniel L. Sudakin, Laura Power, and Luc de Montigny, "The Spatial Epidemiology of Cocaine, Methamphetamine and 3,4-methylenedioxymethamphetamine (MDMA) Use: A Demonstration Using a Population Measure of Community Drug Load Derived from Municipal Wastewater," *Addiction*, Vol. 104, No. 11, 2009, pp. 1874–1880.

Beetham, Tamara, Brendan Saloner, Marema Gaye, Sarah E. Wakeman, Richard G. Frank, and Michael Lawrence Barnett, "Admission Practices and Cost of Care for Opioid Use Disorder at Residential Addiction Treatment Programs in the US," *Health Affairs*, Vol. 40, No. 2, 2021, pp. 317–325.

Bellware, Kim, and Robert O'Harrow, Jr., "Trump Said Solving the Opioid Crisis Was a Top Priority. His Drug Office's Track Record Suggests Otherwise," *Washington Post*, October 3, 2020.

Bernstein, Scott E., and Darcie Bennett, "Zoned Out: 'NIMBYism,' Addiction Services and Municipal Governance in British Columbia," *International Journal of Drug Policy*, Vol. 24, No. 6, November 2013, pp. e61–e65.

Botvin, Gilbert J., and Kenneth W. Griffin, "Life Skills Training: Empirical Findings and Future Directions," *Journal of Primary Prevention*, Vol. 25, No. 2, 2004, pp. 211–232.

Brothers, Sarah, Adam Viera, and Robert Heimer, "Changes in Methadone Program Practices and Fatal Methadone Overdose Rates in Connecticut During COVID-19," *Journal of Substance Abuse Treatment*, Vol. 131, 2021.

Burgard, Daniel A., Jason Williams, Danielle Westerman, Rosie Rushing, Riley Carpenter, Addison LaRock, Jane Sadetsky, Jackson Clarke, Heather Fryhle, Melissa Pellman, and Caleb J. Banta-Green, "Using Wastewater-Based Analysis to Monitor the Effects of Legalized Retail Sales on Cannabis Consumption in Washington State, USA," *Addiction*, Vol. 114, No. 9, 2019, pp. 1582–1590.

Carlo, Andrew D., Brian S. Barnett, and Richard G. Frank, "Behavioral Health Parity Efforts in the US," *JAMA*, Vol. 324, No. 5, 2020, pp. 447–448.

Carlson, Robert G., Raminta Daniulaityte, Sydney M. Silverstein, Ramzi W. Nahhas, and Silvia S. Martins, "Unintentional Drug Overdose: Is More Frequent Use of Non-Prescribed Buprenorphine Associated with Lower Risk of Overdose?" *International Journal of Drug Policy*, Vol. 79, 2020.

Castiglioni, Sara, ed., *Assessing Illicit Drugs in Wastewater: Advances in Wastewater-Based Drug Epidemiology*, Luxembourg: European Monitoring Centre for Drugs and Drug Addiction, 2016.

Castiglioni, Sara, Noelia Salgueiro-González, Lubertus Bijlsma, Alberto Celma, Emma Gracia-Lor, Mihail Simion Beldean-Galea, Tomáš Mackuľak, Erik Emke, Ester Heath, Barbara Kasprzyk-Hordern, et al., "New Psychoactive Substances in Several European Populations Assessed by Wastewater-Based Epidemiology," *Water Research*, Vol. 195, 2021.

Child Welfare Information Gateway, *Parental Substance Use: A Primer for Child Welfare Professionals*, Washington, D.C.: U.S. Department of Health and Human Services, Administration for Children and Families, Children's Bureau, January 2021.

Christie, Chris, Charlie Baker, Roy Cooper, Patrick J. Kennedy, Bertha Madras, and Pam Bondi, *The President's Commission on Combating Drug Addiction and the Opioid Crisis*, Washington, D.C.: U.S. Government Printing Office, November 1, 2017.

Cicero, Theodore J., Matthew S. Ellis, and Howard D. Chilcoat, "Understanding the Use of Diverted Buprenorphine," *Drug and Alcohol Dependence*, Vol. 193, 2018, pp. 117–123.

Commission on Combating Synthetic Opioid Trafficking, *Commission on Combating Synthetic Opioid Trafficking: Final Report*, Washington, D.C., February 2022.

Corbie-Smith, Giselle, Stephen B. Thomas, and Diane Marie M. St. George, "Distrust, Race, and Research," *Archives of Internal Medicine*, Vol. 162, No. 21, 2002, pp. 2458–2463.

Davidson, Peter J., and Mary Howe, "Beyond NIMBYism: Understanding Community Antipathy Toward Needle Distribution Services," *International Journal of Drug Policy*, Vol. 25, No. 3, May 2014, pp. 624–632.

Davis, Corey S., and Derek Carr, "Over the Counter Naloxone Needed to Save Lives in the United States," *Preventive Medicine*, Vol. 130, 2020.

Ehley, Brianna, and Sarah Karlin-Smith, "Kellyanne Conway's 'Opioid Cabinet' Sidelines Drug Czar's Experts," *Politico*, February 6, 2018.

Enos, Gary, "Denver Initiative Should Reduce Need for Police on Some Emergency Calls," *Mental Health Weekly*, Vol. 30, No. 25, 2020.

Europol, "Massive Blow to Criminal Dark Web Activities After Globally Coordinated Operation," press release, July 20, 2018.

Formica, Scott W., Katherine M. Waye, Allyn O. Benintendi, Shapei Yan, Sarah M. Bagley, Leo Beletsky, Jennifer J. Carroll, Ziming Xuan, David Rosenbloom, Robert Apsler, et al., "Characteristics of Post-Overdose Public Health–Public Safety Outreach in Massachusetts," *Drug and Alcohol Dependence*, Vol. 219, 2021.

Frank, Richard G., Keith N. Humphreys, and Harold A. Pollack, "Policy Responses to the Addiction Crisis," *Journal of Health Politics, Policy and Law*, Vol. 46, No. 4, 2021, pp. 585–597.

Health in Justice Action Lab, *Overdose Crisis Reporting Style Guide*, Boston, Mass.: Northeastern University School of Law, 2019.

Hoge, Michael A., John A. Morris, Allen S. Daniels, Gail W. Stuart, Leighton Y. Huey, and Neal Adams, *An Action Plan for Behavioral Health Workforce Development: A Framework for Discussion*, Cincinnati, Ohio: Annapolis Coalition on the Behavioral Health Workforce, 2007.

Howley, Lisa, Alison Whelan, and Tannaz Rasouli, "Addressing the Opioid Epidemic: U.S. Medical School Curricular Approaches," *Association of American Medical Colleges Analysis in Brief*, Vol. 18, No. 1, January 2018.

Humphreys, Keith, Chelsea L. Shover, Christina M. Andrews, Amy S. B. Bohnert, Margaret L. Brandeau, Jonathan P. Caulkins, Jonathan H. Chen, Mariano-Florentino Cuéllar, Yasmin L. Hurd, David N. Juurlink, et al., "Responding to the Opioid Crisis in North America and Beyond: Recommendations of the Stanford–*Lancet* Commission," *The Lancet*, Vol. 399, No. 10324, February 2022, pp. 555–604.

Isaacson, J. H., M. Fleming, M. Kraus, R. Kahn, and M. Mundt, "A National Survey of Training in Substance Use Disorders in Residency Programs," *Journal of Studies on Alcohol*, Vol. 61, No. 6, 2000, pp. 912–915.

Jalal, Hawre, and Donald S. Burke, "Carfentanil and the Rise and Fall of Overdose Deaths in the United States," *Addiction*, Vol. 116, No. 6, 2021, pp. 1593–1599.

Jalali, Mohammad S., Michael Botticelli, Rachael C. Hwang, Howard K. Koh, and R. Kathryn McHugh, "The Opioid Crisis: A Contextual, Social-Ecological Framework," *Health Research Policy and Systems*, Vol. 18, No. 87, 2020, pp. 1–9.

Kahan, James P., John Setear, Margaret M. Bitzinger, Sinclair B. Coleman, and Joel Feinleib, *Developing Games of Local Drug Policy*, Santa Monica, Calif.: RAND Corporation, N-3395-DPRC, 1992. As of May 25, 2022:
https://www.rand.org/pubs/notes/N3395.html

Karamouzian, Mohammad, Carolyn Dohoo, Sara Forsting, Ryan McNeil, Thomas Kerr, and Mark Lysyshyn, "Evaluation of a Fentanyl Drug Checking Service for Clients of a Supervised Injection Facility, Vancouver, Canada," *Harm Reduction Journal*, Vol. 15, No. 46, 2018.

Kennedy-Hendricks, Alene, Colleen L. Barry, Elizabeth Stone, Marcus A. Bachhuber, and Emma E. McGinty, "Comparing Perspectives on Medication Treatment for Opioid Use Disorder Between National Samples of Primary Care Trainee Physicians and Attending Physicians," *Drug and Alcohol Dependence*, Vol. 216, 2020.

Kerman, Nick, Alexia Polillo, Geoff Bardwell, Sophia Gran-Ruaz, Cathi Savage, Charlie Felteau, and Sam Tsemberis, "Harm Reduction Outcomes and Practices in Housing First: A Mixed-Methods Systematic Review," *Drug and Alcohol Dependence*, Vol. 228, 2021.

Killian, Carolin, Jakob Manthey, Sinclair Carr, Franz Hanschmidt, Jürgen Rehm, Sven Speerforck, and Georg Schomerus, "Stigmatization of People with Alcohol Use Disorders: An Updated Systematic Review of Population Studies," *Alcoholism: Clinical and Experimental Research*, Vol. 45, No. 5, May 2021, pp. 899–911.

Kilmer, Beau, *Reducing Barriers and Getting Creative: 10 Federal Options to Increase Treatment Access for Opioid Use Disorder and Reduce Fatal Overdoses*, Washington, D.C.: Brookings Institution, June 2020.

Kilmer, Beau, Jirka Taylor, Jonathan P. Caulkins, Pam A. Mueller, Allison J. Ober, Bryce Pardo, Rosanna Smart, Lucy Strang, and Peter H. Reuter, *Considering Heroin-Assisted Treatment and Supervised Drug Consumption Sites in the United States*, Santa Monica, Calif.: RAND Corporation, RR-2693-RC, 2018. As of May 25, 2022:
https://www.rand.org/pubs/research_reports/RR2693.html

Krawczyk, Noa, Bianca D. Rivera, Victoria Jent, Katherine M. Keyes, Christopher M. Jones, and Magdalena Cerdá, "Has the Treatment Gap for Opioid Use Disorder Narrowed in the U.S.? A Yearly Assessment from 2010 to 2019," *International Journal of Drug Policy*, August 4, 2022.

Krieger, Maxwell S., William C. Goedel, Jane A. Buxton, Mark Lysyshyn, Edward Bernstein, Susan G. Sherman, Josiah D. Rich, Scott E. Hadland, Traci C. Green, and Brandon D. L. Marshall, "Use of Rapid Fentanyl Test Strips Among Young Adults Who Use Drugs," *International Journal of Drug Policy*, Vol. 61, 2018, pp. 52–58.

Lagisetty, Pooja A., Ryan Ross, Amy Bohnert, Michael Clay, and Donovan T. Maust, "Buprenorphine Treatment Divide by Race/Ethnicity and Payment," *JAMA Psychiatry*, Vol. 76, No. 9, 2019, pp. 979–981.

Lofwall, Michelle R., and Sharon L. Walsh, "A Review of Buprenorphine Diversion and Misuse: The Current Evidence Base and Experiences from Around the World," *Journal of Addiction Medicine*, Vol. 8, No. 5, 2014, pp. 315–326.

Mann, Brian, "Opioid Crisis: Critics Say Trump Fumbled Response to Another Deadly Epidemic," NPR, October 29, 2020.

Mee-Lee, David, Gerald D. Shulman, Marc Fishman, David R. Gastfriend, and Michael M. Miller, eds., *The ASAM Criteria: Treatment Criteria for Addictive, Substance-Related, and Co-Occurring Conditions*, 3rd ed., Chevy Chase, Md.: American Society of Addiction Medicine, 2013.

Meinhofer, Angelica, Erica Onuoha, Yohanis Angleró-Díaz, and Katherine M. Keyes, "Parental Drug Use and Racial and Ethnic Disproportionality in the US Foster Care System," *Children and Youth Services Review*, Vol. 118, 2020.

Morreale, Mary K., Richard Balon, Rashi Aggarwal, John Coverdale, Eugene Beresin, Anthony P. S. Guerrero, Alan K. Louie, and Adam M. Brenner, "Substance Use Disorders Education: Are We Heeding the Call?" *Academic Psychiatry*, Vol. 44, No. 2, 2020, pp. 119–121.

Murphy, Sean M., Jake R. Morgan, Philip J. Jeng, and Bruce R. Schackman, "Will Converting Naloxone to Over-the-Counter Status Increase Pharmacy Sales?" *Health Services Research*, Vol. 54, No. 4, 2019, pp. 764–772.

National Alliance to End Homelessness, "SOAR Works to Increase Access to Benefits," blog post, July 11, 2016. As of October 1, 2022:
https://endhomelessness.org/blog/soar-works-to-increase-access-to-benefits

Nilson, Chad, *Collaborative Risk-Driven Intervention: A Study of Samson Cree Nation's Application of the Hub Model*, Ottawa: Public Safety Canada, 2016.

Nolan, Michelle L., Sindhu Shamasunder, Cody Colon-Berezin, Hillary V. Kunins, and Denise Paone, "Increased Presence of Fentanyl in Cocaine-Involved Fatal Overdoses: Implications for Prevention," *Journal of Urban Health*, Vol. 96, No. 1, 2019, pp. 49–54.

Pardo, Bryce, Jirka Taylor, Jonathan P. Caulkins, Beau Kilmer, Peter Reuter, and Bradley D. Stein, *The Future of Fentanyl and Other Synthetic Opioids*, Santa Monica, Calif.: RAND Corporation, RR-3117-RC, 2019. As of January 2, 2020:
https://www.rand.org/pubs/research_reports/RR3117.html

Peiper, Nicholas C., Sarah Duhart Clarke, Louise B. Vincent, Dan Ciccarone, Alex H. Kral, and Jon E. Zibbell, "Fentanyl Test Strips as an Opioid Overdose Prevention Strategy: Findings from a Syringe Services Program in the Southeastern United States," *International Journal of Drug Policy*, Vol. 63, 2019, pp. 122–128.

Pennsylvania Opioid Command Center, *Strategic Plan 2020–2023*, Harrisburg, Pa., undated.

Penzenstadler, Louise, Ariella Machado, Gabriel Thorens, Daniele Zullino, and Yasser Khazaal, "Effect of Case Management Interventions for Patients with Substance Use Disorders: A Systematic Review," *Frontiers in Psychiatry*, Vol. 8, 2017.

Pfefferle, Susan G., Samantha S. Karon, and Brandy Wyant, *Choice Matters: Housing Models That May Promote Recovery for Individuals and Families Facing Opioid Use Disorder*, Washington, D.C.: U.S. Department of Health and Human Services, Office of the Assistant Secretary for Planning and Evaluation, June 2019.

Public Health Agency of Canada, *A Primer to Reduce Substance Use Stigma in the Canadian Health System*, Ottawa, 2020.

Public Safety Canada, "The Hub – Community Mobilization Prince Albert (CMPA)," webpage, 2014. As of April 6, 2021:
https://www.publicsafety.gc.ca/cnt/cntrng-crm/crm-prvntn/nvntr/dtls-en.aspx

ReThink Health, "What Is ReThink Health?" webpage, undated. As of November 24, 2020:
https://www.rethinkhealth.org/about/

Saloner, Brendan, Emma E. McGinty, Leo Beletsky, Ricky Bluthenthal, Chris Beyrer, Michael Botticelli, and Susan G. Sherman, "A Public Health Strategy for the Opioid Crisis," *Public Health Reports*, Vol. 133, Suppl. 1, 2018, pp. 24S–34S.

Schuler, Megan S., Andrew W. Dick, and Bradley D. Stein, "Growing Racial/Ethnic Disparities in Buprenorphine Distribution in the United States, 2007–2017," *Drug and Alcohol Dependence*, Vol. 223, 2021.

Smart, Rosanna, Courtney Ann Kase, Amanda Meyer, and Bradley D. Stein, *Data Sources and Data-Linking Strategies to Support Research to Address the Opioid Crisis*, Washington, D.C.: U.S. Department of Health and Human Services, Assistant Secretary for Planning and Evaluation, Office of Health Policy, September 2018.

Smart, Rosanna, Bryce Pardo, and Corey S. Davis, "Systematic Review of the Emerging Literature on the Effectiveness of Naloxone Access Laws in the United States," *Addiction*, Vol. 116, No. 1, January 2021, pp. 6–17.

Stein, Bradley D., Andrew W. Dick, Mark Sorbero, Adam J. Gordon, Rachel M. Burns, Douglas L. Leslie, and Rosalie Liccardo Pacula, "A Population-Based Examination of Trends and Disparities in Medication Treatment for Opioid Use Disorders Among Medicaid Enrollees," *Substance Abuse*, Vol. 39, No. 4, 2018, pp. 419–425.

Stone, Elizabeth M., Alene Kennedy-Hendricks, Colleen L. Barry, Marcus A. Bachhuber, and Emma E. McGinty, "The Role of Stigma in U.S. Primary Care Physicians' Treatment of Opioid Use Disorder," *Drug and Alcohol Dependence*, Vol. 221, 2021.

Strang, Lucy, and Jirka Taylor, *Heroin-Assisted Treatment and Supervised Drug Consumption Sites: Experience from Four Countries*, Santa Monica, Calif.: RAND Corporation, WR-1262-RC, 2018. As of May 25, 2022:
https://www.rand.org/pubs/working_papers/WR1262.html

Takahashi, Lois M., "The Socio-Spatial Stigmatization of Homelessness and HIV/AIDS: Toward an Explanation of the NIMBY Syndrome," *Social Science and Medicine*, Vol. 45, No. 6, September 1997, pp. 903–914.

Taylor, Jirka, Allison J. Ober, Beau Kilmer, Jonathan P. Caulkins, and Martin Y. Iguchi, "Community Perspectives on Supervised Consumption Sites: Insights from Four US Counties Deeply Affected by Opioids," *Journal of Substance Abuse Treatment*, Vol. 131, 2021.

Tempalski, Barbara, Risa Friedman, Marie Keem, Hannah Cooper, and Samuel R. Friedman, "NIMBY Localism and National Inequitable Exclusion Alliances: The Case of Syringe Exchange Programs in the United States," *Geoforum*, Vol. 38, No. 6, 2007, pp. 1250–1263.

Tupper, Kenneth W., Karen McCrae, Ian Garber, Mark Lysyshyn, and Evan Wood, "Initial Results of a Drug Checking Pilot Program to Detect Fentanyl Adulteration in a Canadian Setting," *Drug and Alcohol Dependence*, Vol. 190, 2018, pp. 242–245.

Vanderplasschen, Wouter, Richard C. Rapp, Jessica De Maeyer, and Wim Van Den Noortgate, "A Meta-Analysis of the Efficacy of Case Management for Substance Use Disorders: A Recovery Perspective," *Frontiers in Psychiatry*, Vol. 10, No. 186, 2019.

Volkow, Nora D., "Stigma and the Toll of Addiction," *New England Journal of Medicine*, Vol. 382, No. 14, 2020, pp. 1289–1290.

Wandersman, Abraham, Pamela Imm, Matthew Chinman, and Shakeh Kaftarian, "Getting to Outcomes: A Results-Based Approach to Accountability," *Evaluation and Program Planning*, Vol. 23, No. 3, 2000, pp. 389–395.

Washington State Institute for Public Policy, *Buprenorphine (or Buprenorphine/Naloxone) Maintenance Treatment for Opioid Use Disorder*, Olympia, Wash., updated December 2019a.

Washington State Institute for Public Policy, *Methadone Maintenance for Opioid Use Disorder*, Olympia, Wash., updated December 2019b.

Whetten, Kathryn, Jane Leserman, Rachel Whetten, Jan Ostermann, Nathan Thielman, Marvin Swartz, and Dalene Stangl, "Exploring Lack of Trust in Care Providers and the Government as a Barrier to Health Service Use," *American Journal of Public Health*, Vol. 96, No. 4, 2006, pp. 716–721.

The White House, "Biden-Harris Administration Expands Treatment to Underserved Communities with Mobile Methadone Van Rule," press release, June 29, 2021.

Overview of Synthesis Exhibits and Ideas

In Table A.1, we provide an overview of ideas to mitigate various aspects of the opioid crisis shown as exhibits in boxes throughout the chapters and explain how they relate to the recommendations within each chapter.

TABLE A.1

Overview of Synthesis Exhibits and Ideas

Exhibit Title	Idea	Primarily in One Component?	Policy Level	Evidence Statement	Discussed in Chapter(s)	Related to Chapter Recommendation (see Table B.1)	Primary Owners (could be others)
1. Supporting individuals as they move across ecosystem components	1A. Support individuals with comprehensive case management	No, across systems	State and/or local	Evidence emerging	Synthesis (Ch. 14)	4B	State and local health, human services, and criminal legal agencies, either directly or through grants to NGOs
	1B. Merge individual-level data across multiple systems	No, across systems	State and/or local	Although studies have shown how data can be used, we are unaware of studies demonstrating the effects of such use	Synthesis (Ch. 14)	2A, 7C, 10C, 11C	State and/or local departments of health and social services; criminal legal agencies

Table A.1—Continued

Exhibit Title	Idea	Primarily in One Component?	Policy Level	Evidence Statement	Discussed in Chapter(s)	Related to Chapter Recommendation (see Table B.1)	Primary Owners (could be others)
2. Coordinating across components and addressing different priorities	2A. Improve systems-level coordination on opioid policy at the federal level	No, across systems	Federal	No empirical studies of effectiveness			President of the United States, ONDCP
	2B. Cultivate, identify, and support system stewards	No, across systems	State and/or local	No empirical studies of effectiveness		4B	State and local health, human services, and criminal legal agencies, either directly or through grants to NGOs
	2C. Create opioid policy gaming exercises	No, across systems	State and/or local	No empirical studies of effectiveness			State and/or local executive officers (e.g., governor, mayor), NGOs, and philanthropic organizations

Table A.1—Continued

Exhibit Title	Idea	Primarily in One Component?	Policy Level	Evidence Statement	Discussed in Chapter(s)	Related to Chapter Recommendation (see Table B.1)	Primary Owners (could be others)
3. Addressing legal consequences and stigma associated with drug use or possession	3A. Increase education for the media and decisionmakers in use of nonstigmatizing language	No, across systems	Federal, state, local, nongovernmental	No empirical studies of effectiveness			Federal, state, and local governments; NGOs
	3B. Increase preclinical and clinical training related to treatment of SUDs	Yes (medical care)	Nongovernmental	Emerging evidence of effectiveness	Medical Care (Ch. 5)	5B	Medical schools, residency and fellowship programs, preclinical training programs, and postclinical training and internship programs
	3C. Make it easier for individuals with low-level drug convictions to expunge or seal these offenses from their criminal records	Yes (criminal legal system)	Federal, state, local	No empirical studies of effectiveness for drug offenses	Criminal Legal System (Ch. 6), Child Welfare (Ch. 10), and Income Support and Homeless Services (Ch. 11)	6D, 10F, 11B	Federal and state legislatures and courts
	3D. Consider reforming drug possession laws and/or how they are enforced	Yes (criminal legal system)	Primarily state and local, but could happen at the federal level	No empirical studies of decriminalization in United States beyond cannabis, and we are not aware of any that measure effects on stigma	Criminal Legal System (Ch. 6)	6E, 8A	Federal and state legislatures; criminal legal agencies

Table A.1—Continued

Exhibit Title	Idea	Primarily in One Component?	Policy Level	Evidence Statement	Discussed in Chapter(s)	Related to Chapter Recommendation (see Table B.1)	Primary Owners (could be others)
4. Preventing non-prescribed opioid use and escalation to OUD	4A. Increase referrals and access to quality mental health care	No, across systems	Federal, state, local, nongovernmental	No empirical studies of effectiveness	Medical Care (Ch. 5)		HHS, CMS, state and local health departments, health care providers, and insurers
	4B. Reduce barriers to nonmedication treatments for chronic pain	Yes (medical care)	Federal, state, local, nongovernmental	No clinical trials of effectiveness	Medical Care (Ch. 5), Employment (Ch. 12)	5A, 12A	HHS, CMS, state and local health departments, health care providers, and insurers
	4C. Take steps to reduce unnecessary prescribing of opioid analgesics	Yes (medical care)	Federal, state, local, nongovernmental	No clinical trials of effectiveness in preventing misuse or escalation	SUD Treatment (Ch. 4), Medical Care (Ch. 5), and Employment (Ch. 12)	5A, 12A	HHS, CMS, state and local health departments, health care providers, and insurers
	4D. Enhance efforts to offer evidence-based skills training and drug prevention	Yes (education)	State, local, nongovernmental	Empirical studies provide some evidence that such programs can decrease use of other substances; we are not aware of empirical studies of reducing opioid misuse	Child Welfare (Ch. 10), Education (Ch. 13)	10B, 13A	State departments of education, local school districts, and NGOs

581

Table A.1—Continued

Exhibit Title	Idea	Primarily in One Component?	Policy Level	Evidence Statement	Discussed in Chapter(s)	Related to Chapter Recommendation (see Table B.1)	Primary Owners (could be others)
5. Identifying individuals who need treatment, increasing access to effective treatment, and making treatment more effective	5A. Promote interagency collaboration and care integration	No, across systems	State, local, nongovernmental	Growing evidence about the effectiveness of such approaches	SUD Treatment (Ch. 4), Medical Care (Ch. 5), Criminal Legal System (Ch. 6), Harm Reduction (Ch. 8), First Responders (Ch. 9), Child Welfare (Ch. 10), Income Support and Homeless Services (Ch. 11), and Education (Ch. 13)	4B, 5C	State and local departments of health, social services, and criminal legal agencies; NGOs
	5B. Develop local networks of service providers to identify individuals who could benefit from engaging in multiple services and develop an outreach and engagement plan	No, across systems	Local and nongovernmental	No evidence of effectiveness in the United States, but some from Canada		4B, 4C, 5B, 5C	State and local departments of health, social services, and criminal legal agencies; NGOs
	5C. Increase capacity for quality SUD treatment in specialty settings	Yes (SUD treatment)	Federal, state, local, nongovernmental	Clear evidence of MOUD effectiveness in general, no clinical trials of capacity expansion	SUD Treatment (Ch. 4) and Medical Care (Ch. 5)	4A, 5B	HHS, CMS, state and local health departments, health care providers, insurers, and medical schools

Table A.1—Continued

Exhibit Title / Idea	Primarily in One Component?	Policy Level	Evidence Statement	Discussed in Chapter(s)	Related to Chapter Recommendation (see Table B.1)	Primary Owners (could be others)
5D. Increase access to quality MOUD in primary care settings	Yes (medical care)	Federal, state, local, nongovernmental	Clear evidence of MOUD effectiveness in general, no clinical trials of increased access in primary care settings	SUD Treatment (Ch. 4) and Medical Care (Ch. 5)	4B, 5B	HHS, CMS, state and local health departments, heath care providers, insurers, and medical schools
5E. Reduce barriers to effective OUD treatment for individuals involved in the criminal legal system	Yes (criminal legal system)	Federal, state, local	Existing evidence of effectiveness	SUD Treatment (Ch. 4), Criminal Legal System (Ch. 6), and First Responders (Ch. 9)	4C, 6A, 6B	BOP, DEA, state and local criminal legal agencies, and state and local health departments
5F. Implement and enforce laws and regulations requiring true parity in coverage of SUD and OUD services	Yes (SUD treatment)	Federal, state	Some evidence to suggest that parity matters	SUD Treatment (Ch. 4) and Employment (Ch. 12)	4A, 12B	HHS, DOJ, and state attorneys general, and state and local health departments
5G. Change laws so that Medicaid benefits are not terminated as a result of incarceration	Yes (criminal legal system)	Federal, state	No empirical studies of effectiveness, but there is evidence that access to Medicaid can improve outcomes for this population	Criminal Legal System (Ch. 6)	4C	Federal and state legislatures

Table A.1—Continued

Exhibit Title	Idea	Primarily in One Component?	Policy Level	Evidence Statement	Discussed in Chapter(s)	Related to Chapter Recommendation (see Table B.1)	Primary Owners (could be others)
6. Reducing the probability that an overdose is fatal	6A. Increase market surveillance so that people who use drugs and public health and public safety practitioners know what is being consumed or purchased, especially in areas at risk of synthetic opioid exposure	No, across systems	Federal, state, local	No empirical evidence of effectiveness	Illegal Supply (Ch. 7) and Harm Reduction (Ch. 8)	7C	Federal, state, and local health and criminal legal agencies
	6B. Increase funding for community provision of naloxone	Yes (harm reduction)	Federal, state, local, nongovernmental	Emerging evidence that increased access and training is associated with fewer fatal overdoses	Harm Reduction (Ch. 8), First Responders (Ch. 9)	9A	Federal, state, and local health departments; NGOs
	6C. Increase community provision of drug content testing services	Yes (harm reduction)	Federal, state, local	No empirical studies of effectiveness on reducing overdoses	Harm Reduction (Ch. 8)	8B	HHS, state and local health departments, and state legislatures
	6D. Reduce state and federal barriers to local experimentation with or implementation of SCSs	Yes (criminal legal system)	Federal, state, local	Most international studies on SCSs are positive, but there are relatively few high-quality studies with strong comparison groups	Criminal Legal System (Ch. 6), Harm Reduction (Ch. 8)	6C, 8C	DOJ, state legislatures, and state and local health and criminal legal agencies

Table A.1—Continued

Exhibit Title Idea	Primarily in One Component?	Policy Level	Evidence Statement	Discussed in Chapter(s)	Related to Chapter Recommendation (see Table B.1)	Primary Owners (could be others)
6E. Law enforcement could clearly communicate that individuals will not be arrested for patronizing or working at SSPs or places where individuals can test the content of their drugs	Yes (criminal legal system)	State, local	No empirical studies of effectiveness	Criminal Legal System (Ch. 6), Harm Reduction (Ch. 8)	8B	State and local health and criminal legal agencies
6F. Introduce an emergency response system for reporting suspected drug overdoses	Yes (first responders)	State, local	No empirical studies of effectiveness	First Responders (Ch. 9)	9C	State and local health and criminal legal agencies; first responder agencies
6G. Get creative about disrupting the supply of illegally produced synthetic opioids	Yes (illegal supply)	Federal, state, local	No empirical studies of effectiveness about the effect of disrupting web transactions	Illegal Supply (Ch. 7)	7A, 7B	Federal and state criminal legal agencies

Table A.1—Continued

Exhibit Title	Idea	Primarily in One Component?	Policy Level	Evidence Statement	Discussed in Chapter(s)	Related to Chapter Recommendation (see Table B.1)	Primary Owners (could be others)
7. Addressing nontreatment needs of individuals using opioids for nonprescribed purposes	7A. Build on efforts to revise laws and other policies that make it harder for those with drug convictions to access services	No, across systems	Federal, state, local	Studies documenting barriers; we are not aware of studies evaluating the removal of these barriers	Criminal Legal System (Ch. 6), Child Welfare (Ch. 10), Income Support and Homeless Services (Ch. 11), and Education (Ch. 13)	6D, 10F, 11B	Federal and state legislatures; federal, state, and local health and human services agencies
	7B. Support research and data-collection efforts to learn more about the size and characteristics of this population and how it is changing	No, across systems	Federal, state, local, nongovernmental	Surveillance is critical for understanding the problem and evaluating interventions	People Who Use Opioids (Ch. 2), Criminal Legal System (Ch. 6), Illegal Supply (Ch. 7), Child Welfare (Ch. 10), and Income Support and Homeless Services (Ch. 11)	2A, 7C, 10C, 11C	HHS, DOJ, NGOs, state and local health and criminal legal agencies, and philanthropic agencies
	7C. Expand integration of the Housing First model with OUD treatment	Yes (income support and homeless services)	State, local	Emerging evidence with respect to SUDs	SUD Treatment (Ch. 4), Income Support and Homeless Services (Ch. 11)	4E, 11E	State and local human services, housing, and health agencies
	7D. Consider expanding SOAR	Yes (income support and homeless services)	Federal	No empirical studies of effectiveness	Income Support and Homeless Services (Ch. 11)	11A	Federal legislators, HHS (SAMHSA)

Table A.1—Continued

Exhibit Title	Idea	Primarily in One Component?	Policy Level	Evidence Statement	Discussed in Chapter(s)	Related to Chapter Recommendation (see Table B.1)	Primary Owners (could be others)
8. Mitigating the burdens that opioids impose on family members	8A. Help family members cope with the stress and other psychological consequences of having a family member with OUD	No, across systems	State, local, nongovernmental	No empirical studies of effectiveness	Family (Ch. 3), SUD Treatment (Ch. 4), Child Welfare (Ch. 10), Education (Ch. 13)	3B, 3C, 3D, 3F, 4D, 10D, 13B	State and local health and human service agencies (directly and via funding support to NGOs)
	8B. Provide additional support for those who serve as informal caretakers	No, across systems	State, local, nongovernmental	No empirical studies of effectiveness	Family (Ch. 3), SUD Treatment (Ch. 4), Child Welfare (Ch. 10)	3B, 3F, 4D, 10D, 10G	State and local health and human service agencies (directly and via funding support to NGOs)
	8C. Amend punitive state laws regarding drug use in pregnancy	No, across systems	State	Some empirical evidence regarding the effects of such laws	Child Welfare (Ch. 10)	6E, 10F	State legislatures
	8D. Increase access to naloxone and trainings on how to administer it	Yes (harm reduction)	Federal, state, local, nongovernmental	Emerging evidence that increased access and training is associated with fewer fatal overdoses, but this evidence is not specific to families	Family (Ch. 3), Harm Reduction (Ch. 8), and First Responders (Ch. 9)	3E	Federal government, state and local health and criminal legal agencies, first responder agencies, NGOs
	8E. Consider amending the Adoption and Safe Families Act	Yes (child welfare)	Federal	No empirical studies of effectiveness	Child Welfare (Ch. 10)	10E	Federal legislature

587

Table A.1—Continued

Exhibit Title	Idea	Primarily in One Component?	Policy Level	Evidence Statement	Discussed in Chapter(s)	Related to Chapter Recommendation (see Table B.1)	Primary Owners (could be others)
9. Improving the data infrastructure for understanding people who use drugs, drug consumption, and drug markets	9A. Introduce a community behavioral surveillance program	No, across systems	Federal, state, local		People Who Use Opioids (Ch. 2)	2A	HHS, state and local health agencies
	9B. Use wastewater testing to track and possibly measure drug consumption, including that of synthetic opioids	No, across systems	Federal, state, local		People Who Use Opioids (Ch. 2)	2A	CDC, state and local health agencies
	9C. Resurrect some version of the Arrestee Drug Abuse Monitoring program	No, across systems	Federal, state, local		People Who Use Opioids (Ch. 2)	2A	DOJ, ONDCP, state and local criminal legal agencies
	9D. Improve analyses of data collected by the DEA	No, across systems	Federal		Illegal Supply (Ch. 7)	2A	DEA
	9E. Validate the NSDUH and add questions specific to synthetic opioid use and the consequences of opioid use for families	Yes (people who use opioids, families)	Federal		People Who Use Opioids (Ch. 2)	2A	HHS

NOTE: BOP = Bureau of Prisons. CDC = Centers for Disease Control and Prevention. CMS = Centers for Medicare & Medicaid Services. DEA = Drug Enforcement Administration. DOJ = U.S. Department of Justice. HHS = U.S. Department of Health and Human Services. NGO = nongovernmental organization. MOUD = medications for opioid use disorder. NSDUH = National Survey on Drug Use and Health. ONDCP = Office of National Drug Control Policy. OUD = opioid use disorder. PWUO = people who use opioids. SAMHSA = Substance Abuse and Mental Health Services Administration. SCS = supervised consumption site. SOAR = Social Security Insurance/Social Security Disability Insurance Outreach, Access, and Recovery. SSP = syringe service program. SUD = substance use disorder.

Overview of Chapter-Level Considerations

In Table B.1, we provide an overview of the main ideas presented in each chapter.

TABLE B.1

Overview of Chapter-Level Considerations

Chapter	Idea	Primarily in One Component?	Policy Level	Informs Synthesis-Level Exhibit Ideas (see Table A.1)
2. PWUO	2A. Improving data collection on PWUO, their families, and related relevant community-level indicators	No, across systems	Federal and nongovernmental	1B, 7B, 9A, 9B, 9C, 9D, 9E
3. Family members of individuals with OUD	3A. Enhancing family members' ability to support their loved one obtaining and engaging in treatment and ongoing recovery	Yes (SUD treatment)	State, local, nongovernmental	
	3B. Expanding treatment options that directly involve families	Yes (SUD treatment)	State, local, nongovernmental	8A, 8B
	3C. Helping families navigate multiple systems involved in addressing SUD in their families	No, across systems	State, local, nongovernmental	8A
	3D. Preparing families of those with OUD for the many nontreatment challenges they will face	No, across systems	State, local, nongovernmental	8A
	3E. Providing families with naloxone and training about how to use it	Yes (harm reduction)	State, local, nongovernmental	6B, 8D
	3F. Devoting resources to help family members deal with their stress	No, across systems	State, local, nongovernmental	8A, 8B
	3G. Developing, evaluating, and disseminating more and better programs that help children being raised in a household with a parent with SUD	No, across systems	State, local, nongovernmental	

Table B.1—Continued

Chapter	Idea	Primarily in One Component?	Policy Level	Informs Synthesis-Level Exhibit Ideas (see Table A.1)
4. Specialty treatment system for OUD	4A. Ensuring parity of coverage for OUD and adequate reimbursement for OUD treatment in both the private and commercial insurance markets	Yes (SUD treatment)	State	5C, 5F
	4B. Supporting the development of networks linking primary care providers and SUD treatment experts	No, across systems	State, local, nongovernmental	1A, 2B, 5A, 5B, 5D
	4C. Better integrating the criminal legal system and the SUD treatment system	Yes (criminal legal system)	Federal, state, local	4E, 5B, 5E, 5G
	4D. Expanding the availability of family-friendly treatment options	Yes (SUD treatment)	State, local, nongovernmental	8A, 8B
	4E. Expanding OUD treatment integration with the Housing First model	Yes (income support and homeless services)	State, local	7C
5. Medical care	5A. Balancing the goals of effective pain treatment and prevention of opioid misuse	Yes (medical care)	Federal, state, local, nongovernmental	4B, 4C
	5B. Expanding access to OUD treatment	No, across systems	Federal, state, local, nongovernmental	3B, 5B, 5C, 5D
	5C. Promoting interagency collaboration and care integration	No, across systems	State, local, nongovernmental	5A, 5B

Table B.1—Continued

Chapter	Idea	Primarily in One Component?	Policy Level	Informs Synthesis-Level Exhibit Ideas (see Table A.1)
6. Criminal legal system	6A. Reducing barriers to community corrections–based OUD treatment	Yes (criminal legal system)	Federal, state, local	5E
	6B. Reducing barriers to jail- or prison-based OUD treatment	Yes (criminal legal system)	Federal, state, local	5E
	6C. DOJ could allow local experimentation with SCSs	Yes (criminal legal system)	Federal	6D
	6D. Addressing the collateral consequences of a drug conviction	Yes (criminal legal system)	Federal, state, local	3C, 5G, 7A
	6E. Revisiting drug possession laws	Yes (criminal legal system)	Federal, state, local	3D, 8C
7. Illegal supply and supply control	7A. Getting innovative about supply disruption	Yes (criminal legal system)	Federal	6G
	7B. Rethinking supply-side deterrence in the fentanyl era	Yes (criminal legal system)	Federal	6G
	7C. Improving data-collection efforts, especially when it comes to markets for synthetic opioids	No, across systems	Federal, nongovernmental	1B, 6A, 7B
8. Harm reduction and community-initiated interventions	8A. Contemplating reforming drug possession laws	Yes (criminal legal system)	Federal, state, local	3D
	8B. Law enforcement could clearly communicate that individuals will not be arrested for patronizing or working at SSPs or places where individuals can test the content of their drugs	Yes (criminal legal system)	State, local	6C, 6E
	8C. DOJ could allow local experimentation with SCSs	Yes (criminal legal system)	Federal	6D

Table B.1—Continued

Chapter	Idea	Primarily in One Component?	Policy Level	Informs Synthesis-Level Exhibit Ideas (see Table A.1)
9. First responders	9A. First responder agencies could serve as naloxone distribution centers	Yes (first responders)	State, local	6B
	9B. Expanding the scope of and raising awareness of Good Samaritan laws	Yes (first responders)	State, local, nongovernmental	
	9C. Introducing a dedicated non-911 emergency number	Yes (first responders)	State, local	6F
	9D. Providing training for and supporting the resiliency of first responders	Yes (first responders)	State, local, nongovernmental	
10. Child welfare	10A. Exploring the effectiveness of safe care planning and other nonpunitive strategies to support children and families	No, across systems	Federal, state, local	
	10B. Increasing funding for prevention services and supporting their implementation	No, across systems	State, local	4D
	10C. Collecting indicators related to behavioral and substance use outcomes for youth and employing evidence-informed interventions to support the well-being of this vulnerable population	No, across systems	Federal, state, local, nongovernmental	1B, 7B
	10D. Increasing support for family-oriented treatment	Yes (SUD treatment)	State, local, nongovernmental	8A, 8B
	10E. Considering amending the Adoption and Safe Families Act	Yes (child welfare)	Federal	8E
	10F. Addressing the intersection between criminalization of drug use and child welfare	No, across systems	Federal, state	3C, 7A, 8C
	10G. Improving the level of support provided to kinship caregivers	Yes (child welfare)	State, local, nongovernmental	8B

Table B.1—Continued

Chapter	Idea	Primarily in One Component?	Policy Level	Informs Synthesis-Level Exhibit Ideas (see Table A.1)
11. Income support and homeless services	11A. Improving access to SSDI and SSI, e.g., via SOAR	Yes (income support and homeless services)	Federal	7D
	11B. Mitigating the consequences of a drug-related criminal record	No, across systems	Federal, state, local	3C, 7A
	11C. Improving information and research on welfare/ TANF populations and their use of opioids	No, across systems	Federal, state, local	1B, 7B
	11D. Developing OUD treatment and prevention strategies specifically targeted to the TANF and TANF-eligible populations	No, across systems	State, local, nongovernmental	
	11E. Implementing a Housing First approach to address the intersection of the opioid crisis and homelessness	Yes (income support and homeless services)	State, local	7C
12. Employment	12A. Balancing pain management needs and prescribing risks, expanding non-opioid pain management therapy	Yes (medical care)	Federal, state, local, nongovernmental	4B, 4C
	12B. Closing loopholes in state and federal parity laws	Yes (medical care)	Federal, state	5F
	12C. Revisiting employers' drug-testing or zero-tolerance policies, mitigating unintended consequences of anti-discrimination laws	Yes (employment)	Federal, state, nongovernmental	
	12D. Developing and implementing programs focused specifically on promoting employment among workers in OUD recovery	No, across systems	State, local, nongovernmental	

Table B.1—Continued

Chapter	Idea	Primarily in One Component?	Policy Level	Informs Synthesis-Level Exhibit Ideas (see Table A.1)
13. Education	13A. Implementing community school model	Yes (education)	State, local	4D
	13B. Implementing trauma-informed school approaches	Yes (education)	State, local	8A

NOTE: DOJ = U.S. Department of Justice. OUD = opioid use disorder. PWUO = people who use opioids. SAMHSA = Substance Abuse and Mental Health Services Administration. SCS = supervised consumption site. SOAR = Social Security Insurance/Social Security Disability Insurance Outreach, Access, and Recovery. SSDI = Social Security Disability Insurance. SSI = Supplemental Security Income. SSP = syringe service program. SUD = substance use disorder. TANF = Temporary Assistance for Needy Families.